W9-CRL-801

HENDRICKS CHAPEL

Hendricks Chapel, c. 1997.
Photograph by Steve Sartori. Courtesy of Syracuse University.

HENDRICKS CHAPEL

*Seventy-five Years of Service
to Syracuse University*

Richard L. Phillips *and* Donald G. Wright,

with contributions by Lawrence Myers, Jr., James B. Wiggins,
Robert S. Pickett, *and* Thomas V. Wolfe,

SYRACUSE UNIVERSITY PRESS

Copyright © 2005 by Syracuse University Press
Syracuse, New York 13244–5160

All Rights Reserved

First Edition 2005
05   06   07   08   09   10   6   5   4   3   2   1

The paper used in this publication meets the minimum requirements of
American National Standard for Information Sciences—Permanence
of Paper for Printed Library Materials, ANSI Z39.48–1984.∞™

Library of Congress Cataloging-in-Publication Data
Phillips, Richard L. (Richard Lee), 1934–
Hendricks Chapel : seventy-five years of service to Syracuse University / Richard L. Phillips
and Donald G. Wright ; with contributions by Myers, Lawrence, Jr. . . . [et al.].— 1st ed.
p. cm.
Includes index.
ISBN 0–8156–0827–6 (hardcover : alk. paper)
1. Hendricks Chapel (Syracuse University)—History. 2. Syracuse (N.Y.)—Church
history. I. Wright, Donald G., d. 1994. II. Myers, Lawrence, Jr., 1935– III. Title.
BR561.S97P45 2005
277.47'66—dc22

2005007768

Manufactured in the United States of America

This book is dedicated to the memories
of Dr. Donald Wright, Chancellor William Tolley,
and Chancellor Melvin Eggers
and to Kenneth Shaw, who retired as Syracuse University's
tenth chancellor only last year.

Their guidance, understanding, and support
of the presence and functioning of a chapel
in the heart of a major university campus
have been critical in making Hendricks Chapel
the excellent campus ministry and
university support organization that it is today!

Donors

Anonymous (2)

William and Valerie Alston

A. Lawrence Baner and Mary Ann Baner

Jean L. Baum

Douglas and Sari Biklen

Guthrie S. and Louise Birkhead

Wesley H. Bradley and family, in honor of the Rev. William H. Bradley

Goodwin and Barbara Cooke

A. N. Culberston & Co., Inc.

Virginia B. and Robert F. Dewey

Wallace D. Finley and Mary Peace Finley, in memory of Kathryn
    Beth Drexel

Don Forsberg

Samuel and Judith Gorovitz

Robert D. Grant

Hans and Mary Louise Hartenstein

Frank R. Heath

Nahmin and Leah Horwitz

Nansie and Robert Jensen

Grant A. Krafft

Bob Laubach

Donald A. and Joyce P. Marchand

Lawrence Myers, Jr., and B. J. Myers

Anis and Nawel Obeid

Dave F. Pieratt

Dave F. Pieratt, in memory of Hazel M. Pieratt

Cindy Phillips

Helen R. Phillips

Kenneth and Betsy Long Phillips

Hazel and Bill Phipps

Robert S. and Jane Pickett

Richard and Ethel Phillips

Marjorie B. Pierson

John and Mary Prucha

Fritz and Frances Traugott

Gershon and Dina Vincow

Phyllis C. Wright

Rod Zetko

Syracuse University Departments

Chancellor's Office, Kenneth A. Shaw

Academic Affairs, Deborah Freund

Auxiliary Services, Peter B. Webber

College of Arts and Sciences, Eric Holzwarth

Food Services, David George

Hendricks Chapel, Thomas Wolfe

Housing, Meal Plan, & ID Services, David Kohr

Human Services/Government Relations, Eleanor Ware

Project Advance, Frank Wilbur

Religion Department, Richard Pilgrim

Student Affairs, Barry Wells

Undergraduate Studies, Judith O'Rourke

WAER, Joe Lee

Contents

Appendixes

Illustrations

Preface

FIRST I WANT TO CONVEY to the readers the story of how this book came into existence. Following that story is an orientation on both the book's structure and how the content from several other writers is distributed.

When I came to Syracuse in the summer of 1961 to do graduate work at Syracuse University (SU) I went to work at University Methodist Church, later University United Methodist Church, at the corner of University Avenue and East Genesee Street. I was associate minister. The senior minister at that time was the Reverend Dr. Donald G. Wright. Our relationship blossomed into a friendship that was to last until Wright's death on June 29, 1994.

This friendship very much included Don's wife, Bernice (Bunny), and the two sons still living at home. Bunny was teaching at SU and was soon to become the dean of the College of Home Economics. I have a very happy memory of, for a short time, team-teaching a course in the Syracuse public schools with her. Bunny was later to die from cancer, a great loss to the family, university, and community.

Don, I learned much later, had been a student at SU when Hendricks Chapel was constructed in 1929–30. He was a key member of the Chapel Board during the first year of its existence. Bunny at the time was employed by the chapel as a counselor to women students. Don's professional career sometimes took him from Syracuse, but well over the last half of his ministry was back in Syracuse. He retained a keen interest in the chapel, its people and programs, from his student days until his death. He also saved many of its routine documents. His collection is now in the SU Archives.

When I returned to Syracuse in 1981 to assume the deanship of Hendricks Chapel it was no real surprise when Don came to my office and presented me with a copy of a large manuscript on the history of the chapel. Don was commissioned to write it by Dean McCombe and Chancellor Eggers after his own retirement. He used his own very numerous items saved from personal years, the SU Archives, and the staff and resources available in the chapel itself. In 1980, as McCombe moved to Florida, Jim Wiggins encouraged Wright to complete his work on the manuscript. The manuscript covered the history of religious-life programs at SU from before Hendricks Chapel was built until the end of the deanship of Dr. Charles C. Noble, the memorial service for Noble in the late sixties, and a section on the deanship of Jack McCombe.

On many occasions both in my office and in his home Wright and I talked

Jack McCombe, then dean, and Donald G. Wright looking at Wright's manuscript on the early history of Hendricks Chapel, January 1980. Photograph courtesy of Syracuse University Archives.

about his manuscript, which had been typed by a person who is now a dear friend, Don's second wife, Phyllis. Don always started the conversation with two concerns, one about the work itself and one about his desire for me to edit, add chapters, and publish it. He had not, he constantly reminded me, written it in a form that was publishable. Wright and McCombe had given copies to several people, and the manuscript was also placed in the chapel archives. In addition, Don wanted me to know that it contained many mistakes, from spelling to organization and sentence and paragraph structure. Editing it would be a major effort, which he wanted me to be fully aware of. "Would you," he asked many times, "be willing to undertake the project?"

My standard response was that I was very interested in doing what he suggested but that I could not undertake it along with the duties I had just assumed as the fourth dean of Hendricks Chapel. Having been well acquainted with Charles Noble and only slightly (at that time) acquainted with Jack McCombe, the second and third deans, I knew the workload was far too great for me to take on such a research and writing effort. As the years passed Don did not let me forget, and I always assured him that I had not forgotten, his request. "When I retire" eventually became my standard response. Early in my deanship I had read the manuscript twice, and I knew preparing it for publication and adding chapters would be major undertakings.

Early in 1994 Don knew he was living his last days (and doing so with dignity and grace), and I visited him, though not regularly enough. On one such occasion he expressed concern about the project and asked me to promise to "edit, add, and publish." He received my promise but again with the qualifier "after I retire." Had it not been for Don's persistence and his good nature about the project this book would never have existed through my efforts, and thus I again tip the hat of genuine friendship and collegiality to him!

Soon after my 1999 retirement I began editing Don's manuscript and researching the holdings on Hendricks Chapel in the Syracuse University Archives and in the chapel office and storage areas. That work involved many trips back to Syracuse and many hours processing more than 150 boxes of files and records in the archives as well as many boxes still in the chapel, most of which I then sent to the SU Archives. The research phase was 99.9 percent completed by the fall of 2002.

Except for chapter 41, the first forty-four chapters of this book are from Don's manuscript, with some editorial changes made by me and editorial comments given as footnotes. Additional information provided by Don, including many lists of the officers on the Chapel Board and its committees year by year, has been placed in appendix A. Minor editorial corrections to spelling, grammar, and organization are not noted, and any errors caused by such editing are my responsibility.

This book contains, in addition to the chapters written by Don Wright and by me, others written by colleagues vitally involved in the chapel's history. Professor Larry Myers, a retired member of the faculty at Newhouse at SU, provided chapter 41 on the relationship between campus radio station WAER and Hendricks Chapel over many years. Dr. James Wiggins was interim dean for eight months between the third and fourth deans, and he wrote chapter 48 to describe that transition. Dr. Robert Pickett served as interim director from mid-1995 through mid-1997, while I was on leave serving as director of the Syracuse University's Study Abroad program in Strasbourg, France. My account of the two years I spent in France constitutes chapter 59, while Dr. Pickett recorded his two years as interim director in chapter 60. Finally, the fifth and current dean of Hendricks Chapel, Dr. Tom Wolfe, has provided chapter 63 about his first years in office, recording the beginning of the current phase of Hendricks Chapel's history.

Each section of this book exhibits the individual writing styles and perceptions of its contributors. They complement one another but do not try to follow the same guidelines for writing. Each should be understood as an effort that stands on its own.

An Added Note to Readers

In writing about my own years as dean I sought and received advice on several aspects of style. Everyone I asked agreed that I should write in the first person, indicating clearly my own observations and experiences. I have followed that advice in the chapters concerning my deanship and my own experiences in other capacities at Syracuse University. However, much of the book was written by others, and in those sections my role has been only that of editor. Any editorial comments I have added to those sections, while still in the first person, have been placed in footnotes so as not to interfere with the voice of the author; they end with my initials, RLP. Of equal concern was the style I should adopt in relating history. I decided to follow the practice of editor Joan Peyser in the book *The Orchestra: Origins and Transformations* (New York: Charles Scribner's Sons, 1986). In her introduction she describes her approach to relating historical information as follows: "An effort has been made to find a middle ground between pedestrian listings and lofty philosophizing" (3). I like that technique, took it as good advice, and have tried to follow it. It is very different from the chronological organization adopted by Don Wright in the first portion of the book and I trust lends a good touch of variety to our respective content regarding the history of our common subject.

There is much more to the history of Hendricks Chapel than these pages can communicate. In fact, more information has been left on the cutting table than has been included. I take, as I am sure Don Wright would also, full responsibility for the decision making that undoubtedly left content some readers would have liked to see included still residing in archival holdings.

Acknowledgments

SYRACUSE UNIVERSITY PRESS AGREED, early in the planning process, to be the publisher of this book, and because of that arrangement I was able to research and write without the worry and effort of finding a publisher, for which I am very grateful. The staff at SU Press has been very helpful (and patient), and for their many kindnesses I am most grateful. Special thanks are due to Peter Webber and Mary Selden Evans for their coordination efforts on this book.

For the green light, moral support, and some financial support for putting the research on disks I thank the SU administration. From Chancellor Kenneth Shaw, Senior Vice President Eleanor Ware, and my successor, Dean Tom Wolfe, I have received much encouragement and from the chapel staff much assistance in being sure all documents and material relevant to the chapel's history were made available to me.

To former secretary to the dean and outstanding staff member Mary Farnsworth I am indebted for putting, during her retirement, my research dictation on computer disks so it could be better utilized in the actual writing. This was possible because of a grant arranged by V. P. Ware.

Several short papers and reports were used as resources and when used are noted. To the first secretary of the chapel, Marjorie Pierson; Jack McCombe, the third dean, now deceased; and several former staff members and former chaplains I am indebted for their efforts to get in writing some portion of the history of the chapel. Along with Don Wright, Marjorie Pierson was a student at SU during the construction of the chapel; she and her late husband, Ted, were marvelous supporters of the chapel, including our Jewish ministry. Marjorie and I had many visits about Hendricks Chapel.

The readers join me in benefiting from Don Wright's mighty effort in documenting well over the first third of this history. I am personally grateful for Don's insistence that I do the project. Don's widow, Phyllis, has made all of his working papers and documents available to me, and they are now in the university archives. A big thanks to Ethel, my spouse, for typing the Wright manuscript after I edited it.

Other former students and "chapelites" have added materials to the records in the archives that have been very helpful. All are destined for the archives as this book goes to press.

To Director Edward L. Galvin and Assistant Director Mary O'Brien of the SU Archives a very heartfelt thank-you. They and almost every member of their staff helped in some way during my research in their shop. What very helpful people they all are. At times the sixth floor of Bird Library seemed to be my home away from home!

Before undertaking the writing I visited on two occasions with John Robert Greene, author of other works concerning SU's history. Those visits were very helpful; my thanks to him.

During the research phase I tape-recorded interviews with about a dozen persons who have had close contact with some portion of the history of the chapel. (These tapes are now in the SU Archives.) Such persons are noted in the text when content from those interviews is used. For their time and candid responses to my questions I say thank you.

To the Iliff School of Theology in Denver (my theological alma mater) a big thank-you for the loan of an office for a few months in which to park my computer so that I might work at this project in semi-isolation but with an excellent library immediately available. Other sites for my writing were our home in Boulder, Colorado, and our cabin in Missouri.

Chief among my research helpers is the same person who has lovingly pressured me to get this project behind us, my wife, Ethel. No bigger thanks do I owe anyone for loyal help, wise counsel, and solid encouragement than her. As during my deanship and in this project, she is my coworker and chief supporter.

The SU Press engaged Annette Wenda to edit the entire work. For her excellent work I am certainly grateful. The final proofreading of the text was done by Ethel and me and by a professional proofreader. It was fun, but the greatest joy was in finishing it.

All materials generated during this project, including research disks and tapes, will be placed in the SU Archives about the same time as the publication of this book.

A huge expression of appreciation to the departments and offices at SU and the many, many individuals who donated to the publication costs associated with the production of this book. They are acknowledged in other pages.

Introduction

DONALD G. WRIGHT

FOR COUNTLESS STUDENTS who attended Syracuse University since 1930 it surely must seem that Hendricks Chapel has always been at the center of the campus. Many older alumni can recall the days before this handsome structure graced the campus. Some of us saw its construction and its early operation, myself included.

Our purpose here is to record, with some detail, the history of Hendricks Chapel because of the unique, profound, and widespread influence it has had in the lives of a very large number of students during its existence.*

The establishment of Hendricks Chapel was a logical development. At work was the same religious spirit that motivated the founding of Syracuse University. There could have been no doubt in the mind of the donor, Senator Francis Hendricks, that the roots and early history of Syracuse University had been dominated by men and women who were committed to the kind of education that was inspired and guided by the Christian faith and that the whole enterprise was a work of divine Providence. Dr. W. Freeman Galpin, writing in *Syracuse University Pioneer Days* after the chapel had become a significant part of campus life and had developed a multifaceted approach to the religious life of a large number of students, reminds his readers how this came about: "It should always be remembered that the light burns brightly largely because of past efforts of Syracusans, who in founding the University on the hill—close to the stars—proclaimed that this institution was and always should be a Christian University dedicated to God and Man."

So, a program of faith had always been the practice before Hendricks Chapel came into being, even before the university was relocated to Syracuse. In early times prayer meetings were a daily occurrence, and both faculty and students were expected to participate. Very early those students whose faith or denomination was different from that of the founders were excused from attending services. Now and again references show that attending chapel was not universally popular, and some students repeatedly sat in the back seats and quietly studied, snoozed, or found ways to not attend at all. Nonetheless, this was not typical, and chapel services went on.

---

*This introduction, and the first forty-four chapters of this book, with the exception of chapter 41, were written by Donald G. Wright in the late 1970s.—RLP

There are some who still remember that Dean Frank Smalley, with a few faculty members, would conduct chapel each morning on the top floor of the Hall of Languages with simple exercises of religious devotion.

Such devotional meetings, however, were held only on weekdays. On Sundays, students were expected to attend a local church for morning and evening services and often an evening prayer meeting on a weekday.

As a part of their strategy, the leaders of the Methodist Episcopal Church not only relocated the academy to Syracuse but, at the same time, established a church at the opposite (north) end of what is now called University Avenue. The cornerstones of both the Hall of Languages and the University Avenue Methodist Episcopal Church were laid on the same day by largely the same people, who saw the two institutions as performing in different ways their respective expressions of the Christian faith. Thus, the establishment, some sixty years later, of Hendricks Chapel was a natural fulfillment of the religious spirit that motivated the founding of Syracuse University.*

*Most of the passages quoted by Donald G. Wright in the chapters he wrote are from chapel brochures, *Daily Orange* clippings, and campus publications. They are all drawn from Wright's papers, which are held in the Syracuse University Archives but have not yet been numbered or labeled. In addition, Wright used material provided by Marjorie Bronner and some from McCombe's writings.—RLP

HENDRICKS CHAPEL

1. The Chapel and the University

HENDRICKS MEMORIAL CHAPEL was the gift to Syracuse University of Senator Francis Hendricks in memory and honor of his wife, Eliza Jane. Senator Hendricks had served as president of the Board of Trustees of the university and was greatly interested in its affairs. Born in Kingston, New York, on November 23, 1834, he came to Syracuse in 1861 to establish himself in the business of photographic supplies. During his life in the city he developed widely diversified interests in both banking and government. Hendricks held a variety of posts in both local and state government, including those of mayor of the City of Syracuse in 1880–81 and senator in the New York State legislature between 1886 and 1891.

Francis Hendricks was a trustee of Syracuse University from 1902 until the time of his death in 1920. He was also a trustee of the State College of Forestry beginning in 1915. In 1919, he gave Syracuse University a five-acre tract of land located at the corner of Raynor and Irving Avenues, which came to be known as Hendricks Field. He also gave generously to the College of Medicine, which was at that time part of Syracuse University.

Senator Hendricks had a summer home in the Berkshires, not far from Williams College in Williamstown, Massachusetts. As Marjorie O. Bronner of the class of 1931 reported in 1934, Hendricks "had formed the habit of quiet meditation in the beautiful little chapel of Williams College. Leaving the chapel one afternoon, he turned to his niece and said quietly that it was his purpose to provide in his will a similar opportunity for Syracuse students in memory of Mrs. Hendricks." * Francis Hendricks's great interest in Syracuse University, combined with his commitment to its religious heritage, gave him the determination that it, too, should have a chapel. In his will Hendricks set aside $500,000 for that purpose. That actual construction did not begin until nine years after his death was a source of some concern to many in the community. A change in leadership and the development of a master plan for the campus were responsible for the delay.

When Charles Wesley Flint came to Syracuse University as chancellor in 1922 the provisions of Senator Hendricks's will were made known to him. One of Dr. Flint's first concerns was to find a proper setting for the building of a new chapel. Before Flint's term, Syracuse University had built new buildings as needed, with-

---

*Marjorie O. Bronner, "The Story of the Religious Program at Syracuse University," *Syracuse University Alumni News,* February 1934.

1

out any overall campus design. As a result, its campus sported a variety of architectural styles. To remedy this, Chancellor Flint resolved to initiate a complete design for the total university, with Hendricks Chapel as its center. At the December 1922 meeting of the Board of Trustees he asked for a "general plan for the Development of Syracuse University." While the location of the chapel would be central to the plan, Chancellor Flint also had in mind the locations of other buildings that he knew would be needed as the university grew. John Russell Pope was given the responsibility of developing this plan, and in June 1927, four and one-half years later, a plan was presented to the Board of Trustees at its spring meeting and adopted. Key to the total design was the central placement planned for Hendricks Chapel, at at the west end of what was then called the Old Oval.

Once the plan was adopted the building of the chapel got under way. Plans were drawn, the site cleared, test borings made for the foundations, and the contracts awarded. I came to Syracuse University as a freshman in 1928 and therefore witnessed the early stages of this process. The building then occupying the site planned for the chapel was the women's gym; to make way for the erection of the chapel, it was lifted up on blocks and moved south in the direction of the stadium, where it remained for some years before it was finally torn down.

Plans for the new chapel, designed in the Georgian colonial style, were executed by John Russell Pope and his associate Dwight James Baum, an SU graduate of the class of 1909. The contract for its building was awarded to the A. E. Stephens Company of Springfield, Massachusetts, for the sum of $596,539, the lowest of nine bids. The company was known in the community, for it had recently completed the construction of the Syracuse Memorial Hospital, located not far from campus on Irving Avenue.

At some point during the construction it was discovered that no provision had been made for offices or rooms for student activities. A number of years later, looking back, Dean Charles Noble made a wry comment about this fact in a letter he wrote to John P. Thomas. "When Hendricks Chapel was built the architect was more interested in the outside of the building and in the main room for worship than he was in the other rooms which were to be provided. In fact, he apparently gave no thought at all in the original plans for office space for the staff and the lounge rooms where the students might hold group activities."* Fortunately, Dean Powers, who was on campus for most of the time during construction, caught this omission and called it to the attention of a foreman. The lower floor was hastily redesigned; however, it had to be done within some rather severe limitations that might not have existed had the architect been more aware of the breadth of the chapel program.† Even within the main room there were problems. Whitney Trousdale, who had come to be Dr. Powers's assistant, later recalled his

*Noble Correspondence, box 2.—RLP
†A classic illustration of form over function.—RLP

discovery that no provision had been made for seating a choir in the worship area. A hasty consultation with Chancellor Flint, who in turn conferred with the architects, resulted in the designing of curved choir stalls around the organ console, allowing seating for a sixty-voice choir. Long afterward, at the instigation of Dean Jack McCombe, the downstairs area of the chapel was redesigned to provide additional usable space.

Once the land was cleared and the foundations laid, the time came to lay the cornerstone. This event occurred late in the afternoon of June 9, 1929, one year and one day before the date of dedication. It was also nine years and one day following the death of the donor, Senator Francis Hendricks. Dwight James Baum, of Pope and Baum, the architects, served as master of ceremonies, while Bishop Adna Wright Leonard, resident bishop of the Methodist Episcopal Church, spoke at the event. Chancellor Flint filled the copper box that was to go into the cornerstone with appropriate mementos, many of which concerned the university. These included a program of the ceremony of the day; a Bible; a copy of the *Daily Orange,* the student newspaper; newspapers from the city; views of Syracuse University and the area as it was then; and the design of plans for the future. One special memento was a set of three test tubes from the Department of Bacteriology marked "From the past to the present, 'Pax Vobiscum.' " Chancellor Flint and Kathryn Hendricks, niece of the donor, spread the mortar with a special ceremonial trowel, and masons slid the large cornerstone into place, thus enclosing the hermetically sealed copper box. In his remarks, Bishop Leonard outlined the purpose of the chapel: "It is the plan of the Chancellor and trustees to erect here a chapel whose architecture shall speak of the eternal, and whose throbbing life within shall be an authority in the spiritual realm interpreting life in spiritual terms"* By the end of the summer of 1929 the shape of the chapel could be seen; by the following spring the building was enclosed and the roof was on, signalling that the chapel would be ready for dedication by June 1930.

During construction, Chancellor Flint gave his attention to the kind of leadership that the chapel would require to fulfill the expressed purpose of its donor, Senator Hendricks. To reinforce his own judgment, Dr. Flint conferred with a wide variety of church leaders and formed a student committee for consultation so that the man selected for the leadership position would be well qualified. Certain necessary characteristics became evident immediately: Someone with a genuine ability to relate well to students was important, as was the almost paradoxical requirement that the new leader have both youthful vigor and mature experience. Along with those requirements he must have both a broad understanding of religion and firm convictions of personal faith. As Bishop Leonard had suggested at the ceremony of the laying of the cornerstone, "It is fitting what whoever shall

*Quoted in Bronner, "Story of the Religious Program."

Hendricks Chapel under construction, December 2, 1929. Photograph by Jasper T. Crawford, courtesy of Syracuse University Archives.

have charge of this chapel shall have spiritual as well as intellectual insight, that his words shall be words of religious authority."*

There seems to have been no question that, because of the nature of its religious founding and its continuing relationship with the Methodist Episcopal Church, the leader selected for the chapel program would be chosen from the personnel of that denomination. How the selection process was carried out, however, and who was included in the list of candidates, is not known.

Suffice it to say that on August 15, 1929, the Reverend William Harrison Powers, D.D., a Methodist minister then serving as the superintendent of the Syracuse East District of the Central New York Conference of the Methodist Episcopal Church, became the "chaplain" of Syracuse University. All Methodist ministers are appointed to a position by their bishops, and this appointment was no exception; even though he would be employed by the university and the announcement came from the university, Dr. Powers was granted this ministerial assignment as a special appointment from his denomination.

Dr. Powers was an alumnus of Syracuse University's class of 1914 and had re-

---

*Quoted in Bronner, "Story of the Religious Program."

ceived an honorary doctorate of divinity from his alma mater in 1925. On his graduation from Syracuse University he had been appointed to serve the James Street Methodist Church of Syracuse. At the Methodist conference in fall 1921, Powers was appointed to serve the First Methodist Episcopal Church in Ithaca, New York. He also served as the director of the Wesley Foundation for Methodist students at Cornell University. This post revealed and developed his talents as he ministered from within the university community to townspeople, students, and faculty. The fact that he was chosen on four different occasions as chaplain for Cornell's commencement exercises demonstrates his reputation and influence.

Under Powers's leadership that church became one of the outstanding college churches in the country, drawing a larger proportion of students into its membership than any other Methodist church serving students. In 1925 Powers received an honorary doctorate of divinity from Syracuse University. Chancellor Flint, in his citation, spoke of Powers's "combination of energy, executive ability, and spirituality which have made you a good minister of the gospel and given you success in interpreting its truths to your congregation, which includes many of the university faculty of our great sister institution in Ithaca." *

Both as an undergraduate and later, Powers had taken part in many extracurricular activities on campus, joining several honorary fraternities, notably Theta Beta Phi (honorary philosophical), Theta Chi Beta (honorary religious), and Pi Gamma Mu (honorary social science). His membership in the varsity debate team led to his election to the national honorary debating fraternity Delta Sigma Rho.

In addition to serving his churches, Dr. Powers early found his way into leadership roles within his denomination. At a time when many ministers were not graduates of theological schools he was active in ministerial education. At one point, Dr. Powers held the position of dean of the Graduate School of Theology for the Central New York Conference and supervised its curriculum. In addition, he was invited to lecture at similar schools for other conferences within the Methodist Church. In 1928, his colleagues in the conference elected him to the General Conference of the Methodist Episcopal Church for that year, the church's highest legislative body. He served as vice president of the New York State Council of Churches and as a trustee of Cazenovia Seminary (of which he was an alumnus), and in 1933 he became its acting president for several weeks.

When Dr. Powers was appointed chaplain of Syracuse University in 1929, Chancellor Flint assigned him three broad areas of responsibility. First, he was to serve as the pastor of Hendricks Memorial Chapel (when completed)—the church of the university—ministering to all students and faculty as their religious interests allowed. Second, he was to serve as the administrator of religious programs on campus, centered in the chapel and developed campuswide. And third, he was to

*Quoted in Bronner, "Story of the Religious Program."

serve as the university's religious representative in its relationships with religious bodies within the community and beyond. It is noteworthy that Dr. Powers soon came to the deep conviction that was to direct and ultimately mark his work at Syracuse University: that if the programs were to develop properly the chapel must have general status. Dr. Powers was determined to prevent the chapel from becoming a kind of stepchild, with second-class standing among other organizations on campus. He was committed to the idea that just as this new building was located geographically at the center of campus, so the programs located within its walls should include top-level leadership of students, faculty, and administration. As a corollary to this conviction, Powers believed that the leader of Hendricks Chapel should have a level of authority, responsibility, and status equal to that of other administrative officials. As at many other universities, he asserted, the leader of Syracuse University's religion programs should be granted the title of dean. Although this goal was yet to be realized, in keeping with Powers's reputation, the *Syracuse University Alumni News* of October 1929 reported: "Since he had been distinctively successful in inspiring and guiding students in self-expression as it relates to social and religious work it is felt that students at Syracuse University have a real friend and counselor who will inspire and encourage them to develop on the campus of Syracuse University one of the strongest programs in the country."

Soon after Dr. Powers arrived on the campus he established a temporary office in the Men's Gymnasium. He very soon gave serious thought to those individuals who would be associated with him in the Hendricks Chapel program. His first appointment was of the Reverend Whitney M. Trousdale, a man he had known as a student at Cornell University. Trousdale graduated from Cornell in 1925 and then went on to Drew Theological Seminary, graduating from there in 1928. He won a fellowship that enabled him to be a student the following year at the American Institute of Archaeology in Jerusalem, with further study at Cambridge University in England and the University of Berlin in Germany. At Cornell, Trousdale was president of the Cornell University Christian Association, a varsity debater, and a member of Delta Sigma Rho, the honorary debating fraternity. He was also affiliated with Kappa Delta Rho, a social fraternity.

On September 3, 1929, Trousdale was appointed assistant to both Dr. Powers and Donald Watt, director of personnel for Syracuse University. He was given the general title of men's student counselor. Already on campus in the dean of women's office was Mabel C. Lytton, who was appointed as religious adviser to women students. Dean Lytton had graduated from Ohio Wesleyan University and then earned a graduate degree from Teachers College at Columbia. Before coming to Syracuse she had been dean of women at Washington State Teachers College and assistant dean at Boston University. She had a marked interest in religion and, incidentally, was the sister-in-law of Dr. Samuel McRae Cavert, for many years the executive of the Federal Council of Churches in America. Before her appointment to the Hendricks Chapel staff, Dean Lytton had already served as adviser to the campus YWCA.

2. Before Hendricks Chapel

ALTHOUGH MANY OF THE STRANDS woven together to form the Hendricks Chapel program are now obscured by time, several elements can and should be identified. The most pervasive and generalized element was the Methodist Episcopal Church, which played a large part in the chapel program not only because Syracuse University was founded by that church but because those Methodist roots were still very evident in the life of the university community when the chapel came into being. This backdrop generated a favorable climate of mind, heart, and spirit that contributed to the acceptance of the chapel and its program. Another contributory element was the nurturance of religion in the student programs of neighboring churches. This created a corps of committed persons when the chapel needed leadership.

Other elements contributing to the Hendricks Chapel program included organized programs of religious activity already thriving separately in Syracuse well before the chapel existed; four of these in particular made key contributions to the new program when it was launched: the YMCA, the YWCA, the Syracuse-in-China program, and the Student Church.

The groups with the longest history were the YMCA (Young Men's Christian Association), founded November 1, 1880, and the YWCA (Young Women's Christian Association, founded in the spring of 1884. Through their national organizations, these groups had for years promoted student religious activities on many college campuses and provided state, regional, and national support structures.[*]

The Syracuse University YMCA had employed secretaries, one of whom was a student named William P. Tolley who later became chancellor of Syracuse University. The last secretary was Charles Carlton. By the fall of 1928 the YMCA had largely ceased to function, though it did sponsor the Freshman Camp for men that year. When Dr. Powers was appointed chaplain of Syracuse University in August 1929, he occupied the largely unused offices of the YMCA in the Men's Gymnasium.

The YWCA, on the other hand, had been and continued to be very active on campus. Like the YMCA it had an employed secretary, whose office was in the

[*]There are many campuses in the United States today that continue to use the "Y model" of campus ministry, Washington University in St. Louis being a good example.—RLP

basement of the library. When the new chaplain came to campus he found the YWCA strong and active. It was one of the more prestigious campus organizations, attracting outstanding women leaders to its program. The presidency of the YWCA was one of the coveted leadership positions in the university. As we shall see, the YWCA continued, almost intact, in the new program. It was the organization through which most women related to Hendricks Chapel. Only very much later did it change its name to the Women's Chapel Association (WCA).

The third established organization was Syracuse-in-China (SIC), a mission program working from Chongqing (then Chungking), China. Later, it also became a constituent of the chapel program. Its beginnings and early history are included here, for they are a fascinating and unique part of the history, not only of the chapel program but also of the university itself.

Syracuse-in-China's origin goes back to the Student Volunteer Movement. In the fall of 1915 Leon Sutton and Gordon Hoople, both students at Syracuse University, attended a YMCA convention in Kansas City at which one of the speakers was Dr. Hume from Yale-in-China in Changsha. Both Sutton and Hoople were student volunteers and found the talk very interesting. On the train home they discussed the possibility of starting a Syracuse-in-China program, knowing that not only Yale but Harvard and Amherst also had units there. As Dr. Sutton relates it, the conversation went as follows: "Hoople was a Geology major and I was pre-med. Hoople said, 'If I changed to pre-med would you consider it?' I said, 'Sure,' not taking it very seriously. About a week later he told me that he had made the change. So that was the real starting point." Sutton continues:

> We began to recruit potential members of the unit, though none of this group actually got to China. Hoople and I studied together through our medical course and never gave up the idea but it was not until our internship at the Brooklyn Hospital that things began to crystallize. We talked with members of some of the other Units in China and were advised to make a connection with one of the Church Mission Boards for reasons of security and permanence. The Methodist Board had just what we were looking for, a Hospital which had been vacant for seven years plus a High School and Church which needed a transfusion. Soon after that the Board found a man who would finance a trip to West China for inspection by one of us. Dr. Hoople was the logical choice. He got a leave of absence from the hospital and was gone several months, took many pictures, etc.
>
> By that time our internship was nearly ended (1921) so we went to Syracuse and got together a group of alumni who might form the nucleus of an organization. I recall that Henry Phillips acted as Chairman. Gordon showed his pictures and we presented our plan. Syracuse University had a financial drive on at the time so the chances of raising money for our project seemed poor. We had expected this and asked if we could raise $30,000 in the next three weeks would they agree it could be done. They agreed. Hoople went to Boston and I to St. Louis. We got

about $33,000 in pledges over the next five years. Syracuse-in-China was organized and recognized by the university.

The Methodist Board would pay our salaries (I, with wife and baby, got $1,500 a year and a house). Syracuse-in-China was to raise additional funds for remodeling the hospital and equipping it. Before we left the Brooklyn Hospital the staff raised a fund of over $3,000 for unscheduled items.

The original group consisted of Hoople and myself, two nurses from Brooklyn, Flora Richardson and Mabel MacLean; two teachers for the High School, Bill North (William R.) and Lillian MacDonald, both of the latter were Syracuse graduates. The next year, 1922, a secretary, Betty Heller and a pharmacist, Ralph Blanchard came out. Miss Heller was also a Syracuse Alumna.

This fascinating story, told firsthand by Dr. Sutton in a letter, gives an intimate picture of the way in which Syracuse-in-China began. During the 1920s the program had its home base and support in Syracuse through an alumni organization. When the chapel opened in the fall of 1930, one of the staff positions created was that of executive secretary of Syracuse-in-China. At that point undergraduates as well as alumni began getting involved in this mission project.

The fourth organized program and antecedent of the chapel structure was called the Student Church. Although it did not continue intact as a specific entity within the Hendricks Chapel organization (as did the YWCA and Syracuse-in-China), its style, spirit, and ideals significantly influenced the kinds of programs that emerged in Hendricks Chapel. The Student Church was not a large program, but it had many of the key elements that would serve as a prototype for what was to come. In her account of the history of Hendricks Chapel, Mrs. Theodore Pierson (writing before her marriage as Marjorie Bronner of the class of 1931) gives a very clear account of this part of the religious life on campus in which she participated as a student:

In the fall of 1927 there was no truly organized religious program on campus, as there had been in the early days of the university. Daily chapel had quietly died. The churches in the university area had various programs for students and these met with differing responses. On campus the Y.W.C.A. and the Y.M.C.A. were still organized and performed a number of activities as has been described. But for all practical purposes there was no interdenominational or interfaith program. This was a time of emerging pre-ecumenism and a few religiously oriented and sensitive students became concerned about the lack of any such programs. They were interested in a religious organization that would transcend the limits of any one denomination or faith group.

In the fall of 1927, Gordon Halstead, a senior at the university, talked with the Rev. Norman Vincent Peale, then the young minister of the University Avenue Methodist Episcopal Church and who later became very well known. They gathered together a group of faculty and students which included Dr. Iva L. Peters, Dean of Women; Miss Mabel Lytton, her associate; and students Ruth Stafford, Helen Honsinger, Dominic Rinaldo, and John Leininger. The group discussed the possibility of worship services under the complete direction of the students. Some of those on the committee had attended the Student Volunteer Convention on their Christmas Vacation, where as one committee member expressed it, "The drive of the convention was no longer to Christianize the world, but to bring all religions together in a process of sharing by which the best elements of each should be made available for all." With this the committee abandoned any idea of establishing a denominational church as being too restrictive and chose the Crouse College Auditorium as a place not associated with any single denomination. Early in 1928 others were recruited to share in this emerging program; they included Wilton Chase, Ivan Gould, Nathalie Herman, Phyllis Leonard, Margaret Crossby, Marian Diamond, Mary Gilmore, Rolland Chaput, Howell Fuller, and Willard Salter. This entire committee planned the first service which occurred Sunday evening, February 12, 1928 with Dr. John Hart, pastor of Episcopal students at the University of Pennsylvania as speaker. During the year, four other services were held with Mr. W. Y. Chen, Dr. Robert Milliken, Patrick Murphy Malin of the Y.M.C.A. and Mary Mildred Welch of Boston University as speakers.*

The next year (1928–29), biweekly Sunday morning services were introduced at eleven o'clock, and a widespread group of speakers representing various denominational and faith groups came to address the Student Church. Added features were a meeting of interested persons each Monday evening and a Sunday afternoon discussion with the speaker of that morning's service. Various committees were established to do the work of planning services and engaging in social outreach. In fall 1928, the *Daily Orange* commented: "A student church should not confine itself to worship. It should combine the three functions of inspiration and worship, expression and instruction, some of which functions now exist on campus." Marjorie Bronner points out that it was interesting to note, in light of subsequent developments, that in one of the meetings of the Student Church committee the appointment of a chaplain was recommended.[†]

In the spring of 1929 the committee formulated the following statement of purpose: "The Student Church is definitely an experiment in religious unity. While many groups have been discussing this problem, here a definite attempt has been made to provide a service at which members of all races and creeds could forget the differences which have separated them and come together in a common worship of God in whom they all believe."[‡] So this group of students struggled on. Lack-

---

*These remarks come from a manuscript by Marjorie Bronner in the university's archives: Marjorie O. Bronner, "The Student Church" (manuscript), 102, Donald Wright Papers, Syracuse University Archives.—RLP

[†]Could this have been a key in the university's appointment of Powers?—RLP

[‡]Bronner, "The Student Church," 3.

ing in experience in conducting religious worship, they made up for it in study and hard work. Worshiping in a place hardly ideal for services, they made it as attractive as possible. Curtailed by less than adequate funds for their programs, they made do. Their offerings were occasionally assisted by a few generous gifts, and after the chapel program was established the university began to give some financial help. Opposed by some who did not quite see their vision of an inclusive religious group, they maintained their ideal and carried on.

The Student Church laid the foundation of three important aspects of the chapel program that was to follow: practical interdenominational and interfaith cooperation; a dynamic interpretation of religion in contemporary, basically liberal, terms; and voluntary and active student initiative and responsibility.

3. Hendricks Chapel as a Fledgling Campus Entity

IN RETROSPECT, the academic year 1929–30 at Syracuse University appears to have been the point at which most of what was to come coalesced. Hendricks Chapel was becoming a reality. Under the creative leadership of the Rev. William Harrison Powers, D.D., who arrived on campus in August 1929, the whole configuration of the chapel began to emerge. By the time the fall semester began he was beginning to make the contacts and establish the relationships that would set the chapel program in motion, even though the opening was nearly one year away. It is my own perception that Dr. Powers was very much aware that something new and significant was about to be born at his alma mater and that the kinds of decisions and choices he made would set the course for Hendricks Chapel for a long time to come.

Whereas his time in Ithaca had given Dr. Powers much valuable and successful experience in dealing with a university community, there was something uniquely compelling and challenging in knowing that into his hands had been placed an opportunity that had never occurred before on any university campus in the United States. Dr. Powers was to break new ground, and he knew it. The erection of a new chapel gave the occasion for extensive planning and organization. In all these endeavors he had strong support from the administration of Syracuse University and from the local Methodist Church authorities.

As he watched the chapel building rise in the center of the campus, Dr. Powers's mind was busy, seeking to formulate a program that would fulfill the highest potential for religious activity at Syracuse University. Just as Hendricks Chapel itself had been placed "at the heart of the campus" geographically, Powers committed himself to developing a religious program deserving of likewise being "at the heart of the campus." He was zealous in his determination that what happened under the aegis of Hendricks Chapel would be neither peripheral nor second-class.*

In many institutions of higher education religious activities were often treated either as fringe programs or as stepchildren. Consciously and with deliberation Dr. Powers sought to ensure that chapel activities would have equal status to whatever else happened on the campus. The other key to the conceptual framework in which he projected the program was that it would be comprehensive and include all the religious activities of the student body.

Although it is impossible now to reconstruct all the processes of mind and heart motivating the development of the chapel program, it is very clear to me that the elements discussed above were the dominant ones in the mind and heart of Dr. Powers. So he began his work of listening, consulting, counseling, interviewing, and acquainting himself with a large number of students, faculty, and administrators. At first, he gathered information. He wanted to know and be known by the young men and women who were the decision makers in the student body. He wanted to discover faculty interest for possible later involvement. Powers was sensitive to the ongoing programs of a religious nature that would become vital elements in the overall chapel program, including the Student Church, YWCA, Syracuse-in-China, and traditions such as the Freshman Camp for men. As it turned out, these programs were ready for the kind of leadership he and Hendricks Chapel would provide.

The problem of relating the emerging programs at Hendricks Chapel with vital and ongoing programs for students in the neighboring churches was more complicated. As has been noted earlier, the establishment of University Avenue Methodist Episcopal Church was a part of the denominational strategy to provide for the churching of those individuals associated with Syracuse University and its surrounding community. At first, those associated with the university were predominately Methodist in their religious affiliation. As the university grew this predominance slowly diminished, but at the time of the building of the chapel it was still a very strong factor. In order to provide ministerial leadership for Methodist student work, the Central New York Conference of the Methodist Episcopal Church assigned the Reverend Webster Melcher to be its first pastor to Methodist students at Syracuse University in the fall of 1928—two years before the chapel opened.†

*Wright, as a student member and officer of one of the first chapel boards, was able to witness firsthand the work of Powers and to share in his vision and organizational effort.—RLP

†This appointment was the start of a denominational structure and style of campus ministry that were soon incorporated into the chapel organizational style of overall campus ministry and the start of an arrangement that continues to this day.—RLP

From his office in University Church, Melcher gave direction and leadership to the Sunday evening fellowship group, often numbering as many as 150 students. He shared in the services of the church with Dr. Norman Vincent Peale, then the pastor of the church, and also visited many of the students in their living centers. On occasion, he would also share in student activities in other Syracuse Methodist churches, notably Erwin, First, and Furman Churches, giving them assistance when requested. At University Church Dr. Peale attracted students to both the morning and evening services by his very popular preaching. A Kollegde Klan, an organized Sunday-school class taught by Dr. Minnie Mason Beebe, a professor of history, attracted many students. The church choir, directed by Professor Howard Lyman, gave students who wanted to sing an opportunity to participate in a large and first-class organization.*

Though not as large or as well organized as the work of University Church, other churches had programs for students. Mention has been made of Methodist churches, but both Park Central Presbyterian Church and Grace Episcopal Church also had organized student programs. During this period, Dr. Bernard Clausen of First Baptist Church attracted great crowds with his popular preaching—especially on Sunday evenings.

It was at this point that the dream of Dr. Powers for uniting all student religious activity under the sponsorship of Hendricks Chapel faced a most formidable and sensitive problem. It was not without apprehension that those people who had an investment in student programs in the surrounding churches viewed the development of the chapel. It was not always easy for those churches with ongoing programs (some of them developed over many years) to accept the changes with equanimity. As it turned out, for the most part, over a period of time acceptance did take place and most of the student-related activities did come to the campus.†

On campus, the new building was being completed, and Marjorie Bronner Pierson reports that one Monday afternoon the Student Church committee was taken on a special tour through the uncompleted interior of the chapel building, which was then a yawning void, full of ladders, planks, and scaffolding. She relates they felt a great sense of space but little of the beauty that was to come. Yet it was possible to see the size and shape of the exterior of the building with its awe-inspiring dimensions and to imagine that the interior would be equally impressive. Like many exciting times it was full of expectation and uncertainty about the future.

---

*Wright, much later, became the senior minister of University Methodist Church. This position, added to his student experiences with Hendricks Chapel, gave him a keen interest in the history of its relationship with local churches.—RLP

†As local church attendance declined in the decades after World War II, many churches, some to this day, tried to attract students with special programs, even sometimes special staff, and saw themselves in competition with Hendricks Chapel.—RLP

By the end of the calendar year, Dr. Powers believed that his preliminary work had been completed, and so it was that on January 8, 1930, with the reconvening of the university after the Christmas recess, the announcement was made of the appointment of the first Hendricks Chapel Board. This board was composed of members of the administration, faculty, and students. Those persons already in staff positions were considered ex-officio members of the board. The membership was as follows:

Members Ex-Officio

Charles W. Flint, chancellor of the University
William H. Powers, university chaplain
Whitney M. Trousdale, assistant to the chaplain

Deans and Directors

Mabel C. Lytton, associate dean of women
Karl C. Leebrick, dean of liberal arts
Harold Butler, dean of fine arts
Donald Watt, director of personnel

Faculty

George Wilson, head of the Department of Philosophy
Herbert Shenton, head of the Department of Sociology
Clyde Wildman, professor in the Bible Department
Helene W. Hartley, professor in the Teachers College

Student Representatives

Glen Loucks (class of 1930), representative of the Men's Senate
Dean Henderson (1930), representative of the Men's Senate
Alice Evans (1930), representative of the Women's Senate
Nancy Ferguson (1930), representative of the Women's Senate
Marion Diamond (1930), representative of the Convocation Committee
Ewart Blaine (1930), representative of the Convocation Committee
Ivan Gould (1930)
Dorothy Flood (1931)
Marjorie O. Bronner (1931)
Douglas Petrie (1930)
Ellamae Merrick (1930)
John Leininger (1930)*

---

*Later listings of such memberships are contained in appendix A.—RLP

The makeup of the board is indicative of the thinking that Dr. Powers projected in terms of distribution and status of those people who were to be in leadership roles in Hendricks Chapel.

Chancellor Flint was an ordained minister in the Methodist Episcopal Church. The deans and directors were sympathetic to the religious program and certainly carried influence with their colleagues. Dr. Wilson and Dr. Wildman were both graduates of Boston University School of Theology. Dr. Shenton and Dr. Hartley were committed church persons. Among the students there were two representatives each from the Men's and Women's Senates, which were the governing student bodies of the time. Others were acknowledged student leaders holding other high-level positions on campus and membership in the class honor societies.

Almost half a century later, as this book is being written, it may be difficult to realize the quality and scope of leadership represented in this group. In addition to being members of the Chapel Board, one or more of these students held significant leadership positions in the following campus organizations: the Athletic Governing Board, Student Senate, Convocation Committee, editorships of both the *Daily Orange* (student newspaper) and the *Onondagan* (yearbook), Student Union, International Relations Club, Pan-Hellenic Association, Boar's Head (dramatic society), Sociology Club, YWCA, Syracuse-in-China, and the Student Church. In addition, many of the students held memberships in prestigious social or academic honorary societies, including the Monx Head, Men's Junior Class Honorary, Phi Kappa Alpha, Tau Theta Upsilon, Men's Senior Honoraries, Eta Pi Upsilon, and Women's Senior Honorary; one was a recipient of the Junior Medal, symbolizing the outstanding women of the junior class. Among the members a number had been elected to Phi Beta Kappa and Phi Kappa Phi in recognition of academic excellence. Marjorie Bronner Pierson has identified all of them in her excellent account. The purpose here is to underline the fact that this leadership group of students was of the highest quality and widest scope.*

The new Chapel Board was organized with Dr. Powers as its chairman and students as vice chairman and secretary, who along with Whitney Trousdale and Dean Mabel Lytton constituted the executive committee. Each student, with a faculty or staff adviser, was assigned to one of the committees responsible for the wide variety of activities that came under the work of the Chapel Board. The board held three meetings that spring. Committees listed that first year included music, worship services, selection of speakers, women's student conferences, discussion groups, social service, the relations between Hendricks Chapel and city churches, social relations, and the supervision of Syracuse-in-China. The Student Church services continued that year, and plans were formulated so that with the opening

---

*The organization and style of the student governance structure continued to characterize the chapel's overall operation until the 1950s, when the student climate evolved into very different patterns and attitudes.—RLP

of the chapel in the coming fall the program would be ready to go. In a sense, this first Chapel Board was a transition group, but it gave a clue to the quality and style of what was to develop.

At the close of the 1929–30 academic year, the work of the Student Church came to its conclusion. The student initiative and interest that led to its founding were strong contributing elements in the program that was being born. At the final pre-Hendricks Chapel service on May 17, 1930, the chairman of the Student Church paid tribute to Dr. Powers, who through the year had provided the leadership that had brought the program to this new stage:

> We are very sorry that Dr. Powers cannot be with us this morning on account of illness. Dr. Powers has been one of our choicest friends, and one of the rarest personalities that we have learned to know in our university experience. I believe I am expressing the sentiment of the students when I say that no finer man could have been secured for the position of Chaplain next year. I know it is the regret of many seniors that they will not be able to work with Dr. Powers as he has formulated the student program.*

During the spring of 1930, construction work was proceeding at a furious pace so that the chapel would be complete enough for dedication at commencement, which had been set for June 8, 1930. However, this had to encompass the alterations in the original building design made to incorporate some rooms for student activities and for offices on the floor below the auditorium. The process was further complicated by the nature of the heating arrangements, planned to provide an even distribution of heat at floor level. This involved building a plenum under the central portion of the main floor; any visitor to Hendricks Chapel today can readily see, underneath the pews, a multitude of small covered openings that send out heat.† The rooms downstairs were built around this central area and received some light from the outside windows. The *Daily Orange* of March 1, 1930, described Dr. Powers as noting "that there will be three very commodious and beautiful rooms on the floor below. The west room (32'6" X 34') will be equipped as a combination Board and social room. Here the Chapel Board will have its regular meetings. Dr. Powers will have his private office here, and a secretary's office adjoining it."

The boardroom had a large table and enough chairs to allow a sizable group of people to gather for meetings. Dr. Powers's office was fairly modest, having a desk, some chairs, and bookshelves. According to the same *Daily Orange* article, "The women's social room will be on the north, the size of which is 33'1" by 39'. Off

---

*Bronner, "The Student Church," 14.
†These heat tubes were removed in the 1985 remodeling of the chapel.—RLP

this room will be the private office of Dean Mabel C. Lytton, Religious Advisor to Women, and that of Miss Florence S. Kunz, Executive Secretary of Syracuse-in-China. The men's social room will be on the south side and will be 25'9" by 39' in size. Off this room will be the private office of the Rev. Whitney Trousdale, Student Counsellor for men."

Let me add some comments. The original arrangement of the rooms downstairs is very clear in my memory. Dr. Powers's office and the office of his secretary were indeed fairly modest. The other offices—an afterthought on the part of the architects—were tucked into very odd leftover spaces and lacked ventilation and outside light. The rooms downstairs were very tastefully furnished. The boardroom, Dr. Powers's office, and the Women's Social Room, later known as the Colonial Room and still later as the Noble Room, were furnished with Stickley furniture made in nearby Fayetteville.* The Men's Social Room became better known as the Men's Student Lounge and was furnished with Kittenger furniture made in Buffalo.

Even though these rooms had not been part of the original plans, the initial impression of them was one of attractiveness, and they proved to be very useful for a variety of functions. Until their redesign in the early McCombe years, however, it must be said that the offices were really never very satisfactory, even though they got a great deal of use.[†]

The exterior of the chapel and the auditorium were very impressive, and the description that follows obviously represents the conceptualization and the language of the two architects who designed the structure:

> The style is Georgian Colonial in type, with an auditorium seating 1450, making it third in size among university chapels of this country. The building is cruciform in plan. It faces the old oval, where it was placed as convenient to other buildings on the campus, and with the intention of later adding a large auditorium it its rear.
>
> The first floor level is raised nearly a full story height above the grade. Approach consists of a generous flight of stone steps with flanking buttresses, through six large Ionic columns of stone, to an open portico roofed with beamed and coffered ceiling, and crowned by a stone cornice and pediment, the tympanum containing the carved seal of the university.
>
> Entrance to the building is from the portico through one large central and two smaller flanking doors, pedimented and trimmed with stone, to a large vestibule which is woodwainscoted and paneled, with marble floor. A circular-

---

*The Stickley desk used by Dean Noble, and presumably by Powers before him, was used by Dean McCombe in his home office at 315 Berkeley Drive. I had the desk refurbished by Stickley in the early eighties, and it again became the desk in the dean's office in Hendricks Chapel.—RLP

[†]Even modern adjustments, such as exhaust fans in the windowless offices, have not taken care of the problems associated with the original oversights of Pope and Baum.—RLP

headed window at either end gives daylight and air to the vestibule. Provision is made here for memorial busts and tablets.

Entrance also may be had at grade level by means of four stair halls in re-entrant angles of the building. These stairs serve as student communication to basement, first, and balcony levels; all interconnected for best circulation.

Leading from the vestibule are three doors into a cross-corridor, which serves as a sound protection and cross connects two of the main stairs.

On the auditorium side of the corridor is a wood paneled screen extending from the floor to the plaster ceiling beneath the rear balcony above, and contains three circular-headed doorways, the central one being ornamented at the head.

The auditorium proper is in the form of a cube, sixty feet on all sides, with three appendages or arms containing balconies and the fourth semi-circular with domed and coffered ceiling, forming the chancel or rostrum. This accommodates a choir of sixty voices, seated in rows in front of six Corinthian columns.*

Behind the columns loosely draped is a deep rich red satin curtain with an applied pattern of gold, concealing the tone opening of the chamber containing the large concert organ. An echo organ chamber in conjunction is located opposite this opening on the rear balcony wall.

The whole interior is plaster and wood, and is attractively assembled in effect. The walls are wood-trimmed at openings, such as door and windows. The doors in the auditorium are leather-covered and studded with bronze nails. Two large groupings of windows, of Palladium motif and specially treated in wood, together with three large semi-circular clerestory windows, give direct light and air to the auditorium.

The ceiling is ribbed and coffered, and gives additional soft light from the eye of the dome by means of a circular ceiling sash with amber glass in the center. The three clerestory windows also contain the same glass; the others being of clear plate.

Extending around the auditorium, over the columns and pilasters, is a Corinthian cornice in the frieze of which, for the entire length, is an appropriate inscription in gold letters of Biblical quotations. Above the cornice, in four pedimented niches at the splays, are ornamental plaster urns. Below these, just above the first floor wainscot line, are four more niches of plaster to receive memorials, surrounded by small ornamental wood columns and rounded pediments.

The seating throughout is colonial in character, and of special design, with deep cushions which carry out the color scheme of the rostrum curtain. At one side of the rostrum is a very fine pulpit, the gift of the 1918 Class, and on the other a reading desk to match.

The color scheme entails an oyster white for walls, ceiling, painted wood, and furniture, with brown solid mahogany trim, rails and rests. The floor is of special composition tile in soft dark green tones in the auditorium and balconies, and of

*With the addition of chairs the choir area was expanded to accommodate a choir of approximately eighty-eight voices.—RLP

wood, carpeted for the rostrum. Acoustics have been given special consideration in the design and selection of materials.[*]

This description is essentially correct except for a few minor details. An early perspective drawing shows the chancel or rostrum area without the choir stalls, and that area was never carpeted. In the fall of 1930, when the organ was installed, the console was placed in the back of the area and surrounded by the choir pews. At a later date this arrangement was altered, but the visitor to Hendricks Chapel today will find the auditorium essentially unchanged from its original design.[†]

4. Dedication "To the Worship of Almighty God"

Not that we have lordship over your faith but are helpers of your joy.
—*II Corinthians 1:24*

God is a spirit, and they that worship Him must worship Him in spirit and in truth.
—*John 4:24*

Ye shall know the truth, and the truth shall set you free.
—*John 8:32*

IN THE SPRING OF 1930, by the time commencement was at hand, the chapel was ready enough that it could be dedicated and its first dean installed. The *Syracuse University Alumni News* of July 1930 carries a fairly complete account of the day's events; the dedication was in the afternoon and the installation in the evening. My recounting of what took place will rely heavily on that source supplemented by some other material, including what was provided by Marjorie Bronner Pierson. It is not noted who wrote the story in the *Alumni News*, but there are parts of it that require quoting in rather great detail.

A ceremony, fitting in simplicity, dignity and quiet splendor the structure which it sought to unite, marked the dedication of the Hendricks Chapel to the preserva-

---

[*]*Syracuse University Alumni News* 11, no. 10 (July 1930): 5 and 6.—RLP

[†]The renovation of 1985 kept the original plan in place and even completed some of the raised panel motifs around the stage that had not been completed in the original construction.—RLP

tion and promotion of the "moral and spiritual welfare of the generations of young men and women at Syracuse University." Attended by leaders of many of the principal religious bodies of this country, the service marked one of the most striking of modern instances of the union of all creeds for the one purpose which actuates them all—the worship of Almighty God.

Throngs filled the auditorium on the afternoon and evening of June 8, 1930 for this highlight of the sixtieth Commencement of Syracuse University. The afternoon sun illuminated the white walls and colorful red and gold hangings and smiled on the gathering of clergy, laymen, students, and alumni who had come from far and near to participate in the ceremony of dedication.

Symbolic of what we have come to know since of the ecumenical and inter-faith spirit which marked the character of the new chapel were a group of eight representatives from eight principal denominations and faith groups, each a leader in his own religious organization. Those participating from this group were as follows: Rt. Rev. Charles Fiske—Bishop of the Central New York Diocese of the Protestant Episcopal Church; Rev. Frederick Knubel—President of the United Lutheran Churches of America; Bishop Adna Wright Leonard—Bishop of the Central New York area of the Methodist Episcopal Church; Rev. Cleveland B. McAfee—Moderator of the General Assembly of the Presbyterian Church in the U.S.A.; Prof. William Lyon Phelps—Professor of English at Yale University and honorary pastor of the Calvary Baptist Church in New Haven, Connecticut; Fred B. Smith—Moderator of the General Council of Congregational Churches; Rabbi Stephen Wise—Rabbi, Free Synagogue, New York City; Most Rev. Daniel J. Curley—Bishop of the Syracuse Diocese of the Roman Catholic Church. Each received an honorary degree as part of the ceremony.

This assemblage was indeed a star-studded group of ecclesiastical officials, and Vice Chancellor Graham characterized them as "one of the most significant which has ever gathered in this county," as Marjorie Bronner Pierson recounted. The *Alumni News* continued with Graham's comments: "Absorbed in the peace and beauty of its whiteness, its blood-red and gold hangings, its deep-toned mahogany, the audience, filling to capacity its deep-cushioned benches, listened to the majesty of an old, measured Oxford hymn, then to Dr. Bernard Clausen, as he read the scripture."

There is a fascinating account of this reading that was written several years later by Ernest J. Bowden in his column in the *Syracuse Post-Standard* (the Syracuse morning newspaper). As nearly as I can place it, this account was written during the summer of 1948:

> While at Hendricks I took another look at the foot-high letters under the dome. They are a reminder of the late Dean Powers who chose them to express the spirit of the chapel organization he set up and to which he gave the crowning years of his life.

But they are also a reminder of the most dramatic touch that I ever saw there, or in any other place of worship. For obvious reasons it didn't get into the record when it happened. When the building was dedicated, a number of ministers were invited to take part. Rev. Dr. Bernard C. Clausen was the outstanding preacher of Syracuse and could not be overlooked, but he was spectacular. Conservative folk were a bit afraid of him; so he was given the very minor assignment of reading the scripture.

Now I don't want to belittle the public reading of the Scriptures, for there are times when it can become a great experience. But on an occasion of that kind it is a reverential chore, and in a life-time of public meetings, I have never seen a man who could make it anything more—except Clausen.

He did his part modestly, without fireworks. Then suddenly he became electric. Stepping back from the lectern, he fixed his eyes on the frieze that runs under the dome and read its text with voice and style that made them luminous: "Ye shall know the truth, and the truth shall make you free. . . . Not that we have lordship over your faith, but are helpers of your joy. . . . God is a spirit, and they that worship Him must worship Him in spirit and in truth."

Bowden concludes, "It is the only part of the dedication that I remember."

If not quite so dramatic, there were other parts of the service that were deeply significant. The Reverend Lucius Bugbee offered a prayer, and the principal speaker of the day was Bishop Adna Wright Leonard, who was introduced by Chancellor Flint. Flint cited him as "the representative of the denomination whose early initiative and early sacrifice made possible Syracuse University; a member of the denomination which seeks no denominational advantage or favor because of the service it has rendered."

Bishop Leonard pointed to the need of religion in motivating knowledge:

The purpose of planting a place for religious worship like this in this university is evidence of the fact that without religion, knowledge may be a detriment, morality may become a dissipation, and the highest aims of life utterly frustrated, unless from a religious motive we understand that life does not consist in the abundance of things that we possess—rather in what we are. May this be the motive of this chapel in its fullest expression—to recognize all other faiths, though this be the expression without apology to the Christian faith; God helping us and this institution to be able to see from the standpoint of the One who went about doing good and who was "the way, the truth, and the life"; to say to the oncoming generations We're keeping an honest watch ahead.

Then followed Fred B. Smith, a Congregationalist, who said, with disarming frankness, "I am a former asbestos merchant, and to mingle me with all these ecclesiastics is a good deal of a strain, all in one day. In my judgment, this is the greatest hour in the history of the university thus far." He then went on to point out the advantage and popularity of education but warned that education without godliness is self-defeating. "Many institutions in the country today calling themselves universities and colleges are engaged only in the colossal business of turning out a lot of 'clever devils.' So I thank God that in this university I love so much, this afternoon, dedicating a chapel, . . . here upon this sacred spot religion shall not die out."

In presenting the Reverend Cleveland B. McAfee, moderator of the Presbyterian Church, as the next speaker, Chancellor Flint noted that Senator Hendricks was a member of the Presbyterian Church. McAfee responded that he was glad that the Presbyterians were behind the establishment of the chapel. He pointed out that religion is something to be lived, and in order to have its proper influence with students religion cannot be presented "in a vague, general way. It has to be done by making religion atmospheric, pervasive. I hope that all religions will come here, but you will not help them best if there is any temporizing about the Christian convictions. I plead that this chapel, dedicated to the Christian Faith, may be so soundly and definitely Christian that every man who comes here will find his religious life deepened and strengthened by it."

To the Reverend Albert C. Fulton, pastor of the First Presbyterian Church of Syracuse, the home church of the donor, fell the privilege of making the presentation of the chapel.

> I have the privilege of presenting what I believe to be the purpose and expectation of Francis Hendricks in giving Syracuse University this memorial chapel. It is not possible to analyze and portray the full intention of Senator Hendricks in making this generous gift, though it is significant that a man of his practical experience and eminent success in the world of banking and politics should embody the essential and final idealism of his life in this temple of religion. . . . [H]e saw, with that clear discernment which made him the wise counselor in what ever conference he might be called, that there must be a citadel and a shrine which would shelter and proclaim the soul-life of it all, and it pleased him to set it forth in the impressive beauty which surrounds us here in this memorial.

Dr. Fulton went on to speak of the inspiration that Senator Hendricks had found in the chapel at Williams College:

> And it was there that he planned this chapel for Syracuse University. What would minister to the life of an eminently practical man, a man wise in experience and who had come to the years that bring the philosophic mind, would minister to the lives of others, and at a time when for them life was not receding, but emerging.
>
> It was as though he was appraising life and giving prominence to his understanding of its essential values and setting it forth in this symbol of the spiritual

and eternal. . . . In assigning this generous gift to this lofty purpose he has unconsciously set forth his hopes and affirmed his faith, the full measure of which will be realized in the complete dedication of this house of prayer, to the worship of God and the service of man.

The pastor turned then to Chancellor Flint and said, "And, Mr. Chancellor, I hereby instruct, on behalf of the donor, that Mr. Dwight James Baum now transfer the key of this chapel to the President of the Board of Trustees."

Baum, who with John Russell Pope planned this memorial, rose in his place beside Chancellor Flint and handed the key to Fred B. Smith, saying, "Mr. Chancellor, it is a great honor to present this master key to the institution. We hope that it will serve many generations of students." He turned to Smith and said, "I give the master key over to you."

Smith responded:

The late Francis Hendricks was a wonderful and staunch friend of Syracuse University. Syracuse has been greatly benefited by his wisdom. He was deeply interested in the future university. He was also interested in the campus and in Hendricks Field. But the one thing that was uppermost in his mind, was the fact that this institution was founded under Christian auspices. And he gave this beautiful building to better their purposes. On behalf of the trustees of Syracuse University I accept this Chapel.

Then slowly, impressively, Chancellor Flint pronounced the dedicatory declaration: "For the Worship and service of Almighty God, for the Diffusion of the Spirit and Ideal of Jesus Christ; for the Moral and Spiritual Welfare of the Generations of Young Men and Women at Syracuse University; to God the Father and to American Youth His Children, We Dedicate this Chapel."

Following this pronouncement came the conferring of honorary degrees upon the religious leaders who came as representatives of their national religious bodies. Fittingly climaxing the solemn service came the dedication hymn by William Cullen Bryant of Williams College:

> Thou whose unmeasured temple stands,
> Built over earth and sea,
> Accept the walls that human hands,
> Have raised, O God, to thee.

The benediction was pronounced by Dr. William H. Powers, who, later in the day, was to be installed as the first dean of Hendricks Chapel.

5. Installation of the First Dean

THE INSTALLATION of the Reverend William Harrison Powers, D.D., as dean of Hendricks Chapel took place at half past seven in the evening on June 8, 1930, the same day the chapel was dedicated.

Dr. Powers's original appointment was to the chaplaincy of Syracuse University, but the commitment had been made that when the chapel was complete he would become its first dean. The purpose of this plan was quite clear: it was intended to give the position of the professional leadership of Hendricks Chapel the status and level of support accorded the several academic deans on campus. A precedent for this action had been set at other universities, most notably Princeton and the University of Chicago. Now the time had come to fulfill this commitment and to emphasize the significance that Syracuse University accorded the religious program at the "heart" of its life.

On this day, as the brilliant sunshine of the afternoon slowly faded into twilight, people once again filled the 1,450 seats in the auditorium of the new structure. After a hymn was sung, an invocation and Scripture reading were given by two ministers from the city of Syracuse, respectively the Reverend Ray Freeman Jenny of Park Central Presbyterian Church and the Reverend Robert Bruce of Plymouth Congregational Church. Then, with quiet dignity, Vice Chancellor Emeritus Smalley presented Dr. Powers to Chancellor Charles Wesley Flint, who gave the charge to the deanship by saying:

> This afternoon we dedicated the chapel to the service and worship of Almighty God, to the diffusion of the spirit and ideals of Jesus Christ and to promote the moral and spiritual welfare of the generations of students at Syracuse University. We now install you, William Harrison Powers, son of Syracuse, ordained Christian minister, to the deanship of the chapel for the same purposes then expressed.
>
> You will superintend the worship and service of God in this place, you will endeavor to diffuse the spirit and ideals of Jesus Christ. Superior to any sectarian bias and apart from any denominational appeal you will seek unalloyedly to serve for moral under girding and for spiritual development all the students of all religious associations equally, in the recognition of the singleness of the religious problem and in the confidence that whatever enriches the spiritual level of one group will lift the level of all.
>
> You are inducted into this office, not that you may in the remotest degree exercise lordship over the faith of any, but that you may be a fellow helper toward the truth that makes free, toward the peace that passeth understanding and toward the joy that fadeth not away.
>
> You will provide out of your own intellectual and spiritual life and out of the

inner life of inspirational leaders of all denominations, messages which will enlighten the minds and stir the souls of the students, to the end that the highest things, the things that are eternal may have their due place in the life of Syracuse University.

As a human instrument and representative of human instrumentality I install you in this office, but it is not by the might of appointment, not by the power of office that you will succeed. May God himself anoint you for the tremendous task now devolving upon you.*

To this charge, the new dean responded to the chancellor with obvious sincerity, voicing his thoughtful vision for the task ahead.

While I am deeply conscious of the honor bestowed upon me this hour I am also conscious of a sense of deep obligation to be true to the implications of its bestowment. This day of great rejoicing will soon echo only in memory. Soon a host of youth will find their way into the life of this university and the hum of curricular and extra-curricular activity will begin. The chapel has been located where cross the crowded ways of youth. But it will take something more than a beautiful Georgian Colonial college chapel to make them pause and turn their minds to sincere worship and spiritually triumphant living. To this task you as executive head of this institution have called me and those associated with me in a definitely religious field.

You have given me this night a name and an honor, but neither a name nor an honor can continue to live unless it becomes the by-product of a character, a consecration and a valid performance. The terrific pressure of this necessity humbles and yet challenges me.

To your leadership, my dear chancellor, I pledge my loyalty; to my colleagues administrative and faculty, I pledge my sincerest cooperation and to the oncoming student life I pledge my most earnest purpose to teach and practice religion so that my office and ministry as dean of Hendricks Chapel may be translated into a beautiful spirit of sincere and helpful friendship.

In the words of the significant Scripture quotations on the frieze of this auditorium I purpose to be not a dominator of credal rationale, but to share with others the joy of Him who said, "These things I have spoken unto you that my joy might remain in you and that your joy may be full." In the belief that "God is Spirit" I shall join audibly and silently with those of all faiths while we "worship Him in Spirit and in truth."

With the great Master teacher of the ages we shall seek to know the truth believing that as we under His teaching find the truth in ideas and ideals we shall experience the only real freedom human personality can know.

Believing in a God of patience and love, believing in the broadminded and sympathetic spirit of my colleagues on the hill and believing in the fine character and purposes of the youth of this generation and especially in that youth which in so short a time will again cover our campus, I pledge myself to do all that human strength will permit and an honest purpose shall inspire to honor the name and place I now hold in the life and destiny of Syracuse University.

The speaker for the installation service was the widely known and highly re-spected professor William Lyon Phelps of Yale University. His sermon was entitled "The Courage of Ignorance," and excerpts from it appeared in the *Alumni News* of July 1930.

As Sunday, June 8, 1930, came to its close, something new had been added to the life of Syracuse University. A new chapel now stood at the heart of the campus and a new dean had been installed to direct its program. It was a day that was to in-augurate a whole new era in the life of Syracuse University.

6. The First Year of Service, 1930–1931

WITH THE OPENING of the university term in the fall of 1930, students who had been away from campus for the summer came back to see the new chapel that was now dedicated and virtually complete, standing impressively at the west end of what had been called the Old Oval. Beyond what they could see in terms of the building, however, was the fact that Hendricks Chapel was ready to welcome them and share with them in programs and activities of wide-ranging religious concerns. Under the leadership of Dean Powers and his staff and with the input of the Chapel Board of the previous spring term, the comprehensive plan to involve any student so inclined in its life was ready to be put into operation. The doors of Hen-dricks Chapel were open now, and students not only could see what the interior of the building looked like but also were given an opportunity to discover what activ-ity was alive inside.

Almost all programs previously scattered among various locations on campus now had a common home and the cohesion afforded by the leadership of the chapel's professional staff. Dean Powers, who had moved his office from the Men's Gymnasium to his new quarters, located on the lower floor just off the Chapel Boardroom, was the key figure in program development. He was at once dean and administrator, worship leader and preacher, staff director and coor-dinator, and counselor and friend to any and all students. The Reverend Whitney

Trousdale, whose office had been located in the Administration Building, now centered his activities in his new office off the Men's Social Room, located on the south side of the lower floor of the chapel. Dean Lytton, who was working both as religious adviser to women and as adviser to the YWCA, now operated from her new office, located off the Women's Social Room on the north side of the chapel's lower floor.

At this time, two new members of the chapel staff made their appearance. Bernice Meredith joined the staff as executive secretary of Syracuse-in-China to coordinate and promote interest and support for this overseas outreach mission of Syracuse University. Meredith, who had graduated from SU in 1929, had been an outstanding campus leader in her undergraduate days, serving, among other leadership and honor roles, as head of the Women's Student Senate; president of Eta Pi Upsilon, the women's senior honorary; and May queen.*

Professor Earl D. Stout was chosen as director of Hendricks Chapel music and as such was the organist and director of the chapel choir. Stout also had impressive credentials. He was a graduate of Syracuse University in the class of 1916. After serving on several music faculties—at Pennsylvania State Normal School and as head of the Music Department at Southwestern University—he was called back to his alma mater in 1924 to be professor of piano. He had also been the organist and choir director at Plymouth Congregational Church and later at the First Methodist Church in Syracuse. For three years previously, he had directed the Men's Glee Club at Syracuse University, winning it recognition as an outstanding music organization.

During his first year Dean Powers's daughter worked with him as his secretary, with an office adjoining his own. Thelma Powers was a graduate of Cornell University, where she had had an active undergraduate career and had prepared herself with secretarial skills for her job at Hendricks Chapel.

I was a member of the first Hendricks Chapel Board to function in the new chapel building. Its members had been selected the previous spring; after the chapel's dedication, they prepared to help the staff and faculty launch or continue the university's religious activities from its new location. This Hendricks Chapel Board was a functional one, with each student being given a specific area of responsibility and a staff or faculty adviser. Those individuals composing the student membership of the Chapel Board had been chosen because of their leadership either in an established program or in one projected as a new religious activity sponsored by the chapel. Three members of this new board—all seniors—were students who had served on the earlier board the previous spring; one member, Marjorie Bronner, held memberships in Phi Beta Kappa, Phi Kappa Phi, and Eta Pi Upsilon

*After marrying Donald G. Wright, she joined SU's faculty, serving as dean of the College of Home Economics (renamed the College for Human Development) between 1964 and 1973.—RLP

and had been active in the university's religious life from the days of the Student Church.* She took on the responsibility for the daily-chapel services. Her experiences in the Student Church gave her the background to handle this task. Dorothy Flood, vice president of her class and a member of the Women's Student Senate and Eta Pi Upsilon, the women's senior honorary society, continued as secretary of the board. Ewart Blaine, now the editor of the *Daily Orange* and chairman of the Convocation Committee and of Phi Kappa Alpha, the men's senior honorary society, was put in charge of publicity—a highly appropriate assignment.

The new members selected were the two student chairmen of the board. The women's student chairman was Margaret Iglehart, a senior, the daughter of missionaries to Japan, president of the YWCA, and a member of the Cosmopolitan Club and Eta Pi Upsilon. I was the men's student chairman. At that time a junior, I was the son of a Methodist minister; an active student on campus in athletics, drama, and music; the manager of the lacrosse team; soloist and first president of the chapel choir; and a member of Corpse and Coffin, the men's junior honorary society. I later became a member of Phi Kappa Alpha, the men's senior honorary society. We presided alternately at meetings of the Chapel Board under the direction of Dean Powers. Other new members of the board were Marjorie Farley, who was active in the Women's Congress, the Student Union, the University Chorus and Glee Club, the Liberal Club, and in debating; Irwin Hannum, a member of the American Society of Chemical Engineers, the Men's Student Senate, and the band; Helen Laidlaw, a junior who was active in the YWCA (and would become its president), sang in the chapel choir and university chorus, and later became a member of Eta Pi Upsilon; and Mildred David, whose activities reflected her two chief interests of music and international relations: she sang in the university chorus and Glee Club and belonged to the Cosmopolitan Club and Syracuse-in-China (eventually becoming its president).

Later, two more members were added to the board: Brewer Burnett and Joseph Hogben. As reported by the *Daily Orange* of October 27, 1930, they were nominated at a Chapel Board meeting held Friday, October 23, and their names were sent to the chancellor of the university for appointment. Brewer Burnett, a junior, was a justice of the Student Court and sang in the Glee Club. In his senior year, he would become men's student chairman of the board. Joseph Hogben was a distinguished scholar and a member of Phi Kappa Phi.

I find it noteworthy that three members of this Chapel Board later became Christian ministers. Burnett became a minister in the Presbyterian Church; Hogben became a priest in the Protestant Episcopal Church, serving as a missionary to the Ute Indians; and I became a minister in the Methodist Church, later returning to Syracuse to become minister at the University United Methodist Church.

*See appendix A.—RLP

The opening of Hendricks Chapel in fall 1930 set off a series of exciting events that together generated a feeling that something new and significant had come to the Syracuse University campus. The programs planned in the spring and summer of 1930 and sponsored that fall by the Chapel Board now got under way. As far as can be determined, the first of these was the renewal of the Freshman Camp for men. Freshman Camp had been conducted by the Student Union in 1929 at the YMCA camp at Sandy Pond on Lake Ontario. In fall 1930, the Freshman Camp for men was held at Lake Moraine, near Hamilton, New York, at the site owned by the Utica YMCA. Ewart Blaine was student chairman, and the Reverend Whitney Trousdale was adviser. Approximately seventy-five to eighty men attended. Transported to the camp by bus from the Syracuse University campus, they spent the weekend becoming acquainted and receiving an orientation to campus life.

About the same time, the Chapel Board set up a booth at the local railway station to welcome new students and to help direct them to the campus and their living quarters. Volunteers also answered any immediate questions the arriving students had.

The week of September 16 was Freshman Week, and the chapel planned many activities and opportunities for orientation for the incoming students. Freshmen women were invited to the Big Sisters Tea in the Women's Lounge of Hendricks Chapel, held between three to five o'clock in the afternoon of Thursday, September 18. The tea was sponsored by the Chapel Board through the YWCA under the chairmanship of Marion Wilner. Notices in the *Daily Orange* and elsewhere that week also invited new students to tryouts for the chapel choir, to be held in the studio of Professor Stout at Crouse College. Anyone—student or faculty member— would be eligible to sing in the choir and would be given one credit hour for faithful participation. A later notice in the *Daily Orange* announced that those singers accepted into the choir should come to Hendricks Chapel Friday evening for the first rehearsal. The publicity release for Hendricks Chapel had focused on the choir and the fact that a full-tuition scholarship would be given to each of four students selected as soloists. There were sixty-three singers in the choir. The soloists were Hope C. Johnson, soprano; Dorothy E. Dudley, contralto; William C. Bedford, tenor; and myself, bass.

My recollection of that first rehearsal is quite clear. Professor Stout handed out the music. There is no way that I can document it, but I am quite sure that the first music rehearsed was the anthem "The Sun Shall Be No More Thy Light by Day." I remember being impressed with how well the rehearsal went, as the members were mostly music students with good voices and good music-reading ability. This rehearsal was indeed a genesis: the first of an almost countless number of times that great sacred music would be rendered by the special quality of the student voices of the Hendricks Chapel Choir. Even though it had not had many opportunities to practice, the choir was ready when Sunday arrived, and we performed well.

Hendricks Chapel's first regular worship service was held at eleven o'clock on Sunday, September 21, 1930. The day before, the *Daily Orange* had announced the event with an editorial; headlined "Go to Church," it urged students to take advantage of this new religious facility on campus, commenting, "The Chapel, and the inauguration of student services on the Hill tomorrow, make us feel that a definite and adequate religious program has at last become a part of our college life." On Saturday evening the first wedding was held in the chapel—the first of many services held to unite students in marriage. On that evening, September 20, with Dean Powers officiating, Mary Isabel Bacon became the bride of Frederick William Hagy.

On Sunday morning the Hendricks Chapel auditorium was well filled. Dean Powers presided over the service. Professor Stout played the new organ, the choir sang its anthem, and Hope Johnson, the soprano soloist, sang "How Beautiful upon the Mountains." Chancellor Flint, a minister in the Methodist Episcopal Church, preached the sermon "The University in Relation to the Student's Religion." He based his sermon on the Scripture words from the frieze, "Not that we have Lordship over your faith but are helpers of your joy" (2 Cor. 1:24). Dean Powers had worked with enormous diligence and searched the Scriptures carefully to find passages that would epitomize his philosophy of what the Hendricks Chapel program ought to be. I have no doubt that Powers consulted with Chancellor Flint about the content of his first service, and this theme was chosen to be the first presented in the chapel. The following Sunday morning Dean Powers would preach on another one of these Scripture passages.

The next of the so-called first events in the new chapel occurred the very next morning, Monday, September 22, 1930, when daily chapel was inaugurated. Marjorie Bronner had responsibility for these services. She was assisted by Dean Powers and the other members of the staff. The services were held each weekday at half past eight and lasted twenty minutes. The service included a hymn, Scripture, prayer, and a brief meditation or sermonette delivered by the worship leader. No one knew how well the services would be supported; the venture was made in faith. An editorial in the *Daily Orange* on October 1, 1930, indicated how things were going in this new religious enterprise: "Religion forms a large part of the college life of the average student, if the attendance at daily-chapel services is any indication. According to Dr. Powers, dean of the new Hendricks Chapel, the response of the student body during the first week has been highly gratifying, considering the fact that the project is an experiment and on a purely voluntary basis."

Over its the first year, the publicity given to Hendricks Chapel events in the *Daily Orange* was widespread, detailed, and favorable, which was not surprising: Ewart Blaine, its editor, was very active in the chapel programs, and with all the new activity going on the chapel generated considerable "news." Before the weekend there would be a story about the upcoming chapel service on Sunday morn-

The late Donald G. Wright, senior minister of the University United Methodist Church, in 1992. Wright was a student at Syracuse University when Hendricks Chapel was being built in 1929–30 and served on the first Chapel Board. Courtesy of Phyllis Wright.

ing, announcing who the preacher would be and any special features of that service. Then, very often, there would be a follow-up story on the main features of the sermon and almost always a small box on the front page about the daily-chapel service.

On Sunday, September 28, at the second worship service, Dr. Powers preached his first sermon as dean. Entitled "Freedom through Truth," it was based on the second of the three Scripture passages inscribed on the frieze, "Ye Shall Know the Truth and the Truth Shall Make You Free." Among his remarks about the chapel, Dean Powers commented: "Here the students of all creeds and no creed, of all races and nationalities may find the true essentials of a universal religion. Truth, then, is first of all 'idea' producing freedom from ignorance, error and superstition. It is 'ideal' producing freedom from a restricted universalism; it is 'idealism' as a universal religion producing freedom from the artificial barriers of religion, racial boundaries and social caste."

The third Sunday morning, October 5, was given over to dedicating the new chapel organ. A generous gift from Kathryn Hendricks, Senator Hendricks's niece, it was installed after the chapel was dedicated. Early in 1930, a committee that included Dr. George Parker, head of the Organ Department; Dr. Harold Butler, dean of the College of Fine Arts; and Dean Powers ordered an organ from the Aeolian Company of New York City. This company had built many concert and church organs, and after deliberations and comparisons with three other organ companies the committee settled on the Aeolian organ. Once installed, it became the largest organ on campus, being one-third larger than the organ in Crouse College. It had four manuals and approximately five thousand pipes with an echo chamber in the rear of the balcony. An additional feature was the concertola attachment that could be set to play organ compositions without manual assistance, a kind of modern and sophisticated player-piano arrangement. Instead of the usual organ case for the pipes and chests, the fixed installation was just behind the columns on the platform and was screened by grilled wainscoting and a silken curtain.

The organ was ready for use at the first chapel service in September, but its dedication came both during the worship service on Sunday, October 5, and at a dedicatory recital held the following Wednesday evening. At the Sunday service Professor Stout played a special series of compositions for the prelude and then the Hallelujah chorus at the conclusion as a special number before the postlude. Dean Powers preached a sermon titled "Music and Worship," after which Chancellor Flint led the congregation in a responsive dedicatory affirmation, concluding with the following words:

> For the comfort of the sorrowing, for the strengthening of the weak, the cheering of the weary, the stirring of the soul to repentance, the swelling of the chorus of praise and for help in the singing of God's praise, we, Thy children in Divine presence, grateful for our lofty inheritance and for the love which prompts the gift, do joyously dedicate this organ to the service of God and the service of mankind, in the name and spirit of Jesus Christ, our Lord and Master.

On Wednesday, October 8, Firmin Swinnen played the dedicatory recital. Swinnen was a distinguished Belgian organist who, at the time, was the concert organist for Pierre DuPont of Wilmington, Delaware, who owned an Aeolian concert organ. Swinnen was also the concert organist for the University of Delaware. One dollar general admission and fifty cents for students was asked for the recital. Ushers were women of the Chapel Board under the leadership of the women's student chairman, Margaret Iglehart. Swinnen played a variety of organ pieces chosen especially to display the organ's versatility. He began with the brilliant Tocatta and Fugue in D Minor by Bach and concluded with his own transcription of the largo and finale from Dvorak's *New World Symphony*.

Sunday, October 12, was the occasion of the first guest preacher at the morning worship service. Dean Powers had announced that although he would be the regular preacher, in order to fulfill his commitment that the chapel would be a place for those individuals of all religious persuasions he would bring preachers from various denominations and faith groups to the Hendricks Chapel pulpit. The first of these preachers was the Reverend Dr. James Gordon Gilkey, minister of the South Congregational Church in Springfield, Massachusetts, a widely regarded speaker to students across the country.

By this time the inaugural year's activities at Hendricks Chapel were well under way. Although there would be considerable development ahead, the main outlines of its direction and scope were beginning to appear. Early that fall the chapel had published its first brochure, *Information Concerning the Religious Program at Syracuse University, 1930–31.* On the cover an artist's drawing of the new chapel building was presented along with a listing of the chapel staff. Contained inside the brochure were sections dealing with the gift of the chapel, its dedication, and the purpose for its establishment followed by a more detailed description of the staff. There was a section written to give students "some idea of the varied program of Hendricks Chapel." Mentioned here were Sunday worship, daily chapel, and the quiet hour at four o'clock in the afternoon when organ music would be played and students might come in for meditation and reflection. The makeup of the Chapel Board was described but not listed. There was a brief mention about activities of the chapel program, including "religious discussion groups, campus and inter-university conferences, extension work in religion and social service, and such other types of activity as may be provided by the Y.W.C.A., the Oxford Fellowship and the Syracuse-in-China Committee."

Considerable space was given in this initial publication to "church and chapel relations," a noteworthy inclusion because, especially at the beginning, it was one of the two principal problem areas that appeared with the establishment of Hendricks Chapel. It has been indicated previously that many of the nearby churches (some far more than others) had ongoing programs of worship and religious activity for university students. To be confronted by a well-staffed religious program, centrally located on campus, and with the announced intention to meet the religious needs of all students at Syracuse University meant considerable accommodation on the part of the nearby churches. They responded to the situation in different ways and with varying degrees of concern. There is no doubt that Dean Powers saw the development of the chapel program as the center of religious activity, but he was also aware of those people who had an investment in student religious programs and who believed that chapel could but should not take the place of church. A section of the first chapel brochure entitled "Church and Chapel Relations" contained the following statement:

> With Hendricks Chapel on the university campus, the student is immediately faced with the question, "Where shall I have my church affiliation during my college days?" In answer to this question, it may be said that as far as the dean of the chapel and his staff are concerned, a student is given absolute freedom in deciding whether he shall affiliate with Hendricks Chapel or with the local church of his denomination. The ultimate purpose of the entire program is that the student shall align himself with either the chapel or the local church during his sojourn in Syracuse and after graduation he shall immediately transfer his affiliation to the church of his faith in the community where he shall reside.

The next section of the brochure, entitled "The Local Church," had a slightly more positive emphasis:

> The churches of Syracuse are very fortunate in the quality of leadership which their clergy provide. Many of the pulpits of these churches are filled by as able men as can be found. The spirit of friendship on the part of the church members is an attractive feature of the church life. Priest, Pastor, Rabbi unite in offering to the student opportunities for worship and fellowship of the finest kind. Every student should have at least some contact with the church of his particular faith.

Following this section was a full page listing Syracuse's eighteen Protestant churches, three Roman Catholic churches, and one Jewish temple, with their locations and the times of their services and other activities.

The *Daily Orange* of September 18, 1930, printed the following announcement:

> At the invitation of the Dean, clergymen representing eight different religious groups will have their representatives in the office rooms of the chapel during Freshmen registration. Each student will receive one appointment card introducing him to the clergyman of his own faith and he can then meet the religious leader for the informal conference.
>
> In addition Dr. Powers has invited each of these clergymen to make use of the chapel offices for a half a day each week in order that he may have more immediate contact with the students who wish to consult with him.

After the Hendricks Chapel program had been in operation approximately four months, Ernest Bowden, in the *Syracuse Post-Standard,* wrote the following column about the chapel:

> One question remains to be settled—shall it be another church, in competition with the services of the city or shall it be an inspirational center, giving every other church a sense of reinforcement? A great deal depends on the attitude of the churches. But Dean Powers is emphatic in his own view and purpose. He couldn't accommodate a quarter of the students if he wanted to. His ideal is to develop a spirit of religious enterprise that shall send them out eager to take their share of work in every church within range.

This euphoric comment did not really confront the issue involved or settle the problem that remained throughout the early life of the chapel. With its coming, a whole new situation was created, and we shall follow its development in the succeeding years.

The other principal issue that developed very early in the life of Hendricks

Chapel was the question of just how and for what the chapel building was to be used. It was not difficult for anyone associated with the university in those days to know why any number of individuals and groups, not related to the chapel, looked with hungry eyes upon the facilities provided by this new structure. Their hope was that within this spacious and attractive building there would be room to house their special interests. Space, such as the chapel provided—even with the social rooms in the basement as an afterthought—was in extremely short supply on campus. This situation had existed for a long time and would continue to do so for many years to come. It was inevitable that there would be great demand both for the use of the social rooms and for the large seating capacity of the main chapel. To be sure, there was the Crouse College auditorium that was used primarily for musical events and some dramatic productions, but there was no campus theater building for drama or a student union building to house a wide variety of student recreational and social activities.

Either in anticipation or more probably because requests had already come in, the first decision made when the first Chapel Board met was to make a statement about the use of the chapel. The *Daily Orange,* on March 6, 1930, reported the following:

> During the first session of the chapel board, the question was raised as to whether the chapel would be used for other than religious purposes. Dr. Powers stated that since it was the wish of the donor that the chapel be used for religious purposes only and due to the fact that its employment for other functions would detract from the significance of the religious nature of the chapel, it is probable that the chapel would not be used for things unrelated to religious development.

Of course, the matter did not end there, and, as a matter of fact, it has never completely ended—as Dean Powers and his successors would discover. There was a very powerful emotional appeal written soon after the chapel opened. In the report of the Firmin Swinnen dedicatory recital, after the review was given of the organ concert, the writer made the following concluding remarks: "We left the auditorium mourning over the fact that concerts and dramatic presentations are not to be given in the chapel which would be an ideal setting for them. If mourning will do the cause any good, we would wear black for the rest of the school year and write only tragedies."

Requests poured in until, in response, the following editorial appeared in the *Daily Orange* on October 13, 1930, entitled "Chapel or Auditorium?"

> In connection with the new Hendricks Chapel there has arisen some unfortunate and misconceived notions as to the purposes for which the edifice is to be used. Certain individuals on the campus, piqued because their own particular interests

are not to be served by accommodations in the building, have been prone to describe the attempt which is being made to keep the chapel what it was intended to be—a place of worship. The Dean of the chapel has already permitted considerable latitude in his definition of what he considers "religious purposes." Rooms have been provided in the basement for various student enterprises that bespeak this broadmindedness. It should be remembered, however, that the man who provided approximately $700,000 for the chapel did so with the proviso that it should be dedicated to devotional uses. Even if for no other reason the memory and hopes of this great man should serve to keep the chapel from becoming a playhouse or common auditorium. We hope the time will come in the near future when Syracuse University will have the kind of a building for various student presentations and activities which it deserves. But let us not confuse this need with the object of Hendricks Chapel.

It can be said again that this editorial did not settle the issue, and from time to time the question would rise again, particularly as the university faced very great pressures over the uses of space that taxed its limited facilities.

One regular feature of the fall season at Syracuse University was the Alumni Weekend. Many graduates would come back—usually for a football game and associated social activities—to meet old friends and to remember their college days. The fall of 1930 had something new in store for the returning alumni, most of whom had not seen Hendricks Chapel and the changed appearance of the Old Oval. In order to set off the new chapel properly, tons of earth were brought in to landscape its approach, which many of the older graduates remembered as a dry, dusty, and fairly unkempt area. Now the approach was green with growing grass that set off the new building and added considerably to its appearance.

It was thought that something special might be arranged to give the returning alumni a chance to experience the new chapel. A special program was set up for Saturday morning that would be brief and completed well before the afternoon football game got under way in Archbold Stadium. Daily chapel was held at half past eight, and at half past ten that morning a special service was held featuring selections by the choir and organist and remarks by Chancellor Flint and Dean Powers. A special tour of the building was arranged for anyone who cared to participate.

As the fall semester moved along there was a growing and steady movement of traffic around the chapel as it began to be an integral part of university life. The Chapel Board met regularly, presided over by its student chairmen, heard reports, formulated policy, and planned the innovations that came with frequency in that first year. There is an interesting report that came out of the Chapel Board meeting of October 24, 1930. It was decided to let all on campus know that membership on the Chapel Board had certain standards that were delineated as follows: "Student members of the Chapel Board must be in good standing in their college, they must not be on probation, ineligible, or rate below a 'c' average."

The services of worship on Sunday morning, once begun, continued with strong student, faculty, administration, and community support. At each service, except for vacation periods, the chapel was "comfortably" filled, and it was estimated reliably that in that first year the average attendance was approximately one thousand at each service. In addition to Dean Powers, other clergymen well known for their ability to speak to students were invited to occupy the pulpit, and the list for the year was a very distinguished one. Aside from Dr. Gilkey, others included Dr. George B. Cutten, president of Colgate University; Bishop Adna Wright Leonard, the presiding bishop of the Methodist Episcopal Church; Dr. John Timothy Stone of the Presbyterian Theological Seminary in Chicago; Rabbi Ferdinand Isserman of St. Louis; Dr. Henry Hallum Tweedy of the Yale Divinity School; Dr. Charles Jefferson of the Broadway Tabernacle in New York City; and Kirby Page, one of the leading social prophets of the time. Here was a sampling of the widespread denominational and faith groups' representation considered important by Powers and others.

From the beginning, the choir, under the direction of Professor Stout, lived up to the high expectations and established an outstanding reputation. The choir, together with the organ music by Professor Stout, gave a notable lift to the worship service. The number of singers allowed to participate in the choir matched the seating capacity of the choir space—approximately sixty-three, including the four soloists.

Two special innovations by Dean Powers added distinction to the services at Hendricks Chapel almost from the beginning. Ushers, under the direction of Wellington Truran that first year, were chosen from among the most prestigious campus leaders and included many of the outstanding campus athletes. Fraternities, sororities, and students from various campus living centers were invited to attend the services in a group and were welcomed in special fashion. A note in the printed program indicated their presence.* Student input into the planning of the Sunday services was reasonably minimal, though suggestions for speakers were welcomed. The ushers, however, were selected by the students.

The daily chapel was much more the product of students, and Marjorie Bronner Pierson, who was chairman of the Daily Chapel Committee the first year, tells us that its success was largely the result of student effort:

---

*This practice remained the pattern for chapel attendance until the mid-1960s, when chapel attendance stopped being counted in the Greek Supremacy Trophy competition. According to Dean Charles Noble, that change is what brought the era of the "full chapel" on Sunday mornings to a close. Of course, this change was only a part of a much deeper social and cultural change about which more will be said later.—RLP

Responsibility for inviting speakers, planning the order of service, and presiding on the platform was theirs alone—of course with the assistance and advice of a staff member whenever it was needed. Many hours were spent in pouring over books of prayers, in culling out hymns and poems, and fitting all the elements into a complete service; and many, many were the hours spent at the telephone inviting speakers, checking and re-checking on topics, and appointing student leaders. Proudly, yet how timidly these boys and girls mounted the platform to confront a congregation in this first attempt to lead public prayer. It was an experiment to entrust the leadership of a service to inexperienced students, but perhaps their very naiveté and resultant sincerity contributed to its success. At least, the plan ceased to be an experiment and became a settled policy. The Daily Chapel Committee subsequently became one of the most active and successful on the Chapel Board.

Whereas the chapel program was purposefully student oriented, an attempt was made late in the fall of the first year to involve faculty in meaningful religious discussion. Early in November, the Faculty Forum on Religion was announced, the purpose of which was to confront the most perplexing religious problems of the faculty. Professor Raymond F. Piper was named chairman, Dean Powers as ex-officio; other members were Captain Albert Tuttle, Dr. R. K. Brewer, Dr. Helene Hartley, and Dr. Ernest Reed. Dean Ernest Griffith was the first speaker, and 650 invitations were sent out. Dr. Floyd Allport and Dr. Ross Hoople were other speakers during the year.

There was other faculty involvement in the chapel programs and activities. It has been mentioned that faculty constituted a substantial part of the Chapel Board. Faculty board members, in addition to the staff, served as advisers to the students in the fulfilling of their committee responsibilities. At other times they participated as discussion leaders in the fraternities, sororities, and dormitories.

There is one very special event that requires mention here, for it involved the administration, faculty, and students in the outstanding social event of the Hendricks Chapel year. Under the expanded leadership of the Social Committee (Helen Laidlaw was the chairman) of the Chapel Board, a faculty reception was planned. This event was held on December 10 and was announced as a formal affair, though a note in the *Daily Orange* indicated that it would be quite proper for one to come in informal dress. This occasion was, however, to be a very "dress-up" event and was held just prior to the Christmas vacation. The guest list was a formidable one and included the following persons (listed here to help readers recall the names of those persons in top positions at Syracuse University at that time), as reported in the *Daily Orange:*

Chancellor and Mrs. Charles W. Flint, Vice-Chancellor and Mrs. William P. Graham, Dean Iva L. Peters, Dean Eugiene Leonard, Dean Mabel C. Lytton, and Dean and Mrs. K. C. Leebrick, Dean and Mrs. Harold L. Butler, Dean and Mrs.

Ernest S. Griffith, and Dean and Mrs. Harry Ganders have also been invited to attend.

Others listed are Dean and Mrs. Herman Weiskotten, Dean and Mrs. Paul Andrews, Dean and Mrs. Hugh Baker, Dean and Mrs. Louis Mitchell, Dean and Mrs. Rueben Nye, Dean A. L. Macleod, Mr. and Mrs. Burgess Johnson, Dr. and Mrs. Wharton Miller, Professor and Mrs. Frank N. Bryant, Dr. and Mrs. William E. Mosher, Professor and Mrs. Hugh Tilroe, Dean and Mrs. William Bryan, Mr. and Mrs. M. B. Brockway, and Professor and Mrs. Earl Stout.

Students as well as members of the faculty have been extended invitations to attend this reception, which is being planned for the purpose of further acquaintance among the board members.

In the reception line were Chancellor Flint and his wife, Vice Chancellor Graham and his wife, Dean and Mrs. Powers, Dean Lytton, Whitney Trousdale, and the student chairmen, Margaret Iglehart and me. A program of music was planned by a committee headed by Ruth MacDonald of the Social Committee. Ruth Hobler played several piano selections, and vocal numbers were presented by Hope Johnson and me. Later in the evening refreshments were served in the Colonial Room, which was decorated in a Christmas theme. The event was a very gala affair and served to bring the top leaders of the campus to Hendricks Chapel to share a notable social event.

Another activity involving faculty and administration was reported in the spring 1930 *Syracuse University Alumni News* by Dean Powers after the chapel program was well under way. Theretofore, student counseling had been based largely on the goodwill, inclination, and talent of faculty who were so disposed. With the coming of the chapel, however, counseling students became an organized concern, and within a short time there was both a men's student counselor and a women's student counselor on the Hendricks Chapel staff. Dean Powers saw student counseling as one of the prime needs to be met through the chapel program.

> There is probably nothing that means so much in constructive helpfulness as student counseling. To find these your people and to know them so well that they are willing to tell you their innermost needs, ideals, perplexities, and confusions opens a way of possible helpfulness to them, the ultimate value of which is immeasurable. Increasingly, provision must be made to meet these personal, human needs. The Chapel staff . . . are doing the best they can to meet these needs; but what are four religious counselors among five thousand students? Only the fact that other deans and professors are willing to give extra time to work of this kind accounts for our ability to touch the problem in even a limited way.

That first fall semester of the life of Hendricks Chapel, here reflected on from a distance of nearly one-half a century, was an impressive configuration of religious activity that made a genuine imprint on the life of the campus. A great many things were happening simultaneously, but not haphazardly. They were well coordinated through the Chapel Board by students, their faculty advisers, and, above all, the staff under the leadership of Dean Powers. On December 7, 1930, the *Daily Orange* reported on a recent Chapel Board meeting in which Dr. Powers had estimated reliably that at least five hundred students were currently engaged in activities associated with the chapel, not only as worshipers but also in the work of committees and projects.

Mention has already been made of the Freshman Camp for men held prior to Freshman Week on campus. It was a kind of preorientation to the life of the university. Freshmen women did not have a camp, but the YWCA sponsored a "big-sister" program whereby a freshman woman was assigned to an upper-class female student. During the summer prior to her entrance to the university the new student would receive correspondence from her big sister. During the beginning of the school year she would receive assistance on a one-to-one basis from her big sister as needed. During Freshman Week, freshmen were invited to a tea held at Hendricks Chapel and a bit later in the fall semester to a series of Sunday afternoon gatherings. These events were designed to make new freshmen feel at home both at Syracuse University and at the chapel. They were told something about the chapel program and given an opportunity to become acquainted with each other in an informal and friendly setting.

Later, a variety of other opportunities were made available to students in the form of discussion groups and get-acquainted sessions. Staff and selected faculty were invited into the fraternities, sororities, and dormitories to consider religious problems and to explain the chapel program and the purpose of its selected activities. In her account of the period, Marjorie Bronner speaks of the selected group of campus leaders whom Dean Powers invited into his home and where, sitting around the fireplace, "certain vital religious problems" were discussed under his inspiring leadership.

She notes that one student who had been privileged to participate in these discussions wrote to Dean Powers after graduation, saying, "I should like you to know that the hours spent in our discussion groups at your home were among the most delightful in my college career. Believe me when I say that you have been an inspiration." What we see developing here is the initiation of what has become one of the chief characteristics of the Hendricks Chapel program through the years. In the early days the sessions were called discussion groups; however, the name assigned does not matter very much. What does matter is that at the beginning those individuals who shaped the chapel program made it possible for students to come together in pleasant surroundings, to meet one another in a friendly atmosphere, and with intelligent leadership to grow in their understanding of the content and implications of religion in their lives.

·　·　·　·

EXPLICIT ATTENTION NEEDS to be called to the contribution made by the YWCA in the beginning year of Hendricks Chapel. The YMCA was phased out at the end of the 1920s, but the YWCA remained very much alive, with strong campus status and support among women. The transition into the chapel program was accomplished smoothly and without difficulty, for although the YWCA retained a good measure of autonomy it also became a strong constituent element in the total Hendricks Chapel program. Its president, Margaret Iglehart, became the women's student chairman of the Chapel Board and its adviser for the first year. Previously, Dean Mabel Lytton of the chapel staff had been adviser. The YWCA was organized very thoroughly and widely supported by those people who participated in its life. It had a continuous schedule of activities. The *Daily Orange* for the academic year 1930–31 is replete with stories of events sponsored by the YWCA.

The YWCA was organized into what were called the first and second cabinets, which consisted of officers and committee chairmen with backups in every position. Early in the fall, on October 14, a "sign-up" session was held at which time the committee chairmen explained the scope and function of their particular part of the program. Women were encouraged to sign up for the particular committee or activity in which they were interested. This event was very successful, for when an additional period for signing up was announced a couple of weeks later, 485 women had already expressed their intention to serve in some capacity. Mentioned in the *Daily Orange* account of these meetings were the following activities or committees: "social service work, World Fellowship Committee, little sister group, discussion groups, Silver Bay, Freshman Committee, and membership and publicity committee."

A regular feature of the YWCA program was the meeting of a discussion group at five o'clock each Wednesday afternoon, with Florence Fenner as its chairman. That fall, the names of Professor Dwight Beck, Dr. Helene Hartley, and Dean Eugiene Leonard appeared as speakers. In the spring, a series was held on the relationship of the arts to religion and included members of the faculty knowledgeable in the fields of poetry, music, painting, and architecture and who also had an interest in religion. In addition to their welcoming tea during Freshman Week, the Big Sister Committee continued helping "little sisters" become oriented on campus, climaxing their fall activity with a big costume party for Halloween in Archbold Gymnasium. Prizes were awarded for skits given by various sororities and living centers. At the beginning of the second semester, with more new young women on campus, the Big Sister Committee spread its attention to include the new students.

The Social Service Committee also had wide-ranging activities, and in her account of that year, Margaret Iglehart, president of the YWCA, reports:

> The members of this group work with the unfortunate classes of society, the sick, and the infirm. They carry a breath of health and good cheer into the monotonous

days of the little invalids in the children's wards of the three hospitals near the university. Gay holiday parties, absorbing games, and fascinating story hours give life and color to the grim hospital room and overpower pain with gayety and fun. They carry through games, stories, Sunday School classes, a spirit of love and individualism to the little orphans brought up in an environment of communality. They adopt "grandmothers" in the Old Ladies' Home and renew their youth for them to bring to life the spirit of their own granddaughters. They work in the missionary centers where part of the foreign population receives its religious training and recreation. Finally, they visit the institution for the blind and help entertain, and by writing letters and reading, to serve the residents.

She added that their own lives were enriched by this unselfish service to others.

The World Fellowship Committee, often in cooperation with Syracuse-in-China, sought to promote international understanding through both discussions and attempts to know and assist the foreign students on campus to feel more at home in Syracuse. During the spring semester this committee was active in helping set up the April Conference on World Relations for New York State Colleges and Universities. More will be said later about the conference that was held for women each June at Silver Bay. The YWCA had a special committee that selected the delegates and worked to prepare for the conference a good part of each year. Early in the second semester a combination of committees hosted one hundred girl reserves from high schools in the surrounding area on their weekend visit to the campus.

We have already spoken of some of the activities of the Social Committee in connection with the formal Christmas party for administration, faculty, and students held at Hendricks Chapel. It was the group that gave the teas and receptions (including one for the choir) that helped bring about a good feeling of fellowship. Most of its activities were carried out in the chapel in what had been originally designated as the Women's Lounge. Just whose idea it was and when it happened is unclear, but it was not long before that room became known as the Colonial Room, later yet the Noble Room. It provided an attractive setting for many delightful social occasions.

On April 15, 1931, after the new YWCA officers had been elected and the committee chairmen selected, the old and new cabinet members met for dinner at a facility called the Home Colonial, which was a good place for such an event in those days. They could look back on their first year of participating in the chapel program with genuine satisfaction, knowing they had played a very vital and extensive part in its development. Though other events including the Women's May Day Breakfast were yet to come, it had been a good year.

Like the YWCA, Syracuse-in-China had had a life of its own in prechapel days but easily made its transition to a mission outreach program of the Chapel Board.

Bernice Meredith had come on the Chapel Board as head of the Syracuse-in-China student organization. This selection led to some changes because, until that time, interest in this project had been generated largely among the alumni. It was determined that in this first year there would be no fund-raising. Efforts would be made to secure interest and give information about the unit in Chongqing, China. There would be activities that would relate to overseas mission projects, the whole matter of international relations, and the more intimate projects that would build friendships with the foreign students on campus.

A good portion of the support for Syracuse-in-China came from the Methodist Episcopal Church. On September 29, Dr. T. Brumbaugh from the Mission Board of the Methodist Episcopal Church spoke to the Syracuse-in-China student organization in the Chapel Boardroom.

On October 10, a meeting of the student groups was held at which time plans for the organization's program were made for the coming year. Regular meetings would be held on the first Friday of each month to reach out to the foreign students on campus and have programs emphasizing international problems. Additionally, whenever possible, when visitors from overseas or representatives of mission organizations were on campus, special meetings would be held to give them a hearing.

One very important event that first year was the visit of Dr. Max Gentry, the physician who had been in charge of the hospital and medical program of Syracuse-in-China at Chongqing, who was back in Syracuse on furlough. He had been in the field for five years and was able to bring firsthand knowledge of the program to all who were concerned with it. The program was hardly ten years old then, and from the records it is interesting to note that he spoke of the progress achieved in getting help from the Chinese in the running of the program. He also made the comment, notable in light of subsequent history, that communist activity, though on the increase, had not disturbed the basic quiet of the country.

During the year, Matias Cuabra, from the staff of the Student Volunteer Movement, visited the campus twice. He came first for a supper meeting for the student organization and then later for a conference on world relations held in Syracuse.

On April 1, 1931, a joint meeting was held with students and alumni at which Robert Van Wagner of the class of 1921 and president of the Alumni Association attended. It must be remembered that two of the medical doctors who had initiated the Syracuse-in-China program were back in Syracuse: Dr. Gordon Hoople and Dr. Leon Sutton. The student group, therefore, had strong support from the alumni.

THOUGH HENDRICKS CHAPEL was focused on the campus of Syracuse University it had ties to state, regional, and national student religious organizations under the developing Student Christian Movement. Frequent visitors to Syracuse were Ray Sweetman of the New York State YMCA, which had a New York State Student Council, and Katherine Duffield of the National Board of the YWCA, who had responsibility for work among the colleges and universities of New York State. On a regional basis there was the Middle Atlantic Field States Council, which comprised a large geographical area. On a wider scale still, during the Christmas vacation of 1930 Dean Powers and the two student chairmen of the Chapel Board attended the national Faculty-Student Conference in Detroit that drew delegates from all over the country.

Over the weekend of December 5, 1930, fifteen students from Syracuse University were delegates to the New York State Student Conference held at the Seneca Hotel in Rochester. Attending were more than two hundred delegates from colleges and universities within the state. I was chairman of the conference.

Over the weekend of April 24–26, the Chapel Board of Syracuse University hosted an intercollegiate conference on world relations. This event was the first intercollegiate one of its kind since the establishment of the chapel program. Every effort was made to ensure that all those individuals attending would feel the new surge of enthusiasm that marked programs of religion on the Syracuse University campus. Mildred David was the student chairman, and Dean Powers was very much involved with advising her about the overall program. The theme of the conference was "How Can We Live Together?" Representatives, including both students and faculty, from sixteen colleges and universities within the United States and other countries came to take part in the program. The discussion leaders were drawn mostly from Syracuse; a notable exception, in light of her subsequent career, was Dr. Georgia Harkness of Elmira College. The principal speaker was Francis Miller, president of the World Student Christian Federation, who addressed the conference twice, at its opening session on Friday night and at the Sunday morning chapel service.

The other intercollegiate event, the Silver Bay Conference for Women, was held after the close of the academic year in the second and third weeks of June 1931. The conference was held at Lake George, New York. This conference had been going on for several years, and Syracuse University had its usual complement of selected attendees chosen by the YWCA.

SOME HAPPENINGS during the first year of the life of Hendricks Chapel do not fit so easily into the broad categories discussed above but are worthy of mention because they were part of the overall chapel program. One such happening occurred on June 15 when an organ concert was given by the twenty-three-year-old musician Fernando Germani, a young Italian prodigy who held the chair of organ at St. Cecilia Academy in Rome and had been described as the "successor to Bossi."

An organizational meeting was held in February to draw together those men and women on campus who intended to make religion their vocation. At registration time it had been noted that fifty individuals had signified they intended to go into some form of religious service. On the evening of Tuesday, February 17, a general invitation was extended to any who might be interested to share in such a group. Brewer Burnett was the student chairman of the event, Professor Dwight Beck was named as faculty adviser, and the Reverend Lloyd Foster of the First Methodist Episcopal Church in downtown Syracuse was the speaker.

About this same time, the Lenten Program of Hendricks Chapel was announced. That first year the program was a fairly modest one and consisted primarily in using the daily-chapel period for special speakers coming in from the city and beyond. This first venture into a Lenten program on the part of the chapel had a certain tentativeness about it. At that time the season of Lent was not given the importance among most Protestant denominations that it has since developed. Beyond that aspect was the fact that the chapel, with its emphasis on universalism in religious life, was not quite ready to emphasize this specific season of Christian devotion.

During the first year of his deanship, Dr. Powers was occupied primarily with the chapel and its program and with his duties as leader and preacher at the Sunday morning worship service. But from time to time he was invited to preach at other college and university chapels and at churches as well. He was also invited to represent Syracuse University in intercollegiate religious associations. He was always ready to interpret the chapel and its program to the people of the city of Syracuse as opportunity afforded. In this activity he was ably assisted by the Reverend Whitney Trousdale, the men's student counselor, who did considerable preaching and speaking both in churches and at special events for young people.

One additional task that Dean Powers took on during this particular year and would continue in the years after was the recruitment of students for the university. Most of this recruiting would take place over a supper meeting in a church to which high school youths would be invited and where Powers would tell of the opportunities at Syracuse University and Hendricks Chapel's program in particular. He would then answer questions regarding their going on to higher education. Since this period was a time of economic depression, many of the inquiries had to do with the kinds of financial assistance available that would make college a possibility for those individuals with meager resources.

THE SECOND SEMESTER of the college year always goes very quickly, and it was not long before Lent, Easter, and spring vacation were all in the past, along with the student elections. Attention began to focus on the year ahead. When the new Chapel Board was elected, an announcement appeared in the *Daily Orange* on April 11, 1931, listing the new members.* Previously, Dean Lytton, who came

---

*See the list of board members for 1931–32 in appendix A.—RLP

to the campus in 1927, had announced her resignation. Her departure would leave a place vacant on the chapel staff. She had been associated with the YWCA as adviser before the chapel building opened and then served as the chapel's women's religious adviser, participating in the first-year program.

Two notable events served to climax the first year of Hendricks Chapel's life. The first event occurred on Sunday, April 19, when following the morning worship services the new and the old Chapel Boards including staff and faculty made their way to the cabins on the Hazard estate at Cazenovia. Following a picnic dinner, devotions were held. The afternoon was then spent reviewing the year and then making plans for the coming year. Although it was usually still cool this time of the year in central New York, it was warm enough this day that groups could gather outside. A good measure of critical analysis and creativity was brought forth in the discussions held away from the campus. The view was that an even better job could be done the second year. After supper the groups made their way back to the Syracuse University campus.

The concluding formal event of the year was the Chapel Board dinner held on Sunday, May 17, at the Drumlins banquet facility. This event was the crowning celebration of those individuals currently associated with the Hendricks Chapel Board and the ones who were to lead it in the coming year. Karl C. Leebrick, dean of liberal arts, presided. The invocation was given by Bishop William Fraiser McDowell, who had been the preacher at the morning worship service. It was a time to look forward and to look back and to speak words of appreciation and gratitude. Marjorie Bronner, who had been on the Chapel Board for two years and was active in the Student Church before that time, was chosen to speak "in retrospect." Ralph Laidlaw, a new member of the Chapel Board for the coming year, was asked to speak "in anticipation." Dean Powers then spoke in appreciation to all who had made a contribution to the chapel in its initial year, paying special tribute and saying farewell to Dean Mabel Lytton. Appropriately enough, dinner ended with the singing of the Syracuse University alma mater.

Two other events occurred in the chapel late that spring that need to be noted here. The first event was the memorial service for Dr. Frank Smalley who had died on April 2, 1931. He had been associated with Syracuse University for more than fifty years. On the last day of May, a service was held for this very beloved dean who, as Marjorie Bronner wrote, "had watched the university grow from one lonely building set in the middle of a pasture on the outskirts of town" to its present size. She concluded, "It was altogether fitting that he should be honored in the house of worship that formed the most recent addition to the campus."

The second event was a happy one for the first dean of Hendricks Chapel and his wife: the marriage of their daughter, Thelma, to Dr. Paul Von Hasler. The young couple was married in Hendricks Chapel by Thelma's father at four o'clock on the afternoon of June 6, and, like many a bridal pair before and after, they held their reception in the Colonial Room on the lower floor.[*]

BY THIS TIME the first year in the life of Hendricks Chapel was over—and a first year never comes again. The newness of the building, the innovations of programs in a new setting, and the basic acceptance by the university community of this expression of organized religious activity had been exciting experiences. Before the fall of 1930 no impressive chapel building had stood at the heart of the campus; now there was one, a stately and beautiful fixture for all to see and enter. Out from this building flowed a multifaceted program encompassing areas of religious concern that its donor, Senator Francis Hendricks, would never have imagined. Yet, at the same time, what was done was basically faithful to the religious purpose for which he gave this generous gift. What was begun that first year would be developed and modified over the tenure of Dean William Harrison Powers and his successors. However, the basic course had been set, and Syracuse University would never again be the same.

As these words are written, almost half a century has passed from that first year, and a sense of nostalgia brings vivid memories of those early days when the dream was new and exciting, with a bright sheen upon it. If in some respects it was an "impossible dream," nevertheless something very substantial had taken place in the life of Syracuse University—and for those people who were a part of it, it is and always will be remembered with deep gratitude and great gladness.[†]

7. New Opportunities, 1931–1932

THE FALL SEMESTER of 1931 began with the knowledge that Hendricks Chapel was an established part of Syracuse University campus life. At the beginning of the previous year, great dreams and plans had been made and launched with hope and expectation, and in its first year the chapel had become an integral part of the university and important to the life of the campus, especially to its students. Looking back, it is clear that during that first year of Hendricks Chapel the pattern was set for what was to follow during the years of Powers's deanship. Although there would continue to be changes in chapel personnel, program devel-

[*]Years later it was my privilege to meet Thelma, the only member of the Powers family I have personally known.—RLP
[†]Don Wright, on many occasions, related to me verbally how much it had meant to him to be a student and in a leadership role during that first year of the chapel's existence.—RLP

opment, expansion, and exploration in other directions, the basic model had been formed, set into motion, and well accepted.

When the second year in the life of the chapel began, the program had been prepared and was ready to go. The resignation of Dean Mabel Lytton the previous spring had opened the position of women's religious adviser at the chapel. Dr. Powers asked Bernice Meredith, who had served the previous year as executive secretary of Syracuse-in-China, to assume additional duties as the women's student counselor. Her task was to be the chapel staff person responsible for the various women's activities under the Chapel Board, to give personal counseling as needed, and to assist Dr. Powers in the overall program of Hendricks Chapel.

With the marriage the previous June of his daughter, Thelma, Dr. Powers found himself without a secretary. Marjorie Bronner, who had graduated the previous spring, filled this position. Being a member of the Student Church Committee and a member of the first two Chapel Boards, Bronner was well qualified, both by her special interest and by her experience, to serve in this position.

This year the chapel had, for the first time, four denominational pastors. (They were not chapel staff, but they associated with the staff.) These four men were supported by their own denominations and had the responsibility of ministering to the special needs of students who were of their particular religious persuasion. These pastors were the Reverend Webster Melcher of the Methodist Episcopal Church, the Reverend David Braun of the Presbyterian Church, the Reverend Charles Patterson-Smyth of the Protestant Episcopal Church, and the Reverend Bernard Clausen of the Baptist Church. Most held other positions as well.

For the 1931 academic year, the Chapel Board again included both elected representatives of student organizations and other persons serving as members at large.* Also on the Chapel Board were representatives of both the administration and the faculty. With the beginning of the college year a considerable amount of activity was generated on the part of the Hendricks Chapel organization. A successful Freshman Camp for men was held under the leadership of Webster Keefe, president of the senior class and a member of the Chapel Board. The YWCA sponsored the welcoming Big Sisters Tea for incoming freshmen women.

On Sunday, September 27, Chancellor Flint inaugurated the Sunday morning chapel services. He was the preacher that day, and his sermon title was "Prove All Things." Waiting to greet the worshipers that morning was a new worship center on casters, which greatly enhanced the beauty and dignity of the chapel auditorium and completed the furnishing of the pulpit area. The chapel choir had grown to more than ninety voices, and additional chairs were brought to the choir area to accommodate them.

Daily-chapel services began the next morning at eight thirty. Later that fall an

*See the list of board members for 1931–32 in appendix A.—RLP

alteration was made. The early morning devotions would feature music on Tuesdays and Thursdays and speakers the other weekdays.

Dean Powers preached at approximately half of the Sunday morning services this year. The remaining Sundays were filled by outstanding speakers from a wide variety of denominational and faith groups. In her account Marjorie Bronner Pierson quotes two of the guests who spoke that year: "In glowing tribute to the beauty of the service Rabbi Philip Bernstein of Rochester wrote, 'I have rarely attended a religious service in which the spirit was so beautiful and the atmosphere so inspiring.' Bishop Francis J. McConnell of the Methodist Church spoke of the student response to these services. 'I have never spoken where I have seen such a large percent of the audience students.'"

As the academic year progressed, once again the chapel became an active, busy place. The YWCA, with Helen Laidlaw as its president, and a full complement of committees constituting a very full program for women welcomed the freshmen women during orientation week through the Big Sister program. There were "sign-up" times at the chapel when those students who were interested could request a chapel committee assignment. For the first time in several years a fund drive for the YWCA was launched because of reduced support from Syracuse University. Once a week, a speaker and discussion were planned for members and interested friends of the YWCA.

Syracuse-in-China, under its president, Mildred David, was active also. In the *Daily Orange* of October 16, a story appeared giving a short history of the organization and named Dr. Hoople, Dr. Sutton, Leland Henry, and Buliel Collins as the ones who instigated the idea of a mission in China in 1916. The story reported on the work then being done in Chongqing and announced that the student organization, though only two years old, was now a part of the total Hendricks Chapel program.

In the previous year no financial support was required because Hendricks Chapel was being funded by Syracuse University. Now, however, a fund drive was instituted by mail to Syracuse University alumni to solicit aid for the Syracuse-in-China program. Mountains and mountains of letters were addressed to alumni in an appeal for funds. This project was accomplished with the aid of student volunteers who helped Bernice Meredith, the chapel executive secretary, with the details.

On the last weekend in October, a large delegation of students, along with members of the chapel staff, journeyed to Kingston, New York, for the New York State Student Conference. This conference was sponsored by the New York State Student Council of the YMCA—of which I was its chairman. It was supported also by the New York State section of the National Board of the YWCA. One of the outstanding speakers at this conference was William Pickens, field secretary of the National Association for the Advancement of Colored People (NAACP). When it was found that Dr. Pickens's schedule would allow him to be in Syracuse the following week, an all-university assembly was hastily planned by the Chapel Board. On Thursday, November 5, Dr. Pickens gave an excellent presentation on interracial relationships.

About that same time—on November 1—the initial Sunday evening worship service was held in Hendricks Chapel. The Reverend W. Harold Beales of London, England, was the speaker. He had come to Syracuse at the invitation and urging of the Reverend Whitney Trousdale, the men's student counselor. Trousdale had known Beales at Cambridge University in England where the two men had met while Trousdale was a student at Cambridge. At that time, Beales was the student minister of the Wesley Chapel. In 1929 he had given up his position there to go to London to work with graduates of Cambridge University. He became adviser to twenty groups of persons whom he had known as students in prior years. (Some of them had been in groups for discussion of theological questions while they were undergraduates.) It was this ministry that had attracted Trousdale to Beales, and when it was learned that Beales was coming to the United States for the Methodist Ecumenical Conference in Atlanta, Georgia, in the fall of 1932, he was invited to come to Syracuse University. He came and was able to spend five days in Syracuse and spoke not only on Sunday evening but also at several daily-chapel services. Following his presentation in Hendricks Chapel on Sunday evening, approximately one hundred students remained to talk with him. Out of this session came the formation (in collaboration with Trousdale) of four groups of students (with approximately one dozen students in each group) known as the Cambridge Groups. The requirement for belonging to one of these groups was one's commitment to take Jesus Christ seriously and to take the group seriously. To take Jesus Christ seriously meant for one to accept him at least as a historical person and to venture on the idea that his teachings were relevant to the everyday problems of campus life. To take the group seriously meant one's faithful attendance at weekly two-hour sessions and participation in the group projects. The four groups later expanded to six, and those students who participated in the groups found them to offer a vital and meaningful experience. The groups continued throughout Trousdale's ministry on the Hendricks Chapel staff.

The year 1932 marked an awareness of the necessity of fund-raising. The reason was very clear. The pervasive influence of the deepening economic depression was being felt in a variety of ways. Many students had to drop out of college from economic necessity, and others were having a desperate time staying there because of decreased family financial support. In response to this situation and originating at a Chapel Board meeting, the Student Emergency Loan Fund was proposed. The idea was accepted and implemented in cooperation with the Men's and Women's Senates. With Dean Powers as adviser, the project became a campuswide enterprise. The appeal was first made to the students, and by Christmas that year $1,701 had been raised. The need was great, so the effort was continued. Two silver teas were held at the chapel. The second tea was held on January 24, and more than four thousand invitations were sent out by a Chapel Board committee under the chairmanship of Helen Loggie to alumni and friends in the community asking them to support the loan fund. As a result of these and other efforts, an additional sum of $1,274 was realized. The administration of the loan fund was given to a committee headed by Dean Powers. In many cases the aid it gave to students proved to be the difference between their staying in college or going home. It is noteworthy that although this effort had been initiated by the Chapel Board, it was widely supported by the entire university community—students, faculty, alumni, and friends.

Other special human needs were met during this academic year of financial hardship. The Social Service Committee of the YWCA raised $150 as Christmas approached. The money was to be used for helping needy families in the Syracuse area. Later, though it was not the direct result of the work of the Chapel Board, Dr. Powers read a letter aloud during a worship service that was sent from Sammy Sebo. Sammy was a patient in the Saranac Tuberculosis Sanitarium. He had been an outstanding football player for Syracuse University just a few years before and had contracted tuberculosis and gone to the Saranac sanitarium for treatment. Now his friends had taken up an offering to help him with the expenses he incurred, and this letter was his way of expressing thanks.

With what might be called the regularization of many of the Hendricks Chapel programs during the first year of its life, the second year gave opportunity for some new and special activities. One was to give more emphasis to the special days of the Christian year. On Sunday morning, December 18, an augmented choir of one hundred voices sang Christmas carols, and Dr. Powers preached a special sermon on the meaning of Christmas. A large contingent from a number of fraternities, sororities, and living centers attended the service as a group. A festival atmosphere pervaded this service, which was held just before the students left campus for home to celebrate the holidays.

Lent, Holy Week, and Easter were also marked with an emphasis that brought special features to Hendricks Chapel celebrations. During the season of Lent, a special program was prepared, printed, and distributed. It was a listing of the daily-chapel speakers. On Holy Thursday the chapel choir, with soloists, presented Stainer's *Crucifixion*. The following day, Good Friday, a three-hour service of devotion was held. The speakers that day used the theme of "The Seven Last Words of Christ." Easter was a special day of celebration with music, a message by the dean, and a festive atmosphere of celebration in worship.

On Mother's Day, an invitation was issued to the students to bring their parents to the campus and to attend the morning worship service at Hendricks Chapel. Many of the students and their parents attended.

Earlier in the year, the bicentennial of the birth of George Washington on February 22, 1732, was noted. Chancellor Flint began a three-day observance with a sermon that Sunday morning titled "Religion, 1732–1932: Some Contrasts." Professor Albert Bushnell Hart, a historian from Harvard, closed the celebration with an address on George Washington the following Tuesday noon in Hendricks Chapel.

Two distinguished religious leaders from overseas spoke on special occasions at the chapel during the year. Archbishop Athenagoras, metropolitan for the Greek Orthodox Church in North and South Americas, addressed a vesper service on Thursday afternoon, May 12. Professor Perley Place presided, and some of the service included reading parts of the liturgy of the Greek Orthodox Church.

At the conclusion of the academic year, during commencement weekend, Bishop Chih Ping Wang, bishop of the Methodist Episcopal Church in Chengdu, China, and a graduate of Syracuse University, preached at a special June 5 vesper service.

In January 1932, largely under the influence of Dr. Powers's gracious wife, the Hendricks Chapel Guild was formed. Its purpose was to be a kind of women's auxiliary to Hendricks Chapel. The *Daily Orange* expressed its purpose as being "to bring about a closer bond of faith and understanding between the student body and faculty and administration." Guild membership was composed of the wives of Syracuse University administrators and faculty, along with some women faculty members. The officers of the new organization were: honorary president, Mrs. Charles W. Flint; president, Mrs. William H. Powers; vice president, Mrs. William P. Graham; secretary, Mrs. Leslie Bryland; and treasurer, Mrs. Ernest Griffith. Their meetings were held every second Monday of the month, and in a very quiet and effective way the Hendricks Chapel Guild helped set a tone and create an atmosphere that brought about a good relationship among the various segments of the Syracuse University community.

Another new venture for the Hendricks Chapel Board in the spring of this academic year was to establish deputation teams. This activity had been carried out for some time by students of the Methodist Church, and for that reason the Reverend Webster Melcher, pastor to Methodist students, was asked to conduct a seminar on February 17 for those persons interested in sharing in this outreach ministry. It was explained at the seminar that groups of students would be invited to spend a weekend at various churches to meet with young people and conduct worship and personal interviews about college life. The churches would pay the weekend expenses. Over the years many churches benefited from this student ministry.

During the year the Faculty Forum on Religion continued its series of meetings. Their topics related to religion and its special relevance to those individuals in the teaching profession. Professor Ross Hoople of the Department of Philosophy was chairman of this forum. There were five meetings during the year. Among the speakers were Professor Herbert Shenton, head of the Department of Sociology, and Professor Ismar Peritz, a distinguished biblical scholar.

An outstanding concert of sacred music was presented by the Hendricks Chapel Choir of Handel's oratorio *Solomon*. It was presented on Wednesday evening, April 20, under the direction of Professor Earl Stout. The Syracuse University Symphony Orchestra accompanied the production under the direction of Professor Andre Polah. Bruce Foote, later to become professor of voice at the University of Illinois, sang the title role of Solomon. Others with solo roles were Dorothy Dudley as the queen of Sheba, Hope Johnson and Mildred Leinbach as the two widows, and me as the high priest. Harry Romanelli was the narrator. This performance was the first time *Solomon* had been presented in Syracuse and only the second time it had been sung formally in the United States. The performance was well received, and a repeat performance was given on Friday evening, May 8.

On April 18 the *Daily Orange* printed the list of those persons who were proposed for appointment by the chancellor to be members of the Hendricks Chapel Board for the next academic year. Wednesday evening, April 27, the second annual banquet of the Chapel Board was held in the Men's Student Lounge. I presided and greetings were brought by Dean Eugiene Leonard and Professor Dwight Beck. Brewer Burnett, who had been men's chairman that year, spoke for the retiring Chapel Board members, and Annabel Nichols spoke for the new Chapel Board members. Dean Powers expressed his appreciation to those individuals who had served and presented the "shingle" to the graduating seniors.

The academic year was not quite over, even though final examinations and commencement would soon be at hand. Several items, three being associated with the YWCA, deserve mention. First, there was a change in the name of the Big Sister program. In the coming fall it would be know as the "Big Chum" program. The change was occasioned by the national "Big Sister" movement, which objected to its name being used for a collegiate program. Another project for the year ahead was to plan a Freshman Camp for women. The camp had been proposed by Bernice Meredith, the Hendricks Chapel women's student counselor, approved by the dean of women, and scheduled for the weekend before Freshman Week the coming fall. The third activity was the conference at Silver Bay, on Lake George, which convened on June 1. The YWCA sent a large delegation of women from Syracuse University to join with other delegates from colleges and universities in the eastern part of the United States.

On commencement weekend, a special edition of the daily-chapel services was held at eight thirty on the mornings of Friday and Saturday for the benefit of returning alumni. The baccalaureate service, held in Hendricks Chapel on Sunday, signaled that the year at the chapel was over. It had been a good year, and the forecast was for an equally good year ahead.*

---

*It was at this 1932 commencement that Donald G. Wright graduated from SU, completing his very active student years in the areas of religious life, choir participation, and leadership in the formative two years of Hendricks Chapel.—RLP

Another innovation was that for the duration of summer school, Sunday morning worship services were held in Hendricks Chapel at nine o'clock.

8. Establishing Traditions, 1932–1933

THIS COLLEGE YEAR began with one new feature at Hendricks Chapel and one new person added to the chapel staff. The new staff member was Helen Laidlaw, a graduate of the class of 1932 and president of the YWCA her senior year. She came to be the student loan counselor and to assist Bernice Meredith in some of her duties. The new program at the chapel was the first Freshman Camp for women, being held at the same time as the long-established men's camp. The camps were held on the weekend just prior to the opening of Freshman Week. The site selected for the Freshman Camp for women was the Huntington Club Camp at Bradley Brook Reservoir. Thirty-two freshmen women attended the camp. Adelaide Ayling was the student chairman, and a full program of orientation, getting acquainted, and recreation was enjoyed by those women who attended. The weekend began on Friday, September 16, and continued until after dinner on Sunday. Not very far from this site, the men's camp was held, with the Reverend Whitney Trousdale as staff adviser and Herbert Ross as student chairmen.

Once back on campus, those students who had attended the two camps were joined by many other students for the activities of Freshman Week. Choir tryouts were announced by Professor Stout, who let it be known that one credit hour was allowed for participation if one became a member of the chapel choir. The big- and little-sister program, now renamed the Big Chum program, was launched during Freshman Week by the YWCA. At this time the older undergraduate women on campus took the incoming freshmen women under their care on a personal basis, assisting them in making their initial adjustment to college life.

When the first Sunday morning Hendricks Chapel service was announced, Dean Powers had said, "This is a place where all unite, regardless of our religious creeds. This is the place where we try to find something in common—one for all and all for each." *

---

*Here we see a continuation of the "interfaith" conduct of worship. This position worked well before Hendricks Chapel was built, and Powers continued to embrace that spirit. It was the age of the "social gospel," a time when Jesus' teachings and example were emphasized more than other aspects of Christian theology. In the flyers and programs of the daily services, as well as in the Sunday services, we find a decidedly Christian content paired with an openness to others in the context of a noncon-

At that first service on September 25, Chancellor Flint presided. Dean Powers preached on the theme "Life Is Like That." The chapel choir sang with Professor Stout at the organ. The next day the *Daily Orange* had both an announcement about the beginning of the daily-chapel services and an editorial titled "Daily Chapel Habit," which suggested that though it was a voluntary program, many students had and would find the twenty minutes time well spent if they established the habit of attending at eight-thirty each morning. In addition, each Tuesday and Thursday afternoons at four o'clock vespers were held. They were of a contemplative nature, with music played or performed, reminiscent of the chapel experience of donor Francis Hendricks while he was a student at Williams College in Williamstown, Massachusetts.

Another innovation this academic year was Sunday morning Bible classes held at ten o'clock in the chapel, concluding in time for the worship service. Professor Ross Hoople led a group of interested sophomores and upperclassmen in "ideals and difficulties of the Old Testament." The Reverend Whitney Trousdale taught a class for freshmen men on the "ethics of Jesus." For the freshmen women, Bernice Meredith led a group in "the teaching of Jesus."

This year there was further extension of the discussion-group method to involve students in dealing with religious ideas. Programs were structured in a variety of ways, but the overall purpose was to show the relevance of religion in life. Though the form and the topics varied, it is accurate to say that this theme was pervasive. The YWCA had long used the "speaker followed by discussion" format for their meetings, and they continued this model in their weekly late afternoon series under the general heading of "What I Believe about God." This kind of program was extended into the freshmen cottages. At this point in the history of Syracuse University most of the freshmen women lived in "cottages." These quarters were residential homes, adjacent to the campus, that had been adapted for students. Once a week, at an early evening hour after supper, students were invited in a selected number of these cottages to involve themselves in a discussion of a religious topic. These discussions were sponsored by the YWCA under the leadership of Margaret Short. For the men of the Chapel Board, a men's forum was held in the Men's Student Lounge, under the leadership of Trousdale. Also, as adviser, he set up six Cambridge Groups for eighty interested students. The groups were established following procedures used the previous year when the program was first initiated.

As Marjorie Bronner points out in her manuscript "The Student Church": "A unique experiment and marked success was the week-end conference led by Dean Powers in the spring on the subject, 'The Quest for God.' It furnished a stimulus to thought and a valuable supplement to the religious and philosophical back-

---

version spirit. It is a style of community worship that has largely disappeared and is unlikely to resurface, except in rare and specifically planned events, in the foreseeable future.—RLP ground of the picked group of twenty men and twenty women who met with him to consider this quest!"

At one of its early meetings that year the Chapel Board set aside Friday night for denominational groups' meetings, and rooms in the chapel were made available to them. There may have been others, but during the year the Methodists, Presbyterians, and Christian Scientists are recorded as having had meetings in Hendricks Chapel. On Sunday, October 31, at three o'clock, the United Lutherans of Syracuse held a Reformation Day service in the main chapel. There was a mass choir from their churches and a speaker whose theme was "Luther or Lenin?"

Referring to denominational groups prompts the recording here of the information given out after the beginning of the academic year by the registrar of the university, Keith Kennedy. Kennedy noted that there were 1,368 freshmen registered, with the religious distribution as follows: Methodists, 299; Roman Catholics, 285; Presbyterians, 183; Jews, 173; Episcopalians, 115; Baptists, 83; Congregationalists, 64; Christian Scientists, 29; and Unitarians, 10. Other groups represented were Armenian Apostolic, Evangelical, Greek Orthodox, Disciples of Christ, Universalists, and Dutch Reformed.

This year was a time when economic depression was felt with increasing severity in every phase of American life. On November 7, in response to the needs of many students and as a result of the success achieved the previous year, a drive to secure money for the Student Emergency Loan Fund was once again initiated. Dean Powers announced that monies collected for the loan fund the previous year had been able to keep many students from having to leave campus and college and helped them over the most difficult spots. Benjamin Moses of the Chapel Board was student chairman, and students, alumni, and residents of the city of Syracuse were asked to contribute. The chapel again sponsored silver teas, and though the money came "very hard," it was believed to be a worthwhile program and would be reinstituted another year.

One month after this loan-fund appeal got under way, the university announced drastic budget cuts and a widespread attempt to effect economies in the light of dwindling resources. These days entailed genuine hardship for large numbers of Americans, and the effects were acutely felt on the Syracuse University campus. The YWCA, as it had the year before, raised money at Christmastime for fifty-five needy children in the city. In addition, Syracuse-in-China held meetings throughout the academic year to keep its visibility high as an important outreach concern of Syracuse University and its community. Efforts were made to raise funds through a letter-writing appeal to the alumni.

Very soon Christmas was at hand, and Hendricks Chapel, now in its third year, was beginning to establish its own traditions. One was having a special Christmas service before the students' departure for home and the holidays. On December

18, there was a morning service of worship with special Christmas music. Houses again attended as a body. There were Christmas decorations throughout the chapel, and the sermon, "The Deeper Meaning of Christmas," was delivered by Dean Powers. That same evening, the first mystery play was presented in Hendricks Chapel. It was produced by the chapel choir and the Drama Committee. Titled *A Mystery for Christmas,* it was written by Howard McKinney. It was in the form of a medieval pageant based on a fifteenth-century biblical play that portrayed the birth of Jesus. Appearing, among others, was Gordon Alderman, then a student, who was later to make his mark as a well-known Syracuse television personality.

On the second Sunday in February, special attention was given to the composer Felix Mendelssohn. His music was sung and played, and Dean Powers preached a sermon titled "Mendelssohn the Man."

The following week, on Friday evening, poet Edwin Markham came to read some of his works in the sanctuary of Hendricks Chapel. Markham was at that time eighty years old and still in vigorous health. He made an impressive figure as he read aloud his works.

Over the weekend of February 25, Syracuse University hosted a conference on disarmament. The opening session was held in the chapel. Participants came from thirteen colleges and universities in New York State.

On February 28, there was a camp reunion for the freshmen who had participated in the camps the previous fall. In addition to recounting their experiences and enjoying their renewed fellowship, the students made comments that were helpful in formulating plans for the camps that would be held the next fall.

In March, after considerable discussion, the Hendricks Chapel Board announced that what had been the YWCA would now have a new name. Thenceforth, it would be known as the Women's Chapel Association. It would parallel the Men's Chapel Association and thereby prevent the duplication and overlapping that had previously existed. It might be noted here that some name changes were also taking place on the state and regional levels. The YMCA and the YWCA had been the major organizations doing student Christian work on college campuses for many years. Now the Student Christian Movement was emerging to combine the functions of the YMCA and the YWCA and would be more inclusive. The SCM, as it became known, retained its relationship with the YWCA on the state and national levels.

On March 28, the *Daily Orange* announced the new Chapel Board for the coming fall. The members were installed in a dignified and impressive service at Hendricks Chapel on Palm Sunday, by Chancellor Flint.

Holy Week featured special daily-chapel services and a presentation by the chapel choir under the direction of Professor Stout of Maunder's *Seven Last Words of Christ.* A three-hour service of devotion was held on Good Friday, April 13. These programs were much the same in form as the year before. However, this year a service of communion was celebrated following the chapel choir presentation on Holy Thursday. It was made clear that there was no connection between the two events. The communion service was open to those persons who wanted to stay or for those who wished to come for communion only. Dean Powers was in charge of the service and was assisted by seven ordained ministers, some of whom were professors at Syracuse University. As far as I know, this occasion was the first communion service held at Hendricks Chapel. In subsequent years communion would continue to be a part of Christian worship.

Sunday, April 23, following the morning worship service, a chapel reunion dinner was held at Drumlins. It was a large affair, as former members of the Chapel Boards were invited along with the new and old Chapel Boards of the year to come and the year past. Included were the first and second cabinets, faculty members, and staff. Ivan Gould, who had been the student chairman of the Chapel Board in the year before Hendricks Chapel was completed, attended and brought some comments to the group. The students who had served were given their shingles, and Professor Stout was presented with a new academic hood.

On May 28 at the Hendricks Chapel worship service, the Reverend Whitney Trousdale gave his valedictory in a sermon titled "A Young Man's Faith." Following the service, in the Colonial Room, a surprise presentation was made to Trousdale in the form of a written statement of appreciation containing fifty-two signatures, including those of the chancellor, staff, faculty, and students.

It had been announced earlier that Trousdale would become associate minister of the Third Presbyterian Church in Rochester, New York, in September. Trousdale had served four years at Syracuse University and Hendricks Chapel and was the first member of Dr. Powers's staff. Single, young, eager, and enthusiastic, Trousdale had shared, at most every step, the development of programs for the first three years of Hendricks Chapel's life. Many young men who had come to him for personal counseling had been helped.

An editorial in the *Daily Orange* the following week said: "There are many young men on this campus who would have no philosophy had they not had 'Whit' Trousdale to thrash it out with. Although Mr. Trousdale may be going on to a bigger job, although Syracuse may be losing his active service, we can never lose the loyal work he has done here during the past years."

In later years, in the midst of a distinguished career in the ministry, Reverend Trousdale would come back to Hendricks Chapel to preach and be greeted by his many friends. In compiling this history of Hendricks Chapel, gratitude is expressed to him for lending me an invaluable scrapbook.

That next weekend at Hendricks Chapel was commencement and the closing of the regular college year. As in the year before, special early morning services were held in Hendricks Chapel at nine o'clock through the first session of summer school.

9. Gaining Recognition, 1933–1934

THE FOURTH YEAR in the life of Hendricks Chapel began with the opening of the 1933–34 academic year at Syracuse University. Program plans had been so well organized the previous spring that when fall came all was in a state of readiness. There was strong acceptance, support, and participation on the part of the college community for the chapel program. To be sure, the effects of the economic depression were great. One sign was that the Monday edition of the *Daily Orange* was omitted. It was not a time to add to the Hendricks Chapel staff, so there was no replacement for Whitney Trousdale. Dr. Powers was still at the helm, having decided not to accept the proffered presidency of nearby Cazenovia Seminary. He had been, for a short time this past year, the acting president while continuing as dean of the chapel.

At the Methodist Conference early in October, the Reverend Webster Melcher was assigned to the Canastota Methodist Episcopal Church. This appointment brought to a close the valuable ministry that he had made to the Syracuse University students of his denomination over the past five years. He had been designated as student minister in 1928, well before Hendricks Chapel opened. Though primarily based at the University Avenue Methodist Episcopal Church, his duties embraced whatever student activity took place in the other Methodist churches that were near the campus. In the years of transition after Hendricks Chapel opened, Melcher made a notable contribution as the minister to students of Methodist affiliation. Methodist students constituted the largest number of any of the denominational groups enrolled at Syracuse University. Melcher had brought skills and talents that were most helpful in the formative days of Hendricks Chapel's life, and he would be greatly missed.

Replacing Melcher was the Reverend Leland Barnes, a graduate of Syracuse University in the class of 1930. He had completed his formal education for the ministry at Drew Theological Seminary.

The freshman camps were the initial activities sponsored by the Chapel Board. This year was the second women's camp, and 23 first-year women attended. The men's camp enrolled 68 freshman. For both groups it was a good start to campus orientation. The Women's Chapel Association began their Big Chum program during Freshman Week. Professor Stout scheduled tryouts for the chapel choir, and the daily-chapel services were soon under way. At the end of Freshman Week, the Chapel Board held a planning meeting at Seventh Heaven, the Powers's cottage on Cazenovia Lake. This meeting was under the leadership of the student chairmen, Benjamin Moses and Annabel Nichols, who, interestingly enough, would find a place on the chapel staff one year later. The response of the freshmen prompted Powers to say that "indications point to the fact that more interest in the chapel program is being shown by this freshman class than any since I have been Dean." After completing their sign-ups, the Women's Chapel Association announced that 520 women had responded. Later it was reported that 200 men were active in the Men's Chapel Association.

On the basis of the enthusiasm shown, a series of weekend conferences were instituted for members of the incoming class. After a personal conference with a member of the chapel staff, a freshman would receive an invitation to share in a group discussion with Dean Powers and a member of the staff or a faculty member on the general topic of the place of religion in college life. Each initial session consisted of 20 men and 20 women. The sessions were scheduled on Friday evenings, with follow-up sessions on Saturday afternoons. An informal supper was provided on Saturday, giving students an opportunity to become better acquainted with each other. The gatherings proved to be a valuable experience for many who participated.

In response to many requests, Dean Powers agreed to form continuation groups to meet once each week throughout the academic year for more detailed consideration of the problems raised in the initial conferences. When asked what questions they would like to discuss, the students suggested a wide variety of subjects, including religion and life, prayer, religious unity, God, immortality, the Bible, and other topics that related to faith and its relation to campus life and the world situation. With their selected topics, group members launched into serious and intense study until the end of the academic year. They then made plans to continue the following year and to keep going until all graduated three years in the future.

Upper-class conferences were organized on the same pattern, with Professor Dwight Beck as the leader. The student chairmen were John Hafer and Margaret Short. From these conferences, continuation groups were also formed; however, it was noted that the enthusiasm of the freshmen was hard to beat. John Hafer, after graduation, was to serve in the administration of his alma mater. He later became president of Emerson College in Boston.

Five discussion sessions on more specific religious topics were held during the first semester. Representative leaders of three religious faiths—Rabbi Benjamin Friedman for Judaism, Father Aubrey Seiter for Roman Catholicism, and Dr. Lloyd Foster for Protestantism—led discussions about the meaning of faith for their particular religious persuasions. Dean Powers led the last two summary sessions.

In the middle of April on a Sunday afternoon, students were given an opportunity to hear about three great religions of the East. Representatives of each faith spoke on Sikhism, Islam, and Confucianism.

Still another innovation during this year was the special Chapel Board Lecture Series, under the general heading of "Civilizing Forces in the Life of Today."

Leaders in five fields of specialization were asked to come and discuss the relation of religion to their particular activity. Those who spoke were Arthur Henderson, Jr., a prominent English barrister, whose lecture was titled "Religion and Politics in 1933"; Channing Pollock, a well-known dramatic critic, playwright, and producer, whose theme was "Does Modern Drama Represent Life?"; Jerome Davis, an economist and sociologist, on "Religion and Economic Justice"; Kirtley Mather, a professor of geology at Harvard, on "When Religion and Science Meet"; and James Gordon Gilkey, pastor of the South Congregational Church in Springfield, Massachusetts, on "Modern Religion for Normal People."

The series was well attended by students and participants from the city. A modest admission fee made the series self-supporting. Unfortunately, Dr. Gilkey could not come because of a severe snowstorm. His place was taken by Dr. Lloyd Foster, pastor of the First Methodist Episcopal Church in Syracuse, who discussed the contemporary crisis in Russia. He had visited Russia the previous summer.

There were other public celebrations during this academic year. Dr. Ralph W. Sockman came to the Syracuse University campus for an Armistice Day service on November 11 at eleven in the morning. Classes were excused so that interested students could attend the lecture, titled "The Next War." Sockman was to return to campus often as a guest speaker and preacher.*

In October Professor Raymond Piper spoke at a chapel vesper service on his trip around the world. He especially made reference to his visit to the Syracuse-in-China enterprise in Chongqing. Later in the year, commenting on his visit, Piper said, "Syracuse can well be proud of this work being done by the unit in China."

At Thanksgiving time Professor Stout brought the freshmen and regular chapel choirs together, a total of 120 voices, to sing for the first time. At Christmas there was a special service at the regular worship hour. In the evening a pageant in medieval style was again presented. It was one that came from the nativity cycle of the York Mystery Plays and was accompanied with music by a quartet and directed by Elizabeth Clark.

On January 17 one of the *Daily Orange* reporters wrote a story that appeared on the front page with the caption "Secret Doings of Chapel Choir Revealed by Female Character." It was suggested, humorously, that if a hymnal appeared to be a bit bulky during the processional, it might contain an extra insert in it like *Dracula* or a love story for reading during the Sunday service. Other diversions included writing the weekly letter home or reading through the hymnal. It was also inferred that some of the girls thought that the processional was a beauty parade, for in the robing room a girl would ask, "Does my hair look alright?" or "Does my dress hang below my gown?" Practically everyone, the reporter continued, who comes to choir practice in the Colonial Room comes because it is so much fun. If

*He was certainly one of the leading voices occupying Protestant pulpits in those days.—RLP

you are a man, not a gentleman, you will sit in a large easy chair; if you are a woman, you will sit in a reclining chair. The report added, "If you have any idea of joining our happy circle make sure you bring a pencil, some paper, and a book. And make sure your boy-friend joins too!"

A more serious concern was the continuing need for emergency funds for students who were facing financial problems. So, once again, late in the fall a drive for the Student Emergency Loan Fund was launched. The goal this year was fifteen hundred dollars. At the beginning of the campaign, Helen Laidlaw, the loan-fund officer, indicated that in the previous year more than three thousand dollars was loaned and reloaned to 275 students to tide them over their specific financial needs on a short-term basis. Appeals were made to all the living centers, letters were sent to off-campus students, an all-university benefit dance was sponsored on Colgate Weekend, and two silver teas were held at Hendricks Chapel. Toward the end of the academic year the WCA conducted a clothing drive for the students in Baxter Seminary in the Cumberland Mountains of Tennessee.

Holy Week, with services on Holy Thursday and Good Friday, was appropriately celebrated and was followed by a joyous Easter service.

On Mother's Day, invitations were again sent to parents to attend the special service, and a number of living centers attended as a body.

Other special events that year were a service in March dedicated to the music of George Frederick Handel, with the choir singing his music. Dean Powers preached on "Handel—Man of Destiny." The Annual Hendricks Chapel Spring Concert was presented on the evening of May 11. There was an admission charge of thirty-five cents.

Sometime earlier, the Reverend Lloyd Hickman from the cast of the play *Green Pastures* was in Syracuse and came to address a group in the Colonial Room of Hendricks Chapel.

By this time in its history, the Hendricks Chapel program was gaining recognition both locally and regionally. In a write-up in the *Daily Orange* of December 20, it was named the "outstanding undergraduate achievement in interfaith cooperation." Letters were being received constantly from those former students who had participated in the program and from those individuals viewing it as a model. As a result, Dean Powers was named, in the spring of the academic year, to a national committee of thirty members to evaluate student religious life on college campuses in the United States. In this regard, a caption appeared that read, "Chapel Dean Says System of Worship on Syracuse Campus Is Most Advanced."

Dean Powers was invited to Yale to lead a series of seminars for seminary students who were interested in a career in student religious work. Even with such successes the program was under continuous evaluation, and toward the end of the year Frederick Shippey, the student chairman of worship who would later become an outstanding church sociologist, requested his committee to study ways in which the worship services in Hendricks Chapel might best be conducted.

On Sunday, April 22, Chancellor Flint installed the new Chapel Board at the morning worship service, at which time all faculty members and all alumni who had served on the Chapel Board were made honorary Chapel Board members. Following the service, a banquet was held in the University Commons. The previous Friday and Saturday, the old and the new Chapel Boards had met together to discuss, review, evaluate, and plan. The theme was "Follow the Gleam." The purpose was to see what the program had achieved in the current year and then make plans for the year ahead.

With many projections for the year to come, the academic year closed for 1933–34. The nine o'clock Sunday morning chapel services continued through the end of the first summer school session.

10. New Year, New Themes, 1934–1935

THE HENDRICKS CHAPEL PROGRAM in the academic year 1934–35 was vital, strong, varied, well established, and with fewer innovations than in the preceding years. There were the inevitable changes in student and staff leadership; however, the basic patterns had been set and, having proved themselves, needed little alteration. The account of this year, then, need not include retelling in detail many of the events that were merely repeats from past years. This is not to say, however, that this year was a carbon copy of the previous years.

While Marjorie Bronner, Dean Powers's secretary, took a leave of absence for a year to study personnel work at New York University, Annabel Nichols took her place. Benjamin Moses served in a special capacity as a graduate assistant.

Many outstanding speakers alternated with Dean Powers in the pulpit at Hendricks Chapel in the worship services.

Freshman Camps were growing in acceptance. The Freshman Weekend discussions, which had such a fine beginning the previous year, were again conducted. Continuation groups were set up for any who wanted to continue the progress they had made the year before in the exploration of religious subjects. Get-acquainted social activities were held in Hendricks Chapel on Sunday afternoons. The yearly sign-up for both men and women brought many new recruits to participate in the various chapel programs.

Four of the student committees provided genuine outreach concern; the Social Service Committee took as its purpose "to put religion into practice on and off campus." The men participated in the Americanization League, Syracuse Boys' Club, Dunbar Center, Onondaga Orphans Home, and YMCA. The women worked in the hospitals, especially with children, and some of them adopted a "grandmother" in the Home of Aged Women. The women also went to the orphanage to read stories to the children, and they also visited with working girls in the Sagola Home.

Another outreach program was the work of the Deputation Committee. During the college year members of this group visited more than thirty churches in the Syracuse area. They developed a peace action play that was presented on appropriate occasions. They often spent the entire weekend in one of the churches where they would lead youth groups and participate in the worship service. In addition, they visited the Auburn Prison.

The World Relations Committee took as its theme for the year "Let Us Know Our Fellow Men." This group sought to relate to the foreign students on campus by holding formal and informal meetings where students could come together to provide mutual understanding and friendship.[*]

Syracuse-in-China shared a concern for the overseas students on campus, as well as focusing on bringing information and support to the unit in Chongqing. Nelson Ma, a man from China, was on the Syracuse University campus that year. He delighted in cooking his native meals for guests who would then sit and discuss China. After serving in China for ten years, Lillian MacDonald was furloughed. She had gone with the original group and returned now to the United States. During the month of November she was in Syracuse and stayed at the home of Dr. and Mrs. Gordon Hoople. She had served with Dr. Hoople while he was in China. During this month she made herself available on both a formal and an informal basis to provide information about Syracuse-in-China. She had brought with her some Chinese students whom she introduced to the Syracuse community.

Late in the fall in what had now become an annual effort, the Hendricks Chapel Board again launched the Student Emergency Loan Fund. This year, the goal was a total that would represent a gift of twenty-five cents from each Syracuse University student. Approximately twenty-three hundred letters were sent asking for aid; however, it was still a difficult time to raise money. The loan-fund organization struggled to raise even a minimum amount of money to meet the needs of many students who desperately needed a few dollars as a bridge to take them over some financial emergency.

Late in October, it was believed that there was enough interest to form a club for students interested in the ministry. Frederick Shippey was elected president of the group, and Allen Best was elected the treasurer. Professor Beck and Professor

---

[*]This paragraph and the next chronicle the chapel's ongoing work with SU's international students, which eventually took a more formal shape. Still later, an office to provide services to international students was established. The Office of International Students continues to support SU's international students.—RLP

Wilson acted as the advisers. Meetings were held in Hendricks Chapel on the first Thursday evening of each month.

The Christian Festival of Christmas and the Easter season were again celebrated appropriately. At the Christmas Sunday service, students from twenty-nine living centers came to the service as groups, including sixteen fraternities and sororities. That evening the medieval-style play that had first been given in 1932 was again presented.

On Palm Sunday the chapel choir presented the oratorio *The Holy City* by Gaul. On Holy Thursday they presented *From Olivet to Calvary* by Maunder. Following the music on Holy Thursday a service of communion was again made available to those worshipers who wished to participate. Dean Powers asked Professor Beck and the Reverend David Braun to assist him in the communion service. He also had Allen Best, Ernest Fowler, Phillip Pitcher, Frederick Shippey, James Skillen, and Ray Terry, all students from the preministerial student group, share in the service.

An innovation that was to be repeated in later years was the sunrise service at six o'clock on Easter. It was sponsored by the Friendship League of the University Avenue Methodist Episcopal Church.

During this academic year two men who were active nationally in youth programming came to campus and to Hendricks Chapel. They were T. Z. Koo, who was Chinese and was associated with the World's Student Christian Federation, and Sherwood Eddy, a veteran of the student movement and an interpreter of world events.

A conference to establish the Student Christian Movement in New York State was held in Syracuse on February 10, with representatives from ten colleges and universities attending. Dean Powers was chairman of the conference, and Bernice Meredith, Leland Barnes, and Lester Rounds were the delegates representing the program at Syracuse University. Meredith was quoted as saying, with regard to the proposed reorganization of student religious work in New York State, that "the organization may be said to be a fellowship of students interested in common ideals, and in the social and religious order." This organization reflected a movement that was taking place on a national level.

Although Roman Catholic students had participated on an individual basis in the Hendricks Chapel program for many years, there was no official representation of this large group of students at the conference. Catholic students were the second-largest group on the campus. The Newman Club, the student organization of the Roman Catholic Church, had been in existence for some time now and had a priest as its adviser. From time to time the group had met in space provided in Hendricks Chapel. On April 6 a joint statement was issued by Bishop Duffy, the Roman Catholic bishop of the Diocese of Syracuse, and Chancellor Flint. They announced that the Reverend Gannon Ryan would be the adviser to Roman

Catholic students at Syracuse University and that he would have an official connection with the chapel. Previously, the only affiliation a Roman Catholic priest
had had with Syracuse University was in the person of the Reverend James J. Ban-
non, who was moderator of the Newman Club. Having a full-time Catholic chaplain was something Dean Powers had wanted for a long time. It would make even
more inclusive the religious representation at Hendricks Chapel. As we shall see
later this path was not the direction of Ryan's orientation.

The new Chapel Board was announced on March 6 and installed by Chancellor Flint in a chapel service on Sunday morning, April 7.

A more personal event took place on Saturday, May 25, 1935. Bernice Meredith, who had been a member of the Hendricks Chapel staff since the chapel
opened in the fall of 1930, was married to me, the first student chairman of the
Chapel Board. Bernice, or "Bunny" as she was known to a host of friends on campus, had had a vital and creative part in the Hendricks Chapel program almost
from its very beginning, and she was given a citation on her departure. Following
her departure, the Silver Bay delegation was led by Adelaide Ayling as staff adviser.
Years later Bunny would come back to Syracuse University to become a member of
the faculty and then the dean of the College of Home Economics. This college
would, under her leadership, become what is now known as the College for
Human Development.

As in previous years, the nine o'clock Sunday morning services of worship continued through the end of the first summer school session.

11. Integrating Programs, 1935–1936

THE FALL SEMESTER of the academic year 1935–36—Hendricks Chapel's
sixth—did not differ substantially from that of previous years. A few events near
the beginning of the year, though, did lead to change, most notably the election of
Chancellor Charles Wesley Flint as a Methodist bishop, which marked the end of
an era for both Hendricks Chapel and Syracuse University.

Staff changes also brought some shifts in emphasis and perspective. The marriage of Bernice Meredith the previous spring had taken from the staff someone
who had played a creative part in the development of the chapel program since its
beginning in the fall of 1930. Her place as women's student counselor was taken by
Mrs. Adelaide Ayling Webster, who had been a campus leader and an active participant in the chapel program as an unmarried undergraduate. Also new to the staff
was Ethel Armstrong, who became executive secretary of Syracuse-in-China. Marjorie Bronner returned to her position as secretary to Dean Powers after spending

the previous academic year studying in New York City. In the denominational post of minister to Methodist students, Lloyd Stamp replaced Leland Barnes. Stamp, who had graduated from both Cornell University and Yale Divinity School, came to Syracuse from a teaching post in philosophy at Colgate University.

Despite these changes, the year began with a well-established series of events designed to integrate new students, including chapel open houses, held on Sunday afternoons, and freshman orientation camps. Enrollment in the women's camp remained stable, while enrollment in the men's camp reached a high of 130 attendees. Sign-ups were scheduled to allow interested students to join one or more phases of the widely diversified Hendricks Chapel program.

In October, a series of lectures was given by Professor Ismar Peritz, the former head of the Department of Bible Studies and a very able biblical scholar. Although born a Jew, he had converted to Christianity. The year 1935 marked the four hundredth anniversary of Miles Coverdales's translation of the Bible into English. Professor Peritz gave four lectures in Hendricks Chapel to put that event into perspective.

These lectures presaged the later announcement of the regular Hendricks Chapel Lecture Series. Speakers for the year were to include Lloyd Douglas, the minister-turned-author whose books were receiving a great deal of attention; George Sokolsky, a commentator and lecturer, who spoke on the question "Can Democracy Survive?"; Cornelia Stratton Parker, a well-known novelist, whose lecture was entitled "Life Begins at 6 A.M."; the poet Louis Untermeyer, who addressed the subject of "The Poet as a Philosopher"; and Dr. Eugene Swann, a noted physician and psychiatrist, who discussed "Patterns of Marriage." In January, a special lecture at the chapel was given by the Arctic explorer Vilhjalmur Stefansson.

Another noteworthy chapel event was the conferring of honorary degrees on two outstanding churchmen who were visiting Syracuse to address a convocation of ministers. In a chapel service held on December 8, 1935, Chancellor Flint conferred the degree of doctor of sacred theology on Ivan Lee Holt, a bishop of the Methodist Episcopal Church South and president of the Federal Council of the Churches of Christ in America. The degree of doctor of letters was conferred on Richard Roberts, moderator of the United Church of Canada.

The Armistice Day convocation was held in the chapel on November 11. Dr. Ernest Griffith returned to speak. Once the head of the Lower Division at Syracuse University, he had left to become dean of the Graduate School of Public Affairs at American University.*

Again this year the Hendricks Chapel Board sponsored a financial drive for the Student Emergency Loan Fund, with Marjorie Bronner serving as the loan-fund

*The events described in this chapter demonstrate that within a few short years of its construction the chapel was being used for a much broader range of activities then religious programming alone.

counselor. The fund provided a stopgap, a life-saving source for those students who had nowhere else to turn when awaiting their scholarship checks or other financial aid. Dr. Powers was able to get time on WSYR Radio to appeal for contributions to the loan fund. The goal that year was fifteen hundred dollars, and the effort came very close to meeting the mark. The fund's student chairman that year was John Connor. He would later become first president and then board chairman of the Allied Chemical Company. He also served for a time as the U.S. secretary of commerce.

Christmas was celebrated with special decorations. It had become a tradition for the choir to bring special music to the holiday celebrations. This year, the one hundred-voice chapel choir sang "Christmas Day," by Holst, among other selections. Twenty-eight houses and living centers attended the service as groups, and Dean Powers preached. His sermon title was "Merry Christmas, Neighbor."

One noteworthy event in the new year was Marjorie Bronner's marriage to Theodore Pierson on January 18, 1936. Marjorie Bronner had very deep and continuous roots in Syracuse University. As a student she had served on and chaired the Student Church Committee before the construction of Hendricks Chapel. She had been a member of various Chapel Boards before and after the opening of the new building. She had graduated with honors in June 1931, having been elected to Phi Beta Kappa, and in fall 1935 had become secretary to Dean Powers. Until mid-spring 1937, Marjorie Bronner, now Pierson, had made steady, creative contributions to the success of Hendricks Chapel.*

Early in the second semester, a fascinating innovation occurred that made history, in light of all that has happened since in the field. As a result of a large number of petitions on the issue, Syracuse University, with a kind of reluctant wariness, allowed a noncredit course on the subject of marriage to be held in Hendricks Chapel. Dean Powers was named chairman of a committee to set up the course, which was scheduled to be held in the Colonial Room. The initial enrollment was 150, and with more and more students wanting to participate the course was moved to the main chapel. The whole enterprise elicited considerable interest and attention. Interestingly enough, when the marriage course was offered the following year it had a very bland, noncontroversial title, The Art of Living. A start had occurred, however, and at least some of the fears that originally accompanied this daring departure seemed to have been allayed by the very tentative and carefully considered presentation of the subject matter.

A little later in the spring, the proliferation of the many chapel activities

*The Piersons were key supporters of both the Jewish campus ministry and the chapel in general. Both Ted (until his death) and Marjorie were active members of the synagogue near the campus, the Temple Society of Concord. Their friendship and help have been great gifts to the chapel and to all five chapel deans. Marjorie moved away from Syracuse in 2004.

brought the need to do some rather careful thinking about how to integrate the programs. To reduce schedule conflicts, a plan was conceived and adopted by the Chapel Board. The plan outlined a new meeting schedule for the various chapel groups and committees for the next academic year. The plan stipulated that with each freshman continuation group, there would be a member of the freshman commission. Out of these groups would come candidates for appointment to the Hendricks Chapel Board. Dean Spring of the College of Forestry, commenting on this plan of reorganization, said, "The plan outlined by Dean Powers is an excellent organization and permits flexibility in its operation."

During the year, outstanding preachers came to the pulpit of Hendricks Chapel on Sunday morning. Two who were returning to Syracuse were Whitney Trousdale, who had been on the chapel staff at its beginning, and the Reverend Lloyd Foster, who at First Methodist Church had been a helpful and cooperative clergyman in the formative days of the chapel program.

Two other notable speakers came for special events sponsored by the chapel. Toward the end of February Kirby Page led a weekend conference, "Pacifism and the Class War," and preached on Sunday in Hendricks Chapel. His sermon was called "The Sermon on the Mount." On April 3, Toychiko Kagawa, who was regarded as one of the great Christians of the world for his work with the poor in Japan and who was making a tour of the United States, spoke in the chapel. Chancellor Flint presided at this meeting, and Dean Powers, in describing Kagawa, called him the "greatest living Christian" in the world.

Holy Week and Easter were celebrated much as before. On Holy Thursday, the chapel choir sang *From Olivet to Calvary* by Maunder, and a communion service was held as in previous years. University Avenue Methodist Church, First Methodist Church, and the chapel cosponsored a five o'clock Easter sunrise service at Prospect Hill.

On Mother's Day, a special service was held, and the members of Eta Pi Upsilon, the women's senior honorary society, served as the ushers. That same evening, the chapel choir under the direction of Professor Stout gave their annual concert and presented the Requiem Mass by Mozart.

The first major event in the chapel sponsored by the Roman Catholic students was a retreat weekend beginning on Thursday evening, May 7. The retreat was well attended and concluded on Sunday morning with three hundred students attending mass, followed by a communion breakfast.

Shortly after Easter, on Sunday, April 19, Charles Prouty Shed of Yale University, a leader in religion in higher education, was the morning preacher in Hendricks Chapel. He installed the new Chapel Board members at that service. Dr. Powers had worked closely with Dr. Shed, conducting seminars for him at Yale, and he would do so again. Following the service, the annual Hendricks Chapel Reunion Banquet was held in the North Room of the University Commons. It was attended by old and new Chapel Board members, members of the chapel choir, alumni, and interested faculty. John Connor was the chairman.

On May 13, the Syracuse papers and the *Daily Orange* headlined the announcement that Chancellor Charles Wesley Flint had been elected bishop in the Methodist Episcopal Church at its General Conference in Columbus, Ohio. In the initial announcement there was some speculation as to whether the chancellor would accept this top position in the Methodist Episcopal Church. It soon became clear that he would do so. After fourteen years of service as the head of Syracuse University, Chancellor Flint would be leaving to assume his new position. With the conclusion of his leadership of Syracuse University, an era in the life of Hendricks Chapel came to an end. The program would go on and with strength, but it must be remembered that it was under the guiding hand of Chancellor Flint that Hendricks Chapel had achieved its current influence and importance to the university. As a committed Christian minister, he made the decision to locate the chapel building at the "heart of the campus" and had made it central to the life of Syracuse University. He had sought and found Dr. Powers and had given him the status of dean. As the administrative head of the university, he had set an example of active support and participation in its developing programs. While striving to cope with a severe national economic depression and the problems of a university in debt, Chancellor Flint never flagged in his efforts to provide Hendricks Chapel with its share of the too few resources that were available.

As the years unfolded, it would become apparent that Chancellor Flint's vision and guidance in using the generous gift of Senator Francis Hendricks made both a creative and a lasting contribution to future generations of Syracuse University students. Students would probably never realize how much they were in his debt for the contribution of the chapel and the influence it would have on their lives as students at Syracuse University.

At commencement, already consecrated as bishop in the Methodist Episcopal Church and assigned as resident bishop of the Atlanta area, the university conferred upon Bishop Flint the honorary degree of doctor of laws.

The commencement issue of the *Daily Orange* contained a report on a meeting of the Alumni Group of Syracuse-in-China. The group announced that in cooperation with the Women's Foreign Missionary Society of the Methodist Episcopal Church, construction was under way on the Syracuse-in-China campus in Chongqing of a seventy-five thousand-dollar school building. The campus would now include two hospital buildings, two schools, and one church. At the meeting, Professor Beck was elected president, Mrs. Perley Place was elected vice president, and Charles Carleton was elected treasurer. Ethel Armstrong was the executive secretary and a member of the Hendricks Chapel staff.

Again, the nine o'clock Sunday morning worship service would be held throughout the first session of summer school.

12. A New Chancellor Takes Office, 1936–1937

WHEN THE ACADEMIC YEAR began in the fall of 1936 there was a new leader in the office of the chancellor. Following the departure of Charles Wesley Flint the responsibilities of the chancellorship fell to Dr. William Pratt Graham. Dr. Graham was designated as acting chancellor while a committee was formed to seek a permanent leader. Dr. Graham had served for many years as Syracuse University vice chancellor and was familiar with the total program of both the university and Hendricks Chapel, where he was known as a strong supporter.

Because of the interim nature of Dr. Graham's leadership there would be few departures in the day-to-day operations of the university during this academic year. It seems very clear, now, that Dr. Graham had given Dean Powers assurance that he would continue the support of the Hendricks Chapel program. It is interesting to note that Dr. Graham was the first Syracuse University chancellor who was not an ordained Methodist minister. He was, however, a committed churchman of that denomination, holding his membership at the University Methodist Episcopal Church. What changes that did occur in the chapel program this year were ones that had been projected the previous spring in response to the need to reorder a program that had been growing constantly since its inception in 1930.

By this seventh year of operation, the Hendricks Chapel program had assumed a vital role in the orientation of Syracuse University students as they arrived on campus to begin their college life. During the Freshman Weekend of two days and two nights, some two hundred men attended the Freshman Camp and forty women attended their own camp. The chapel was swarming with students during its open house; approximately seven hundred attended.

The Big Chum program attracted eight hundred women. This program gave the first-year women an opportunity to find help in adjusting to college life. They were assigned to an upper-class student who met with them on a one-on-one basis. During Freshman Week, an opportunity was given for those students interested in doing so to sign up and thereby indicate their choice of the kind of participation they would like to have in the chapel program.

On Thursday of the opening week on campus, daily chapel was held at noon. On the following Sunday morning the first worship service was held. The chapel choir sang, and Dr. Powers preached on the subject of "Religion, Elected or Required?" He gave the freshmen an overview of the Hendricks Chapel program and its traditions. He indicated his conviction that it was a laboratory for those individuals of all faiths to work and worship together. Outstanding speakers were soon announced for the academic year, notably Bishop Flint, former chancellor of the university, now the bishop of the Atlanta area of the Methodist Church; Dr. Lloyd Foster; Dr. Henry Hallum Tweedy; Dr. Jesse Bogue; Dr. Augustus Seimlem; Rabbi Philip Bernstein; Dr. Lester White; Dr. Harrison Franklin Rall; Bishop Francis J. McConnell; Adna Wright Leonard; and Albert Beaven.

The Sunday afternoon teas began and provided a comfortable setting for students, faculty, and staff to meet and get to know each other on an informal basis.

Returning members of the Chapel Board and other friends were saddened upon hearing of the accidental death of Dorothy Webster, who would have been vice chairman of the Chapel Board. On October 11 a special service was held at the chapel in her memory, and the Dorothy Webster Memorial Library was established in Hendricks Chapel.

In October, though not the direct enterprise of the Chapel Board but appropriate to its purpose, a lecture series was given in the chapel on Tuesday evenings. It was sponsored by the Departments of Bible and Sociology of Syracuse University and the Syracuse Council of Churches. The lectures were given by Professor Emeritus Ismar J. Peritz, a distinguished scholar and former head of the Bible Department. His topics were titled "Bible, Religion, and Democracy"; "Woman's Place in Church and Ministry"; "Marriage and Divorce in Bible Teaching"; and "The Biblical Ideal of the Family."

In November, the Hendricks Chapel Lecture Series began with the following persons as featured speakers: Dr. Howard W. Haggard of Yale spoke on "Medical Fads and Superstitions" on November 10; Phyllis Bentley, a noted author, spoke on "The Modern Drama" on December 8; and Chancellor Joseph M. M. Gray of American University in Washington, D.C., spoke on "Wanted, a New Renaissance" on January 12. The fourth of this series was a debate between Dr. Helgo Culemann, a German exchange professor who defended National Socialism in Germany, and Count Raoul de Roussey De Sales, an American correspondent for the *Paris Le Soir,* who opposed it. In February, Dr. William Pickens of the NAACP, a previous visitor to Syracuse University, lectured on "Abraham Lincoln, Man and Statesman" on the eve of the Great Emancipator's birthday.

As had been the custom in previous years, classes were excused for the special Armistice Day service that was held in Hendricks Chapel on November 11 at eleven o'clock. Dr. Harold Speight of Swarthmore was the speaker, and approximately twelve hundred students and nonstudents attended.

A very special event was the coming of the president of the United States and former governor of New York State, Franklin Delano Roosevelt, to lay the cornerstone of the new building for the medical school. The medical school was, at this time, one of the colleges of Syracuse University. It was later given to and incorporated into the state university system. At the ceremony Dean Powers gave the invocation.

In this academic year it was announced that the Maxwell School of Citizenship building would be erected on the "front line" of buildings on the university campus between the Administration Building and Crouse College.

Early in the fall a series of weekend conferences were held for freshmen, after which any who wished to participate further were placed in a continuation group. The initial conference weekends were led by Dean Powers, the Reverend Lloyd Stamp, the Reverend David Braun, Father Gannon Ryan, Rabbi Irwin Hyman, and Benjamin Moses.

Upperclassmen groups were formed at Hendricks Chapel according to the students' expressed inclinations. A rotation system was established so that it would be possible for a student, by the time he or she was a senior, to have participated in most of the major areas of Hendricks Chapel concerns.

A marriage course that had been requested the previous year and developed under the chairmanship of Dean Powers was continued. Because of its innovative nature the course had received a good deal of attention beyond the campus. The *Syracuse Post-Standard,* Syracuse's morning newspaper, had carried an article on the matter. The magazine *Woman's Home Companion* had a feature article, the *Toronto Star* had dispatched one of its reporters to cover it, and the *National Parent-Teacher Magazine* had taken note of the course. It seems quite apparent that the academic authorities at Syracuse University were wary about continuing a course in marriage. For one thing, the subject matter was regarded as being interdisciplinary and, hence, did not fit into any one college. After the repeated requests of students, however, a noncredit course was projected for the second semester under the title Personal Relations. The sessions were held in Hendricks Chapel, and approximately 780 students enrolled.

The economic depression was still a vital factor in the lives of students. The university had been awarded a grant of $7,300 in the work program of the NYA to aid needy students, but it was necessary to raise additional funds. On November 18 a drive to secure $2,000 was launched with the hope of reaching the goal by Thanksgiving. Since 1931, when the fund had been started and administered by Hendricks Chapel, $4,326 had been distributed for emergency needs. The fundraising effort encountered very hard going, and the results were not as good as they had been in previous years.

Marjorie Bronner Pierson, in her account, reports that the Christmas service this year was especially lovely and meaningful. Dean Powers preached on the topic "Keeping the Christ in Christmas." The music was a great addition to this special service and was presented by the chapel choir and soloists under the direction of Professor Stout. Instead of having the mystery play or pageant, a vesper service of carols and other Christmas music was held in a candlelight setting.

Although Easter would not be celebrated on campus this year, as the students were on spring break, events in the Christian year leading to Easter were well marked. A series of Lenten services beginning on February 10 were held each Wednesday evening in the chapel. The series began on February 10 and was sponsored by the Seabury Club with their adviser, the Reverend Charles Patterson-Smyth. Vesper services were held each Sunday afternoon in Hendricks Chapel, and the daily-chapel services for that period were planned to complement the vesper services. On Holy Thursday, the chapel choir and soloists presented the oratorio *The Seven Last Words* by DuBois. Following this program a service of Holy Communion was celebrated for those individuals who wished to remain. It was led by the Reverend Lloyd Stamp and the Reverend David Braun, assisted by several ministerial students. In addition, a Good Friday service was held.

A sad note was struck when word was received in early January of the death of Dr. Herbert Shenton. He had been head of the Department of Sociology and a friend and supporter of Hendricks Chapel. Dr. Shenton graduated from Drew Theological Seminary and was an ordained Methodist minister. He had later pursued an academic career of great distinction. After a private funeral service in his home, a special memorial service was held in Hendricks Chapel on January 17, with Chancellor Graham and Dean Powers participating.

Syracuse-in-China had an active program going all through the year, often in conjunction with the World Relations Committee. This year a substantial gift was made to the work by Mrs. George Maxwell. When Syracuse-in-China was organized, her husband was the first president, and Mrs. Maxwell's gift was in his memory. Dr. Maxwell died in 1932, and his wife's gift made possible the Syracuse University School of Citizenship that bears his name.

A special event this year was the arrival in Syracuse of the Reverend William McCurdy, director of the Lewis Memorial Institutional Church and the Syracuse-in-China unit in Chongqing. He had served there for twenty years and was home on furlough. From April 7 to April 24 McCurdy was the guest of Dr. Leon Sutton in Syracuse. Dr. Sutton had been one of the first to serve in the hospital in Chongqing. McCurdy brought recent firsthand knowledge of the Syracuse-in-China unit, and he spoke on a variety of occasions, including daily chapel. One impressive report was that the hospital in the year before he returned home had served 2,136 inpatients and 52,000 outpatients.

An innovation of the chapel program this year was that the principal officers of the Chapel Board were elected by the student body. On March 6 the candidates were announced, and in the general student elections of Wednesday, March 10, William Nichols was elected chairman of the Men's Chapel Association, Carol Simons was elected chairman of the Women's Chapel Association, Kathryn Benner was elected secretary-treasurer of the Chapel Board, Edwin Cubby was placed in charge of the Men's Freshman Camp, and Katherine Ford was put in charge of the Women's Freshman Camp. The other officers of the Chapel Board were elected by the outgoing officers, and all were installed on April 11 at the Sunday morning chapel service. This occasion was followed by a banquet at Schrafft's, with Benjamin Moses as toastmaster. Added guests this year were alumni representatives J. Winfred Hughes and Charles Lee, Jr. A special guest was Rabbi Earl Stone, who had been active on the Chapel Board in 1933–34. Rabbi Stone would later serve a short time as the chaplain to Jewish students at Hendricks Chapel.

It was not long before commencement time was at hand. In those years commencement was held on Monday morning with a meeting of the trustees preceding the ceremony.

On Saturday, May 29, in a large headline the *Daily Orange* announced that Dr. William Pratt Graham, the interim chancellor, had been elected chancellor of Syracuse University. This quiet and reserved scholar announced that he would serve for one year or until his successor was chosen.

That same day the graduating class held their class exercises in Hendricks Chapel, with Dick Dower presiding. The next morning Dean Powers delivered the baccalaureate sermon in Archbold Gymnasium. On Monday morning the newly named chancellor presided over the graduation exercises of the class of 1937. The academic year on campus was over, and a new chancellor had been installed. For Hendricks Chapel, however, the activity was not over.

Early in December, Katherine Duffield and Ray Sweetman, field representatives of the New York State Christian Movement, had come to Hendricks Chapel from New York City. They brought word that this year the conference at Silver Bay, which for many years had been for women only, would now be for men as well. From June 14 through June 20 a delegation of twenty-six women and six men from Hendricks Chapel attended the first coeducational conference at Silver Bay on Lake George, with Benjamin Moses as staff adviser.

13. A Series of Endings and Beginnings, 1937–1938

IN THE FALL OF 1937 Dean Powers could feel secure with Dr. William Pratt Graham, a trusted friend of Hendricks Chapel, as chancellor of Syracuse University. There would be no need for any discontinuity in the basic pattern of activity that had marked the chapel program.

Although the years had brought some changes, they were evolving and developmental in nature, with each year building on the foundation of previous years. As this semester began there were some staff changes and shifting of office space. Marjorie Bronner Pierson, who had been Dean Powers's secretary since the chapel had opened, with the exception of the one year she spent studying in New York City, had retired. Other than Powers, she had been at Hendricks Chapel longer than anyone. During the six years of her service she had taken on the responsibility of staff adviser to some of the student groups and was also, for a time, the administrator of the Student Emergency Loan Fund. Her service, support, and enthusiasm had been invaluable to Hendricks Chapel.*

Dean Powers chose Mariam Decker as his new secretary. Flower Sheldon became the loan-fund secretary. Some reassignment of space was made to accommodate them at the north end of the Chapel Boardroom. A glass case was installed in the Colonial Room to hold the books contributed for the Dorothy Webster Memorial Library.†

As the students came to college this fall the chapel performed its special part once again in the human relations' side of orientation. The Freshman Camps were well supported, the chapel open houses gave newcomers a chance to become acquainted, and the Big Chum program for women provided personal attention to first-year women. Daily chapel got under way at the noon hour on Thursday of Freshman Week. Dean Powers began a series of Sunday morning sermons using the overall theme "I Believe." Opportunity was given, as in previous years, for sign-ups where students could indicate the areas in which they wished to work on Chapel Board committees and projects. A new feature of the Sunday chapel service was the attempt to incorporate elements from the Hebrew liturgy into the Sunday morning worship.

Tryouts, under the direction of Reverend Lloyd Stamp of the chapel staff and Professor Sherman Kennedy from the School of Speech, were set up for students interested in leading the daily-chapel services.

In October Dr. Ismar Peritz, professor emeritus of the Bible Department, again gave a series of lectures at Hendricks Chapel. He spoke under the general title "The Lordship of Jesus Newly Restated."

The Hendricks Chapel Lecture Series began on November 9 when Raymond Moley, a member of President Roosevelt's "brain trust," gave a presentation on "Minding America's Own Business." The series continued with a lecture by Katherine Smith, a blind lecturer and journalist. Her topic was "Political and Educational Trends in South America." She delivered the lecture at Hendricks Chapel on December 14. On January 25 Reuben Markham, a foreign correspondent of the *Christian Science Monitor,* was the speaker. On March 8 the series presented

---

*Perhaps no other person so well exemplified the interfaith nature of the chapel's overall operation than did Marjorie Pierson, both as a student and as a staff member. She was a superb example of the position that knowing others' faith can result in the strengthening of one's personal religion.

†This library was to continue to be located in the chapel well into McCombe's deanship when it was moved to Chapel House and later integrated with the other university libraries.

Dr. Henry C. Link, director of psychological services from New York City and well known for his book, *A Return to Religion.* As a special added lecture, Professor Howard Hansen of Vassar College came to speak on the subject "Choosing a Mate." Carol Simons presided at this lecture, and Dean Powers gave the introduction. The final feature of this series was a chapel choir concert that was presented on May 1. The program featured one hundred voices and soloists under the direction of Professor Stout.

The annual Armistice Day celebration was held at eleven o'clock on November 11 in Hendricks Chapel. The speaker was Professor Charles Beard, an outstanding American historian from Columbia University.

Two new Syracuse University buildings were dedicated in November. The first was the new building to house the Maxwell School of Citizenship, which was built between the Administration Building and Crouse College. Among the dignitaries, and the most notable, was former president Herbert Hoover, who came to take part in the ceremony. Ten days later the new Medical School Building on Irving Avenue was dedicated.

Two men, long associated with Syracuse University, died during this academic year. The first was "Old Doc John" Cunningham, who had come to work when the Hall of Languages was being built. He had become a fixture on campus over the years. His funeral was held in Hendricks Chapel and presided over by Dean Powers. The death of Old Doc John removed from the campus one who had been associated with the university almost from its beginning. Later in the year, word was received of the death of Coach James Ten Eyck, one of the most distinguished and beloved of Syracuse University's coaches. He had made the university nationally known with his winning crew teams. Ten Eyck's funeral service was also held in the chapel, and again Dean Powers presided. Chancellor Graham brought words of tribute to Coach Ten Eyck during this service, which was attended by many of the men he had coached. The John Masefield poem "Sea Fever" was read.

The fund drive, which had become an annual event, was launched for the Student Emergency Loan Fund. This year the goal was again set at fifteen hundred dollars; Emerson Facler was the chairman. The faculty women and faculty wives lent helpful support to the drive. Just before Christmas break it was reported that four hundred dollars had been raised. Much later in the academic year, Phi Kappa Alpha, the men's senior honorary society, announced that it would sell flowers to help the fund. This effort was not permitted, as it was forbidden for any group to sell anything on campus for any reason.*

The New York State Student Christian Movement Conference was held at the

*Because of the not-for-profit status of SU, and for other seldom-stated reasons, this policy remains in place today. Even so, it must be observed that there have been over the years many exceptions, some approved and some not approved.

Cutler Union Building at the University of Rochester from November 5 to November 7. The theme was "Christian Citizenship and Its Responsibilities." Students from many colleges in New York State and a number of student representatives of the Hendricks Chapel Board attended.

Christmas Sunday was celebrated with 640 attending the worship service from fraternities, sororities, other campus residences, and the community. Dean Powers preached a sermon titled "I Believe in the Spirit of Christmas." The chapel choir provided outstanding music. One of the musical numbers that was sung almost every year by the chapel choir on Christmas Sunday was the anthem "Christmas Day" by Holst. Holst had incorporated into this musical presentation a number of familiar Christmas carols. Their sequences were arranged in such a way as to suggest the effect of groups of carolers on Christmas Day passing a certain spot. A group from the choir would sing a carol, and then another group would sing a carol. For many years this presentation remained a fixture in the chapel choir repertoire for Christmas Sunday.

As in previous years, the pulpit was occupied about half the Sundays by Dean Powers and at other times by outstanding speakers brought in from outside. This year the list included, among others, Bishop Francis J. McConnell of the Methodist Episcopal Church, Dean Emeritus Charles R. Brown of Yale Divinity School, Harold Roupp of Minneapolis, Amos Thornburg of Wilamette Methodist Episcopal Church in Illinois, and President Albert W. Palmer of the Chicago Theological Seminary. In addition, Dean Powers invited the Reverend Charles Patterson-Smyth once again to the pulpit. He was now the rector of the Emmanuel Protestant Episcopal Church in Elmira, New York. Patterson-Smyth had served as adviser to Episcopal students at Syracuse University. The Reverend David Braun, now the pastor of the Swarthmore, Pennsylvania, Presbyterian Church and former adviser to Presbyterian students at the university, was also invited to preach.

Another special speaker this academic year was Mary McLeod Bethune, president and founder of Bethune-Cookman College in Daytona, Florida. She spoke to the World Relations continuation group in the Colonial Room on February 11.

Slowly but surely the course in marriage, which was heavily supported by the students, was making its way into the regular college curriculum. It was still a committee project, however, with Dean Powers as chairman. Other committee members were Blair Knapp and Dean Eunice Hilton. It was decided that the course would be "lodged" in the curriculum of the College of Home Economics and would consist of a series of six lectures. The course would be an elective three-hour credit course open only to upperclassmen. The course sessions were divided; the 83 men met in the Men's Student Lounge, and the 90 women met in the Colonial Room. Later in the year, a campuswide poll was taken at which time 80 percent of 1,119 men voted in favor of keeping the marriage course. Earlier it had been given a decisive vote by the women, with 644 in favor to 44 against. It is interesting to note here that the Lutherans, recognizing the value of this kind of course to meet the needs of the students, provided their own series with sessions on friendship, courtship, and marriage.*

As it had in the past, and would do many times in the future, the chapel provided a gathering place for religious groups from outside the campus. This year it housed a conference on Christian unity for pastors of the churches of Syracuse and vicinity. The conference was on February 14 and 15. Both Dean Powers and Chancellor Graham spoke to the group.

A notable innovation on the part of the Roman Catholic students was a series during Lent arranged by the Reverend Gannon Ryan, counselor to the Roman Catholic students. The series was scheduled for Friday evenings beginning with the ceremony of the Stations of the Cross. This devotion would be followed by a lecture given by the Reverend Francis of Buffalo on the subject "The Passion of Our Lord and Savior Jesus Christ."

In the spring Ethel Armstrong, secretary of Syracuse-in-China, released the contents of a letter she had received from Mrs. Gentry of Chongqing, China. As a result of the revolution in China, Chongqing had become the capital of the country, and the Syracuse unit was busier than ever, as the city was swarming with refugees needing medical and educational assistance. The letter indicated that for the time being the unit had adequate supplies.

On March 29 a meeting was held in the Chapel Boardroom to elect the men's and women's student chairmen of the Hendricks Chapel Board for the coming academic year. Newell Rossman and June King were elected. Shortly thereafter forty additional members of the Chapel Board were chosen by the retiring board members. All these men and women were installed during the following Sunday worship service by Chancellor Graham.

The Chapel Board banquet was again held at Schrafft's. The theme was "The Hendricks Chapel Special," featuring Helen Laidlaw Smith as alumni speaker. The banquet was also the last event of the Chapel Board for Dean Karl Leebrick, who had been a member of the first Chapel Board. He was leaving Syracuse University to become president of Kent State College in Ohio.

Mother's Day had developed into a very special day at Hendricks Chapel. It is recorded that seventeen hundred persons attended the service this year—which

---

*At this time, Hendricks Chapel was facilitating a cocurricular course on human sexuality and marriage, as were campus ministry programs and campus churches all over the country. In most cases the academic side of the schools soon incorporated these courses. It is of some interest to those of us in campus ministry that religious programming often took the lead (as it had a century and more earlier in the development of the science curriculum) in the so-called controversial areas of human learning and advancement. This is not to say that religion, in one or another, or several of its forms, did not drag its feet as more and more "modern" curricula graced our academic institutions.

seems to have stretched the capacity of the auditorium. Many houses again came as a group, and many of the students were accompanied by their parents.

Dean Powers announced that more than twelve hundred students had been involved in the Hendricks Chapel program during this academic year. Their influence, he said, had created a unifying effect on the campus. Before the end of the year the chapel's Social Service Committee, under the leadership of John Oliver, had a drive for clothing to be distributed by the Community Chest through its agencies in Syracuse. Oliver would later become an official in the United Nations.

A group of twenty-five women had signed up for the Big Chum program for the next fall. Cochairmen Clark Hunt and Ann Harrington of the Deputation Committee had appointed ten men and ten women to plan for the coming academic year. They projected that next year at least twice as many students would be involved in visitations to churches.

In June another Hendricks Chapel delegation attended the Silver Bay Conference on Lake George that was sponsored by the New York State Student Christian Movement.

14. Gathering Shadows, 1938–1939

THE LARGEST NUMBER of students to ever enroll, to date, at Syracuse University arrived in the fall of 1938. The tuition had been raised from $335 to $375, and sixty-six hundred students paid the higher fee for their matriculation to the university. Hendricks Chapel, through its many activities and with its accumulated experience, was ready to greet the new students and make them feel at home. Realizing that a university the size of Syracuse could be overwhelming to an incoming freshman, the chapel was prepared, with programs specifically designed to extend a welcoming hand on both a group and an individual basis as freshmen students made their transition into college.*

*Still today Hendricks Chapel maintains a helping role with the welcome and orientation of new students. Official SU student services programs and admissions staff have, however, taken over many of the roles and tasks assumed by the chapel during the 1930s, 1940s, and 1950s. In our current society, in general, the roles once performed by "religion" have been incorporated into schools and government agencies, thus leading to the so-called secularization of American society. Here again Hendricks Chapel reflects the reality of general society. I am not one who thinks the "secularization" process is an all-negative development. It could just as well be called the "sacralization" of our society. For those of us who see no real dividing line between secular and sacred the issue becomes, Who does what role most effectively at what time? Of course, this is not to say that proprietary issues are not of critical importance to all of us at one time or another. "We are all in this together" is not always an easy position to maintain.

During Freshman Week, Hendricks Chapel had special teas to welcome new-comers and to acquaint them with faculty, staff, Chapel Board members, and each other. The Big Chum program enabled a coed to know she had someone to turn to for information, even personal counseling and help.

Freshman Week camps were held for both men and women. This year the men's camp became one day and shifted from Lake Moraine to Camp Ten Eyck at Green Lakes State Park. Daytime activities were held, and buses brought the men back to campus at night.

It was announced that approximately two-thirds of the entering class were ex-pected to sign up to participate in weekend conferences. These conferences were to give individualized orientation to the Hendricks Chapel program and to pro-vide the means for any student, who so desired, to participate on a continuing basis. Each weekend in the fall, about forty-nine men and women would spend concentrated time from Friday evening through Saturday exploring the meaning of religion for them in their college life. These conferences generally followed the discussion method. After the conferences the students could find their way into a continuation group or a committee project of their choice. Dean Powers always led some of these conferences and was assisted by the Reverend Egbert Hayes, the Reverend Lloyd Stamp, and Benjamin Moses.

During Freshman Week, daily chapel began on Thursday at noon. Finla Craw-ford, the new dean of liberal arts, was the first speaker. The first Sunday morning Hendricks Chapel worship service was held on September 25 and began at 10:50 with the chapel choir singing and Dean Powers preaching. A little later, tryouts would be held for those students who were interested in leading the daily-chapel services.

Very early in the fall semester, the annual Hendricks Chapel Lecture Series was announced. In an enthusiastic comment about it Dean Powers said, "This is un-doubtedly the greatest series of lectures the Chapel has ever offered." It was a bar-gain, too, for students paid one dollar for the entire series; all other persons paid two dollars. On the lecture schedule were Dr. Stuart Chase, an economist, who would speak November 8 on the subject "The Tyranny of Words." On December 13, Senator Gerald Nye of North Dakota spoke on "Some Important American Problems." In January Dr. Gerhard Schacter of Prague, Czechoslovakia, lectured on the subject "Central Europe Today." On the fourteenth of February the Amer-ican poet Carl Sandburg came to talk and read poetry under the caption "An Evening of Carl Sandburg." In March Dr. Alfred H. Griggs took as his topic "Democracy and World Crisis." The final lecture, also given in March, was by Jack McMichael, cochairman of the National Intercollegiate Christian Council. Out of college but two years and eligible for a Rhodes scholarship, he had decided instead to journey to China to see what was going on there and then to lecture on his ex-periences and impressions.

Noteworthy in the university and the chapel during this academic year were two concerns that were manifest throughout the campus and the university community. The first was the economic depression that was still very real. Tuition had been raised, and financial hardship was still a critical factor in the lives of many students. Ethel Armstrong let it be known early in the semester that the chapel had a lending library of textbooks that had been founded four years earlier and now contained approximately ninety volumes that were available to students in need. For the sixth year the Student Emergency Loan Fund set out to secure funds. This year the drive began earlier than usual, in October, and the goal was three hundred dollars higher than the fifteen hundred dollars raised the previous year. The drive was conducted under the leadership of Dorothy Skerrit and Newell Rossman. It was revealed that the previous year an impressive amount, nine thousand dollars, was able to be loaned on a revolving basis.

The second concern that appears again and again, as these days are reviewed in retrospect, was the darkening shadow of impending war. The academic community was alert to all the portents of another world war that seemed far too evident to be ignored. Concern about the preservation of peace appeared in some of the sermons preached by Dean Powers. Dr. Max Gentry, from Syracuse-in-China, was home on furlough and spoke in the chapel on October 16 about the conflict in China. His belief was that the Japanese had used the threat of communism as an excuse for the invasion of the mainland. Dr. Schacter, Dr. Griggs, and Jack McMichael, in their presentations in the lecture series, dealt with the issues of the current war in Asia and the possibility of war in Europe.

Armistice Day was marked by a mass meeting in Hendricks Chapel on November 11 at eleven o'clock in the morning. Classes were again excused to allow students to attend this service. The meeting was addressed by Dr. Walter H. C. Leves of the University of Chicago.

So ominous did the prospect of war appear that on April 27 a special peace convocation was held in Hendricks Chapel. The Reverend Dr. Ray Freeman Jenny addressed the group, and, again, classes were excused to allow students to attend.

Included here for no relevant reason except that it was a campus event of great importance, in the fall semester on a certain Saturday the Syracuse University football team defeated Colgate for the first time in fourteen years. The celebration was not missed at Hendricks Chapel.

In the *Daily Orange* of December 1 and December 2, there appeared two articles about Hendricks Chapel and its personnel. The first article dealt with the founding of the chapel and its donor and indicated something of the scope and purpose of its programs since its founding. The article indicated that on the chapel staff were the dean, the men's student counselor, the women's student counselor, a chapel secretary, the student loan fund counselor, and the executive secretary of Syracuse-in-China, along with the organist and choirmaster for the Hendricks Chapel Choir. It also stated that the following denominational or faith groups had clergy representatives serving their constituents and were associated with Hendricks Chapel: Methodist, Episcopal, Presbyterian, Protestant Episcopal, Jewish, Roman Catholic, Lutheran, and Baptist. Others had less formal representation but were available as needed.

A more generalized observation needs to be made here about a trend in chapel programming and activity. Steadily and surely, the religious pluralism of Syracuse University began to assert itself more self-consciously and would continue to do so in the future. There were often separate denominational or faith group meetings, conferences, and events. Probably the strongest manifestation of this religious pluralism was the announcement in February by the Reverend Gannon Ryan of the purchase of property adjacent to the campus. A St. Thomas More foundation would be established on the property with a building and facilities to serve Roman Catholic students at Syracuse University. At the same time attempts were constantly alive to foster understanding and cooperation among all the religious groups.

The Interfaith Committee of the Chapel Board sponsored a series of five weekly meetings beginning on February 15. The purpose was to help students understand the beliefs and practices of the various religious faiths represented in the Hendricks Chapel program. The following speakers took part in this endeavor: Rabbi Irwin Hyman, the Reverend Gannon Ryan, the Reverend Lloyd Stamp, a Mr. Samuel for the Christian Scientists, and the Reverend Egbert Hayes. Following the presentations there was time for questions and discussion.

Other events of note this academic year included the Christmas celebration. At the morning worship service on December 11 Dean Powers preached on the subject "Always Christmas." Many houses again attended the service in groups. In the evening, with soft lights and special music by the chapel choir, a tableau was presented under the direction of Florence Perry, the loan-fund counselor.

The Deputation Committee, which had been expanded the previous year, had organized prior to the close of the college year the previous spring and was able to respond to invitations to visit churches on many weekends. This project was under the combined leadership of Clark Hunt and Ann Harrington.

In the month of March a feature of one of the Sunday morning worship services was the work of Professor William Berwald, who had been a member of the faculty of music at Syracuse University for forty-seven years and a member of the committee that had selected the first organ for Hendricks Chapel. He was chairman of the Organ Department in the College of Fine Arts. His compositions both for organ and for choir were played and sung during this service.

The New York State Student Christian Movement Conference was held this year on the Syracuse University campus. It was attended by students from twelve colleges and universities in New York State. Syracuse, as always, was well represented at this conference. Among other items of business, plans were made for the student conference at Silver Bay, now coed, which would take place from June 14 to June 21.

As happened each year, student elections were held for the various offices on the Hendricks Chapel Board. On Tuesday, April 4, Clark Hunt and Helen Coonrod were elected men's and women's student chairmen. Thomas Van Loon (prominent later in the life of Hendricks Chapel) was elected vice chairman, Marjorie Bock was elected secretary, and George Krablen and Betty Blanchard were elected to lead the next year's Freshman Camps. Later, thirty-six other persons would be selected for positions on the Chapel Board. This year an office of chairman of public relations was added to the Chapel Board. The total group was installed at the chapel service on Sunday morning, May 7. Following the service the traditional banquet was held with old and new board members, alumni, faculty, and staff participating. Dean Powers spoke words of appreciation to the graduating students. Newell Rossman (later to have a long and distinguished SU career) spoke for the retiring Chapel Board, and Helen Coonrod spoke for the incoming board.

This spring word was received from Kansas City, the seat of the General Conference of the Methodist Episcopal Church, that Bishop Charles Wesley Flint, former chancellor and under whom the chapel had been built, was to be assigned to a newly created episcopal position. The new position would be in the Syracuse episcopal area, and his headquarters would be in Syracuse. Prior to this time the office of the bishop had been located in Buffalo. With this change, Bishop Flint would be returning to the city where he had served for such a long time as chancellor of Syracuse University.

Later in the spring it was announced that Adelaide Ayling Webster would be retiring as women's student counselor. Ethel Armstrong would take over this position. She had been the executive secretary of Syracuse-in-China and would begin her new duties in the fall.

15. Resisting Pluralism and Separatism, 1939–1940

EARLY IN SEPTEMBER 1939 the *Daily Orange* carried an article written by Dean Powers in which he described the purposes and program of Hendricks Chapel. The article included comments about the conferences for freshmen that would be held on five weekends in the fall where there would be an opportunity for the students to discuss "The Place of Religion in Student Life." In addition, the freshmen would be given the opportunity to involve themselves in the chapel program through the continuation groups. In terms of philosophy, Dean Powers indicated that "probably the most significant feature of Hendricks Chapel is its interfaith (not nonsectarian) character." After this comment he listed the various committees of the Chapel Board, including Worship, Deputation, Social Relations, Music, Social Service, Syracuse-in-China, Special Programs, and World Relations. These committees were under the direction of the Chapel Board and included students from all of the major faith groups under this "umbrella" arrangement.*

As Hendricks Chapel began its tenth year, a parallel and related series of religious activities continued to emerge. This was an increasing emphasis on organization and programming within the denominational or faith groups. It arose out of a general theological emphasis on church and churchmanship and a recognition of the reality of the depth of religious pluralism in the nation and on its college campuses. At Syracuse University, the most obvious example occurred the previous spring when the Reverend Gannon Ryan announced the establishment of the St. Thomas More Foundation. Through the appointment of increasing numbers of denominational student pastors and the strengthening of denominational student work at national levels, this trend toward both religious pluralism and separatism became increasingly evident on campus.

In addition to this internal fact of the religious life on the Syracuse University campus, there were the ominous beginnings of World War II in Europe. As the conflict came closer, student life was increasingly affected.

The program of Hendricks Chapel during this tenth year would not be very different from the years immediately preceding this one. Carol Simons, who had been secretary to Dean Powers, was married during the summer. The Freshman Camps, Freshman Week orientation teas, the sign-up for Chapel Board work, and tryouts for the chapel choir all went on as usual. Daily chapel began, and the sequence was under way once more.

On Sunday morning, September 24, Chancellor Graham welcomed the freshmen to Hendricks Chapel, and Dean Powers began a series of sermons on "The Great Teacher Answers Life's Questions."

In response to the beginning of hostilities in Europe, an overflow crowd assembled in Hendricks Chapel on September 28 to discuss U.S. neutrality. War fever was running high. The Reverend Dr. Ray Freeman Jenny of the Park Central Presbyterian Church was the principal speaker and leader.

---

*The term *umbrella* was used early in connection with the operation and programs of Hendricks Chapel. It remains in use as a structural administrative term, indicating that Hendricks Chapel is not just a building but a concept, under which all religious life programs on campus, even those housed in other facilities, falls.—RLP

On October 7 the Hendricks Chapel staff joined with the Syracuse Council of Churches to inaugurate a series of vespers on Saturday evenings at seven o'clock over radio station WFBL. Dean Powers was the first speaker, and the Chapel Quartet provided the music.

The Hendricks Chapel Lecture Series was announced early in the fall with the following speakers: Dr. Hu Shih, Chinese ambassador, on November 14; H. R. Knickerbocker, a foreign news correspondent, on December 12; Bertita Harding, an author, on January 9; Louis Adamic, an author, on February 13; and Robert Frost, the American poet, on May 7.

Special speakers at Hendricks Chapel during the fall semester included the Reverend Dr. James Robinson of the NAACP, who spoke under the auspices of the World Relations Committee. He urged students to "make the Negro student feel normal and confident on campus." Rabbi Hyman, in speaking on November 12, said that the "anti-Semitism of today is not an end, but a means; a tool in the hands of strong political leaders." R. H. Markham, a correspondent for the *Christian Science Monitor,* spoke on "Various Attempts at World Unity" at a special lecture in the chapel on November 28.

The coming of Christmas brought special activities. Kent Larrabee and Doris McHale cochaired a drive that distributed two hundred empty barrels to the various living centers to be filled with used clothing. The clothing was then distributed to the needy by the Salvation Army and the Red Cross. A feature of the Christmas program this year was a tableau by Rinehardt supervised by Professor Editha Parsons and directed by Paul Scanlon. More than one hundred students participated in this production, which was presented on Sunday evening, December 10.

Although it has been emphasized that much of the Hendricks Chapel program followed successful and well-established patterns, there were always innovations. This year, the outstanding innovation was the campuswide Religious Emphasis Week, which was held from February 4 through the eleventh. It was sponsored by the chapel staff and the Chapel Board. An attempt was made to make a pervasive impact on the total campus community through large meetings and a wide range of discussion groups and personal interviews. The Reverend Dr. David McLennon of Toronto was the featured leader, and Rabbi Earl Stone, active on the Chapel Board in his undergraduate years, returned to participate in the program.

In addition to the Sunday morning worship service and the daily-chapel services, a special all-campus convocation was held in Hendricks Chapel at eleven o'clock on the morning of Wednesday, February 7. Classes were excused to allow students to attend. Both Chancellor Graham and Dr. McLennon spoke. General discussion groups for the women were led by Mrs. Graham, wife of the chancellor, and for the men by the Reverend Gene Bartlett, who would later become president of the Colgate-Rochester Divinity School. All of the staff and denominational pastors participated as well, and a large number of meetings were held in the living centers. For those individuals who requested them, personal interviews were scheduled.*

Another new activity, small in scale, was the inauguration in February of the "Family Campus Tours." The tours took students to those parts of the campus with which they were least familiar. The first tour was to the College of Forestry. Four tours in all were planned to both show the buildings and give the history of the programs.

In April the kitchen in Hendricks Chapel was open for lunch for women students who lived off campus.† Though not new, it was announced that the Dorothy Webster Memorial Library was available to students during the hours of eleven in the morning until noon and from two until three in the afternoon each day. This memorial library now contained some 186 volumes that were available to students.

A religious census for the year was taken, and 6,381 students reported their religious preferences. The results were the following: Protestant, 4,800; Roman Catholic, 1,300; Jews, 500. These figures represented the major faith groups. Within the Protestant category, listed in numerical order, were Methodist, Presbyterian, Episcopalian, Lutheran, Baptist, Congregational, and all others. Dean Powers, in commenting on these figures, said that Syracuse compared favorably with other colleges in the United States in the number of students expressing a religious preference.

Some of the speakers visiting the Syracuse University campus during the spring semester included R. Babu Lai Singh of India, a friend of Gandhi; Dean Howard Thurman of Howard University; the Reverend Dr. Christopher Mc-Combe, a Methodist minister from New York City and an uncle of the third dean of Hendricks Chapel; and D. T. Miles of India, who would later become well known through his work in the World Council of Churches. They spoke either at a Sunday morning worship service or on some special occasion.

During Lent a series of services was sponsored by the student organizations of the various Christian denominations. These worship services were held on Friday evenings. The Roman Catholics had their own series on Wednesday afternoons. They followed these services with a retreat during Holy Week. As a special feature, the Reverend Dr. William Orchard, a well-known Roman Catholic churchman from England, spoke in the chapel on March 5.

On Palm Sunday, Dean Powers preached a sermon titled "Cheers, Jeers, Tears." During Holy Week special emphasis was given to the daily-chapel services

---

*Intense programming known as Religious Emphasis Week may have originated at SU. From this time until well into the 1970s, such programs were normal fare for college campuses across the United States and are still held today, particularly in smaller, religious schools.—RLP

†Such programming for nonresident students and for community outreach was nothing new and was an important part of the chapel's philosophy of operation.—RLP

held at the noon hour. The three-hour Good Friday worship service was led by Dean Powers, the Reverend Egbert Hayes, the Reverend Lloyd Stamp, and Professor Dwight Beck. There was a special vesper service in the evening, followed by a communion service led by Powers and Stamp.

Elections for the principal officers of the Chapel Board were scheduled for April 9, the same time as the general campus elections. Clark Hunt and Helen Coonrod indicated that all students who had participated in Hendricks Chapel programs were eligible to vote. Arnold Fellows was elected as men's student chairman, Marion Covell as the women's student chairman, Shirley Weingrad as secretary, and Douglas Cagwin and Lucille Baker as men's and women's commissioners for Freshman Camps. On the following Thursday, at a meeting of the Chapel Board, the remainder of the board was selected for the coming year.

The tenth anniversary of Hendricks Chapel was celebrated with much joy and gratitude at the worship service on Sunday, May 5, 1940. It was a high point, indeed, and perhaps the most meaningful occasion in the young history of the chapel. The Reverend Lloyd Stamp presided, and Chancellor Graham installed the new officers of the Chapel Board. Yours truly, the Reverend Dr. Donald G. Wright of the class of 1932 and student chairman of the Chapel Board for 1930–31, also took part in the service. The chapel choir under the direction of Professor Stout sang, and many old friends filled the pews that day. Dean Powers preached a sermon called "Three Families," which he described as one's own personal family, the university family, and the family of God.

The service included a memorial to Dwight James Baum, class of 1909, who had helped design the chapel building. Kathryn Hendricks, niece of the donor, Senator Francis Hendricks, was present. Professor A. E. Johnson wrote the following poem for the occasion, "In Memoriam: Dwight James Baum '09, 1886–1939":

> If ever there were sermon writ in stone
> How eloquently here his praise is sung;
> He will be present when ourselves are gone;
> Already is his timeless soul among
> The unborn generations who shall come
> Into this blessed place, and find their home.
>
> O Master who all workmanship commands,
> Whom, if we do not serve, we build in vain,
> We need not here commit into Thy hands
> Thy fine apprentice nor his works again;
> He built immortality—Who then shall now
> Receive him O Arch-Builder, if not Thou?

Following the service, more than two hundred people attended a banquet at Drumlins. Included in this group were the Chapel Boards, incumbent and returning; parents; friends; alumni; and staff. At the dinner program, Douglas Petrie, class of 1932, told of the "life of living" that the chapel had brought: a broader religious appreciation and an opportunity to develop his personal faith and to fulfill it in service. Clark Hunt, the retiring men's student chairman of the Chapel Board, discussed the work of the seventeen committees and also paid tribute to Dean Powers, "not only as director of one of the finest religious programs on any campus, not only as Dean, but as a friend of literally thousands of students." Marion Covell, the new chairman of the Women's Chapel Association, spoke of the plans for the coming academic year. She announced two new activities: working at Dunbar Center and the publication of a chapel news sheet.

Bernice Wright (my wife, Bunny), who would later become dean of the College of Home Economics, spoke. She described the work and growth of Hendricks Chapel activities during the past ten years. As Bernice Meredith, she had been a member of the chapel staff during its first five years and thus spoke from much personal experience. The College of Home Economics later became the College for Human Development, owing in large part to the efforts of Dean Wright. An additional speaker this day was Chancellor Graham, who reviewed the concern and support for the chapel program by the administration.

The day was truly a memorable one. It gave a special occasion to celebrate all that Hendricks Chapel had meant for the first ten years of its life in service to God and to the university community. It also gave the opportunity to acknowledge the leadership of Dean Powers and all those individuals who had been associated with him in making the years successful. In retrospect, it can be seen to represent the zenith of the dreams that Powers had for the life of the chapel and its comprehensive programs. Even in the midst of economic depression the program had prospered. It would never be quite the same again—no organization could repeat those ten years.*

World War II was not far off, with all the dislocation that it would bring. As noted earlier the beginnings of the proliferation of denominational and other faith groups had begun. The nurturing and fostering of religious life on campus had been achieved in a remarkable way. In his tribute in a scroll presented to Dean Powers on this occasion, Chancellor Graham called him "the man who made Hendricks Chapel what it is today." This tenth anniversary provided everyone involved an occasion to celebrate all remembrances with joy and gratitude.†

---

*Wright is certainly accurate here. Hendricks Chapel came on line at a unique time in the history and spirit of American religion. Had it been constructed ten or twenty years one way or the other its present character would certainly have been very different.—RLP

†World War II and its aftermath proved to be a "divide in history." So massive were the changes that our society and our institutions were changed forever. The first ten or eleven years of Hendricks

16. Dr. Powers Takes a Sabbatical, 1940–1941

AFTER SPENDING eleven years in formulating the program and guiding the life of Hendricks Chapel, Dean Powers took the academic year 1940–41 away from the Syracuse University campus. Though it was not announced as a sabbatical for him, it did serve the same purpose. Dr. Powers was appointed as honorary fellow and lecturer in the Department of Religion and Higher Education at the Yale Divinity School. He filled in for Professor Clarence Shedd, who had developed an outstanding program of ministry in Christian higher education, a program that attracted many students to Yale. Although Powers would be back to Syracuse University on special occasions, the Reverend Lloyd Stamp was appointed assistant minister of Hendricks Chapel. He, in turn, was most ably assisted by Ethel Armstrong in directing the programs of the new academic year.

As the year opened Hendricks Chapel engaged in many of its proven programs that were especially helpful to students coming to the campus for the first time. Freshman Camps were held. Teas, open houses, and the Big Chum program gave students who participated a chance to quickly become a part of college life and establish personal relationships as well as receive helpful information. Daily chapel began during Freshman Week at eight thirty. It shifted back to the noon hour when too many conflicts materialized with the early hour.

The first Sunday worship service was held on September 22. Dean Powers was present for this service and gave a sermon titled "Religion and Education."

Approximately 850 students signed up to participate in chapel committees. Other students, after tryouts, were selected to lead the daily-chapel program. Tryouts were also held for the chapel choir by Professor Stout. A total of 67 students were selected for the choir.

Speakers for the Hendricks Chapel Lecture Series were chosen, as follows: Mme. Genieve Tabouis, a French journalist whom Adolf Hitler had attacked by name. She spoke November 12 on "How France Collapsed." Carlos Davito, former Chilean ambassador, was announced for December 10, but his place was taken by Prince Paul Sapieha of Poland, who had escaped after the fall of his country and now resided in the United States. Grant Wood, a well-known American artist, spoke February 14 on the topic "Regional Art." Bertha Damon, American author of "Grandma Called It Carnal," was the speaker on February 11. Dr. James

---

Chapel history remain a remarkable "era." Even so, as Wright has noted, Hendricks was already an evolving and progressing entity at SU and would continue to be so.—RLP

M. Hebron, an outstanding criminologist, was scheduled for March 11. Pierre Van Passen, a well-known journalist, spoke on April 29 on the topic "Crisis in Western Civilization."

Special events in the fall semester included the Syracuse-in-China Sunday. The Reverend Chester Rappe of the Methodist Board of Missions was the speaker. He described the work being done in Chongqing, which was then the provisional capital of a war-ravaged nation. As a result of his visit, funds were requested to help the refugees who were pouring into Chongqing and depleting the resources of the Syracuse-in-China unit.

The Armistice Day observance, which had been a feature of the campus program in previous years, was discontinued this year. The previous year 500 students were excused from classes to attend this special service in the chapel, but only about 200 attended.

On Sunday, November 3, Dean Raper led a memorial service for those individuals in the university community who had died. The Reverend Lloyd Stamp was the speaker. The service was followed by communion.

During the fall a wide variety of activities took place for Lutherans, Roman Catholics, Christian Scientists, Methodists, Presbyterians, Episcopalians, and others, continuing the trend of the proliferation of denominational activities. Though affiliated with the Hendricks Chapel program, they were not always housed in the chapel building, a continuing evolution of the "umbrella" concept.

As in the previous year, there was a collection of used clothing. Empty barrels were placed in the living centers for collecting the clothes, which were then distributed to those persons in need.

Christmas Sunday was observed on December 15. Dean Powers returned to preach on "Preparation for Christmas." That evening a Christmas pageant, *The Nativity,* was presented and supported with music under the direction of Professor Stout.

While he was at home for the Christmas season, Dr. Powers announced that Hendricks Chapel would sponsor a hymn contest for which a prize of ten dollars would be given for the hymn chosen and then designated as the official hymn of Hendricks Chapel. Professor William Berwald had agreed to write the music.

Early in January two distinguished Christian leaders visited the campus and spoke to groups in the chapel. On January 4 Dr. E. Stanley Jones spoke in the afternoon as well as the next morning in daily chapel. Muriel Lester, founder and director of Kingsley Hall in London, spoke on the desperate needs of people in wartime Britain.

As the second semester opened, the Reverend Lloyd Stamp announced that continuation groups for all but freshmen would be discontinued. In their place, for sophomores and upperclassmen, there would be a series of discussion groups held over eight weeks and to be completed before Holy Week. The topics selected were

"The Relation Between Religion and Science," "The Teachings of Jesus in the Life of Today," and "Personal Devotions and Worship."

The Chapel Board again sponsored Religious Emphasis Week, which began on February 23. The theme was "Has Religion the Answer?" The program was under the leadership of Dean Thomas Graham of the Oberlin Graduate School of Religion. Participating in an interfaith discussion program were Tracy Ferguson, Father Gannon Ryan, and the Reverend Lloyd Stamp. Dr. Edwin Dahlberg of the First Baptist Church spoke at daily chapel, and in the evenings there were "fireside discussion groups" in many of the living centers. In announcing the series in editorial fashion in the *Daily Orange,* the Reverend Lloyd Stamp was quoted as saying, "Coming in a winter of a campus-wide sense of discontent and uncertainty, religious emphasis week will endeavor to engender in students a spirit of confidence natural to a religious outlook on life."

During Holy Week each faith group had events appropriate to its tradition. Each afternoon there was a special service of devotion in Hendricks Chapel. The Roman Catholics sponsored a retreat, and Rabbi Irwin Hyman conducted a Passover service in the chapel.

In the student elections held on April 5, Warren Bartholemew and Barbara Hopkins were elected chairmen of the Men's and Women's Chapel Associations. Harriet Whitney was chosen as secretary. Later that week twenty-three other persons were named as members of the first cabinet of the Chapel Board. Two weeks later a second cabinet was named. These newly elected officers were installed at the Sunday morning worship service on May 4. This day was designated as Parents Day for the students. Dean Powers returned to preach, and his topic this day was "The Divine Dilemma." Following the service a Chapel Board banquet was held in the Mizpah Hotel for the incoming and outgoing boards.

The academic year concluded with Dean Powers returning to campus for the final Sunday morning worship service held in Hendricks Chapel on May 23.*

17. Carrying on in the Face of War, 1941–1942

DEAN POWERS RETURNED to a campus that was increasingly apprehensive about the war in Europe and Asia. Before the year was over the nation was deeply

---

*Pearl Harbor was still several months away, but a war-torn world had already had a significant impact on life at Syracuse University and Hendricks Chapel.—RLP

involved in the war. In one sense, the program of Hendricks Chapel would go on as developed over the previous years. Even after the attack on Pearl Harbor, on December 7, an attempt was made to keep up the normal flow of events. As time went on, however, the war effort had a profound effect on the university and was a pervasive and underlying influence in almost every aspect of Syracuse University life.

Initially, this effect was seen in the decreased enrollment of 5.7 percent, as men who would otherwise be in college now became involved in the war effort. Jobs that had been scarce during the Great Depression became available in defense industries. Prices rose. Even so, a few months before the attack on Pearl Harbor, Syracuse University opened as usual, and the chapel again played an important part in freshmen orientation. The Freshman Camps were held, there were orientation teas and open houses, and the Big Chum program got under way. Orientation conferences were led by Dean Powers, the Reverend Lloyd Stamp, and the Reverend Egbert Hayes.

The Hendricks Chapel Lecture Series was announced with five distinguished visitors. Later, other names would be added to round out the list. The first list was as follows: Thomas R. Ybarra, a news correspondent, was scheduled for October 24 to speak on "Friends and Foes in Latin America." John T. Whitaker, a foreign correspondent for the *Chicago Daily News,* was scheduled for November 11. Richard Lahey, of the Corcoran School of Art at Goucher College, was scheduled for December 9. Hallet Abend, chief correspondent for the Far East for the *New York Times,* was to be the lecturer on February 10. André Maurois, the eminent French historian, was to speak on the subject "The Writer and the Reader." The two added lecturers were Dr. Haridas Muzumdar, a disciple of Gandhi, speaking on April 14, and Dr. John S. Badeau, dean of the American University in Cairo, scheduled for April 21.

Reflecting the concern of the university community about maintaining peace with the war going on in Europe, World Peace Week was sponsored by Hendricks Chapel. It was to begin on Sunday morning, November 9, just before the traditional Armistice Day service. The preacher was Dr. Liston Pope of the Yale Divinity School. His sermon title was "Things That Belong to Peace." On November 16 students were invited to an interdenominational service held at the Park Central Presbyterian Church. The featured speaker was the Reverend David McLennon from Toronto, who had been the leader at the first Religious Emphasis Week. He spoke on the problems that the postwar world would face.

The *Daily Orange* was not published on Mondays, so it was Tuesday, December 9, that this student newspaper first carried the large caption concerning the attack on Pearl Harbor. It read "Student Status Unchanged" and explained that Chancellor Graham sought to reassure students about what would happen as a result of the declaration of war by the United States. Despite his assurance, change would take place, as became ever more evident in the days just ahead.

Campus life did go on. A Freshman Camp reunion was held, to which the two hundred men who had attended the camp prior to the opening of the fall semester were invited. Charles Lee, the alumni field secretary of Syracuse University, showed moving pictures of the event. The names of Professor Ross Hoople and Professor William Davidson, stalwarts of the program, appear along with Eric Faigle, Leslie Bryan, and Dean Knapp as distinguished members of the faculty.

In late November the Reverend Egbert Hayes helped in the establishment of a cooperative house for interracial living on campus. Also, for the first time, the Chapel Country Dance was held in the Colonial Room. The dance was complete with hillbilly costumes, country music, and skits. Warren Jenks and Peggy Street were the cochairmen of this dance.

Christmas Sunday was observed on December 14, and Dean Powers preached on "Christmas Signs Missing." In the evening Ethel Armstrong Shaffer as adviser, Virginia Lamphere as director, and Professor Stout as musical director presented, along with the choir, a pageant titled *The Child Jesus* by Clokley and Kirk. This pageant was preceded by a brief worship service.

This year, as before, clothing was collected in the living centers. The clothing was distributed by the American Friends Service Committee for war refugees.

At the beginning of the second semester, it was announced that there would be five interest groups sponsored by the chapel for those students who wished to participate. These groups were listed as: Dominant Personalities in Judaism, Catholicism, and Protestantism, to be led by the Reverend Lloyd Stamp; Building a Christian Home, with Dean Powers as the leader; World's Living Religion, with Professor Raymond Piper as the leader; the Bible as Devotional Literature, with Professor Dwight Beck as leader; and Science and Religion, under the leadership of Professor J. Theron Illick.

Earlier in the semester, the *Daily Orange* featured a ten-article series about the religious organizations formally represented on campus. The comment was made that "Now, as ever, students need faith." The articles began on February 10 and concluded on February 21. Excerpts from the ten articles follow:

1. Dr. Powers stressed that the religious program at Syracuse University had two unique features: it was interfaith but also had its diversity expressed in a cooperative venture through the chapel.

2. Rabbi Irwin Hyman indicated that it was his purpose to help "inculcate in Jewish students a reverence for and understanding of the Religion of Israel, and to work cooperatively in Chapel programs."

3. William Ward, the Lutheran counselor, stressed that "the work of the Lutheran Church is very clearly stated—it is to make disciples (Christians) of men. But it believes that the Church is one and hence seeks cooperation with others."

4. Father Gannon Ryan spoke of his appointment to the chapel ministry in 1935 and pointed to the programs for Roman Catholic students held at the St. Thomas More Center, in Crouse College, and in Slocum Hall.

5. The Reverend Egbert Hayes spoke about the history of the Presbyterian Church and his denomination's desire to be a part of the cooperative ministry of Hendricks Chapel.

6. The Reverend Bradford Tite of the Protestant Episcopal Church indicated that that church body had been a part of the chapel program since 1931. He also mentioned the organization of the Seabury Club for Episcopalian students and the ministry provided through Grace Church, which was located near the campus.

7. The Reverend Gene Bartlett, the Baptist minister on campus, spoke of the history of his church and its founding in the United States by Roger Williams. He said he welcomed the cooperative ministry of Hendricks Chapel and believed that it was the hope of the future.

8. The Reverend Lloyd Stamp reviewed the long history of the Methodist Church as founder and participant in the life of Syracuse University and its ministry to students long before the establishment of Hendricks Chapel. He also spoke of its clear commitment to the cooperative interfaith program of the chapel.

9. Alfred Harry Rapp, the Congregational adviser, reviewed the history of his denomination in the life of the United States and pointed out that it was the oldest denomination in America, dating back to the Pilgrims of 1620.

10. Chancey Whitney Sampsell gave the history of the founding of the Christian Scientists under Mary Baker Eddy and stressed the importance of "the spiritual understanding of practical problems."

About a month later, Dean Powers commented that "there seemed to be more interest manifest in religion on the Syracuse University campus during this time of national crisis, even though students did not always go to church."

The Reverend Charles Noble, then minister of the First Methodist Church in Syracuse, spoke at daily chapel on February 23, 24, and 25. As far as it is known, this appearance at Hendricks Chapel was his first. It preceded his distinguished ministry as dean of Hendricks Chapel that would begin a few years later.

The Chapel Board sponsored several special events in the spring semester. A special China Night was held to raise money for war relief carried out by the Syracuse-in-China unit in Chongqing. Cochairmen of the event were Violet Fisher and Lyman Hale. In April, under the leadership of Margaret Moon and Philip Han, a reception in the chapel was held for students from South Africa.

In March the Reverend Dean Richardson, then pastor of the Irwin Methodist Church, led a meeting of students considering a religious vocation.

On Palm Sunday Dean Powers preached on "The Drama of Holy Week." On Easter morning the Syracuse Junior Council of Churches sponsored an early service in Hendricks Chapel at a quarter to seven for the youth of the community.

During this period it was made known that the chapel still needed donations for hymnals. Each hymnal cost one dollar, and twelve hundred dollars was needed. Before the semester was over it was announced that Ruth Van Ness, a magna cum laude graduate of the class of 1939, had won the Chapel Hymn Contest and that her hymn would be placed in the new hymnals.*

Elections were held for the Chapel Board for the coming academic year. Thomas Banfield and Doris Perry were elected as men's and women's student chairmen. Sally Brown was elected secretary.

Jack McCombe, who had succeeded to the chairmanship of the Chapel Board for the current year, was the toastmaster at the Chapel Board banquet, held on April 28. He had established himself as an outstanding debater. He would later become the third dean of Hendricks Chapel. Speakers for the banquet were Donald Shetland; Mary Winstreet, retiring vice chairman of the Chapel Board; Thomas Banfield, the newly elected men's student chairman; and Dean Powers.

Despite the outbreak of war and all the dislocation it brought to campus life, Hendricks Chapel had carried on its programs. An article in the last issue of the *Daily Orange* described the outstanding events on campus during the past year. In a kind of prophetic note the concluding sentence read: "And nobody knows what next year will bring."

18. Changes in Leadership, 1942–1943

THE APPOINTMENT of a new chancellor of Syracuse University came during the summer of 1942. On August 9 Dr. William P. Tolley, of the class of 1922, the president of Allegheny College, became the chancellor of Syracuse University. He was known to be the youngest college chancellor in the country. Chancellor Tolley was on hand at the opening of the academic year. An ordained Methodist minister, Tolley would have a long tenure in office and was a strong participant in and supporter of Hendricks Chapel.

Dean Powers was beginning his fourteenth year at the university, and there were changes in staff. Ethel Armstrong Shaffer finished long and useful service on the staff as women's student counselor. Her place was taken by Agnes L. M. Gasch. The Reverend Lloyd Stamp continued as assistant minister of the chapel and as Methodist counselor. Eleanor McCurdy, whose husband had been the minister of the church in the Syracuse-in-China unit, became loan-fund counselor and secretary of Syracuse-in-China. Professor Earl Stout, who had been organist and director of music at the chapel since its opening, left his position and was suc-

---

This hymn continues, on rare occasions, to be used. Van Ness, who was living in California, visited the chapel during my deanship. She was given special recognition, and the Hendricks Chapel Choir led the congregation in singing her hymn.—RLP ceeded by Professor Leon Verrees. Mary Alice Gates was office secretary. The Reverend Egbert Hayes was the adviser for the Presbyterian students, the Reverend Gannon Ryan for the Roman Catholics, William Ward for the Lutherans, the Reverend John Schroeder for the Baptists, and Rabbi Irwin Hyman for the Jewish students. These men, along with the Reverend Lloyd Stamp, constituted the religious counselors on campus. In December the Reverend James Rockwell became rector of Grace Church and adviser to Episcopal students.

Concurrently, with the coming of a new chancellor, there was tremendously increased involvement of the university in the war. In almost every issue of the *Daily Orange* during the year several references were made to the steady Allied invasion and to how the war was influencing the life of the university. Registration was larger than expected, and at first there was an attempt to keep things as normal as possible. The inexorable pressure of events, however, affected almost all aspects of student life. Many men left college to enlist in the armed forces.

The university opened with its usual patterns, including the Freshman Camps, the orientation teas and receptions for new students in the chapel, and the beginning of daily chapel at noon. The first regular Sunday morning worship service was held on September 27. Chancellor Tolley participated in this service.

An editorial in the *Daily Orange* on October 8 titled "Chapel Offers Work for All" stressed the importance of attending chapel for worship and participating in the various activities to serve God and fellow students.

Religious Emphasis Week came early this year, beginning during the week of October 5. I and my wife, Bernice, were honored to be asked to be the leaders. During the week we spoke at daily chapel and led discussion groups. The following Sunday I spoke at the Sunday morning worship service, and Bernice spoke at a special vesper service at four o'clock in the afternoon. This service was followed by a reception and tea.

Over the weekend a New York State Student Christian Movement Conference was held at the First Presbyterian Church in Syracuse. Ray Sweetman and Katherine Duffield of the SCM staff were present.

On the following Sunday twelve hundred new chapel hymnals were dedicated. The editor, Professor Henry Hallum Tweedy of Smith College, was the preacher

*By now it had become well established that denominational and faith-based counselors, later called chaplains, served alongside the chapel staff in a collegial manner. Already this arrangement was called a guest-host relationship. The Hendricks Chapel staff, including the dean, was paid by the university. The chaplains were salaried and supported by their denomination or sponsoring agency and "hosted" by Syracuse University. Whenever possible Hendricks Chapel provided the chaplains with offices and programming space. Some services were also provided, one being a formal relationship to Syracuse University, which included an SU ID card. Office and programming space and the SU ID card were provided without charge. It has long been my position that SU receives far more service from the chaplains than the costs involved on the part of the university.—RLP

of the morning. Included in the hymnal was the prizewinning hymn written by Ruth Van Ness of the class of 1939. It was sung during the dedicatory service.

Continuation and interest groups began the week of October 20. A series for freshmen titled "Religious Resources for College Living" was conducted by the Reverends Lloyd Stamp and Egbert Hayes. Other interest groups included such titles as "The World's Living Religions," with Professor Raymond Piper; "Toward a Better Understanding of the Far East," with Eleanor McCurdy; "Experiments in Cooperative Living," led by Professor Norman Whitney; and a series led by Dean Powers that discussed marriage problems.

The Hendricks Chapel Lecture Series for this academic year was devoted to speakers who would discuss the Atlantic Charter and the four freedoms. Dr. Carl Hambro of Norway was scheduled to speak on October 27 on "The Atlantic Charter." Judge Florence Allen of Cleveland, of the U.S. Circuit Court, was to speak on "Freedom from Fear" on November 10. Professor Roland Bainton of the Yale Divinity School was to speak on the topic "Freedom of Religion" on December 8. Norman Cousins, the thirty-year-old editor of the *Saturday Review of Literature,* was assigned "Freedom of Speech and of the Press." He would speak on February 9. Dr. Waldo Emerson Stephens had as his subject "Freedom from Want" on March 1. An editorial in the *Daily Orange* urged attendance at these lectures, and it was announced that all military servicemen would be admitted free of charge.

The inauguration of Dr. William Tolley as chancellor of Syracuse University was held on November 14. It was an impressive service, though purposely kept simple because of wartime conditions. Sharing in the program of installation in Hendricks Chapel were Bishop Charles Wesley Flint and Dr. William Graham, both former chancellors. The principal speaker was Ezra Edmund Day, president of Cornell University.

The raising of a "war chest" was completed before the Christmas holiday season. By December 11 seventy-two hundred dollars had been pledged. This amount was reduced somewhat in collections because some of the men making pledges left campus for the armed forces.

In the pre-Christmas period Syracuse-in-China sponsored a sale. The proceeds from the sale were primarily used to help a Chinese student studying in the United States. The clothing drive, which had been established several years before, was launched again. This year the clothes were given to the Salvation Army for distribution.

Christmas Sunday was celebrated on December 13, and Dr. Powers preached on the subject "A Christmas Letter." A pageant, *The Child Jesus,* was presented in the evening and was directed by Muriel Rosebrook.

During the early part of the second semester, continuation discussion groups were held much as they had been held in the first semester. The topics this time were "Towards a Just and Durable Peace," "The Church in the War Period," "The Post-War World," "Social Adjustments in the War Period and the Post-War World," and "Marriage and the Home in the War Period and the Post-War World." On Monday evenings in February there was a series of book reviews held in the chapel that dealt with problems of peace and future planning.

In reading the accounts of student activities during this period, one is struck by the pervasive activity that the war effort produced. There were war bond sales, stamp sales, references to the draft status of the men on campus, and questions as to whether they could finish the year. There were blackouts, the presence of servicemen and women on campus, and calls for the donation of blood. There was also the playing of the Crouse College Chimes by women, which had traditionally been done by men. Despite all of this activity, campus life went on as best it could.

Elections of Chapel Board leaders were held on Friday, February 26. Richard Hudson was elected chairman of the Men's Chapel Association; Richard Thompson was elected vice chairman. Margaret Chase was elected chairman of the Women's Chapel Association and Violet Fisher as secretary. Soon the entire Chapel Board was selected and announced. The installation service was held on Sunday, April 11, at four o'clock in the afternoon.

Late in March it was decided that the religious programming for the chapel for the remainder of the semester would be planned by the denominational and faith groups.[*]

The Lenten theme was announced as "Resources for Living in This Time of Chaos." During Holy Week Rabbi Benjamin Friedman conducted a seder in the Men's Student Lounge celebrating the Jewish Passover. On Good Friday, the Episcopalians conducted an evening service, and confessions were heard in the St. Thomas More Center. A service of the Stations of the Cross was held in Crouse College for the Roman Catholic students.[†] Servicemen on campus were given passes to attend the services of their choice. On Easter Day Dean Powers preached on the subject "Immortality Now."

During the week following Easter it was announced that the Reverend Lloyd Stamp, the associate minister of Hendricks Chapel and religious counselor to Methodist students, would be leaving at the end of the semester to become minister of the United Congregationalist Church in Rochester, New York. He had served in many capacities at Hendricks Chapel since 1935.

---

[*]Here we see the first withdrawal by the Office of the Dean from involvement in things increasingly considered the domain of the chaplains.—RLP

[†]This is Donald G. Wright's first mention of Roman Catholic services in Crouse College Auditorium. Crouse College was used for both Sunday services and special Roman Catholic services until the construction of the Alibrandi Center adjacent to the St. Thomas More facility. That expansion came in 1993.—RLP

Early in May an article appeared in the *Daily Orange* titled "Dean Powers Finds All Corps Interested in Religious Activities." The article pointed out that many of those students in the military programs participated in chapel programs, attended the all-university worship service on Sunday mornings, and shared in some of the activities of the chapel program. The men expressed appreciation for the counseling services offered at the chapel. Dr. Powers is quoted as saying it was "a great privilege to serve them."

Commencement came early. Chancellor Tolley spoke at the baccalaureate service in the chapel on Sunday, May 9. The next day at commencement, Doris Perry, who had been the chairman of the Women's Chapel Association that year, graduated as valedictorian of the class.

A "third semester" began on May 17 and continued through August 28.

19. Loss of a Great Leader, 1943–1944

BY THE FALL of 1943 the involvement of the country in the war was having its effect on every facet of life within the nation. Syracuse University was not excluded from this pervasive influence. Great numbers of young men who otherwise might have been pursuing their academic careers were in the armed forces or in training. At Syracuse University were units for the U.S. Air Corps and the Women's Army Corps.* Syracuse cancelled its intercollegiate football schedule.

The university opened, nevertheless, and Dr. Powers began his fifteenth year, fourteenth at Hendricks Chapel. The Reverend Lloyd Stamp had left the university, and in his place came the Reverend Thomas Van Loon. Van Loon was a Syracuse graduate who had been active in the chapel program while a student. His theological training was at the Yale Divinity School. Doris Seward became the women's student counselor.

A list of those speakers who were to preach in the chapel was announced. The speakers included some of the great clergymen of the United States. They would alternate with Dean Powers and other members of the clergy on the staff at the Sunday morning worship services. Very early in the year, Dr. Frank Laubach, who had become well known for his "Each One Teach One" literacy method, made a

---

*Syracuse became a center for military language training programs, chiefly the Russian language program. Syracuse also had several other special contracts with the military for educational programs. More about these programs will be discussed under the deanship of Charles Noble.—RLP

visit to the campus. He spoke in the chapel at four-thirty on September 17. Later, Laubach Literacy would establish its world headquarters in Syracuse. Frank Laubach's son Robert, a Syracuse graduate, became head of the organization after his father's death.

An editorial in the *Daily Orange* on September 27, titled "Vital Chapel Work Begins," said that those students who wanted to help in the war effort could ill-afford not to share in the work the chapel was sponsoring. This activity included volunteer work in community centers, hospitals, schools, and other social agencies whose workforce had been diminished by those individuals who had gone into national service. During this year the chapel set up a branch social service center in which volunteers would gather to be useful as needed—especially to the military service personnel on campus.

Early in the fall it was announced that Dean Powers would become the civilian head of chaplains for military personnel on campus. He would be assisted by Rabbi Benjamin Friedman and the Reverend Gannon Ryan for Jewish and Roman Catholic personnel, respectively. They would be assisted by the denominational ministers: the Reverend James Rockwell for Episcopalians, the Reverend Egbert Hayes for Presbyterians, the Reverend Alfred Rapp for Congregationalists, the Reverend Robert Romig for Unitarians, Arthur Hooper for Christian Scientists, the Reverend Christian Jensen for Lutherans, and the Reverend John Schroeder for Baptists.

The Big Chum program continued helping young women to make their adjustment to campus life, with some special emphasis concerning social relationships with the men in the Air Force Training Program.

Though not as complete as in other years, the Hendricks Chapel Lecture Series was held in late fall and winter. The speakers were as follows: on November 3 Ruth Bryan Owen, daughter of William Jennings Bryan, spoke on "New Horizons for America"; on December 7 Dr. Nathaniel Peffer lectured on the results of the Cairo Conference; and Dr. Ralph Sockman, minister of the National Radio Pulpit and a well-known Methodist minister, spoke on "The American Way," on January 11. The concluding lecture in the series was given on February 8 by Paul Gallico, a novelist, sportswriter, and now war correspondent. His topic was "The Profession of Writing."

The Student Christian Movement was still active statewide, and over the weekend of October 22–24 a conference was held in Cortland, New York. There were representatives from Syracuse and other colleges of New York State.

A special Thanksgiving Day service was held on November 25 with the Reverend Dean Richardson, minister of the Irwin Methodist Church, as the preacher. Students Richard Grant and Ruth Kent aided in the service.

A Christmas pageant was presented with music under the direction of Professor Verrees. For the first time a speaking choir participated in the service.

I must report a very distressing portent that began to appear at the heart of the chapel's life. Early in November Dean Powers developed a severe case of shingles, a painful and debilitating disease that immobilized him and kept him away from chapel activities. At first he was treated in Syracuse, but soon he sought help in the prestigious medical facility at Clifton Springs. Unfortunately, he did not respond to treatment there. It was suggested that perhaps the warmth and sunshine of the South would help him. A recent graduate of Syracuse provided a place in Florida for the Powerses. The trip was made, but it too failed to restore his strength and the Powerses returned to Syracuse.

When Dean Powers was first ill it was thought his illness was temporary and that he would soon be back to work. The staff and the denominational chaplains carried out the program that had been planned. It was difficult without the active participation of the dean and the increasing dislocations caused by the war. Thomas Van Loon became the key person providing the necessary leadership.

On Sunday, January 23, an all-university conference was held under the title "Suggestions for a Better Syracuse." Chancellor Tolley took a leading part. A visiting leader was Dr. Halford Luccock of Yale. From Syracuse University Dr. Helene Hartley, Dr. Maurice Troyer, Dr. Walter Taylor, Dr. Eric Faigle, and Dr. Floyd Carlson served as discussion leaders. Captain Dunkleberger, the campus air force chaplain, made a special effort to participate. Ray Sweetman and Katherine Duffield, staff members of the Student Christian Movement of New York State, also participated in the conference. An effort was made to secure the participation of the entire student body, including those individuals in the service programs, in the conference.

An interesting editorial in the *Daily Orange* at the beginning of Lent, on February 23, asked whether the students were irreligious. The editorial pointedly indicated that in this special and crucial time in the nation's history what happened in the Lenten period would give the answer in very practical terms. A challenge was issued to the students to live their faith.[*]

In the early spring a special interfaith convocation was held on Thursday, March 16. The leadership was provided by Rabbi Joseph Zeitlin, the Reverend Gannon Ryan, and the Reverend Harry Taylor.

During Holy Week a three-hour Good Friday service was held in Hendricks Chapel. Participating were the Reverend Thomas Van Loon, the Reverend Dean Richardson, the Reverend James Rockwell, Professor Dwight Beck, and the Reverend Egbert Hayes.

---

[*]It is obvious that some falloff in chapel participation was taking place. Donald Wright and I talked about it. We both believed the disruption of the war and Powers's illness were important factors in the drop in participation in regular chapel events, the drop in some cases causing the cancellation of events.—RLP

Earlier, elections for the Chapel Board were held. On April 16 Chancellor Tolley installed these new officers. Following the installation a banquet was held in Drumlins with Wynne Cotton as toastmistress and Dick Thompson as toastmaster.

Dr. Powers's health continued to decline. When college opened in the fall of 1944 there was a brief hope that he would return to the chapel. It was thought he would recover his strength over the summer and resume his duties in the fall, and this hope was reported in the *Daily Orange*. But it was not to be. Despite a great variety of attempts to reverse the deterioration of his health, nothing seemed to help. The reasons are still not clear, and Dr. Powers was but in his middle fifties. To be sure, he had given of himself to the limits of his strength, and perhaps beyond, to fulfill his dream for Hendricks Chapel. It is not inconceivable that he spent his physical and emotional resources to the point of irrecoverable exhaustion.[*]

After being ill and away from his work for almost a year, and perhaps realizing that he could not return to full leadership in the chapel, Powers requested retirement from the ministry in the Methodist Church. On October 9, 1944, at a special session of the Central New York Conference held in Phoenix, New York, his request was granted.

On November 20, at the fall meeting of the trustees of Syracuse University, Powers's resignation from the chapel was accepted, and he was named dean emeritus. This event was announced in the *Daily Orange* on the following Tuesday with an editorial expressing regret for his leaving and commending him for his leadership and vision both in developing the program at the chapel and in the pioneering efforts he had made in the field of cooperative religious programming.

About the middle of December, Powers became so ill with pneumonia that he was taken to University Hospital. After being there two weeks he died at half past eight on the morning of December 30. His wife and daughter were at his bedside.

Immediately upon his death, scores of tributes both public and private poured forth in appreciation for all he had accomplished in his ministry, especially his leadership as dean of Hendricks Chapel.

Services for Dean Powers were at two o'clock on January 3 at Hendricks Chapel. His body lay in state prior to the service. Taking part in the service were Bishop W. Earl Ledden, resident bishop of the Methodist Church; the Reverend Dr. Dwight Beck, head of the Department of Biblical Literature at the university; the Reverend Charles Noble of the First Methodist Church in Syracuse; the Reverend Dr. George Y. Benton, district superintendent of the Methodist Church; Chancellor Tolley; and the Reverend William Montgomery of the First Wesleyan Methodist Church. Pallbearers were Dr. Eric Faigle, Dr. Leslie Bryan, the Rev-

---

[*]While Powers was away from his duties, Thomas Van Loon was officially appointed to administer the chapel on his behalf. His title was "chief of staff" of Hendricks Chapel.—RLP

erend Thomas Van Loon, the Reverend Clark Hunt, the Reverend Lloyd Stamp, and Benjamin Moses.

A private committal service was held in the Morningside Mausoleum, as it was in the winter. Later, Dr. Powers's body was permanently laid to rest in Oakwood Cemetery, across the street and within view of the house in which the Powerses had lived during his tenure as dean of Hendricks Chapel.

20. Summary of Dr. Powers's Deanship

TO CAPTURE IN WORDS all that Dr. William Harrison Powers's deanship at Hendricks Chapel meant during the fifteen years he served at Syracuse University is a formidable task. It will be approached in two ways. First, it is fortunate that we have Dr. Powers's own words on his philosophy of what he did. They appeared in a 1938 article he wrote for the *Journal of Religious Education*. The article was written when the program at the chapel had matured and was in full bloom and before the war years caused their dislocations. In the article Dr. Powers describes the details of the program, which have been well explored earlier. What is most useful is the motivating philosophy that he shares in the article. I will quote Dr. Powers, and then an attempt will be made to measure the goals and programs in terms of what was accomplished.

> From the very beginning certain fundamental principals have been observed. In the first place a university should make adequate provision in leadership, physical equipment and finance for the development of the moral and spiritual life of its students. This demands nothing less than a complete religious program. In the second place, along with this provision, the only limit placed upon student activity and leadership being the extent to which they are willing to accept and discharge such responsibility. After considerable thought on the part of the chosen leaders the following purpose and aims were adopted. Its purpose is to aid every student: (1) to come to a full and creative life through a growing knowledge of God; (2) to make this life possible for all people; (3) and in their search for an understanding of Jesus and endeavor to follow Him.
>
> Its aims are:
> (1) To promote a sincere spirit of tolerance and cooperation.
> (2) To include activities fitted to all types of personality.
> (3) To develop the comradeship of faculty and students.
> (4) To make possible the sharing of viewpoints and convictions on important questions.

(5) To foster the highest relationship between men and women.

(6) To develop individual and social integrity.

(7) To increase the scope of religious knowledge.

(8) To develop mastery over the forces of life.

(9) To insure a richer, more abundant life.

While it was perfectly obvious that an organization should be developed, there was the uniform acceptance of the basic principle that organization should always be considered as a means and not as an end. . . . The very first group set up for the beginning of the program decided unanimously that neither constitution nor by-laws would be adopted, but that near the close of each academic year a careful survey and appraisal of the work of that year would be made and from this study and its implications a program would be adopted for the succeeding year. This has been done every year since the chapel work was started and has proved to be a very wise procedure.

Dean Powers then went on to outline the makeup of the Chapel Board, consisting of both faculty and students, and the personnel constituting the chapel staff and to list the denominations or faith groups that had counselors at the chapel. He laid out the program in some detail, listing the three emphases of worship: Sunday morning services and the daily chapel, the discussion groups, and the committee structure. He pointed out the importance he attached to counseling as a function of the chapel staff. At the conclusion of the article, Powers made the following evaluation of the work of Hendricks Chapel:

It is said that religious work must be done many times purely on faith, almost with a complete absence of visible results. Yet it is possible for us to chronicle certain results which have been produced by this extensive and intensive but definitely religious program. Perhaps as significant as anything in this connection is the campus wide respect in which the chapel program is held. The maximum degree of participation is another result. More students are active in the chapel program than in any other student activity on the Syracuse campus. Far beyond anything dreamed is the preparation for later leadership through this program. The leadership in the churches of city, village and countryside is augmented every year by students who have had four years experience in this very productive laboratory of religious life. A different type of alumnus is being produced who thinks of his Alma Mater not in terms of a winning football team, a delightful social life or any of these passing phases of what is called collegiate, but who thinks of that institution on the campus which was to him a helpful friend from the first day of his Freshman year to the day of his graduation. Citizenship is more prized because of its opportunities of unselfish service through the training received in such a program as that of Hendricks Chapel. One of the surprises in connection with this work has been the degree to which it has developed as an inducement for students to come to Syracuse University. In the decision of more than twenty-five percent of this year's Freshman class to choose Syracuse University, the Hendricks Chapel program was definitely one of the decisive factors.

A comment on this last point is in order. Dean Powers and some members of his staff had played a significant part in recruiting students for Syracuse University. One needs to recall that this era was still a time of economic depression and also that Syracuse University served the populations of the towns and villages of upstate New York as well as reaching out to other sections of the country. In the years before she was married, Bernice Meredith recounted the excursions that she and Dean Powers had made on what she called the "meat-loaf circuit" of churches. On a given evening ministers, usually, though not always, of Methodist churches would bring their high school youth together to hear the story of Syracuse University. Both Dean Powers and his associate would tell of the work of Hendricks Chapel in these discussion sessions. In addition, in many instances the dean would be able to help a young man or woman with inadequate financial resources who was inclined to think that college was an impossibility. Such young people were helped to find the necessary loans or scholarships that would make college possible. Although this is not the sole reason that young people chose Syracuse University, these recruiting expeditions could not help but be a factor in their decision.

Dean Powers concluded the article as follows:

> Syracuse University aims not only to train the mind but to give to the individual experience with guidance in all phases of life. Hendricks Chapel provided for the students of Syracuse University the opportunity for religious and social growth and experimentation. The place the Chapel holds in the minds and lives of the students, in the respect of the faculty and in the memory of alumni tells the story of its significance to present day college youth.

It may be recalled that early in this book a quotation was given from Dr. Galpin's history of the university in which he spoke of the zealous belief of the founders of the university that theirs was a task under divine Providence. It seems appropriate to make the same comment about the giving of the chapel and the establishment of its operation under the first dean. Some less theologically disposed persons might be inclined to describe what happened as a fortuitous set of remarkable circumstances that came together in the history of the university to produce the chapel and its program. It can be recalled that Victor Hugo once said, "Greater than the tread of mighty armies is an idea whose time has come."

It is appropriate to note that the following elements, unique in time and place, made Hendricks Chapel possible:

• the founding of Syracuse University by committed churchmen who believed in a Christian concept of education;

• this foundation, in turn, provided the motivation for Senator Francis Hendricks to donate the money for the building of a chapel to house a religious program for all faiths;

• an administration at the university under Chancellor Flint, an ordained minister, who saw this donation as an opportunity to produce a master plan for the campus with the new chapel located at its heart;

• a university administration, faculty, and student body who were sufficiently inclined toward religion and the creation of community to give the chapel a good start;

• it was a time in religious history in the United States when religious liberalism had minimized the differences in theological belief and made cooperation possible;

• it was also a time of economic depression in both the nation and the world that had deflated the euphoric optimism of the preceding decade and prompted a search for resources and values that would be enduring;

• Syracuse University had no student union or similar facility or program, which left a vacuum that was filled in large measure by chapel activities;

• and, finally, Dean Powers proved to be the right man in the right place at the right time.

In the Book of Esther in the Old Testament, Mordecai says to Esther, "Who knows whether you have not come to the kingdom for such a time as this?" (4:4b, RSV). In one sense, a superficial look at Dr. Powers's qualifications might raise the question of whether he really was the right man to become the first dean of Hendricks Chapel: He neither had a brilliant mind nor was a great scholar. He was a graduate of Syracuse University, but he did not go on to earn a theological degree. (His alma mater honored him early with the doctor of divinity degree.) What, then, was it that made him so uniquely able to bring about through his leadership such extraordinary results at Hendricks Chapel? Three qualities of mind and heart stand out.

The first quality was expressed by Dr. Beck at Dean Powers's funeral service. He emphasized that Powers was "first of all a man of deep devotion to his God." It was this quality of life that had led him into the ministry and was the rock that formed the foundation on which he based all that he did at Syracuse University. This devotion impressed and inspired his collegiate hearers, so they listened and responded to his effective preaching.

The second quality was Dean Powers's great and natural skill in human relationships, or, as Dr. Beck phrased it, his "great capacity for friendship." Friendship was only part of a larger talent that included Powers's ability to lead people, his confidence in the potential of youth, his concern for the welfare of others, and his broad tolerance of human differences.

The third ingredient was his vocational consciousness. Dr. Powers was aware

William H. Powers, first dean of Hendricks Chapel, served from 1930 to 1944. He had studied as an undergraduate at Syracuse University, and in 1925 Chancellor Flint granted him an honorary doctorate in divinity, praising his "combination of energy, executive ability, and spirituality." Photograph by Steve Sartori of oil portrait. Courtesy of Syracuse University Art Collection.

that in coming to Syracuse University to be the first dean of a new chapel he was given a uniquely privileged opportunity to make history. In accepting this challenge, he gave all the resources of his life that he could command with single-minded purpose. He insisted that there should be no mediocrity in the program and that it should receive the status from Syracuse University and the community that he believed it deserved.

When it came time for Dean Powers to lay down his responsibilities, his contribution to Syracuse University's life through Hendricks Chapel had made a profound difference both in the lives of many students and to the university itself.

With penetrating insight Dr. William P. Tolley, chancellor of Syracuse University, spoke the following words at the funeral service for Dean Powers. With the quoting of these words, we bring the history of Hendricks Chapel under its first dean, the Reverend William Harrison Powers, D.D., to a close.

Fifteen years ago the walls of this Chapel were slowly rising toward the sky and the dreams of a great architect were being made real in brick and stone. As the builders were busy with their work a vigorous and winsome preacher called from Ithaca to be the first Dean of Hendricks Chapel was also busy with his plans. He envisioned here a new kind of religious program, unlike that on any other campus. He dreamed of a Chapel that would transcend all differences of creed, all distinctions of faith, and that would unite all students and faculty in love of God and their fellow men. He thought of himself not as Dean of Methodists or Presbyterians, not as Dean of Protestants or Catholics, not as Dean of Christians or Jews, but as Dean of religion for every student in the university. But he also knew that an institution as broad as the universe should plan a religious program for universal needs. He knew that education needed a new dimension—the depth of the resource of religion. He knew that the minds and emotions and wills of men needed the nourishment and help provided only by religious faith. He wanted to Minister to that need without sectarian limitations.

He was happy in the location of the Chapel. Because religion is in the very center of life, he knew the Chapel should be where it is—in the very center of the campus. He liked to remind us that Hendricks Chapel is the heart of the university and pumps its life-giving strength to every other building.

It was he who helped select the scripture on the walls, and made a place for the star of David as well as the Cross of Christ in the chancel. It was he who built an inter-faith program with Jews as well as Christians on the Student Chapel Board.

Whether his dream of interfaith unity has been fully achieved here in the university is not a question that need trouble us. What is significant is the path he made, the bridge he built, the way he made plain by precept and example. If Syracuse University has a mental climate friendly to religious values, if it is tolerant of other races and faiths, if it is more concerned with fundamental unities than diverse differences, we can thank Dean Powers. The program of Hendricks Chapel is his program. From the beginning this Chapel has been the lengthened shadow of a man.

21. The Close of War Brings Changes, 1944–1945

THE DEATH OF DEAN POWERS at the end of 1944 not only marked the conclusion of his ministry at Hendricks Chapel, but also made evident gradual but steady changes in the chapel program as its planners sought to respond to significant shifts in the student body at Syracuse University brought about by the disruption of the war years.

One major shift was an increasing religious, ethnic, and cultural pluralism on campus. When Dr. Powers came to Syracuse University first as its chaplain and then as the chapel's first dean, the university's roots in the Methodist Church were still a dominant factor in the religious affiliation of students, faculty, and members of the administration. Thus, Dr. Powers was able to bring the programs of most denominations represented on campus, hitherto operating from separate locations, under the aegis of the chapel as part of its total program. It was his dream to find the common elements in a diversified student religious community and unite them in a comprehensive program under the auspices of Hendricks Chapel. For most of his deanship this concept prevailed and was effectively implemented.*

The era immediately surrounding World War II was a time when a liberal theology prevailed in the United States, dominating the philosophy of the student religious movement of the YMCA and the YWCA and also finding expression in the Student Christian Movement (SCM), in turn affiliated with the World Student Christian Federation (WSCF). In this atmosphere, theological and church differences over interfaith matters were often minimized. Although it is not part of our story, it is significant that early leadership of the ecumenical movement found one of its principal sources in the World Student Christian Federation. In these years student bodies were predominately, though not exclusively, Protestant.

It was within this context that the program of Hendricks Chapel was conceived and initiated. Denominational activities were seen as part of the larger, inclusive whole. At this time, however, this ecumenical approach was not shared by the Roman Catholic contingent. In the long years before Vatican II, the Roman Catholic Church saw its position as unique and even exclusive, an attitude that found local expression during Dr. Powers's tenure in the Catholic denomination's establishment of the St. Thomas More House and its peripheral relationship with the chapel program.

Thus, though it may not have been as clearly apparent then as it is in retrospect, the year 1945 marked the beginning of considerable change in the program of Hendricks Chapel. Before the year was out the war would be over, a new dean would be appointed and installed, and a burgeoning of the postwar student body would tax all available university facilities—changes that would prompt the chapel to place growing emphasis on the activities of the denominational groups.

While the coming end of the war would increase enrollment, its toll had already altered the makeup of the student body by fall 1944. The university wel-

*Indeed, it had been part of Francis Hendricks's "design" for the chapel and the expressed wish of earlier Syracuse University leadership.—RLP comed its largest-ever female enrollment that semester, and Hendricks Chapel moved to respond. The first week of daily chapel featured speakers from the dean of women's office, including Deans Eunice Hilton and Marjorie Smith. These speakers were arranged by Shirley Bowman, chairman of the Daily Chapel Worship Committee. The shift in demographics also prompted a special plea for more male singers for the chapel choir.

When, in fall 1944, Chancellor Tolley realized that Dean Powers would not be able to resume his direction of the chapel, he asked the Reverend Thomas Van Loon, the Methodist student counselor, to act as chief of staff until a new dean could be selected, allowing the program to proceed steadily and without interruption. In the absence of Dr. Powers, the Reverend Thomas Van Loon preached at the first Sunday chapel service on September 17, 1944, with the Reverend Egbert Hayes conducting the service.

Although the war was still on, the chapel was a very busy place that fall, its central role reflected in a headline from the *Daily Orange* that read, "Hendricks Chapel to Begin 15th Year as Campus Center." Among the programs projected for the academic year were special services for Thanksgiving, Christmas, and Holy Week; a week of religious on-campus emphasis, called Embassy Week; an intercollegiate conference to be held at Elmira College in mid-October, and a trifaith weekend in January 1945. Outstanding guest preachers were announced, including the president of Souchan University in China; Bishop W. E. Ledden of the Methodist Church; Dr. David McLennon of Toronto; Ruth Seabury of the Board of Foreign Missions of the Methodist Church; Dr. Eugene Bartlett of the First Baptist Church of Columbia, Missouri; Dr. R. H. Espy of the National YMCA Council; and Dr. E. Franklin Frazier of Howard University in Washington, D.C.

As the semester got under way, the chapel issued its usual invitation to all students to participate in the chapel program by signing up to serve on one of its committees. By the end of the first week, 575 students had indicated their willingness to serve. Soon the program was in full swing. Early in September a tea was held for the student deans to acquaint them with what went on at the chapel. A book drive was sponsored to secure reading material for prisoners of war. Daily chapel was conducted each weekday at noon.

Distinguished leaders in the Christian world came to campus as guests of the Chapel Board. These included Dr. Winburn Thomas, executive secretary of the Student Volunteer Movement, and Dr. E. Stanley Jones, the well-known missionary and evangelist. Methodist bishop Carleton Lacy of China was the Sunday morning chapel speaker on October 22, and the members of Syracuse-in-China attended as a body.

In November the Worship Committee prepared for Thanksgiving by publishing and distributing a devotional guide, *Things We Have to Be Thankful For*. In December, students preparing to leave campus for their Christmas vacation were cheered by carol singing on the chapel steps, followed by the annual Christmas pageant. Sadly, Dean Powers was to die before their return to campus.

Upon their return, students learned of Dr. Powers's death in the January 9, 1945, edition of the *Daily Orange,* which carried not only the news story about his death but an editorial honoring him. Entitled "Father of Hendricks Chapel," it recalled the tenth anniversary of the chapel, when Dr. Powers was presented with a scroll inscribed with words of praise by then-Chancellor Graham, who characterized Dr. Powers as the "man who made Hendricks Chapel what it is today."

The chapel staff, chosen by Dr. Powers, believed that their best tribute to him would be to carry on. They rose to the challenge not only by maintaining existing programs that had proven successful in the past but by bringing into being several new programs planned under his leadership.

The first of these new undertakings was a five-week series of discussion groups. A letter was sent out to all chapel committee members, both faculty and students, inviting them to attend the discussions on Tuesday and Thursday evenings beginning in mid-January. The overall theme was "Extra-curricular Problems Facing College Students Today." Participants could choose among four specific topics: "Toward a Living Peace," "Practicing Christianity," "The Men Who Made Our Faith," and "What Can We Believe?" A committee made up of both students and staff planned and supervised the program. Students Grace McCarthy, Ruth Tannenhaus, Ruth Bisgrove, and Marjorie Tonks served, along with staff members Doris Seward, the Reverend Thomas Van Loon, and the Reverend Egbert Hayes.

Among the established programs repeated this year was Embassy Week, an attempt to engage the student body by setting up meetings in their living centers. This year, it was planned for the week beginning on Monday, February 26, when participants would consider the question, "What must we do to have a true brotherhood of men?" Speakers were drawn from both the faculty and the community.

At the beginning of March, the chapel hosted an interracial weekend led by Dr. James Robinson, pastor of the Church of the Master in New York City. This program included discussion groups and a sermon by Dr. Robinson in the chapel on the following Sunday morning.

Later that week Ray Sweetman from the New York State Student Christian Movement visited campus and spoke to students at the chapel about the upcoming Silver Bay Conference, planned for the beginning of the summer. He was on his way to the New York State SCM conference that was held in Rochester the following weekend, March 9–11. Accompanied by Doris Seward and the Reverend Egbert Hayes, a delegation of Syracuse students attended the conference and returned impressed by what they had seen; as a result, periods of meditation were scheduled in the chapel. During Lent, Roman Catholic students were invited to a retreat, likewise held in Rochester, by the Reverend Gannon Ryan.

On the Friday before Easter the *Daily Orange* announced the list of cabinet members for the following year.* On Easter Sunday, the chapel held a sunrise service at 6:30, with Bishop Earl Ledden as the speaker. This was followed at 10:50 by the special Easter morning service, preached by the Reverend Harold Ehrensberger, editor of *Motive*, the Methodist student magazine.

The substantial program carried out during the spring semester was a tribute to the dedication of the student officers and staff of the chapel, under the coordinating leadership of the Reverend Thomas Van Loon. Despite the continued dislocations caused by the war and the death of Dean Powers, they had done well.

Before the semester was over the death of President Franklin Roosevelt on Thursday, April 12, would not only shake the world but also have reverberations on campus. As the academic year came to a close Eleanor McCurdy and Doris Seward concluded their service on the chapel staff.

22. Dr. Charles C. Noble's First Year, 1945–1946

FROM AN HISTORICAL PERSPECTIVE, the highlight of the summer of 1945 was the end of the European phase of World War II. I remember very well the hastily assembled victory parade in Newport, New Hampshire, following the announcement of cessation of hostilities. After what we know as V-J Day, solemn services of thanksgiving were conducted in churches everywhere.

As students arrived to begin the 1945 fall semester at Syracuse University, they were greeted by the chancellor as the first postwar student generation. Despite the disruption of the war years, which had created all kinds of difficulties, the university had remained open and adapted well. Now, suddenly, a whole new set of circumstances was emerging that would profoundly affect campus life. Coping with these rapid changes would be a major concern of the university administration.

One major decision facing Chancellor Tolley was the selection of a new dean for Hendricks Chapel in the wake of Dean Powers's death. Tolley was committed to maintaining Hendricks Chapel as a vital and central part in the life of Syracuse University. Moreover, he understood that this goal required the chapel to be flexible, constantly adjusting its program to stay current with the times. The high national reputation of the religious program at Syracuse University gave Dr. Tolley a wide field for his choice of a new dean; the position was much sought-after, attracting people with superior qualifications. Dr. Tolley also had another advantage

*See appendix A.—RLP

in his search: his own position as an ordained minister of the Methodist Church, which gave him wide contacts and brought him many suggestions for candidates.*
After considering candidates from across the country, however, Dr. Tolley found his new dean within the Syracuse community.

One day, as he rode with some friends belonging to the First Methodist Church of Syracuse, Dr. Tolley asked about their pastor. His friends praised their minister, commenting on his unique appeal to young people. Struck by this, Dr. Tolley asked more questions. By the end of the conversation, he intuitively felt that "he had found his man." After further inquiries and clearing his choice with Bishop Ledden, Dr. Tolley made his decision. Soon the university announced the appointment of the Reverend Charles C. Noble as the new dean of Hendricks Chapel.

The *Syracuse Herald-American* was the first to carry the news in its September 9 edition, with the headline, "Rev. Noble New Hendricks Chapel Dean." This was followed by a similar announcement on the following Tuesday in the *Daily Orange*. Both accounts revealed that the new dean would be unable to take up his duties at the university until November 15, because of present commitments.

In the meantime Hendricks Chapel was sharing the excitement that marked the end of the war. Although a new dean had been chosen, the Reverend Thomas Van Loon would continue as chief of the chapel staff. Beryl Ball was named women's staff chairman, filling the position vacated by Doris Seward, who had resigned. Margaret McKinnon was named as the loan counselor, and Dr. Alice Gregg as the new executive secretary for Syracuse-in-China.

Supplementing the central chapel staff and aiding them in varying degrees were the faith leaders and denominational pastors: the Reverend Charles Schmitz, Baptist: the Reverend James Rockwell, Episcopal: the Reverend Christian Jensen, Lutheran; the Reverend Thomas Van Loon, Methodist; Arthur Hopper, Christian Science; the Reverend Alfred Rapp, Congregational; the Reverend Ellsworth Reamon, Universalist; the Reverend Robert Romig, Unitarian; the Reverend Gannon Ryan, Roman Catholic; and Dr. Milton Barron, a member of the Department of Sociology, for the Jewish ministry. The Reverend Egbert Hayes, who had very actively served as the Presbyterian pastor, had left the university during the summer, and his replacement was not made until the following April.

The student officers of the Chapel Associations had been elected previously and were on campus and ready to serve. For the women, Ruth Bisgrove of the pre-

---

*Throughout his chancellorship Tolley not only was a great supporter of Hendricks Chapel but also gave much advice and even direction regarding its operation. He continued this pattern into his retirement. My first awareness of his love of Hendricks Chapel came while I was a graduate student. During the early 1960s I became a member of the Tolley tennis group and thus came to know "the Iron Chancellor" very well.—RLP vious year had become Mrs. Hoffstra and was the chairman, with Lois Parmalee as vice chairman and Alice Webster as secretary. For the men, Russel Parker was chairman, with Ellsworth Stone as vice chairman and Chester Galaska as secretary.

During the week of September 4 registration and orientation activities proceeded. That first week the Big Chums were active, and the next week sign-ups for chapel activities would be made. On Sunday, September 9, the first Sunday chapel service of the semester, Dr. Georgia Harkness of the Garrett Biblical Institute of Evanston, Illinois, was the preacher. Responding to the times, her sermon was "A Time for Greatness." Chancellor Tolley presided at the service. Roman Catholic masses were held in Crouse College at nine thirty and eleven.

On Tuesday of the following week, at the Chapel Board meeting, with Charles Noble present, the Gold Chapel Cup was presented to the members of the first cabinet of the Chapel Board to emphasize the very special commitment that they had made to the chapel and to its program. Before the week was over 675 students had signed up for chapel activities, and it was noted that of this number 263 had specified that they would be interested in serving on the Syracuse-in-China Committee.

Dr. Dwight Beck, professor of religion, was the preacher for the Sunday chapel service on September 16. In making the announcement about the Sunday morning chapel service the *Daily Orange* began what was to become a quite regular practice of announcing the denominational evening meetings as well. For this Sunday it was noted that the Canterbury Club would meet at Grace Church at six in the evening for the Episcopalians, the Pilgrim Fellowship for Congregationalists at Plymouth would also meet at six, Baptists were invited to the First Baptist Church at five, Methodists assembled at University Church at five thirty, and the Westminster Fellowship for Presbyterians was scheduled for five forty-five at the First Presbyterian Church. It was also announced that the Sunday chapel speaker for the next week would be the Right Reverend Malcolm Peabody, bishop of the Episcopal Diocese of Syracuse.

Thomas Van Loon let it be known that the chapel would be open each day from eight to five for private meditation. On September 19, in the Colonial Room, Syracuse-in-China had its first meeting. Laura Coman and Romayne Brown were in charge of the meeting, and the first and second cabinets of the Chapel Board were presented. Dr. Alice Gregg, the new executive secretary, was also introduced. Plans for the fall program were announced. Kitty Blanchard would head the Chinese Supper Committee. Ruth Ross and John Shaver would chair the Christmas sale, and James McCurdy would head the clerical work group.

On that same evening the Interfaith Council met and was addressed by Professors Barron, Piper, and Illick. On Friday Dr. Frank Laubach, a world-famous missionary and apostle of literacy, spoke to the World Relations Committee to plead for a hunger-free world.

Later in the month Romayne Brown was named to the first cabinet for Syracuse-in-China, and the chapel staff gave a tea for the head residents of the houses to acquaint them with the chapel and its activities. On October 10 Syracuse-in-China sponsored a Chinese supper; the cost was sixty cents and open to the first eighty-five people who came.

Each year there had been some kind of financial drive to collect funds to help students with emergency loans. This year in October, with Franklin Callender and Joan Ward as chairmen, the Victory Chest Drive was announced, with a goal of $10,000 for temporary loans to aid veterans. After considerable time and effort and cajoling on the part of the *Daily Orange,* the final amount collected was $8,417.32. Though the drive did not quite reach its goal, the money was a considerable help to those students caught short of cash in emergency situations.

Among the chapel events occurring before the arrival of the new dean was one a bit different from the usual run of programs. On Friday, October 9, Dr. Benjamin Leighton of Cornell University led a fun fest for chapel members. A fee of ten cents was charged, and the affair was sponsored by the Deputation Committee. The next Sunday Dr. Halford Luccock, professor of preaching at the Yale Divinity School, was the preacher at the morning service and not untypical of his style was his sermon topic, "Sleeping Through a Revolution."

On the weekend of November 14–16 sixty-eight Lutheran students gathered at the chapel for the annual New York State Lutheran Student Association meeting. Marge Freitag, a Syracusan, was elected vice chairman of the group.

The Chinese Shop, with John Shaver as chairman, was opened on November 16 in the chapel and would continue until Christmas with Chinese articles for sale. Profits were to benefit the projects of Syracuse-in-China.

Although Dean Noble's appointment was announced in September, he was unable to take up his duties until mid-November. In the initial months of the fall 1945 semester, therefore, the chapel's staff and students filled in, planning and initiating a full program of activities, which were in full swing when the new dean arrived.

Charles Casper Noble was born in the Salvation Army Headquarters on Pennsylvania Avenue in Washington, D.C., on January 1, 1898. During his childhood, as a son of Salvation Army officers, he moved fairly frequently when his parents accepted assignments for service. Communities in which he was raised include Peoria, Illinois, and Kansas City, Missouri. By the time he was high school age the family had their home in Newton, Massachusetts, a suburb of Boston, and he graduated from Newton High School in 1916.

He might have gone to college that fall, but he had his heart set on going to Williams College and he was lacking some of their high entrance requirements. He spent a year at Wilbraham Academy taking classes that made it possible for him to enter Williams in 1917. At this period of its history, Williams was considered to be a college that served students who were financially well off. This fact, however, did not deter Charles Noble, and though the money that he brought to college was meager, by working as well as studying he was able to remain in college and graduate in 1921. He was active in campus affairs, becoming a member of Phi Gamma Delta fraternity, president of the Williams Christian Association, a leader in the college glee club and choir, a member of the varsity baseball squad, and a member of the senior honorary society.

Remembering that it was in the Williams College Chapel that Senator Hendricks found the inspiration to make the gift that made possible the chapel bearing his name at Syracuse and that it happened about the time Charles Noble was a student, the question naturally arises as to whether Charles ever saw a distinguished older man make his way across the Williams College campus to spend some quiet moments in the chapel. It is an interesting speculation for which there is no answer. It seems possible—at least there was proximity!

By the time Noble had graduated from college his decision to enter the Christian ministry was firm, and in the autumn of 1921 he entered Union Theological Seminary in New York City. While a student he served churches in surrounding communities. Upon his graduation in 1924 he was appointed to serve the Van Nest Methodist Episcopal Church in the Bronx, where he also became a member of the New York Annual Conference of the Methodist Church.

At the conclusion of his first year of ministry he journeyed to Aurora, Missouri, to marry Grace Myra Kepner, who had been head of the Department of Expression and Dramatics at Drury College in Springfield, Missouri. The young couple had known each other for ten years prior to their marriage, having gone to high school together in Newton. Grace had gone to Abbott Academy in Andover and then the Curry School of Expression in Boston. Grace had an aunt and uncle in Newton, and their home was the meeting place for Charles and Grace when he was in college and theological seminary.

At the Methodist Conference session in 1927 Noble was appointed to the King's Highway M.E. Church. Three years later he became minister of the First M.E. Church in Hartford, Connecticut. He served three years and then was assigned to Christ Church (Methodist Episcopal) in Glens Falls, New York. This post was to become his longest pastorate in a local church; he was there seven years. In addition to being the pastor of the church he became a very active community member. He served as director of the YMCA, president of the Ministerial Fellowship, and president of the Rotary Club during his time in Glens Falls.

In the spring of 1941 he was called to become the minister of the First Methodist Church in Syracuse, which brought him to the city in which he would spend the remainder of his life. Here too, in addition to serving as minister of a busy church, he reached out to serve in other areas. He became the editor of the Methodist Conference newspaper, chairman of the Social Service Committee of the Council of Churches, a Rotarian, director of the New York State YMCA, and chairman of the Civic Lenten Services.

Throughout his ministry Noble had a special interest in the field of mental health. While in Hartford he had served as president of the Hartford County Society of Mental Hygiene, and later in Glens Falls he had been a member of the committee that conducted a weekly clinic in neuropsychiatry at the Lake George Foundation. In Syracuse he became a member of the Onondaga County Mental Hygiene Association and director of the American Red Cross clinic for returned veterans.

When the Nobles came to Syracuse they were the parents of three daughters. The year Noble became dean his eldest became a freshman at Syracuse University after graduating from the Emma Willard School in Troy, New York. During his last year at First Church Syracuse in the year 1944–45, the future dean taught part-time at Emma Willard in the field of religion.

When the announcement was made in September that the new dean would be the Reverend Charles C. Noble, he gave an interview that provided both his reason for accepting the post and some of his ideas about what he hoped to accomplish in his new position. In accepting the deanship he said that it was his belief that the postwar world was in a state of disintegration and that it needed unity. "It is my opinion that no one field such as philosophy, science or economics can do this. The world needs 'oneness' around which to build. To me, the way to find this is through the will of God." He stressed his intention of continuing the program established by Dean Powers. He also indicated that he would like to see more denominational workers at the chapel. "They must bring the meaning of religion before their groups and weld them into a harmonious working whole."

He hoped to visit other campuses and was "keenly interested" in examining their activities in promoting courses that would help students think through their philosophy and religion for life. He indicated that he had a number of projects in mind to be discussed and worked out with students. He also expressed his desire to become better acquainted with members of the faculty so that the program of the chapel would be coordinated with the rest of the university.

Though he was able to attend meetings and functions on an occasional basis, Noble did not assume his full responsibilities until much of the semester had passed. On Sunday, November 25, he was installed as dean at the morning service of worship.

The installation service was preceded by special music prior to the 10:50 A.M. chapel worship hour. The service began with a procession of participants in full academic attire and included members of the Board of Trustees, the University Senate, and other members of the faculty and administration; representatives from colleges and universities in upstate New York; and the principals of the installation service. The new dean was presented for installation by Vice Chancellor Finla G. Crawford to Chancellor Tolley and Bishop Earl Ledden of the Methodist Church, who shared in the act of installation. Also assisting in the service was Rabbi Benjamin Friedman of the Temple Society of Concord and the Reverend Thomas Van Loon, Methodist chaplain and interim head of the chapel staff.

Following his formal induction the new dean preached a sermon titled "Religion's Part in Civilization's Battle." The service was broadcast over radio station WSYR. Among the things he said in his sermon were the following: "In this welter of world forces, we, of Hendricks Chapel must share the broad faith of our Jewish-Christian heritage, faith that God is the center of all being and human experience. Without a unifying sense of one eternal purposeful God, a university will at best become nothing more than a multiversity." Following the service an informal reception was held for the Nobles in the chapel's Colonial Room.

That afternoon the newly installed dean was again back at the chapel for the second annual Chapel Convocation. The first half hour was a time for the dean to get acquainted with staff and the cabinets. The next segment was an hour devoted to four discussion groups, each with a faculty leader and student chairman. They were arranged so that each committee or commission had an assigned group to attend. The first was listed as "Hebrew-Christian Association," and the leader was Professor Dwight Beck with Peggy Nass as student chairman. The Interfaith Commission, the Worship and Music Committees, and the ushers were assigned to this section. The second group had as its topic "World Relatedness," with Professor Carl Bye as leader and Romayne Brown as student chairman. This group was composed of the World Relations Committee, Syracuse-in-China, and the Graduate Commission. The third group was led by Professor Ross Hoople with Betty Burdett as student chairman. Its subject was "Growth of Persons" and sharing in it were the Freshman Commission, the House Representatives, and the Deputation Committee. "Social Responsibility" was the topic of the fourth group, led by Professor Milton Barron with Helen Spiner as student chairman. Making up this group were the Social Service, Social Relations, and Campus Relations Committees. Following the discussion groups supper was served at a cost of twenty-five cents, and the evening concluded with an interfaith vesper service conducted by the newly installed dean. The student chairman of the convocation was Marjorie Ehrenreich.

Noble had been formally installed by leaders of the university administration and religious community in the presence of a worshiping congregation. In his sermon he had set forth some of his dreams and aspirations for the chapel. In the afternoon he had been able to share with the chapel family, staff, students, and some of the faculty as they confronted their work together. It had been a good day launching the career of a new dean who was to lead Hendricks Chapel for years to come.

THERE WAS NOT MUCH TIME before Christmas vacation, but the chapel schedule was full. During the next week it was announced that there would be a new chapel committee, Chapel Service, to keep a record of all chapel activities. Named as cochairmen for the first cabinet were Margery Knapp and Art Blackburn, and named cochairmen for the second cabinet were Dorothy Harley and

Malcolm Coleman. Shortly thereafter the World Relations Committee and chapel representatives from each living center announced that food would be sent abroad for the hungry and needy in the postwar world.

The next Sunday the season of Advent started. Noble preached on "Hope in a Hopeless World," and Professor Verrees and the choir provided Christmas music. In the evening the annual Christmas pageant was presented in candlelight with a series of tableaus. The theme was "Meditation at Christmastime." The choir sang before curtain time, and the production was sponsored by Zeta Phi Eta and directed by Helen Bishop.

The following Sunday Professor Douglas Steer of Haverford College, a member of the Society of Friends, was the speaker, with Noble presiding. The following Tuesday, the last daily chapel was held, and Dean Noble spoke on the timely subject "Christmas and Examinations."

The chapel Christmas service, held on Sunday morning, December 16, was a first for Noble. As always it was a very special festival with music by the choir and a message appropriate to the day titled "Stars over Syracuse." Before the week was over most students were on their way home for the Christmas recess, and after the first round of active participation in the life of the chapel the new dean would get ready for the new year and his first full semester as dean.

With the opening of the 1946 spring semester the first portents of what would happen to the size of the student body began to appear. Chancellor Tolley had earlier made it clear that Syracuse University felt a moral obligation to provide educational opportunities for those individuals who had been denied it by their participation in the war effort. Although the great flood of students was yet to come, the pressure was already beginning to be felt, and in Syracuse home owners responded to appeals to make rooms available as the need arose. When the count was complete 7,405 students had registered for the second semester, an all-time high for SU to this point. Along with the increase in numbers there would be other changes as well. Many more married students would become a part of the student body, and housing and other provisions would need to be made for them.

As usual, early in the semester sign-ups were conducted in the chapel for either new arrivals on campus or those students who had not indicated their desire to participate in the chapel program in the fall.

The first Sunday morning of the new year found Noble in the pulpit preaching on "Getting Down to Business," with Van Loon presiding. Masses were held at Crouse College at nine thirty and eleven o'clock, and the Congregationalists, Episcopalians, Lutherans, and Methodists announced open-house receptions for the evening. The second Sunday Noble presided with the Reverend Albert Butzer of Buffalo in the pulpit. Well-known guest preachers were a tradition at Hendricks Chapel, one that Noble was to continue.

After his appointment to the university it was necessary for the dean to find a place to live. Fortunately, he was able to secure a house on Ostrom Avenue, within easy walking distance of the campus. The house was near the corner of Euclid, and over the years countless numbers of students found their way there to accept the hospitality of the dean and his gracious wife, Grace. An early January event in the Nobles' home was the entertainment of all the presidents of the living centers.

This year the student-affairs division of the university highlighted the awarding of the Chapel Cup. It was given to the living center that showed the greatest participation in chapel activities. Earlier, a new point system had been worked out by two math majors, Harriet Hoffman and Philip Dunning. The contest was to close on March 15, and this year two cups were to be presented. One would be given to a men's house and one to a women's house.*

During the semester, in addition to all of the regular activities of Sunday morning worship, daily chapel, and the various activities sponsored by the committees and commissions of the Chapel Board, four special emphases were added. The first was an interfaith discussion held in the chapel lounge on February 13 that followed the sermon on the previous Sunday by Rabbi Philip S. Bernstein of Rochester, "Plain Talk about Brotherhood Today." The questions for the discussion were "How far can Jewish-Christian relations go? Is Hendricks Chapel the answer?" Margaret Nass, head of the Chapel Worship Committee, was chairman, and staff adviser was Beryl Ball, women's student counselor.

Sunday, February 24, was designated as Interracial Sunday, with Dr. James Robinson, pastor of the Church of the Master in New York City, as the morning preacher. In the afternoon discussion groups were held with various campus leaders. Following supper, Dr. Robinson spoke at a meeting sponsored jointly by the NAACP of Syracuse, the Interfaith Committee of the chapel, and other campus organizations.

On Sunday, the last day of March, the third Chapel Cooperative Conference was held. It was sponsored by the Hendricks Chapel Association, with the announced purpose of dealing frankly with sexual behavior standards. Methodist bishop Fred Corson of Philadelphia preached the morning sermon, asking the question "Are Christ's Standards Obsolete?" In the evening, following a supper, a discussion was held on the topic "Morals: Today and Tomorrow." Freshman Weekend followed on April 6, and in his sermon on Sunday morning Noble preached on the question "Are We Still Expendable?"

During the first week in April a tea was held by the chapel staff to welcome the newly appointed Presbyterian counselor, the Reverend Wilbert B. Smith, Jr., who had come to replace the Reverend Egbert Hayes.

Earlier in March elections had been held for the student officers of the Chapel

*Noble was to say in later years that the points for chapel participation were the key to a full chapel.—RLP

Associations. David Bauer was elected men's student chairman and Romayne Brown women's student chairman. Student chairmen of committees and commissions were announced later. These student leaders would come back to a campus literally overflowing with students that would tax their abilities and the facilities of the university. Dean Noble had already made a place for himself not only at the chapel but also in the total life of the university, which would prove providential for the challenging years ahead.

When commencement weekend came Noble preached the baccalaureate sermon for the first time. In doing so he reached not only the students but also the larger university family in a way that would make him an effective spokesman for his adopted alma mater, a role that would continue for almost a quarter of a century, not only in Syracuse but in the entire northeastern part of the United States as well.

23. Meeting the Challenges of Triple Enrollment, 1946–1947

THE ACADEMIC YEAR that began in September 1946 was an extraordinary one for Syracuse University and for Hendricks Chapel. Though World War II had been over for more than a year it was at this time that the tidal wave of GI Bill students hit the campus in full force. Some institutions of higher learning set quotas above which they would not admit students from the flood of returning veterans. Syracuse did not set limits. Chancellor Tolley had made it clear that the university would admit any qualified veteran who wished to enroll. So come they did, men hungry and eager to get an education and make up for the time that they had spent in military service. Others came who might never have had the chance for a college education but who, under the GI Bill, were given the opportunity.

From a student body of a little more than five thousand in the fall of 1945 the numbers soared to more than fifteen thousand before registration was over in 1946. Space was in great demand. Living quarters had to be found, and expanded places to eat had to be provided. Classroom space was needed. Qualified instructional personnel were short. The university had anticipated that the student population might double, but when it tripled the logistical problems were immense. The government helped. After all the living facilities were filled around campus, barracks space was found at the state fairgrounds, in Baldwinsville, and in Mattydale. Transportation to and from these locations was worked out. University dining rooms were expanded and hours extended, and the commercial establishments on Crouse and Marshall Streets became very busy. As soon as they could be secured from the government, temporary prefabricated classrooms were set up on almost any space available.

To be more specific about the makeup of the student body, the final registration figure was 15,228, with 10,516 of them men; 90 percent of this number were veterans. Furthermore, though no statistics are available, a significant number of veterans were married, as were some of the other students.

Hendricks Chapel had also anticipated a large influx of students and sought to be ready for them when they arrived. By this time Noble's orientation was over, and he was the established chief executive officer of a multifaceted program.

After its installation in the spring of 1947, the new Chapel Board had begun to make plans. They held meetings with the retiring board, the staff, and faculty advisers. Just before the opening of the fall semester they held a Chapel Board retreat at Casawasco, a Methodist conference center thirty-five to forty miles away, where they got acquainted and reviewed and polished their plans for the various committees and commissions for the coming year.

At registration each student was asked to fill out a religious preference card in duplicate; one copy was given to denominational counselors, and the other was kept in the chapel office. Each new student was given a carefully prepared booklet, *Getting at the Heart of Things*, a guidebook to Hendricks Chapel. It included a message from Noble, greetings from the chapel organization cochairs, an explanation of Chapel Night, and the opportunity for sign-ups. There were descriptions of the various committees and commissions. There were announcements of events to come, such as "Meet Your Faculty," special weekends, hospitality at the Nobles' home, a snack and fellowship every Thursday from four to five at the chapel, and the announcement of a couples' club. Syracuse-in-China was highlighted, and a proposed program, "A Veteran Views His World," was projected. There was a list of the religious counselors for each faith and denominational group and an account of their programs and times of meeting. Under the heading "At Your Disposal" the resources of the chapel were described, including the use of the Dorothy Webster Memorial Library, study in the Colonial Room, or an opportunity for leisure in the lounge, the latter two rooms described as "among the most popular on campus." There was an explanation of the Student Emergency Loan Fund and an invitation to invite chapel staff into the living centers. At the bottom, on the cover, two events were listed: Freshman Sunday, September 15, and Chapel Night, Thursday, September 26.

Freshmen had arrived early for a special SU orientation, and though the schedule was much as it had been in prewar days, no Freshman Camps were held because no place of sufficient size was available. Great emphasis was placed on Chapel Night. Posters had been displayed at places where students congregated and in their living centers. The *Daily Orange* carried a write-up about Chapel Night, and it was announced at the convocations for men and women as a part of Newcomer's Daze Week.

Upon arrival for Chapel Night everyone was given a name tag with one half of a college name on it like "Cor" and "Nell." The object was to find the person with the other half. The place was jammed, with more than nine hundred attending. Student members circulated to talk up the chapel. Football coach Munn gave a short talk on "The Part of Religion in a College Student's Life." The student chairman spoke, and Dean Noble introduced the committee members. Two students told the attendees what the chapel meant to them. Opportunity was given for signing up, and refreshments were served. After the rug was rolled up there was dancing in the Colonial Room and in the lounge. Those individuals who liked to sing gathered around the piano.*

The theme of the evening was "Rah, Rah, Syracuse," and when it was over students left reluctantly and those persons who had planned it believed that the programs of the chapel had been well launched. At the retreat for planning it had been emphasized that "the whole challenge of our year at Hendricks Chapel lay here at the beginning." Hence, Chapel Night and Chapel Sign-Up were greatly emphasized as "a reliable barometer of the future of the Chapel program." At the retreat two slogans had been adopted: "Every Syracusan—a Chapelite" and "to make Chapel, campus conscious and campus, Chapel conscious."

A further concern was a genuine attempt to promote a sense of unity among the faith leaders and groups and to provide a more adequate plan and structure to bring this goal about. The guideline was the expressed expectation that the denominational chaplains and counselors would devote one-third of their time to the overall program of the chapel.

Earlier I noted that there was a strong effort to have each student fill out a religious preference card at registration time. When registration was over the report (though unofficial) for fall semester 1946 by the chairman, Rosalind Glickman, was as follows: Roman Catholic, 1,833; Jewish, 1,688; Methodist, 1,418; Presbyterian, 1,119; other Protestants, 2,797; others, 363; and no preference, 394, making a grand total of 9,612.

Here is how carefully and thoroughly the Chapel Board was organized. At the top was the Executive Committee made up of the two cochairs, Romayne Brown and David Bauer; the two vice chairs, Jeanne Marge and Edward Hanna; two secretaries, Claire Smith and Philip Dunning; and this year for the first time two recording secretaries were added, Rosalind Glickman and Arthur Andrews. All were students.

This leadership group was very active in initiating, supervising, and coordinat-

---

*Noble was known to play both the piano and his accordion for such singing and other events. —RLP ing a whole host of different programs under the chapel umbrella. The multiplicity of activities leaves one a bit breathless. These days were highly intense and busy times at Syracuse University, and it was generally believed that at its very heart was Hendricks Chapel. The leaders sought, with great energy, to be equal to the challenge placed upon them.

They had begun the year in September with the retreat for the whole board and staff at Casawasco. They had set up a special "Bluebook Committee" to revise and improve the chapel guidebook for freshmen. They made reforms in the standards for the awarding of the Chapel Cups, making participation in the interfaith groups count toward the award. In the same spirit they broadened and lengthened what had been Embassy Week, both giving it a broader interfaith base and stretching the week to a longer period. They established the Watch and Ward Committee to supervise the use of the chapel rooms and to monitor the activities so that the whole complex operation could proceed decently and in order. The increased size of the student body made such careful stewardship of the chapel space and resources a necessity.

Through the vice chairs the Executive Committee supervised and trained members of the second cabinet, assistant leaders who were being groomed for larger leadership roles. Weekly meetings were held with the second cabinet to keep them informed and up-to-date on what was going on and also to give them training and skills in leading meetings and discussion groups.*

In the late 1940s most of those individuals who were associated with the chapel program were members of chapel committees or commissions. At the time of the sign-up one person was allowed to serve on two committees and one subcommittee. Many, of course, took only one responsibility. Here, to illustrate the workings of the chapel, is a description of the projected function of each committee and its personnel. With this one year's example we can see the rather enormous sweep and diversity within the most active and prestigious organization on campus.† An attempt has been made here to group committees so they can be seen not only in their uniqueness but also in their relatedness.

We begin with the Worship Committee. The Sunday service of worship (known as University Worship) was largely under the direction of the dean. Beyond the Sunday service the principal responsibility of the student committee, with chairs Dorothy Schambacher and Robert Fehlman (with the Reverend James

---

*In some ways one can look back upon this time as the "golden years" of student leadership. From the 1960s on, student leadership was of a considerably different style, and by the early to mid-1960s the intensity of chapel participation began to fade. By the mid-1970s, patterns of student participation that exist today were emerging.—RLP

†This pattern characterized many years of the chapel operation under Deans Powers and Noble.—RLP

Rockwell as staff adviser), was the presentation of daily chapel. Emphasis was placed upon quiet, directed meditation with music and reading, including hymns and litanies. At the beginning of the semester there were special speakers. Participating in the first week, which began on October 1, were Academic Dean Frank Piskor, Dean Eunice Hilton, Dean J. Theron Illick, and the Reverend Thomas Van Loon. If there were special services, such as Thanksgiving, this committee played a role. A speech clinic was held for students needing help in presiding at the daily worship services, and an altar guild took the responsibility both to understand and to take care of the symbols of worship that were used. It was suggested that the committee prepare a devotional booklet as a guide for personal meditation. The committee met once a week.

The Music Committee was chaired by Irene Engle and Richard Stover. Professor Verrees, who played the organ and directed the choir, was staff adviser. Under their direction was the music for all the regular services and for special occasions. Each Sunday morning the choir, made up of 120 voices (filling a space designed for 88 voices), sang an anthem. It had been announced that academic credit was to be given for participation in the choir. Credit for participation in the choir had been given in the very early years, so this announcement was a resumption of that practice. The choir was organized and had three soloists. The president was Dominick Lamaccia, Charlotte Rutty was secretary-treasurer, and Sue Shaw was social chairman.*

The Chapel Ushers Committee consisted of 26 men divided into two groups, each performing their task every other Sunday and at any special services in the sanctuary. Fred Wolk was chairman, and the Reverend Wilbert Smith, Jr., was adviser.

A fairly recently established committee was Chapel Service, which was created to do a wide variety of housekeeping chores to keep things going. The members provided the free snacks at an all-chapel fellowship time each Thursday afternoon. They supervised chapel social functions, receptions, and teas and provided refreshments for them. They had charge of the Dorothy Webster Memorial Library and kept a scrapbook and lists of people participating in the chapel. In their hands were the sign-up process and the supervision of the elections. It was also projected that they might find a way to hold some social events for the whole official chapel family. The student cochairs were Esther Stevenson and Robert Young. Beryl Bell was the adviser.†

It was the purpose of the Campus Relations Committee, with Helen Budd and

---

*The chapel choir was to remain the best-known choir within the university and often made tours as well as singing at other university events.—RLP

†The importance of these functions continued even after student leadership styles changed. During the 1970s, 1980s, and 1990s most of these responsibilities were handled by paid chapel staff members.—RLP

Clyde Jones as cochairs and Bell and Dean Noble as staff advisers, to get all the publicity possible for the chapel's programs and events. They devised several ways of doing this task. Stories of events were provided for the *Daily Orange,* and it was hoped that a special weekly column might be established to list the activities of the chapel. The downtown newspapers were also alerted to special events. Posters were put up both in public places on campus and in living centers to announce chapel programs and activities. A chapel publication, *Chapel Chimes,* was planned and issued in the second semester. It was distributed on campus and made available to interested alumni and to other colleges and universities. In conjunction with the Chapel Service Committee and to improve faculty-student relationships a series of coffee hours were held.

The primary aim of the House Representatives Committee was to provide a conduit between each living center and the chapel. Each week a meeting would be held at which all chapel news was announced, and mimeographed materials were made available to be taken back to each house for posting. This committee also kept the records for the awarding of the Chapel Cup. The committee's adviser was Van Loon, and the student cochairs were Geraldine Matingly and Robert Lindsey.[*]

Although the idea of Freshman Camp had to be abandoned, the idea behind it continued to flourish through the Freshman Commission. Early in the first semester there was a freshman orientation course, with members of the faculty as leaders. Usually there was a faculty panel, a breakup into smaller discussion groups, and a social hour to conclude. The first topic was "What's the Big Idea?"—what to expect out of college, with Dean Noble leading. "Friendships—Fatal or Fruitful?" dealt with fraternities and other campus relationships and was led by Professor Herman Boyle. Dean Frank Piskor led the group asking the question "Are 24 Hours a Day Enough?" which had to do with the planning of personal time. "Dating, Drinking, Dealing," focusing on morality, was another topic for Noble. "Prayer, Piety, and Popularity" had to do with building a philosophy of life, for which Vice Chancellor Finla Crawford was the leader. "How's Your Health?"— keeping fit mentally—was discussed by Dean Eric Faigle.

In the spring semester the Freshmen Commission planned weekly meetings, to which they invited campus leaders to speak and lead discussions. Among the topics were sexual morals, interfaith relationships, prejudice, cribbing, and how to develop a pleasing personality. Beryl Ball and Dean Noble were advisers and Marcia Taylor was student chair of the Freshman Commission.[†]

---

[*]Noble attributed the high Sunday attendance at worship to the work of the committee and the value placed on the "cup." His preaching deserved much of the credit also.—RLP

[†]In the year 2005 the chapel continues to be charged with responsibility for programming for all students in areas dealing with questions of purpose, meaning, values, ethical concerns, morality, relationships, and social responsibility. Students still generate many of the issues and questions that be-

Though not listed officially as part of the Chapel Board committees, a kind of ad hoc Senior Commission developed later in the year. Its purpose was to help seniors get ready for the world beyond college. Senioritis was alive and well even then!

Among the veterans coming to the university were men seeking graduate degrees. The chapel sought to be helpful to them through the Graduate Commission. Some of these students were identified both in a religious preference card at registration and at the chapel sign-up time. Early in the fall a reception was held for graduate students, and later, for any who were interested, an after-dinner coffee period was held that focused attention on world religions. A social event at Halloween drew one hundred graduate students together. A group of about twenty-five participated in a deliberately informal and unstructured program, and a special attempt was made to reach out to the international students on campus. From March into May Dean Noble led a seminar for them on "The Anatomy of Spiritual Power," which focused on the relationship of religion to personal growth and development. Mary Winhurst and Warren Scott were chairs of the Graduate Commission, and Beryl Ball was the adviser.*

The work of the Interfaith Committee can probably be understood only in terms of the history and context in which it sought to function. After their experiences in the war many of the veterans were not convinced that faith differences were vitally essential, and they were often impatient with those persons who emphasized exclusivity. The history of the chapel is replete with both successful and not-so-successful attempts at interfaith cooperation. At the fall retreat at Casawasco, the Chapel Board decided great efforts should be made in this area. In fairness and objectivity, it needs to be remembered that prior to Vatican II the exclusive posture of the Roman Catholic Church made cooperation in all interfaith ventures a very limited or surface one. At Syracuse University the establishment of the St. Thomas More House symbolized a philosophy of student ministry, and its leadership provided very little support for interfaith cooperation. This history is not surprising given the times and the Methodist origins of the university and the dominant Protestant position in the operation of Hendricks Chapel, even as it reached out, somewhat ahead of the national trend, hopefully and generously to

---

come the basis for programs, but the programmatic follow-up is largely staff and chaplain facilitated.—RLP

*At this time SU did not have a special office for assisting international students, and the graduate population was just beginning to grow. For years the chapel was the chief source of assistance for many of the everyday needs of international students. Noble gained an excellent reputation for "saving" such students, who suffered everything from homesickness to cultural confusion and financial difficulties. It did not take any of the SU students long to discover that Noble was not only friendly and helpful but also a first-class problem solver.—RLP

other faith groups. The advisers to the Interfaith Committee were Noble and Rabbi Earl Stone.* The student chairs were Wilma Jepson and John Shaver.†

Early in October, under the leadership of Father Ryan, Rabbi Stone, and one of the Protestant counselors, a series was begun titled "Areas of Appreciation of the Three Faith Cultures." Three weeks were given to each faith, first to explore its history and culture, second to understand its liturgy and religious holidays, and third to see its influence on culture and society. These meetings were held on Wednesday afternoons. They began with a tea followed by a presentation and discussion. In the spring another series was held with such topics as "Church and State," "Religion and Segregation," and "Religion and Education." In evaluation it was confirmed that the response to this committee's work was not very good. Somewhat later the formation of the Interfaith Council would try to find a better structure for interfaith cooperation.‡

Syracuse-in-China had long been a fixture on campus, with its own staff and widespread alumni support. Student support for the organization was also strong, and in 1946 118 had signed up to serve its program. Its stated aims were cultural interchange, with a special relationship with West China Union College. Subcommittees consisted of Program, Dramatics, Chinese Supper, Far Eastern Courses Promotion, and the Chinese Christmas Sale. In late October Ruth Hoople, executive secretary, escorted a group of students to Toronto, where, as in previous years, they visited the Chinese Department of the Royal Ontario Museum.

"The largest aim and achievement" for the year was the sending of a Syracuse University representative to teach English at West China Union College. Funding for this aim came through money from the Campus Chest, an annual fund-raising

---

*Stone would later have a long and very distinguished ministry in Denver.—RLP

†It is only fair to say that I differ from Donald Wright on the connection between exclusivity and the St. Thomas More House. In later years and under different leadership the relationship between Hendricks Chapel and this ministry was excellent, productive, and rewarding. Thus, my position is that leadership was the key and not the fact of a separate facility. In fact, the growth in the percentage of SU students who were Roman Catholic accelerated after World War II, and we would not have been able to provide enough space for the ministry were it not for the separate facility.—RLP

‡Francis Hendricks's dream and stipulation of a chapel that would serve all faiths were not compromised, even though the dream, perhaps somewhat naive, did not take the form some had hoped. Indeed, in different periods of the history of the chapel the style of being "a house of worship for all" manifested itself in different ways. Without doubt, many envisioned a melting-pot faith where all could fellowship and worship under one banner. Fortunately, from my point of view, that effort never came to dominate or define the Hendricks Chapel ministry to the campus. The expressed need for the integrity and unique content and style of each of the world's religions was always espoused and practiced along with major efforts at cooperation in programming and shared expressions of spirituality. As the university became more and more multicultural, nationally and religiously, the chapel found itself on a strong foundation to serve everyone. Indeed, it served then and serves now as a model for other campuses.—RLP

project. After two years the representative would return to Syracuse, and it was be-lieved that "the effects of his stay will do much to further the cultural tie we are striving to have." Kenneth Brock was president of the association, and the cochair was Ruth Ross.

The World Relations Committee focused its programs on knowledge and ac-tion. In the postwar period world affairs were very much on the minds of students, and many of them with war experience had lived among people from very different cultures. One program included ten discussion meetings with speakers and films. Included were such topics as atomic energy, the United Nations, world relief and rehabilitation, the CARE Program, Russia, India, and the Zionists in Palestine. These meetings were well attended, with about forty present at each. In Novem-ber the committee mobilized the campus to collect both clothing and food for the world's needy. This drive was repeated in February, and the goal was to secure a ton of food to be sent overseas for the hungry. The Reverend Donald Prigge, a Syracuse graduate who had returned to become the Lutheran counselor, was the adviser to this committee whose cochairs were Marilyn Baum and George Daigneault.

It was the purpose of the Deputation Committee to send out to area churches and organizations that would receive them a group, usually of four people, who would spend the weekend, usually in a church, working with their youth. Though the format would vary, it usually consisted of a social program on Saturday evening. On Sunday they would teach in the church school and participate in the morning service of worship. In the afternoon they would have a hike or some other social event. They had individual conferences to talk about college, and on Sunday evening they would conduct a short worship service followed by discussion groups. The host church would take care of their transportation and provide for their needs while they were in the parish. The first semester was spent largely in training, and preparation, and about ten teams went out during the second semester. The *Daily Orange* carried a story on one of these teams when it reported that over the first weekend in March a team of coeds conducted a deputation visit to Adams Methodist Church and because of storms, not uncommon in that area, were stranded there for four days. There was committee frustration with so many of their number willing to participate and too few churches willing to invite them.* Dorothy Laird and Ralph Beane were cochairs, and the Reverend Thomas Van Loon was the adviser.

Another service opportunity was open to those individuals who wished to be-come assistant teachers in Sunday schools. This was accomplished in locations close enough to the campus to be carried out each Sunday morning. Eva Teich-man was the chair of this committee, and Beryl Ball was the adviser.

*It is not uncommon for committees (even great organizations) to create wonderful, powerful programs for which there is simply not enough expressed need. The deputation-team idea is a great one, but such efforts must always be based on demand and be a good fit with the times.—RLP

Two other service opportunities were open to students, the Personal Social Service Committee and the Group Social Service Committee. The first was for those students who wished to be useful on a one-on-one basis. There were opportunities to tutor or visit with shut-ins, the elderly, the blind, or those individuals who might simply like to have some contact with a student. Others could go to the hospitals to help feed patients and read or write letters for patients. In addition, patients in homes for the elderly and the Elmcrest Rheumatic Fever Hospital for children had need of this kind of personal service. Patricia Younkins was chair of the Personal Social Service Committee, and the Reverend Charles Schmitz was the adviser. The Group Social Service Committee, with Ruth Tannenhaus and Elton Ridge as cochairs and Ruth Hoople as adviser, sought to place 115 of their number in the following group work agencies in the city: the Girl Scouts, Jewish Community Center, Neighborhood House, Boys Club, and Salvation Army.

The foregoing is a brief description of the principal functions of the various committees and commissions of the Chapel Association. They were varied, vigorous, and comprehensive and involved a large number of students. Having laid out the organizational structure it may be helpful now to record some of the major functions and events of this remarkable year (1946–47) in the life of the chapel, though some have already been listed.

SUNDAYS THIS YEAR had a unique flavor about them. Other aspects of campus life might slow down, for there were no classes and the library was open only part of the day, but the chapel flourished. Roman Catholic masses were held at Crouse College at nine thirty and eleven. At ten-fifty there was a service in the main chapel with an overflow choir, popular sermons from either Dean Noble or a visiting preacher, a competent ushering staff, and pews well filled. Usually several of the living centers, including fraternities and sororities, would attend in a body (spurred at least in part by competition for the Chapel Cup). Sometimes special events would take place in the afternoon, but the early Sunday evening hours were reserved for the meetings of the various faith groups. Most of these meetings would begin with a light supper, which was a great attraction, as this meal was generally omitted in the living centers and dining halls on Sundays.

The main chapel was used for all kinds of other university-wide assemblies because it was the largest available meeting place on campus, which remained true for many decades. Some of this usage had very little to do with the chapel program as such. This function became accepted as a necessity, but it was a departure from the intent of Francis Hendricks. The pressure of an increased student body made the need great. Interestingly enough, it made the chapel an even more central part of the campus and of SU traditions.*

*There was not a larger auditorium on campus until the construction in 1984–85 of the Schine Student Center with its Goldstein Auditorium. First Manley Field House (1961) and then the Carrier

Armistice Day was celebrated with two events. At the morning service Dean Noble spoke about the needs of the Campus Chest and used the topic "A Cavalcade of Suffering" as his theme. Later in the day a veterans' convocation was held, at which time the Reverend James Claypool, D.D., a high-ranking naval chaplain and author of *God on a Battlewagon,* was the speaker. His subject was "The Veteran Views the World."

Because of an area coal strike many of the students who would ordinarily have gone home for the Thanksgiving weekend were not able to do so because many of the trains were not running. As a result a special Thanksgiving service was held in the chapel, and Dean Noble's address was titled "A Way to Say God."

The annual Christmas pageant, again with Zeta Phi Eta in charge, was presented on Sunday evening, December 15. A cast of forty, including soloists and the choir, presented *Pageant of Holy Nativity* by Leonard Young and David McKay Williams. It was the first time this work had been performed in Syracuse. The production was directed by Rosemary Sinnett, assisted by Doris Knoepke. The narrator was George Billick, and the soloists were Vera Ford, George Angell, and Dominick Lamaccia. Prior to the pageant the combined chapel faith groups met to sing carols on the steps of the chapel.

Following the Christmas recess Hendricks Chapel announced the formation of the Religious Coordinating Council. For practical reasons this step was strategically designed to deal with a problem that went back to the beginning days of the chapel.

As has been stated earlier it was the dream of Dean Powers that the program of Hendricks Chapel would be broad enough to be religiously inclusive. This hope grew out of a liberal Protestant theology that characterized the university. For most religiously interested students in the 1930s (as well as the school as a whole), it posed few problems. Furthermore, when the chapel was built the Methodist influence was dominant at the university within the students, faculty, and administration.

The liberal Protestant hegemony was, by the second half of the 1940s, diminishing, and society was moving in the direction of an increasingly diversified religious population. Even in the ecumenical movement that was gaining momentum at the time (note the formation of the World Council of Churches in 1948 and the National Council of Churches in 1950), the emphasis on ecclesiastical structure brought with it an awareness of the religious pluralism with which such movements and organizations had to deal.

In the new policy statement that was printed in the *Hendricks Chapel Guide*

Dome (1980) began to house some university functions such as commencement, the first-year students and their parents for the chancellor's opening of each academic year, and other special programs, but they were never really considered auditoriums.—RLP

Book it was noted that "we are now making an honest recognition of the three-fold division of the faith-groups, and to use it as an asset and not a liability." The Religious Coordinating Council was the structural way this policy statement was implemented. The council consisted of the dean of the chapel, the Roman Catholic chaplain, the Jewish chaplain, and the chairman of the newly created Protestant Council. In an editorial in the *Daily Orange* it was said that "the traditional spirit of religious tolerance and fellowship at Syracuse has been given new impetus by this reorientation of Chapel emphasis."

The Protestant Council was part of the reorganization of the operating procedures for the chapel. It was made up of each resident Protestant chaplain and two students from each denominational group. Its purpose was to become an agency where the common concerns of Protestants could be integrated and implemented in the overall chapel operation. It was in fact the arm of the Student Christian Movement (a national effort) on the Syracuse campus.

The officers of the Protestant Council were Robert Young, chairman; Lucy Cummings, secretary; Beatrice Nann and Everett Jennings, Religious Coordinating Council representatives; and William Wilson, representative to the Chapel Board. The Reverend Thomas Van Loon was the chairman of the Protestant Council and along with Beatrice Nann and Everett Jennings represented it on the Religious Coordinating Council. For the Lutherans, Marguerite Freitag and Robert Young were the student representatives, and the counselor was the Reverend Donald W. Prigge; Ann Noble and Everett Jennings were the students for the Methodists, and Van Loon was the counselor; for the Unitarians Shirley Huber and Barbara Brooks were the students, and the Reverend Glenn Canfield was the counselor; for the Episcopalians Lucy Cummings and William Wilson were the students, and the Reverend James A. Rockwell was the counselor; for the Presbyterians Beatrice Nann was the student, and the counselor was the Reverend Wilbert B. Smith, Jr.; for the Baptists Jean Brown was the student, and the Reverend Charles H. Schmitz was the counselor; the Congregationalists and the Inter-Varsity Christian Fellowship were represented by Edith Lloyd and William Matthews, with Professor Catherine Condon the counselor.

The officers of the Jewish Student Fellowship were Ethel Greene, president; Ruth Tannenhaus, secretary; and Elliott Gross, treasurer. Rabbi Earl S. Stone was the Jewish chaplain and along with two students represented the Jewish Student Fellowship on the Religious Coordinating Council.[*]

As stated earlier, the year was a vigorous and comprehensive one at Hendricks Chapel, a veritable beehive of activity involving a very large number of students. For Dean Noble it was a year of intense activity. It was agreed that he seemed to be

[*]Donald Wright fails, in his manuscript, to state how the Roman Catholic students were represented on the new Religious Coordinating Council!—RLP

everywhere at once, rushing in and out of meetings, speaking to this group and that group, spending long hours in personal counseling, and with Mrs. Noble regularly entertaining students in their home. Other staff and religious counselors were busy also, both in terms of the programs they assisted the students in sponsoring and in the many hours of counseling they gave to students who sought their help. There is no way the counseling can be measured except to say it was an important part of the chapel's service to students and almost endless hours were invested in response to widespread personal problems.

The gathering of the Chapel Board at Casawasco in September for a retreat and planning conference had proved so valuable that another one was held between semesters, both to review what had happened and to plan ahead. One problem that had to be dealt with was the resignation of some of the committee chairmen who, owing to the many pressures upon them, did not believe that they could adequately fulfill their jobs and asked to be relieved. Sign-ups were held on January 16 and again on February 16, and a number of new recruits to the chapel program were enlisted. On Sunday, February 9, Dean Noble greeted and welcomed all newcomers to the university as the second semester got under way.

It has been noted that there were a large number of married students on campus, and to take note of their presence a tea was held for them on Washington's Birthday, with Mrs. Noble and Margaret McKinnon in charge.

The next week a series of student-faculty coffee hours began. They were held each Wednesday evening and would continue throughout the semester. Also, before February was over, the New York State Student Christian Movement Conference to be held at Geneseo was announced by Philip Dunning with the theme "The Outreach of Christian Belief." The newly formed Protestant Council announced a series of courses to be held during Lent with the general theme "Religion—Elective or Requirement?" The courses were scheduled each Monday and Tuesday afternoon under the leadership of the Reverend Thomas Van Loon, the Reverend Wilbert Smith, Jr., and the Reverend Donald Prigge and were scheduled as follows:

February 25: "What Can and Ought to Be Done to Strengthen Religion?"
March 10: "What Protestants Believe" (Part 1)
March 11: "What Protestants Believe" (Part 2)
March 17: "How Did the Protestant Church Start?"
March 18: "The Protestant Witness Today"
March 24: "Pathways to Truth"
March 25: "Roadblocks to Pathways to Truth"
March 31: "Sunday Worship—Required or Elective?"
April 1: "Getting the Most from Worship"

For Roman Catholics an Easter retreat began Sunday morning, March 23, with masses at Crouse College at nine thirty and eleven and on Sunday, Monday, and Tuesday evenings at seven thirty at Hendricks Chapel.

Even in the midst of all the furious activity there was time for humor, and on April Fools' Day the *Daily Orange* carried a story about a new set of regulations at the Sunday morning service, "promulgated by Dean Noble." In order to keep the chapel pure, the article stated, men and women were to be seated separately, with women ushers for the women's section. Furthermore "echo" prayers were to be featured between sections of the chapel, very much like the athletic yells in the stadium. The article was a clever spoof and full of fun.

In keeping with the Easter season, the chapel choir presented the cantata *The Seven Last Words of Christ*.

After the Easter break, the Chapel Board in conjunction with the Men's and Women's Student Governments sponsored the first annual Campus Leadership Conference. It was held over the weekend of April 25 at Casawasco. Officers of the administration and leaders of twenty campus organizations were invited. The explosion in the campus population and the multiplication of organizations that were formed to respond to their interests produced a very confusing if not sometimes chaotic situation. The conference was an attempt to bring some order to the new reality. Discussions were held about the philosophy and techniques of leadership. Information was presented about the functions of the university in relation to students, such as financial aid, the alumni office, and so on. This face-to-face meeting of the campus leaders and members of the administration provided a forum for the constructive resolution of many problems, and not only was it pronounced a great success but there was also a determination to hold such an event each year.

By the beginning of May the college year was already coming to its conclusion. On the second of May campus elections were held, including the officers of the Chapel Associations. On May 7, Romayne Brown and David Bauer installed the new members of the Chapel Board. In another week the second cabinet had been selected.

On May 8 it was announced by Beryl Ball that the Student Christian Movement summer conference at Silver Bay on Lake George would be held from June 17 to June 20, and those individuals who wished to attend could register through her office.

On Sunday, May 11, there was a memorial concert by the chapel choir for Professor Leon Verrees, who for several years before his death had been the conductor of the choir. Dean Noble took part in the service, and Professor David McCloskey conducted the music.

Dean Noble addressed the graduating class on June 1 at the baccalaureate service in the chapel. His subject was "Crisis or Evolution?" and in answer to those persons looking for pat and quick solutions he said, "We shall move from the present chaos to our ideal future only as we keep taking the next rational steps."

By this time the 1946–47 academic year (the year of SU's greatest expansion) was over, and an extraordinary year in the life of the chapel had been completed. As a kind of postscript, the very thoughtful cochairmen of the Chapel Board, Romayne Brown and David Bauer, sat down, reflected on what had happened, and wrote down what the year had meant as they had seen it. It is contained in a bound volume, held in the SU Archives, which they titled *A Year at Hendricks Chapel.**

24. Settling into a Rhythm, 1947–1948

BY THE FALL OF 1947, even with a continuing rise in the number of students, the campus began to get used to its new situation. Hendricks Chapel reflected this same mood. If the year before had been very full with hasty innovations that sometimes bordered on a frantic effort to respond to tremendous needs cropping up almost every day, this year the whole university community knew more about what to expect, and even if it did not take it all with ease it managed to take it in stride. As far as the chapel was concerned, a new dean had established his place, patterns of operation had been set, and some of the pressures of innovation were diminished.

The basic structures of the Religious Coordinating Council and the Protestant Council were continued. This year marked the coming of the first full-time Jewish chaplain, Rabbi Luitpold Wallach. Serving the Episcopalians was Elizabeth Riley, a laywoman. Later in the year, Bishop Malcolm Peabody indicated that an ordained Episcopal priest would be appointed to this position. As in other years there were several part-time religious counselors.

Prior to the opening of the college year the Chapel Board met for a planning conference at Casawasco to prepare for the year, and they would return again for a shorter session just before the second semester resumed.

Chapel Night was held on September 24 following the Men's Convocation, at

---

*Even the first year of Hendricks Chapel cannot compare to the excitement and the stress and strain associated with the year 1946–47. It was, without doubt, the most challenging and perhaps most productive year the chapel has ever known. Noble was more than just busy. His popularity had grown to legendary proportions, and his time was in demand both on and off campus. Chancellor Tolley and Dean Noble had become great friends, and Tolley started to facilitate some R&R time for Noble when he saw his energy wane.—RLP

which time the representatives of the three faiths spoke on "The Place of Religious Activities in College." The chairman of the evening was George Daigneault, who presented Dean Noble to those individuals in attendance. The Chapel Boardroom was open for anyone seeking information about the chapel, and outdoor dancing was held in the paved area adjacent to the chapel.

On Sunday morning a special service was held for the incoming class with a welcome by Chancellor Tolley and Dean Noble preaching on "Never Take It for Granted."

Chapel was always a busy place, with programming and activities going on most of the time. But Sundays were special. There were no classes, only the realization that they would be meeting the next day and that it was important to be ready. The now decidedly Protestant Sunday service at Hendricks began at ten fifty. A large choir, under the direction of Professor David McCloskey, rehearsed before the services and continued to overflow the space originally built for them. Roman Catholic masses were celebrated in Crouse at nine thirty and eleven.

Sunday evenings were reserved for the denominational group meetings. They usually began with supper at five thirty followed by program and fellowship. Occasionally there would be a large meeting either in the afternoon or later in the evening. It is important to recall that each Friday a Sabbath-eve service was conducted by Rabbi Wallach for students of Jewish faith. Also, each weekday a twenty-minute daily-chapel service began at noon under the sponsorship of the Worship Committee. It is not difficult to see that there is an emerging pattern, once established, that was continued throughout the postwar years and in modified form to the present day.

By this time Dean Noble had established himself as a popular preacher and speaker. Some of the sermon topics preached this year give an insight into what it was that brought students and other members of the university community to Sunday morning services. For Freshman Sunday it was "Never Take It for Granted." Later titles were "Survival of the Fittest," "Making the Best of a Bad Bargain," "Yearning for God," "Achieving a Balance in a Dizzy World," "High Obligation of Brotherhood," and "When the Unexpected Happens." Dean Noble was not only popular in his own pulpit but also frequently invited to speak at other college and university chapels, as well as churches and public events throughout the northeastern United States. When Noble was not at Hendricks as preacher his place was taken from time to time by the full-time denominational chaplains, Van Loon, Smith, and Prigge, and also by distinguished visiting clergymen. Special guests for this year were Bishop G. Bromley Oxnam, the Reverend Dr. Harold Case, Dean Charles Gilkey of Chicago, the Reverend Dr. Lloyd Foster, T. Z. Koo of the World's Student Christian Federation, and the Reverend A. Grant Noble, chaplain of Williams College, highly regarded leaders all.

The meeting of Syracuse-in-China on October 6 outlined plans for the coming year, including the showing of Chinese films, parties, plays, chopstick suppers, the Christmas sale, and speakers on the Orient. Of special note was the fact that Donald Flaherty was now at West China Union College in Chongqing as the first student representative from Syracuse, and his letters, which gave glimpses of his life there, were eagerly read at the meetings.

Interfaith discussions and activities were high on the agenda of the chapel program. On October 17 the Reverend Jim Smith began a series on the topic "Explaining Protestantism." Later there would be two sessions each on Roman Catholicism, Judaism, Buddhism, and Islam. It was projected that later topics might include intermarriage, discrimination, a possible world faith, and modern ethics. During the latter part of March and into April a series of programs on intermarriage was held. It began with Professor Barron of the Sociology Department speaking on "Religious Intermarriage and Society." Later the Reverend Jim Smith spoke on "Intermarriage and Religion," and the series concluded with a talk by Dr. Marion Welcher of the University Health Service speaking on "Intermarriage and the Family."

Early in November the annual appeal for the Campus Chest was launched. The purpose of this chapel fund drive was to make one financial appeal for a variety of human needs and cares, including the Student Emergency Loan Fund, Syracuse-in-China, the World Student Fund, tuberculosis, and cancer. The goal was thirteen thousand dollars, and it was given wide publicity by the *Daily Orange* with a special edition, endorsements by the religious faith leaders, and continuing reports on its progress. When all the results were in the reported total was eighty-five hundred dollars, of which eight thousand dollars was distributed to the respective causes.

Some special events of the chapel year included the celebration of Armistice Day with a service at noon on November 11 to honor the Syracusans who had lost their lives in World Wars I and II. It was sponsored by the Religious Coordinating Council.

On Thanksgiving the new full-time Jewish chaplain, Rabbi Luitpold Wallach, spoke at the service held in the chapel. His topic was "What Do We Owe to the Pilgrims?" Participating in the service were Dean Noble and student worship leader Robert Smith.

Much later in the year, on Sunday afternoon, May 23, the Hendricks Chapel Choir and soloists presented Brahams's Requiem under the direction of Professor David McCloskey. A portion of this music had been sung earlier on Sunday, April 25, in memory of Professor Leon Verrees who had directed the choir for six years before his death.

Established in the previous year under the instigation of the Chapel Board, the Campus Leadership Conference had proved to be of such value that it was repeated again this year. As in the year before, the conference was sponsored by the

Chapel Board and Men's and Women's Student Governments and included all the major campus organizations. The conference was held the weekend of April 25 at Casawasco and included faculty and administration as well as students. This event became a fixture on the campus calendar for many years to come.*

As the year drew to a close and the students were looking forward to summer, other special activities were held in the chapel. The first of these events, sponsored by the Protestant Council, was a program called "Invest Your Summer" and asked for volunteers for work camps in the devastated areas of Germany, Holland, and France. For those students who could not go to the work camps, an opportunity was available to help those individuals suffering from the effects of the war by giving to the clothing drive—the second of the year. A special appeal was made to students packing to go home to be sure to give what clothes they could for those persons in need.

A summer conference sponsored by the New York State Student Christian Movement, to be held at Silver Bay on Lake George, was announced for June 16 through June 23. Sign-ups were to be made with the Reverend Jim Smith, who would lead the delegation from Syracuse and also participate as one of the conference leaders.

This year was one full of vigorous activity at Hendricks Chapel in a postwar period when religion still lived in a hospitable atmosphere. With the installation of the newly selected Chapel Board on Wednesday evening, May 29, Senior Sunday on June 6, and the baccalaureate and commencement the following weekend, a good year in the life of SU and the chapel had come to a close.

25. The Chapel and Choir Reach New Heights, 1948–1949

"CHAPEL WELCOMES NEWCOMERS" was the headline in the first edition of the *Daily Orange* as college opened in the fall of 1948. Beneath the headline was a description of the services available to students in the chapel and a special invitation to attend Chapel Night on Wednesday evening, September 22, to hear more about the program and to get acquainted with its leaders. A sign-up day was also announced for September 28, when students could register to participate in specific chapel committees and activities. In the article there was an endorsement

---

*It even popped up in the 1980s and 1990s on an irregular basis. Often the student leaders were unaware of the history of the chapel's role on campus.—RLP

of the chapel program by Rabbi William L. Schwartz, himself a newcomer, in which he said, "Under the wise guidance of Dean Noble every religious group on the campus is encouraged to make its distinctive contribution to the life of the University."

It was also announced at the beginning of the year that there was no Methodist chaplain, for Thomas Van Loon, who had made such a distinctive contribution during the illness of Dean Powers as well as after the arrival of Dean Noble, had left the campus for a church in western New York. Late in September Dean Noble announced that the Reverend Arthur Hopkinson, Jr., was to be the new Methodist chaplain. Hopkinson had served as a student pastor in Amherst, Massachusetts, and at Iowa State University in Ames. He was the preacher at the October 10 Sunday morning service in Hendricks Chapel, preaching on "Attitudes That Matter." Hopkinson was to serve in this Methodist chaplaincy role for many years.

Early in the fall the Jewish High Holy Days were at hand, and Rabbi Schwartz arranged services that filled Hendricks Chapel. Rabbi Benjamin Friedman of the nearby Temple Society of Concord, a Reform congregation, was the speaker.

The previous May the officers and committee chairs of the Chapel Association had been installed and were now busy with their tasks.*

A very special arrival on campus in the fall of 1948 was Dr. Arthur Poister, who came to head the Department of Organ in the College of Fine Arts and to direct the choir and play the organ at the chapel. His coming to Syracuse was the result of a decision by Chancellor Tolley that he wanted to see this position filled by the most qualified person who could be found in the country. At the time Professor Poister was head of the Department of Organ at the Oberlin College Conservatory, one of the most prestigious colleges of music anywhere. A native of Ohio with degrees in music from the Conservatory of Music in Chicago, he had had a distinguished career at the University of Redlands and the University of Minnesota and had been at Oberlin for ten years. Among his teachers had been the world's best, Josef Lhévinne in piano and Marcel Dupré in organ.

Dr. Tolley had asked Professor Poister to come to Syracuse to counsel him on what needed to be done in order to create the kind of program that Dr. Tolley envisioned, and a visit had been arranged. Poister, it is said, suggested that both of the organs on campus were out-of-date and needed to be replaced and that more adequate instruments would be needed for practice by students. As a result of their consultation Dr. Tolley asked Professor Poister if he would be willing to come to Syracuse to implement his suggestions, were they to be followed. Fortunately, this almost ideal arrangement appealed to Dr. Poister, and after some encouragement he agreed to come. Though it is not, strictly speaking, chapel history, it is impor-

*See appendix A.—RLP

tant to point out that the concert organ that was installed in the Crouse College Auditorium by the Holtkamp Organ Company of Cleveland was the kind that did not exist anywhere in the United States, and its creation, design, and installation created a prototype that was later built for other locations. The coming of Dr. Poister also made possible a new Holtkamp organ for Hendricks Chapel. With the arrival of Poister a period of almost two decades of great choral and organ music began, which not only brought great distinction to the university but also filled the lives of students in the choir with experiences that they would cherish as long as they lived.*

Early in the fall it was announced by Father Gannon Ryan that the masses at Crouse College would be expanded and that they would be held at nine, ten, and eleven on Sunday mornings. This expansion reflected the national situation that found Roman Catholic students coming to college in numbers never before seen.

Attesting to the number of married students with children, the chapel offered a baby-sitting service to those students who wished to attend service there. The second cabinet was in charge, and volunteers were recruited to help with child care. In later years an informal agreement was reached with local churches that students with children would be directed their way.

Because of the heavy use of the chapel by many people for a wide variety of events, the chapel was in need of a good cleanup. Saturday, October 20, was set aside, and volunteers were asked to come and give as much time as they could to help. Tall men were especially requested to help clean the tops of the high windows.

On the second weekend of October the chapel was host to the New York State Student Christian Movement Conference, which drew about two hundred students from various parts of the state. Dr. Roland Bainton, a well-known church historian from the Yale Divinity School, was the principal conference leader.

"From Syracuse to Syracuse" was the theme of the Campus Chest drive that began on November 1. To dramatize the effort that was being made, the students in Syracuse, New York, were directing special aid to the people of Syracuse (Siracusa), Sicily, as well as helping with a variety of other needs. It seems to have worked, for this drive was one of the most successful Campus Chest drives ever, with a little more than twelve thousand dollars raised.

Arising out of a suggestion made at one of the Casawasco Conferences and given its name by Dean Noble, the Skeptics Corner started in December. Meeting in the Nobles' home and beginning with about ten students, this group was both to grow and to continue for a long period of time. The idea behind it, as originally

*Indeed, the Poister years at Hendricks Chapel and the School of Music are looked back upon as golden years by everyone who had any contact with them. Later in their professional lives at least two of Poister's students would follow him on the organ and in working with the Hendricks Chapel Choir.—RLP

formulated by the Interfaith Committee, was to have an "entirely honest, undogmatic and cosmopolitan discussion of ethical values." In a sense the name of the group was a misnomer, but it did give the students a chance to examine their own beliefs in a free, permissive atmosphere. Some of the topics discussed were the "effect of the analytical sciences on religion, the power, uses and fundamentals of prayer, and the possible steps toward a healthy life, both spiritually and materially. The tie between psychology and religion was one of the most absorbing concepts considered."* Some of the sessions were recorded and edited, and from time to time the material was used in the *Chapel Chimes* and broadcast each afternoon on the university radio station WAER. The sessions attracted considerable attention, and by the next year the average attendance was forty-five. In commenting on the program Dean Noble said, "Only in this way can critical thinkers be helped on the road toward their own liveable, workable philosophy." The *Alumni News* of December 1949 carried an article on the Skeptics Corner by Richard Petrow, and the information given above is largely from that article.

December was a full month on the chapel schedule. Advent vespers were held each of the four Wednesday evenings before Christmas. The theme was "The Light of the World." To inaugurate the Christmas season on campus the chapel and the Outing Club cooperated in a joint venture on Friday evening, December 10. It began on the chapel steps with a huge crowd of student carolers who sang and then made their way to a Christmas tree that had been set up and decorated in the middle of the campus. At a given signal the lights were turned on. Dean Noble spoke and more carols were sung, symbolizing that the Christmas season had now begun. About this time a special service celebrating Hanukkah was held for students of the Jewish faith at the nearby Temple Society of Concord. Christmas Sunday at Hendricks Chapel was December 12, with Dean Noble preaching on "Miracles for Moderns." In the evening the annual Christmas pageant was presented under the auspices of Zeta Phi Eta, with Nancy Callahan as director. At both the morning service and for a half hour before the pageant the superb chapel choir under the direction of Professor Poister provided the music. Though many students were away for the Christmas break, quite a number remained on campus, and Sunday services continued at the chapel during the vacation.

The outstanding chapel event of the second semester was the first All-Chapel Banquet held Thursday evening, February 17, in the new Sims Dining Hall. Under the sponsorship of the Chapel Board, with Alice Reid and John Ballentine as cochairs, its purpose was to provide an occasion when members of all the faith groups could come together for an evening of celebration. Chester Winters was the student chairman, Dean Noble was toastmaster, and Chancellor Tolley was the

---

*Dean Noble was to become identified with the increasingly popular Skeptics Corner for years to come. He considered it one of his most successful ministries.—RLP

principal speaker, choosing as his subject "The Place of Religion on the Syracuse Campus." Choirs from each of the faith groups provided music. Incidently, Professor Poister had revived and reorganized the Jewish choir at the beginning of the year. In his remarks, Dean Noble said that the event was "evidence of the universal spirit of religious cooperation of Hendricks Chapel," and Father Gannon Ryan, who did not always find it possible to join in interfaith ventures, expressed the hope that this annual event would become one of the great traditions of the university.

Under the sponsorship of the Jewish Student Fellowship a Sabbath-eve service marking Brotherhood Week was held in the chapel on February 25. The Reverend Dr. Henry Hitt Crane was the guest speaker, and participating in the service were Rabbi Schwartz, the Reverend Arthur Hopkinson, and the Reverend Wilbert Smith. Music was provided by the combined Hendricks Chapel and Jewish Choirs.

Although we have noted many activities of the various chapel committees and commissions, the whole year was full of numerous meetings and events sponsored by other segments of the increasingly inclusive chapel program. The World Relations Committee offered students many opportunities to hear speakers to help them understand events that were happening in various parts of the postwar world. Syracuse-in-China had its usual full program, and it needs to be recalled that 1947 was the year of the communist revolution in that country. Nonetheless, it was decided to send a second representative to teach there for the coming year, and out of many applicants Tom Scott was selected.

The Human Relations Committee sought to help students with the changing patterns of interpersonal relationships, especially in the area of sexual relationships. Sessions were held to help students deal with changing values in this part of their lives. Perhaps no topic is more important or a more predictable "ticket" on any campus, yesterday or today.

Interracial concerns were continuing to emerge. The NAACP had been formed on campus, and when the Reverend Dr. James Robinson, an outstanding black preacher, came to the chapel on Sunday, March 13, practically all the fraternities on campus attended as a body. Many of them were attempting to deal with the discrimination clauses imposed on them by their national associations.

The newly formed Committee on Overseas Relief, under Chairman Robert Troyer, asked that each living center send at least one package overseas and at the end of the semester appealed for ten thousand pounds of clothing.*

Lent and Easter were celebrated as usual, and the first weekend in May was Spring Weekend when the Chapel Cups were presented to Chi Sigma for the women and Sigma Nu for the men as a result of their excellence in chapel participation. On the same weekend John Ballentine, cochairman of the Chapel Board,

---

*Here again we find Syracuse, often a leader in such matters, part of a national emphasis on sending help, often clothing, to war-torn and struggling international locations.—RLP

and Robert Sturgess, president of the Protestant Council, were elected to the men's senior honorary society, Tau Theta Upsilon, signifying their leadership on campus. The next year Ballentine became chairman of the Campus Leaders' Organization. The next weekend a chapel interfaith picnic was held at Onondaga Lakeshore Park from three to eight in conjunction with the intercollegiate crew races.

Sunday morning, May 15, the Reverend Ivan Gould, at that time with the Pennsylvania State Council of Churches, delivered the morning sermon. Gould was the student chairman of the Chapel Board the year before the chapel was opened. At four o'clock the Hendricks Chapel Choir, under the direction of Professor Poister, presented an a cappella concert of sacred music. A spring choir concert was to become a tradition that provided the choir with two major campus concerts each year.

The year was now fast drawing to a close, and exams and commencement would soon be at hand. Dean Noble, it seems, was busier than ever, and it is pleasant to record that Williams College, where he had studied and worked to support himself in his undergraduate years, conferred on him the honorary degree of doctor of divinity at their commencement on May 21.

26. The Chapel Celebrates
Its Twentieth Year, 1949–1950

ON SEPTEMBER 21, 1949, the *Daily Orange* proclaimed in banner headlines, "Doors Open Wide at Chapel Tonight." Chapel Night was the big event to let newcomers especially as well as other interested students know about the chapel and its programs. Of course, students were urged to sign-up for participation in the chapel committees and programs. The same issue of the *Daily Orange* had an editorial stating that this event was something that should not be missed, "for the Chapel is the heart of the campus—both figuratively and literally."

Those students attending this Chapel Night were greeted by Chancellor Tolley, Dean Noble, John Hess, and Betty Ruth Scott, the latter two cochairmen of the Chapel Board and presidents of the Men's and Women's Student Governments, respectively. The Reverend Arthur Hopkinson, Jr., gave the invocation, and Rabbi William Schwartz pronounced the benediction. Following the formal program students circulated around the building where booths had been set up as information centers for various areas of the chapel program, and questions were answered about specific committees and commissions. Just outside the building, those individuals who wished to do so were invited to join in dancing.

A week later the chapel was open from nine to five, and those persons who had not yet signed up were able to do so. John Hess, one of the student chairmen, said, "You have a place in the Chapel and the Chapel has a place for you. But it's up to you to come and find it." This appeal brought a good response. When the sign-ups were complete a new record had been set, with a total of 1,285. The Human Relations Committee led in number with 195, closely followed by Social Service and Music, the latter including the choir.

To get ready for Chapel Night and other all-chapel activities, an All-Chapel Planning Conference had been held September 12–16 at Casawasco, with more than 70 students and counselors participating. Introduced to the group were Mary Lent Ayer, Dorothy Neiman, the Reverend John Cook, and George Daigneault, new members of the chapel staff and counselors for the United, Lutheran, and Episcopal groups and men's adviser, respectively. Attending the conference was Ray Sweetman, the New York State Student Christian Movement director. The officers of the student board on whom the responsibilities would rest for this year had been elected and along with committee and commission chairs had been installed.*

Even though the total number of students was down from the record influx that jammed the campus in the immediate postwar period, the university was still a bit overcrowded. Religious interest continued to be strong, reflecting the so-called religious boom that was characteristic of the whole country in the ten years that followed World War II. The post-World War II chapel, with Noble as its dean, had become a solid fixture in the life of Syracuse University. This year was the twentieth anniversary of the chapel's presence on campus.

Some basic program patterns were now in place that would be repeated for most of the period of Dean Noble's leadership. Some of them, like the Sunday and daily-chapel services, Syracuse-in-China, the Student Emergency Loan Fund, and the continuing stream of students who came for counseling, antedated his coming to the chapel. The Sunday morning services at the chapel enjoyed great support during this time. Dean Noble was a very popular preacher, and when he was not in the pulpit clergymen of national reputations or one of the full-time denominational chaplains would give the sermon. Professor Arthur Poister was not only one of the nation's outstanding organists but also a superlative director of a choir of 120 voices. They poured out their hearts and voices in great choral music. The Jewish Sabbath-eve services were held each Friday evening, and the Roman Catholic masses were held each Sunday morning at nine thirty and eleven in the auditorium of Crouse College. Though daily chapel's hours had varied, it was now at noon and continued to provide an opportunity for daily devotion.

Some of the sermon titles used by Dean Noble during the year were "God's Troubadours," "Living Victoriously under Pressure," "God's Greatest Weak-

*See appendix A.—RLP

ness," "Is Our God Big Enough?" "Why Bother with Life's Jerusalems?" (for the Freshman Weekend), and near the end of the second semester "How to Finish Strong." Visiting preachers were Dean Charles Gilkey of the University of Chicago Chapel, the Reverend Peter Shih on Syracuse-in-China Sunday, Bishop Fred Pierce Corson, and the Reverend David McLennon, who had often been to Syracuse from Canada and was now on the faculty of the Yale Divinity School.

In addition to its regular program, Syracuse-in-China had some special features this year. In October it was host to the New York State Regional Conference of the World Student Service Fund. Don Flaherty, who had been the first student representative to go from Syracuse to teach at West China Union College returned to campus. His presence on campus gave members firsthand information about what was happening in that part of China. Word received from the current representative, Tom Scott, indicated that the Chinese had welcomed communism's arrival.

At the sign-ups nearly two hundred students indicated their preference to serve on the Human Relations Committee. Not long after it was decided that it should be divided into three subcommittees: Interfaith, Social Hygiene, and Skeptics Corner. Late in October the Social Hygiene Committee announced a five-part series on sex that would meet Mondays, Tuesdays, and Thursdays on the topics "Dating Behavior," "Choice of a Mate," "Understanding Our Sexual Biological Selves," "Factors Contributing to Marital Success," and "Responsibilities of Parenthood." Interestingly enough, the day after this series was announced the Interfaith Committee held a panel discussion on intermarriage. So many students responded to the Social Hygiene Committee series that a second one was held in March.

Another October event was the launching of the Campus Chest, which the year before had raised twelve thousand dollars. Included in the appeal were Syracuse-in-China and the Student Emergency Loan Fund.

Just before the Christmas break, a new committee, the Committee on Overseas Relief (COR), with David Rosen and Mary King as cochairmen, urged each living center to send one food or clothing package overseas for the world's needy. About this time, the International Students Committee was formed, and Chet Seymour was appointed to provide a guide service to students who wished to know more about the chapel facilities.

Following the plan that had been instituted the year before, the second annual Brotherhood Service was held in the chapel on the Friday evening before the Colgate football game. Norman Zankel and Betty Ruth Scott were cochairs of this event, and Dr. Ralph W. Sockman, a well-known Methodist minister from New York City, was the speaker. The other part of this interfaith expression came on Sunday, February 27, at the morning worship service when Rabbi Julius Mark of the Temple Emmanu-El of New York City and former chaplain with the Pacific fleet was the speaker.

Although the NAACP had been organized in Syracuse at an earlier date, the civil rights movement was just beginning on campus when on December 15 the organization held a rally at the chapel. Franklin Williams, assistant counsel for the national organization, came to speak at the four o'clock meeting that received endorsements from Chancellor Tolley, Dean Noble, and Rabbi Schwartz. In an editorial the *Daily Orange* proclaimed that "the Chapel was a proper setting for such a meeting." In February the Student Union hosted a gathering marking Negro History Week. Early in the second semester the chapel staff publicly backed student efforts to eliminate discrimination clauses imposed on some fraternities by their national organizations.

Advent was celebrated with three special candlelight services on Wednesday evenings. There were music, meditation, and prayer with the theme "The Light of the World." The annual Christmas pageant depicting the nativity was held Sunday evening, December 18, under the sponsorship of Zeta Phi Eta and directed by Billie Howells. Prior to the pageant there was carol singing on the steps of the chapel. The pageant drew a *Daily Orange* editorial comment that "Christmas at Syracuse would not be the same without it"—yet another confirmation of the power of tradition.

The weekend before the second semester opened 130 members of the chapel community once again went to Casawasco for a two-day retreat and planning session. As the semester opened sign-ups were encouraged for students who were new or had not previously participated. It had been previously announced that once again the Chapel Cups would be awarded to the living centers whose members had contributed the most to the chapel.

The interfaith All-Chapel Banquet was the outstanding feature of the second semester. This year it took on special significance because it marked the twentieth anniversary of the opening of the chapel. Tickets were priced at $1.20, and it was held in the new Sims Dining Hall. Endorsements of the banquet were received from Senator Lehman, Charles Wilson of General Electric, and Assistant Secretary of the Treasury Foley. The speaker was Dean Harry Carmen of Columbia College of Columbia University and a graduate of Syracuse in the class of 1909. The chairman was Merph Smith, and the affair was regarded as a great success.

When the chapel elections were held in April, Merph Smith and Billy Coulter were elected student cochairmen of the Chapel Board. On Sunday afternoons during Lent, Professor Niel Richardson gave a series on "The Life of Jesus." The first All-Chapel Picnic was held Sunday afternoon, May 7, at Elmwood Park, with Tink Wilson as chairman. There was recreation, eating, and a candlelight service at the close.

On June 3, after traveling across the country to deliver the baccalaureate address at Stanford University, Dean Noble was back at Syracuse to do the same and to participate in the first televised graduation at Syracuse University. This event brought to a close the twentieth-anniversary year in the life of Hendricks Chapel.

27. Religious Schism on Campus, 1950–1951

WHEN SYRACUSE UNIVERSITY opened its doors to the entering class in the fall of 1950 it was a college generation away from the postwar population explosion that occurred in 1946. This year the freshman class numbered about eighteen hundred. In the previous year it was twenty-eight hundred. What had been problems of an expanding student population became problems associated with a diminishing student population. Religious interest and participation remained strong, and as an editorial in the *Daily Orange* of September 27 suggested, "Chapel, year after year, offers an activity outlet to a greater percentage of the Syracuse undergraduates than any other organized source." The chapel year was launched on the basis of proven programming patterns, including the religious preference cards at registration and Chapel Night with its presentation of the chapel program followed by a recreational time.

Sign-up days again offered students the opportunity to indicate their interest in a chapel committee or activity. Guidebooks were again distributed. In the 1950 edition are these words:

> The University desires an adequate and inclusive ministry for all students. To further this objective, a full time administrative staff is provided at Hendricks Chapel. In addition, all churches and religious fellowships are invited to appoint chaplains who lead their groups in the planning and implementation of religious services and social programs, conduct extensive counseling services, and lead study groups on their religious heritage. The chaplains also share in the overall administration of the Chapel and assist in advising the committees of the Student Board.

The guidebook noted that two student committees were new this year. The Personnel Committee would advise the Chapel Board in selecting and recruiting the best leadership for the various programs. The Design and Decorations Committee was created to give as much professional help as possible to the decorations for special chapel events.

Worship services were scheduled as the year before, with the Roman Catholic masses at Crouse College at nine thirty and eleven on Sunday mornings, the Jewish Sabbath-eve services at the chapel on Fridays, and the Protestant service on Sunday mornings at ten fifty, with a nursery for those individuals who wished to leave their children there during the service. A daily-chapel service was again held weekdays at noon.

During the year the Brotherhood Services emphasizing the relationship between Jewish and Christian students brought Dr. Ralph W. Sockman once again to speak on the eve of the Colgate football game. Later in the year, on the last Sunday in February, Rabbi Abba Hillel Silver of Cleveland was the preacher in the Sunday chapel service.

A brief announcement in the *Daily Orange* of October 17 said that Melvin Eggers had been appointed an assistant professor of economics, having come to Syracuse from Yale with service in the war as a Japanese language expert. Many years later he would become chancellor of the university.

At midsemester the weekend Chapel Convocation was held at Casawasco with the theme "Faith for the Future." After a fall filled with chapel events, the Christmas season was at hand. A weeklong celebration was planned by the Chapel Board in conjunction with the Outing Club and Lamda Chi Alpha. It began with a candlelight march on the campus, with carols sung along the way, on the evening of December 9. Festivities included the lighting of the Christmas tree and a folk festival at Sims Dining Hall. During the week a contest was held to determine the winners of a decorating contest at the living centers. The Committee on Overseas Relief sponsored a clothing caravan on Saturday, December 16, and on Sunday the seventeenth there were religious services and the annual pageant in the evening. The pageant was produced by Zeta Phi Eta, and the choir participated. Before the pageant there was carol singing on the steps of the chapel.

For two years previously the All-Chapel Banquet had proved to be an effective expression of interfaith cooperation, so plans were well under way for the third by the beginning of the second semester. The invited speaker was Professor Kirtley Mather of Harvard.

The announcement of his coming proved to be a time bomb. Not long after the start of the semester Father Ryan was visited by a zealous anticommunist who told him that Dr. Mather was a member of organizations listed as subversive. As a result Father Ryan told Dean Noble that he would have to withdraw Roman Catholic participation if Mather was permitted to speak. When this pronouncement became known, a vigorous and acrimonious debate engulfed the campus and soon extended all over the country. The relationship of the Roman Catholics to the chapel had never been a very intimate one, and cooperation was limited. Even so, until this time there had been no open conflict. Now it burst wide open! A disappointed Dean Noble felt very much let down and finally asked Dr. Mather to speak at the Sunday morning service in the chapel, which was jammed with students and others, rather than to address the banquet. The *Daily Orange* came down hard on the "informer," stating that the assumption of "guilt by association" was intolerable and at the end of a long editorial concluding, "If Syracuse backs up again, it fails as a University." The Reverend Walter Welsh wrote a letter to the *Daily Orange*—there were many such letters—saying, "In principle, however, the 'All-Chapel Banquet' will be held on a low common denominator of collusion to pacify a smear organization no matter how redeeming the substitute speaker may be."

For two weeks Father Ryan remained silent and then sent a long letter to the *Daily Orange* complaining that he had been both misrepresented and persecuted and suggested in words published by the *Syracuse Herald-Journal* and sent over the Associated Press wires that "religious cooperation on the Syracuse Campus was dealt a mortal blow by the Dr. Kirtley Mather incident." And indeed it had been, for now more than ever the Roman Catholic student program at Syracuse went its separate way. The final word arrived sometime later, sent by Dr. Mather who, having read what Father Ryan had written, wrote that he believed himself to have been unfairly judged and that he considered himself a loyal American citizen. The whole controversy was a very unfortunate chapter in the religious life of the Syracuse campus, and the religious schism it exacerbated would take a long time to heal, never completely realized under Ryan's chaplaincy.

A positive interreligious achievement was the dedication of a new scroll and ark in the chapel on Sabbath eve on May 11. The Sefer Torah was presented by M. H. Rudolph and B. G. Rudolph in memory of their parents, and the ark was given by Mr. and Mrs. Al Markowitz in memory of their son, Rubin, who had died of injuries suffered in World War II. In the procession were Rabbi Hyman, Dean Noble, Theodore Pierson, Tracy Ferguson (both members of the Temple Society of Concord and great supporters of both Hendricks Chapel and Syracuse University), officers of the Jewish Student Fellowship, the faculty of the Bible Department, and presidents of the Jewish fraternities. The service was conducted by Rabbis Schwartz and Hyman and guest cantor Pinchos Spiros. Following the dedication a tea and reception were held under the sponsorship of the six Jewish women's sororities. The ark still remains in the south wing of the main chapel. The scroll is kept in another safe place.

In addition to the special events recorded above, a full program was carried on in the chapel during the academic year. If there had been moments of difficulty, there had been, as usual, an almost overwhelming number of good moments in the lives of the students, providing confirmation of the editorial in the *Daily Orange* at the beginning of the year. A new slate of officers had been elected in April and other cabinet members selected and installed who would be ready to carry on the next fall.

Dean Noble was the preacher at the baccalaureate held at Hendricks Field on Sunday, June 3, at ten thirty. How he had the strength to do it is a wonder, for the day before a new record had been set when seven wedding services were conducted in the chapel, with Dean Noble officiating at six of them—certainly confirmation of his popularity on campus.

28. Education, Democracy, and Religion, 1951–1952

THOUGH THE COMMUNIST REVOLUTION had swept across China, causing the severance of diplomatic relations with the United States in the fall of 1949, it was not until the summer of 1951 that Tom Scott arrived back on the Syracuse campus. He had been sent as the second Syracuse student representative of Syracuse-in-China to teach at the West China Union College. The first part of his journey back to the United States was described as a harrowing escape. Before he was allowed to leave he was placed on trial as a reactionary but being an American citizen was given permission to return home. His journey was full of delays and difficulties as he made his way by foot, bus, train, and boat, first to Chongqing, then to Hong Kong and freedom, and then slowly back to the United States.

One of his longer stops was in Bangkok, Thailand, where he explored the possibility of a student representative from Syracuse teaching at Chulalonghorn University. Early in December, after Scott's return to campus, a representative of that university came to Syracuse. After conferring with the Syracuse-in-China organization it was announced that now that mainland China was closed to Americans, the next student representative would be sent to Chulalonghorn University in Bangkok, and the name of Syracuse-in-China would be changed to Syracuse-in-Thailand.

Thus, worldwide communist activity had a direct bearing on the religious situation on the Syracuse campus. In addition to the China situation, the alliance between Russia and the United States had broken up after the end of World War II. This breakup set up a vigorous response, especially through the U.S. House of Representatives' Un-American Activities Committee. It reached hysterical intensity in what came to be know as McCarthyism, which used the "guilt by association" philosophy to label any form of dissent as being subversive and communist inspired or related. It had been this, later discredited, hysteria that had initiated the protest of Father Ryan about Professor Kirtley Mather the year before. Early in April 1952 there was a McCarthy-generated investigation at Syracuse with the purpose of discovering subversive activity. It is not my purpose to go deeply into this controversy, which in retrospect was not a happy one, except to say that it was this kind of thinking that broke up almost all interfaith cooperation between Father Ryan and others on the Syracuse campus.

Father Ryan publicly declared that the chapel was "off-limits" for Roman Catholics. The program of the St. Thomas More House was expanded and intensified and became more isolated. Dean Noble did what he could to foster a relationship. In his report to the chancellor at the end of the year he noted that the tensions between the Roman Catholics and Syracuse University had increased and said that in response, the Protestants "are combining a spirit of brotherhood with a frank and unapologetic propagation of the traditional emphasis on the democratic spirit of Christianity." It was evident that the programs at Hendricks Chapel suffered no diminution of life or student participation because of Ryan's stance.

Though it would not be quite accurate to characterize them as routine, there were many elements in the chapel program that were repeated year after year during Noble's leadership. Among them were the planning conference at Casawasco at the beginning of each semester; Chapel Night to introduce all newcomers to the chapel program; the days of sign-ups; the worship services, including one on each Sabbath eve for Jewish students; Roman Catholic masses at Crouse; the Protestant service in the chapel with the superb choir under the direction of Professor Poister; preaching by the dean, the chaplains, and other outstanding preachers from various parts of the nation; and a nursery for children. Daily chapel at noon for a twenty-minute period continued as in the past.

Firmly established were the two Brotherhood Services, the first one on the Sabbath eve of the Colgate football game with the perennial speaker being Dr. Ralph W. Sockman, and the second being on a Sunday morning with a rabbi preaching. This year Rabbi Benjamin Friedman was the preacher.

The celebration of Christmas had developed its own set of traditions, the earliest of which was the pageant under the direction of Zeta Phi Eta and the caroling on the steps of the chapel that preceded the program. This year the pageant was under the direction of Janet Bolton. It was done in pantomime with a verse-speaking choir, and the scenes were adapted from "The Last Room," a story by A. E. Johnson. The pageant came at the conclusion of Christmas week, which had begun eight days before with the lighting of the Christmas tree on the quad. The Outing Club had put the tree in place. The contest for the best-decorated living center sponsored by Lamda Chi Alpha continued. On Sunday morning Dean Noble would preach, and the choir, now one of the best in all the land, would sing, thus bringing two very popular chapel entities together to provide a powerful Sunday service at Christmastime or any time.*

Both in the pre-Christmas period and at the end of the second semester, the Committee on Relief organized a clothing caravan to pick up clothing for the world's needy.

In addition to the more established programs, each year brought its own special features. One of them this year was the New York State Student Christian Movement Conference held at Vassar College. It was notable for the leadership of

---

*The popularity of both Poister and Noble certainly helped keep the image of Hendricks Chapel at a very high level.—RLP

Reinhold Niebuhr and Theodore Gill and its theme, "In Christ—History's Hope." *

Nearer to Syracuse the Reverend Walter Welsh, the Episcopal chaplain, led a one-day retreat. It was open to all Protestants and was held at the Pompey Community Church on Saturday, November 3.†

Before the Christmas break the Reverend Wilbert Smith, the Presbyterian chaplain and one of the mainstays of the chapel staff, announced that he would leave at the end of the academic year. His replacement was to be the Reverend Arnold Nakajima.

Shortly into the second semester, on February 24, the All-Chapel Banquet was held, and though there was no participation on the part of the Roman Catholics, attendance was good, with 550 attending. The speaker was Charles Taft, president of the National Council of Churches and a candidate for governor of Ohio.

The second semester also produced a significant first event that had long been talked about. The Faculty Advisory Committee invited Dr. Joseph Sittler of the Chicago Lutheran Seminary to come to Syracuse for a four-day consultation with the faculty. The relationship of education, democracy, and religion was the theme, a most appropriate subject for the times. It was well publicized and was a great success.

Sensitive to the growing awareness that educational opportunities for black youth were limited, the Chapel Board wrote to twenty-four area black high schools telling them of the opportunities at Syracuse, bidding them welcome and advising them of financial assistance that would be available to them. There is no report of the results of this effort.‡

In March a series of events took place. One of them was the annual financial campaign for the Campus Chest, which set a goal of $10,000. In the fall the Cam-

*Here we see the first evidence of neo-Orthodox Protestant theology, but still within a liberal tradition, beginning to be found on the national student scene. Niebuhr and others were intent on correcting what they saw as some of earlier liberalism's excesses, especially an overly optimistic view of human history and human potential. This particular movement in American Protestant theology did not have much impact on religion at SU. Noble disassociated himself from it in important ways, and it had largely run its course by the time McCombe became dean. With minor exceptions, chapel leadership from Powers to the present has been solidly in the so-called liberal camp of Christian thought. —RLP

†The existence of and participation in such regionally, nationally, and internationally focused events demonstrated the expansive outlook that characterized both SU and its students and the national scene in the early 1950s. There was perhaps no time in our recent history when American religion, particularly most Protestant expressions of it, was more optimistic and forward looking. The postwar surge in interest in religion and social problems found, as it did elsewhere, fertile soil in the Syracuse "garden."—RLP

‡Chancellor Tolley was well known for his outreach to various underrepresented groups in the student population. He was often criticized for his efforts in such matters.—RLP

pus Carnival had raised $750 for this cause, but support had dwindled, and despite great effort on the part of the sponsors, the campaign netted a disappointing $4,400.

Always popular were the sessions on social hygiene (that is, human sexuality), and this year registration was limited to fifty students for the four-part series. The topics and leaders were: "Are You Ready for Marriage?" by Dean Noble, "Premarital Dating" by Barbara Griggs, "Should We Plan Our Children's Birth?" by Gladys MacLean, and "Will You Use the Whip?" by Dr. Helene Hartley.

The All-Chapel Assembly was held on Saturday, March 29, from one thirty to five thirty at the ski lodge at Sky Top on the south campus. The subject was "Religion on Campus: Beware of Dare." Some suggestions were made for a new structural organization for the chapel operation. Election of chapel officers was held on April 3, and special services were held in Lent, leading up to Palm Sunday before the Easter break.

At the close of the year Dean Noble reported that an average of 4,260 students had been in the chapel each week for some purposeful activity and that sixteen major committee projects had been carried out.*

29. "Questing on a Common Road," 1952–1953

"HENDRICKS CHAPEL'S BASIC PURPOSE is still to relate students and faculty powerfully to God." This Dean Noble quote described the chapel's reason for being, late in the spring of 1953. To accomplish this purpose required a full and varied program. The statistics are available that may give us insight into the numbers and differentiation of students served in this year of the chapel's life.

Below is what might be called a constituency count of the various faith and denominational groups for this year, along with the name of the chaplain or adviser. These numbers were undoubtedly secured at the time of registration, when the students who were willing to do so filled out religious preference cards. As we can see, in some instances the numbers were rounded out.

| Greek Orthodox | Father Michael Harmand | 72 |
| Methodist | Reverend Arthur Hopkinson, Jr. | 800 |

*See appendix A.—RLP

Presbyterian	Reverend Arnold Nakajima	800
United		
Congregationalists		
Dutch Reformed,		
Evangelical,		
and Reformed	Ruth Hoople	250
Lutheran	Marilyn Pflueger	370
Episcopal	Reverend Walter Welsh	
	and Reverend Roswell Moore	560
Unitarian	Reverend Robert Zoerheide	100
Universalist	Reverend Ellsworth Reamon	32
Christian Science	Florence Hartman	35
Baptist	no counselor but served	
	by Reverend George Middleton	30
Friends	Norman Whitney	17
Inter-Varsity		
Christian		
Fellowship	Lawrence Walker	not available
Jewish	Rabbi William B. Schwartz	1,500
Roman Catholic	Reverend Gannon Ryan	1,200

The combined participation of these groups in the Sunday evening meetings was approximately 500 each week. Attending some form of worship each week were 2,800 students, including daily chapel, which averaged between 50 and 75. The average weekly attendance at various meetings in the chapel was 950 students. The statistics for staff activity show that 4,200 visits, meetings, counseling sessions, hospital calls, and the like were compiled during the year.

What is reflected here is not a homogeneous program but a great variety of religious and quasi-religious activities. Some students participated in Chapel Board programs only; others were involved solely in their faith or denominational events. Still others attended worship or some of the special events. Then, of course, there were those students who gave an enormous amount of time, energy, and devotion to many aspects of the chapel's life. Whatever the degree of participation, the chapel was the creative and energizing hub around which a tremendous amount of activity took place, which in turn furnished not only the inspiration but also the energy for the organizational structure that made it all possible.*

Before the year was over it was decided to eliminate the second cabinet and find other ways to develop students for chapel leadership posts. In the course of my

*See appendix A for student officers.—RLP

account of the life of the chapel I have not said very much about the second cabinet, which was established by Dean Powers to facilitate leadership development in students training for the Chapel Board and to give each member of the board an understudy. Times had changed, and it was clear that this kind of arrangement had outlived its usefulness. Little has also been said about the Faculty Advisory Board (FAB), in existence for several years, which was a group of interested members of the faculty who met from time to time with the dean and his staff.* The FAB for this year was as follows: Dean Marjorie Smith, Dean Eunice Hilton, Dean Robert E. Stone, Dean Robert Oxnam, Professor Floyd E. Carlson, Professor H. Niel Richardson, Professor Raymond Piper, Professor Dwight Beck, Professor William P. Gormley, Professor Reginald D. Manwell, Professor Harry Hepner, Professor Stuart C. Brown, Professor Byron Fox, Professor Phillips H. Bradley, Professor Kenneth Kindlesberger, Professor Guthrie Birkhead, and Dean John S. Hafer.

The basic patterns of programs for this year were much the same as they had been in years past. Along with the established and proven activities there were always some innovations. This year a chapter of the National Organization of the Fellowship of Reconciliation was formed, with Professor J. Theron Illick as faculty adviser. A new face at the chapel in the fall was the Reverend Arnold Nakajima, who had come to be the full-time chaplain for Presbyterians.

The format for the daily chapel was slightly altered when the Jewish students began to share in its planning. Previously, there had been one Jewish daily-chapel service a week, and this practice continued. The daily-chapel services were now planned by both the Christian and the Jewish groups. The Reverend Arthur Hopkinson, Jr., was the adviser.

The new program that had the widest effect on the campus was the first Casawasco retreat for the house representatives, which was held the first weekend of October. Attended by one hundred students, its purpose was to strengthen the lines of communication between the chapel and each of the living centers. It proved to be a great success.

During this year long and descriptive letters were received by Syracuse-in-Thailand from Tom Gill, who had arrived in Bangkok the previous June to be the Syracuse-in-Thailand student representative. He was teaching English at Chulalonghorn University.

When Professor Poister came to the university in 1948 a commitment was made to him that in addition to a new organ at Crouse College there would also be a new one in the chapel. Working with his friend Walter Holtkamp, Poister shared in designing an instrument appropriate to the chapel. One notable feature was the desklike console that would give Professor Poister full view of the choir. It was, when finished, an impressive instrument, with 3,567 pipes and three banks of keys,

---

*The purpose of the board was to be the eyes and ears for the dean and thus help the chapel be as effective a part of the university as possible.—RLP

with all the appropriate stops and couplers that gave it the distinction of being one of the great church organs in the country.*

Early in the second semester it was announced that Rabbi William Schwartz, who had been at the chapel since 1948, would be leaving to take a rabbinical position in Helena, Arkansas. Rabbi Schwartz had made a very valuable contribution to the Jewish fellowship, which he had revitalized. In a time of interfaith conflict he had demonstrated that one could be true to one's own convictions and at the same time cooperate in interreligious affairs.† Under Rabbi Schwartz's leadership a Jewish choir had been formed, a new ark and scroll had been presented and dedicated, the High Holy Days had been celebrated on campus, and the Brotherhood Services had been initiated. In all of these activities he helped to integrate the Jewish program into the total spiritual and cultural life of the university. On February 20 a farewell service was held for him and was attended by many students, faculty, and staff, including Chancellor Tolley. The reception that followed in the Colonial Room was sponsored by the Syracuse Chapters of B'nai B'rith and Jewish Women.

Just before Rabbi Schwartz departed he participated in the All-Chapel Banquet, which Dean Noble described as the "star event of the entire season." The speaker was Dr. Mordecai Johnson of Washington, D.C., the first black president of Howard University. The program also included talks by chapel officers and selections by the choirs. Attendance at the event reached an all-time high.

Great effort was put into raising funds for the Campus Chest, and when the drive was over the amount collected was $4,808.36, topping the previous year's figure. To this amount was added the $600 raised at the Campus Carnival.

A special committee was set up at the chapel to support students who were conscientious objectors to war. Committee members were the Reverend Arthur Hopkinson, Jr., Robert Laubach, Dean Frank Piskor, Dean Marjorie Smith, Roland Smith, the Reverend Walter Welsh, Professor Norman Whitney, Dean Robert, and Dean Noble.‡

On April 17 Chapel Board elections were held, with Patricia (Rusty) Roden and Deane Lavender elected as cochairmen for the coming year.

In the account of this year in the life of the chapel it may appear that many of the usual fixtures were omitted, but it is not so. This year was full, with a huge program. In addition to all the new and special activities, the usual solid core of events and activities that marked the chapel program from year to year were as demanding and as productive as ever.

---

*That organ and console are still in Hendricks Chapel and still one of the great church instruments in the country.—RLP

†This conviction was to remain a philosophical and theological cornerstone for the operation of the chapel to the day of this publication.—RLP

‡The need to respond to current events—local, national, and international—is probably nowhere on campus more keenly felt than in the life of Hendricks Chapel. The effects of the Korean War were no exception.—RLP

On the inside front cover of the *Hendricks Chapel Guide Book* for the year is printed a poem called "What Is Chapel?" that reflects how one student, Marcia Moskowitz, caught up in the life of the chapel, communicated what it meant to her.

> To some a place where friends are met
> To some a place to chat: and yet
> A spot where placidness and rest
> Can supplement excessive zest.
>
> Each noonday twenty minutes spent
> In worship bring a deep content
> Where boy meets girl at Thursday tea;
> Where friendship lasts without a fee.
>
> A counselor will hear your woe
> Concerning lover, friend or foe
> Here, others join a group to lend
> A hand, or just to be a friend.
>
> Here, "international" is thought
> To be a word which means one ought
> To aid his neighbor, Human need
> Means more than color, race or creed.
>
> Work is done by Christian, Jew
> And those with no sectarian view.
> The test is no set thought or code,
> We're questing on a common road.
>
> Philosophies are made each day
> Through living in a Chapel way.
> Human traits are not thought odd
> Because they seek a living God.

30. Ministering to SU's Postwar Population, 1953–1954

TO UNDERSTAND THE HISTORY of Hendricks Chapel, its role must be examined in the context of the times of each student generation. Clearly, World

War II had been a turning point in American life, deeply affecting not merely life on campus but life in general. Chancellor Tolley had made it known that Syracuse University would do its best to meet the educational needs of the men who had served in the armed forces. The GI Bill gave financial support to all qualified veterans, among whom were a considerable number who, had they not served in the war, might not have gone to college. At Syracuse, as I have pointed out, the campus exploded with sheer numbers in the falls of 1946 and 1947, and the university mobilized itself to take care of them.

During this period the chapel was a veritable hub of activity—a kind of creative catchall—ministering to a great number of students with a broad array of human and spiritual concerns. The four years from 1946 to 1950 were the most crowded and intense. After that the pressure began to ease as the numbers being registered began to diminish and the academy had developed the resources required to serve the increased numbers. This gradual diminishment of numbers continued through the fall of 1952.

In September 1953 the trend reversed yet again, and when registration figures were tabulated there were more students in the entering class than the year before. This year also marked the beginning of a building program that would add many new buildings to the campus. The first addition was the Women's Building, which was dedicated on Colgate Weekend.

In the midst of and in a sense at the very heart of the new "wave" was Hendricks Chapel. Its basic programs established patterns of serving needs but were responsive to changing times and were never quite the same in any two years.

After many years of attempting to find some formula for interfaith cooperation with Father Ryan and the Roman Catholics, the 1953 *Hendricks Chapel Guide Book,* given to all newcomers, bluntly stated, "Although the Roman Catholic program has been omitted at the direct request of the Reverend Gannon F. Ryan and his student leaders, a place is reserved for them when circumstances may open up channels for renewed participation."

The chapel now operated with three basic constituent structures: the Chapel Board, the Jewish Student Fellowship, and the Protestant Council. During this year the chapel continued many of its well-established programs but, as always, added some new ones. At the opening of each semester the usual planning conference for chapel leaders and another for housing representatives were held at Casawasco.

Regular repeated events were Chapel Night for newcomers, the sign-up days, the distribution of the *Hendricks Chapel Guide Book,* and the many meetings of the committees and commissions of the Chapel Board. There was the Sabbath-eve service for Jewish students, the Roman Catholic masses at Crouse on Sunday mornings, the Sunday chapel service for Protestants with the superb choir under the direction of Professor Poister, and a nursery for young children of married students. Daily chapel was again held each weekday at noon.

Even without the participation of the Roman Catholic students, there were major interfaith events during the year. The first occurred on the Friday before the Colgate football game when at eight thirty, after the pep rally, a Sabbath-eve service was sponsored by the Jewish Student Fellowship with the Reverend Dr. Ralph W. Sockman of New York City again the speaker. In February the Christians reciprocated by inviting the Jewish students to a chapel service on Sunday morning to hear Rabbi Edward Sandrou of Cedarhurst, Long Island, preach the sermon. This year the advisers to the Jewish Student Fellowship were Rabbi Hyman of Syracuse and Professor Fred Krinsky of the Maxwell School, Rabbi Schwartz having left the campus the previous February.

The social hygiene series on sex and marriage again proved a popular part of the chapel program and was well supported. New this year was a mental hygiene series under the leadership of the student cochairmen, Everett Gertner and Beverly Darrow. The topics of the series are listed as follows: "You and Your Emotions," "Frustrations in Campus Living," "Parents and What to Do with Them," "Military Service and You," "Should the Atomic Age Scare You?" and "How to Make Grades and Influence Deans." To keep the group to a manageable size, each session was limited to forty students.

Late in November Dr. William Stuart Nelson, dean of Howard University in Washington, D.C., was a guest on campus, having come to study the program and philosophy of Hendricks Chapel.*

The Christmas season was once again celebrated with a configuration of events and programs that included the setting up and lighting of the Christmas tree and the contest for the best-decorated living center. The Sunday morning service in the chapel featured special music by the choir, and in the evening there was the singing of carols on the chapel steps before the Christmas pageant under the direction of Zeta Phi Eta.

The most creative innovation in the chapel program this year was a three-day conference on religion that came to be known as Footprints. It was organized under the leadership of students James Carr and Elizabeth Goddard with staff assistance. The leaders of the conference were the Reverend Dr. A. Powell Davies of Washington, D.C., whose topic was "The Nature of Man"; Professor E. G. Homrighausen of Princeton, who spoke on "The Nature of God"; and Rabbi Joseph Fink, whose subject was "The Nature of Truth." The conference included four sessions for students, with an attendance of between sixty and one hundred for each one. It also included a faculty colloquium on Sunday evening, March 5, asking the question, "What are the claims of religion?" The conference was designed to reach the whole university community with the purpose of stimulating thought

---

*From its beginning Hendricks Chapel has served as a model of a style of campus ministry that many have used in developing their own campus religious-life programs.—RLP

on religion and philosophy, and this general format would be repeated for several years to come.

Father Gannon Ryan in his sermon on Sunday, March 7, publicly asked the question as to whether Syracuse University was a nonsectarian university or a church-related institution, addressing his question to the administration. The question, of course, was rhetorical and displayed his own feelings about the religious policy and background of the university.*

On April 25 Professor Albert Outler, a leading Methodist scholar from the Perkins School of Theology of Southern Methodist University, came to lead a three-day conference on religion for the faculty. The major question addressed was "What are our obligations to our students as reflecting our personal, moral, and religious convictions?" A committee consisting of Professors J. Theron Illick, Stuart G. Grown, and U. V. McKenn arranged for Outler to meet with various groups of faculty in separate sessions. He spoke on the general theme "The Implications of Religion for a University Faculty" and then addressed the discussion to specific disciplines in which the various faculty members were involved.

On Monday evening, May 10, the chapel choir, having reached outstanding stature as a musical organization under the direction of Professor Poister, gave its spring concert.

In June the New York State Student Christian Movement Conference, now called the Champlain Conference, met at Silver Bay on Lake George. Syracuse had the largest delegation of any college or university in the state. Officers and members of the Chapel Board were elected for the academic year 1953–54.†

The official name for the former Syracuse-in-China and Syracuse-in-Thailand programs became Syracuse-in-Asia (SIA) and would be so for the remainder of its life. It did not have the power or charm of the original program but remained a viable part of the chapel operation. Later it would pass to the Maxwell School.

From the beginning of his tenure Dean Noble's suggestion of a Chapel Board retreat at Casawasco before the college year began had drawn an enthusiastic response. This year the event lasted for five days and was organized around the theme "The Source of Values," with attention being paid to experience, religion, revelation, and metaphysics. The core group of those persons attending included the Chapel Board officers and committee and commission chairmen, the dean and

*By this time the university had formally separated itself from Methodist control and identity and had declared itself a nonsectarian, private, independent university. Thus, Ryan was on firm ground with his concern about what he viewed as continuing Protestant, if not Methodist, hegemony in the operation of the religious-life aspects of the campus. Later, professional Roman Catholic leadership on campus reversed almost completely the "Ryan style," but some concern will always exist regarding this issue. As we shall see later, a study in 1979 and 1980 of the chapel's operation made some changes designed in part to answer the religious-equity question.—RLP

†See appendix A.—RLP

his staff, the chaplains and counselors, and special resource persons who were brought in.

Advancement of qualified student leadership within the chapel organization was normal. Committee members with both leadership ability and continuing interest would soon move up to greater responsibilities. For many years this process included a position on the second cabinet—for two years now a thing of the past. Now, elections were held each spring, usually in March, from a slate drawn up in a nominating process from the most able and active of the chapelites. Four students, two men and two women, were nominated to become cochairmen. Four others were nominated to become secretaries. Election was by those individuals eligible to vote because of their involvement in the chapel. The top four vote getters became the cochairmen and the co-vice chairmen. The next four top vote getters became the secretaries and the comptrollers. The committee and commission chairmen were appointed in a consultative process, except for the officers and representatives of the Protestant Council and the Jewish Student Fellowship who were elected by their members.*

31. Clarifying the Philosophy of Hendricks Chapel, 1954–1955

THIS YEAR a rather ambitious program was used as an orientation vehicle to help new officers understand the workings of the chapel. These sessions were held each Tuesday afternoon in the fall under the leadership of Arthur Kinney. At the first one Dean Noble said, "The purpose of Hendricks Chapel is to lift the opaqueness in a student's religious life and give him light and the opportunity to express his interest in religiously motivated activities and experiences." In the next session James Fellows, cochairman of the Chapel Board, speaking about its function, said, "The Hendricks Chapel Board is a group of people religiously motivated and with a personal concern for one's own relationship with God, seeking a means of expression in religion with other people." Vice President Frank Piskor, in his talk about the place of the chapel in the university community, said, "We rely on the chapel to nurture a concern for values, to develop a concern for human relationships, such as international student groups, and to remain sensitive to student needs."

---

*See appendix A for those officers and representatives elected for the 1954–55 academic year.
—RLP

The training session that received the most attention was the one called "The Religious Policy of Syracuse University," with the chancellor as the scheduled leader. Tolley was called away and the Vice Chancellor Finla Crawford spoke in his place. Dr. Crawford used some of the material prepared by Dr. Tolley, and it was obviously a carefully worded statement, especially in light of the questions that had been raised about religious policy on campus, notably by Father Ryan. The first point made was that policy of any kind can be made only by the chancellor and the Board of Trustees. Dr. Crawford went on to differentiate between the traditions of private and public higher education in the United States, noting that in private schools and colleges there were both religious and nonreligious institutions. He pointed out that there was a greater degree of freedom for those institutions in the private sector. Syracuse University had been founded by the Methodist Church but had had a long policy of nondiscrimination on the basis of religion, race, or national origin and thus SU was not greatly affected by the recently enacted state regulations concerning discrimination and the oath of allegiance. He concluded by saying that Syracuse University presented ample opportunity for students to be active in the religious group of their choice and that no student was required to take a course that would conflict with his religious faith.

The campus radio station WAER had, for one year, carried *Chapel Chimes,* a fifteen-minute program each afternoon at 5:15.* This broadcast was abandoned after the first year of its inception. This year the Radio Committee set up another broadcast on WAER, this time a half-hour program on Sunday evening. The first part of the program was a review of the dean's sermon of the morning, and the second part was an interview with freshmen about their perception of chapel activities. Later, the Sunday sermons were broadcast live.

Activities in the first semester at Hendricks Chapel followed the patterns of other years. They had been reviewed and refined at the Casawasco planning retreat before the opening of the college year.

The always popular social hygiene discussion groups were scheduled for both the first and the second semesters and covered the full range of relationships between the sexes, including dating, mate selection, marriage, family planning, parenting, and all the moral and physical problems of sex faced by college-age men and women.

The annual Brotherhood Service, sponsored by the Jewish Student Fellowship, was held on the Friday night of Colgate Weekend, and Dr. Ralph W. Sockman was again the speaker.

As Christmas approached the Syracuse-in-Asia Committee announced that it would have twelve hundred articles for sale and that the proceeds from the sale,

*See chapter 41 by Lawrence Myers, Jr.—RLP

added to an allocation received from the Campus Chest, would be used to support Donald Magnin as the student representative in Thailand for the year.

A new addition to the annual Christmas pageant was the participation of a string quartet directed by Professor Louis Krasner, which played *Christmas Prelude* by Corelli. The pageant was directed by Rosemary Sinnett and was based on "The Last Room," a Christmas story written by Professor A. E. Johnson. Two days after Christmas Marilyn Pflueger, who had been the Lutheran counselor, was married, and her place was take by Evelyn Christenson.

In the second semester the annual Hendricks Chapel banquet was held on Sunday evening, February 20, with Dr. Buell Gallagher, president of the City College of New York, as the principal speaker.

The success of Footprints the year before had been so great that Footprints II was scheduled for March 6–8 with Dr. Mordecai Johnson, president of Howard University; Dr. Henry Steele Commanger, an author and historian; and Dr. Paul Harris, a member of the Society of Friends, as leaders. The topic for this year's program was "The Relation of Religion and Philosophy in International Affairs," and it drew wide support from students and faculty. The question might arise here as to whether this program should be included as a part of the history of Hendricks Chapel, for strictly speaking it was not. Dean Noble had promised a group of students that Footprints would not become a part of the chapel program. Nonetheless, the whole idea arose, as Noble put it, "over a cup of coffee," and it would never have come about had it not been for the chapel sponsorship making possible strong university-wide support.*

On the last day of March, Joan Bosworth and John Husband were elected cochairmen of the Chapel Board for the coming year. Late in April the officers of the Jewish Student Federation conducted a Sabbath-eve service at which Dr. Fred Krinsky, assistant professor of citizenship at Maxwell, was officially installed as associate rabbi and chaplain for Jewish students.†

I have mentioned the personal role taken by Dean and Mrs. Noble in using their home for the benefit of students and faculty. Day after day and night after night, teas, receptions, meetings, Skeptics Corners, visits, and counseling sessions were held. Many students would long remember the warm and personal attention

*Though probably not the first such cooperative sponsorship, the chapel soon became a key instigator and cooperator in such jointly sponsored programs and remains so at the time of this publication.—RLP

†Krinsky was an eminently effective lecturer in religion, political science, and citizenship. He was to finish his academic career in California but always held close ties to Syracuse University, returning on the fiftieth anniversary of the chapel to present a lecture. He lectured several other times at SU, even after his retirement. He was a very close friend of Ted and Marjorie Pierson, who often (even after Ted's death) financed his visits and lectures as well as hosting him while he was in Syracuse.—RLP

they received as they would make their way to the Noble home on Ostrom Avenue, just a few short blocks from the chapel and campus. Soon the Nobles would move to a university-owned house on Berkeley Drive, just about five blocks away. More will be said about that house later.

32. "Joy in the Struggle," 1955–1956

FACULTY AND STAFF who met at Casawasco in September 1955 to get ready for the chapel program were to be involved in a particularly significant year. They could have been aware of this fact, though there is no indication that they took note of it. They were intent on looking ahead, and so it seems probable that none realized that twenty-five years earlier, a quarter of a century, the chapel was dedicated and its doors opened to students. It might have been asked then, as we ask it now, in the intervening years, if the dream of Senator Hendricks had been fulfilled, a dream he had while experiencing peace and quiet in the chapel at Williams College. Hendricks wanted such a place for Syracuse University and gave the money to make it possible. Surely, the prodigious amount of activity with its highly diversified character would have astonished him. He would have taken great satisfaction in knowing the chapel had indeed become "the heart of the university" and that it was religious faith and outreach that were the central motivating powers behind all that had happened in the building that bore his family name. He could have taken satisfaction too in knowing that literally thousands of students' lives had been influenced by participation in the kind of life the chapel had made possible for them.*

For these twenty-five years religion, as housed under the "umbrella" of Hendricks Chapel, had been vital, constructive, and respected at Syracuse University. As these words are written the question arises as to whether any other major university in the United States had as effective a religious-life program on campus. More will be said of this question later.

What those individuals assembled at Casawasco in those autumn days could not know, though they might have had some slight intimation of it, was that precisely at this time social historians dealing with religion saw the beginning of the end of the so-called post-World War II religious boom. Hospitality to religion had been widespread in the post-World War II years among most segments of U.S. society. I have recorded the times when it was all the chapel could do to provide an

---

*He would have been especially pleased that the chapel, through its programming, had become a "house of prayer" for all the world's people. An equally interesting question would be to discover what, if any, would have been his disappointments.—RLP

adequate variety of programs and activities as students swarmed in and out of its doors. Gradually, the tide of interest in religion began to turn, as would soon become evident.

Another anniversary was not forgotten but was celebrated at the time of the Brotherhood Banquet in February: the ten years that Charles Noble had served as dean of Hendricks Chapel. His arrival on campus in November 1945 had coincided with the ending of World War II and the influx of returning veterans. He had plunged into his task with enthusiasm and zest and with what seemed like an almost inexhaustible amount of energy. To honor him, Chancellor Tolley presented him with a silver tray on behalf of the university. Included as part of the appreciative inscription were the words "Joy in the Struggle," the title of one of Dean Noble's most popular sermons. The Reverend Arnold Nakajima presented him with a book of clippings and photographs titled "A Guy Called Noble," which had been put together by Milton Shefter, chairman of the banquet. In addition, a pair of silver candlesticks was presented on behalf of all "chapelites" by Jane Sheckels, cochairman of the dinner. More than one hundred letters were assembled from people beyond the university community with whom Dean Noble had worked. The principal speaker at this event was the seventy-one-year-old veteran socialist Norman Thomas. By any standard of judgment, during these ten years, the dean had been the most active and visible leader at Syracuse University.

Organizationally, the chapel had become a kind of cooperative federation, with a steering committee furnishing the glue to hold things together. The Chapel Board included members of most of the faith and denominational groups, with the exception of the Roman Catholics. In addition, there were the Jewish Student Fellowship and the Protestant Council, which had representatives on the Chapel Board. Within the Protestant Council were representatives of the various denominational fellowships who carried on their own meetings and programs while cooperating with others in some of the larger events. In the *Hendricks Chapel Guide Book* for the year the officers were listed not only for the Chapel Board but for all the organized religious groups.

In his report to the chancellor Dean Noble wrote: "Like everything else at Syracuse University, Hendricks Chapel is a dynamic, changing entity which creates problems for itself by refusing to coast along on tradition and established conventions." This year a research committee was formed and charged with the task of formulating a plan for a more efficient organization of the whole program, with specific attention being given to better communication, less duplication of effort, and a more accurate nomenclature. This call for change did not include the elimination of the well-supported programs that had become perennial highlights of the year.

This year there were three Casawasco Conferences, one before the beginning of each semester for the leaders of the various segments of the chapel program and one for the house representatives, who were stimulated by the theme "If I Were Running Syracuse University." Early in the fall a reception was held for the dean of women's and the dean of men's staffs to acquaint them with the chapel. Chapel Night and the days for sign-ups were held, and both drew a good response.

The Jewish-Christian Brotherhood Services were held. The first was the traditional Sabbath-eve service held on Colgate Weekend, with Dr. Ralph W. Sockman returning for the eighth year as the speaker. The second was the Sunday morning service on March 4, with Rabbi Philip E. Bernstein as preacher.

Sunday morning worship continued to draw a large congregation of worshipers from both the university and the wider Syracuse community. The preaching of Dean Noble and a superb choir of 120 voices under the direction of Professor Arthur Poister proved to be an irresistible combination. Usually Dean Noble preached twice a month, each full-time chaplain once or twice during the year, and outstanding visiting preachers filled the remainder of the schedule. There was also a daily chapel each weekday at noon. The Jewish Student Fellowship sponsored, in addition to the Brotherhood Service, the special religious holiday celebrations for Jewish students and a regular Sabbath-eve service.

The Protestant Council or one of the member denominational groups planned for special services during Advent and Lent and participated with the Chapel Board in sponsoring the Christmas pageant.

Syracuse-in-Asia drew support from a wide and varied constituency, which made it possible for its representative in Thailand, Donald Magnin, to continue his second year. Monetary support also came from the Christmas sale and Campus Chest.

The Protestant Council also served as a conduit through which students related to the Student Christian Movement on the state, regional, and national levels and to the International World Student Christian Federation. Footprints III, though not an official part of the chapel program, received its chief guidance from the council. The name "Footprints" was derived from Longfellow's words "Footprints on the sands of time" and promoted campuswide emphasis dealing with philosophical, psychological, theological, and political questions. Among the leaders this year was the well-known Quaker leader and author Dr. Elton Trueblood.

For many years the chapel had requested more space be made available for its proliferating programs, and when Mrs. Huntington Crouse gave her home at 400 Comstock Avenue to the university, it was determined that it would be made available for use by the chapel. The announcement of the gift and its designation was made early in the year, and at the All-Chapel Assembly on Wednesday, May 2, it was formally opened. It was to be used for teas, get-togethers, and Sunday meetings and for the remainder of the academic year would be open from three to ten o'clock with the hope that during the next year its use and hours could be expanded. Operating it proved taxing for both staff and budget.

Chapel elections were held on April 12, and all chapelites who had attended at least half of the meetings of their committees for fellowships were eligible to vote. Dorothy Campbell and Donald Williams emerged as the new cochairmen for the coming year.*

33. Secularization on the Rise, 1956–1957

LONG BEFORE the word *ecumenism* had entered into the vocabulary of church relationships, attempts were being made by the people of God to find ways in which they could cooperate. Prior to Vatican II this participation was usually exclusive of Roman Catholics. At city, county, state, national, and world levels the conciliar movement with its formation of councils of churches was becoming operational. The areas designated for cooperation were in the realms of faith, order, life, and work. Almost at the same time, particularly in the United States, the denominations were becoming more aware of their own distinctive identity. As they began to interact, they began to try to understand who they were in relationship to the beliefs and practices of the other churches with which they were cooperating. Inevitably, this understanding was reflected in the religious situation at Syracuse University and in Hendricks Chapel. Dean Powers came to the chapel in a liberal theological era and believed it should not be too difficult for people of differing persuasions to come into a cooperative arrangement under one organizational structure. It seemed quite possible to him that with a wide degree of toleration, all religious groups could work together in this liberal framework. In many respects it worked, especially at the beginning. As time went on the reality factor of increasing religious pluralism on campus created problems. The first of these problems had to do with Father Gannon Ryan, the Roman Catholic chaplain. Father Ryan rigorously defended the long-held doctrine of the exclusiveness of the Roman Catholic Church.

The response of the Jewish student religious community was very different. They found the liberal religious leadership of the chapel, for the most part, to their liking. It left them free to celebrate their faith according to their own beliefs. They found many areas in which they had no difficulty in cooperating with Hendricks Chapel and other religious groups. By and large and in varying degrees the Protestants worked together. They often had differences, but for the most part their

*See appendix A for a full listing.—RLP

agreements outweighed their disagreements. Some of the differences were focused on order, or the way a church celebrated its worship, most notably between the liturgical and nonliturgical churches. The strongest and most numerous of the denominational groups were the Methodists, the Presbyterians, the Episcopalians, and the Lutherans, who each formed core-group ministries. Their chaplains found ways not only to serve the students within their own denominations but also to cooperate in a broad chapel program.

Yet the program could never be tied up into a neat package; there always seemed to be loose ends. When the ambiguities became too great then some alteration in the structure would take place with the hope that it would help solve any problems inherent in such diversity.

A wide consensus developed in the fall retreat of 1956 at Casawasco that there needed to be a better way to organize the chapel program. The Protestants decided they would broaden the base of the Protestant Council and gave it the name the United Protestant Assembly. It was agreed that a study needed to be made of the total chapel program.

At the winter Casawasco retreat, held in February, agreement was reached that the entire interfaith program with all its components would be placed under the Executive Committee of student officers. Final authority for determining chapel policy would rest with the Casawasco Conferences or the All-Chapel Assemblies. Eligibility for the "assembly" was to be based on participation in one of the fellowship groups, a service committee, or an activity group of the Chapel Board. Thus, the new Chapel Board would consist of the five officers of the Executive Committee, the cochairmen of the service committees, and the twelve presidents of the fellowship groups. Ex-officio were members of the staff, the chaplains and counselors, and the Faculty Advisory Board. The general organizational pattern sought to bring all the decision makers into one body, and great hopes were invested in the plan.

The officers of the 1957–58 Executive Committee were Dorothy Campbell and Donald Williams, cochairmen; Carol Curtis and Paul Ackerson, vice chairmen; Marilyn Swanson, secretary; and Elizabeth Cougler, treasurer.

While all this reorganization was going on most of the usual programs and activities continued much as they had in recent years. Most of the religious fellowships met early Sunday evenings, usually sharing a meal before their program. The Sunday morning worship service with Dean Noble, a visiting clergyman, or chaplain preaching was held at 10:50. The superb choir of 120 voices under the direction of Professor Poister provided the music and added greatly to the service. Jewish worship was held each Sabbath eve in the chapel by the Jewish Student Fellowship. Daily chapel was now from 12:30 to 1:00 each weekday with a varied program.

There were also special events that had become part of an all-chapel program.

For the ninth time Dr. Sockman came to preach at the Brotherhood Service on the Friday night of Colgate Weekend, and later in February Rabbi Arthur Lelyveld was the preacher for the Sunday morning Brotherhood Service.

This year a great many Hungarian displaced persons came to the United States. A considerable number of them were sponsored in Syracuse. In November a special drive for clothing and food was made on campus by the Chapel Board to help them get settled.

Special holidays were marked. In the fall the Jewish holidays were celebrated and then later Advent and Christmas with the traditional pageant. Though most students were home during the Christmas break, Hendricks was host to about two hundred students who came for a conference sponsored by the northeast region of the United Christian Council.

Syracuse-in-China, now Syracuse-in-Asia, had come into the chapel program when the chapel opened in 1930 and had always maintained its own alumni group. This year, in January, the decision was made to identify completely with the chapel program.

In an effort to be as broadly ecumenical as possible, Dr. George N. Shuster, president of Hunter College and a well-known Roman Catholic layman, was invited to be the speaker at the Brotherhood Banquet. The theme chosen for the affair was "Each Apart, yet Each a Part." This visit, however, did not mitigate Father Ryan's opposition to Hendricks Chapel programs. At the time of the Footprints conference, which this year was specifically separated from chapel sponsorship, Father Ryan urged Roman Catholic students not to participate. Without strong chapel support the program floundered. The theme had been "College Freedom," and the leader was Dr. Harry Gideonse, president of Brooklyn College. The response was embarrassingly poor, leaving its future in doubt.

On March 25 it was announced that the Social Service Committee had signed up sixty volunteers to work with the Volunteer Center in Syracuse and were assigned to help in programs at the Cerebral Palsy Clinic, the Girl's Club, Percy Hughes School (for handicapped children), and the Syracuse Day Nursery. Most of the people helping were freshmen.

Earlier in the month the Jewish Student Fellowship had sponsored a conference for ten upstate colleges around the theme "The Role of Campus Judaism" with the hope that it might become an annual Purim event. Well-known scholar and author Will Herberg gave the principal address, "The Face of Religion in America Today." With one exception the chapel fellowships shared in this part of the conference.

Crouse House, which was now available for chapel activities, became a very busy and active place during this year. In his report Dean Noble said that more than 1,000 students a week used it for some kind of campus function. At the beginning of the second semester, in conjunction with the International Student Office, the overseas students reorganized themselves, and each Wednesday evening they met at Crouse House with an average attendance of 150.

From one point of view the most significant happening at Hendricks Chapel in the year 1956–57 was the restructuring that consolidated the program under one comprehensive organization.* During the second semester the University Student Opinion Service interviewed 196 students about their religious attitudes and participation. Sixteen said they were not interested in responding; the 116 remaining said that before coming to college they had been active in religious groups. When asked if they were active in any religious organization on campus, 129 answered no. They were asked why. The answers varied and included "drifting," "no time," "poor organization on campus," "MSF [Methodist Student Fellowship] too big," "more of a need at home," and "organization seems too big and impersonal." On the other hand, students who were active reported that they had more time than they did at home, that they found great emphasis on religious activity on campus, and that participation in religious programs was a good channel for excess energy.

When students were asked what they thought the main functions of the chapel were, they replied: fellowship (89), service (60), discussion and debates (61), worship (129), study (15), and counseling (86). This study was interesting, for while the headline in the *Daily Orange* announcing it proclaimed a lack of interest in religion on campus, it was obvious that out of the 180 students responding, 51 were involved and participating in some form of chapel activity. The study did, however, indicate a slacking off of religious interest and participation from the early postwar years when the chapel was strong, vigorous, and prestigious. The study indicated that on the Syracuse University campus as in American life in general the trend was toward a creeping secularization that would be increasingly manifest in the years to come.

34. The Acquisition of Chapel House, 1957–1958

THE FALL RETREAT at Casawasco had long been the place for chapelites to get "geared up" for the coming year. In the fall of 1957 Dr. Hans Hoffman came to supplement the staff and chaplains on the theme "The Meaning of the Chapel in University Life." As usual it was well attended, and this year under the new plan

---

*Shifting student interest and widespread disinterest in religion were beginning to be major factors at the chapel.—RLP

of organization for Hendricks Chapel it included all the fellowship groups that were related to the chapel program. The Chapel Board no longer occupied a dominant position in the chapel organizational structure, but still represented a wide spectrum of religiously concerned students.[*]

At this point in the chapel's history it is interesting to note that programs that were originally initiated by the chapel in response to students' needs had been taken over by other campus entities. We have previously mentioned Footprints, which was chapel inspired and supported but later became campuswide in its appeal and support. The Campus Chest had its birth in response to needs for emergency student loans and support for Syracuse-in-China (which had become Syracuse-in-Asia). The Social Hygiene Committee of the Chapel Board, which dealt with discussions on sex and marriage, became legitimated as credit-bearing courses in the College of Home Economics. The chapel committee that first reached out to the growing numbers of students from overseas became a university-sponsored service for international students. One short-lived chapel function was its cosponsorship of the student leaders' conference at Pinebrook, which later became an annual program under the direction of student government. All of these activities in whole or in part had their genesis in the programs of Hendricks Chapel and therefore made their contribution to the total life of Syracuse University. This generative trend continued to characterize the avant-garde nature of the chapel on the SU campus, as did the fact that programs shifted to bases of operation other than the chapel.

This year several staff changes took place. The Reverend Arnold Nakajima, who had been the Presbyterian chaplain for five years, accepted a position as assistant executive secretary of his denomination's Board of Christian Education starting in October. The Reverend Dugald Chafee of the East Genesee Presbyterian Church took his place, on an interim basis, for the remainder of the year. Nakajima was invited to return to Syracuse to speak at the Annual Brotherhood Service of Friday evening, November 15. In addition, the Reverend Jack White became the Episcopalian chaplain and Sheila McDorney the counselor for Baptist students.

Dean Noble inaugurated the first noon daily-chapel service, speaking on "Jesus Goes to College." It was decided that each Wednesday a full Protestant service of worship would be held, including choral participation by a volunteer choir of about twenty-five. Each week the service would be under the leadership of one of the denominational fellowships, reflecting their particular style and form of worship.

Casawasco was not available for a fall conference of chapel representatives, so they assembled for two days in late October at the Lisle Conference Center. There they decided to organize discussion groups to be held each Thursday afternoon to

[*]See appendix A for the 1957–58 student leaders.—RLP

deal with such campus problems as drinking and helping overseas students and to seek more widespread understanding of four major religious groups: the Jesuits, Protestants, and the Jewish and Eastern Orthodox faith groups.

Syracuse-in-Asia had decided on two crucial matters during the year. Dr. Gordon Hoople, a local physician, had been one of the founders of Syracuse-in-China as well as a participant in China as a medical missionary. He headed a committee to reorganize the effort that was now called Syracuse-in-Asia. The reorganization brought it more fully within the Hendricks Chapel program. In addition Karl Schultz had not been able to complete even his first year in Thailand, having been called back home because of his military draft situation. This absence left SIA without a student representative for the current year in Asia. For this and other reasons it was decided to explore the possibility of finding a new college in Asia. All of this upheaval did not curtail the activities of the local Syracuse-in-Asia organization. The Christmas sale was conducted with good financial results, and later in the year a drive was launched to secure books to be sent to the impoverished libraries in several Asian locations.

During the traditional holiday season the Jewish Student Fellowship, under the leadership of associate Rabbi Fred Krinsky, sponsored its first Hanukkah service. The United Christian Council set up a special late-evening Advent service that included the ringing of the Crouse College chimes.

Three new fellowship groups emerged during the year, reflecting both the increasing religious pluralism and the presence of larger numbers of overseas students on campus. By this time there were enough students at the university to form Hindu, Muslim, and Buddhist groups.

The chapel never seemed to have enough space to carry on its many activities, and Dean Noble was always begging the administration for more space. From time to time projections had been made for an additional building adjacent to the chapel that would expand its capacity. When Crouse House became available it gave some relief to the crowded conditions at the chapel but was away from the center of the campus and though extensively used proved difficult to administer and thus was only a stopgap facility. When it became known that the Beta Theta Pi house on Comstock Avenue would be available, Dean Noble was quick to request the use of it. On November 7, 1957, the *Daily Orange* carried a story that showed a picture of the building and announced that it would indeed become Chapel House. By the second semester it was in operation, with offices for chaplains, several rooms for meetings and services, kitchen facilities, and a dining room. Its proximity to the main campus and its space made it a valuable adjunct to the chapel.

During the winter Casawasco retreat it was known that Chapel House was available, and program plans were made to utilize the space. Crouse House had previously been used by overseas students and was now given over more fully for their use. The theme of this Casawasco Conference was "Why Bother with Religion?" It began a very busy semester for the chapel.

The Universal Day of Prayer for Students promoted by the World Student Christian Federation was celebrated at the Sunday morning chapel service on February 16, with Methodist bishop Frederick Newell of New York as speaker. An attempt was made to involve as many of the Christian students from overseas as possible in the service.

Ash Wednesday occurred on February 19, and a great variety of services were held during Lent. Services at noon on Wednesdays were sponsored by the various denominational fellowships. They were better attended than the regular daily-chapel services. A communion service was celebrated each Wednesday morning at six thirty by Dean Noble. The Episcopalians conducted a daily communion service at seven in Chapel House.

On the first Sunday evening of Lent, the Annual Brotherhood Banquet brought Dr. Hurst Anderson, president of American University in Washington, D.C., to be the speaker. The theme for the evening was "One World Without One Mind." In order to give students more chance to participate, follow-up meetings were held in the Chapel Boardroom the next day at four and seven o'clock. Dr. Peter Bertocci, professor of philosophy from Boston University, was the speaker and discussion leader.

Footprints V was held March 3–5 with the theme "What Has Happened to America?" It had never been a chapel program per se but had always drawn heavily on the chapel for leadership and participation. Leaders were astronomer Dr. Harlow Shapley, John Ciardi, and Gordon Hall, a researcher whose field was the study of hate groups that had used smear tactics to gain their ends and achieve their disruptive influence on American life.

The decision to establish the Hillel Foundation at Syracuse University beginning in the fall of 1958 caused a significant alteration in the organization of Hendricks Chapel. For many years those alumni who were influential in directing the program for Jewish students at Syracuse were not hospitable to the idea of having a unit of Hillel on campus. But after the conference of the previous year that brought together Jewish students from various upstate colleges and universities the decision was made to establish a unit of Hillel with a relationship to the national organization. This year a similar conference was held at Syracuse, focusing on the tenth anniversary of the establishment of the State of Israel. Abba Eban, Israel's representative to the United Nations, was the speaker, and his keynote address was open to all the chapel groups. When the time came for the Jewish Student Fellowship to elect officers it was understood that students elected for the following year would be officers of the Hillel Foundation. A tie vote for president was resolved by naming Robert Secor president of Hillel Foundation for the first semester and Elaine Robinstein president for the second semester.

Elections were also held for Chapel Board and the United Christian Council. Hugh Gregg and John Cooley were elected cochairmen of the Chapel Board, and Jeane Harris was elected president of the United Christian Council.

35. Innovations and New Pressures, 1958–1959

THE PROGRAM at Hendricks Chapel was certainly recognizable because of its continuity from year to year, but each year also brought innovations and changes. The fall of 1958 had more changes than had occurred in some other years. To be sure, the master plan that had been worked out to include as many of the programs and activities under the direction of one inclusive decision-making body was still in effect.*

The first full year of the operation of Chapel House, the arrival of Hillel on campus, the change in the content of the Casawasco Conference, and some changes in program names and emphases caused many new pressures and changes at Hendricks Chapel. New chaplains brought change as they mixed with the old guard. Three new full-time chaplains began their work during this year. Bishop Peabody appointed the Reverend Robert C. Ayers as chaplain for Episcopalians. The Reverend David Engel became the Presbyterian chaplain. For Jewish students there was both a new organization and new professional leadership. What had been for years the Jewish Student Fellowship now became the B'nai B'rith Hillel Foundation at Syracuse University with a full-time chaplain, Rabbi Louis Niemand. Hillel would continue many of the activities of the former Jewish Student Fellowship but would try to give its students a broad historical and cultural understanding of their faith and attempt to make the entire campus aware of Jewish traditions.

In previous years an almost constant theme of the chapel was the request for more space. More programs, the proliferation of activities by the faith and denominational fellowships, and an ever increasing student body, both in diversity and in size, created the need for more space. In addition, the lack of student-union facilities meant the chapel had for many years done what it could to function in a way to

---

*Even so, Noble was not a dean to rest overly much on tradition. By this time he was fourteen years into his role and eager to keep up with the times. Students now were different from the students in the late 1940s. In the late 1950s the social climate was changing, and Syracuse University was expanding, with new buildings going up and more being planned by an imaginative administration. —RLP

fill this need. From time to time suggestions had been made that an annex might be constructed adjacent to the chapel. When Chapel House came on line the previous year it was seen as a godsend, and it was well utilized.

In previous years the Casawasco Conference had focused its attention on theological or religious themes and concerns. This year the emphasis was on campus leadership, with an opening address by Vice President Piskor. Student leaders from other colleges were invited to participate, and representatives from Utica, Cornell, and Mount Holyoke attended. Dean Noble reviewed Jean-Paul Sartre's *No Exit,* and workshops were held on race relations, Skeptics Corner, denominational and faith fellowships, and social action. This meeting was the twentieth Casawasco Conference to be held.*

In an article designed to acquaint new students with the place of Hendricks Chapel on campus, the October 1 issue of the *Daily Orange* described Dean Noble as the coordinator of a chapel program that affects "more students than any other category of activities other than the academic ones" and that it was one of the most extensive religious programs in any U.S. university. Dean Noble described his job as senior chaplain and "an accredited friend at large to everyone on campus" and as administrative officer responsible to the chancellor and the Board of Trustees for providing ministries to the various religious groups. The story then went on to say that Dean Noble was preacher, counselor, and policy maker and that he was influential on campus and was a nationally known speaker. Dean Noble was known to be liberal in his theology with an interest in the social implications of the Gospel and a belief in the positive potential in man as a coworker with God. This position was in contrast to the pessimism of current existential philosophy and neo-orthodoxy theology.

Daily chapel was opened in early October by Dean Noble noting that it was the oldest nonacademic continuing Syracuse University tradition. The Sunday morning services with the outstanding choir continued to attract large numbers of worshipers. The majority were students and faculty, but the chapel in these years also attracted many people from outside the university community who found the preaching and the music to their satisfaction.

Chancellor Tolley, when he was in the city, was a regular attendant at the chapel services.† One Sunday when Dean Noble was absent and the preaching was not up to standard, Tolley made some notes that he forwarded to the dean upon his return. It will be remembered that Dr. Tolley was both an ordained minister and a believer in the pursuit of excellence. In his comments he wondered why the preaching in the dean's absence could not be better, why the living centers wor-

---

*The content of this conference was an indication of the changes taking place on the campus and in society.—RLP

†In fact, he wrote many years later that he never missed a Sunday service at Hendricks Chapel when he was in town.—RLP

shiping as a group were no longer identified, and why the ushers were a bit sloppy in dress and demeanor. He also mused that perhaps the coeds did not have money enough to properly cover their heads with hats, and he was concerned with the appearance of the bulletins in which the order of service was printed. As a result some changes took place. A new bulletin was prepared with a beautiful colored picture of the chapel on the cover and more attention was given to general appearances. There seems to be no indication, however, that the young ladies of the university ever took seriously the scriptural dictum that a woman's head be covered in church!

For the annual Parents Weekend a Federated Protestant service was held for students and their parents on Sunday morning, and in the evening the parents were invited to participate in the fellowship group meetings. Each week the *Daily Orange* carried what was called a "Chapel Roundup" in which all the events both of the chapel and of the fellowship groups were listed. Of special significance this year was the return for the tenth time of Dr. Ralph W. Sockman for the annual Brotherhood Service, this year for the first time under the sponsorship of Hillel rather than the Jewish Student Fellowship.[*]

It has been previously pointed out that many of the programs initiated by the chapel had been taken over by other groups on campus, such as Footprints and the Campus Chest. Early in November it was explained that the Student Emergency Loan Fund, established by the chapel in Depression days under Dean Powers, was now funded and operated as a university fund, with the chapel retaining a key role. To obtain a loan a student was required to make application at the chapel, then to his academic dean, and finally at the treasurer's office. Members of the board administering the program were the dean of the chapel, the deans of men and women, representatives from Men's and Women's Student Governments, and the university secretary of student finances.

In December Syracuse-in-Asia had its traditional Christmas sale. What was new was the fact that for this year the student representative, Louise Crawford, had gone not to Thailand but to Formosa. From time to time her communications were received and read at the Syracuse-in-Asia meetings and on occasion also reported in the *Daily Orange*.

Christmas was celebrated with the pageant, singing of carols on the chapel steps, and the lighting of the campus Christmas tree. The pageant was directed by Zeta Phi Eta, and music was provided by the chapel choir. On the Sunday following the pageant and immediately before the holiday break the annual Advent serv-

---

[*]At this time SU was becoming a major national football power, soon to win national championship honors. It was now in every way a "big time" school, taking on more and more of the characteristics of a nonsectarian academy. The university had officially become a nonsectarian, private university earlier in the 1950s but at the same time continued ties with the Methodist Church and continued to pay homage to its Methodist heritage.—RLP

ice sponsored by the United Christian Council made up of the Protestant and Orthodox faith fellowships was again held. The first semester closed with the "Mourner's Corner," a coffee period that gave students a chance to relax and talk between their exams.

The midwinter Casawasco retreat, held at the beginning of February, featured Professor of Philosophy Maurice Friedman of Sarah Lawrence College. The topic selected was "The Image of God and the Image of Man in Contemporary Culture." Following Professor Friedman's presentation a student panel responded.

This year saw the traditional Brotherhood Week changed to International Week. The noted pacifist A. J. Muste came to campus and led off the celebration of the week with an address called "Morality and International Relations." Each afternoon coffee hours were held with faculty present to discuss the issues raised. The week concluded with a miniature World's Fair, which included a fashion show, folk dances, and music that reflected the customs, costumes, and traditions of many different countries.

Three special celebrations or events, one for each of the faith groups, took place during the spring semester. The first occurred in March around the Hebrew festival of Purim when the Hillel Foundation at Syracuse was host to an intercollegiate conference to which fifteen neighboring colleges sent representatives. The speaker for the conference was Dr. Marshall Sklare who spoke about Jewish youth in the United States.

In April the chapel sponsored a campus conference called "God and History: Today and Tomorrow." William Stringfellow, a well-known lawyer and Episcopal layman, gave the keynote address with follow-ups by members of the faculty and chaplains from Hobart, Cornell, and Brown Universities.

Also in April a banquet was held at the Hotel Syracuse to celebrate the twenty-fifth anniversary of Father Gannon Ryan as Roman Catholic chaplain at the university. Many students, alumni, and clergy from the city attended. Speakers were the Reverend William Donaghy, S.J., president of Holy Cross College, and Chancellor Tolley.

In May a new venture was held in the chapel in the form of an experimental, nondenominational religious service that included a jazz band, poetry reading, and a lecture by Leonard Weinberg titled the "Relationship of Jazz and Sex to the Spirit." The moderator of the service was Muggzie Gutt, who said it was an attempt to integrate modern expression into a religious service. As might have been expected from such a radical departure from tradition, the service drew widely varied comments.* The next year saw even more drastic change in the chapel's operation.†

*Such events certainly put the stamp of validation on the changing nature of campus life and campus religious life.—RLP

†See appendix A for the Chapel Board 1958–59 officers.—RLP

36. Seeking Diversity within Unity, 1959–1960

IN HIS REPORT to Chancellor Tolley at the end of the 1959–60 academic year, Dean Noble aptly described what had happened during this year at Hendricks Chapel:

> Religion on this campus, as on most campuses in America, is undergoing the same critical questioning being leveled in every area of student life. A cautious, reserved spirit has replaced the collegiate enthusiasm which once we knew. . . . Reexamination, reorientation and reorganization have marked the past year at Hendricks Chapel. Tensions mounted within the student board from the very beginning of the year and eventuated in a complete overhauling of the administrative and promotional machinery. The experiment of having all departments of chapel activity under one tent, which has been tried for two years, was judged a failure and detrimental to the best interests of all parties concerned. An entirely new "set-up" resulted.*

Seen in historical perspective, from the very earliest days of the chapel's life when Dean Powers sought to place all religious activity within the chapel program, a slow but steady erosion took place almost every year. Yet efforts never ceased to find an organizational vehicle that would meet the needs of diversity within unity. The latest effort in this direction, which Dean Noble has described above, was a major task for the year.

The radical nature of the trend toward separatism at SU and in society became apparent at the traditional Casawasco planning conference held before the opening of the university in the fall and attended by students, staff, and faculty. The Brotherhood Services, so long a fixture, were discontinued. The All-Chapel Banquet was terminated. Even the Casawasco Conferences, so dear to past student generations of "chapelites," were suspended. Some of the usual Sunday evening meetings, sponsored by the denominational fellowships, took on different forms and structures. Each religious group on campus seemed intent on establishing its unique and independent identity in terms of its program, worship, and activity. Nothing quite as divisive had occurred at Hendricks Chapel since the Roman Catholics had decided to go their own way at an earlier time.

What was left? Despite the tendency of each religious fellowship to do its own

*SU Archives, DGW materials.

thing and to go its own way, there was still enough momentum in some of the Chapel Board service committees to do a number of significant things. Much of what was done centered around the Sunday morning Protestant worship service, which continued to be well supported in spite of the fact that many of the denominational fellowships had their own services of worship at some time during the week to emphasize what they regarded as their unique understanding of what the worship experience was all about. Dean Noble's popularity and the supremacy cup probably saved the Sunday service.

At the Sunday morning service Dean Noble was the preacher on alternate Sundays. Usually on one Sunday a month one of the full-time male (all were male) chaplains occupied the pulpit. The remaining Sundays of the year out-of-town clergy men were guest preachers and included the following: Dr. Wayne Oates of the Southern Baptist Theological Seminary; Dr. Joseph Sitler of the University of Chicago; Dr. Daniel Hill of Howard University; Dr. Lloyd Foster of Newark, New Jersey; Professor William Muehl of Yale Divinity School; Dr. Colin Miller of Hamilton College; Dr. George Morgan of Rensselaer Polytechnic Institute; Dr. Murray Cayley of Rochester, New York; Professor J. A. Sanders of Colgate-Rochester Divinity School; the Reverend Bradford Abernethy of Rutgers University; President Vernon Grounds of the Conservative Baptist Theological Seminary of Denver; and Dean James McLeod of Northwestern University.

A key part of the appeal of this service was the great organ and choral music provided by Professor Poister and the superb choir of 140 voices under his direction. The ushers for this service had their own committee, and the Stewardship Committee was responsible for the expenditure of more than eight thousand dollars that was raised through the offerings at the service.

Other service committees were able to keep their activities going. Daily chapel continued under the direction of the Worship Committee. The Human Understanding Committee conducted panels on campus drinking and in March and April brought Ethel Nash of Chapel Hill, North Carolina, to lecture and lead discussions on love, sex, and marriage. In quite a different field the same committee sponsored International Week, featuring a lecture by Dean Harland Cleveland on "Religion and the World Situation" and an International Night at Sims Hall that attracted a thousand students. The Public Relations and Radio Committees, though operating separately this year, publicized chapel activities with a weekly radio program on the university station and a revival of *Chapel Chimes*. By year's end they planned to merge their efforts for the coming year.

The House Representatives Committee was discontinued, with the thought that what efforts were made in this direction could best be made among the incoming freshman class. The Reception Committee continued its long tradition of having an open house with coffee and cookies one afternoon a week for students who wanted to drop in at the Colonial Room. Once each week students would trudge up to Dean Noble's home for the weekly discussion of his Skeptics Corner.

Not only were students served, but they also took it upon themselves to serve. The Social Service Committee secured seventy volunteers to give time and talent in downtown agencies under the auspices of the Council on Social Agencies.

Syracuse-in-Asia had a good year. The Christmas sale raised twenty-eight hundred dollars, a program on Far Eastern affairs was well received, and Carol Eaton was chosen as the student representative to teach at Tunghai University in Taiwan for the following two years. The library in the Chapel Boardroom was augmented by books from the Jewish community, and the combined collection was open-shelved for student use.

The chapel staff presented a forum series that had an enthusiastic response. In December Dr. Leo Pfeffer spoke on "Church and State." In January Dr. Stringfellow Barr's topic was "The Campus Is a Comedy." In February, as part of International Week, Dean Harland Cleveland spoke on "Religion and International Affairs," and in April, Professor Paul Holmer concluded the series with a lecture on "The Problem of Religious Knowledge." Fellowship groups including Hillel, the Campus Christian Fellowship, and the Methodists brought a variety of speakers to campus.

It was pointed out earlier that the traditional Casawasco Conferences were discontinued; however, other conferences were held. Two were held for the total chapel leadership and also two each by the Methodists, the Lutherans, the Episcopalians, and the Campus Christian Fellowship. Three Student Christian Movement Conferences were attended by students from Syracuse at the state level, and a delegation attended the National Youth Conference at Miami University at Oxford, Ohio, during the Christmas recess.

Although there was less cohesion in the chapel program, the individual efforts on the part of staff and chaplains remained undiminished. Counseling sessions, speaking engagements, discussion group leadership, advising committees, and leadership of the fellowship groups provided a constant input into the lives of students on the part of the professional leadership.*

This year's account would not be complete without a brief description of the operation of Chapel House under the direction of Don Skinner. When Dean Noble asked the university for its use, he indicated that the need for more space was a critical necessity for chapel activities. In addition to providing office space for the chaplains and a guest room for visitors, more than 450 fellowship meetings and approximately 125 other meetings were held there during the year. It also provided a place for study, particularly during the examination period, where sustained by coffee and cookies on a pay-as-you-go basis students had a quiet place in which to concentrate.

---

*The trend was more and more away from strictly student leadership to more professional leadership, not that such leadership had been absent during the previous thirty years of the chapel's life. —RLP

In May a chapel constitution was adopted. In essence it gave more autonomy in the decision-making process to the various groups and ministries that were part of the total chapel program, though now operating more independently. These groups included the service committees and the sanctuary committees as well as the religious fellowships.

Though this year had been one of considerable change and reorganization, in his report for the year Dean Noble noted: "Increased understanding has developed within the Chapel staff this year. Paradoxically this has been largely the result of a continued study of differences. The heightened awareness of separatism has appeared to make for a kind of ecumenicity." *

---

*Wright's characterization of the 1950s centers on the now well-established dean, Charles C. Noble. Noble had become known in many places in the northeastern part of the United States as "Mr. Syracuse." It is fair to say that his "fame" exceeded even that of Chancellor Tolley, except in academic circles. Noble's popularity as a speaker for graduation ceremonies, ministerial conferences, retreats, and celebrations of many types had become legendary. His storytelling ability combined with an easy speaking manner and a message always directed to his specific audience and full of relevant content made him the subject of rave reviews.

Noble's sermons are a prime example of why he was so popular. His preaching was excellent and popular, which is by no means the whole story of a filled chapel for the services every Sunday. Charlie was known and respected on campus for his mind as well as his humor and speaking ability, but a thing called the Supremacy Trophy helped ensure a full chapel. More about the trophy later in the discussion of the mid-1960s, when chapel attendance became a problem and in many ways a headache, and for many also a heartache.

As the 1950s wore on it became obvious to all who paid attention to such things that Noble had to begin to marshal his energy owing to the hectic and taxing nature of his many involvements. In fact, Chancellor Tolley later began to send Charlie on "command" vacations to get some badly needed R&R. Often the vacation was in Florida in midwinter. Even there, as well as at the Noble summer camp in New England, his work did not stop, as many letters testify. His letters frequently refer to the many phone calls to conduct routine business and to make arrangements for his speaking engagements. It was from the distance of New England in the summer that Noble did much of the preparation and communication necessary, working with staff and chaplains, to prepare for the fall semester, which he frequently said was "just around the corner."

By 1961, when I first became acquainted with Charlie, he was visibly tired much of the time, even if still always very spirited in conversation and in work. Of course, it helped his spirits that he was an immensely popular figure on campus and in Syracuse. Noble's reputation and popularity were not confined to central New York and New England. As a ranking staff person from the New York State Council of Churches told me, the dean of Hendricks Chapel was second only to the cardinal in New York City for being well known as a religious figure in the region. Noble wore that distinction without any sign of an air of importance, but at the same time he enjoyed having the reputation he did.

Don Wright knew Noble well, even before his deanship at SU began. In Wright's account of the Noble years it is clear that the chapel programs, even after Charlie's first few months, had the stamp of his personality and style. If one phrase could be used to mark that style it would be the "idea and practice of collegiality."

Under Noble's deanship the chapel became a source of pride for virtually everyone on campus and reached a nationwide reputation in campus ministry that has not been matched, perhaps not even approached, at SU and rarely in the country since that time. Chancellor Tolley was fully aware of

37. Decreasing Centralization, 1960–1961

WITH MUCH OF THE COHESIVENESS of the chapel program dissipated the year before, a pattern had been set for the operation of Hendricks Chapel that would continue as long as Dean Noble remained at the university. Whereas in the years before there had been a strong central core of chapel activity surrounded and supported by the denominational and faith fellowships, the reverse now seemed to emerge as the basic pattern. Now there was a basic collection of almost independent fellowship groups, which on occasion joined in the cooperative efforts of the total chapel program. This separatism was ascribed to the tendency toward resurgent churchmanship, of denominational consciousness, and of unique theological identities and liturgical practices. Dean Noble was not happy with these developments and in his report for the year lamented that "there still seems very little that we can do together." *

There were, however, some campuswide religious events. Outstanding for the year was the visit to the campus by the distinguished theologian Professor Paul Tillich, who came to give two major lectures with a follow-up luncheon and coffee-hour discussions. In his two-day visit to the university it was estimated that at one time or another he reached more than two thousand students and faculty.

Another campuswide activity was International Week, which had been established two years earlier as an outgrowth of the brotherhood emphases. With the increasing number of students from overseas at the university, this event featured a festival in which many nationalities and cultural groups set up booths in Sims Hall to show costumes and artifacts unique to their way of life.†

In the new constitution adopted last year, the Sanctuary Board was established, with primary responsibility for the Sunday morning Protestant service. The

---

Noble's reputation and successes and promoted them with pride. Even in the late 1960s, when a conflict between these two popular figures had dampened the relationship, Tolley was fully aware of what an effective colleague he had in Noble and for a variety of reasons kept Noble in harness long past the normally required age of retirement. That subject will be treated more fully later.—RLP

*Yet another reason for an increase in "denominationalism" was the social changes affecting church attendance. Under such conditions the "circle the wagons" mentality that develops tends to highlight specifically denominational thinking and practice.—RLP

†The chapel's concern for international students and an international forum has been both historic and current, perhaps Syracuse-in-China being the first structural evidence; the International Student Office now under the administration of Student Affairs is another example. Even so, the international emphasis continued under Dean McCombe, myself, and now Dean Wolfe. Cooperation between Hendricks Chapel and the International Student Office is very good.—RLP

board had committees for music, ushers, worship, and stewardship. The service was still known as "the University service" of worship, though increasingly was so in name only. Despite the multiplication of other worship opportunities, the service continued to attract substantial numbers. The preaching was good, often excellent, and the choral music was superb. The board also had the responsibility of budgeting the approximately nine thousand dollars in offerings that were received at the services. This year, for the first time, the board initiated a discussion period following the service in the Colonial Room where those persons interested could discuss with the preacher of the morning any questions or comments they wished to make. Although this discussion period did not attract large numbers, the people who participated were enthusiastic. Daily chapel was also a responsibility of the board and this year consisted largely of organ music provided to stimulate individual meditation during the noon hour. The board also took responsibility for a forum series and in March sponsored an event on Africa at which three university professors spoke, followed by discussion.

Under the Chapel Board, though it did not meet as such, several committees continued and instituted new programs. In the previous year the House Representatives Committee was dissolved, but in its place was born the Freshman Representative group, which met, found the experience worthwhile, and continued to meet. The Social Service Committee sponsored "Operation Volunteer" and secured more than one hundred students to serve in the downtown social agencies. The Thursday afternoon open house in the Colonial Room and the Skeptics Corner were open door opportunities for any students who wished to share in them. Syracuse-in-Asia continued to provide students with a present-day mission vehicle. The Radio and Public Relations Committees sought to keep the student body informed of chapel activities. An almost nostalgic Casawasco Conference was held for the chapelites who wished to attend, and though it had neither the impact or support of previous years it proved worthwhile for the individuals who attended. Gone were the days when it was a planning session.

Both to clarify and perhaps to counteract the separatist nature of various elements associated with Hendricks Chapel, Dean Noble prepared a statement on religious policy for the university. It was primarily for the staff but also for any who might be interested. It is quoted here in full because it provides insight, both into the life of the chapel at this time and by implication into the issues involved with those persons who may have had different ideas about its place on campus. It is found in the dean's report to the chancellor for the year 1961.

Syracuse University is non-Sectarian, with a grateful recognition of its Methodist beginnings. Because of its Protestant inception, it insists upon religious freedom and welcomes all religions to the campus. Experience has shown that most students continue in their inherited religious culture while they are at the university. The university does not encourage proselytizing although realism must recognize that some students will move from one religious group to another as their minds are changed by the process of learning.

The Chancellor and the Trustees appoint a Dean of the chapel to act as chaplain and coordinator. On the one hand, he ministers to the religious needs of the community through preaching, counseling and representing the Religious policy of the university, especially by inviting all denominations having constituents on the campus to send chaplains and counselors for service on the religious staff. It is the dean's responsibility, as far as coordination can be effected, to aid the various chaplains and counselors in whatever cooperative efforts they desire to pursue in making a common impact upon the Campus.

When religious and church groups appoint chaplains to maintain their characteristic ministries, the university voluntarily undertakes to provide accommodations, within the limits of its resources, where these religious guests may conduct their program. Complete autonomy and freedom to work and worship according to their tradition is afforded these chaplains and their constituents. All religious groups who accept the hospitality of the university, with the exception of the Roman Catholic Church, are expected to clear administratively through the dean of the chapel's office. This does not obligate them to participate in any joint or cooperative enterprises.

The university's service of worship Sunday mornings is the responsibility of the chapel Dean. Attendance is voluntary. It is supported financially by the offerings received at the service. Visiting preachers occupy the pulpit at the invitation and discretion of the dean, and student activities and committees related to this university service are under his jurisdiction. The university recognizes the right and duty of all to worship at times and places of their own choosing, to hold their own creeds and observe their own sacraments.

The basic task of the religious ministries and activities at Syracuse University is the enhancement of the growth of the members of the university community in ethics, idealism, psychological maturity and spiritual experience.

Counseling resources are provided by the dean and the chaplains to supplement services found elsewhere on the campus.

A major function of the religious groups and the chaplains in the cooperative activity is to provide projects which implement our social concerns and our awareness of campus and world needs.

The chapel strives quietly and continually to exercise a constructive criticism of campus culture in the light of the religions represented, especially the Jewish-Christian values of our western culture.

It is the policy of Syracuse University to improve and increase the space provided for religious programs, chaplain's offices, worship centers, study rooms, meeting and dining facilities.

This statement speaks for itself. Probably the most important word in it is *guest,* which sought to clarify the status on campus of the various religious fellowships, some of whom were wanting unrestricted freedom. The statement still breathes the hope that there could be some kind of orderly and cooperative impact of religion on the campus community—a hope dear to Dean Noble.

Chapel House at 711 Comstock Avenue continued to be an important adjunct to the chapel as a center for religious and other meetings of campus-related groups. Here space continued to be provided for offices for the chaplains and rooms for meetings and worship. In his report for the year Don Skinner estimated at least twenty meetings and six worship services were scheduled each week, in addition to one hundred students who used the facility for study. He found scheduling a problem because of the many requests made to him for the use of rooms for meeting places, especially during the evening hours. Traffic was heavy and maintenance was difficult. Furthermore, the space occupied by the house was considered to be one of the prime sites for the construction of the new library that had long been a dream of Chancellor Tolley. Yet for the time being Chapel House proved to be a very useful building as an overflow facility for chapel activity.*

38. Turbulent Times, 1961–1962

THROUGHOUT THE DECADE of the 1960s Hendricks Chapel and its program was under pressure for a variety of reasons. It was in the second half of the decade that college campuses across the United States came alive in political protest. The assassinations of the two Kennedys and Martin Luther King, Jr., the struggle for civil rights, and the trauma of Vietnam sparked protest after protest as the conscience of American students responded to what they perceived as violations of human rights and dignity. There was also the ebbing tide of organized religious interest that followed the ten-year religious boom after World War II. It was in the context of these events and this mood that students lived out their lives, and it is little wonder that all of it was reflected on the Syracuse campus during this period.

At one period following World War II the chapel, with its powerfully cohesive program, attracted more students than it could manage. Now the situation had changed, and the focus of campus ministry was largely in the hands of the faith or denominational fellowship groups.†

The Chapel Board and its service committees still attracted participants, but they were fewer in number and less comprehensive in scope. The services spon-

*It was in the summer of 1961 that my family moved from Denver to Syracuse so I could continue my graduate work.—RLP

†It must be remembered that just as many students may have been served in this decentralized structure as had been before, but decreasing centralization made everything look smaller.—RLP

sored by the religious fellowships, however, were of the utmost importance, for they provided a context of faith and personal guidance to help the many students find a place for religion in their lives. In addition, the chaplains constituted a counseling corps of great value to their constituents. Further, there was a partial ecumenicity that developed when the Presbyterians and the United Church of Christ joined their campus ministry to become the United Campus Christian Fellowship. They were later joined by the American Baptists when chaplain Norman Keim came on campus in 1961.

At registration every student was given an opportunity to fill out a religious preference card. This year the compilation broke down as follows: Protestants, 39 percent; Jewish students, 22.3 percent; and Roman Catholics, 22.2 percent. The percentage choosing not to respond was 8.9.

Early in the fall it was announced that the Reverend Arthur Hopkinson, Jr., Methodist chaplain since 1949, would be leaving Syracuse to serve on the staff of the Commission on Chaplains of the Methodist Church in Nashville, Tennessee. At that time he had served longer than any other denominational chaplain and was well known on campus. He left campus on November 1 with no replacement. The position was open until February, when Vernon Bigler came from Indiana to take his place as Methodist chaplain.

Early in the fall it was also announced that Dean Noble, at the invitation of the air force, had agreed to visit air force personnel in Greece, Turkey, and Crete. He would be gone from campus from October 10 to November 21. Interestingly enough, this trip was his first one overseas. His schedule was a grueling one, and on his return he was described as a "tongue-wagging" champion. Noble was never at a loss for words—almost always perceptive and helpful words and always with plenty of humor.

Before he left the *Daily Orange* carried a two-page photographic essay showing the multifaceted nature of his work. Underneath each picture was one of his best-known quotations:

• We are not created as problems to be solved, but as lives to be lived.

• We become strong by grappling with problems bigger than ourselves.

• We may not belong to the other fellow's church, but we belong to his God.

• Achievement comes through constant wooing of our goals.

• To keep the treasured values and relationships of life, we must treat them as elusive.

On his return from overseas Dean Noble said that he was both proud and not so proud to be an American.

Early in December, because of increasing numbers attending the eleven o'clock service in Chapel House, the Reverend Robert Ayers, the Episcopal Church chaplain, made it known that Gifford Auditorium, a new and larger facility, would better suit the needs of his congregation. This assertion produced a controversy that lasted about three months. Chancellor Tolley denied permission for the change on the basis that the hour would conflict with the service at Hendricks Chapel. Father Ayers contended that this was not the case because the people he served would not be attending the service at the chapel. He pointed out that Episcopalians did not all consider themselves Protestant. He also pointed out that the Roman Catholics had been celebrating mass at Crouse College on Sunday mornings at the eleven o'clock hour for many years. The *Daily Orange,* citing the policy of the university of being tolerant of all religious faiths, got into the discussion, mainly asking for a more complete explanation from the chancellor. After a rather prolonged period of controversy, the February 16 issue of the *Daily Orange* carried a full statement by Chancellor Tolley in which he reaffirmed the freedom of religious expression as a policy of the university. Citing the proliferation of religious practices on campus and the inability of the university to accommodate them all, Tolley declared the time between ten thirty and noon on Sunday morning was reserved for the Hendricks Chapel service, the only exception being the Roman Catholic mass at Crouse. Though some discontent remained, this statement settled the issue, and the *Daily Orange* in an editorial declared it did not wish to pursue the issue any further.*

A significant cooperative venture by the various segments of the chapel occurred in February and March when a distinguished group of three theologians visited the campus to discuss the "Religious Situation in Contemporary America." These three religious leaders represented each of the major faith groups: Jewish, Roman Catholic, and Protestant. The first theologian was Dr. Will Herberg, a well-known author and a member of the faculty of Drew University. The second was the Reverend Father Gustave Weigel, S.J., of Woodstock College in Maryland. The third was Dr. Martin E. Marty from the *Christian Century,* the influential nondenominational weekly religious journal.

In his midyear report Dean Noble reported that there were 611 students participating at that time in Chapel Board committees, including the Freshman and Upper-class Skeptics Corner, Public Relations, Social Service, and the Sanctuary Board, which included committees on music, ushers, and stewardship. In addition, there was an infirmary visitation program and some informal attempts to relate to the many international students at the university. During the year special study groups were held under the auspices of Hillel, the United Campus Christian Fellowship, the Methodist Student Fellowship, the Lutherans, and the Inter-Varsity Christian Fellowship.

The coffee corner that had been set up in the lounge for the purpose of pro-

*Tolley had proved himself to be a traditionalist at this point. As a result of personal discussions with Tolley many years later I believe he had two strong motives. First, he wished to perpetuate the tradition of an "all-university" service at eleven o'clock on Sundays, which he never ceased to believe was possible. Second, he was, I think, operating under the perception that in this action he was protecting his dear friend Noble and trying to strengthen Charlie's ministry to the university.—RLP viding an informal setting for faculty-student discussion did not work out as planned. For one thing many faculty resisted. More important, no one seemed to want to make the effort to keep the place picked up and tidy. For a while, as an altruistic gesture, Eta Pi Upsilon, the women's senior honorary society, undertook the task, but they soon gave up. An editorial in the *Daily Orange* on April 19 complained that it was a dirty-looking mess that was a disgrace and the people who used it ought to keep it picked up and looking good.

On Good Friday the chaplains cooperated to sponsor a three-hour service in the chapel, which gave a glimpse of the kinds of projects that could secure cooperative effort. The service was divided into the seven traditional segments, and the following persons participated: the Reverend Norman Keim, Don Skinner, the Reverend Robert Ayers, Patricia Howland, the Reverend Vernon Bigler, the Reverend Paul Bosch, and the Reverend David Engel. Norman Keim and David Engel were chaplains for the United Campus Christian Fellowship assisted by Patricia Howland. Don Skinner was the director of Chapel House. Vernon Bigler was the Methodist chaplain, Paul Bosch the chaplain for the Lutherans, and Robert Ayers the Episcopalian chaplain.

Chapel House had another year full of meetings and events, and at midyear its first floor with kitchen facilities became the noontime temporary faculty club.

A midwinter Casawasco Conference was held from January 31 to February 2 with Dr. William Mueller of Goucher College as leader. The theme was "The Prophetic Voice of Modern Fiction" and was open to all chapelites. Dean Noble saw to it that Casawasco did not get dropped from its close chapel ties.

Visiting preachers at the Sunday morning chapel services during the year included: Chaplain Theodore Speer of the United States Military Academy at West Point; President Herbert Gezork of Andover-Newton Theological School; Bishop W. Ralph Ward of Syracuse; Professor William Muehl of Yale Divinity School; the Reverend Russell Bishop of Shaker Heights, Ohio; Chaplain James Kelly of the United States Naval Academy at Annapolis; and Chaplain Bradford Abernethy of Rutgers University.

The account of this year comes to a close with the news that during the month of June, two men long associated with Hendricks Chapel received honorary degrees. The first was Dean Noble, who was awarded the honorary degree of doctor of laws at the commencement of George Williams College in Chicago. The other was the degree of doctor of sacred theology that was conferred upon Dr. Ralph W. Sockman of New York, the outstanding Methodist minister who had, ten times, been the speaker at the Brotherhood Service at the chapel on the Colgate football weekends. Interestingly enough, this year Syracuse terminated its football schedule with Colgate after many years of intense rivalry.[*]

---

[*]Following the SU football national championship year of 1959, the strength and prestige of the program far outstretched any football plans at Colgate or within their conference. The university

39. Continuity with the Past, 1962–1963

BY THE EARLY 1960s Hendricks Chapel had become a collegial program in which the faith and denominational fellowships served the principal group and personal religious needs of their constituents. A list of the religious groups that were organized on campus indicates both their multiplicity and their diversity. They were:

B'nai B'rith Hillel Foundation	Rabbi Louis Niemand
United Campus Christian Fellowship	
Presbyterian	The Reverend David Engel
Baptist	The Reverend Norman Keim
Evangelical United Brethren	
United Church of Christ	Patricia Howland
and Disciples of Christ	
Christian Science	Advisers P. Lachlan Peck and
	David L. More
Eastern Orthodox	The Reverend Alexander Warneke and
	the Reverend Michael Harmand
Episcopal Church	The Reverend Robert Ayers
Friends	Mr. and Mrs. Gene Gilmore
Inter-Varsity Christian Fellowship	
Liberal Religious Fellowship	
Unitarian and Universalist	The Reverend John Fuller
Lutheran Church	The Reverend Paul Bosch
Methodist Student Fellowship	The Reverend C. Vernon Bigler
Moslem Fellowship	Professor Fazlellah Reza
Roman Catholic Church	Father Gannon Ryan; later The
	Reverend Charles Borgognoni
Unitarian Campus Club	The Reverend John Fuller*

When the religious census was taken at the time of registration the breakdown was not very different from the year before. The percentages of religious prefer-

---

sought to achieve at the highest level of collegiate football and this year, with the construction of Manley Field House, had positioned itself with a new coach and a stellar freshman class to do the same in basketball.—RLP

    *In addition, there was still a Chapel Board, whose officers are listed in appendix A.—RLP

ence were Protestants, 37.9 percent; Roman Catholics, 21.1 percent; and Jewish students, 20.9 percent. Not responding were 9.4 percent of the students. Although this leaves just over 10 percent of students unaccounted for, it still represents the fact that four-fifths of the students indicated at least minimal religious interest.

Some of the faith and denominational fellowships were much more highly organized and comprehensive in their programs than others. In the first fall issue of the *Daily Orange* on September 20, the United Campus Christian Fellowship placed a large paid advertisement telling of its program, which in addition to its regular Sunday evening meetings included a special worship service each week at Chapel House, outside speakers, study courses, and opportunity for counseling. At the bottom of the ad it was indicated that the local campus organization was affiliated with the World Student Christian Federation, the Student Christian Movement in New York State, and Hendricks Chapel.

Hillel was also very active. The opening of the college year coincided with the Jewish High Holy Days, and every effort was made to let the Jewish students know of the special services that were held for them at the chapel.

The Methodist Student Fellowship, which was perhaps the largest religious group numerically, also sought to relate to students in a very comprehensive way.

The Chapel Board was largely responsible for activities in social service in the downtown agencies and the worship services at the chapel.

In the welter of all this diversified religious activity Dean Noble acted in two capacities. To the extent possible, he sought to be the catalyst that kept the chaplains in communication. In addition to being the major preacher at the Sunday morning services in Hendricks Chapel, he was a campus legend. When a drive was conducted asking students to give blood for the blood bank, he was the chairman and 557 pints were collected.

On Parents Weekend, when seven thousand parents visited the university, he was one of the speakers, talking on "High Potential Living," and hosted a reception in the Colonial Room of the chapel for them. When it was discovered at neighboring Cornell that an unmarried man and woman were living together, it unleashed considerable discussion on the Syracuse campus. Commenting on this situation Dean Noble said, "While we cannot force upon the student our preconceived pattern of morality we have a duty to make his life at Syracuse morally attractive."

During the fall term students and some professors began to get involved in civil rights protests. Protests began in Syracuse when it became clear that the city was planning to move great numbers of minority people out of their homes in the Fifteenth Ward, just west of the Syracuse campus, with no provision for their relocation. Staff chaplains organized a service of prayer at the chapel on Tuesday, December 4, at noon to "bring together those concerned over discrimination in housing in this city." Participating in the service were the Chaplains Engel, Howland, Bosch, Niemand, Ayers, Bigler, and Dean Noble. Graduate student and teacher Eduordo Mondlane, later to become head of the Mozambique Liberation Front in Africa, spoke. This event would be but the beginning of a long series of protests in the struggle for civil rights.

On Monday, December 3, Dr. Gordon Hoople, chairman of the Board of Trustees of the university and founder of Syracuse-in-China, opened the Christmas sale in the chapel. The event celebrated the fortieth anniversary of SIC/SIA, for it was in 1922 that Dr. Hoople had gone to China. Carol Eaton, who had been the student representative teaching at Tunghai University in Taiwan, was now back on campus, and in her place overseas was Nannette L. Williams, who was serving the first year of her two-year term.

"Hill Mourns Father Ryan" was the headline in a box appearing in the *Daily Orange* on December 6, announcing the death of the Roman Catholic chaplain the day before, at the age of fifty-eight. He had begun his work at Syracuse when Dr. Powers was dean, on April 2, 1935. Ryan had been honored by his church by being made a monsignor in 1960. Tributes came from many sources, including Chancellor Tolley, who spoke of his long service to Roman Catholic students at the university. Dean Noble said, "He was the senior chaplain of us all." In an editorial in the *Daily Orange* perhaps the key words were "strong willed and determined." It spoke of his service to students and the establishment of the St. Thomas More House, but it also did not gloss over his break with Hendricks Chapel and his insistence on the exclusiveness of the Roman Catholic Church. It would not be helpful to elaborate upon the series of conflicts that he had had both with the chapel and with the university administration. Both by nature and by his perception of his church in the days before Vatican II he believed it was his duty to pursue a separate course for Roman Catholic students that left very little room for any kind of cooperative endeavor in religious affairs on campus. It was one of Noble's frustrations that he could not bring Ryan into a more collegial relationship with the other chaplains and the chapel.

Although Father Ryan's death was sudden and had come without warning, the Roman Catholic bishop of Syracuse, Bishop Foery, believed the position should not be vacant for an extended period of time and on December 12 appointed the Reverend Fr. Charles Borgognoni to take the place long occupied by Father Ryan. Father Charles, as he would come to be known, was a native of Canastota, New York, and had his training at Our Lady of Pompei Church in Syracuse, where he had earned a reputation for his work with young people and where he had established the Pompeian Players, a theater group. Before his retirement Father Charles had become both an SU and a community figure of some stature.

The Christmas season, with its traditional tree in front of the chapel, was celebrated. The pageant, which had been a longtime tradition, had given way to the annual Christmas Choir Concert, and this one, the third, took place on Sunday evening, December 16, at seven thirty. Prior to the concert the denominational groups gathered on the steps of the chapel to sing carols, a tradition that continues to this day.

This year, Easter came at a time when more of the students remained on campus, as spring vacation was scheduled for another time. To provide for all who wished to worship two services were held on Easter Sunday morning, one at nine thirty and the other at eleven. Dean Noble preached, and the outstanding choir sang special Easter music under the direction of Professor Poister.

In June there was a change in the leadership of the Hillel Foundation. Rabbi Louis Niemand was succeeded by Rabbi Earl Jordan. Rabbi Jordan had been active in Hillel as a student at Boston University.

In June Dean Noble, having reached the age of sixty-five on January 1 of this year, would ordinarily have been scheduled for retirement according to established university policy. Chancellor Tolley, however, believed that in Dean Noble and Professor Poister he had chapel leadership the university could ill-afford to lose, and upon his recommendation to the Board of Trustees Dean Noble's retirement was postponed until June 1964.*

The years between June 1963 and June 1967 might be described as bonus years for Hendricks Chapel, for the university, and for Dean Noble. Though Dean Noble was to retire in 1964, Chancellor Tolley asked for another year and then another until Dean Noble remained as dean until June 1967. Dr. Arthur Poister, organist and director of the chapel choir, also remained at his post until April 1967. Thus, the team that had made the all-university Sunday morning service so popular and significant was to continue for four years beyond normal expectations.†

Dean Noble's presence on campus, with his great personal popularity, provided a stabilizing force during a period of student unrest, and it also provided continuity with the past and a known and predictable quality of life for the present.

40. The Late Noble Years, 1963–1967

DURING NOBLE'S FINAL YEARS there was little forward movement in programming because the tide of religious organizational interest was receding,

---

*In those days trustee action was necessary to continue university employment for anyone beyond age sixty-five.—RLP

†It is widely known that Tolley, born in 1900, also delayed his retirement with trustee approval. Good company?—RLP

not only at Syracuse University but throughout the nation as well. This period was a time for holding on, not for innovation. By this time the programs housed in the chapel and the Chapel House had become widely diversified. There was a minimum of cohesion and cooperation among the faith and denominational staffs and fellowships. It was not so much that they were at odds with each other—in fact, there was considerable cooperation—as it was that each group believed itself to have a unique ministry in terms of its operational methods and form and style of worship. The Chapel Board was a nondenominational, or multidenominational, vehicle that planned and participated in the all-university Sunday morning service, secured volunteers to work in the downtown social agencies, and officially sponsored Syracuse-in-Asia.

In these years, as students came to college in the fall, a two-page illustrated announcement proclaimed the totality of religious activity on campus. A welcome on behalf of all the chaplains was extended to students by Dean Noble. His message stressed two points: first, that Syracuse University was a place where religious and moral values were important, and second, that in the diversity of religious programs there was a place for everyone who wanted to participate.

Part of his message in the fall of 1964 reads as follows: "The first Board of Trustees of Syracuse university in 1870, envisioned a great university, which in character and philosophy would exemplify our (American) tradition of equality and freedom. Ever since that time, Syracuse University has endeavored to further religious idealism as an integral part of education, and to foster morality."

The next year he said, "In some schools, a person who manifests interest in religion may be called a 'square,' but not at Syracuse University. Here we are definitely concerned with moral and spiritual values, and the programs and personalities described in this brochure prove the point."

During these years there were changes in the leadership of the fellowship groups. Rabbi Earl Jordan had succeeded Rabbi Niemand in June 1963, but his stay was short, and he in turn was succeeded by Rabbi Milton Elefant the next year. The Reverend David Engel left the campus in January 1964, and the next fall his place was filled by the Reverend Harvey Bates as cochaplain with Norman Keim of the United Christian Campus Fellowship.

On campus for these years were the following religious fellowships:

• Hillel Foundation, with up to three thousand Jewish students and Rabbi Elefant as adviser.

• Roman Catholics, with the Newman Club centered at the St. Thomas More House with up to three thousand students and Father Charles Borgognoni as adviser.

• The United Christian Campus Fellowship comprised the Baptists, the Disciples of Christ, the Presbyterians, and the United Church of Christ. The advisers to this group were the Reverend Norman Keim, a Baptist minister, and the Reverend

Harvey Bates, a Presbyterian minister. The students in this group numbered about fifteen hundred.

• The Methodists were served through the Methodist Student Fellowship, of which the Reverend Vernon Bigler was adviser, and it numbered about fourteen hundred.

• The Episcopalians numbered approximately eight hundred and were served through the Canterbury Club, with the Reverend Robert Ayers as chaplain.

• The Lutherans numbered about five hundred, and the Reverend Paul Bosch was their pastor.

All of the above fellowship groups were served by full-time chaplains. In addition, there were other organized groups, the largest of which was the Inter-Varsity Christian Fellowship. Listed also were three hundred Eastern Orthodox Christians, including members of the Russian and Greek Churches. There were seventy-five Christian Scientists and a like number in the Liberal Religious Fellowship made up of Unitarians and Universalists. The Society of Friends numbered fifty. From the Eastern religions there were seventy-five Muslims, forty Hindus, and thirty Buddhists. During one of these years the members of the Wesleyan Methodist Church organized an informal group.

These statistics came from information voluntarily given by students at registration. During these years there was a student trend of either making no response or giving no religious preference. In spite of this tendency, however, Dean Noble commented that 85 percent did indicate a religious preference and that it was his estimation that about one-third of students doing so made some kind of an affiliation with a religious group.

In addition to the fellowship groups the Chapel Board had ongoing committees that included Public Relations, Social Service, the Sanctuary Board, Skeptics Corner for both freshmen and upper-classmen, Syracuse-in-Asia, and Special Programs.

What glue there was to hold things together came through the office of the dean of the chapel. Noble chaired the University Religious Council (URC) made up of all the chaplains and advisers and the student leaders of the various fellowships and their faculty advisers. Noble also conducted the meetings of the Chaplains Council, which met regularly. Each of these groups provided a vehicle for communication and on occasion for joint programming and action.

Each week, for the first three years of this period, the *Daily Orange* had a section titled "Chapel Roundup," usually published on Fridays and giving a comprehensive scheduling of all the religious activities on campus. Most of the large groups had a Sunday evening meeting, usually including a supper and a program with a speaker and discussion. The Roman Catholics and the Jews had their own distinctive services of worship. Whereas many of the members of the denominational fellowships attended the all-university service of worship on Sunday morning, most of the groups had special services of worship at some other time in the week. Those services focused primarily on their particular tradition of celebrating Holy Communion.

It was during this period that the student protest movement began to accelerate and gather force. Civil rights became an issue in the nation, in the Syracuse community, and at Syracuse University. Early in the fall of 1963, shortly after the opening of the college year, the Chaplains Council took out a quarter-page advertisement in the *Syracuse Herald-Journal,* the afternoon newspaper, protesting discrimination in housing in the Fifteenth Ward of the city. In this protest they joined forces with the Congress of Racial Equality (CORE), the NAACP, and the Syracuse Interreligious Council of Religion and Race. The following signed their names to the advertisement: the Reverend Robert Ayers, the Reverend Vernon Bigler, the Reverend Charles Borgognoni, the Reverend Paul Bosch, the Reverend David Engel, Patricia Howland, Rabbi Earl Jordon, the Reverend Norman Keim, Mark Sullivan of Chapel House, Lewis Torman of the chapel staff, and Dean Noble.*

At the forefront of the discussion of the form that the protest should take was the issue of civil disobedience. Some saw it in terms of conflict between the laws of God and the laws of men. As the issue heated up in the community after a long hot summer, CORE and those individuals associated with it thought there needed to be a large mass meeting of protest that would involve members of the university. The administration found itself in the middle on the issue and asked that the meeting be held off campus. This request was agreed to, and on the evening of September 25 at half past seven, the University Methodist Church was filled with individuals who had come to give vent to their feelings. (Phillips was associate minister at the time, and I, Don Wright, was the senior minister.)

Speakers were Dean Stephen Bailey; William Chiles, director of relocation for the City of Syracuse; Dr. George Wiley of CORE; and the Reverend David Engel of the Chaplains Council, who had set up the meeting. All the speakers stressed the importance of the community taking action to end discrimination in housing. The issue arose as to how it was to be done. Dean Bailey warned that it was important to use legal means to make whatever protest was believed necessary. He argued in effect that the "end is prefigured in the means" and that violence and civil disobedience tend to feed upon themselves. This point of view was generally unpopular with those attendees who thought that the situation was so grievous that any means ought to be used to overcome it.

The situation became so volatile and was so closely connected with the Chaplains Council that the chancellor became alarmed as to what might happen the

---

*At this time I was a graduate assistant teaching in the Department of Religion. Several of my colleagues engaged in a demonstration. Jim Hunt, a colleague, was arrested, and I was allowed to visit him in jail. It was a time of great local tension.—RLP

next Sunday morning at the all-university chapel service when the Reverend Vernon Bigler, the Methodist chaplain, was scheduled to preach. Dr. Tolley asked Dean Noble to cancel his out-of-town appointment and occupy the Hendricks Chapel pulpit, which meant, of course, that Vernon Bigler was asked to withdraw. He did so, but it complicated an already difficult situation by adding the charge that the freedom of the chapel pulpit was being abridged. Later, when things had quieted a bit, Bigler was given his opportunity to preach. His sermon was "Unrighteous Religion" and dealt with the issues of the civil rights protest in religious terms.*

The next spring on April 14, the Reverend Ralph Abernathy, a coworker with Martin Luther King, Jr., in the Southern Leadership Conference, came to campus to speak at a meeting sponsored by the United Campus Christian Fellowship. Student protest was in the air all across the nation, and in its last issue of the year the *Daily Orange* carried the headline, "Syracuse University 1963–64 Was the Story of the Protest," indicating that protest was the common key to the mood of the year. What it could not know was that there would be more and more turbulent protest to come.

A year and a half later, on February 19, 1965, "A Vigil to Protest Viet Nam" was held on the steps of Hendricks Chapel. As far as can be ascertained, it was the first public action at the university expressing opposition to the Vietnam War. At first the protests were initiated primarily by faculty and graduate students but would become a movement of enormous proportions and consequences before it was over.

During the 1965 spring vacation a group of twenty-four students with financial support from the fellowship groups and CORE and under the leadership of the Reverend Harvey Bates went to Jonesboro, Louisiana, to help rebuild two churches that had been burned because they had become centers of voter registration.

On May 5, 1965, James Farmer, the national director of CORE, came to Syracuse to give support to picketers at the Niagara Mohawk Power Corporation. The issue was discrimination in employment. At the time of the picketing it was alleged that only five of the fifteen hundred employees of the utility were black.

In the early fall of 1966 the maintenance workers of the university called a strike for higher wages and the right to organize a union. The university contended that the workers had no legal right to strike or to organize a union because private universities were exempt from the provisions of the law that applied elsewhere. There had never been a union of any kind at the university, and it was the fear of the administration that having one would open the door to internal strife and to financial trouble and difficulty for the future. As the strike wore on the workers were

*Bigler and I became good friends. He was a bright and calm part of the events, decidedly a voice of reason.—RLP

given the support of the Syracuse University Chapter of the American Society of University Professors. On October 4 the following statement by the Chaplains Council appeared in the *Daily Orange:* "It is the sense of the Chaplains Council at Syracuse University that among the basic rights of working men is the right to organize and bargain collectively for the common good." Though he did not initiate it, Dean Noble associated himself with the statement. As a result, there unfolded one of the most poignantly personal and painful chapters in chapel history.

In what he viewed as a very critical issue for the future of the university, Chancellor Tolley thought that he had been let down by a very close personal friend. Tolley had been, for many years, the best supporter in the administration the chapel had ever had and had attended its services whenever he was in town. Now he believed he could no longer do so. This produced a wound in friendly and outgoing Noble that never completely healed.*

Of course, life went on in that last year of Dean Noble's service to the university. Despite the fact that his health was deteriorating, when it was announced that he would be preaching, the old charisma returned and students and townspeople came to hear him as well as to listen to the great organ and choral music by the chapel choir under the direction of Dr. Poister.

The fellowship groups continued their programs, but staff and chaplains' meetings became increasingly infrequent and less meaningful. The end of a year was approaching, and it became known that this year would be Dean Noble's last at Hendricks Chapel. He turned sixty-nine on January 1, 1967, and the chancellor, aware of and sensitive to his health problems, would not again recommend extension of his tenure.

In April 1967, Dr. Arthur Poister, whose association with Dean Noble and the chapel had made such an outstanding contribution through organ and choral music, retired from his position. At a special convocation in April, Syracuse University awarded him the honorary degree of doctor of humane letters, and Chancellor Tolley read the following citation:

> Arthur William Poister, preeminent among American organists, extraordinary teacher, able composer and choral leader, yours is the gift of eloquence in music, called by Longfellow the universal language of mankind. A native of Ohio, you showed early promise as a concert pianist and organist at the American Conservatory in Chicago where you studied under Josef Lhévinne, William Middelschulte, and Leo Sowerby. This promise was confirmed in Europe where you perfected your skills under Gunther Ramin, Karl Straube, and Gunther Raphael in Leipzig and the incomparable Marcel Dupré in Paris. As a member of the faculty at the

---

*I had left in the summer of 1966 to begin teaching at Baker University in Kansas, so I was not present during these events. Tolley, in later years, told me that he regretted his "mistake" and the painful separation it caused as much as anything he did in his administration. "Charlie was right," indicated Tolley in a personal conversation, "in supporting the workers."—RLP

Charles C. Noble, second dean of Hendricks Chapel, served from 1945 to 1967. Taking office just after World War II and serving into the turbulent 1960s, he stressed the need for " 'oneness' . . . through the will of God." Photograph by Steve Sartori of oil portrait. Courtesy of Syracuse University Art Collection.

University of Redlands in California, the University of Minnesota and Oberlin College, you built an international reputation as a brilliant recitalist and foremost interpreter of Bach. As the chairman of our department of organ since 1948, you have helped to train the leaders of a whole new generation of concert organists. Equally notable has been your contribution to campus life. Your unforgettable concerts on the magnificent Holtkamp Organ in Crouse College, your inspired direction of the Hendricks Chapel Choir, your warmth and wit in the classroom and your devotion to students, colleagues and friends have enriched the lives of countless Syracusans and made us proud to claim you as our own.

On May 9 at the annual Flint Awards Banquet at Graham Hall Dean Noble was the principal speaker, urging everyone present to dream great dreams. A little less than a month later Dean Noble delivered his twenty-first baccalaureate sermon in the chapel, and it would be his last. On June 3, 1967, at the 113th commencement of Syracuse University, he was awarded an honorary doctor of laws degree by his adopted alma mater. Chancellor Tolley read the following citation:

> Charles Casper Noble, beloved Dean of Hendricks Chapel since 1948, your wisdom and warmth have earned you an enduring place in the affections of generations of Syracusans. One of the great preachers of our time, your eloquence in the pulpit and your gift for working with young people fitted you perfectly for the post you have served so well. You have been an incomparable force for good in this community of students and scholars.

The awarding of this degree was, in a very real sense, the culmination of Dean Noble's relationship to the university, though he carried on until the arrival of his successor, the Reverend Dr. John H. McCombe, Jr., in September. Even in poor health Dean Noble was in demand as a speaker and as a religious and civic leader. At the opening of the Protestant Church Center on October 8, a cooperative venture under the leadership of the New York State Council of Churches, he was asked to speak. Honors continued to come his way, and the university conferred on him the title of dean emeritus of Hendricks Chapel. His health continued to deteriorate, and in February, just prior to his participation in a funeral service at the chapel, he suffered a stroke and collapsed, and was taken to the hospital and later to the Hill Haven Nursing Home.

Late in May 1968 after the remodeling and redecorating of the office area of the chapel, what had formerly been known as the Colonial Room was rededicated as the Noble Room, and a portrait, painted by A. Henry Nordhausen, was unveiled by Harry R. Freeman, the student president of the University Religious Council. Through facilities provided by the New York Telephone Company, Dean Noble was able to listen to the ceremonies from his bed at the nursing home.

Five weeks later, on Monday evening, July 1, 1968, Noble died. Having touched so many lives over a long and useful career, but especially the twenty-two years he spent at Syracuse University, brought many tributes to his career, his multifaceted ministry, and his person. During the 1980s and 1990s anyone on campus who knew him still viewed the chapel in "Charlie Noble" terms.

On Wednesday afternoon following his death, his family gathered together for a private service at which the Reverend Dr. Ellsworth Reamon spoke words of comfort and appreciation about his longtime friend.

On the afternoon of July 11 a public memorial service was held for the entire Syracuse community at Hendricks Chapel under the leadership of Dean McCombe. Speaking for the university, Vice President Frank Piskor said, "Charles Noble was a true example of the whole man. He was a great leader of the faculty and the students. He possessed a heart and mind that appreciated and understood his fellow man. We have learned from his humor, his loyalty and his spiritual greatness to endeavor to live at his level of quality."

Bishop W. Ralph Ward of the Syracuse area of the Methodist Church said, "Dean Noble was one of God's unique and wonderful persons and a good minister of Jesus Christ. The world is better because he lived. Life is better because he chose to live among us. . . . But above all he preached hope and his warm transcendent faith in God, led Charles Noble to serve persons of all kinds. His was an inclusive ministry."

Speaking for the student body, Charles R. Hicks, president of the student government, declared, "We students were fortunate to share his friendship—it has been an honor for every student, for you see he trusted us and never doubted us. He could see more good in people than they could see in themselves."

The service was brought to a close by members of the University Religious Council distributing roses to each one who was present, and as the crowd dispersed the chimes of Crouse College played the alma mater. "Mr. Syracuse" was gone, and proper note had been taken. Thus passed from service to Syracuse University a man who was loved, listened to, and respected as few had ever been before, during, or after on the Syracuse campus.

Because he richly deserved a long and happy retirement it was unfortunate that it was short and painful, though he would never have enjoyed a prolonged period of inactivity. Chancellor Tolley in his concise and formal citation, which has been quoted, paid him high tribute. Perhaps even more poignantly he wrote to Mrs. Noble these words: "Charlie was incomparable. There was none his equal as a preacher and a man. . . . His influence lives in all who know and loved him." *

41. Hendricks Chapel and Radio Station WAER

LAWRENCE MYERS, JR.

IN THE 1930s the consideration of radio broadcasting as a subject for academic study was relatively new in university circles.† Nevertheless, Syracuse Uni-

---

*The tributes to Charlie in this chapter are very much on target. One had only to be with him for a brief time to realize what a wonderful and magnetic person he was. More than anything I remember his brilliant public prayers and his very keen sense of humor.—RLP

†What follows are citations not included within the body of the manuscript, additional information, and excerpts from letters, e-mails, or conversations with alumni who were involved in various ways with WAER programming relating to Hendricks Chapel. The designation LM refers to my initials. I served the inaugural and six additional years as faculty manager of WAER and later was chairman of the Radio-Television Department for twenty years.

versity had achieved stature through the pioneering efforts of Kenneth G. Bartlett, a young professor who eventually became vice president for public affairs. He taught an introductory radio course in 1932. Experimental broadcasts originated from Crouse College. In collaboration with the two existing Syracuse radio stations, WSYR and WFBL, a "radio workshop" was established in 1938. Educational and public service programs utilizing university faculty resources were provided to those stations from a two-studio complex in the basement of Carnegie Library. In 1943, in collaboration with Northwestern University and Stephens College, a national academic honorary, Alpha Epsilon Rho, was established. In the mid-forties Syracuse University was the only eastern educational institution accredited by the Council on Radio Journalism, and one of nine schools or departments that was a charter member of the University Association for Professional Radio Education.*

In the spring of 1947 Radio House was constructed immediately south of Carnegie Library. This specially designed prefabricated building on a permanent concrete slab contained studios, control rooms, classrooms, and faculty offices to support not only an expanded educational curriculum but also an experimental FM radio station that had been authorized by the Federal Communications Commission (FCC) to the General Electric Company. Following spring and summer test periods and visitations by FCC officials, a construction permit was issued to Syracuse University, and the station, WAER, began its first formal broadcasting that autumn.†

I was appointed faculty manager by the Radio Department. In turn, a student staff was appointed by the faculty to create a schedule of programs to be broadcast

---

Alumni who provided information are Kathryn Griffin Barr, Katherine Bell Beckwith, Phyllis Lavine Berk, Sylvia Macy Bloom, Wallace Bradley, Susan Perry Browne, Richard Case, Hugh Cleland, Phyllis Perkins Cohen, Carl Eilenberg, James Fellows, Judy Gregg Fernald, Dugald Gillies, George Hamilton, Joel Heller, Marlene Buksbaum Herwitz, John Hottenstein, Ted Koppel, Don La Mont, Jerry Landay, Alan Lapides, Don Lloyd, James Mailler, Ralph Malvik, Robert Martindale, Nancy Hoehle McClelland, John McFall, Peter Moller, Florence Parise, Ransom Place, Richard Purtan, Inez France Reedy, Florence Reif Richman, Norman Ross, Enid Roth, John Soergel, Kenneth Sparks, Elliot Spiro, Jason Squire, Michael Styer, Robert Vivian, Milton Wallach, and Bette Bartlett Weinheimer.

Other assistance was provided by the National Public Broadcasting Archives, University of Maryland; Ohio State University Manuscript Archives; E. S. Bird Library, Syracuse University (microfilms, *Daily Orange*); and S. I. Newhouse School of Public Communications, Syracuse University.

Daily Orange, Mar. 4, 1949. This issue describes in considerable detail the history of radio broadcasting at Syracuse University, including a long feature article, editorial, poem, cartoon, feature on Kenneth Bartlett, and four photographs.

†"The Low Power Educational Station," in *Education on the Air* (Columbus: Ohio State University Press, 1950), 230–32; "Problems of Low Power FM," in *Education on the Air* (Columbus: Ohio State University Press, 1949), 228–30. During the experimental phase pending FCC approval, beginning in April 1947, the station operated with the call letters WJIV.

regularly Monday through Friday from 4:00 P.M. to 10:00 P.M., thereby avoiding interference with the university's academic schedule.

A daily program from Hendricks Chapel was proposed by student Judy Gregg.* The station staff approved of the idea, as did the Hendricks Chapel Board, and WAER installed a telephone line from its studios to the chapel to enable programs to originate from that location. Gregg was appointed director of the series for the station.

The concept may well have been the most ambitious program series on WAER's schedule. Crude wire recorders then in existence could not be edited, and tape recorders had not yet been invented! Transporting heavy, cumbersome equipment to the chapel from the WAER studios added a physical dimension to the task.† Thus, creating five programs each week that were to be presented "live" from a remote location presented significant challenges.

Religion played an important part in the lives of many students. A news item in the October 1, 1947, *Daily Orange* ran the headline "Chapel: The Heart of the Campus" when describing the formation of a 160-voice chapel choir. (Daily twenty-minute services were held each noon.) Thus, it was not surprising that on October 6 at 5:15 P.M. when WAER began its major fall schedule, people tuned to WAER first heard: "From the heart of the campus, it's *Chapel Chimes.*" These

---

*"The idea for *Chapel Chimes* originated in a small Methodist church in Brooklyn. A letter had gone out asking for suggestions for WAER programming (1947). I regret to say that my thoughts wandered during the church service. I thought of a radio program from Hendricks Chapel featuring a voice of an imaginary and invisible person, 'Chapel Chimes.' When I suggested this on returning to college I was asked to do a sample program. Apparently it was a success in the eyes and ears of the Program Director (Gerald Adler) and I was asked to do a program for the following day, and then the next until we were a five days a week program. At that point I wrote a script for the following day's show. It was quite a week" (Judy Gregg Fernald, letter to LM, Aug. 20, 2003).

†"I traveled to the chapel frequently, on foot, as either the program announcer or engineer. From a personal standpoint, I will never forget lugging those hundreds of pounds of heavy remote boxes, mikes, and cables from Radio House to Hendricks, and assume those who did it have suffered in later years from 'stretched arm syndrome' " (Norman Ross, letter to LM, June 1, 2003).

"When I started at WAER, I learned that the engineers received an hourly wage, so I asked for an engineering job. There were no other women doing that but nobody wanted to give that as an excuse for turning me down. Instead I was told that the engineers had to carry all the equipment to the remote location and they doubted I could do that. I asked them to try me. So they loaded me up with microphones, stands, and a wire recorder and asked me to meet them at Hendricks Chapel. I dragged the stuff out of Radio House. It must have weighed a ton. Fortunately, a group of forestry students were heading to the quad from their classes—each one a young Paul Bunyon—and must have seen my look of distress as they passed me. Two of them stopped and asked if they could help. I explained that I was trying to get all the equipment over to the chapel. They said they'd be happy to help, picked up everything and walked me over. I got the job. By the way, I was never sent out on another remote and I never played the recording of the Star Spangled Banner at the wrong speed!" (Enid Roth, letter to LM, Aug. 25, 2003).

words, together with the chiming of Hendricks Chapel's bells, were WAER's daily introduction to the program devoted to chapel personalities, interfaith worship, and education.

The following spring the *Daily Orange* published a long feature describing the program. Its banner headline read: "Chapel Personalities Shine on WAER 'Chimes' Show."* "Chapel personalities" was the theme of the Monday program. Persons active in various chapel programs told of their work. Monday also was used to describe special projects and drives. "Campus fellowships" was Tuesday's theme, when members of the various religious groups acquainted listeners with their activities. Wednesday was devoted to interviews with foreign students. More than twenty nations were represented during the year.† Thursday was "interfaith day," with writings from the major religions on various themes such as love, faith, peace, and charity. On Friday the dean of Hendricks Chapel, Charles Noble, spoke. Typically, as the program was being introduced, Dean Noble would quietly ask the producer what the subject was for that day. He then proceeded to present an inspirational message for the next twelve minutes. When given a thirty-second warning signal, he would conclude his message on the second! It never ceased to impress, amaze, and fascinate the student producers.‡

On May 9, 1948, Hendricks Chapel announced that Judy Gregg and her colleague Nancy Phillips, who had been prime movers during the year, had been appointed as coordinators of the Radio Committee to oversee production of the *Chapel Chimes* radio service the following year. Additional support was provided by the Interfaith Committee. The action was reinforced when the 1948–49 senior staff of WAER was announced and included Judy Gregg as assistant program director. Subsequently, Nancy Phillips was appointed assistant program director for WAER for 1949–50, thus ensuring continued interest in the program.

WAER leadership, by design, changed each year, as most senior staff members graduated and new student officers were selected to take their places. As the *Chapel Chimes* series developed, the format became even more diverse, with programs devoted to music, readings from the Bible, appearances by clergy, and dramatizations of biblical stories or stories with some spiritual association. Typical of the latter were "The Story of the Prophet Elijah," "The Macabee," and "The Story of the Holy Bible."§

*Referring to *Chapel Chimes,* Judy Gregg Fernald in her Aug. 20, 2003, letter to me wrote: "Dick Clark was our regular announcer for about a year."

†*Daily Orange,* Apr. 8, 1948.

‡Fernald, letter to LM, Aug. 20, 2003.

§Additional credits for programs mentioned in the text, as gleaned from various issues of the *Daily Orange,* are: "The Story of the Prophet Elijah" (Bob Synes, writer; Milton Wallach, producer; Sylvia Macy, Gerry Sperling, and Dan Logan, principal actors; broadcast Dec. 8, 1949); "The Macabee," the story of Hanukkah (John Nelson, writer; Milton Wallach, director; Dan Logan, Jerry Landay, Gerry Sperling, Enid Roth, and Charles King, actors; broadcast Dec. 15, 1949); "The Story

Generally, broadcasts originated in the sanctuary of the chapel before an audience, although the dramas were sometimes produced from either Studio A in
Carnegie Library or Studio C in Radio House.* No matter from where produced
or the theme of a particular day, the identification line for the program was: "As a
man thinketh in his heart, so is he." †

The authorized radiated power of WAER at its inception was a mere two and
one-half watts, barely sufficient to cover the city of Syracuse, although the power
was increased with FCC approval to one thousand watts on April 10, 1951, accompanied by a full-page advertisement in the *Daily Orange*. Nevertheless, the
impact of its programs reached well beyond the campus and city. In the spring of
1948, the annual American Exhibition of Recordings held at the Institute for Education by Radio conference at Ohio State University honored a drama, "Estrel-
lita, the Little Star," with a First Award in the "Special One-Time Broadcasts"
program category. Written by John Nelson and directed by William Volpe, the citation accompanying the award read: "For originality of concept and sincerity of
acting and production, for a pleasurable fifteen minutes of unsentimental whimsy
designed for children but equally pleasing to the most child-like of all adults anywhere on the sunny side of ninety." ‡ The program was broadcast on December 13,
1948, as a Christmas special on *Chapel Chimes* and repeated four days later. The
program was also rebroadcast the next two years.

---

of the Holy Bible" (Inez France, writer; Wallace Bradley, producer; Will Lape and Robert Martindale,
narrators; broadcast Apr. 4, 1954).

*"The program was presented 'live' in Hendricks Chapel in front of an audience composed of
students and anyone else who cared to drop in. It provided the WAER staff with an opportunity to do
a real 'remote' and show off their stuff in front of their fellow Syracusans. It must have had some influence. . . .

"I have been telling a story about *Chapel Chimes* for years and hope it is fitting for your work.
One day the program was presenting a student-written radio play based on a Biblical theme. The actors were all students and some of them were nervous about this 'live' public performance. A microphone placed on the chapel s stage had the dual purpose of feeding both the public address system and
the WAER transmitter. Without the public address system, few in the audience could hear the pro-
ceedings. About midway through the performance the PA system failed and the actors had to raise
their voices to be heard in the back of the sanctuary. I'm sure the people listening at home thought
that the actors were just hamming things up. The nuances of radio acting were simply thrown to the
winds.

"And then it happened. In a stentorian voice one of the actors read his next line with increased
gusto. 'What does the mighty Goliath have to say?' he intoned. There was no answer. He repeated in
a louder voice, 'What does the mighty Goliath have to say?' The reply came from a confused and
shocked Goliath who thought his comment could not be heard by anyone except perhaps the cast. He
was right to a degree. No one in the sanctuary heard him, but the people listening did. 'Jesus Christ,'
the befuddled actor whispered not quite off-mike. 'I lost my place in the script.' So much for the
mighty Goliath" (Joel Heller, e-mail to LM, Aug. 17, 2003).

†Milton Wallach, letter to LM, Aug. 23, 2003. "As a man thinketh" (Prov. 23:7).

‡*Education on the Air* (1949), 423.

In addition to that award the program series *Chapel Chimes* received a distinguished Honorable Mention award from the Institute for Education by Radio. The recognition follows: "Planned-produced by the Syracuse University Radio Center. Length: 15 minutes; Script, J. Gregg, N. Phillips, J. Nelson, and S. Hinden; Talent, University faculty and students; Directors, J. Gregg, N. Phillips, J. Nelson, E. Becker, W. Volpe. Broadcast Monday through Friday 5:15 to 5:30 P.M., E.S.T., over station WAER, Syracuse." The citation read: "For a well-planned series designed by a University group to promote an understanding of all religious faiths." *

The following year another dramatic program appropriate to be incorporated within the *Chapel Chimes* format, "For This I Die," received an Honorable Mention award from the Institute for Education by Radio conference in the "Special One-Time Broadcasts" category.† Written by Milton Wallach and Jerome Landay and directed by Nancy Phillips, it dramatized the story of Amnan Berman, a former Syracuse University student who left school to join the Israeli Air Force after the 1948 partition of Palestine. In the course of the war, he was shot down and killed. The judges caught the essence of the religious message. The citation accompanying the award read: "For a highly appealing and deeply moving tribute to courage. The program's utter simplicity and complete sincerity make it as powerful as a Biblical parable. It is a thought-provoking piece of writing and production with universality of appeal." ‡

Chapel Chimes continued as a daily feature at 5:15 P.M. for four years. In the fall of 1951 the daily effort was replaced by a half-hour version each Thursday at 5:00. The program's title changed to *Chapel Topics* in 1952 and then to *Chapel Highlights* in 1954, but the concept of the program continued as before. The various student fellowships comprising the Protestant Council and the Jewish Student Fellowship took turns presenting the programs; at times they joined together for group presentations.§ Advancing technology in the form of tape recording and editing permitted greater flexibility in program production. Although Sunday worship services were not broadcast, they could now be recorded and edited for later playback.#

---

*Ibid., 420.

†"I don't remember the source of the story ('For This I Die'). It was either something I read in a local paper or given to me by a fellow student, Bernie Hirsch. I remember taking a draft with me when I went for a visit during summer vacation. In any event, it turned out to be one of the best things I ever wrote, a fact substantiated by its award winning status" (Wallach, letter to LM, Aug. 23, 2003).

‡*Education on the Air* (1950), 460.

§Don La Mont, letter to LM, Aug. 14, 2003.

#"On occasion (1954) we rebroadcast portions of the Hendricks Chapel Sunday service. The premise was that many busy students 'unable' to attend services could hear Dean Noble's great sermons and Arthur Poister's magnificent organ music. I can recall being cramped up hidden away in a tiny area on the pulpit side, and taping several services. Dean Noble was always gracious, cooperative and supportive of our efforts. I felt he certainly knew about our tiny listening audience but was being

The final name change for the program occurred in 1956 when, after two years, *Chapel Highlights* morphed into a half-hour program, *In Spirit and in Truth.* The title was adapted from the longer Scripture emblazoned high around the rotunda of the chapel: "GOD IS A SPIRIT & THEY THAT WORSHIP HIM MUST WORSHIP HIM IN SPIRIT & IN TRUTH." *

Under its newest name and format, the producer or one or more coproducers continued to be asked to serve on the Chapel Board. As such, they attended board meetings and acted as conduits for information, comments, or requests.† *In Spirit and in Truth* became a regular feature each Sunday evening at 7:00.‡ In 1957 WAER entered the program series in the competition held annually by the Institute for Education by Radio-Television. In the "Religious" category, it received the coveted First Award.§ The program found its niche and continued as a regular Sunday feature until its termination in 1965.

Thus over a span of years, the creators of *Chapel Chimes* and its sequels, *Chapel Topics, Chapel Highlights,* and *In Spirit and in Truth,* won four national awards for religious programming—two for individual dramatic programs and two for the concepts of the parent program series—a feat never achieved by any other educational radio station. The venture demonstrated a remarkable collaboration between a university's radio station and its interfaith chapel programs.

During the formative decade of WAER, one person stood above all others in ensuring continuity between the radio station and Hendricks Chapel. Dean Charles C. Noble was much in demand for every conceivable Syracuse University

---

the kind and loving 'father' to us 'kids in radioland' " (Robert Martindale, e-mail to LM, Aug. 15, 2003).

*"God is a spirit" (John 4:24). "That beautiful inscription around the rotunda was one of the many things that made my chapel worship experiences so rich and treasured. My Dad died suddenly when I was a freshman. I had to be in Hendricks Chapel on Sundays to make it through the week. Looking up at that 'inscription' hundreds of times, I felt His presence" (anonymous alumnus).

†Kathryn Bell Beckwith, letter to LM, Sept. 4, 2003. Beckwith and Don La Mont were WAER producers and members of the Chapel Board during the academic year 1956–57 when the new title was adopted.

‡"I recall a flub that happened on *In Spirit and in Truth.* In early December 1956 the Jewish Student Fellowship presented a Hanukkah program, 'Chanukah, the Festival of Lights.' The announcer for the JSF program was delayed and the on-duty announcer was asked to voice the program's opening. In his best Frank Gallup announcer's voice, he checked the copy and in his best unaware Hebrew introduced the 'Cha-nuk-a, the Festival of Lights.' No one had told him the 'c' was silent. After the cast gained its composure and pronunciation explained (it's pronounced Han' A ka') the program continued and we entered the holiday that year with a little more awareness and brotherhood than before" (La Mont, letter to LM, Aug. 14, 2003).

§"I was on the Chapel Board both my junior and senior years. I served as the chapel 'rep' both years and as producer of *In Spirit and in Truth* during the 1956–1957 academic year. It was a memorable time. In 1957 *In Spirit and in Truth* received a 1st place Ohio State award. I remember feeling really good about the effort we invested in the program" (ibid.).

activity. During the 1947–48 academic year, not a week went by without the *Daily Orange* featuring Dean Noble in some activity. The same could be said for his interest in WAER. Some representative examples follow.

During the fall semester of 1948 WAER, following a Drama Department presentation of *All My Sons,* produced a discussion from the stage that included a philosopher, Milton Williams; a sociologist, Milton Barron; a political scientist, Samuel Solomon; and a theologian, Charles Noble.*

Skeptics Corner, a discussion group that met weekly at Dean Noble's house, was occasionally recorded, edited, and presented the following week on *Chapel Chimes.* A typical example on February 21, 1950, was "Can Religion Remove Chaos in the World?"

On United Nations Day, October 24, 1950, at 11:55 A.M., WAER joined with the three major networks in broadcasting the dedication and ringing of the Freedom Bell in Berlin. Following the worldwide broadcast at 12:05 P.M., to complete the local radio presentation, Dean Noble spoke on the significance of the ceremony.

When WAER broadcast the Brotherhood Banquet from Sims Hall in 1954, it was preceded by a specially recorded introduction by Dean Noble.

WAER originated an annual award presented to the most valuable player in the Syracuse-Colgate football game (an important event in the early 1950s). The panel of judges consisted of the sports editors of the *Syracuse Post-Standard* and the *Syracuse Herald-Journal,* the SU athletic director and athletic publicity director, the chancellor or vice chancellor, a prominent alumnus, and Dean Noble.

On October 1, 1954, the *Daily Orange* announced that *Chapel Highlights* would be broadcast on Sundays at 6:45, immediately preceding *In Spirit and in Truth.* The first program featured highlights of Dean Noble's sermon on September 26.

Other instances of cooperation between Hendricks Chapel and WAER abound.

From the late forties until the mid-fifties the football rivalry between Syracuse and Colgate was intense, sometimes resulting in vandalism. As an approach to ameliorating the situation, Hendricks Chapel instituted the Brotherhood Service in 1951, which WAER broadcast on the Friday evening preceding the game.

Periodically, when permission by speakers was granted, guests such as poet Karl Shapiro, author Ayn Rand, and media guru Marshall McLuhan, who were speaking before a general university audience in the chapel, were broadcast by WAER.† The station also provided coverage of other special occasions such as the

---

*Daily Orange, Apr. 14, 1948.

†"I was on the Hendricks Chapel Board. It consisted of a group of students representing various campus activities. Lucille Stitzenberger and I were on the Radio Committee and coordinated and developed radio projects with WAER. I recall initiating several remotes from the chapel, always opening the programs with 'From Hendricks Chapel—the heart of Syracuse University—WAER presents. . . . ' The program I especially remember featured the English department's Miss Mary Marshall" (Ransom Place, letter to LM, Sept. 26, 2003).

service of Thanksgiving and dedication of the *Revised Standard Version of the Holy Bible* on September 30, 1952.*

Whereas the sanctuary of the chapel was regularly used for large lectures and special presentations by distinguished visitors to the university, several significant broadcast events occurred that enabled Hendricks Chapel and its associated programs to receive special national recognition.

On January 23, 1949, at 10:30 A.M. the Sunday worship service was broadcast nationally by the Columbia Broadcasting System (CBS) on its *Church of the Air* series. Bishop W. Earl Ledden of the Syracuse area of the Methodist Church spoke, and the chapel choir furnished the music.†

On three consecutive Sundays in December 1959, the 140-voice Hendricks Chapel Choir was featured by the National Broadcasting Company (NBC) on its program *Great Choirs of America.*

For four consecutive years (1953–56) Syracuse University was invited by NBC to participate in *College Quiz Bowl.* Teams of four SU students challenged and were challenged by similar teams from other universities. WAER coordinated the local effort that was broadcast nationally from the stage of Hendricks Chapel.‡ A local version, *Syra-Quiz,* was created, pitting sororities, fraternities, and living centers against one another. The program was broadcast from the stage of the chapel for seven years.

To herald the Christmas season on December 15, 1953, WAER, in conjunction with Hendricks Chapel, produced "Christmas, USA." The program featured campus luminaries and featured skits, original seasonal songs, sacred and popular, a 50-voice glee club, and a drama, "Gift of the Magi." A special dress rehearsal was presented the Sunday preceding the broadcast at the Veterans Hospital. All proceeds went to the annual Christmas Seal Drive.§

---

*Phyllis Lavine Berk, letter to LM, Sept. 19, 2003.

†When the Sunday service from Hendricks Chapel was to be broadcast on CBS on January 23, 1949, an article in the *Daily Orange* read, in part, "The regular service has been moved up from 10:50 to 10:30, which will enable the students to get an early start on their studying."

‡"Although the College Quiz Bowl was broadcast before my time (1961), I remember the event because NBC never removed its line from the chapel, and when I was broadcasting from there the line still was 'live' and had cue on it. Someone then called NBC Operations and a few days later the line was distinctly quiet" (Alan Lapides, letter to LM, Sept. 8, 2003).

§The "Christmas USA" radio program from the chapel to aid the annual Christmas Seal drive was written by Lanny O'Kun and Bill Angelos, narrated by Will Lape, and produced by Randy Place. Featured soloists were Louise Orlando, Lorraine Smoral, Fred Greisinger, Ken Sparks, and Lorraine Peters. The Boar's Head dramatic society provided the actors. The glee club was composed of 50 members from fraternities and sororities. Gil Katz, WAER's publicity director, was quoted in the *Daily Orange:* "No one is obligated to contribute, but let's fill the chapel."

"We were rehearsing the Christmas Special with the entire cast a week before airtime. Dean Noble dropped by for a few minutes. To him, it must have looked terribly disorganized. On his way out, the Dean shook his head and said: 'This will never come together.' The old saw is true. We were

In the 1950s, WAER's programming included Syra-Quiz, a local quiz show drawing its contestants from the university's sororities, fraternities, and living centers and broadcast every Tuesday from Hendricks Chapel. This show was broadcast in March 1956. Compliments of Elliot Spiro; courtesy of Lawrence Myers, Jr.

In the fifties the Christmas pageant produced by the women's speech honorary soceity, Zeta Phi Eta, in conjunction with Hendricks Chapel, was broadcast by WAER from the chapel. The programs featured poet-in-residence A. E. Johnson's adaptation of "The Last Room" and the Hendricks Chapel Choir under the direction of Arthur Poister.*

After nine years, *In Spirit and in Truth,* the longest running weekly program in the station's history, left the air. In its place a significant event occurred on Sunday, September 26, 1965, when WAER signed on the air at 10:45 A.M. The Hen-

---

too young to know it was impossible to put a show like that together in just four weeks" (Place, letter to LM, Sept. 26, 2003).

Daily Orange, Dec. 10, 1947. In an interesting sidelight relating to the producers and participants in the first pageant, major student responsibilities were carried out by Doris Knoepke, Jean Mason, Doris Kittel, Joyce Belanger, Nancy Callaghan, and Alicia Panages, with assistance from Bob Faselt and Chet Gould. All were academic "radio majors" and staff members of WAER.

dricks Chapel worship service was broadcast "live and direct."* From the station's beginning WAER had operated under a general guide that no university activities should interfere with the Sunday morning worship periods. An informal agreement with the chapel to broadcast the weekly worship service modified the policy, and direct broadcasts continued for years to come.[†]

The various chapel programs created from 1947 to 1966 demonstrated a significant collaborative effort between the radio station and the various Protestant and Jewish student fellowship organizations. During this period relatively few members of other faith groups attended the university, and no specific programming was created for them, with a single exception of a short series on the Bahai faith in 1948. However, one large group on campus, seemingly overlooked, was the Catholic faith. Programs emanating from the chapel were not shared with them. "It was not a time of ecumenical efforts, and the Catholic students remained at the St. Thomas More Chapel located on Walnut Place rather than join the Jewish/Protestant programs at Hendricks Chapel."[‡]

Conditions changed in the 1960s as personnel and attitudes changed. For example, the Sunday service carried by WAER on September 29, 1968, featured a person with no ministerial credentials. Professor Michael Sawyer, a popular professor of constitutional law, was the speaker. It marked the first time that a lay Roman Catholic spoke at a regular Protestant service. Other speakers that followed during the fall semester were Rabbi Milton Elefant, Jewish chaplain; Father Charles Borgognoni, Roman Catholic chaplain; Professor Donald Meikeljohn, director of public affairs and citizenship in the Maxwell School; and Professor Charles V. Willie, chair of the Sociology Department. The Reverend Dr. John H. McCombe, Jr., dean of the chapel, explained that their "visitations" were "part of the ecumenical spirit of the chapel." "Change" was clearly in the wind. On October 6, an experimental folk communion was led by Methodist chaplain Frank A. Halse, Jr.[§]

During the weekend of October 18–20, the station broadcast a continuous program of folk music. The question arose: what to do on Sunday morning with-

---

*"In *Feedback*, a dittoed publication put together by WAER staff at the end of the broadcast year, on the page titled 'The Dubious Engineering Awards the year 1966–67,' H___ B___ is commended 'for making the Sunday morning Hendricks remote despite circumstances and hangovers which would have kept any sane man in bed' " (Dugald Gillies, e-mail to LM, Sept. 29, 2003).

"Just received word from Jason Squire that Feb-May 1969 WAER program schedule shows Hendricks Chapel services broadcast from 11 AM to noon" (ibid., Sept. 30, 2003).

[†]James Fellows, a former member of the Chapel Board, program director of WAER, and subsequently faculty member of the Radio Department, wrote that "during my time at Syracuse University (1951–1963) I don't recall that Hendricks Chapel services were ever regularly broadcast" (e-mail to LM, June 16, 2003).

[‡]La Mont, letter to LM, Aug. 14, 2003.

[§]*Daily Orange*, Sept. 27, 1968.

out interfering with traditional religious programming at 11:00 A.M.? An easy solution was found. Father Charles Borgognoni celebrated a folk mass from Crouse College, which WAER carried. Then, from 3:00 to 5:00 that afternoon, a folk concert was aired live from Hendricks Chapel.*

On Sunday, November 3, 1968, WAER broadcast a special "celebration of man under God" featuring seven religious faiths uniting in the chapel worship service. Originating from discussions by students who wanted to "expose the heartbeat of all major traditions under a common theme," a planning committee composed mainly of international students was formed. From this committee emerged a program for the first such celebration. Representatives of Buddhist, Christian, Hindu, Jain, Jewish, Islamic, and Sikh faiths explained their unique, yet common, approaches to monotheism. The congregation ended the celebration singing "No Man Is an Island."[†]

This brief recount of a generally overlooked activity at Syracuse University has been confined to a period from 1947 until 1969. In retrospect, one is impressed by the extent to which two Syracuse University organizations, the newly established radio station WAER and the venerable and revered "heart of the campus," Hendricks Chapel, worked together in common cause.[‡] Beyond offering practical experience for radio students, the relationship attempted to offer spiritual enrichment and education to those persons, students, and general audience members alike who wished to benefit from the various offerings.[§]

Daily Orange, Oct. 18, 1968.

[†]*Daily Orange,* Oct. 25, 1968.

[‡]"I shall always treasure the friendships, fellowship and fun we had when FM was more of an 'experiment.' Yet we took those responsibilities seriously and made honest efforts to broadcast 'quality' and not worry about 'quantity' (of listeners)" (Martindale, e-mail to LM, Aug. 15, 2003).

[§]The following three chapters were originally put together as an internal Hendricks Chapel paper by history graduate student Jerald S. Cohn at the request of Dean McCombe (memo from Jack, August 17, 1976, in the Donald Wright holdings in the archives, yet to be numbered). Wright's editing hand and that of several others, including mine, bring it to its present form. I have been told that Darrell Fasching oversaw the project, but I could find no confirmation in the files or the archives. In the memo McCombe indicates the paper was created to go with Don's manuscript on the history of Hendricks Chapel.

A letter to Wright from McCombe also dated August 17, 1976 (also in the Wright materials), states that Jack had sent copies of the first draft to Don and to most of the chaplains and staff members asking that they read and supply additional information. Jack's final sentence in that letter is: "I will then edit and present the draft to you for your finishing touches." Jack indicates in the memo that the original was not adequate coverage, so I must assume a good deal of editing and rewriting took place, which would help explain why Cohn did not get a byline on the final draft. I have talked with Don's widow, Phyllis, who typed the paper for Don's manuscript. She is not sure how much editing Don did on the paper but believes that he did do some editing. She also remembers that Don was reluctant to write too much about McCombe's deanship owing to the fact that it was still in progress, and at that point no one knew how long it would last.

The paper as it appears in Don's manuscript is not divided into chapters but does have the basic

42. Dean McCombe's Early Days, 1967–1969

DEDICATED IN 1930, Hendricks Chapel quickly became the spiritual center of the Syracuse University campus. Though a Methodist minister of a Methodist-related institution, it was the goal of Hendricks Chapel's first dean, William H. Powers, that the chapel become a symbol of the kind of religion possible in a university. To Dean Powers this meant a chapel run primarily through student initiative where cooperation among the various religious faiths would eventually lead to a universal religion. Although Dean Powers's idealistic conception was never fulfilled, under his leadership and that of his successor, Charles C. Noble, Hendricks Chapel did administer vigorous student programs with a high degree of interfaith cooperation.[*]

During the later years of Noble's deanship the chapel began to show signs of institutional evolution. Student participation began to wane. The various faith groups, which had proliferated in number, began more and more to go their own way. Perhaps most significantly, by the 1960s student attitudes and values had changed considerably from those of the 1930s, 1940s and 1950s. In their search for social and self awareness, young people were becoming increasingly disenchanted with institutional religion.[†]

It was this kind of environment that McCombe faced. Dean Noble retired in 1967, and that August, from a list of more than thirty candidates, the Reverend Dr. John H. McCombe was chosen as his replacement.[‡]

Jack McCombe, a Syracuse University alumnus, class of 1942, and former Hendricks Chapel Board copresident, brought broad experience to the chapel deanship, experience that combined Christian ministry with international experience. He began his career in the diplomatic service attached to the United States Embassy in Mexico. It was there that McCombe decided that he could best serve humanity as a Christian minister. He received his bachelor of divinity degree from Union Theological Seminary in New York City and a Ph.D. degree from the National University in Cuzco, Peru. Following seminary McCombe became a

---

headings inserted in the paper with essentially the same wording I have used in dividing it into chapters 42, 43, and 44 of this book.—RLP

[*]Summary of research done on Hendricks Chapel under Deans Powers and Noble. For Dean Powers's conception of the chapel, see the *Daily Orange*, Mar. 11, Apr. 7, and Sept. 29, 1930.

[†]See Hendricks Chapel Annual Reports for the years 1959–60 and 1960–61, SU Archives, Hendricks Chapel Reports and Minutes, box 239.

[‡]Memo, "Candidates for Deanship," Hendricks Chapel, Records of the Chancellor's Office: William P. Tolley, box 59, Candidates and Deanship File, SU Archives.

Methodist pastor in New York City from 1951 to 1959. In 1959 he joined the American Bible Society and did work for them in Japan for three years. He returned to New York City in 1961 and was an executive secretary of the American Bible Society when appointed to the deanship of Hendricks Chapel.[*]

Dean McCombe came with an innovative mind that understood the changes occurring on the college campus. McCombe believed that for the chapel to remain a significant part of the university it would have to keep pace with the times. He once explained, "To stay alive and vital the Chapel must experiment; otherwise it becomes a caretaker of religion." Under McCombe experimentation and change were the order of the day. The chapel would become a virtual laboratory of religion.[†]

Such a flexible approach to religious activities implied a very broad understanding of the purpose of religion in society. Dean McCombe spoke of "the secularization of religion as one of the best things to have happened to the Church since the Reformation," and he indicated that "helping a student to discover himself in an all night bull session, could be just as religious as a prayer session."[‡]

In order to make the chapel an effective instrument, Dean McCombe believed that cooperation among the religious groups was essential. This aim, of course, was also one of the goals of both Powers and Noble. Because of the commitment of Dean Powers and Dean Noble to interfaith cooperation, by the time McCombe returned to Syracuse University it had one of the largest staffs of denominational counselors in the country. Approximately fifteen chaplains and part-time advisers worked with the Chapel, including the following ministries: B'nai B'rith Hillel, the Episcopal Church, the Evangelical Commission, the Christian Science Organization, Lutheran Campus Ministry, Inter-Varsity Christian Fellowship, the United Methodist Church, Newman Association, Orthodox Christian Fellowship, Society of Friends, Student Religious Liberals, and the United Campus Christian Fellowship. Moreover, the Newman Club and the B'nai B'rith Hillel Association were reported to be among the largest and most active in the country.[§]

The dean's vision for increasing the unity among the disparate faith groups was the creation of an ecumenical spirit. Joint participation in the development of chapel programs would be engendered through a new ethos of interfaith understanding. It would be characterized by a complete respect for the authority and

[*]Memo, American Bible Society, ibid.; *Daily Orange,* Sept. 15, 1967.
[†]Bruce Frazer, "The Campus Shift to Religion at Syracuse University," *Weekly Observer,* Mar. 1, 1970, 9; personal interview with Dean McCombe, June 1976; *Daily Orange,* Dec. 16, 1969.
[‡]Frazer, "Campus Shift," 8–10.
[§]"Hendricks Memorial Chapel: Religion on Campus, Present and Future Needs," files of Hendricks Chapel; *Daily Orange,* Dec. 12, 1969.

traditions of each religion. Through mutual understanding would come a willingness to work jointly in the promotion of religious activities of the campus.*

The administrative arm of ecumenical development was to be the University Religious Council. It consisted of two student representatives and a chaplain from each faith group holding membership in the Chaplains Council.† The activities of the URC perhaps best illustrate the nature of the work done by Hendricks Chapel during the early years of McCombe's deanship.

As expressions of the ecumenical spirit, the University Religious Council, under the dean's leadership, promoted a number of interfaith religious services. In May 1968, for example, Hendricks Chapel held an ecumenical communion service using a combination of Protestant and Catholic liturgies and a jazz band. Another service brought together seven major religious traditions of the East and West—Buddist, Christian, Hindu, Jain, Jewish, Islamic, and Sikh—for an hourlong celebration, "All Men under God." Each religious tradition was allowed to express its unique features through scriptural readings, symbols, and prayer.‡

To further unite the religions on campus, the URC backed an effort to interest the university in constructing an interfaith center attached to the chapel. Such a building would have lessened the overcrowding in Hendricks and would have enabled the Protestant, Jewish, and Catholic faiths to hold their services under the same roof.§

Although the interfaith center never became a reality, the chapel itself underwent its first major renovation since its construction. The ninety thousand-dollar chapel refurbishment was funded entirely through Dean McCombe's efforts in securing personal contributions from friends and trustees of the university. Besides repairing the chapel sanctuary, a major remodeling job was done on the lower level. Expanded facilities were provided for Hillel, the Chapel Boardroom, and the dean's office. In addition, a fifteen thousand-dollar sculpture of Christ, *The Corpus,* was given to the dean's office, a donation of its sculptor, Doris Caesar. The seven-month chapel refurbishment was carried out as a tribute to former dean Charles Noble. The renovated Colonial Room was renamed the Noble Room, and a large portrait of the former dean was hung above the room's fireplace mantel.#

With a seating capacity of more than one hundred, the renovated Noble Room was made into a minicenter for the arts, with art exhibits and musicals held

Daily Orange, Aug. 1, Sept. 26, 1968.

†"Hendricks Memorial Chapel," 7; *Daily Orange,* Sept. 26, 1968.

‡*Daily Orange,* May 3, Sept. 25, 1968; "Hendricks Memorial Chapel," 8.

§"Hendricks Memorial Chapel"; memo, McCombe to Tolley, Jan. 4, 1968, Hendricks Chapel, Records of the Chancellor's Office: William P. Tolley, box 59, John H. McCombe File, SU Archives.

#*Daily Orange,* Apr. 29, 1968; *Syracuse Herald-American Empire Magazine,* Apr. 6, 1969, 2–4.

there.* Such activity is suggestive of the wide range of social programs the chapel undertook.

In addition to its sponsorship of the arts, the University Religious Council helped to initiate a number of social service programs. One such service was Operation Volunteer, a tutoring program centered in downtown Syracuse. Another was Link, an organization that attempted to further understanding and friendship between Syracuse University students and families of the ghetto.† An educational program for clergymen in the Syracuse area was inaugurated by the chapel in cooperation with the Department of Religion. Clergymen were exposed to six weeks of intensive study in the newest advances in the sciences and the humanities.‡ There was also Film Forum, a program developed by the United Campus Christian Fellowship that brought to the campus a wide variety of films with particular messages to convey. It was the belief of the Film Forum's director, Chaplain Norman O. Keim, that films could be one of the most effective vehicles for communicating with young people.§

The chapel also addressed itself to timely social needs. The chapel sponsored "Rap on Sex," bringing together parents, chaplains, doctors, and thirty newly married couples. This program proved so popular that it again brought to the attention of the university the need for sex education courses. Similar presentations were given on ecology and justice.#

The variety of these programs underscores the flexible and experimental approach of Dean McCombe in his early years in the chapel. Nowhere was the dean's experimental approach more apparent than in the chapel's own services. The Chapel Board, under the dean's direction, remained the organ responsible for the chapel's major Protestant service. The dean sensed that students wished to diverge from the more traditional forms of church worship. Consequently, he permitted the students of the Chapel Board to have more control over the content of the Sunday services. Thereafter, experimental services became more and more common. Such innovations as interpretive dance to represent the Sermon on the Mount, contemporary jazz as a celebration of communion, and an all-music liturgy were introduced into the services. There was also an attempt to fuse religious and social concerns with a "Theology of Ecology" service. In another change, speakers for the Sunday services were no longer drawn predominantly from outside the campus. Effective use was made of faculty and administrators as speakers. Like the rest of the chapel programs, chapel services attempted to move with the times.**

*"Hendricks Memorial Chapel," 10–11.
†*Daily Orange,* Sept. 28, 1968.
‡"Hendricks Memorial Chapel," 10.
§Ibid.; personal interview with Keim, July 1976.
#Bruce Frazer, *Weekly Observer,* Mar. 2, 1970, 8–10.
**Ibid., 9–10; *Daily Orange,* Dec. 1, 1967, Apr. 4, 1969, Feb. 20, 1970; *Syracuse Post-Standard,* Mar. 7, 1969, 7; personal interview with Dean McCombe, June 1976.

43. Coping with Campus Unrest, 1969–1970

IN MID-OCTOBER of 1969 Hendricks Chapel held a "Pilgrimage to Peace" service. As the service began the choir filed in silently, followed by students carrying the chapel's large crucifix sculpture, which was then laid on the alter. This dramatic service was written by a college senior to symbolize the plight of the nation as it observed the upcoming Vietnam moratorium. On October 15, the day of the moratorium, the chapel remained open the entire day as it observed the Vietnam protest.[*]

Hendricks Chapel could not avoid involvement in the growing protest of the Vietnam War, but how far could a college chapel, one that was administratively attached to the university, go in its relation to a nationwide campus protest movement? For the most part the chapel confined its activities to symbolic acts of support and by continuing to serve as a campus meeting place. However, the increasingly obstreperous character of the campus protest atmosphere put the chapel and its dean in a difficult position. In March 1970 four leaders of the nationwide student antiwar movement, David Dellinger among them, were invited by the student body of Syracuse University to speak at Hendricks Chapel. Because of an overflow crowd of more than fifteen hundred people, some who could not get in forced open doors and smashed windows in an effort to hear the speakers. As a result Dean McCombe was called upon to decide whether the chapel should continue to be used for such events. Stating that the chapel exists for the purpose of student involvement, McCombe decided against restricting the use of the chapel. In so doing the dean resisted the alternative of insulating the chapel from the activities of the student activists.[†]

On Monday, May 1, 1970, National Guardsmen opened fire on student protesters at Kent State University. Four students were killed, and nine were wounded. Students in more than 350 colleges, already angered over the bombings in Cambodia, reacted to the events at Kent State by going on strike. At Syracuse University the strikers searched for a place to use as their headquarters. The chapel, at the center of the campus and not strictly an administration building, was chosen by the strikers as their command post with McCombe's blessing.[‡]

Deciding to let the strikers use the chapel was perhaps the most controversial

---

[*]*Daily Orange,* Oct. 10, 15, 1969.

[†]*Daily Orange,* Mar. 7, 1970.

[‡]Description of Kent State affair from Irwin Unger, *The Movement: A History of the American New Left, 1959–1972* (New York: Dodd and Mead, 1974), 186–87; for events in Syracuse, see *Daily Orange,* May 5, 1970.

decision McCombe had to make at Syracuse. The chapel remained open twenty-four hours daily, and the chaplains remained in the chapel to supervise its use and to help stabilize the situation until the strike ended. Eventually, the strike ended without any occurrences of violence. The dean's decision to allow the chapel to be used by the strikers may have been an important factor in the absence of violence on the Syracuse campus.* Nonetheless, some of the more conservative members of the university could not have but resented the dean's action.†

44. Remaining Current in a Changing World, 1970–1976

THE STUDENT STRIKE represented a turning point for Hendricks Chapel. As student protest began to fade and the campus gradually returned to normal, the dean had to reconsider the role of the chapel. This reassessment was spurred by a number of trends that began to appear after the period of student unrest.‡

Student attendance at the regular Sunday service had declined precipitously between 1968 and 1970. This student apathy toward religious services carried over into the workings of the University Religious Council. Student and clerical participation had long made the URC a forceful expression of ecumenism on campus, but over the three years following the 1970 strike the University Religious Council had virtually disappeared as a vehicle for interdenominational cooperation.§

The decline of the URC also reflected a decrease in the number of chaplains on campus. Some of the Protestant churches, distrustful of the university's image as a center for radicalism and suffering from a shortage of funds, withdrew their chaplains from the campus. From a high of fifteen full- or part-time chaplains during the 1960s, the number dwindled to seven.# The chaplains remaining on campus were: the Reverend Robert Ayers, Episcopal Church; Monsignor Charles L. Borgognoni, Catholic Church; the Reverend Paul Bosch, Lutheran Church; Rabbi Milton Elefant, B'nai B'rith Hillel; the Reverend Norman C. Keim, chaplain-at-large; Dr. T. E. Koshy, Evangelical Ministry; and the Reverend George Van Arnam, United Ministries in Higher Education.

---

*Both Michael Sawyers and Chancellor Eggers came to believe and related to me that McCombe's decision to use the chapel was, after all, the correct decision.—RLP

†Derived from personal interviews with chaplains and staff of Hendricks Chapel.

‡Derived from personal interviews with chaplains and staff of Hendricks Chapel.

§*Syracuse Post-Standard,* Nov. 8, 1974, 11; *Long Island Press,* Aug. 30, 1975, reprinted in Hendricks Chapel Annual Report, 1975–76; personal interviews with chapel personnel.

#Hendricks Chapel Annual Reports, 1972–76, files of Hendricks Chapel.

The downturn in student and chaplain input, symbolized by the fortunes of the URC, lessened the effectiveness of the type of interfaith cooperation that had characterized earlier ecumenical efforts at Syracuse University. This was exacerbated by persistant differences among the denominations that simply could not be transcended. These differences impeded the kind of interfaith cooperation Dean McCombe was seeking.

The incident of the Chapel Cup illustrated this problem. To represent the ecumenical spirit of Hendricks Chapel, Dean McCombe commissioned silversmith John C. Marshal to make a silver cup and bowl patterned after *The Chalice of Antioch*. The idea of a Chapel Cup appealed to McCombe as an expression of interfaith spirit, as it could be used by each of the faith groups in its services. The cup and bowl were completed in 1971 at a cost of two thousand dollars, but they were never used as envisioned by Dean McCombe. The chapel cup is now on display within the university art collection.*

As a result of the changes in the religious environment on campus, McCombe endeavored to redirect the activities of the chapel to meet the changing conditions. To help formulate and implement new goals for the chapel he added administrative personnel. His staff included Assistant Dean Darrell Fasching; Secretary to the Dean Marjorie Thomas; organist and choirmaster Brent Hylton; Director of Community Relations Ruth Hall; chaplain intern Ben Bortin; Community House director Michael Dolcemascola; Helen Eichman of the Married Student Ministry; and chapel associates Jean Baum and Kendra Smith.†

Through the combined efforts of the dean, his staff, and the chaplains, chapel programs began to form around three primary goals. First, through the chaplains and the general Protestant, Catholic, and Jewish services, the chapel would remain the center of conventional religion on campus. Second, the chapel would seek to serve the greater campus community by offering programs directed toward personal growth and humanization. Finally, Hendricks would facilitate communication and an exchange of ideas among all segments of the university.‡ In a sense all of these goals were interrelated, and none was particularly new, but Dean McCombe's efforts gave them new prominence. Most chapel programs developed after the strike were oriented toward achieving these ends. A description of some of the activities will show how the chapel was functioning.

As befitting its original purpose, Hendricks Chapel continued to promote reli-

*Memo, McCombe to Tolley, Dec. 14, 1967; memo, McCombe to Eggers, Nov. 2, 1971; report, *The Chalice of Antioch,* files of Hendricks Chapel, Chapel Cup File; personal interview with Dean McCombe, June 1976.

†Hendricks Chapel Annual Reports, 1972–76, files of Hendricks Chapel.

‡"Hendricks: A Rainbow of Ministries under Its Umbrella," *Syracuse University Record,* Nov. 29, 1973, 11; Dean McCombe, "Something Happens to People at Hendricks Chapel," *Daily Orange,* Mar. 2, 1976.

gious activities on the campus. The Chaplains Council met once a month to discuss areas of mutual concern. B'nai B'rith Hillel and the Newman Club were still among the largest in the country. Monsignor Charles Borgognoni reported that Catholic masses drew as many participants as before the strike, and Hillel continued to expand its membership and the scope of its activities. Attendance was also rising in the regular Protestant service. Dean McCombe, in conjunction with the Chapel Board, nurtured this increase by reverting from the experimental format of the prestrike years to a more traditional service stressing continuity and centered around basic liturgical forms. Innovative services did not completely cease, however. In May 1973, the chapel held a baccalaureate service in honor of graduation, and in January 1974, a "Medieval Procession for Epiphany" was performed.[*]

The gradual loss of several chaplains led to some creative efforts by the chapel to maintain an additional clerical presence on the campus and to increase communication with the surrounding churches. The Unitarian-Universalist Churches initiated a chaplain intern program in 1971. When church funds dried up in later years, the chapel agreed to bear part of the cost, and the intern became a regular member of the chapel staff. Chaplain Norman O. Keim had a similar experience. When his church could no longer support him, Keim decided to stay on campus and support himself through Film Forum. Dean McCombe created the position of chaplain-at-large, which enabled Keim to continue his clerical duties in the mode of a "worker-priest." The chapel worked toward improving communication and interaction between the campus and community churches by establishing the liaison position of chapel associate in 1975.[†]

In addition to functioning as a religious center, the chapel directed much of its work toward "humanizing" the campus. The dean and his staff saw this goal as enabling students to discover "each other and themselves." Two chapel programs, Community House and People's Place, were particularly effective in furthering these ends. Community House, formerly known as Chapel House, had become a widely used student-faculty center. Minicourses, fireside dialogues, encounter group sessions, and seminars were offered. There was a food bar, the Orange Place, which served lunch daily. On Friday afternoons students and faculty would unwind with a TGIF wine and cheese party. People's Place served a similar function of providing a place for students and faculty to gather. Semiautonomous and

[*]Report of worship, Hendricks Chapel Annual Reports, 1974–75, 1975–76, files of Hendricks Chapel; personal interviews with Monsignor Charles Borgognoni and Rabbi Milton Elefant, July 1976; "Guidelines for Liturgy," Hendricks Chapel Worship Committee, spring 1974, files of Hendricks Chapel; *Long Island Press,* Aug. 30, 1975.

[†]Personal interview with Keim, July 1976; Hendricks Chapel Annual Report, 1975–76, files of Hendricks Chapel.

run entirely by students, People's Place provided a friendly atmosphere just around the corner from the Noble Room.*

Hendricks Chapel also humanized campus life through its sponsorship of cultural activities. Artists had an open invitation to exhibit their work in Community House and in the Noble Room. Poets brought their work to poetry readings held at Community House. Guest choirs and organists were invited from time to time to give concerts. The chapel's own choir had become "one of the most successful in the country" and gave concerts throughout the country. The chapel choir celebrated its fiftieth anniversary with a concert in the nation's capital and a tour of Europe that included ten cities and seven countries.[†]

Finally, Hendricks had become an important medium for communication and the free flow of ideas. For example, the dean brought together faculty, administrators, and students for lunch in his "Monday Munchies" program. Also, the chapel had, in the prophetic mode of the ministry, kept the campus aware of significant moral and ethical issues. In the spring of 1975 the chapel sponsored Hunger Action Week, designed to raise the consciousness of students to the problem of world hunger. Later, it sponsored programs designed to emphasize and support the university's responsibility for helping faculty and students formulate moral values.[‡]

Through the wide variety of its programs, Hendricks Chapel continued to exercise its role as a central force in the campus experience, demonstrating that the classical and contemporary purpose of religion can make itself relevant to the needs of a college campus. As a result, the chapel became, in the phrase of Dean McCombe, a "cathedral of life" on the Syracuse University Campus.[§]

---

[*]Hendricks Chapel Annual Reports, 1972–76, files of Hendricks Chapel; Dean McCombe, "Something Happens at Hendricks Chapel," *Daily Orange,* Mar. 3, 1976; personal interview with Dean McCombe, June 1976.

[†]Hendricks Chapel Annual Reports, 1972–76, files of Hendricks Chapel.

[‡]Ibid.

[§]With these three chapters Donald G. Wright's manuscript comes to a close. I try to cover other issues of McCombe's deanship in the chapters to follow.—RLP

45. A Closer Look
at the McCombe Years

RICHARD L. PHILLIPS

JACK, AS HE WAS KNOWN to all his friends and associates, was a tall, handsome man with a warm, winning personality. He had the open hand, ready smile, and easy style of relating often associated with persons in the clergy. Both his education and his work experiences gave his life a decided international flavor. By nature he was very gregarious and truly enjoyed himself and others when in a social setting. He loved to use his considerable language skills, particularly Spanish and Japanese. He and Mel Eggers often spoke Japanese with one another. It is said that Eggers's Japanese language skills were a bit better than McCombe's and that they enjoyed sharing that ability.

Jack's spouse, Dory, related in a note to me that she and her daughters drafted following Jack's death that his happiest times were with groups of students and that sometimes faculty gathered at the dean's residence, discussing important matters over a meal. The pleasure was increased when the gathering had an international makeup.

Jack left the deanship of our chapel with very positive feelings toward it, toward SU, and toward Eggers. One needs to see Jack in light of the fact that controversy, even very contentious controversy such as he and Eggers and others in the SU administration had at the end of his career at Hendricks Chapel, did not carry forth in future relationships enough to spoil either life or those very same relationships for Jack. My source of information on this fact is gleaned from his correspondence during and after the time of the controversy and in several conversations with me. So with this introduction I move to some important aspects of his service as dean of Hendricks Chapel in an effort to add to what Donald Wright has already related.

The need for upgrading the chapel facility, particularly the lower level, was acute when McCombe replaced Noble as dean. During the 1960s I visited Noble several times in his office and found it hard to believe that he was not provided with an aesthetically and functionally more appropriate office and meeting space. Jack went to work on this problem immediately, and it did not prove difficult to raise money for the project in honor of Charlie Noble.

The following is quoted from a *Syracuse Post-Standard* article of May 25, 1968:

The $56,000 face-lifting program has been made possible through gifts by Dr. and Mrs. Dwight Beck, the Newman Club through the Rev. Charles L. Borgognoni, Donald MacNaughton, Earle Machold, Mrs. Edward S. Haviland, the Syracuse Jewish Welfare Federation, Mr. and Mrs. Robb Quimby, Charles E. Wilson, Dwight W. Winkleman, T. Frank Dolan, Dr. George Manley, Howard C. Hirsch, DeWitt C. LeFever, Joseph I. Lubin, George W. Lee, Malcom P. Ferguson, Frederick Killian, Mrs. Lindsay Damon and an anonymous donor.

The dean himself was reported to be the chief fund-raiser for the entire project.

As has been noted, the Colonial Room was renamed the Noble Room at the close of this remodeling effort. Unfortunately, Charlie died as the project was being completed. The *Syracuse Post-Standard* of May 25, 1968, reports that he was recovering from "a cerebral vascular incident followed by pneumonia." He was thought to be recovering well but died less than a month later. On May 26 the Noble Room was rededicated and the A. Henry Nordhausen portrait unveiled. Grace Noble was visibly pleased with the renovation project in his honor but was also reported to still be upset about the conflict between Tolley and her husband. Her family members and friends reported to me that she was still hurting from the "wound" for several more years, perhaps right up until her death.

The portrait by Nordhausen of Noble was originally hung over the fireplace in the Noble Room and later moved to the narthex of the main chapel on the opposite wall from the portrait of Dean Powers. (The Noble Room fireplace has since been eliminated.) The student chair of the committee charged with overseeing the portrait preparation was Harry R. Freeman, known by current Syracusans as Harry Freeman Jones. He was very active at Hendricks Chapel at the time. Harry himself painted a mural in the dean's office reception area after he graduated from SU. It continues to greet all who enter the dean's suite. There is a description by Harry that can be read by interested persons.

Sometime in the late 1970s, probably the fall of 1979, the portraits of Powers and Noble were slashed with a sharp object and were later taken to the SU Art Collection for restoration. They were not available for rehanging until shortly after I became the fourth dean. As far as we know the motive for the damage done was never discovered. The restoration work proved to be excellent.

Don Wright noted that McCombe very early revived the effort by Noble to have an addition to the chapel built (which in the original plan could be done on the west side) or to have a separate facility constructed as an interfaith center. His appeal, repeated for several years, was not successful. After the renovation of the offices and meeting rooms in the lower level of the chapel were completed, Jack began to request that the old heat exchangers and piping in the central areas of that level be removed (they had long been replaced in the function of heating the building) so that space could be claimed for program and office use. It was only in his last full year, in preparation for the chapel's fiftieth anniversary and to replace at least part of the space lost from the sale of Community House, that that project was approved.

The chief professional organization for persons engaged in campus ministry at the time was known as the National Association of College and University Chaplains (NACUC) and Jack joined and soon after became an officer. Noble had also been a member. Jack later served as president of the group. He and SU hosted the March 1970 meeting of NACUC. It was a very successful time. Dick Gregory came as one of the speakers, and others included William Sloan Coffin, Jr., from Yale (perhaps the best-known campus clergyman in the country), a representative of Malcom X Liberation, and participants from across the country (see file box 013697 of the chapel archives). Jack was by nature inclusive as well as internationally oriented as both a person and a dean. He participated in such organizations with ease both nationally and worldwide. It was during his deanship that NACUC split into two organizations, the new one called the Association of College and University Religious Administrators (ACURA). I will relate something of the new organization in chapters about my own deanship.

The urgent need to retool Hendricks Chapel for the new and much changed generations of students was foremost in Jack's ministry very early. Meetings of chaplains, advisory boards, and committees were filled (really throughout Jack's years but especially in the years 1968 to 1972) with concern about how to make the chapel relevant to the times. What to do about the administrative structure and the committee setup in the overall chapel picture were the dominant concerns. There is nothing new about these issues being "the" topics of concern because Noble had wrestled with the operational documents and philosophy of the chapel operation throughout his deanship, especially the second half. It seems every change, every new idea, every new committee, lasted only a year or so and then it was back to the drawing board again. Tough times to be serving any institution, especially a campus religious one!

In an effort to promote the chapel the idea of a film took root and in 1969 a twenty-eight-minute film on religion on the campus was produced. Norm Keim was the chair of the committee working with the production company. It was basically an interview-based effort to find out what students thought about religion, why they did or did not participate, and what they thought they needed in this area of their lives. McCombe makes a final appeal in the film for seeing Hendricks Chapel as the place where searching and questioning can take place. In the end no one thought the film accomplished its intended purpose. It was funded by Dewitt C. LeFevre, a layperson who had supported the recent renovation project. Norm Keim, in an interview with me (the tape of which is now in the archives), said the committee lost all control of the project, that the young film group had their own ideas of what to do and simply shut out all chapel-based input. LeFevre himself was disappointed in the final product and offered to fund a corrected and extended effort, but the company was long gone and not interested, so after a brief period of use it died. The film, for unknown reasons, was titled *The Newest Testament*. Interestingly enough, LeFevre, a Methodist layman, was upset that the film did not give Jewish and Roman Catholic interests any real treatment and that the academic study of religion was largely ignored. As with so many big efforts to deal with big problems this costly one flopped.

Jack was of course not only the dean but also the head of the Protestant worshiping community with services on Sunday mornings and a choir and organist of some reputation. Both the music and the services had a great history. Suddenly, what Noble had predicted and indeed feared for his late years happened. It happened so suddenly that getting a handle on it quickly was not possible. Almost all at once the Sunday morning congregation was no larger than the choir! What to do? It was not McCombe's preaching, which all agreed was very good, and it was not the music; it was just that few people were coming. Noble had heard and now McCombe was feeling the impact of the student comment, "The loneliest place in the world is the shower on Sunday morning." Jack was to spend great energy and much worry over this issue for the rest of his deanship. Even after intellectually realizing that student participation had forever changed, there lingered the fond hope that something could be done, some way could be found to rekindle a participatory spirit and habits to go with it. After all, places could be found where the chapel was still full on Sunday, so why not here again? I will return to this dilemma, this reality, again.

One of the great traditions of the office of the dean started with Powers and has continued right up to the present. A dean's discretionary fund, now known as the Dean's Benevolence Fund, has allowed the dean to assist students with a wide range of emergency needs. Each of us has had the ability and the joyous experience of making it possible for students to stay in school who would otherwise have had to drop out. Sometimes books could be made available when they simply could not be afforded. A trip home for the funeral of a parent or grandparent even qualified for the fund to be opened. As far as I know most of the money during the McCombe and Phillips years came from rental to graduate students of rooms over the double garage of the dean's residence. The university provided the heat, lights, and water and ignored the potential income, so it could be deposited in the fund. I do not know if this practice was used under Noble. Other funding came from students who payed back the money, sometimes many years after having benefited from a grant or loan. Sometimes an unexpected gift came from out of nowhere, as it were! Jack continued the fund throughout his deanship, as I did during mine. I do not know about the other deans. I had to begin to pay bills for such things as tuition, travel, books, reading glasses, and even food directly and to discontinue giving cash or checks directly to students. Not hard to read the why of this practice! After the sale of the dean's residence in 1995, the fund has been kept up by annual deposits from the university as arranged by the chancellor.

The next chapter is a more focused treatment of the times during which Jack served and the built-in difficulties with which he had to deal. Following that chapter is my own on the McCombe-Eggers controversy.

46. McCombe in Trying Times

THE DESCRIPTION in chapter 40 of Noble's final months, and in chapters 42–44 of the subsequent appointment and tenure of John McCombe as Noble's replacement were put together by Don Wright from several available documents. The primary source was a paper written by a graduate student (with staff help) (see chapters 42, 43, and 44) that was considered for publication but was never published. Several copies are in the archives. Wright also relied on other primary sources, notably the annual reports submitted to the SU administration by staff members, including McCombe, over several years. While he was on the chapel staff Darrell Fasching appears to have had primary responsibility for the annual reports. These reports too reside in Syracuse University's archives, though not in any particular order.

Wright's chapters constitute a very good summary of the third deanship of Hendricks Chapel. However, the availability of considerable additional material not accessible by Wright, together with the hindsight provided by the additional passage of time, has prompted me to attempt a further description of McCombe's tenure through the 1970s and 1980s in the context of the cultural changes of that era and their impact on the Syracuse University environment. I have based this account not only on the archival materials, but on personal memory, limited personal contacts with McCombe, and interviews I conducted with chaplains and others who were here during those years. The SU Archives contain a great deal of material from the McCombe years: the dean and his staff did not skimp on the volume of materials sent to the archives, and those papers were supplemented by several file boxes of materials concerning that period sent to the archives from the chapel files while I was dean.

Long before his death I had promised Don Wright that I would complete the history project he had started. To prepare for this task, I wrote to McCombe asking that he draft his own account of his years of service as dean of Hendricks Chapel. Jack said he was interested in doing so and would put it in his plans sometime soon. Sadly, Jack died too early in his senior years, and when I contacted his widow, Dory, to see if he had indeed written about his deanship, no such manuscript was found, despite diligent searches by Dory before her death and by the McCombes' children.

Jack, as I shall call McCombe in these pages, came to Syracuse University as the third dean of Hendricks Chapel at a difficult time—a time when the conflicts and unrest of the wider world were impinging on, and changing, the once-protected world of Syracuse University. Jack arrived with the cards stacked against him, yet he worked tirelessly to overcome the difficulties confronting him.

. . .

THE FIRST DIFFICULTY facing McCombe had been in the making for years: the unqualified success of the first two deans. Neither Powers nor Noble (even given Charlie's dispute with Tolley) ever had any serious conflicts with the university administration over either their ministries or their management of the chapel. Added to this span of thirty-seven years of virtually unqualified success was the difficulty anyone would have faced in succeeding Noble. Charlie was not only a hero and a legend at SU, even before he reached retirement, but also a personality loved and, yes, adored throughout the area. The sheer strength of his personality made him unequaled as a leader. People did not have to be coaxed to follow his lead; doing so was natural. In fact, it was almost impossible not to follow him in either his work or his leisure. The way Chancellor Tolley extended Noble's tenure is only one indication of his worth; Syracuse University and its people did not want to lose the services of this remarkable clergyman. Noble was a hard act to follow; any successor to such a figure will be hampered by too many built-in expectations.

A second difficulty facing McCombe was the change then occurring in the religious habits of Americans, including the habits of those individuals coming to college campuses. Even as early as the closing years of Powers's deanship, in the mid-forties, the intensity of student involvement in Hendricks Chapel committees and projects had begun to decline. Noble contended with this problem increasingly throughout his deanship, although it did not become a public issue until his final years. Even when Charlie retired, the image in the community, including the SU community, was that on Sunday the chapel was full. It is not possible to overstate the concern McCombe and others at SU felt over the falling away of student, staff, and faculty participation in organized, traditional religious activity, including worship attendance—or the energy and determination they put into combating it. The image of a thriving chapel with a full Sunday service was one that Chancellor Emeritus Tolley never gave up. Just over a year before his death, he wrote me a note after attending chapel, telling me the dean should again become the preacher at the chapel, that we should again have music of the Poister excellence, and that if we did all these things right we would again have the fullest chapel in the land. He also admitted he could not stop playing chancellor, at least where the chapel was concerned. Until his last years in office, Chancellor Eggers likewise did not find himself able to abandon his conviction that if we only did it right—if we just had great enough preaching, commanding enough music, and the right approach to advertising—we would again have a full chapel. Yet the times were against us.

As I reflect on McCombe's years I am increasingly convinced that many people blamed him for this problem, seeing him as failing to maintain the patterns of religious participation known to the campus before his time. This feeling was still current, if diminishing, when I became the dean in 1981, a testimony to the human resistance to change. To illustrate this resistance and show how slowly images shift on such matters, I can testify that even when I retired in 1999, many important persons on SU's campus continued to assume that the dean was still the ministerial head of the Protestant community and still preached on Sundays to a chapel almost, if not completely, full.

McCombe himself struggled with the realization that he was expected to maintain a chapel persona that had not been a reality even for Noble. Charlie, on several occasions, remarked to me that if it were not for the Supremacy Trophy, the chapel would appear as empty as it appeared full because of the trophy. Charlie came to the realization that it was very hard to preach to a group of students who were in chapel on Sunday morning for reasons other than either worship or to hear a sermon. Of course, this is not to say that there were not many students who still came for those purposes—but Charlie knew full well that they would not fill the place.

It is my perception that the religious difficulties that developed between Jack and Eggers were in large part based upon Eggers's belief that if Jack just knew how to appeal to the students of that day, the chapel would be, if not full, at least a large, bustling congregation. My own view, however, is that in the 1970s and 1980s, no dean, however charismatic, and no course of action could have revived the pattern of participation characterizing the first third or more of the chapel's history.

The third difficulty confronting Jack was what we categorically refer to as student unrest. By the late 1960s, well before he took office, student activism was already upsetting American institutions and disrupting their established ways of doing things. From the early 1960s antiestablishment rhetoric and behavior were making their mark on the United States. The opt-out attitude, the Beatniks, the hippy movement, and certainly the Vietnam War demonstrations were maturing before Jack ever became dean of the chapel. When Jack, seeking to calm rising emotions and channel student passions, encouraged SU students to center their demonstration efforts in Hendricks Chapel, no one could have predicted the havoc their antiestablishment behavior would wreak on the chapel's image.

In 1970, as newspapers and magazines spread images of striking students at Hendricks Chapel, people became very upset. Well after I became dean there were people telling me they would never again give money to Hendricks Chapel after seeing that "the university" allowed beer in the chapel and allowed people to swear, drape their feet over the pews, and even sleep in the sanctuary. Such intense feelings died only slowly. Hindsight is a helpful thing, for soon most of the administrators who had to deal with the demonstrators—and with the police—came to realize that the fact that McCombe allowed the students to use the chapel as the "headquarters" of the uprising may well have been a key factor in preventing the demonstrations from exploding into violence. "Jack was right," Mel Eggers told me much later, "in giving the students a neutral base of operation." Nevertheless, the chapel image paid a heavy price for its role, both within and outside of SU, and Jack was strongly criticized by many for his generosity with the chapel facility.

Institutions almost always react to given situations in terms of perceived self-interest. Charlie Noble had discovered this when Tolley reacted harshly when Charlie joined with the chaplains in support of the unionization efforts of the Physical Plant workers. Even so, Charlie did not pay the heavy price for his action that Jack paid in 1970—in terms of lost support, lost respect, and a loss of overall goodwill. Moreover, Tolley, like Eggers, took a different view from a distance. The "Iron Chancellor" told me the greatest regret of his administration was his conflict with Charlie over that issue. "Charlie was right in supporting the workers," Tolley told me on more than one occasion.

The necessity of change in the chapel was the fourth reality that Jack confronted as he undertook his deanship. That the evolving changes in cultural and student life made it impossible to ever replicate the deanships of Powers and Noble seems obvious today, but in the late 1960s and early 1970s, resistance to change and experimentation was strong. At the time, it was easy to view Jack's experimentation, described so well by Don Wright, as a departure from success rather than a search for ways to serve a new and different generation of students, staff, and faculty. It even got Jack into trouble with the facilities-planning folks when he began to discuss changing the interior of the chapel-seating plan.

There were other realities confronting Jack's administration that I will mention in passing. Chapel House, which had its roots with the first annex (detailed elsewhere) arrangement for more room for chapel programs and which was later called Community House, was both a budgetary and an administrative bomb. During the 1970s its operation, mostly by design, became very freewheeling and as a result more and more difficult for the chapel to administer. When, late in his administration, Jack let the former fraternity house go back to the administration for sale to another fraternity there were unfortunate political as well as budget issues for which Jack received criticism. By then, however, there was an administrative circle closing in on Jack based on issues other than any direct religious considerations.

Denominational funding of campus ministry and trends for religious organizations to tend more to their own internal matters both had, from the standpoint of traditional SU practices, a negative impact on our campus, including Jack's deanship. Interdenominational and interfaith cooperation faltered during much of this period, even when funding was available. Although the Roman Catholic and Jewish ministries on campus maintained their good relationships with the chapel and each other, Donald Wright has noted that American Baptist money was withdrawn from Chaplain Norm Keim, prompting him to turn to other work, especially his Film Forum, to remain at SU. Jack, Father Charles, and Rabbi Elefant continued to work together cordially but for several years the United Methodist Church failed to provide any money to support its chaplaincy. This lack resulted in a layperson, Jean Baum, becoming a part-time representative and Jack himself picking up what was always an unofficial United Methodist representation. The thin ranks of

denominational chaplains, combined with a continuing decline in student participation, prompted Jack to experiment with part-time specialty chaplaincies—but
this effort backfired, getting him in trouble with several administrators.

Of considerable importance was a shift in reporting that took place during the
first half of Jack's deanship. Just what prompted it I am not sure, but Mel Eggers,
shortly after Chancellor Corbally's brief tenure, shifted the line of administrative
responsibility for the chapel to Mel Mounts, vice president for student affairs. This
move closed off a main channel for direct communication about the chapel to the
chancellor and consequently to the the SU community as a whole. This was aggra-
vated by considerable differences between McCombe and Mounts in terms of personality and administrative style. Communication between them deteriorated,
becoming sparse and mostly contentious, as the letters in the files of each amply
demonstrate. This and other aspects of Jack's dealings with the central administration were often strained and sometimes produced ill will. By the end of Jack's first
decade, for example relations with both the Physical Plant and Facilities Planning
were very strained. Jack reports that he had to fight for everything he needed for
his residence (at 315 Berkeley Drive) and had equal trouble in getting routine
maintenance at the chapel, including adequate custodial service. The strain was felt
on both sides of each relationship, and during the interim before I took office as
the fourth dean the committee appointed to administer the chapel, chaired by Jim
Wiggins, did a great deal to clean the slate.

Corbally and Eggers (and Graham) were the only chancellors before Shaw
who were not clergy, although Eggers was known as an active churchman. The
consequently lower degree of interest at the top in the operation of the chapel was
a huge change from conditions under Tolley, who never missed attending Sunday
services in the chapel when he was in town. Nevertheless, this somewhat lower
level of interest in the chapel, its personnel, and its overall operation should not be
taken as lack of support. Both Corbally and Eggers demonstrated keen interest and
often participated in chapel-generated programs, as did Shaw after them. For the
most part the relationships between Jack and the two chancellors under whom he
served were cordial and even very friendly. So, the changed nature of interest at the
level of chancellor, while worth noting, was essentially a minor development. I
have found its importance often overstated by members of the clergy.

The last of the issues I will mention concerns Jack's style of religious practice.
It was no more widely different from his predecessor's than Noble's was from
Powers's, but it was a style not identified with the traditional approach characteristic of the chapel's previous history. As Don Wright has so clearly written, the style
of religious practice before McCombe was well within the liberal Protestant mainstream, characterized by general piety. Even though Jack shared the same basic liberal theology, he was more inclined to use traditional liturgy. A good example was
the use of the Apostles' Creed that Mel Eggers found himself unable to live with as

part of Hendricks Chapel services. In light of the cultural drift already noted, this style resulted in fewer and fewer members of the university's staff, faculty, and administration coming to the chapel for their experience of worship. By the same token it began to draw to the chapel those students and others who tended to be comfortable with a more liturgical approach. It was for this reason and I think also the fact that Paul Bosch (Lutheran clergy) and then Darrell Fasching (Roman Catholic layman), who were both very liturgy oriented, became during the last portion of Jack's deanship the staff persons most centrally involved in planning the worship services. The Lutheran chaplain on campus, Paul Bosch, sometimes doubled as a staff person, even substituting for Jack as chief administrator of the chapel during some of Jack's longer absences.

While the difficulties described here prevented a smooth and uniformly peaceful tenure for Jack, they did not make life impossible for him, nor did they result in an unhappy or unproductive deanship. Although it was a troubled time in the history of both the chapel and the university, Jack's service at Hendricks Chapel was in no way a failure. Moreover, I know from personal visits with both McCombe and Eggers that each in retrospect thought he had responded poorly to some of the issues that came to a head in 1979 and that both felt very good about their relationship once the issues were settled. Later I will quote Eggers's tribute to Jack, given just before the McCombes moved to Florida.

So, though by no means a failure, Jack's deanship was set in times of struggle and change in the life of both the chapel and the university. He was faced with cultural and religious changes that produced immense changes in religious participation. At the same time he was faced with expectations that the life of the chapel should go forward with little noticeble change. My own belief is that had not the structual changes of 1979 and 1980 taken place with a new definition of the role of the dean and the chapel, the fourth deanship would have been faced with equally difficult times.

47. The Eggers-McCombe Conflict

THE 1979 CONFLICT that resulted in the termination of the McCombe deanship is known by most as a direct conflict between the dean and the chancellor. Indeed, this issue must receive special attention in this book both to set the record straight especially for those individuals who believe it was a personal conflict and to give a much broader view of events and issues. The archival material is wealthy in resources dealing with the matter, especially the perspectives that reached the campus and local newspapers. Of greatest value, however, is the corre-

spondence, now in the archives, from both the chapel and many university administrators. Also of significant value to me were interviews and conversations with
persons who were serving on the Chapel Board before, during, and after the public conflict, many centrally positioned SU administrators, Hendricks Chapel staff
and chaplains, and both Eggers and McCombe (both have now died).

After the story broke about Eggers's comments to McCombe in a memo from
Eggers dated September 9, 1979, most of the news focused on the conflict as a
matter of religious practice, even theological in nature. Indeed, that conflict did
exist between them, but this detail was not the key to understanding what had
been developing for two, even three, years in the relationship between McCombe
and several members of the central administration. Eggers told both McCombe
and me that he had made a mistake in writing that memo, of even entering that
topic into discussion between them. "I was wrong in doing that," Mel told me
more than once. Even so, here is the Eggers memo in question:

> I thought your sermon was fine and the choir was splendid. The rest of the service
> needs attention.
>
> The apostle's creed does not belong in an ecumenical service. Anyway, I
> doubt that anyone in the chapel, including you, could say it honestly. I certainly
> could not. There probably is no creed on which there could be agreement so I
> suggest leaving that segment out altogether.
>
> The prayers were much too long. It is not necessary to identify everyone who
> could benefit from God's grace.*

This memo goes on with a few more suggestions, less weighty, and then ends with
Mel's comment that the service was, overall, too conservative and traditional for
an ecumenical service in the Hendricks Chapel of that day. Mel indicated to me
that he saw himself writing as a lay member of the "congregation" with some suggestions and that his relationship with Jack was such that that would be the spirit in
which Jack would read it. This situation is a prime example of how difficult it is for
the top administrator to communicate personal and institutionally unofficial concern and suggestions in written form. A conversation with Jack, I believe, would
never have reached the fever pitch of reaction that followed. Owing to the special
circumstances associated with rank in an institution, this exchange simply could
not be viewed by Jack as a normal layman-to-clergyman conversation containing
mere suggestions. Even so, the opinion that Eggers was attempting to curtail freedom of the pulpit, as perhaps feared by McCombe and as was charged by some, I
have come not to share.

If Mel and Mildred Eggers were still living I might not have quoted the memo

---

*McCombe 1975–81 folder, box 010324, SU Archives.

here, but I believe it important now for the record. Mildred never attended a chapel worship service again while Jack was the dean, and she remained pained for many years about his deanship and this specific conflict.

Don Wright wrote about a memo from Tolley to Noble that Tolley sent on February 15, 1959. This Tolley memo is similar in critical analysis concerning what had happened in a Sunday service but much more directive in word and tone than was Eggers's. Noble's response four days later: "Dear Bill: I have your directive of February 15 and shall take appropriate action. As ever, Charlie."* If Jack's other university relationships had not already become a problem, I think Jack would have had a similar response for Eggers.

In the paragraphs below we will see that Eggers later made his position on this matter public and stated his "real" reasons for requesting Jack's resignation. The conflict, in my view, really resulted from McCombe's concerted efforts, over several semesters, to bring a more powerful and more comprehensive campus presence and ministry from Hendricks Chapel to everyone at SU. What follows is an attempt to deal as fairly as I can with these issues, some aspects of which have already been discussed.

That the issue of Jack's problems as dean predates this September memo is clear from reading the copies of letters contained in archival files. Jack had begun to search for other employment opportunities the year before. He knew things were coming to a head. Eggers, for his part, had started writing to United Methodist officers in the summer of 1979 asking for information about how the appointment process in the church would work for a clergyman serving in a role as a university employee. The wheels were spinning on both sides as to how to bring Jack's deanship to a peaceful close. Let's look at some of the reasons this was the case.

There is an old saying that when there is trouble in the administrative ranks there is probably a budget issue at the bottom. Indeed, since 1976 the chapel had been running serious budget deficits. Two reasons are easy to document; there were others but to my knowledge none that even suggests the possibility of malfeasance. In fact, throughout all of the troubles not one person even suggested any problem with Jack's honesty or integrity. He was well known as richly blessed with both.

Community House had, by the mid-1970s, become an administrative nightmare. So many (too many) segments of the university used it and saw themselves as "owners," with the right to use it as they pleased. Custodial service to the building had become weak, often nonexistent. At one point a memo went out telling all who had offices in the building or who had meetings there that they would have to clean up, even take trash to the Dumpster, because no money was available for cus-

*Contained in box 001533, SU Archives.

todial care. For a period of three years the expense of operating Community House matched almost exactly the chapel's budget deficit, usually around twenty-five thousand dollars each year. But that deficit would have been much greater had there not also been some income (largely from rented space) associated with the Community House operation.

We have already discussed Jack's venture into multiple part-time chaplaincies. He had done so on the basis of two assumptions, neither of which proved to work out in the overall experience. By way of review, these positions were created so the chapel could better serve several of the campus's minority populations, specifically women, internationals, and African Americans. By the mid-1970s Jack's intense search for a new focus—indeed a new identity—for Hendricks Chapel was the motivating factor in much chapelwide thinking, dreaming, and then experimentation. This experiment was to have paid for itself by drawing in outside grant money, funding that Jack was sure such innovative university chapel programming, ministry, and service would bring to his doorstep. After a year of trial and much grant writing, however, no outside help had materialized. The experiment had failed, not only from a budgetary perspective but also in terms of morale: the elimination of the part-time positions before their incumbents really had a chance for a good start resulted in some very unhappy people.

Mel Mounts, the student affairs vice president responsible for administrative oversight of the chapel, was put in the awkward position of having to answer for experimentation that he obviously had not favored from the start. His relationship with Jack had been deteriorating for several semesters; this latest crisis plunged it from the level of friction to serious and openly expressed disagreement. It was during this period that Mounts assigned an associate, Peter Baigent, to work hand in hand with Jack, on a weekly basis if necessary, to control the budget. Peter continued working with me into the first months of my deanship to help me understand the budget, which by then had returned to relative health and was once again directly under the office of the chancellor. But I get ahead of the story.

The elimination of the part-time chaplaincies opened the way for the appointment of John Jones, who had been serving as one of the three half-time chaplains, as a full-time chaplain. His duties are dealt with elsewhere. Mounts and McCombe had a major conflict, resolved but I dare say not forgotten by either, over this appointment. Mounts contended that it had not been approved from either a budget or a hiring perspective. The record of communication in this matter is reported only in Jack's notes as having been resolved verbally in a meeting between the two of them. I found no other documentation on that particular point. McCombe carried the day with the strong claim to Mounts that verbal approval had been given by Mounts for hiring Jones full-time. A disgruntled Mounts agreed to let the appointment stand, but stated that if the position went beyond a second year it would have to be filled through an official national search process. To me the record indicates that no high-ranking SU administrator expected McCombe to be in office for another two years.

Here, to illustate this expectation, I jump ahead. Eggers later revealed some of his reaons for seeking Jack's resignation. The following letter from Eggers, dated November 20, 1979, is typical of his response to the scores of letters he received on this matter. Mel told me he responded to every letter he received on the conflict.

> I am pleased to know of your continued interest in Hendricks Chapel, but it is clear that you have received a garbled version of what I said or did.
>
> While I did request that Dean McCombe resign as dean, I did not make that request as an alternative to changing the Protestant worship service. There will always be a Protestant worship service and it will be what the Protestant minister makes it.
>
> My action with respect to Dean McCombe was based on a judgment of his skills and performance as an administrator. The standards by which a dean is judged are different from those by which a minister (or professor) is judged.
>
> I also believe the chapel can contribute much more to the welfare of the students, faculty, staff of the university, and the general community than is now the case. A committee is examining the role of the chapel. I do not wish to substitute "Monday Munchies" or anything else for traditional denominational worship services, nor do I question Dean McCombe's pastoral ministry.
>
> You asked that I reconsider what you called my "rash" decision. I will; and in the same spirit, I ask you to reconsider your letter.*

Returning to the budget, with Jones now full-time and with Community House in its last year, the budget overrun continued into the next year. In all fairness, the overrun also reflected the severe university-wide budget reduction of 1976–77, in which the expenditures of the chapel were not cut nearly as much as the budget was cut. This issue was yet another significant reason for Mounts's displeasure with Jack.

Starting in the 1975–76 academic year, Fasching and McCombe, others on the chapel staff, and most of the chaplains initiated some intense programs on ethics. The considerations were quite technical, as a very fine paper prepared by Fasching demonstrated. Many faculty were involved, and the issues being addressed had a decidedly international flavor. Several special guest speakers were brought to the campus. Such programming was popular across the nation in the aftermath of the Vietnam War and the intense student activism that arose from it.

Mounts thought the program too expensive and did not believe it was appropriate for the chapel to generate and oversee such an effort. He expressly referred to it as more of a faculty matter, not a subject for the chapel to host. As a result he

*Melvin Eggers Records, Hendricks Chapel, SU Archives, box 012875.

specifically instructed Fasching and McCombe to discontinue such programming at the chapel and focus only on strictly religious practice—that is, worship services and pastoral-type service to the campus. Here, in my estimation, Mounts took a more seriously restrictive administrative action than any taken by Eggers, especially considering that Eggers's memo had only suggested, rather than ordered, some changes to be made. This action by Mounts is the only instance I have found in the entire history of the chapel in which the university administration gave the chapel specific instructions to modify programming that had always been part of the stated purpose of the chapel and part of the responsibility of the dean.

I submit that such programming was distasteful to Mounts not simply because of budget issues but because he was just plain unhappy with Jack. I believe sometime during that year the administration, chiefly Mounts and Eggers but with others in agreement, had decided that McCombe was to be squeezed enough to sting him into resigning. Just think, if one of the positions for which McCombe applied had come through before September 1979 the conflict would have been avoided and the separation would have been accomplished with fine words of lavish praise! Even as it was there was much very sincere praise of McCombe by Eggers as well as others during the leave-taking.

There is one additional issue, a very sensitive one, still to be taken into account. During the 1978–79 academic year, some unrest, if not dissatisfaction with McCombe's deanship, had surfaced among the chaplains. Even some who had served on Jack's staff in the 1970s were unhappy. As far as I can tell the unhappiness concerned Jack's administration and his increasing absences from the chapel and did not indicate any personal dislike for Jack. I will mention three examples.

In an interview with one of the chaplains I was told that by this time most of the chaplains had lost respect for Jack and the way things were going. That year, for example, there were almost no meetings of the boards and committees of the chapel and little in the way of relationships between staff and chaplains. Everyone was in agreement that the situation was serious and troubling to all.*

In the correspondence files there is more evidence that the wagons were circling on the dean. Letters indicate that Jack learned that one of the chaplains had gone to Mounts with word that there was trouble in chapel land and that it was time for a move. Jack found out about this "behind the back" report and wrote to Eggers a very strong letter objecting to such an unethical action on the part of the

---

*Two of the graduate students living in rooms at the dean's residence carried over as renters after we were aboard. They confirmed beyond any doubt in my mind that serious tension filled the McCombe air during Jack's last two years at the chapel. In fact, Jack almost died from a bleeding ulcer the last year of his deanship. It was his first and as far as I know last such health problem while dean, but it was very serious. Only a few on the campus ever learned of it; it was several years before I found correspondence related to the illness and his recovery. Jack and I never discussed it.

chaplain in question. In my reading of the material it would appear that the chaplain in question was representing more of the chapel family than just himself. Even so, I agree with Jack; they owed him such a conversation first.

Finally, there was an unhappy group of former chapel staff members. One of the discontinued half-time chaplains was considerably upset and made those feelings known. Another former staff member who had had central chapel administrative responsibility vowed, in a conversation with me, never to give money or support to the chapel again. Over the hiring of Jones and the way the cuts were made in the half-time chaplains the equal opportunity employment office of the university wrote of their unhappiness. The short and the long of it is that the chapel family itself was divided and, in the end, part of the circling of the wagons.

As I have indicated before, Jack was not unaware that all of this activity was happening. To his great credit, after the shock and the pain of the request Eggers made for his resignation began to wear off Jack conducted himself with considerable grace and dignity. I am sure he was greatly relieved that the pressure was off and a positive change in life lay just ahead.

Eggers officially asked for Jack's resignation in November. The press gave a great deal of attention (ink) to the matter, and always the religious issues alone were considered to be involved in the administration's decision making. Only gradually, and for a limited number of people, would this picture change.

Even though Jack's stated reasons for his intention to resign were based on the religious restrictions he believed Eggers was asking for, he was fully informed, beginning in mid-September, of the whole range of concerns. Jack first voiced his intention to resign in a meeting with United Methodist bishop Joseph Yeakel of the central New York area of that church. Yeakel was not only McCombe's ecclesiastical leader in his home church, but he was also on the Board of Trustees of SU. Jack wanted him to be fully informed of his side of the issue within both of Yeakel's roles.*

At the risk of overdoing this particular aspect of the history of our chapel I will comment here on what I consider some of the most interesting aspects of McCombe's last months as dean of Hendricks Chapel. The events seem to me to be a positive ending to the controversy on the part of both Eggers and McCombe.

McCombe encouraged Professor Thomas Green, a longtime School of Education faculty member, often a board and committee worker for the chapel, and a

---

*In the fall semester of 2001 a graduate student by the name of Allison Cuda wrote a paper for Professor Joan Burstyn. It is on file in the archives in a box yet to be numbered as this book is being published. It is an excellent paper and treats the entire matter in a fair and in my view very accurate manner. It is also extremely well documented. Anyone interested in reading more on the various issues involved would do well to seek out the document as well as the account by John Robert Greene in his book *Syracuse University: The Eggers Years,* published by Syracuse University Press in 1998.

member of the Wiggins committee making recommendations to Eggers on the future directions for the chapel, to make a statement in the service of worship in Hendricks Chapel on November 11, 1979. Green had written an insightful letter to Eggers in the infancy of the controversy. Green's wisdom and practical insights are something of a campus legend at SU. The chief reason for and need for Green's statement had to do with the widespread and very wild rumors circulating on campus and in the community. Many of them had to do with the fear that the administration of SU intended to either close the chapel for good or discontinue the Protestant services of worship. In a joking manner Eggers once told me that in the heat of the conflict it once crossed his mind that the chapel could be turned into the campus computer center and thus never risk such a storm again. Eggers said it took only a minute for him to permanently discard that idea! He was, as he related to me, too fond of the chapel to even consider such a move.

Green's statement on that November Sunday is in keeping with his reputation and his skill.* He clearly stated the purpose of the Wiggins committee (known as such only because Professor James B. Wiggins was its chair) in the following part of his address: "to help formulate policies for Hendricks Chapel and provide a plan to provide for a clear presence of Hendricks Chapel in the structure of University administration." A bit later he said, "It is well understood by the Chancellor, as it must be understood by the entire community, that the principle of freedom of the pulpit will remain inviolate in Hendricks Chapel, and that the Protestant expression of the faith will continue to be pronounced in preaching and in worship."

McCombe at this point issued a statement printed in the *Syracuse Herald-Journal* that same day. It was to be the first of many actions by Jack to bring a more positive face to the controversy. Jack endorsed the statement by Green and the committee as being an excellent development and was quoted as saying, "I'm very pleased with their general perspective. I look forward to the increased effectiveness of Hendricks Chapel and its services." Jack made many efforts to defuse the rumor mill as well as to bring healing to the community. When a student or students supporting McCombe wrote on the outside of the big tall doors on the east of the main chapel, "Eggers Need Not Enter," McCombe in a public statement and in a service of worship indicated that Eggers along with all others were welcome to enter at any time and that the sentiment expressed by the graffiti was morally wrong.

Of course, these efforts did not lift rumor from the mix of things going on at the time, but they did, especially for everyone who knew Green, make it clear that the future of the chapel at SU was secure and that the Wiggins committee would not flag in its attention to duty.[†]

*The statement is contained in the Eggers Records, Hendricks box 012875.

[†]A fuller report on the committee's work appears a bit later, including chapter 48, written by Wiggins himself.

McCombe played a role, a rather remarkable and in the end I believe a constructive role, in seeing to it that Hendricks Chapel as it had become known on the campus would continue. After declaring that he would resign, McCombe then qualified his intention. He announced that he would not resign until the chancellor and the university gave assurance that the future of the chapel in the life of the university was secure. This news, if one does not wish to call it some sort of power play, was carried in the press and was surely one of the reasons for Professor Green's statement in the service of worship. In addition to the Green statement on behalf of the committee studying the role of the chapel and the deanship, the chancellor himself assured McCombe and the community that the chapel would continue with his enthusiastic endorsement. Most rumors died as a result, at least the ones speculating that McCombe was being asked to resign to pave the way for the university to close the chapel for good.

McCombe's refusal to resign until the assurance was given accomplished, I believe, two very important things. First and foremost, it assured the community that the existence of the chapel was not in danger. Although it may have moved the chancellor and the committee appointed by him to make this public statement earlier and in ways not planned, I do not for a moment think, given my knowledge of Eggers and the members of the committee, that the future of the chapel at SU was ever in any danger. Now, after studying the archival material on the various aspects of the controversy and seeing the circle of pressure being brought to bear on McCombe over several semesters, I am absolutely certain events bringing McCombe's deanship to a close had within them nothing but intentions to enhance and clarify the role of the campus chapel. Jack had simply lost the support of too many of the SU administrators and at least some of the chaplains.

A second accomplishment of considerable importance to both McCombe and the many who were supporting him and who were in one way or another unhappy about the controversy was the dignity it restored to McCombe himself. He took a strong, principled stand, and made it a powerful stand. Essentially, he said to the community at large as well as the primary actors in the drama that he, McCombe, could be sacrificed but that the chapel in the life of the university could not! It was a form of putting oneself on the line that I believe was part of the healing needed on campus, especially in the relationships of the primary persons involved.

There were efforts on the part of many students, faculty members, and administrators to get Eggers to reverse his request for Jack's resignation. Hundreds of letters and phone calls were received, and the record shows that Eggers answered every letter with a calm, rational statement of his position on the need for a change of deans. (One such answer is quoted earlier in this chapter.) There were also a few letters to Eggers endorsing his action, sometimes with regret about how the events unfolded. The record shows that both Eggers and McCombe after the initial period of "more heat than light" dealt with the aftermath of the whole affair calmly, with a

Jack McCombe, third dean of Hendricks Chapel, served from 1967 to 1980. His innovative responses to changing times arose from his belief that "to stay alive and vital the Chapel must experiment." Photograph by Steve Sartori of oil portrait. Courtesy of Syracuse University Art Collection.

sense of dignity and with concern for the large issues at stake. I think this fact is what made it possible for the two of them to patch things up and to again be good friends.

In the end Jack did a good job of communicating to his supporters that he and Dory were pleased, indeed happy, with the resolution of the controversy. Eggers too seemed content with how the endgame went. In my early conversations with him about this unfortunate bit of history, he always left me with two impressions: first, that he and Jack were friends and things were going well, and second, that this whole matter was settled and that despite its turmoil some good things had happened as a result.

On April 10, 1980, Eggers publicly announced the appointment of Jack to his new position as the regional director of development and alumni relations to be based in Florida. "Dean McCombe is a man of ability and great personal integrity," Eggers stated, "who is dedicated to Syracuse University. It is an important assignment that Dean McCombe is undertaking for Syracuse."* McCombe responded, "I look forward to this new opportunity. Syracuse University has been a most important part of my life since my undergraduate days. It will be rewarding to maintain and strengthen the ties between the university and our alumni and other friends in the South."

My own personal visits with Jack, twice in Florida and several times when he visited Syracuse, demonstrated his lack of any lingering anger, his respect and friendship for and with Eggers, his love of life and of SU, and his gratitude for having served as the third dean of Hendricks Chapel. I doubt the resolution of the controversy could have ended on any higher note for either of the principals than it did.

The same summer Jack and Dory departed for Florida, Mel Mounts also left SU—he for good. What a bit of irony!

48. A Time of Transition, July 1980–April 1981

JAMES B. WIGGINS

THE BACKGROUND for these months was set on November 2, 1979, when then chancellor Melvin Eggers made these remarks to the Board of Trustees: "At Syracuse University we remain proud and respectful to our chapel history and tradition. We will continue to support, encourage, and value denominational worship with all the resources that we have to bring to bear and also we will try with renewed dedication, and as a special priority, to reach those who are a part of our community but who do not have a commitment to a particular faith and who are still searching."†

A week later to demonstrate the commitment made, Chancellor Eggers announced the appointment of a blue-ribbon advisory committee on Hendricks Chapel charged to make recommendations for the future of the chapel at Syracuse University. I was the chairman of the committee that included eleven other members.‡ With the fiftieth anniversary of the chapel on campus looming in 1980, it

---

*For this and other materials related, see Eggers Records, box 012875.

†Minutes of Board of Trustees, November 2, 1979.

‡Lois Black, director of the Office of Affirmative Action; Burton Blatt, dean of the School of Education; Dale Cohen, undergraduate student; Paul Eickmann, associate in Academic Affairs; Frank Funk, dean of University College; Thomas Green, professor of education; the Reverend Vernon Lee, United Methodist clergyman and university trustee; Michael Mooney, graduate student; Professor Michael Sawyer, vice chancellor; Professor Constance Timberlake, College for Human Development;

was a propitious time to have a serious examination of its role on campus. And a conflict between Dean John McCombe and Chancellor Eggers that had erupted in the early fall of 1979 had necessitated consideration of the question by a group with its own independence and clear charge.

Their blue-ribbon committee submitted its report on March 7, 1980, after ten meetings of the full committee and innumerable interviews and conversations with members of the campus community and investigations of the role of chapels on campuses of other independent universities around the country. Seven recommendations with extensive commentary on each were sent to Chancellor Eggers:

• Preceded by a proposed charter for Hendricks Chapel, the first recommendation was that the university's commitment to the work and importance of the chapel be publicly reaffirmed in its fiftieth anniversary year.

• As a manifestation of this commitment, the chapel should administratively be responsible directly to the chancellor.

• A new board of religious affairs should be created to advise the university on issues related to religion on campus.

• In what was the most dramatic change recommended, the dean of the chapel was no longer to serve as the Protestant chaplain to the university, as had previously been the case, but rather "will provide spiritual leadership for the total mission to the University and will be the chief administrative officer of the chapel program, facilities, and personnel. . . . The Dean will actively attend to creating the process and means for Hendricks Chapel to encourage religious inquiry, to voice the concerns of conscience and to be an agent of reconciliation through emphases on excellence and wholeness."

• In consultation with the New York State Council of Churches the university should appoint a Protestant chaplain, preferably a United Methodist in the tradition of the university, "who will be responsible for the Protestant Ecumenical worship service . . . and for the pastoral care of the worshipping communicants."

• Members of the Council of Chaplains, chaired by the dean of the chapel, would continue to be selected and recommended by their respective religious communities. These bodies should propose appointees, but the dean would have final voice before such appointments were final.

• As executive officer of the chapel, the dean should be responsible for the allocation of all resources of the chapel on the principle of the greatest benefit to all the programs of the chapel.

In the following weeks Chancellor Eggers accepted and endorsed the committee's recommendation. As a result, a future continuous with but also different from its past was set in motion for Hendricks Chapel.

---

and Mary Voll, undergraduate student. It was a diligent and committed group that reached complete consensus on the recommendations that emanated from it.

In late May 1980 Vice Chancellor Michael Sawyer invited me to come to his office. Earlier in the spring I had been chosen by the faculty of the Department of Religion and the dean of the College of Arts and Sciences to become the chairperson of the department, effective July 1. Sawyer informed me that Chancellor Eggers had delegated the administrative responsibility for Hendricks to him and that the chancellor and he were putting a search procedure in place to identify the next dean of Hendricks Chapel in accordance with a job description defined by the blue-ribbon committee's recommendations. That was excellent news, I thought. Since, however, Dean McCombe had departed Syracuse for another university assignment, there was nobody in place to be the acting dean of Hendricks until a new permanent appointment could be made. The purpose of the visit came into clearer focus. Dr. Sawyer asked me to become the acting dean.

This request confronted me with a dilemma. The Department of Religion has been a part of the College of Arts and Sciences at Syracuse University since 1895, marking it as one of the first such academic units in a university in the United States. When Hendricks Chapel opened in 1930, its purposes were for worship and promotion and development of religious life on campus. Its dean and the chaplains from various religious communities had clearly served a pastoral role in the subsequent decades. The Department of Religion, despite several requests over the years, had steadfastly insisted that chaplains would not be engaged to teach in the department. This position was taken on the grounds that there was a clear distinction between the academic study of religion that is the work of the department and the practice of religion that is the task of the chapel. The distinction is difficult enough to communicate under the best of circumstances, and the department wanted a clear line of demarcation. I had been among the most adamant about this point.

One does not, however, lightly refuse a request from the chancellor to perform a particular task. When I was absolutely assured that the redefinition of the position of dean of the chapel to be the administrator of the chapel was what was wanted and that I would concurrently be able to perform the duties of being the chairperson of the Religion Department, with considerable trepidation I accepted the appointment.

Beginning the process of changing the perception of the role of the dean both within the structure of the chapel and within the larger university was my challenge. And daunting it was. Few challenges were greater than the relationships with the already serving chaplains from various religious communities and traditions. They had functioned in many respects as independent agents with a very large degree of autonomy during the preceding decades. Now they were being asked to work in a much more collegial and community way.

I convened them on seven occasions, and the conversations began. Members of the Chaplains Council were assured they would be involved in the search for the

Sketch of James B. Wiggins, chair of Syracuse University's Department of Religion, served as interim dean of Hendricks Chapel for several months in 1980 and 1981. Courtesy of Syracuse University.

new dean of the chapel, and they began to hammer out the principles upon which the council would operate. In the subsequent twenty-five years it seems that an ever growing degree of cooperation and often collaboration has emerged among the various chaplains. Real interreligious work is demanding and challenging in many ways, regardless of the venue. A university chapel setting, however, is one of the most promising and auspicious sites within which to pursue such work just because of its setting in a larger institutional context of open inquiry and serious debate. One of the accomplishments of the year that included the chaplains was the beginning of the International Student Thanksgiving Service, largely promoted by Dr. T. E. Koshy, an evangelical Christian, who has devoted much of his distinguished chaplaincy to ministering to international students.

With the departure of Dean McCombe and no one appointed yet to the position of Protestant chaplain, one of the challenges was to provide for the weekly Sunday Protestant worship service without my coming to be regarded as the Protestant chaplain. This need presented both theoretical and practical challenges.

Some of the chaplains from other religious communities pressed the issue of why there should even be such a position and such services. Although to be funded through external monies, the position seemed to some to represent a kind of Protestant hegemony over the other chaplaincies and to place whoever would come to the position in a first-among-equals situation. The primary response was an appeal to the history of the university as having been founded by Protestant Methodists and of the chapel itself in which the three preceding deans had also been the university's Protestant chaplain. Honoring that history, concurrent with making the position dependent on external support rather than direct compensation from the university, was a challenge. When the first newly defined position holder was eventually appointed, he had a real task to establish the role of that position within the Chaplains Council.

At the weekly practical level guest preachers were engaged. The chapel organist and choir director did work far beyond the call of duty in helping plan and execute the Sunday services. The student members of the "congregation," both undergraduate and graduate, put their shoulders to the task. Somehow the work of Protestant ministry got done at a reasonably high quality level that year!

One of the steps made by Chancellor Eggers that year to underscore the changed role of the dean of the chapel was to invite me to the annual retreat for university administrators at the university's Minnowbrook Conference Center prior to the opening of the school year. Interaction with the other university administrators, many of whom I had known for years in the context of other mutual activities at the university, was gratifying. My presence evoked neither outward hostility nor negative response, and many were very cordial in their welcome.

Among the most vivid memories that year in connection with student groups had to do with People's Place, the convenience snack store in the basement of the chapel building, and with the Black Celestial Choral Ensemble (BCCE), a gospel music group. People's Place required regularizing the most minimal sound business practices such as inventory control, cash accountability, scheduling personnel assignments, and relations with the university's food service. Eventually, all was upgraded or institutionalized, and it has remained a great service center provided by the chapel to the campus ever since.

Working with the gospel choir was more contentious and complex. The Hendricks Chapel Choir has been a campus group widely recognized and celebrated dating back to the founding of the chapel. African American student participation in the regular chapel choir had never been extensive. When the celestial-singers group was created, student interest was high, particularly among African Americans. The leaders were aware of the status and prestige of the Hendricks Chapel Choir, and they wanted to achieve parallel status very quickly. For example, they wanted a different, distinct set of choir robes, and they wanted to go on tour, as was the practice of the traditional choir. Observing that Rome was not built in a day had little effect on ameliorating some of the emotions expressed by some members of the group. Discipline in accounting for expenses, in scheduling rehearsals at free times. and other practical skills took work and negotiations. Chaplain John Jones, an African American clergyman who had been appointed by Dean McCombe, proved to be a valuable ally in this work as he assumed much of the administrative responsibility for the affairs of this group. And eventually great progress was made, and that choir has won many friends and performed in many venues since its inception.

Numerous other programs and activities were conducted under the auspices of the chapel that year. Collectively they drew attention to the chapel and under-scored that it is a place open to all members of the SU community and that it exists to serve and challenge the community.

One of the most troublesome discoveries of the year was the great problems be-setting the physical plant of the chapel. So many things called out for attention that only a few could be addressed immediately. In large part owing to the very heavy traffic flow through the building, there was embarrassing filth and clutter all around. With the great cooperation of the janitorial service of the university, a thor-ough cleaning was rapidly accomplished, and a dependable, regular cleaning rou-tine was established. At least the surface appearance was significantly improved. But far more critical problems were identified. An inventory of needs was compiled with an estimated cost of five hundred thousand dollars. The list included replacement of some of the basic mechanical systems for the building and new lighting and sound systems for the sanctuary. This challenge was one of my bequests to the new dean.

Compared with the pace of many searches for appointees to academic positions, faculty and administrative, the search committee for the new dean of Hendricks Chapel moved expediently. Dr. Richard Phillips was selected by December 1980. With that selection secured, plans could take shape for the Jubilee Celebration of the fiftieth anniversary of the opening of Hendricks Chapel. Phillips was soon to be-come the fourth dean of Hendricks Chapel and continued the presence of a United Methodist clergyman in the position. Ruth Hall, wife of one of the professors in the Religion Department, was engaged to coordinate the planning of the events of the Jubilee. Having undertaken his duties on March 1, 1981, on Friday, April 10, 1981, Dr. Phillips was installed in the afternoon, followed by a gala banquet that evening.

Sunday, April 12, was Palm Sunday. "A Service of Thanksgiving and Hope" began at 10:30 A.M. and included three vocal choirs, a bell choir, a brass sextet, liturgical dance, congregational singing of the "Alleluia Chorus," and a sermon by Dean Phillips. In the afternoon the Hendricks Chapel Choir presented its annual spring concert, and the closing Jubilee Reception was held that evening.

The torch was officially passed. With confidence in the quality of leadership that Dr. Phillips would provide in achieving the vision of the role of Hendricks, it was an enormous relief to return to the task of chairing the Religion Department.

49. On Becoming the Fourth Dean of Hendricks Chapel

IN THE SPRING OF 1980 I came to Syracuse on a business trip. I was then the president and executive director of the American Youth Foundation (AYF) headquartered in St. Louis, Missouri. At that time I knew nothing of the problems that had developed regarding what we now call the Eggers-McCombe controversy. I had met Jack McCombe for short but pleasant visits during two different vacation trips to Syracuse but did not know that he was to depart Syracuse and that a good friend, Jim Wiggins, would serve as the interim dean of Hendricks Chapel. I had been teaching in the 1960s in the SU Department of Religion when Wiggins came on the faculty. As colleagues and friends we established a close family relationship. Our sons brought us together even more closely through mutual membership in an organization called Indian Guides.

I left Syracuse in the summer of 1966 after teaching a summer school course at the Chautauqua Institution in western New York. At that time Charlie Noble was the second dean of the chapel, and we, during my five years as a graduate student and fledgling faculty member at SU, had become close friends. It never entered my mind, even once, that I might someday be one of Charlie's successors. We corresponded a few times after I left Syracuse to become a faculty member at Baker University in Baldwin, Kansas. It was a sad day when I learned that Noble had died in the very infancy of his retirement. I continued at Baker for nine years before moving to St. Louis and joining the AYF in the summer of 1975.

That 1980 trip to Syracuse proved to be a life- and career-changing stop. I look back on it with both surprise and appreciation. While in Syracuse I learned of Chancellor Eggers's efforts through the Wiggins committee to reformulate the definition and operation of Hendricks Chapel. I knew Noble had advocated for such action on the part of the university and have since learned that McCombe did so on several occasions while he was dean. The description of the Wiggins committee work and the recommendations it was making to the chancellor filled my ears but not at that time with any deep understanding. Before departing I was asked if I would allow my name to be placed in nomination to become the fourth dean. My only response was that I would talk with Ethel about it and think it over and get back with an answer.

We had had five very good years in Syracuse from 1961 to 1966, but when we left to move to Kansas we did not envision ever moving back to the eastern part of the United States. We were midwesterners by background and in heart and saw ourselves there near both of our families. We were both born in the northwestern part of Missouri and between us had lived in Missouri, Nebraska, Colorado, and Kansas as well as our five years in Syracuse. Moving back to New York had never been on either our dream or our real agendas. It was not an easy decision.

Chancellor Eggers had indicated his intention of accepting most if not all of the recommendations being made by his committee on the chapel, and those recommendations did become the key to our final decision. The role of the chapel in the life of SU was not only to be continued but also to be strengthened in several ways. The role of the dean of Hendricks Chapel was to be separated from direct leadership of the Protestant worshiping community. This change would allow the dean to relate to all campus religious practices on an equal basis. The new dean was to participate more formally and more actively in the entire operation of the university. The chief symbol of the comprehensiveness of the role would be the direct relationship of the chapel deanship to the Office of the Chancellor and not to the Office of Student Affairs. Membership on all four of the central administrative committees of the university was to allow the dean a comprehensive participation and perspective on the workings of the academy and was to include an ethical and moral awareness, perhaps even a prophetic judgment when it was needed. Finally, as Eggers himself informed me, the dean was to function as the chief ombudsman (but not to carry that title) within the university. The anticipated changes at Hendricks Chapel made the job a very attractive package for my personal involvement.

Within a few days after returning to St. Louis we gave our "yes" to a candidacy. After all, five or so more years of Syracuse weather couldn't be that bad! In fact, part of our decision was that if we did move back to Syracuse we would enjoy and take every advantage of the weather, the beauty of central and upstate New York, the wonderful people of the university, Syracuse, and the area and that we would find ways to truly enjoy, if it were to develop, life in a place with such a bad winter reputation. Looking back on it I think we did fulfill rather well that promise to ourselves. As for the five years that developed into an eighteen-year career ending in retirement has suited us just fine, even if it was so unexpected.

Early in the fall of 1980 we were informed that I was to be one of four finalists brought to campus for an interview. The interview was to include the presentation of a short paper on the role of the chapel and the deanship and campus ministry in general. Many meetings, including with all the chaplains, the staff, a number of administrators and faculty members and students, all in addition to the selection committee, were carefully planned by the search committee. My interview visit was scheduled for midfall. All four of the candidates were interviewed within a two- or three-week period. We did not overlap, so I did not meet any of them at that time.

Probably the two most helpful things that happened to me as I prepared for the extended and intensive interview was the chance to meet with Bob Rankin and Merrimon Cuninggim. The latter was a former chief administrator of the Danforth Foundation (DF) of St. Louis and one of the most experienced persons in the country reporting on the campus scene, including campus ministry. Cuninggim's 1994 book, *Uneasy Partners: The College and the Church,* is a wonderful testament to his knowledge and wisdom concerning such matters. In 1980 he was as informed as was Robert Rankin on issues related to campus ministry, its styles and overall practice, including its problems. Between the two of them they were leading authorities on religion on the campuses of the United States.

The relationship between the American Youth Foundation and the Danforth

Foundation was and is one of sisterhood. The AYF came first in the early 1920s and was to be both the programmatic and the philanthropic extension of the Danforth family interests in education, particularly education involving the development of personal potential and character. The Danforth Foundation was created when it was discovered that combining the two functions in one organization was not very practical. During my years as president of the AYF I had many opportunities to share with President Gene Schwilck and the staff of the DF; we even designed and administered several programs shared by the two entities.

This information is all a little more than just of passing interest because Robert Rankin had been with the DF for some time and had just written and edited, along with other important names in campus ministry, a new (1980) publication *The Recovery of Spirit in Higher Education* (Seabury Press). Other editors were Myron B. Bloy, Jr. (unknown to me until much later, he also was one of the four finalists for the deanship of Hendricks Chapel), David A. Hubbard, and Parker J. Palmer. The research and publication of the book was underwritten by the DF. There are several chapters in the book by other prominent names in campus ministry. Bob Rankin and I had become friends, and on October 29, 1980, he gave me a copy of this just-off-the-press book. At the same time I informed him that I was a candidate at Syracuse University. Bob knew its history and the people who had, over the years, been involved. He assured me that I would be well engaged should I receive the appointment as the new dean.

The DF had, ten years earlier, underwritten a similar project that was also a successful effort at a comprehensive treatment of campus ministry throughout the nation. That was the book *The Church, the University, and Social Policy,* and it had been overseen and edited by Kenneth Underwood. I had earlier, during previous service in campus ministry, read the Underwood study. The Rankin book was intended to be an update of the original concept manifest in the Underwood book. Suffice it to say, I devoured Rankin's gift as I prepared for the SU interview. Thus did Cuninggim and Rankin, and Underwood as well, serve to guide my preparation for my interview and also served to guide me in the last eighteen years of my career. I have reread Rankin's book as part of the research for this history and find it still today a very helpful and "up-to-date" tool for campus ministry.

I did not enter the interview in question without some direct experience in campus ministry, and that brief history is the purpose of this paragraph. First, my friendship with Charlie Noble helped a great deal in not only understanding campus ministry but seeing it in operation at SU as well—at a time when SU was at the peak of its national reputation as a leader in the field. Earlier, during my last year (1959–60) of theological education at the Iliff School of Theology in Denver, Colorado, I had served as the associate director of the Wesley Foundation at the University of Colorado in Boulder. We lived in Boulder, and I commuted to Iliff. My next campus ministry experience was at Baker University, starting in 1966. For the first two years of faculty involvement there I also served as chaplain to the school and then in the third year became fully engaged in faculty roles. The work at the AYF between 1975 and 1981 was with older high school- and college-age youth in leadership education programs. Some of that work proved to be at least a cousin to campus ministry.

Now, back to the SU interview in November 1980. By this time those people on campus interested in Hendricks Chapel had had plenty of time to adjust to McCombe's departure (with a few exceptions) and were looking forward to the new look widely written and talked about on campus and in the newspapers. The Wiggins committee's report had been circulating for some time, and for that whole semester the chapel had been under Jim's administration as interim dean. Thus, the interview focused on the future of Hendricks Chapel and almost not at all on the past. Meetings with committees and with the chaplains were serious, with some real depth of content to them and also were more than cordial.

Key administrators involved in the interview process were Chancellor Eggers, Vice Chancellor Michael Sawyer, Dean Frank Funk (he was also chair of the search committee), and Jim Wiggins. On a more casual basis I met with a number of other administrators, with several faculty members, and with about ten students who were in one way or another involved in the chapel programs and committees. My paper was delivered in one of the Bird Library rooms with about seventy-five people in attendance. Other friends from our past SU involvement and the community came by to say hello who were not able to attend the hearing of the paper. The entire interview process was carried out in a very professional way and left no doubt in my mind about the serious manner the campus at large was taking the future of Hendricks Chapel and its role on the campus. I was impressed.

It was a stimulating and pleasurable two days on campus for me. I believe I was well served by being acquainted with the history and program at Syracuse and with the fresh content of Rankin's new book. I left for St. Louis with the feeling that if I did not get the offer, it was not because I had not had a good interview. While there I had even been able to attend a football game in the Carrier Dome in its first semester of operation. Ethel and I then played the waiting game in St. Louis and during a holiday trip to Colorado.

In mid-December we received a phone call from Michael Sawyer informing us that I had been selected to become the fourth dean of Hendricks Chapel. A few details were discussed, and I was then asked if I would accept. I asked for a couple of days to discuss the issue with our family. In two days I returned Sawyer's call, asked a few questions about minor issues we had discussed, and then accepted the invitation. In that same call a January date was arranged for us to come to Syracuse to meet with Virginia Denton of Facilities Planning so that some needed work could begin on the dean's residence at 315 Berkeley Drive in preparation for our

Dr. Richard L. Phillips at the time of his inauguration as the fourth full dean of Hendricks Chapel, 1981. Photograph by Steve Sartori, courtesy of Syracuse University.

planned late-February move. March 1, 1981, had been agreed upon as the date for my work as dean of Hendricks Chapel to begin. We viewed the move, the changes in the role of the dean and the chapel, and the work I was about to undertake in very positive terms. I did then and still do at this writing believe the tasks inherent in the position were tasks well suited to my skills, interests, energy, and orientation to service and to my commitment to higher education and ministry. These issues had become both in practice and in philosophy the marks of my career to that point. I do believe it was a good fit, one from which I probably benefited more than did the university.

Thus, a United Methodist clergyman with two SU degrees returned to become a member of the SU and Syracuse communities for the remainder of his professional career. Each of my predecessors had been Methodist clergyman, yet that affiliation was not a requirement. Indeed, two of the finalists were not members of that church. On the matter of the separation of the role of dean from the role of head of the Protestant ministry, I did make one major decision that was different from the first three deans. I did not become a member of the Central New York Conference of the United Methodist Church. My reasoning was that to associate myself too closely with local United Methodist interests might be seen by the other chaplains at the university as not being as evenhanded as was intended by the new chapel structure. I think that decision was a wise one. I remained on special appointment from the Rocky Mountain Conference of the United Methodist Church at the annual request of Chancellor Eggers, thus keeping my ecclesiastical relationships in proper order.

Dr. Donald G. Wright and I had a long and solid relationship that started in 1961 when I joined him as associate minister at University Methodist Church where he was the senior minister. This part-time position allowed me to support my family, stay out of debt, become well acquainted with the religious community of Syracuse, and develop friendships that to this day are both dear and treasured, all while I was a graduate student at SU. When, two years later, I became full-time faculty at SU we continued our relationship with the church until a new associate could be found.

In the fall of 1980 Don, then retired, was at the presentation during my interview and an enthusiastic supporter of my candidacy. It was later, during the first or second week of my deanship, that he visited my office and presented me with his manuscript on the earlier history of Hendricks Chapel. That manuscript is the basis of the early chapters of this book (see the introduction for more details). Don had not written the manuscript for publication and during that visit asked for the first of many times that I edit and add to it with the goal of publishing the history of Hendricks Chapel. Little did either of us think it would be well over twenty-three years before his request would be fulfilled. The intervening years proved to be very busy ones!

50. Honeymoon, Celebrations, Weddings, and Other Events

THE INTERIM DEANSHIP under Jim Wiggins's leadership proved to be a healthy period of recovery. The months of controversy surrounding the Eggers-McCombe issues had been amicably resolved to the satisfaction of almost everyone, including Jack McCombe. The chapel and all those individuals on campus interested in it and its relationship to the entire university were looking forward, not backward. The central administration had made it clear that the future of the chapel was more than secure; it was to be enhanced in budget and in terms of its roles within the university. Through it all the vast amount of support on the campus for Hendricks Chapel had been demonstrated again and again. It was a very good time to become its new dean.

If any leadership position ever had a honeymoon period for its newly arrived appointee, this one was certainly it. Ethel and I were welcomed by the chapel family and supporters, by old friends at the university and in Syracuse, and by the rank and file of this great university. Ethel, I must add, was already a person of very positive reputation in this community—fortunately, some of it rubbed off on me! Mc-

Combe had come into the position in what proved to be the most difficult of times, whereas I was fortunate to enter in what proved to be excellent if not the best of times.

The first months were spent learning the "territory." They were also tightly scheduled with official events, formal and informal meetings, the reading of files, working on budgets, getting to know the staff and chaplains, and starting my service on many SU committees. Working closely with Vernon Lee and Irving Hill (two officers and clergymen representing the United Methodist Church in the creation of the new and very important interdenominational Protestant chaplaincy at Hendricks Chapel) proved to be both productive and rewarding while at the same time very time consuming. More on this topic later in this chapter.

Getting acquainted with students went more slowly than with the permanent members of the SU community. Those students holding over from McCombe's congregation accepted me with open arms but at the same time did not pull back on their loyalty to Jack. There was only one time that I received what I would call negative feedback from anyone in this group. One student had a very negative reaction when I moved the desk in my office about a foot from where Jack had had it. The message was, "nothing should change." Well, some things did and some things did not, and we got along just fine.

No longer were there the student committees, boards, and chapelwide groups that had characterized the chapel in the days of Powers and Noble, taking at least 60 or 70 percent of Noble's time. Now chapelwide student involvement was limited to a few students on the Hendricks Chapel Advisory Board and a committee here and there. Almost all student relationships had become tied to the individual chaplaincies and not to the central operation of the office of the dean. The exception was the Hendricks Chapel Choir membership. That group was to be one of the focal points of my own regular interaction with students.

This pattern of student involvement was without a doubt the biggest change in the character of the chapel during Noble's later years and McCombe's years. It continued to characterize my years, and I anticipated it right from the start. I had seen the chapel under Noble only during five of the last seven of his years, so I did not notice the change as much as long-term observers like Mel Eggers and Don Wright did.

Key events as noted in the Wiggins chapter during this first half-semester of my deanship included the dedication of the Dankovich Chapel (also known as the small chapel). The invocation that some member of the small-chapel dedication committee had written and that I read is, in part, as follows: "For the worship and service of the Giver and Sustainer of life, for the diffusion of the spirit of compassion, reverence and understanding, for the moral and spiritual welfare of the generations who constitute the community of Syracuse University, to that which binds and holds the family of humanity together, we dedicate this chapel." That weekend included the delayed celebration of the fiftieth anniversary of the building of

Hendricks Chapel and my installation as the fourth dean (these events included Jack McCombe's participation, for which I was very grateful). Jack did not stay for the Sunday events, a mark of his sensitivity and wisdom. That wonderful weekend was truly a celebration of the life and history of Hendricks Chapel.

Filling in as coordinator of the Sunday services at the eleven o'clock service (which Wiggins had done) was helpful for my learning, but I have never been convinced that playing that role was wise, given the need to establish the new separation of the deanship from the leadership of that particular religious community. I did go ahead and attach to that community as my "home" religious community on campus but tried to make it as an attendee and not as a professional clergyman. I was never sure that even that move was wise. The guidelines passed on by the Wiggins committee called for me to preach at this chapel service once or twice a year and to work with the Protestant chaplain in lining up other guests for the pulpit. I look back on it as a vestige of the Charlie Noble image of how these services of worship should be carried out. Hindsight tells me it was probably not wise, but I did stick with it throughout my deanship.

Some of the chaplains who served that pan-Protestant post over the years were comfortable with my participation; others I am not so sure were. My institutional insight told me that no one needed a dean looking over their shoulders, yet I wanted to be supportive. Had I to do it over again I probably would have opted to attend an off-campus worshiping community on Sundays and thus not risk being around and being seen as holding the "dean" card.

In accordance with tradition, we carried out several chapel and even university-wide events through that Sunday service. Two cases in point were the Sunday we dedicated the Place of Remembrance for the students who died in the Pan Am 103 bombing over Lockerbie, with Lockerbie pastor Alan Neal as the preacher. Another was the rededication of the chapel after the 1985 renovation. There were other such times, which may have been appropriate, at least if all the negotiations for doing so were done with sensitivity to the chaplaincy in question. I hope I filled that sensitivity bill.

Although my involvement in coordinating the services that first semester helped my learning curve, it may have delayed the rapidity with which the SU and chapel communities came to understand the separation of the traditional roles of the dean and other changes. Even so, it did not prove to be a major issue. Late in the semester there were the usual end-of-the-year convocations, commencement, and much planning to do for the summer and the 1981–82 academic year. I had been led to believe that summers were a relaxed and mostly down time at the chapel. Right from the first summer that proved not to be the case, except for the fact that there were far fewer students around.

Much time that first half-semester was devoted to getting acquainted with staff members and the chaplains. The full list of the names of persons involved may be found in appendix B of this volume. The staff was most helpful in getting me grounded. Everyone from the secretaries to John Jones and Jean Baum (the program director and informal United Methodist representative on campus) were eager to help. The summer was to see some major changes, but they were for the most part preplanned before I came aboard. I did not come with a clean-the-house mentality and did not make any moves for that reason. The first major staff change and most visible was the previously announced termination of the staff role for John Jones. John and I continued a fine relationship for the next several semesters, even though it was a strained relationship at times. Later John started his own small church in Syracuse and has since died.

Jean Baum, a local United Methodist laywoman and wife of the late Alan Baum, was a delight to work with from her first greeting of welcome to her retirement several years later. Hired by McCombe, Jean had served, as already documented, on the staff in connection with both Community House and programs within the chapel itself. When the United Methodists found themselves without a clergy presence on campus, except for McCombe himself, Jean was asked to be the temporary, informal Methodist "presence" on campus. The arrangements and details were being worked out for the return of a clergy person to again fill the "expanded" chaplaincy. A Methodist chaplain had long been a key presence, in addition to the dean, in the ministries of Hendricks Chapel. With her role for the Methodists Jean began to take on a great deal of student counseling, a role for which she had minimal training but very fine instincts. She continued in that role until we added a trained person for that specialty. Jean was and continued to be the key staff person coordinating chapel events both in and beyond the building itself. She was one of those persons who, by nature, was a facilitator in both ideas and practice.

John Jones, an African American, had first been hired by McCombe as one of three part-time chaplains for special ministry, in his case ministry to minorities, especially African American students and staff. McCombe's hopes for this overall plan did not work out, and Jones was hired full-time when the experiment was dropped just before McCombe's final year in office. The controversial aspects of all of this matter are dealt with in the McCombe chapters. Jones had been told that the budget of the chapel would not carry the full-time position he held in the 1981–82 school year, that notice having come between semesters. Wiggins did consult with me by phone concerning both the budget issue and the Jones position before informing Jones that the position would not continue.

Jones was also a graduate student in the Department of Religion but had not been making good progress toward completing the program. During my first months Wiggins and I worked with Jones to find a way for him to continue his graduate work. We were able to locate other work for him within the university by underwriting a portion of his salary for the first year and gave him much encouragement to complete his doctoral studies. He did work at it for a year or so but in the end did not complete the program.

Because I believed that the chapel had put Jones in a position that could not be continued and because I believed Jones's work and perhaps his future had been compromised by all the controversy surrounding his early roles at the chapel, I continued, through the Hendricks Chapel budget, to give tangible support to his salary and his graduate work for two additional years. When he left the university he told me it was to fulfill his dream of starting a house church and helping it flourish into a permanent congregation.

Jones was easy to like yet somewhat difficult to deal with. He had become, along with his other duties, the first adviser to the Black Celestial Choral Ensemble during its first full year of operation as part of Hendricks Chapel. The BCCE had started as a part of the Office of Student Affairs but owing to its religious nature and purposes was shifted to Hendricks Chapel before it was a year old. During my first visit with the officers of BCCE in the spring semester of 1981, they requested that I appoint myself as their adviser (a formal role required of all student groups at SU) as a replacement for Jones. Their reason: "Rev. Jones and we do not see eye to eye on too many matters." Reluctantly, I fulfilled their request and remained in that role through my deanship. I will later discuss more fully this basically African American choral group in a chapter dealing with several ongoing chapel groups.

Here I risk spending too much ink on the John Jones relationship to Hendricks Chapel. Certainly, other individuals worked there longer and deserve more attention. Even so, this bit of history has some major and lasting administrative importance that deserves my attention and that of at least some of you readers.

First, if McCombe's experiment with the three part-time chaplaincies as staff positions had succeeded as he hoped and dreamed they would, through special grants, the whole nature of the operation of the chapel would have changed. Chaplains and chaplaincies had always before come from sponsorship and financial support from outside the university, not from within. For example, if chaplaincies for special ministry such as for women, African Americans, and international students were generated from within SU, the existing contracted chaplaincies would have complained that Hendricks Chapel and SU were "stealing" at least a portion of those populations from their own established memberships. So much, if such were the case, for the new plan that the dean would deal evenhandedly in all such matters.

Second, if such a practice had come to pass, there would be huge, unwieldy questions. Where would it end? A chaplain for gays? A chaplain for those students with physical limitations? A chaplain for students from New Jersey? And, just as difficult, where would the budget come from to support any such chaplaincies? Personally, I am pleased that Hendricks Chapel is not called upon to staff in quite this manner even while concurring that human needs often point toward the legitimacy for types of special ministry. Organizationally and functionally, I tried to find ways of staffing that would avoid such problems.

In the mid-1990s Vice President Robert Hill of SU served a term on the Hendricks Chapel Advisory Board. An African American himself, he had a keen interest in having every part of SU better serve this portion of our student and staff populations. He asked a specific question early in his membership on the board, and we had an ongoing discussion about it each meeting for several years. Robert requested that I consider hiring on the Hendricks Chapel staff an African American with clergy status equal to the other chaplains specifically to be a chaplain to our African American population at SU. Of course, he understood that budget was a big issue, but I do not think he ever fully understood the issue of what such a chaplaincy would communicate to the established religious organizations already having chaplains and serving their share of those same populations at SU. I took the position that if a number of black churches of Syracuse would join together and agree to underwrite and sponsor such a chaplaincy, then I would do everything I could to make it a working part of all the chaplaincies within the university. I believe that process is the only way such a specialized ministry could result in collegial relationships. I maintained that position regarding specialized ministry throughout my deanship, but of course there had to be exceptions.

To conclude this matter I did hire Millie Woods, a well-known Syracuse laywoman and an African American, very soon after becoming dean. As part-time coordinator of African American programs on the staff of Hendricks Chapel, she could and did help provide special attention to this population but without threat to other chaplaincies and, for the most part, in ways other than established church or quasi-church programming such as the establishment of a congregation. Later in my deanship Millie moved on and was replaced by Francis Parks, who started as a part-time graduate assistant and then, when a volunteer program came into existence (the Students Offering Service), became a full-time staff member with two titles along with, probably, two dozen roles. At this writing Francis continues in these roles at Hendricks Chapel. Although not unhappy with the roles played by Millie and then Francis, Robert Hill did not like it that they did not have ordained status to compare with the other chaplains. Through it all Robert and I remained friends.

Getting acquainted with the chaplains serving SU when I became dean was a rewarding pleasure, and those relationships remained so throughout. Usually on a semiformal contractual basis, Hendricks Chapel has long offered religious bodies and groups the opportunity to have chaplains serving their constituencies on campus. For example, the Hillel ministry serves our Jewish population, the Roman Catholic ministry through the St. Thomas More House serves the Catholic students, and on through the mainline Protestant denominations and more recently the Muslims though the Islamic Society of Central New York, which sponsors their chaplaincy. The Evangelical Christian Campus Ministry led by Dr. T. E. Koshy is the most unique in that it is sponsored by a group of otherwise mostly unaffiliated Syracuse-area churches. On a regular basis there are eight or ten hosted chaplaincies on the campus. Hosting means that we provide meeting space, usually office space and some services such as some remitted tuition to these chaplaincies. In turn, they agree to see themselves in limited ways as being of service to the entire university. A few chaplains have earned advanced degrees through the program, Ondrako, Kobeisy, and Wolfe being three names you will hear more about later.

Two other general types of ministries exist under the umbrella of Hendricks Chapel. Many organizations such as Campus Crusade for Christ, the Navigators, and Chi Alpha are usually not denominationally affiliated and thus do not have religious preference cards available to them. In addition, they provide their own staff members and have long had Hendricks Chapel status for campus ministry. These groups are also present only on the basis of a contract between their sponsoring organizations and Hendricks Chapel. At least in theory no religious organization or ministry can take place without a formal relationship to the chapel. This fact we say makes Hendricks Chapel an umbrella and not just a building. Some small informal groups have slipped past the requirement. We have usually referred to groups like the ones listed in this paragraph as sponsored group ministries.

A third group of organizations are normally generated from within the campus populations. Churches with a very limited number of students are good examples. The Christian Science Church has long had a group, with a faculty member serving as adviser or coordinator of its meetings and activities. Other such groups include the Orthodox Christian (mostly Eastern) Churches, the Mormons, the Society of Friends, the Hindus, and others.* Such groups must be registered and are also provided with meeting space but not with office space.

Yet another type of group can have Hendricks Chapel status. If a group of students wishes to form a study or prayer group with a stated religious purpose, have a faculty or staff sponsor, register with both Student Affairs and Hendricks Chapel, and have student officers responsible for the group, they too can schedule space within the university for their meetings. Obviously, there are such groups for discussion, prayer, and study that form and never do bother to register. They exist and meet on an informal basis. It is a guess that as many as thirty such temporary groupings exist in any given semester.

All of the above registered groups must agree to abide by university regulations, must agree with the aims of education as stated in the purposes of the university, and must agree to follow Hendricks Chapel guidelines. In my time as dean we have had only one group expelled from campus for failure to follow basic requirements (The Way International), and only a few times have groups had their

---

*See appendix C for a complete listing.

rights restricted for one or more violations. Denying the right to schedule space, to advertise, or for leaders to come on campus are examples of restrictions but have rarely been needed. The total number of groups in any year associated in one or more of the official categories ranges between thirty-six and forty-five. All groups with less-than-chaplaincy status were required to reregister every year.

Regarding the acceptance of chaplaincies and the registration of such diverse religious groups I faithfully followed what I call an open-arms policy. If a group wished to form, even sometimes for what I saw as unsound reasons, we welcomed them with open arms and provided the same facilitative services we would for all groups if they would agree to and follow the rules. I found "open arms" a sound philosophy of operation for Hendricks Chapel, even though it did from time to time make for extra, sometimes unpleasant, work. The reader has only to imagine what increasingly can pass for a religious practice and affiliation in today's world. The far-out and ultraconservative groups usually went out of existence in a short time owing to lack of student interest.

Obviously, one cannot become well acquainted with all of these operations in a short time, and maybe not in eighteen years! Even so, I set out to do so as quickly as possible. I held meetings with all leaders and advisers, visited as many of their services or meetings as possible, and took their professional ministers or staff members to lunch or tea as soon as possible. I promised myself I would visit a meeting (usually a service of worship) of each of the larger ministries at least once each year, in some cases twice a year. During my last five or so years I fell far short of this goal. I tried to drop by briefly for some meeting or event of each group within the first few months of my deanship. Some groups invited me to speak regularly, including the Jewish, Roman Catholic, Islamic, and mainline Protestant groups, and when possible I accepted such invitations.

Very soon in my introductory months I discovered a collegiality among and between the chaplains and religious leaders that was truly remarkable. Hendricks Chapel, I soon learned, had a long history with few exceptions of such positive collegiality and respect. Even those of us who found ourselves on opposite sides of very critical theological and social issues accounted for close friendship in a spirit of agreeing to disagree about central matters. Over the years I worked hard at maintaining this atmosphere, and I like to believe doing so was one of my greatest successes. Almost without exception, groups try their very best to serve the needs of their members or constituents and to be a positive presence in the life of the chapel and the university. Normally when problems developed they were problems of operation or problems created by style and not problems of aim and purpose. One example was a group singing hymns in a classroom in a building where other classes were in session, something they had promised they would not do!

Earlier in this chapter I mentioned the work of Jean Baum. She, owing to the Methodist role she played at that time, was one of three persons having three distinctly unique relationships to Hendricks Chapel. The second was Norm Keim. Earlier chapters have documented how Norm's service as the American Baptist chaplain came to an end when the money from that denomination ran dry. That chaplaincy ended long before Norm's formal relationship to Hendricks Chapel came to a close. When I came aboard Norm's title was chaplain-at-large. Mc-Combe had granted him this relationship, and Norm continued to be a valuable part of the Chaplains Council. Indeed, from my own experience and from other reports he was a well-liked and worthy contributor to the deliberations of the council and to the shared events sponsored by the council and a fine addition to the tradition of collegiality. In addition, Norm had continued his directorship of Film Forum, an operation that sometimes provided his entire financial support. Some semesters and some years he was also employed, often only part-time, by the Office of Student Affairs and by the Newhouse School, where he taught some courses in film. The saying around the university was that "Norm has learned to survive in the cracks!" In such a patchwork fashion Norm continued to be a part of Syracuse University until the early 1990s when he retired and took up part-time work in real estate.

The most visible and well-known Hendricks Chapel role Norm was playing when I became dean was in the performance of weddings, and therein lies the first agonizing decision of my deanship. Norm was one of the few clergy persons on campus who was institutionally free and willing to conduct mixed and other weddings not compatible with the rules other chaplains were constrained to follow. He did so much of it that he had become known as the "Marrying Sam" of Hendricks Chapel. Many years weddings became a significant part of his income. Also, Norm was popular with students and worked with many in all of the roles he played in the university; thus, he was often called upon by students to celebrate their weddings for that reason even if they did not fall in the mixed marriage category. I attended two or three of Norm's wedding ceremonies, and indeed he did a fine job in that role.

Slowly at first and throughout that first semester the chaplains came to me to express their concern and usually displeasure at the fact that Norm was still doing weddings, many weddings. Each chaplain believed that some of the weddings (not necessarily the mixed weddings) being done by Norm actually belonged in their ministry and that they too needed that income to offset the low salaries standard for clergy, especially campus ministry clergy. At the end of the semester I made this issue a topic of deliberation at a special Chaplains Council meeting to which Norm was not invited. Everyone was in agreement that Norm, under the banner of Hendricks Chapel, should no longer have any weddings referred to him. The use of Hendricks Chapel for weddings of students who directly asked Norm to do their weddings was not denied, but no more was the chapel staff to refer students to Norm for any weddings. Communicating this decision to Norm as well as the end of his related appointment as chaplain-at-large was one of the hardest tasks of my deanship. I had known Norm only slightly when I was a graduate student and he the American Baptist chaplain. I liked him and I liked him even more in my new role.

Here I digress to an issue involving Vice President Mel Mounts, who left SU the same time as Jack McCombe. Interestingly enough, it may have been a Hendricks Chapel-related person's situation that provided the last straw leading to Mounts's departure. Very briefly, the issue was related to Norm Keim and his operation Film Forum. For several years the Student Affairs division of SU had tried to take over Film Forum. After all, it was probably the only fairly large operation within SU that was owned and operated by an entity other than SU—in this case by Keim himself. Finally, after years of on-and-off negotiations, a deal was struck and Mounts agreed that Norm would remain its director as a member of the staff of Student Affairs. In my interview with Keim I learned that he did legally sign Film Forum over to Student Affairs, and then Mounts went back on his promise to retain Norm as its director. Obviously Keim, was not willing to drop the matter, and soon Mounts was gone.

Taking Keim out of the wedding duties left open the issue of where to refer students, especially ones planning mixed marriages, for clergy officiates. The most difficult of such marriages were, and are, the ones between Jews and non-Jews. None of the rabbis in Syracuse would do such weddings, and Rabbi Elefant, the director of Hillel and our Jewish campus minister, did not want such weddings to take place at all in the chapel. His reasoning, with which I long agreed, was that Hendricks Chapel was, in Jewish terms, his "parish" and that he should have the right to say yes or no to any Jewish person wanting to have a wedding there. As a matter of professional courtesy I functioned in this manner, with rare exceptions, for many years. I saw it as necessary, and he realized that he must tolerate such mixed marriages in Hendricks Chapel if the couple asked one of the other chapel-related clergy to do the wedding as long as a visiting rabbi was not brought in to do or to share the wedding. It was reported to me by the leadership of the Syracuse Jewish Federation that only some five hundred Rabbis in the United States were willing to do such ceremonies and none within 250 miles or so of Syracuse. This guideline for Jewish mixed marriages was in practice at Hendricks Chapel until the late 1990s. Roman Catholic mixed marriages also presented difficulties, but generally they presented problems much easier to resolve than the ones just discussed.

Because I did not have time nor did I want to become the next Marrying Sam on campus and in order to be sure we could serve the SU population in this matter of weddings, I made sure we had other chaplains, individuals other than myself, who were willing to have mixed marriages referred to them (and take any heat resulting from their doing so) that they could accept without violation of their ordination status in their home religious body. There were a total of three of us open to this type of referral. Over the years we all did several such weddings. I also found a small number of clergy who were serving on the faculty of the university who let me know that they, in an urgent case, would be willing to consider doing such weddings. I think it happened only once. So, we could cover the wedding issue without Norm Keim and make the representatives of religions with campus ministry at SU a happier group. The issue of having judges or other qualified public officials do weddings in Hendricks Chapel was also of some concern. This practice was allowed if the proposed wedding in question was outside of the "territory" of any given chaplain. It was also easy to justify if the public official was a relative or close friend of the bride or the groom or one of their families.

This section is expanded far beyond the first months of my deanship but is better dealt with now in an overview of some sixteen years of dealing with wedding issues. So I will now discuss the chaplain-of-record role we created in part to facilitate a fair and helpful distribution of money coming from wedding-related income. The average wedding honorarium for clergy at this time was about one hundred dollars. As indicated that amount was of some real financial help for some of the chaplains. As a result, if a guest clergy or public official was to be brought in for a wedding we instituted the policy that a Hendricks Chapel chaplain would be assigned to be "chaplain of record" and that the fifty dollars received for this service would be added to the charge made to the couple for the use of the chapel for their wedding. Usually, the honorarium to the officiate of a wedding was paid directly by the wedding party. If requested we added it to the chapel fee and in turn paid the clergy. The fifty dollars for the chaplain of record was simply added to the user fee (rental of the building) when an officiate was coming in from the outside.

The chaplain-of-record role was also instituted for another very important reason. We soon discovered that most clergy and officials from the outside needed help in rehearsing and conducting Hendricks Chapel weddings, such as where to find things, what works best at one or another stage of a ceremony, and many other similar issues. The visiting officiate received a letter fully explaining that the chaplain of record was to be a consulting helper in the rehearsal and the wedding and otherwise involved only if asked to do so but was not expecting to do so. This practice worked out very well. I agreed to assign chaplains on the basis of the religious relationship of the bride or groom or both whenever possible and to make a fair distribution of the role in all other cases. For only a few weddings over the years did I find it necessary to appoint myself when others were not available. In a few additional cases, especially for the occasional wedding proving to be difficult for one reason or another (and it is not always the mother of the bride), I sat in the back of the chapel as an observer.

The resulting experiences confirmed my belief that the chaplain-of-record role was both helpful and justified in the Hendricks Chapel setting. There was agreement on the part of the chaplains. We also had a wedding coordinator helping with each rehearsal and each wedding. The coordinator was usually a carefully trained student worker, sometimes a staff member or even chaplain. The fee for the coordinator came from the chapel rental fees, and sometimes they also received a tip from the wedding party. For very small weddings in either the small chapel or some other location, especially when there was no rehearsal, we waived the need for a coordinator. Over the years we had several very effective and very loyal wedding coordinators, probably none more so than David Aitkin, who sometimes continued with that role even after graduation.

Over the years both Chancellor Eggers and then Chancellor Shaw came to me, each more than once, to ask how we justified not allowing Jewish clergy to come to Hendricks Chapel to do mixed weddings (visiting rabbis were not a problem for an all-Jewish wedding) when asked to do so by students and staff of SU. When denied that avenue of securing clergy for a Hendricks Chapel wedding the complaints would come, usually to me first, often directly to the desk of Eggers or Shaw. Eggers did not, over the ten years we served together before his retirement, agree with my "parish" argument as the basis of this restriction, but he did understand it and my wish to continue this professional courtesy and he allowed it to continue. The university took some real heat, often sacrificed some potential donations, over the issue. On more than one occasion inquiry concerning our practice came from government officials as a result of complaints and requests to intervene and have us allow visiting rabbis do such weddings in Hendricks Chapel. These calls came from both New York state and U.S. government officials, at least once as high ranking as a U.S. senator. I must add that they were often joined by prominent Jewish laypersons of Syracuse who did not agree with their rabbi's stance on this matter.

As indicated above, it was late in the 1990s when the issue finally came to a legally based decision that opened a door and closed an informal policy. In 1996–97 the chaplains and staff did a full study of weddings and wedding policy at Hendricks Chapel, both because such a review was needed and because Shaw had asked us to do so. Legal opinion had been sought, and the issue seemed clear that the overall claims of the university that it is open to persons without regard to issues of race, religion, and so on did mean that the SU community should have access to Hendricks Chapel on the same basis as a classroom, a gym, or a dormitory room. We interpreted this ruling to indicate that if, for example, a Methodist could call for a visiting clergy person, perhaps hometown clergy, to do a Hendricks Chapel wedding, mixed or otherwise, so could anyone else who wished to do so. We had almost always allowed this practice in non-Jewish mixed weddings (for Catholics, other ecclesiastical permission had to be sought to bring in an "outside" priest, but doing so was never strictly a Hendricks Chapel issue), and now we saw clearly that a door was to open and a door was to close. The closing of the door that I had long called professional courtesy was another of those painful but necessary decisions. In the end, though it angered local Jewish clergy, including Rabbi Toby Manewith, then serving as the Hendricks Chapel chaplain, they also understood that legally we had no choice. When it was all said and done, I was sad yet I agreed with the new policy. In fact, I really wish we had pushed things to this position the first time Eggers had inquired about the policy. Isn't hindsight wonderful?! Over the years it would have been the best solution to many, many problems we had to deal with over and over again. Even so, weddings, of which there have been so many and of so many kinds over the history of Hendricks Chapel, are one of the most joy-filled involvements any of us have.

NOW I RETURN to those first few months of my deanship. Jim Wiggins mentioned that there were some difficulties associated with overseeing the operation of the Black Celestial Choral Ensemble. The difficulties he alluded to continued to create problems, sometimes minor, sometimes not so minor. I will deal with them in a later chapter on special chapel organizations, but here I should say that I did prize my relationships with BCCE and that over the years the relationship was healthy and rewarding. I was pleased that they wanted me to be their adviser; they honored me in my first weeks in office.

It became clear those first weeks that my institutional peers were to be the other SU administrators and some faculty members. In functioning as a dean in an academic institution there are really no professional peers in your own corner of your university world. Even so, the primary groups for my week-in-and-week-out functioning were the chaplains, religious workers (which we called all the group leaders who did not have chaplaincy status), and the Hendricks Chapel staff members. In terms of experience, formal education, ordination, and certainly wisdom, many of these persons were my peers, and many of those relationships had a close peer quality to them. Even so, as head of the staff, as chair of the Chaplains Council, and as coordinator of almost every meeting I called, I was set apart by role, if for no other reason, from all the rest. When you are at the head of the group and say something like, "Oh, damn," you soon realize that it means something different to every participant. That reality is one of the big prices one pays for assuming the role of dean. Both Wiggins and Eggers had told me to be sure to get to know and relate to individuals in the university outside of Hendricks Chapel for they would be very valuable peers. They were correct, and I am very glad I took that advice seriously.

Regarding this matter, Eggers had briefed me on what he thought the dean of Hendricks Chapel should do with at least part of his time. He wanted me to be present and known in every corner of the university. He wanted me to attend as many events of as much variety as my time would allow. He wanted me to be called upon for everything from public prayers to formal speeches and classroom participation. He made sure my parking permit was good on every campus parking lot.

He wanted chapel-based presence in every campus emergency and in every campus celebration. His concept of ministry, especially to an institution, was that one's presence was a large part of one's ministry. I continue to feel very fortunate that his concept of ministry and mine were so very parallel. Of course, Eggers had one other role in mind, that of being an effective ombudsman for the entire campus. That role started early and was never thwarted, indeed was enhanced at every turn. It could not be effective without a campuswide presence. It was perhaps my most rewarding role and never once in eighteen years was any office door closed to me when I called or knocked to deal with a problem, large or small.

As dean I was frequently referred to as the ethical and moral guardian (or similar language) of the campus. I never liked the sound of that challenge and charge, but Eggers was also clear with me that he expected no less than a wide-awake approach to such matters on my part. We did not ever arrive at suitable language to express this role, which from time to time could be very important. I saw it as very closely related to the ombudsman role. Eggers expressly asked me to let him know through personal contact if I ever saw him performing in a way that violated good ethical standards. In regard to his administration or his person I did so only once. His response was most favorable.

At the same time Eggers was clear about some of his expectations for this dean, he specifically left me free to develop my own work guidelines for both Hendricks Chapel matters and university-wide concerns. At the very first I established my self-rule standards about service in the dean and the ombudsman roles. They are few and simple but proved to be very important. If I was to function, be effective, and have a sound reputation in this classic prophetic function, then I must guide myself carefully. Here is the result.

First, I would never go public with an issue until I had explored it fully with anyone and everyone involved. Second, I would let the right officer of the university know if I might do something that would land me in jail or in some way embarrass the university or the chapel. Third, I would never, as ombudsman, advocate for anyone unless and until I had all the facts of the case. And, fourth, I would not hesitate to let the right university officer know if I saw an issue where moral and ethical concerns were at stake in any university policy, problem, or procedure. I found I liked myself for following these standards.

THE CELEBRATIONS that followed my assumption of duties were well planned, a delight to experience, and a wonderful reintroduction to life at Syracuse University. I shall touch upon each briefly.

Ted and Marjorie Pierson have already been documented in this book. They were long supporters of Hillel, of Hendricks Chapel, and of SU. They were, and Marjorie still is, members of the Reform Jewish synagogue just a few blocks from the chapel. She was a fellow student with Don Wright, the first secretary to Dean

Richard L. Phillips, fourth full dean of Hendricks Chapel, served from 1981 to 1999. During his eighteen-year tenure, he not only presided over the chapel's ministry to the university community, but directed its response to larger events, including the tragedy of the Lockerbie air disaster of 1988. Photograph by Steve Sartori of oil portrait. Courtesy of Syracuse University Art Collection.

Powers, and a very active participant in chapel events and affairs both before and after her graduation from SU. We became, as almost everyone who came to know them did, close friends. Ted's death, too early in his retirement, was a cause for great sadness. It was my honor to share in his memorial service at Temple Society of Concord along with Rabbi Ted Levy.

The Piersons' daughter Rena died shortly after her graduation from SU, her marriage, and the birth of her only child. As Hendricks Chapel prepared to celebrate its fiftieth anniversary, the Piersons donated the funds necessary to reclaim an area formally part of the heating system in the lower level of Hendricks Chapel and to dedicate it as a chapel in honor and memory of Rena. The dedication service became part of the anniversary celebrations and my first such dedication ceremony at SU. McCombe had also been close friends and had worked with them on the planning and construction of this small chapel, and he returned for this and the fiftieth celebrations. Jack had worked hard on the plans and preparation for the fiftieth, so it was a real blessing that he could return and be part of it.

This beautiful and very functional chapel, including accoutrements for several religions, is formally known as the Rena Pierson Dankovich Chapel. Later they created an endowment to cover the costs of permanent maintenance of the facility. Another of my joys is that a friend and SU artist, George VanderSluis, shortly before his death painted the mural that adorns the front wall of the chapel. George described but did not title the mural as "ascension and descension." George was quoted prior to the dedication of the small chapel as saying he would describe the painting as "a oneness." The mural changes a very common four-walled room into a beautiful chapel. As many as four and five events a day have characterized the use of this chapel. From weddings to memorial services, services of worship, prayer meetings, a place for meditation, discussion groups, committee meetings, and regular Alcoholics Anonymous meetings, it has been used most productively. In addition to the continued support of the Pierson family, Marjorie has been helpful to both me and Don Wright regarding portions of the history of Hendricks Chapel. The Piersons are among the many angels that make the whole place so very special.

Ruth Hall, a friend from other times and places, had been on the chapel staff and was asked to be the chief coordinator of the events of the week. Ruth came to Syracuse with her husband, T. William Hall, also a longtime friend, when he came to SU's Department of Religion in 1966, the summer we had moved to Baker University in Kansas. As a member of the department I had, in 1965, placed Bill's name in nomination for the chair. Another "old home week" feel to our return.

Ruth's able hand was everywhere as was that of the whole staff, for the events all unfolded with typical SU excellence and precision. The ceremonial parts, such as the academic procession for my installation, were planned by Pete Cataldi, long the chief designer and marshal of such SU ceremonies as commencement. Pete, a member of the faculty, had been a friend during the 1960s, and I regret that he died shortly after the start of my deanship.

On Friday afternoon, April 10, 1981, the formal installation service and academic procession was held in Hendricks Chapel. My parents had come from Colorado to be present for the pride-filled event. The Hendricks Chapel Choir sang, and an array of administrators and dignitaries, including Bishop Ralph Ward of the United Methodist Church, participated. I had invited my theological mentor from the Iliff School of Theology, Dr. Harvey H. Potthoff, to give the address. Chancellor Eggers issued a challenge and oversaw the formal installation, and I gave an acceptance speech. The full house of smiling faces and the celebratory spirit were indeed memorable and deeply appreciated. My address was based on the passage of Scripture containing the instruction to take the shoes off your feet, for the ground upon which you are standing is holy ground. As I entered the pulpit I took off my shoes, indicating that I did so out of respect for our Muslim colleagues who remove their shoes when entering the mosque for prayer and because I believed the ground upon which I now stood, meaning all of Syracuse University, was holy ground and that I wished to conduct my deanship in that spirit. The most remembered part of the service, as I learned years later, was the removal of my shoes!

Following his experience there, Potthoff told me that he believed I had come to the best campus ministry spot in the country. He still held that view some years later. Harvey may have been being kind, but he was very well informed on campus ministry and had visited and known scores of us so engaged—so I not only took him seriously but before long came to the same conclusion myself.

That same evening the banquet formally celebrating the fiftieth year of the presence of Hendricks Chapel and its programs and people was held in the large dining facility on Mount Olympus. Rabbi Fred Krinsky, formerly from the Maxwell School and once our campus rabbi, returned from California to be the anniversary keynote speaker. His address that night, as well as on two other return trips to Syracuse, was excellent in content and delivery. Others shared appropriate remarks, and I was, as guest of honor, able just to sit back and enjoy the event with Ethel and our family. Events where you are part of the planning and conducting are never quite so enjoyable.

On Saturday some seminars, tours, and supportive events were held, and on Sunday I had been invited to preach in the regular worship service that was, in keeping with the fiftieth celebration, a "Service of Thanksgiving and Hope." That same afternoon the Hendricks Chapel Choir gave its annual Spring Concert under the direction and organ work of Winston Stephens. It was both a wonderful concert and a fitting close to the week of celebrating the past and welcoming the future. If nothing had yet touched the soul of those persons who questioned the university's intentions regarding the future of the chapel on campus, this week surely put negative fears to rest, at least until 1995.

Several of the chaplains seated at the time of my arrival stayed for several years, whereas a few had already been there for years. The most well known in the community was Father Charles Borgognoni, the Roman Catholic director and minister since the death of Father Ryan in 1961. I had known him only slightly in the 1960s. Charlie, as he was known to all of us, had proved to be an excellent choice for that ministry and for the university and the community at large. He had become well known as director and producer of the Pompeian Players and almost single-handedly put on a classic Broadway musical for the entire community every year. Primarily it was a fund-raiser, one of five he had developed over the years to support his ministry, which was supported but not financially by the local Catholic diocese. This production had its beginning while Charlie was a parish priest in the neighboring town of Pompey. Charlie proved to be as delightful to work with as was his community-wide reputation. He was a well-rounded, spaghetti-eating, friarlike country priest with a twinkle in his eye who loved a glass of wine with his meals—Italian meals, if you please! He was also very popular among Roman Catholic students for performance of their weddings. In most of the wedding ceremonies he sang part of the service.

In addition to his special projects like the Broadway musicals he had found his way into the SU athletic programs by asking Coach Ben Schwartzwalder early on if he could sit on the football players' bench for the SU game against Notre Dame. That request turned him into being team chaplain for men's football and basketball, including traveling with the football team to almost all games and to some of the away games for basketball. Charlie relished that role and to the best of my knowledge was an effective chaplain to the teams and was certainly loved by the players and the coaches. His last few years, with failing health setting in, proved to be somewhat of a problem for both the athletic program and the St. Thomas More campus ministry. More on such matters later, but all I need to say here is that from the very start we had a special relationship and I enjoyed working with him a great deal. It is sad that he is alive but "not with us" as this book is written.

Charlie was very ably assisted by a second priest, Father Ed Ondrako. A gentle man, Ed loved students, had a big heart, and had the spirit of a scholar. Ed was more than a blessing to Charlie and the Roman Catholic ministry; he was a real savior in Charlie's years of declining health. Ed earned his doctorate while serving with Charlie at SU. They were a good team: Ed could keep it all together while Charlie did his many mini ministries. Both Ed and Charlie were great supporters of the Chaplains Council and the interfaith events of Hendricks Chapel.

The next chaplain in seniority was Rabbi Milton Elefant, who when he retired had been at Hendricks Chapel for more than twenty-five years. For years Milton had the largest Hillel campus ministry in the country. This fact and its explanation were confirmed to me by the national-level officers of the Hillel organization. Here again I found a relationship of support and mutual goals for student work. Milton asked me to speak at services each year for both Hanukkah and Yom Kippur, a role I found very rewarding and considered a great honor. Milton often involved other rabbis and Jewish leaders to help, and I believe he provided each branch of Judaism with effective ministry. In my section dealing with the bombing of Flight 103 I will mention something of his broader concerns for ministry.

Milton was and is an Orthodox rabbi, meaning that kosher living requirements put certain restrictions on his schedule and his style of conducting his ministry. We all learned to live with that fact, with the exception of campus security and the parking department at SU. He would drive to the chapel before sunset on Fridays and leave his car and walk home until late Saturday or even Sunday morning, when he would walk back to campus to get it. Often, events at SU made such parking difficult if not impossible to work around. I was pleased to be part of the solution to this particular problem. By getting a set of keys to his car I was able to steal it each Friday evening and by some magic leave it in his driveway a few minutes later. We both seemed to enjoy the arrangement, even if it was not a good kosher solution!

Dr. T. E. Koshy, a native of India, was the next in seniority and at this writing is still at Hendricks Chapel in his role as Evangelical Christian chaplain. As mentioned earlier, this campus ministry was unique. McCombe had consented to allow this chaplaincy because several evangelical churches in and around Syracuse were willing to sponsor and at least partially underwrite its costs. Koshy is by nature and interests an internationalist both at heart and in practice. Koshy (as he is called) and his wife, a medical doctor, hosted us many times and for many meals and conversations. Koshy has always been a supporter of the Chaplains Council. Especially early in his chaplaincy, the style and the ministry's evangelical nature created some problems within the university, which I will discuss more fully later. From the start, Koshy has been a positive part of the collegial spirit at Hendricks Chapel.

The Lutheran chaplaincy was filled by Rick Bear as a full-time position. The Lutherans and the Episcopalians have, with limited student populations, been very consistent in providing full-time pastors to their campus ministries at SU. Rick was to be in the position a few more years before moving to Ithaca to serve a congregation in addition to serving Lutherans on the Cornell campus. Rick accomplished something no other chaplain did while at Syracuse and with wonderful results. We provided each chaplain with their religious preference cards during the summer. Most wrote letters of welcome to their constituents in addition to the letter of welcome sent by Hendricks Chapel to all, both new and returning students. Rick had a policy he followed very rigorously: he called personally upon every registered Lutheran student within three days of the start of each fall semester. The remarkable result was that Rick had a higher percentage of participation by his students in his services and programs than did any of the other chaplains. Other brief sketches of chaplains are contained in a later chapter.

One of the most important tasks during the first months was working with Methodists Vernon Lee and Irv Hill in getting the last details of the new interdenominational Protestant chaplaincy set up and funded and conducting a search for someone to fill the position. This position was to be the major chaplaincy to fulfill the new arrangement wherein the dean would no longer pastor what is essentially still the same congregational makeup of students and staff. These two things, the newly defined role of the dean and the new Protestant chaplain, are the two most visible and functional changes from pre-1981 to post-March 1981 as far as the operation of Hendricks Chapel was and is concerned.

With the help of representatives of four mainline Protestant churches and sometimes with input from the New York State Council of Churches, Lee and Hill, and sometimes the resident United Methodist bishop, had been working at the task for several months prior to my arrival. Because we all wanted a chaplain in place for the start of the 1981 fall semester, we worked fast and hard on the tasks at hand. In doing so we probably made two mistakes. By agreement of the other three denominations the Methodists took the lead, financed almost all of the arrangement, and were to have one of their clergy in the role. The other three denominations were and are still today American Baptist, United Presbyterian, and United Church of Christ (Congregational). The Presbyterians agreed to put their financial backing to a similar arrangement at Cornell. After a nationwide search a United Methodist clergyman from Montana and an SU graduate, Bill Kliber, was selected to fill the position and was in fact seated as the fall semester got under way.

The two mistakes, at least the ones that became obvious, had to do with the lack of a clear understanding of the selection and appointment process and the lack of clear guidelines for the reporting to be done by the chaplain, that is, accountability. Lee and Hill were seeing the position as primarily a Hendricks Chapel position underwritten financially by their church, whereas I was seeing the position as being parallel in nature to the other established chaplaincies on campus. We simply failed to ever get clear in all of our minds just how this situation was to work. I take the blame for perpetuating the lack of clarity by playing such a central role in the search and appointment process and by establishing at least one condition with Kliber regarding the appointment. The results were that Kliber was with us for only one year. During the last part of the 1981–82 year Lee, Hill, and I worked hard at closing the gap on such criteria as would govern the chaplaincy.

In short, Kliber and his wife (she was at the time a nurse practitioner in Montana and may still be—Bill has since died) made it clear at the interview that she would probably not join him for the first year if he were to fill the position. There were some vibes connected with the communication about this fact that concerned me deeply. After agonizing over the issue I took what was probably much too paternalistic a stand. With Hill and Lee in agreement, I informed Kliber when we decided he was the person for the job that if his wife, Mary Nell, decided not to join him in one year, then the appointment would be for only one year. I was not going to place the church, the chapel, or myself in a position where we could be seen, by any of the parties involved, as the cause for the breakup of a marriage. I suspected and it proved to be the case that the year apart was seen, at least by her, as a trial separation.

Thus, in the spring of 1982 I asked both Bill and Mary Nell if she would join him by the start of that fall semester. The answer was a firm no. She did not plan to be with him for his second year. At that point I asked for and received Bill's resignation. We were all upset by the turn of events. Bill was understanding but wanted us to cancel the previous one-year stipulation, local Methodists were upset by the slow start and disruption it caused in the new plan, a number of students who had related to Bill's ministry were upset that he was forced to leave, and I was most upset of all for all the obvious reasons and because we now knew about and had to correct the mistakes that had been made in the plan and its first implementation.

Fortunately, the mistakes were mostly of omission rather than commission, and we corrected them with relative ease. From that point on, the chaplaincy was the property of the four denominations, with the Methodists at the lead. I related to this chaplaincy in the same way I did the others (usually a consultant to a search process and also usually in on final interviews), with the final vote of approval for the seating of a new chaplain. The report process and accountability were now finally with the sponsoring religious body or in this case the four bodies.

Lee, Hill, and I have remained close friends through it all and since, and I continued to have a special interest in and was a constituent of this ministry as well as having a special administrative relationship. As indicated earlier, my position included serving as a guest preacher from time to time, helping to line up and underwrite other guests for the pulpit, providing for the "loan" of the Hendricks Chapel Choir for the services of worship, and providing a small budget to help facilitate that portion of the work of this chaplain that by nature and purpose overlapped other Hendricks Chapel operations. The plan was adjusted a bit year by year—after all, it was the working out of a plan and a relationship new to all of us. My biggest disappointment with the package has been that the other three denominations do not share more of the financial burden. If they did, I think it would follow that they would do more in other ways to support the chaplaincy on a regular basis. All that says is that the joint aspect of the ministry was, during my time, more on paper than it was in practice. Nonetheless, it has served us well to have the ministry as a package.

In reflecting, I believe it has worked very well for both the churches and Hendricks Chapel. Without this chaplaincy or something very similar, the newly established role of the dean could not have worked at all. After serving in this chaplaincy for eight and a half years, Tom Wolfe was to succeed me and become the fifth dean of Hendricks Chapel. That fact indicates not only the success of Tom's ministry but also the positive manner in which the new chaplaincy has fitted within the overall operation of Hendricks Chapel.

THIS CHAPTER has been about much more than just my first months as dean but also indicates a theme rather than basically chronological organization I am using in writing about my years. That style will continue in future chapters. Now I must share some of my early reflections.

Working with Vice Chancellor Michael Sawyer as my first line of reporting to the Office of the Chancellor was wonderful. I cannot remember a conversation we had that was not delightful. I knew of and had met Sawyer in the 1960s. He was an honored professor of constitutional law in the Maxwell School. He was beloved by students, was respected and used as a resource by faculty, was witty, had a very comprehensive knowledge of the university, and long was a very important part of the central administration. I am sure it is fair to say that for Eggers there were, during most of his time as chancellor, two people who were close and upon whom he leaned most frequently and heavily in matters of general SU administration. They were Cliff Winters and Michael Sawyer. As each of these three neared retirement, others took their places in that inner circle. Later Eggers shifted the first line of my reporting to Vice President Eleanor Ware, where it remains today. That relationship has also been wonderful, supportive, and facilitative.

I very quickly became aware of the reputation of Hendricks Chapel in the wider world of campus ministry. Calls for information and advice from other schools soon confirmed that reality. In one of my first trips to New York City I was informed by the then head of the National Council of Churches that the dean of Hendricks Chapel was, second to the Roman Catholic cardinal of New York, the most well-known religious figure in the state of New York. If so, I had no question about why: the reputation and work and public speaking of Charlie Noble lives on! I was to learn again and again that though not on top in every measure, Hendricks Chapel is certainly one of the leading campus ministry operations in the nation.

As I assumed my duties both Eggers and McCombe urged me to become involved in one or more of the national-level campus ministry professional organizations. The Association of College and University Religious Administrators (ACURA) was, I was told, the key group for my membership. Within the first full year I participated in three such organizations: the Campus Ministry Association, the National Association of College and University Chaplains, and ACURA, which had split off from NACUC a few years before. ACURA was indeed the one for me, and I later served two and a half years as its president. In addition, Syracuse University is now the holder of the ACURA Archives. The key difference between ACURA and the others is that ACURA is for those individuals who administer the overall aspects of campus religious life, whereas the others are made up primarily of persons who serve as chaplains, pastors, and ministers on the campuses of the country. The meetings and meeting agendas of ACURA differ greatly from the other organizations, and I found it much more helpful given my overall responsibilities.

Of lasting value to me and to any Hendricks Chapel dean was to very early discover the widespread and deep support Hendricks Chapel has from members of the SU community. Even so, I know there are a few who think Hendricks Chapel is an unnecessary expense and occupier of space on campus. From time to time I even found support for some aspect of the Hendricks Chapel operation from such a person. Goodwill and support come not only from those faithful with personal ties to religion and its institutions but also from the unaffiliated and even the non-believers. In fact, three times during my deanship there were efforts to change the reporting relationship of Hendricks Chapel back to the Office of Student Affairs. In one case the effort almost succeeded. In addition to the objections to such a move on the part of the religiously affiliated, considerable and powerful support for retaining the more comprehensive relationship to the Office of the Chancellor came from some very influential nontheists on campus, persons who spoke out about both the importance of the work of the chapel and the importance of it being related to the chancellor. I am not at all sure but that these latter were the voices that saved the day! If Hendricks Chapel is to have a deep, comprehensive role on campus, it simply must report to the only administrator with the ultimate and comprehensive institutional responsibility. In Student Affairs it can too easily be seen by many in the community as limited to a student service. Most of our Student Affairs administration understood this point, but at least a few of them were not deterred in making the effort to have the chapel shifted to their "shop."

My first invocation at a commencement ceremony (May 1981) received many favorable comments and even requests for copies. One parent, a faculty member in Oswego, had a child graduating that year and found my failure to use the word *God* in the invocation a cause for the writing of several nasty letters both to me and to Eggers. My response that I had used the terms *divine* and *Creator* in order to be more inclusive but that I often did and would use *God* in such utterances was to no avail. I had missed an opportunity to bring God before, if not into, people's lives. The negative letters continued. I later learned that such behavior was characteristic of this person and that it was best to ignore the matter. What was rewarding was the response of the central administration of the university and the solid words of support I received from within SU. One quick lesson learned was that there are sometimes better ways to deal with some problems than to try to argue one's own case.

The health of the interfaith spirit of Hendricks Chapel was alive and well, I quickly discovered, and it pleased me very much. Francis Hendricks had directed us to have such a chapel, and I intended to do all in my administration to keep it so, even to improve upon that spirit. Some say I have abandoned my Christian ministry, at least in part, by becoming as closely tied to interfaith matters as I did and as I am. I take just the other side of that issue. First, I understand my Christian faith to move me into the world to seek out and serve my neighbor, both friend and stranger. Second, I find my interaction with believers of different faiths and with persons of no identifiable religious faith to both stimulate and improve my understanding of and commitment to my identification of myself as a Christian. I am, as has been said before, willing to go to Hell for believing as I do. In the present conservative atmosphere there are many who certainly believe that I will. I understand and accept that reality.

Now to a final first-blush perspective. Student interest and participation in institutional religion, I knew full well before coming back to SU, was down, in fact was very low. No new news here, but it was really lower than I thought. When I left the Department of Religion faculty in 1966 to move to Baker University in Kansas I found that 85 percent of the students in my SU classes had some church or synagogue background and knew at least some of the basics of the religious background of their family and that only 15 percent had no such training. By 1981 those figures were reversed. When only 15 percent of the population making up our overall constituency has any tangible background in matters of institutional religion you have to assume you are starting from a religious ground zero in any classroom or generalized grouping of students.

It goes without saying that the "congregations" of each of the chaplains were for the most part made up of only a portion of the 15 percent and that touching the lives of the 85 percent at SU had to take place, if it did at all, in settings that were other than specifically religion based. That challenge was clear and was something we all worked at every week and every semester. It is also the reason Hendricks Chapel has the charge (well expressed by Eggers and by the Wiggins report) to do programming for believers and nonbelievers in matters of morals, ethics, values, cultural problems and change, meaning, and any and all other issues dealing with what we in religion like to call the sanctity of life. From day one the challenges before us were far beyond the time, energy, and resources needed to achieve any full measure of success. Fortunately, that fact did not stop any of us at Hendricks Chapel from doing our best to make whatever progress we could in getting a spiritual awareness before a population largely devoid of same.

I wish it were possible to convince everyone in religious organizations that support for campus work is of critical importance to our future, even if that work does not yield a specific increase in the number of members or constituents they can count in the postcollege years of these seemingly nonreligious students. If indeed life is sacred, then someone must be attending to the store, to the key issues of how and why we live and do as we do. I think the college years are the last place that should be without such storekeepers! Our very presence is critical. In fact, observers of religion have long known that sheer presence is one of the most important aspects of institutional and interpersonal ministry.

51. The Hendricks Chapel Advisory Board

WITH CHANCELLOR EGGERS's implementation of almost all of the recommendations of the Wiggins committee report in late 1980, the stage was set for a rather significant change in the operation of Hendricks Chapel. The search was under way for a new dean; Wiggins, as interim dean, was putting some of the recommendations into practice and the new Hendricks Chapel Advisory Board (HCAB) was set up. Below is a list of the first membership of that board. Most of the members were persons who had served on the Wiggins committee or the dean's search committee or both. With its genesis all other Hendricks Chapel governing boards and committees, except for the Chaplains Council, became history. Don Wright has detailed most of them. McCombe had done some board and committee governance experimentation. It was hoped that this new structure into which I stepped as the fourth dean of Hendricks Chapel would serve the needs of the overall operation in the years ahead, which indeed it did.

Eggers was cautious in setting up the new HCAB. He wanted to keep a more hands-on approach, no doubt in part because of the recent months of both emotional and intense work he and the others had just put in regarding Hendricks Chapel issues. In fact, he made the HCAB officially a committee of the chancellor and passed the role of facilitating the work of the board to the new dean. Even so, final responsibility of the board rested in the chancellor's office. This situation was to be the case for ten years. In 1990, as Eggers was preparing to retire, he shifted the HCAB from his office to the office of the dean of Hendricks Chapel. At the time he said to me, "The new structure works. It is past time to get the Board back into the Chapel where it belongs." He agreed to have a dotted line to the chancellor's office so that the HCAB could, in case of special need, go to the top with one or more concerns.*

The structure for the HCAB reflects the caution of the chancellor as well as his desire to be sure Hendricks Chapel was viewed as a comprehensive, all-university agent and operation. The structure called for two SU trustees, an officer from the central administration of SU, one chaplain from the Chaplains Council, four additional SU administrators, four faculty members, one SU staff member, and four students. The faculty, staff, and students at the College of Environmental Sciences and Forestry (ESF) were eligible for service in these structured categories, and many did serve over the years. At one time we also had a faculty member from the New York State Medical School on the HCAB. Hendricks Chapel did, in several ways over the years, provide space and other services to the upstate medical school and its population.

The makeup of the HCAB, as I see it, reflected the years of changes that had been evolving at Hendricks Chapel. The most obvious was the gradual reduction in student activity and student governance regarding the overall operation. Another way of putting it was that Hendricks Chapel had steadily changed from student-generated and -administered programs for the campus, especially its

*See appendix C for a listing and description.

students, to an operation characterized by professional leadership and program generation for the campus, still especially for students. Now more than ever it was to operate as a two-division setup. The office of the dean was now designed and structured to be responsible for Hendricks Chapel's more comprehensive, that is university-wide functions, and the various campus chaplaincies and ministries to be responsible for worship and other religious-life activities on a more denominational and faith basis. From my perspective, adjustment to this officially new but functionally familiar way of operation for Hendricks Chapel was smooth and with only a few hitches along the way, probably the smoothing out of the interdenominational Protestant chaplaincy the chief source of early problems, problems basically minor in nature. The membership on the HCAB, with its heavy administrative and faculty representation, combined with a light student membership seems to have but confirmed the shifts that had really taken place over years of time.

Starting under Interim Dean Wiggins and carrying into my first year, the members of the HCAB were:

Trustees: Vernon Lee and Margot Northrup
Central Administration: Molly Broad
Faculty: Ralph Ketcham, James Wiggins, Tom Green, and Alan Berger
Chaplains Council: Charles Borgognoni
Administration: Frank Funk, Paul Eickmann, Lois Black, and Lowell Davis
Staff: Norma Jean Hussong
Students: Michael Mooney, Stephen Katz, Suzanne Roth, and TBA
Chair: Frank Funk
Deans: James Wiggins, then Richard Phillips

The members, except for students, were set up in classes of three years, with approximately the same number going off the board each year. The exceptions were the chaplain (to be chosen each year by the chaplains) and the students (a one-year but renewable membership). It was to be a self-perpetuating board with its own nominating committee. With minor adjustments we continued to use the basic structure for the HCAB throughout my deanship. Chief among the changes was to reduce the trustee representation to one. The result was that Vernon Lee served in that capacity throughout the eighteen years, many of them after he became an honorary trustee. The adjustment took place when Northrup went off the Board of Trustees and with Eggers's decision that one representative in this category was enough. Later the administrative and faculty categories were reduced to three members each, and of the four students we endeavored to have one graduate student.

Except for student participation, which was always sporadic, often none was present, the HCAB members were very active over the years and took their advisory role very seriously. We met once a month, twice if in the midst of some business that demanded it. Later in my deanship we decided two or three meetings per semester was enough if there was not special business to which to attend. Summer meetings were very rare.

The term *advisory* was the operative word and not the word *board*. The HCAB was, essentially, without administrative decision-making power. I always informed all new board members that their responsibilities were basically twofold. The first was to advise and council the dean in any and all matters relating to the operation of Hendricks Chapel and their perception of the needs of the campus that Hendricks Chapel might be fulfilling. In this regard, being the eyes and ears for the operation of Hendricks Chapel was of great importance. At times I asked the members to be particularly attentive to one or another issue on campus or within the Hendricks Chapel community. A second role, which I emphasized with the HCAB each year, was to consult with the chancellor if at any time they felt the conduct or administration of the dean needed to come before the chancellor for his consideration. I am unaware if there was ever a meeting with the chancellor for this purpose.

The HCAB regularly heard reports on the operation of the chaplains and any major problems associated with that aspect of Hendricks Chapel. The dean's report always reviewed as complete a range of the dean's activities as seemed called for. There was also a report on any Hendricks Chapel staff matters of importance and then whatever agenda the HCAB had as the business of the day or was generated as a result of reports and discussions. As with many committees, one of our most troublesome agenda items from year to year was to find a time when everyone could schedule ninety minutes for a meeting. We often met at lunchtime, even brown-bagging it sometimes. We rotated meetings to various campus locations, including at ESF, particularly when Jim Heffernan was our chair.

My gratitude for the loyalty, hard work, and conscientious attention to Hendricks Chapel matters by the members over the years is difficult to express. Both Eggers and I wrote letters of thanks to persons when they went off the board. That formality is simply not enough. The goodwill, the hard work, and the very presence of these persons on the HCAB made such a positive contribution to Hendricks Chapel, to SU, and to me and my well-being that no amount of thanks-saying can ever fully express our gratitude.

The list of persons, without student names, below indicates the broad scope of campus interest in the operation of Hendricks Chapel. I take some of the blame for the fact that student participation was so slight that an accounting of the names is both inappropriate and would be misleading. There were a few students who tried to attend meetings and to enter into the discussions, but even they were not terribly regular. I should have done more "promo" work to get the students to be more involved. But I did not and they did not. Such is, at least in part, an example of the student interest changes that have been discussed throughout this book. At the same time I fully understand the lack of the student members' interest, perhaps *toleration* is the better word, in the processes and the discussions of our HCAB meetings.

Special note needs to be made about Frank Funk, who at the time was the dean of SU's University College. Frank was a very central figure on the Wiggins committee, served as the chair of the search committee for a new dean, and chaired the new chancellor's HCAB for its maiden voyage. We became good friends, and his leadership of the HCAB and his vast knowledge of the university and the operation of and the dreams for Hendricks Chapel were critical to my orientation to the deanship and the multiple roles the dean was designed and destined to play. I hope and trust the retirement for Frank and Ruth Funk continues to go well. Thank you, Frank, and Ruth too, who later served on the HCAB.

The following are all members of the HCAB who served during my deanship, some for two successive three-year terms. I have left off the names of the chaplains for the simple reason that the Chaplains Council decided to rotate their membership on the board so that all would serve at least a one-year term while at Hendricks Chapel and SU.* The names indicated by a plus sign (⁺) are persons who at one time or another served as chair of the HCAB.

• HCAB Faculty: Alan Berger, Samuel Clemence (⁺), Willielmina Reubin Cooke, Robert Daley (also School of Medicine faculty), Donald Ely, Judy Foster, Alejandro Garcia, Gerald Grant, Tom Green, Gerald Gross, Howard Johnson, Ralph Ketcham, Mary K. Maroney, David Miller, Pat Cox Miller, Amanda Porterfield, Lois Schroeder, Milton Sernett, Houston Smith, Gary Spencer, Manfred Stanley, Brad Strait, Jim Wiggins (⁺), and Kay Wiggins

• HCAB College of Environmental Sciences and Foresty, faculty and administration: Robert Blackmon, Alan Drew, Jim Heffernan (⁺), Robert Jelinek, Don Koten, Leslie Rutkowski, and Larry Van Druff

• HCAB Administrators: Carol Walker Bell (also known as Carol Simkins) (⁺), Edna Bell, Colleen Bench, Lois Black, Molly Broad, Ron Cavanagh (⁺), Susan Crockett, Lowell Davis (⁺), Paul Eickmann (⁺), Gideon Frieder, Frank Funk (⁺), Ruth Funk, Ed Golden, Scott Greene, Robert Hill, Mary Lou Koenig, Vincent Lamparella, Jane Lillestol (⁺), Jim Morgan, Richard Phillips (as dean), Robert Pickett (as director), Michael Riley, Mary Roberts-Bailey, and Barry Wells (⁺)

• HCAB Staff: Cindy Bates, Norma Jean Hussong, Sue Price, and Susan Ryan

• HCAB Trustees: Vernon Lee and Margo Northrup

• HCAB Chancellor s Office: Jim Gies and Kathryn Lee

---

*See appendix B for a complete listing of the chaplains.

52. Campus Ministry in and Beyond Syracuse University

FROM THE START SU provided for on-campus ministry as well as helping students relate to the local churches and synagogues in Syracuse. The style of campus ministry at SU was very much like the type provided in a great number of private academic institutions. Even so, there were and are significant differences in the characteristics of ministry as carried out on the public and private campuses of the United States. The purpose of this chapter is to briefly review the major styles and to see how SU fits into the broader picture of what was and is going on in other institutions.

Protestant, Roman Catholic, and Jewish campus ministries are probably as old as academic institutions. John Wesley, an Anglican clergyman later to become the founder of Methodism, was himself a campus minister for a time, at Oxford in England. As other faiths began to populate the campuses of the world they too became involved in this specialized ministry.

Many colleges (especially true in the United States) were church created and related, and many remain related today. The United Methodist Church, for example, created more than one thousand colleges and still has some two hundred related colleges and universities in the United States today. From the beginning it was common for church-created and -related institutions to have someone designated as minister to students. In many settings this person was the pastor or a staff member of the church of the denomination located closest to the campus. When the student population grew large enough, someone, often in combination with a faculty role, usually a teacher of religion courses, was appointed to the role. My own second professional experience in campus ministry was at Baker University in Baldwin, Kansas, where I served for two years in such a dual role. My first was at a state school, the University of Colorado in Boulder, where I was associate director of the Wesley Foundation, the Methodist ministry on the edge of the campus. SU became my third service in this particular specialized ministry.

As time passed and private colleges grew, the role of campus minister (known by different titles in different settings) would normally become full-time, usually sponsored by the college itself, often with some financial help from church agencies. That pattern was characteristic of SU during its first years of existence until a growing national movement of YMCA/YWCA campus programs came to SU. It did also in many of the larger institutions, normally the universities with growing diversity in the student body. The Syracuse University experience with the Y style of ministry on campus is dealt with by Donald Wright in earlier chapters. At

SU it was combined with a continuation of the pattern just reported. Funding for the Y ministries was and is a very mixed bag. Funding patterns range from total underwriting by the college to shared (between the college and the YMCA locally or nationally) to totally independent, with the leaders having to raise their own support money.

Overall the style of ministry being characterized in the last few paragraphs is what I call the in-house style. In colleges remaining closely associated with their sponsoring church this form continues to be the dominant style today. Where diversity in the student body demands it there is often supplementation by representatives of other denominations and faiths brought in usually on a part-time basis to minister to "their" students. Financing for such campus workers varies a great deal: sometimes the college picks up the tab, sometimes the affiliated faith group pays a stipend, and sometimes the service is provided on a voluntary basis. Both clergy and laypersons are common in such supplementary arrangements for ministry. In any case diversity has become the common campus reality even in most of the small institutions, and though there is usually a lag in time the campus ministry picture is characterized by efforts to serve this diversity, usually with some success.

State-sponsored schools and private, nonsectarian colleges and universities normally provide us with a different, off-campus style of campus ministry. Even so, many, like Syracuse University, became nonsectarian, most after World War II, but retained the in-house style. SU and others often moved toward a modified in-house ministry without receiving any financial help from the original sponsoring denomination. SU, as a private, independent university, has continued to recognize and pay homage to its original church relationship without any financial support from the church. This pattern is true of many other schools as well. In a modified in-house campus ministry style the school usually hires and pays the salary of a dean or director and provides that person with staff support. The dean or director then works closely with, in our case many, religious groups who provide, on the campus, their own persons and financial support for their particular ministry. This form continues to be the pattern at Syracuse University. I call this a modified in-house style because SU (and others) does not pay for the specific ministries but is the official host of the ministry by "contracting" for its presence on campus, providing meeting space, sometimes office space, and supporting them in having appropriate access to their clientele on the campus. I have found that most of the major universities with a church-related background are involved in some form of modified in-house system in providing for campus ministry. Just a few examples may be helpful: Duke University, Columbia University, Vanderbilt University, Harvard, Yale, UCLA, Southern Methodist University, University of Chicago, Northwestern University, Cornell University (partly private, party public), and Boston University.

Roman Catholic colleges and universities also fall into first the in-house style and then the modified in-house style and are today characterized by providing for diversity, as are those schools originally Protestant sponsored. There has been much less evolution of Roman Catholic and Jewish institutions from the sectarian to the nonsectarian status than is true for their Protestant counterparts. In the Jewish institutions of higher learning the development of diversity within the student body has been, though always present to a limited extent, much slower to develop, but when needed the modified in-house approach is the direction here also. It should be noted that a national organization, the Hillel Foundation, has been active in helping all schools provide ministry for their Jewish students and represents a very helpful and healthy part of the overall campus ministry picture in the United States.

To be successful this in-house or modified in-house style of campus ministry must have the support of the top-level administration of the institution as well as be seen as an important service to the school by the majority of the faculty and other important constituencies. Without such support the ministries will be shunted to the side and campus ministry will begin to be practiced like it is at institutions that allow for such ministries only on the "outside," that is, on the periphery or margins of the campus, state or public institutions being the chief example. During my years as dean of Hendricks Chapel I increasingly came to believe that the modified in-house style is the most capable of providing comprehensive and effective service to the private, independent institution and its students. It is even the style in practice on a few public campuses. If properly supported, as SU does, the modified in-house style can be a great benefit to the institution far beyond its specific service to the religious groupings on campus. Any form of in-house supported programs should always attend to some careful evaluation of the benefits the unit provides the institution in addition to providing a place or places for specifically religious activity. Otherwise, budget concerns may jump up and demand such an accounting. I will speak to this in other chapters as well. I now shift to a quick look at another style, one not part of Syracuse University's history.

I am a firm believer in the separation of church and state. It is one of the realities that makes the United States what it is today and is, I think, a policy that strengthens both church and state in untold ways. That almost all American religious groups are firm supporters of the separation is a very healthy part of our current society. Even so, this separation has resulted in campus ministry of a different style on most of our public campuses. Why so?

State institutions of higher education in our country have, for the most part, not allowed for in-house ministry to take place on their campuses. I will not go into the reasons for this decision nor the wisdom or lack thereof. Suffice it to say that the reality has dictated a style of campus ministry that has characteristically seen campus ministry develop on the edges, the periphery, and beyond the campus proper. That it would develop even if not on the campus proper would be easy to predict given the drive churches have to serve, expand, and preserve their respective clientele. In this style religious groups rent, buy, or build facilities on the edge of the campus and hire or appoint clergy or lay leaders to provide ministry. In some cases the ministries are housed in a nearby church of the denomination. I call this style the off-campus style of campus ministry. In some cases the public institution gives some aid in providing names based on religious self-identification where such information is collected, but in large measure the ministries are conducted without financial or facilities aid, albeit usually with the permission of the public institutions. Often, but not always, the campus administration appoints an officer, usually in the Office of Student Affairs, to deal with issues that arise between the school and the ministries in question and may even provide some sympathetic support, even sometimes space, for their programs and functions. Almost never is any additional state support provided to or for the ministries. In some public schools there is a formal registration process for the off-campus ministries, but normally even that procedure is not performed. One very positive aspect to this style is that the sponsoring church or religious organization must keep close contact with the respective campus ministry and provide it with funds or help the unit itself to raise funds for its ongoing operation. In the in-house style the contact between the campus ministry unit and the original church-sponsoring group frequently becomes a very loose tie. This separation can result in the clergy or lay leadership on the campus feeling isolated and ill-supported, which in turn often diminishes the effectiveness of the ministry itself. Another positive aspect, from my point of view, of the off-campus style is that it has encouraged intergroup relationships among the religious workers (except for the very conservative groups who tend to operate in isolation from other ministries) and has often produced cooperative ministries between religious groups and organizations with similar backgrounds, ministerial philosophies, and social and religious concerns.

In each of these major styles (I have personally worked in the in-house, the modified in-house, and the off-campus styles) there can be found excellent ministries taking place for both the constituents of the religious groups and the academic institutions themselves. None of the styles should be considered the right or the only way to do campus ministry. As with our society in general, the issue of diversity demands that we have diverse ways of ministering to human needs, religious and otherwise. There are hundreds, maybe thousands, of types of ministry taking place within each of these major styles. They range from what has been called the milk-and-cookies type to the guitar-songfest type, the strict Word-and-sacrament type, and the social-service type. Often there is emphasis on more than one type tied to a given ministry. Additionally, in any given religious group we could find in its practices from campus to campus a huge range of types of programs and practices. To outline let alone deal with such a diversity of types of ministry would take hundreds of pages by itself and then some important ways of doing ministry on campuses would probably be left out. The type(s) of ministry taking place on any campus and within any religious group is most dependent on two variables: first, the tradition already established at that place and, second, the character and skill of the leadership assigned.

There are a variety of professional campus ministry organizations where campus ministers who wish to attend can share information, problems, resources, and other concerns as well as helpful interinstitutional relationships. I will deal with them in another chapter.

53. Students and Hendricks Chapel

THIS CHAPTER is the first of four dealing with the people associated with the operation of the chapel. In this chapter I focus on the students and expand upon my earlier first impressions. Then there will be a chapter on the chaplains and workers, both professional and lay, serving SU through the chapel, and a third will deal with the staff members, each chapter covering the years of my deanship. A fourth short chapter will deal with the group ministries during these same years.

As chapelites and the SU administration are well aware, people in contact with people constituted the key to almost all the work of the chapel. Although quantity was not the only key issue, I always wanted as many workers in contact with the SU community as we could have. Of course, the quality issues were also very important. It was essential that staff members understand the basics of working with each segment of the university community and they and the chaplains be skilled in both the general practice of "ministry" to the community and highly skilled in those special ministries we found so important.

The test of my people-in-contact-with-people philosophy came when money became an issue. During the budget reductions in the 1990s there were two major all-university cuts. One was a 15 percent cut, and the other was just over 10 percent. In each case the request from the central administration was to cut both the salary portion of the budget and the operational portion in approximately equal figures. Thus, within fewer than three years we experienced just over a 25 percent decrease in our budget. Some departments and operations within the university suffered even stiffer cuts.

Vice President Eleanor Ware became my first line of reporting when Michael Sawyer retired, and in my direct work with her and Chancellor Shaw I was able to successfully make the case for not making any personnel cuts in the staff at Hendricks Chapel. It was necessary to make my case more than once. I took the position that Hendricks Chapel was unique in the university in that our work was almost all based on person-to-person contact and that we could not give the same amount or quality of service without the full staff. I was willing and did make all the cuts in the operational budget. This reduction meant that we offered fewer high-budget programs and focused more of our energy on low-budget programming. We did so by leaning even more heavily on SU faculty and staff and their skills and expertise in offering programs (for example, a panel on problems in the Middle East, human sexuality, moral and ethical issues, or religious issues both domestic and international) for and with students. We increased the number of programs we cosponsored with other departments and operations, and such efforts had some very good spinoff benefits. We also cut our expenses as much as we could in the regular week-in-and-week-out operation. Here the staff was wonderful and even creative in getting as much done but with fewer resources. We delayed equipment replacement like computers, and we all took great care not to waste anything we could possibly avoid wasting. We were so successful that I doubt seriously if any segment of our university-wide clientele saw any reduction in our efforts or our overall service to the school. Most important, I do not think programs directed at students suffered, and I do not think the work of the chaplains or our staff work with them was diminished. Later we were able to add some resources, thanks in part to generous donors, to return to some high-ticket programs such as bringing to campus nationally known leaders in one or another of our areas of programmatic concern. Now I turn to students and Hendricks Chapel.

To some extent I was surprised that my own interaction and degree of direct contact with students, both undergraduate and graduate, was much greater than I had originally thought it might be. With the dean now separated from ministering directly to the mainline Protestant flock, would I, I had asked myself, have much direct dealing with students? I soon found that several avenues made for a great deal of direct interaction. Chief among them were the following: the Hendricks Chapel Choir, for it remained a program under the dean's direction; the Hendricks Chapel's student employees both graduate and undergraduate (usually between thirty-five and forty-five each semester); the interdenominational Protestant chaplaincy, for there is where I participated on Sundays; the Black Celestial Choral Ensemble of which I was adviser and often rules enforcer; the Hendricks Chapel Advisory Board with four to six students sometimes participating; the dean's Advisory Committee made up of ten to twelve students; the Martin Luther King Celebration Committee, which had the best and most intense student participation of any committee at SU upon which I served with students; the dean's Benevolence Fund, which as a student emergency fund I administered; and a great deal of student counseling that ultimately became a bit too time consuming. My regular appearance in campus events, my recreational basketball and tennis playing (I was for a time sponsor of the Men's Tennis Club), and service in the disciplinary hearings combined with frequent speaking engagements also made for a high level of student contact. On two occasions I was asked to teach the senior honors seminar in the Honors Program, and that relationship with students was very rewarding.

During my years I did notice a definite shift in student focus. In the early 1980s students listed getting an education for self-fulfillment as the highest of their goals. Over a period of no more than six or seven years the focus became decidedly career oriented. Getting a good job and earning very good money moved to the top as students' chief motivations for getting a college education. That shift resulted in a noticeably more serious attitude about class work and study in general, and it also increased enrollment in career-preparatory courses.

Earlier I mentioned the dramatic downshift in student organizational participation that took place during Dean Noble's late deanship and during Dean McCombe's time. During Hendricks Chapel's early years, as Donald Wright related in the first portions of this book, there were literally hundreds of students serving on dozens of committees and boards directly related to the overall operation of Hendricks Chapel. There was also strong student participation in the individual ministries on campus. As student patterns of involvement in organizational matters, religion included, dwindled in the 1950s we gradually found a new and very different style of student participation—some would say lack of participation.

The first shift came with students relating more to the individual ministries and less and less directly with the overall operation of Hendricks Chapel. With the rise of theological trends toward a more neo-orthodox Protestant Christian perspective and a more Orthodox expression of Roman Catholic patterns, we found a corresponding drop in the ecumenical and interfaith practices that so marked the years of Deans Powers and Noble. A new post-Holocaust Judaism likewise tended to draw itself into its own operations and to feel less comfortable in a ministry expressing itself in interfaith terms. Judaism also became more and more concerned about cultural and religious assimilation in the post-World War II years, even to the extent that there was much alarm that if assimilation trends continued, Judaism was in danger of disappearing in the United States.

These trends did not result in a discontinuation of cooperation between religious groups (cooperation was strong, usually at the professional-worker rather than the student level) but certainly shifted the focus of student participation from all-chapel committee participation to working more exclusively within each tradition. This shift combined with a massive move away from standard institutional involvement generally and certainly (including religious involvement and affiliation) followed the general societal trends we called the "dropout" period of the late 1950s and 1960s. Youth involvement fell noticeably beginning with the so-called Beat generation and then fell even more during the hippie period.

Already mentioned in my introductory chapter was the great shift in students' affiliation and education in their families' religious backgrounds. From the mid-sixties to the early eighties we saw a drop from 85 percent to 15 percent of students

with at least some training in the family religious tradition. This drop, in my experience, is a key if not the key indicator of why student participation in institutionalized religion fell so drastically in such a few years. It was a major shift in our
culture, and most observers do not ever see it changing back toward the previous
patterns of identification.

There are three somewhat different ways of looking at this issue without coming to the conclusion that religion is dying in the lives of our current students and
in our society in general. There are excellent new books dealing with the realities
of the matter. I shall mention two after a paragraph on overall participation.

I have little doubt that a smaller percentage of Syracuse University students
participate in overall chapel-related programs and ministries than was true twenty-
five or thirty years ago. Even so, one can make the case that participation is strong
and that numbers of participants are steady even if the percentage is down. If you
add up the numbers of students attending all the religiously generated services of
worship, study and prayer groups, theologically oriented discussion groups, and
fellowship programs offered each semester at SU, it is probably a greater number
than were doing so in the 1930s and 1940s at Hendricks Chapel. After all, in any
given semester, we had more than thirty-five, sometimes as many as forty-five, active ministries and groups. If you add the great increase in interest in spiritual life
in general and the very private activity associated with the spirituality boom we
know is taking place in our society and today's student, it might even be that a
higher percentage of students are religiously active today than was then. There is a
problem in that hard data are just not available for us to know for sure how such
matters stand today. Whatever the situation I am ready to debate with anyone the
claim that there is less interest in religion today than in any prior period of our history. If public polls are to be taken as an indicator, there has never been any
stronger interest in religion or any more traditional belief patterns in our society
than we see right now. Students are no different.

I mentioned two new books. The first I want to briefly look at is by a group of
researchers that includes former Syracuse University professor Amanda Porterfield. She and her colleagues Conrad Cherry and Betty DeBerg published *Religion
on Campus* (University of North Carolina Press, 2001) after extensive research on
four U.S. campuses. They used both standard measuring techniques as well as personal visits and interviews to arrive at their conclusions. Many of their findings are
something of a surprise. They end up siding with other scholars who are challenging the rather standard hypothesis that we have become an increasingly secularized
society. On page 5 of their introduction they quote Peter Berger: "I think what I
and most other sociologists of religion wrote in the 1960's about secularization
was a mistake. Our underlying argument was that secularization and modernity go
hand in hand." The authors go on to note that Berger and others like Rodney
Stark conclude that the opposite is basically the reality. Most of the world, they ob-

serve, including the United States, is very religious. One of the stated purposes of *Religion on Campus* was to test the secularization hypothesis, and the authors end up agreeing with Berger's observations above. What has happened is that when an increasingly pervasive pluralism combines with a precipitous drop in identification with institutionalized religion, it can indeed look like secularization when in reality just the opposite is taking place.

The researchers found religion, both the formal study in academic departments of religion and the practice of campus ministry, to be functioning well, in what is for the most part a very hospitable climate, and engaging students in great numbers at both public and private schools all across America. They conclude that one must include the current "spirituality" in understanding campus religious practice today and that when this is done, "opportunities for undergraduates to practice religion were widely available at all four schools" (275).

They also observe that "coerced religious activity had disappeared" (293). We have seen that trend in almost all but the small private colleges closely tied with a founding church. We certainly saw it take place early in the SU experience with campus ministry.

The final sentence of this book is also worth quoting and speaks to campus-based religion at Syracuse as well as in the schools they studied for their book. "More clearly, our study reveals that the ethos of decentered, diverse, religiously tolerant institutions of higher education is a breeding ground for vital religious practice and teaching" (295).

Differences between this finding and what we find in the early years of religious practice at SU are day-and-night differences, to be sure. Is one better than the other? That question cannot be answered. We simply must realize we live and minister in vastly different times and with much different students.

The second book centers on the issue of spirituality. Its title, *Spiritual but not Religious*, by Robert C. Fuller (Oxford University Press, 2001), almost tells the whole story. I recommend that anyone wanting to understand what working with young people in today's religious climate is all about (some would say what they are up against) should read these two books.

Fuller leads us in a history lesson that demonstrates that noninstitutionalized religion is nothing new in the United States, even if it has become very pervasive today. Perhaps we are as doggedly independent as a nation in matters religious as we are individualistic in our approach to much of life. One simply cannot say that a person is not religious just because they participate in no specifically religious organization. Increasingly, Americans fall into this catchall category of "spiritual" for their religious identification.

Fuller indicates that the vast differences in the unchurched traditions make it impossible to see continuity in the religious worldviews they construct for their personal use. That they are a curious mixture is obvious, where it will lead not so obvious. Fuller has written widely on the topic and expects to continue his research in the area. "Obviously, a great deal more needs to be known about the way that individuals who are 'spiritual but not religious' utilize both churched and unchurched religious traditions in their personal lives" (175).

Throughout my own career I have seen many expressions of this type of spirituality. Some of it has been the basis of good humor, such as comedian Flip Wilson's "Church of What's Happening Now." Some of it has been the source of great distress, such as the sexually oppressive groups we all hear about from time to time. The so-called New Age movement has spawned countless groupings and private practices. Not long ago I learned of a religious group that claimed body piercing as the basis for their religion and one member was suing Wal-Mart for not allowing some of her expression to be worn while she was at work. Most of us can think of countless examples of where private or semiprivate spirituality has taken and will continue to take people. I will forgo citing some examples from our own campus.

One can draw several conclusions from these trends. Most telling, I believe, are the deep hunger and the fervent searching we see in people that lead them to grasp for answers to life's spiritual questions when they no longer find a "home" for those questions in the institutionalized traditions of their families and their own pasts. It is easy, I believe, to see this searching and all of its uncertainties in the students of Syracuse University and almost all of our sister institutions.

In this chapter I have stepped outside of SU and Hendricks Chapel to look at today's student. We are not an isolated retreat; we are very much a reflection of our society even while we reflect upon our society. I hope I have been of some help to people who are trying and will continue to try to make sense, in religious terms, of the persons that Hendricks Chapel is charged with serving at Syracuse University.

THE USE OF ALCOHOL AND DRUGS by students is another reflection of our society. We grapple with the problem all the time, we have programs we hope will help, we provide counseling for those individuals who have been engulfed, we even work with the local bars to try to have them do a more responsible and less degrading job of advertising their presence on the edge of our campus. No one has worked harder at this than Vice President Barry Wells. Will we stop it? No! Will we make an impact in some precious lives? Yes! So, Barry and staff and all at Hendricks Chapel, keep on keepin' on!

When I came to Syracuse University in 1981 we were in the middle of what we called a watering-hole generation. Students, especially on Friday and Saturday nights, lined up around the blocks of Marshall Street waiting to get in the bars, which in turn were having to enforce house-capacity regulations. Sometimes, even in the snow, the wait was hours long. A typical ad went like this: "Come to _____'s and GET SMASHED!" Or "Lose Yourself and Your Troubles, TWO FOR

ONE ALL NIGHT at _____'s. Several of us from Hendricks Chapel made the rounds of the owners after seeing this approach and asked them not to use ads that appeal to that which degrades the human spirit. Each owner said he would like to do as we suggested but that he had to keep up with the competition or lose business. Things did get better both in the lines waiting and in the ads, but the less blatant ads did not last long. Competition was too great. Over the next months the lines of waiting students did disappear, but it was more a factor of student wisdom about waiting and the start-up of more bars.

What is important to know is that the vast majority of SU students do not get drunk, do not stand in line half the night to get into a bar, and do not take drugs. They too are searching for what life is supposed to be and what free-time activities are worthy of their involvement. The chapel and other university-based programs did our best to sponsor a great variety of things speaking to dignity if not the sanctity of life. Vice Chancellor John Prucha once counted and found that more than six hundred extracurricular activities and meetings took place every semester on campus. Practically every department and program on campus was involved in the effort, including, of course, Hendricks Chapel.

Syracuse University has a party-school reputation and that has been true for a long time. Along with others at SU we saw our students as falling into three general categories—broad, rough, and ill defined but I think pretty accurate. In most major universities with which I have any familiarity this shoe also fits. About a third of our students were the party animals. They come to party and have a good time, they did not come to study anymore than necessary, they may have some hope that they will get a degree, but that goal is very secondary to their presence on campus. College is simply where one spends one's middle to late adolescence, not really perceived as a place of research, teaching, and learning. A few of them do pick up the student banner before it is over, but many of them are the first- and second-year dropouts. Hendricks Chapel is rarely a factor in the lives of these students.

Yet another third of our students come because parents and others expect them to be in college, and they have complied. They do not know why they are there, and some never do really figure it out. Some of them join the hard-core party crowd, and some do become what I call real students with academic interests and graduate, even go on to graduate school. In their times of searching the why-am-I-here questions, some become depressed, some drop out a year or more to find themselves, and some become searchers while going through the tunnel of finding a true identity. These students are often the searchers who show up to special chapel programs and often ask the best questions. They may be, as a group, the average American on the college gig. I like to think the sharpest of them make it to the point of embracing the purposes of our institution.

Yet another, the final, third of our students are here because they want to be; they are in pursuit of an education, and they have some sense of themselves as budding scholars. They are fun to teach and fun to visit with, but that does not mean some of them do not party with the best of the party goers. Most of them have already contemplated the possibility of graduate school. When they are inclined (only a minority are) to participate in one or more of the Hendricks Chapel ministries, they are the best leaders and the best workers. They know something about giving as well as taking while on life's voyage. They are very busy to a person, often having committed to far more campus-based involvement than they can fulfill. When they have a focus (as in degree sought or goal for a career) they are great members of the campus community, even if at times a little too narrow in focus. They claim most of the academic honors, make life worthwhile for professors, and usually help others come as far down the road of scholardom as possible. Most campus organizations, including Hendricks Chapel, solicit their participation.

This characterization, as I said, is a rough categorization, and within each of these categories there are students who are on the border of the adjacent group and students who shift, some soon, some late, to one of the other categories. As in most of life, I have found a pattern. Those individuals with whom the first-year students associate as peers are often the most important variables determining which category will claim them by the time they are juniors or even seniors.

That the individuals in each category are asking the essential and age-old religious questions is obvious. If the campus is without some real caring and perceptive leadership in the arena of religion, religious bodies not placing such workers here are missing an opportunity of touching lives at a very critical stage of human development. But, alas, that question is one, you say, that should concern a chapel dean, and it did and does! Too many traditional sponsors of campus ministry have withdrawn into a financial and to some extent identity retreat from any significant outreach to today's college youth.

The variety of students who relate to Hendricks Chapel and its ministries is great. For the most part they are all fun to relate to, sometimes trying but certainly interesting. Those who are there because it is a part of their precollege life and they want to continue (say to go to mass regularly) are bread and butter to any campus minister. Those who are there to search out and explore the deeper questions of faith and life are sometimes delightfully stimulating, sometimes troublesome group members, but I found that every chaplain found rich rewards in working with such students. And some are there because they have been saved, have found the "truth," and a good many in that category have come to believe that they must try their best to bring others to their theological station in life. It is when they also believe so strongly that the ends associated with their evangelizing justify whatever means they use to get to their ends that these truth bearers become a real problem. "You must accept the sister and brotherhood of each religious group on campus and not proselyte from their ranks." How many times and in how many ways have I had to explain that reality to the convert-them-now-oriented possessor of religious truth. You deal with that problem the best you can, but it is always present no matter what resources you bring to bear. The closest I have come to a convincing statement to such persons is to let them know that they can believe and practice, within limits, the religious life they wish because others here respect their right to do so—so they must respect others' rights as well. Though that does not change their beliefs, it usually results in some backing away from their high-pressure tactics of conversion.

I have discovered that a chaplain will seek the involvement of a dean most fervently when some ultraconservative group is known through an ad, a sermon, or a discussion to have said something like, "All Catholics are going to Hell" or "Jews are Christ killers" or "Only with us can anyone be saved." That too will be an ongoing reality in the world of the practice of religion. I do not believe that, in any other arena of human life, feelings run so near the surface and so strongly as they do in religion. I have accepted it, with reservations, as the nature of this profession. Even so, I hold out that reason will someday run as deep.

Students, as a rule, do not have a very mature view of their religious beliefs. But I have discovered that neither do many older adults. For me, one of the marks of religious maturity is the ability to step outside of one's self and look objectively at another's religious beliefs and practices. We work hard at that at Hendricks Chapel. I believe it makes for the best kind of growth in general as well as in religion.

As a whole, students support Hendricks Chapel well. They know we are present for their benefit; they especially sense it at times of either personal or societal crisis. They know, if nothing else, that we are a place of weddings and memorial services and that they too might one day need assistance in one or both of these areas. Once a beer party directly in front of Hendricks Chapel broke up peacefully when I informed the partyers that a special wedding would take place in an hour and that I did not think they would want such a party at the front door of their own wedding.

Over the years I discovered over and over that working with students is a joy. It can also be a cause for frustration and even some aging. I do not go so far as to say students are what campus ministry is all about. Indeed, more than four thousand nonstudents at SU were and are served by the chapel in important ways. For me, they are also a precious part of the clientele! Even so, students are the key to the work of all campus ministry.

54. Chaplains at Hendricks Chapel

I WAS OFTEN ASKED to explain what my job entailed or to give a summary of responsibilities. My answer always started the same. I saw my first and foremost responsibility to support the chaplains serving their constituents within the Syracuse University community. Specifically, I believed that I should help make their respective ministries on campus as successful as possible. As "host" there are many things that the office of the dean can do to facilitate their work. When we provided space free of cost, religious preference lists, photocopy machines, and other services on a cost basis and encouraged cooperative programming that benefited the entire campus, I saw it as my responsibility to make sure the services and the relationships involved were first class whenever possible.

The Chaplains Council together with one-to-one relationships were the chief settings in which this facilitative philosophy was communicated and fulfilled. As a group and with key Hendricks Chapel staff members present, the Chaplains Council meetings were always conducted to achieve several key goals: first to be open to discuss any problems any chaplain might be having in fulfilling his or her ministry, next to create a peer group of mutual respect and concern and to make it clear that our camaraderie was of great importance to me, and finally to plan for as much mutual and cooperative programming for the campus as possible, including from time to time taking positions on the key social concerns of the day. When we were confronted with urgent situations, like the Lockerbie air disaster, it was, whenever possible, our goal to act as a group rather than as separate ministries.

As I got to know the operations of other campuses I came to believe Hendricks Chapel performed extremely well in this regard. The reputation for collegiality within the ranks of the chaplains on our campus was excellent. Many of my peers on other campuses came to view our situation as one of if not the best in the country in this regard. Of course, we had differences of opinion, and not all chaplains could share in every event held on campus. We often saw important theological issues in different, sometimes opposite, ways, but we could, nonetheless, agree to be the closest of friends and colleagues even when on different sides of an issue.

As has been made clear earlier, each chaplain was selected and supported financially from outside the university. Even so, the dean had to give university approval for the chaplain selected to serve on the campus, technically to be renewed on an annual basis. One of the responsibilities of the dean was to work with any religious body supporting a chaplain if, as did happen, it was observed that the person in question might not be serving the best interests of the sponsoring agency or agencies. In my eighteen years I recall only twice having to meet with religious officials outside the university to let them know that all was not well with their ministry on the campus. That task is not a pleasant responsibility, but I must say it is a very important one.

In appendix B the reader will find a listing of all the chaplains who served under the umbrella of Hendricks Chapel from 1981 until 1999, the span of my deanship. In this chapter I will relate some information about how each of the major chaplaincies did their work, some special aspects of some of the individual chaplains, and some of the things we were able to do together. Over the years we at Hendricks Chapel and SU have been blessed with many outstanding chaplains, in terms of both their ministry to a flock and their ministry to and on behalf of the whole university. In a few cases chaplains were called upon to serve in a part-time or quasi-staff relationship as well as with their own chaplaincy. The two persons who did so at very important times in our history were Thomas Van Loon and Paul Bosch.

From Dean Powers's time to the present there have been three chaplaincies that have had numbers of constituents that set them apart from the other religious groups. They are the Roman Catholic, the Jewish, and the so-called mainline Protestant chaplaincies. The exact format of the Protestant ministry has changed from time to time, but the new interdenominational Protestant chaplaincy formed in 1980–81 resulting from the work of the Wiggins committee continues to be the format at the time of this writing.

First I will turn to the Roman Catholic ministry at SU. It has already been well documented that it was, from the start, a key chaplaincy at Syracuse University. Don Wright has well documented the fact that Father Gannon Ryan, a difficult figure in some important ways, died in that office in the 1961–62 academic year and that Father Charles Borgognoni took his place. Borgognoni was to become one of the most popular and well-known figures on the campus and in the Syracuse community within the first few years of his chaplaincy. His tenure was to be long and storied. These few paragraphs cannot begin to do it justice or to cover its rather remarkable range of ministry.

Charlie, as he was known by his peers and friends, was called Father Charles by the students and people who did not know him well. In addition to his roles in all the more traditional duties of a chaplain and priest in the Roman Catholic tradition, Charlie became a community fixture in at least three additional ways. Mention has already been made of his musical theater group called the Pompeian Players. In addition, he became a community presence as the informal but very regular chaplain serving the football and basketball teams. Yet a third aspect of his ministry was that of fund-raiser for the complete operation of the St. Thomas More ministry located in its own facility on the northern edge of the campus. Because they have already been treated earlier in this book, only short mention will be made of the musical group and the athletic involvement in this chapter. As for the fund-raising aspect, there were no fewer than five major annual events to keep the money flowing to support the ministry, which did not benefit from any money from "headquarters." Even so, every Catholic within many miles of Syracuse was touched for support, and many non-Catholics found themselves similarly beloved!

Father Ryan had established the St. Thomas More facility at the corner of Walnut and Adams as the site for the Roman Catholic ministry long before Father Charles took over. Under Borgognoni it grew and had two major additions during his tenure. The apartment where Charlie lived is located in the facility. He was 100 percent involved in his ministry. Owing to the steady growth in the numbers of Catholic students on campus as well as the growth in percentage of participation of those students Charlie soon found it necessary to have a second priest in the ministry. When I arrived that priest was Father Ed Ondrako, a wonderful young priest with just the right temperament for work both with students and with Charlie. Ed was to serve with Charlie until Charlie retired. Both Charlie and Ed were solid, eager, and spirited participants on the Chaplains Council and often hosted our meetings at their facility.

This Roman Catholic chaplaincy was the only chaplaincy either before or during my deanship that was carried out both in Hendricks Chapel and in its own facility. In fact, this factor is probably why the term *umbrella* was first used in connection with the operation of Hendricks Chapel. Throughout these years there were daily masses said in Hendricks Chapel, sometimes Sunday mass, but those masses were, until the 1985 construction of the Alibrandi Center addition to the St. Thomas More facility, usually held in the Crouse College building auditorium. After the construction of the Alibrandi Center, the Sunday services were always there, but daily services still took place in Hendricks Chapel. After Alibrandi came into existence, the need for fund-raising increased significantly, as it proved to be very expensive to heat and to operate. The Alibrandi Center proved to be a wonderful multipurpose facility that the Roman Catholic ministry has always generously made available for other Hendricks Chapel events and in some cases use by Syracuse University as well.

Borgognoni was a wonderful part of the Syracuse sons of Italy tradition so prominently a part of greater Syracuse (he once joked that he was never sure he could trust any non-Italian Roman priest) and a true romantic at heart. He loved everyone, even people who sometimes he did not get along with for a minute or two! A close circle of friends developed around Charlie. These friends were like lifeblood for him. He was not a terribly practical individual. They saw to his recreational needs, to cleaning out his refrigerator from time to time, to taking him on vacations, to tending to more serious needs as his health failed prior to and after his retirement. As of this writing Charlie continues to live in a health care facility in Syracuse. He was retired amid several appropriate celebrations in 1991.

Because he was such a prominent part of Hendricks Chapel and of central New York, some Borgognoni stories are in order. My favorite and a most telling story about the generosity of his spirit and his ministry came at the time of the death of his father. The funeral was in their hometown of Canastota just east of Syracuse. Ethel and I timed our drive to arrive about fifteen minutes before the service and settled in seats near the back. Ed Ondrako had seen us come in, and within three or four minutes he was standing next to us.

"Father Charles would like for you to do the service, Dick. Could you do it?" I responded that I would do anything I could and followed Ed to the robing room just off the front of the chapel. Ed had spoken correctly. Charles wanted me to do the service, not just read a Scripture or say a prayer but to be the clergy presence and leadership. Ed briefed me, gave me the texts, and asked if I remembered how to do the sign of the cross. A quick check revealed that I did and was told that was the first thing to do to get the service under way. I was able to read only the first few paragraphs before we entered, were seated, and the service was ready to begin. Needless to say, it was a tense but rewarding time. Charles is, under these and similar circumstances, a very emotional fellow and prone to cry, so his contribution was short and tear filled. Ed made a few comments also. I have often reflected on the broad and generous spirit of collegiality (in this case with me, a non-Roman Catholic clergyman) Charlie demonstrated on a day that was a very special occasion in the lives of such a strong and traditional Catholic family. I was honored and will never forget either the surprise or his collegial action of the day.

A quick, broad-stroke reflection on the Pompeian Players is in order. Charles, through connections in New York City, was able to use the original sets of most of the Broadway musicals he produced in Syracuse. Often the production companies even paid for the shipping of the sets. Over the years most of the great Broadway shows were performed by the players, with Charles directing the live orchestra from the pit and often prompting the players as well. During the last few productions the costs were great, Broadway in New York City no longer so generous, and the financial benefits to the campus ministry less and less. In addition, Charles was aging and did not have the energy to continue. After the last two productions (as usual we attended), he was so exhausted it was a health risk for him to continue. So a great tradition came to an end. Charles's declining health was by now becoming more and more evident. Bob Pickett often sang in the chorus of the productions and has often told me how very hard Charlie worked at seeing to virtually every detail of each show.

For several years the chaplains all went together to have an interfaith picnic at the New York State Fairgrounds. The last weekend of the fair often falls at the end of the first week of classes of the new fall semester, so a Sunday-afternoon gathering of chaplains and students became a great kickoff to the year and a fun time. We were able to get free admission to the grounds and through Jim Strates of Strates Shows free carnival-ride tickets for all the students. Jim is an SU graduate and a great supporter of Hendricks Chapel. I was even able to arrange with the fair staff to provide a prayer room for the Muslim students to use during the course of the outing.

During the picnic each of the chaplains did some aspect of the cooking and serving of the meal. Several good stories came from it, one involving a graduate assistant on the Hendricks Chapel staff cooking both kosher and nonkosher meat on the same grill. It did not take long to correct that glitch in interfaith sensitivity. Perhaps the greatest laugh came when Borgognoni was dipping ice cream from one of those two-gallon paper containers. Until several of us noticed it Charlie was alternating each dip of ice cream with a lick of the scoop and enjoying the result with some relish. The peals of laughter were not enough to alert Charlie to the problem. We had to tell him that one just does not do that when dipping ice cream for others to eat! He joined the laughter.

"Borgo," as many of his friends called him, was in great demand to perform weddings by members of his congregation. Festive by nature Charles did weddings with a flair that was usually just right for the couple. His beautiful baritone voice almost always graced the ceremony with a song or two, often from the musical *Fiddler on the Roof.* Sometimes he sang the wedding song from that musical with the original words, but sometimes, usually to some raised eyebrows, he modified the text with specifically Christian phrases being substituted for the original words. I am not sure if anyone ever challenged Charlie directly on that freewheeling habit!

During his last three years, even weddings were difficult because Charles's memory was in serious decline. During the last eighteen months or so of Charlie's ministry, Father Ed always stood beside him during a wedding and kept his finger ready to identify just where he should read next. This backup duty started after Charles lost his place near the end of a ceremony, paused for a long time, could not remember where he was, and started the whole ceremony over from the beginning. Even with this handicap in his ministry the love for Charles and his skill in doing weddings kept them coming. It was necessary for someone, usually Ed, to brief each couple about the potential for a "senior moment" during their ceremony.

More than a few times Charles became lost in unfamiliar cities during football or basketball trips. Finally the Athletic Department had to assign a staff member to be with Charles at all times during their trips. On one occasion, at the Big East Basketball Tournament in New York City, Charles became lost on the streets of Manhattan. Eventually, he was returned to the hotel by a police officer along with the suggestion that he be accompanied whenever he went out. I visited with Athletic Director Jake Crouthamel about the problem to see if the danger was too great to have Charles on such trips. Staff help was the answer rather than breaking Charlie's heart with a "no travel" policy. No better example can be found of the love and concern that surrounded Charles throughout his ministry. Jake and I did agree that, after Charles retired, there would not be a successor to his athletics-related ministry.

Several fine celebrations brought Charles's ministry to a close. The 1991 retirement one called "We Love You, Father Charles" was sponsored by the Office of the Dean of Hendricks Chapel and indeed was a tribute of love and appreciation for his long and broadly based service to the Roman Catholic campus ministry and his legendary service to both SU and the greater community. Everyone who worked with or knew Charles would like to add at least a dozen stories to the few I have related in this volume.

It is fair to say that almost all of us assumed that Father Ed would succeed Charles as head priest and director of this ministry. Ed had earned his doctorate while serving at Syracuse University, and he was known and loved by all in Hendricks Chapel and as far as I know from within the Roman Catholic ministry in general. Even so, Charles let his bishop know, some months before he retired, that Ed was not the man for the job, and that communication carried the day. Ed stayed for the introduction of the new chaplain, James Lang, but soon moved on to ministry at Cornell University in Ithaca, later to other priestly service of both teaching and campus ministry.

Charles and I had several good visits after his retirement. One such visit was the occasion for a confession of a particularly sad kind. Charles boldly told me that the worst mistake he ever made was to blackball Ed for the position and that he deeply regretted his action in the matter. "I feel terrible about it," he said, "and I don't know why I did it."

Unfortunately, Charles had but a few months to really enjoy his retirement, for he was soon in a nursing home, and on only a few occasions has his memory allowed him to identify even his closest friends. Many asked if it were Alzheimer's that caused Charles's decline. We do know that there were other health complications, but the final diagnosis is for speculation by each of us.

Father Jim Lang came to us in 1991 from campus ministry at Oswego State University, just north of Syracuse. His experience served him well. He had a great sense of humor and a strong personality. It was soon decided that the budget for the ministry could not sustain two priests, so Ed sought another appointment. They parted, as far as I know, on good terms. Unlike Charles and Ed, Jim was not comfortable with the umbrella concept and role of Hendricks Chapel on the campus and at times openly affirmed that his was a ministry outside of that umbrella. He did become, long before moving to the administrative ranks of the local diocese, a wonderful colleague and a fine member of the Chaplains Council and accepted the historic relationship between the Roman Catholic ministry and Hendricks Chapel. Perhaps the greatest test of Jim's ministry was the powerful Borgognoni tradition and legendary reputation he inherited at the heart of this ministry. I conversed over many lunches with Jim about the burdens associated with being Charlie's successor. Lang was succeeded by an outstanding personality, Father Adam Keltos, in the 1998–99 year. I did not get to know Adam well, as I was soon off to France.

After World War II the Roman Catholic student population grew by leaps and bounds. When I arrived in 1981 it was more than 39 percent of the student body and grew in the next few years to more than 44 percent with the prediction, based on a strong area Catholic population, that it would top 50 percent within a few years. It had not yet done so by 1999. During the 1970s and right up to the year 2000 the Roman Catholic population not only grew but so did the percentage of Catholic student participation, as measured by attendance at weekly mass. The

Roman Catholic ministry was the only one on campus that experienced growth in participation by its campus constituents on a week by week basis. This trend was observed all across the United States, not just at SU. Along with sociologists, all of us at Hendricks Chapel speculated about the cause for the Catholic trends in participation that were counter to what all the other religious organizations were and are experiencing. No firm, supported hypothesis has come forward to explain the trend even though we all have made our more or less educated guesses. Let us just say that the Alibrandi Center and the Roman Catholic ministry were very busy places on the weekends, as often the total count was nearly a thousand attending the four masses.

A word of summary may be unnecessary, but here is one anyway! Hendricks Chapel and Syracuse University are blessed to have such a strong Roman Catholic student presence on this campus and an equally strong Roman Catholic ministry. We are additionally blessed that it has such a wonderful facility as home base. We have been blessed, at least since 1961, with a ministry with both ecumenical and interfaith tastes and sympathies and with wonderful cooperation in such matters. Finally, this ministry extends into the university far, far beyond service to our Roman Catholic population; it indeed ministers to all of us.

We now turn our attention to the Jewish ministry on our campus. Rabbi Milton Elefant became the director of the Syracuse University Hillel ministry in 1963–64. He succeeded several well-known campus personalities, probably chief among them Rabbi Fred Krinsky, already mentioned as a key part of our fiftieth anniversary celebrations, and Rabbi Earl Stone, who moved to Denver, Colorado, where he eventually retired as that city's chief rabbi. I feel most fortunate to have known both of these fine rabbis and to know something of their work in both synagogue settings and in Krinsky's case the academic world. Milton broke a rather traditional pattern of having Reform or Conservative rabbis as campus ministers. As noted in an earlier chapter Milton is an Orthodox rabbi. To be sure, he performed his duties well as the clergy representing all of the branches of Judaism.

Milton and his successors were all troubled by the campus presence of a Lubavitch rabbi by the name of Yaakov Rapoport. The Lubavitch movement is an ultraconservative branch of Judaism with a very rigorous and literalistic approach to their understanding of Scripture and of Judaism and has a very aggressive approach to ministry. As such they are often referred to as the fundamentalist branch of Judaism, a term they do not like. Each of these characteristics just mentioned was to cause numerous problems for Hendricks Chapel, for Milton, and for SU as the years unfolded. Rapoport came to Syracuse just before I arrived on campus as a representative of his branch of Judaism but without any negotiation with Hendricks Chapel, which was to be formalized only a couple of years later. There was only weak Jewish support on campus for this ministry, and few students participated, though enough did, however, to make it a permanent part of the Jewish campus ministry. Although the Lubavitch organization and Rapoport objected, we always considered it as a subministry under the Hillel banner. To have done otherwise would have given away the farm!

This Lubavitch ministry in Syracuse did not meet with the approval of any of the local rabbis. In fact, Rapoport was never admitted to the Rabbinical Council of Syracuse, though he certainly wanted that relationship. So far to the ultraconservative side of Judaism was this rabbi that he once told me he did not even consider Milton, an Orthodox and highly educated clergyman, to be a rabbi. It was only after several years that there were some good relationships with Rapoport, but even then many of the problems continued. Most of the problems involved his failure to follow university rules about such things as parking, his frequent public and print representation of himself as the campus Jewish presence, his habits of misrepresentation in scheduling campus space, his bully-type tactics to get his way, going directly to central offices in the university rather than through channels, his appearance in a fraternity without invitation, in the conduct of certain parts of his ministry in a loud (as in noise) and tacky manner, and his failure to pay his chapel bills until months after they were due. Needless to say, Rapoport was never a part of the collegiality character of the chaplains on campus. In my work with the central Hillel office in Washington, D.C., in telephone contact with the regional Lubavitch office, and in my relationships with other campuses with a Lubavitch presence, I learned that on some campuses their ministry is much more mainstream and largely devoid of such problems. We were just lucky, I guess.

My most unpleasant episode as dean came shortly after a change in our campus Hillel leadership. On each of three such occasions after Milton's retirement Rapoport made moves to claim overall Jewish leadership and to get his ministry removed from the Hillel relationship. When Sivan Kaminsky became the director of our Hillel in 1998, Rapoport made very strong moves, probably partly because Sivan was a lay director of Hillel and not a rabbi. Finally, after some very distressing actions on his part I had to call Rapoport into my office with Sivan and two others included as witnesses, and there I read a list of some twelve issues that were problems associated with Rapoport's conduct on campus and then established rules and guidelines that if violated in the future would forever bar him from coming onto the campus. The message got through because afterward there were no more major problems associated with his ministry while I was dean. This is too much ink for a ministry that accounted for very few constituents and caused much stress. Isn't that almost always the case? It is the problems that occupy so much of our time and energy and not the things that go well, contribute mighty to the common good, and make work a delight day in and day out! Even so, it is only fair to say that there were things about Yaakov and his ministry that I liked. I enjoyed many of our visits.

When I arrived in 1981 Rabbi Elefant had the largest campus Hillel organization in the United States. I verified this fact with the Hillel office in Washington, D.C. Milton had developed a sign-up system for Hillel membership while parents were delivering their children to SU. It worked and as far as we know this technique continued to produce the largest Hillel until Milton retired.

Rabbi Bill Rudolph became the national Hillel director shortly after I arrived at Hendricks Chapel, and through several visits and in telephone conversation over some years of time we became good friends. I had even some hope that Rudolph would come to SU after Milton retired—he was just the kind of campus minister every campus should have. Bill was always helpful to me and to the university in matters related to their ministry here, in matters of perspective about the Lubavitch presence on campus, and in sharing, as a peer, ideas about ministry and higher education. I know of no national organization that was better in touch with its campus ministry units or the philosophy of campus ministry than was Hillel. They were a delight to work with, and I for one was sorry to see the organization changed radically when funds were no longer available to operate in its traditional manner. After it happened, Bill Rudolph became a congregation-based rabbi.

Milton's ministry was full and demanding. I have already related the story of his car and the limitations his kosher practices placed on his ministry. It made his work harder than it might have otherwise been, but he did it with a great spirit. Normally the Orthodox and the conservative services on Friday evenings were together in the main sanctuary of Hendricks Chapel. The Reform services were either in the small chapel or the Noble Room. Others helped each week because Milton could not be everywhere. His High Holy Days services packed the main chapel of Hendricks Chapel, and he always invited me, as dean, to say a few words in the form of a short sermonette. Milton kept his nose to the grindstone but at the same time was always a great part of the Chaplains Council and a great colleague to the other chaplains.

The night of December 21, 1988, found Milton and his wife visiting in New York City. They saw, on the television news, the report of parents gathered in a room at Kennedy Airport, beginning to deal with the reality that their children had died as a result of the bombing of Flight 103 over Lockerbie, Scotland. Milton said he knew immediately that he had to go to the airport. He did and there was able, on behalf of everyone at Syracuse University and Hendricks Chapel, to begin a very special ministry under the awesome weight of a major American tragedy, one that would change life at SU and be a headline-news item in the United States for the next ten years and indeed has continued to make headlines even as I write. This book contains a special chapter on the Lockerbie air disaster.

Milton and Charles Borgognoni were the very best of friends. It was noticeably hard on Milton when Charles's health was failing. Milton was, though never the popularity figure we have seen in Father Charles, well known and respected on campus in his more than twenty-five years of ministry. When he retired we held the party in one of the local Syracuse synagogues, and there were as many local citizens present as campus folks. The tributes to his ministry were excellent, and his send-off into retirement marked, in direct contrast to the retirement of Charles, entry into a long and enjoyable time of life, a time that at this writing continues.

Milton's wife, Channa, was a special Syracuse citizen and a good friend. She was a professional educator and added much to those chapel tasks that she shared from time to time with Milton and to those chapel social events that she attended, as did other spouses. Their commitment to religious Judaism was special to witness and is attested to by the fact that they have four sons, all of whom entered the rabbinate.

Milton was replaced by Rabbi Alan Iser in 1989. Alan was an excellent chaplain and an exemplary colleague at Hendricks Chapel. It was amazing to see how very rapidly he and the other chaplains began to function as peers—it was as if they had been working together for years. With people like Iser coming aboard it is certainly not hard to perpetuate the spirit of collegiality I found so important to the work of Hendricks Chapel.

Here I digress just to boast a little, for Hendricks Chapel and not about me. As I worked in ACURA and other national-level organizations associated with campus ministry it was soon very evident that most places do not have a sense of collegiality with the total cadre of religious-life workers. Everywhere there are the close friends who work as colleagues, but it is rare to find it to include almost all who serve a given institution. Make no mistake, there were always one or two who did not enter into the core collegiality at Hendricks Chapel. I do not believe this situation was true with regard to any of the chaplains or the staff.

Some who were more or less on the outside are noted in these pages. From time to time that isolation caused some friction. Usually those individuals opting out of closer relationships do so because they do not wish to be so identified, sometimes for theological or institutional reasons, sometimes for personal reasons—often it is a combination of both. One example and then back to our chaplains. Paul Jewell served as leader of the Campus Bible Fellowship throughout my deanship. A nicer, more collegial type you could not meet. Even so, Paul was not a member of the Chaplains Council because he represented a group ministry and was not sponsored for a chaplaincy. He was thus not in the circle where the relationships would normally blossom into a collegial expression. In addition, Paul was one who worked alone, and I suspect would not have had it any other way. At SU and Hendricks Chapel there were always a few in the same category as Paul, and I never did find a way, as I hoped I could, to include them more closely in the collegial picture.

Our first female rabbi, Toby Manewith, followed Iser in 1993. She was a fine colleague and worked well with the other chaplains and our staff. In fact, she developed close friendships with almost all of us on the Hendricks Chapel staff. One can only imagine how difficult it was for Rapoport to see his ministry falling under the overall responsibility of a female rabbi. For that matter, there were others who at the time did not accept the concept of a female rabbi, and we dealt with that reality while Toby was here. She left the position to take a similar one at American University in Washington, D.C., while I was serving in Strasbourg.

Sivan Kaminsky, a layman, followed Toby and brought his excellent talents to bear on this very important chaplaincy. Sivan got the ball rolling for a separate new center for the Jewish campus ministry, but it did not become a reality until after his departure. Since Rabbi Manewith we have not had a rabbi in the directorship position. I personally wish it could return to that pattern, but at the same time I affirm that lay ministry is conceptually sound and those individuals who serve in that capacity are just as able though a bit more limited in what they can do than those individuals who are ordained.

Jewish campus ministry on our campus is as old as Hendricks Chapel, indeed even older. It is a key part of the Hendricks Chapel service to Syracuse University and its constituents, and it has been a joy for me to work with each of the persons who have served this ministry. In some ways I regret that it is now housed, like the Roman Catholic ministry, in a separate facility. Even so, it will, I am sure, continue to enrich the overall fabric of the umbrella and continue to be a key part of the collegiality. The other side of the facility issue is that Hendricks Chapel could not house all that in theory it needs to house and Hillel simply did not have enough space for its needs in the Hendricks Chapel building. Thus, I trust we all benefit from the generosity that has made a separate facility possible. Because it was constructed after my retirement I do not have any personal experience regarding its operation.

In my introductory chapter I detailed the start of the interdenominational Protestant chaplaincy, including the story of its first chaplain, Bill Kliber. I will not repeat that content here. With the United Methodists in the lead, they are joined with the American Baptists, the United Church of Christ, and the United Presbyterians in the sponsorship of the ministry. With the exception of part of one academic year, 1987–88, this chaplaincy has conducted the Sunday morning services formerly known as the University Worship Service. That year the Protestant service was moved to the evening. Sunday morning became an experiment with a cultural event rather than a service of worship. I will give some detail to this experiment in another chapter. That year two clergy served the interdenominational chaplaincy. The first semester it was Elaine Cleeton, a United Church of Christ minister and graduate student at the university. The second semester it was well-known and retired Alexander Carmichel who filled the post. They were replaced the next year by Paul Kowalewski; his was to be only a two-year appointment.

As was the design from the beginning the Protestant chaplain worked very closely with the dean on some aspects of the ministry, and I can say with no hesitation that there has been joy in working with each of the clergy who have served in that capacity.* Without this chaplaincy or something very similar the changes of 1979–80 based on the recommendations of the Wiggins committee and put in place by Chancellor Eggers could not have worked. As I look back on the eighteen years I shared with this chaplaincy I believe the principal actors, especially the Methodist officials already mentioned, did an excellent job in putting together a new ministry that has served the constituents of the four denominations, Hendricks Chapel, and Syracuse University extremely well. The fact that Tom Wolfe, who served as chaplain for this ministry for almost nine years, became the university's choice to become the fifth dean of Hendricks speaks not only to Tom's skills but also to the place of that ministry in the life of Hendricks Chapel.

The ministries of Carl Johnson, Paul Kowalewski, and Tom Wolfe each added much to the development and the conduct of this chaplaincy. Johnson and Wolfe were the more comprehensive in their views of the ministry, each doing a great deal of ecumenical and interfaith work as well as cooperative programming for the benefit of the whole campus. Kowalewski had, not long before becoming chaplain, moved from being a Roman Catholic priest to the United Methodist ministry. He was later to shift to the Episcopal priesthood, more of a middle ground between the two. Understandably, his time at Hendricks Chapel was marked more by self-discovery and "feeling his way" than by the more comprehensive approach of the others. Bill Kliber was the first to fill this chaplaincy role, and his short ministry at Hendricks Chapel is recorded in an earlier chapter.

If any newcomers to this chaplaincy want to look at a model for how I see the operation of the role as clergy best conducted in this chaplaincy, they would do well to look at the service of Carl Johnson and of Tom Wolfe. Wolfe's efforts to put the ministry on a stronger financial base are a particularly good model. Both of these chaplains were special friends as well as what I sometimes called "my pastor."

Before moving on it is appropriate to repeat my "wouldn't it have been nice" statement about this chaplaincy. I believe it would be an even stronger ministry if the three denominations had shared the annual cost with the United Methodists. The sense of "ownership" by the others is as a result too weak. I hope the future might bring some corrective to this important problem. I cannot, however, be judgmental, for I did not labor enough in an effort to bring that goal about in the early development of the chaplaincy.

Of more than passing importance is the need to remember that many of the historic Protestant chaplaincies such as American Baptist, Presbyterian, United Church of Christ, and Methodist played extremely important roles at Hendricks Chapel. During all of my deanship most Protestant ministries were tied into the one focused on in the above paragraphs. The Lutherans and the Anglican-

*See appendix B for the names and dates.

Episcopal chaplaincies are the exception. They are usually lumped into "Protestant" (not always accurately), and these two denominations, with only brief exceptions, continue to place full-time chaplains at Hendricks Chapel.

In shopping-center terminology the "anchor" chaplaincies at Hendricks Chapel have always been and are today the Protestant, Catholic, and Jewish ministries. They serve approximately 82 percent of the religious backgrounds of the SU students, faculty, and staff. They are by no means the only important ministries; indeed, I consider each and every campus ministry effort taking place at Hendricks Chapel to be very important. I now turn my attention to some of them.

In chapter 50 I introduced the chaplains who were at the university when I became dean. A brief word in addition to what was said there is in order for some of them, including some who came later in my deanship. Additional information is available in other parts of the book.

I mentioned earlier that Dr. T. E. Koshy was and continued to serve as Evangelical Christian chaplain. McCombe had formalized the chaplaincy relationship with Koshy and his sponsoring churches in 1974. Prior, beginning in 1972, McCombe had asked him to serve as a chapel consultant to international students. Koshy, or Kosh as many of us called him, focused his ministry primarily on international students, which sometimes created some problems, particularly with our International Student Office and to some extent with the Office of Student Affairs. Problems often centered around meeting announcements and other statements and releases that seemed to claim that Koshy's ministry was an official SU ministry to all our international students and sometimes implied that the meetings were officially called by SU rather than specifically by the Evangelical chaplaincy. Another area where problems developed were in his attempt to work with the ISO staff to get names and addresses of international students, something not permitted by university regulations.

I attribute some of the problems generated by Koshy's ministry to a lack of understanding about how such matters work from the perspective of SU and some of the problems to a spirited evangelical Christian approach to the enlistment of membership. Whatever the complexity of the problems, they were manageable, and after the first few semesters they almost completely died out. Koshy and Indira and Ethel and I soon became good friends. The most winning aspect of Koshy's ministry was that he saw service to others as the key to the expression of his own Christian faith. His special focus on international students was tied to his own background.

Koshy's ministry centered around a congregational model. It was really a small evangelical church meeting on campus under his leadership. Over the years it met in several different locations, including Community House, Slocum Hall, and the Hall of Languages, until his congregation built a new facility for the ministry in the southern part of the city, beyond walking distance from the campus. The new church came just in time, for the university finally had to withdraw from providing space for the congregation but delayed the action until the construction of the new facility was complete.

I have visited his campus locations and even preached at one or two of his services. Later I did the same in their new facility. It was a congregation made up of about 60 to 70 percent community members and maybe 30 percent students, many of them graduate international students. The ministry reached far more students through what became know as his Thursday Luncheon ministry. Each week members of the congregation and his small staff would prepare and bring to the chapel a lunch characteristic of some part of the international world. It was provided free of cost and served buffet style to all who came to dine with them. At one point in the early 1990s the Onondaga Health Department stepped in and required that the luncheons meet current specifications for such food service. It was a tense time, but the ministry was able to comply by greatly increasing its equipment and the workload associated with the Thursday efforts.

As this book is written Koshy continues to be the chaplain with senior status as far as years of service are concerned. He is the only person now related to Hendricks Chapel who has served under five different chapel administrators: McCombe, Wiggins, me, Pickett, and Wolfe.

The Lutheran chaplaincy and the Episcopal chaplaincy are noteworthy for many reasons. Perhaps the chief reason is that they have almost always been full-time positions sponsored by the two church bodies. What is so remarkable about that fact is that the numbers of people on the campus who are identified with those denominations are relatively small and it would be easy to understand if the respective officials were to say there were too few folks to warrant the expense of a chaplain. The roles they have played on the campus, in the Hendricks Chapel family, and in the Chaplains Council are far too important and productive for justice to be done in any brief treatment here. In times of need, sometimes times of crisis—such as with Lutheran chaplain Paul Bosch during McCombe's deanship, Methodist Tom Van Loon during both Powers's and Noble's deanships, Methodist Frank Hulse during the student strike and the troubles of the 1970s—these clergymen, to name but a few, came to the fore as leaders of the chapel community. There are a host of others who come to mind, including Harvey Bates, Arthur Hopkinson, and Vernon Bigler, who played roles in Hendricks Chapel far beyond their denominational duties. I will now relate some information about those individuals who did so during my deanship.

Lutheran chaplain Rick Bear has already been mentioned and noted for his pastoral excellence. I do not believe, during my years, that any chaplain had a more loyal and closely knit constituency than did Rick. He was succeeded by Michael Shultz Rothermel, a man of great integrity and talent who played key roles in the ministry to the campus following the bombing of Flight 103. The next full-time

Lutheran was Dr. George Koch, who brought a significant depth of experience and keen interest in the dialogue between science and religion; we even worked together on a conference on the topic. George went on to a Lutheran administrative post in Chicago. Michael and his Lutheran clergy spouse, Marilyn (who served briefly on the Hendricks Chapel staff), left to take up teaching and parish duties in the same city. Unusual and maybe even unique at Syracuse University is the fact that our Lutheran chaplaincy serves all branches of Lutheranism, a feat not unlike having one rabbi serve all branches of Judaism.

Because of our large international population at SU we have always included all of the Anglican Church folks as part of the Episcopal chaplain's responsibility. Robert Ayers served as their clergy chaplain for many years retiring just before I came. Jacqueline Schmitt was one of the early women to be ordained as an Episcopal priest and was chaplain when I arrived. She was replaced by Dennis Winslow for two years, and then there were some short-term and interim assignments until James Taylor came in 1988 and continued to fill the chaplaincy until after I retired. Taylor had had thirteen years of campus ministry at Indiana University and one year at the University of Michigan before coming to Hendricks Chapel. His depth of experience, his brilliant sense of humor, and his wealth of knowledge served him and all of us extremely well. While at Hendricks Chapel he became the "word master" of the Chaplains Council. He retired after his service to Hendricks Chapel and to his denomination. For the last several years of his chaplaincy he also served as pastor to Grace Episcopal Church, a small congregation a few blocks north of the campus.

A very important recent addition to our chaplaincies was the Islamic faith. McCombe, during the last part of his administration, accepted the Islamic Society of Central New York's offer to place a chaplain on our campus. In fact, Jack helped them find property to buy on Comstock Avenue just across from and south of the Women's Building. That move was controversial because many of the neighbors did not want a mosque built in the midst of their homes. When I arrived a local physician, Rafil Dahfir, was president of the society. He was serving as its leader and as the counselor to Muslim students on campus. Friday prayers were held in several locations in Hendricks Chapel until the new mosque was complete.

Soon the Islamic Society was able to hire Ahmed N. Kobeisy as their imam and chaplain to the campus. His letter from me confirming his chaplaincy status at Hendricks Chapel was written on August 7, 1990. As of this writing he continues to serve in both capacities. My work with both Rafil and Ahmed has been most rewarding. The mosque and its program have been a significant part of the religious life of central New York and Syracuse University. Ahmed continues to be a very active part of the Interreligious Council of the area. I continue to treasure my friendship with Ahmed and am very supportive of his ministry.

Three brief stories associated with the Islamic presence on campus are worth relating here. The first involves my sensitivity to the plight of Muslims during Desert Shield and Desert Storm of the early 1990s. As would be expected, tensions were high, and some negative input was directed their way from the community. During much of the year in question I came to Friday prayer at the mosque and stood in back of the service as my own way of showing support. The enthusiastic expressions of appreciation were, as the year drew to a close, far more than anything my witness deserved.

A second involvement was the construction of purification stations in both the women's and men's rest rooms near the Muslim prayer room on that level of Hendricks Chapel. Such stations are often called *wuzus*. They are for ritual and actual washing of the face, hands, and feet before prayer. One of our Muslim students in the School of Architecture designed them, and SU's physical plant and facilities staffs built them. As far as I know they were the first to be built for Muslim students in any school in the United States. Several other schools, including Cornell, came to see them and to build stations of their own.

The third item of interest involved a reaction to the visit and speech of Louis Farrakhan during one of his visits to Syracuse University. His speech took place in the Goldstein Auditorium in the Schine Student Center. Farrakhan and the so-called black Muslims were known for their anti-Jewish rhetoric. Naturally, this visit was of great concern to our Jewish students and community. The black Muslim movement was then not held in high regard by most of the rest of the Islamic world, so the Muslim students were also not happy about the visit. As a result a very unlikely event took place. Our Muslim students stood with our Jewish students on the lawn of the campus across the street south of the Schine Student Center in silent and orderly protest of the visit of Farrakhan and his staff. For me it was a wonderful moment of collegiality. At the same time I supported the right of campus groups to sponsor appearances of controversial speakers, Farrakhan being but one example.

During his very successful tenure Kobeisy used his university-remitted tuition benefits to pursue his doctorate and is now Dr. Ahmed Kobeisy! I am pleased we could support him in this way. On many occasions Ahmed has waived important Islamic tradition and practice to join in collegial expressions with the other chaplains. It continues to be my belief that it is very important for non-Muslims to show support for the Islamic Society and its members and programs when we are nationally and internationally experiencing such deep and troubling tensions.

As will be noticed in appendix B there are a few other chaplaincies that experienced short-term presence. One was the Empire State Baptist, another the Assembly of God, both of very short duration. Yet another was a Pan-Orthodox presence for less than a year. Such efforts usually fail to be long term for one of two reasons: either the money is not found to continue them or the numbers of students attracted to the ministry are too few to warrant continuation. Some of the group ministries will be commented on in a later chapter. These group ministries are often focused on the very students some denominations or religious organizations would like to have served by chaplaincies but simply cannot afford to do so.

The mainline, as we call them, chaplaincies are a wonderful and very productive part of what Hendricks Chapel is and how it serves the university. Without them and their very professional staff people over the years there would really be no possibility of a comprehensive ministry at SU. They deserve much more treatment in this book, but to extend the coverage would require a second volume. What does need to be said here is a word of thanks from Hendricks Chapel and Syracuse University, an expression of thanks that can never really be properly extended. Nonetheless, it is certainly deeply felt.

55. The Hendricks Chapel Staff, 1981–1999

AN OPERATION of any importance and size, as most everyone knows, can be successful only if the staff is well suited to the tasks at hand, has an excellent grasp of the purposes espoused for its functioning, and can have some fun doing what it does. I believe the "fit" must be both a task fit and a people fit. If either dimension is not present the operation and the people within will not lead to a productive result. Just how much my wisdom or lack of it contributed to a great staff during my years I do not know. I do know that I was richly blessed with wonderful and productive people in the staff roles year in and year out.

Lists of the staff working for Hendricks Chapel during my years as dean— minus most student employees and volunteers—form appendix B of this volume. The Hendricks Chapel staff, independent of the university's employment classifications, encompassed several categories of employees: undergraduate students; graduate students (usually graduate assistants); full-time employees; part-time employees; and shared employees. From time to time we also had volunteers working at the chapel.

Semester by semester undergraduate and a few graduate student employees were numerous, sometimes as many as fifty in any given semester. Their primary roles were either as proctors or workers in People's Place, our coffee shop-type operation. These workers are not listed in appendix B. Even so, their importance cannot be overemphasized. As proctors they staffed the front desk at the entrance to the offices in the dean's suite. They were, in many cases, the first contact a visitor had with our operation and thus needed to make an excellent first impression. They also, most of the working day and until ten o'clock in the evenings, were the first persons to answer the telephone calls, again an important first contact with the office. In these roles some training was necessary, and that training, after an introduction each semester by me, was usually done by one of our senior secretaries, sometimes by other staff members.

I offer two quick illustrations to establish the importance of the training. I once listened to a proctor answer the phone, and when the caller asked to be put through to a certain chaplain the proctor at first said, "I don't think he is in the office." When asked another question by the caller the answer was, "Oh, I have no idea where he is." This response is not, I think, the way anyone would want their staff to respond to a caller. The idea of being a public relations officer on behalf of some two or three dozen people associated with Hendricks Chapel does not come naturally to all students; coaching is essential. In People's Place the training was done by the student managers, hired each year by my office and usually drawn from the experienced student staff of this operation.

Added to the proctor duties was the clipping and pasting necessary to build a year-by-year chapel scrapbook, which are held in the SU Archives. Many undergraduates were placed, once they had the necessary experience, in several other key staff responsibilities. Such roles were usually wedding coordinators, People's Place managers, and building monitors. About 40 percent to half of our undergraduates were qualified for the university's work-study program, which was a great help to our budget. It is not possible to relate in such a short space the importance of our undergraduate workers over the years. For many of them it was their first work in a professional setting, and so their great value to Hendricks Chapel was, I trust, more often than not, matched by some learning value for them.

The graduate students who worked at Hendricks Chapel were generally SU graduate assistants (GAs). Through the office of the vice chancellor for academic affairs and the Graduate Office I was able, my first semester, to negotiate three GA positions for Hendricks Chapel. This success meant that graduate credit was awarded to the GA by the university for the major, usually all, portion of their tuition. Hendricks Chapel was then, from our budget, required to pay the GA stipend. GA guidelines called for twenty hours of work per five-day weeks during the two semesters of the academic year. Some summer graduate assistantships were also available.

Our first graduate student assistantship, and one that continued throughout my deanship, was an MBA student from our School of Management hired as our Hendricks Chapel business manager. Usually these appointments were for one year, but several went for either three or four semesters. This program was wonderfully successful. Over the years several officers of the School of Management related to me that this post was one of if not the most helpful GA positions into which their graduate students were placed. It also proved to be a helpful employment experience to have on one's curriculum vita when going out into the world for a career.

GA positions also came from students from the Maxwell School, the Newhouse School, the School of Music, and, rarely, the Department of Religion. Most often the GAs were supposed to assist the person in charge of some aspect of our program. The most frequent utilization was as assistants for general administrative tasks, the operation of our Students Offering Service volunteer program, and the choir and music programs of the chapel. The reader is again referred to appendix B for specific listings of each GA's role on the staff. Titles given to the GAs varied a great deal, the most consistent one being business manager. We did not use all three graduate assistantships each semester, but they were "on the books" when we needed to use them the next time.

The use of GAs was my answer to two concerns. One was to provide a practical working experience for graduate students as part of their education and career preparation. The other was to get the work power built into the chapel operation to achieve the things we wanted in the way of overall service to the campus and to our internal operation while staying within our budget. It was a very productive endeavor in both arenas and also made for many very precious friendships. On three different occasions a person serving as a GA ended up with a part-time or full-time job on our staff. Francis Parks is one and is still on the staff as this book is written. I remember only two GAs who did not work out in a productive and rewarding way. Out of the some forty-six GAs we utilized, that is a winning program! This style of operation for Hendricks Chapel is one that I would work very hard to repeat if, as they say, I had it to do all over again.

To single out specific graduate assistants from the many who served over the years would be very unfair to the rest. Some had more impact on the overall operation of Hendricks Chapel than others—indeed, an administrative assistant certainly should—but all of them contributed mightily to our daily and semester-by-semester operation. Without their youthful enthusiasm and energy, we could not have made nearly the impact on campus that we did. Most are included in the staff lists reproduced in appendix B, lists that for me produce considerable nostalgia as I recall those years.

Several internships are also noted in appendix B. Jack McCombe had accepted an internship program known as Mutuality in Mission, a Central American short-term mission opportunity. That program continued at no cost to Hendricks Chapel for the first two years of my deanship. Neither the program intern nor those of us at Hendricks Chapel ever achieved a good working definition of the role. It ended after a few years, as had been planned from its inception. I do not know how McCombe came upon the program.

Mention has been made of the Unitarian Universalist intern program. It was started by the two Syracuse Unitarian Universalist churches, May Memorial and First Universalist, to provide a chaplaincy program for their denomination on our campus. It involved Unitarian Universalist seminary students taking a year away from their graduate clergy-preparation program to get practical campus ministry experience. Hendricks Chapel was able to offer them the opportunity to take a class or two during the internship and to utilize half of their internship (their work description paralleled the responsibility of a GA) as a Hendricks Chapel staff position. They were a valuable addition to the campus in both roles and a delight to work with. Unfortunately, that program died for two reasons. It became very difficult in the last few years of the internship to find students willing to spend time away from their theological schools, and finally it became impossible for the two sponsoring churches to continue to fund the program. It was an extremely valuable program and provided us with some perceptive and hardworking young theologians and budding members of the Unitarian Universalist clergy.

Most years there were few full-time workers at Hendricks Chapel. In addition to myself as dean there were usually two full-time secretaries, a program officer (first was Jean Baum), and an almost full-time director of music who normally taught organ part-time in the School of Music. My first semester John Jones was full-time, working essentially as a second program officer and aide to the dean.

Nina Sardino and Tione Gausman were the secretaries when I arrived, and both were in the process of moving to other SU positions during my first semester. Nina, the wife of Syracuse chief of police Tom Sardino, and Tione were both very helpful in my initial orientation to the office, and I was sorry to see such rapid turnover in that role. Nina continued to work for the College of Visual and Performing Arts for many years.

Rosemarie McGinnis joined my first full year and stayed with us for ten years until retirement. A more conscientious worker you will never meet. With her help most of the office procedures we used during my deanship were put in place. She and some of her children, while students at SU, were first-class chapelites! A couple of one-year secretaries followed and then, in 1983, Corinne Sopchak joined us for two years before moving to another SU department. The next hiring I specifically looked for a person with long-term interests to join our staff. At that point Mary Farnsworth was to join us for more than fifteen years and worked her way into our hearts as well as many managerial positions.

When Rosemarie retired, Ginny Yerdon, whose husband works at the university, joined us and is still, as of this writing, carrying major responsibilities at Hendricks Chapel. Soon Sue Martini joined, first part-time, and she too is still at Hendricks Chapel. Just before I retired, with the planned retirement of Mary Farnsworth very close to mine, we added Agnes Magnarelli, and she is also still with Hendricks Chapel. I could not have asked for a more dedicated and productive secretarial and clerical staff over the course of my deanship. Mary's work on the tasks associated with this book are noted earlier.

Rosemarie McGinnis became secretary to the dean in 1981, and was a valued member of the Hendricks Chapel "family." Courtesy of Rosemarie McGinnis.

In the academic world, as in most professional offices, there is no question but that the secretarial and clerical staff is the heart of any successful operation. It was certainly true for us, and I want to go on record as being fully aware that whatever positive can be said about Hendricks Chapel between 1981 and 1999 has more to do with that portion of our staff than any of the others of us who labored there! They can indeed leap tall buildings in a single bound!

Both full-time and part-time persons served us in what I call the program staff. Millie Woods, an African American laywoman, was the first program staff person I hired. She developed African American programs. She worked part-time, though more so in pay than in time invested. Without going into detail, the need for special attention to our African American students at SU became the same need at Hendricks Chapel. Millie was sought out because she was well known in the Syracuse community as a successful teacher and committed churchwoman. Her husband, Joe, was serving as a school principal in the Syracuse school system. Both were and I am sure still are today completely committed to education. Millie, until her retirement, served Hendricks Chapel with great insight, great energy, and great results. Her place was taken and her responsibilities assumed by Francis Parks who, after assuming Students Offering Service director duties, became full-time. I have detailed Francis's work in several other chapters.

Just before Jean Baum retired in 1986–87 I received a phone call from a friend and faculty spouse, Nansie Jensen, who said that she was interested in serving on the Hendricks Chapel staff if Jean's position was to be filled. I jumped at the chance to have Nan on the staff. She soon became certified through Onondaga Pastoral Center courses and took over the counseling and the events-coordination roles that Jean had performed so productively during her years with us. Nan followed Jean in producing our biggest annual event at that time, the International Thanksgiving Meal, and later helped plan and coordinate what became Hendricks

Mary Farnsworth became the chapel's longest-serving staff member under Dean Phillips. Courtesy of Mary Farnsworth.

Chapel's biggest event of each year, the Martin Luther King Jr. Holiday Celebration. Nan was a wonderful team person and provided, along with Mary Farnsworth, a lot of what I call the glue that held the Hendricks Chapel staff together and in such a productive mode of operation. My memory of the work of these two, Nan and Mary, is not lacking at another particularly important function. They, more than any staff I have served with, knew how to cover for the dean when he came up short on one or another matter—a skill that I know kept them and others pretty busy over my eighteen years.

As Don Wright has well documented, music at Hendricks Chapel has been a very important part of our identity. It remained true both during McCombe's deanship and mine. When I came in 1981 Winston Stephens, Jr., had been both organist and choir director since 1977. During my first full year he announced his plan to resign and to seek an advanced degree. He was a fine organist and well liked by the members of the choir and the staff. I did not relish the idea of his leaving, but his personal plan was both his and thus my priority for him. As it turned out he took a church job in Florida and owing to some problem or another did not, as far as I know, go back to school. Win had also taught organ classes and gave lessons in the School of Music, so the university knew of his plan to leave. He was considered a part-time member of both the School of Music and Hendricks Chapel. That tradition had been well established by the great Arthur Poister.

The School of Music approached me for a possible cooperative arrangement to have a member of the faculty there become a shared employee. The number of organ students was declining, a trend that continued for many years and may still be the case, which made the idea very appealing. Professor of organ Will O. Headlee was the recommendation, and we soon agreed to the shared arrangement. With Winston's departure in the summer of 1982 Will became the organist and choir director of Hendricks Chapel. Will had played the organ regularly in churches, sometimes doubling in choir work, so although it was not his field, he did have experience. Without his interest and willingness to do both the organ and choir, the arrangement could not have worked financially. Hendricks Chapel thus began to share Will's salary and his work time. He remained SU's official organist and played for any university events calling for organ music.

Will was to continue in this dual role for six years before he began a phased retirement while continuing in his faculty role. Will was an excellent member of the staff, did a wonderful job with weddings, and produced some very good choral results, including tours almost every year. This period, it must be said, was a time when choir members became hard to recruit and students did not have the same love of touring for ten days or so as students had in earlier years. Will also helped raise money for each tour, and that task was not an easy one. Normally we asked each choir member to pay a share of the cost, usually around one hundred dollars, and to help raise the rest. Some budget was allocated to the tour in addition to the normal choir budget, and we all scrambled for donors, even parents. Each choir tour an anonymous donor, now deceased, gave ten thousand dollars toward the expenses of touring. Without that angel of many years we probably could not have toured so regularly.

In the summer of 1988 Dr. Katharine Pardee became our organist and choir director, the first woman to hold the position. We were lucky to find her. I had been given her name as an excellent prospect and had left a message on her answering machine not knowing that she was in England with her husband; she was playing some concerts there. Ian, her spouse, was at the time a physics professor in Rochester, New York. She happened to call in for her phone messages and stopped in Syracuse for an interview and audition as they arrived home from England. Katie was by far the most professional candidate of three finalists.

With time out for the births of three children, Katie was with us for eleven years. She also served in the School of Music, gave organ lessons, and served as university organist when Headlee retired. She and Ian moved to England in 1998–99, thus mandating her departure from Hendricks Chapel. During her final years at Hendricks Chapel Katie reduced her time considerably and did not direct the choir. Touring was also less frequent while she was directing the choir. In 1994 School of Music choral director G. Burton Harbison became the Hendricks Chapel choir director and realized a long-standing dream of uniting all the choral music within the university under one directorship.

Burt, with Katie and her successor, Chris Marx, at the organ, produced some wonderful choral results. He was fortunate in two ways, the obvious one being that he could readily draw from the voices of other choirs in the School of Music. In addition, he came in at a time when student interest in such things as choral performance was picking back up. The touring tradition, though still somewhat reduced, was continued and included two international tours. As of this writing Burt continues at Hendricks Chapel but with retirement planned soon.

One other person must be discussed in this context: Dr. Joe Downing, another excellent organist from our School of Music. Joe served as our substitute organist for many years. Steady and reliable as well as talented, he substituted for weddings when the Hendricks Chapel organist was unavailable and for other events as well. I have another, very gratifying personal connection with Joe. When I retired, the chaplains of Hendricks Chapel commissioned Joe to write a hymn in my honor for the occasion. He wrote both the music and the words and gave it the title "This House Shall Be a House of Prayer for All." I have the framed, autographed copy in our home. The hymn was first performed by our choir at the last Malmgren Concert before my retirement. To my complete surprise, the staff and chaplains had arranged for it to be a program in my honor. The Malmgren Concert program is detailed in a following chapter devoted to several Hendricks Chapel special programs. As for Joe Downing's hymn, it forms appendix D of this volume.

It has been a joy for those at Hendricks Chapel to share music staff with the School of Music over the years, a practice that has not only benefited the chapel musically but also forged close ties between the two university units, generating other mutually beneficial developments. A good example is the harpsichord commissioned by Win Stephens and built from a kit by SU graduate Reed Martin. The Hendricks Chapel budget paid for the kit, and Martin donated his time. After very limited use in Hendricks Chapel it was loaned to the School of Music (probably a permanent loan) for use by a faculty member who was teaching harpsichord. Later, after neither entity had use for it, it was sold by the chapel during Wolfe's early years as dean.

Both graduate and undergraduate students and usually a member or two from the ranks of Syracuse University employees made up the choir. All members of the choir were volunteers. The choir usually contained one or two Jewish members; it also generally included an even greater number of nonbelievers, drawn by their love of music and of singing. I am convinced that that love— the love of music—has a way of overriding at least some questions of religious identity. Each year, almost without exception, one or two members of the choir became our close friends. They were sometimes guests for a meal at the dean's residence, and listening to them always made me wish I had a voice that would have warranted my singing with them!

Though far from being a musician myself I do enjoy, perhaps *relish* is the word, classical music, both church and general, and so my support and my enjoyment were always front and center regarding the Hendricks Chapel music staff and programs. Their recordings continue to provide both great music and great memories.

Most all of the Hendricks Chapel staff, including the business manager, were given some overall programmatic responsibilities. For the first several years I allocated a small budget to each staff person with the charge that he or she study the needs of students and staff as best he or she could and come up with at least one program during the year that they believed would serve the campus community, within or without the religious community. I dropped that practice after seeing that for some staff members this practice was a burden both in terms of interests and time. I did not drop the idea that every staff person should have input into our overall programming, and in fact some outstanding events and programs resulted from such input. The GAs and the chaplains were also key figures in providing such input. I hope none of them ever felt anything other than that they were part of the Hendricks Chapel team, especially in programming terms.

Part-time people are almost always worth far more than they are paid. That fact was true of the Hendricks Chapel part-timers, whether their role was more or less permanent or they were substituting for Katharine Pardee during one of her pregnancies. Sometimes for personal reasons someone wanted to become part-time for a short period of time, and when possible I accommodated such requests. In an operation so diverse as Hendricks Chapel it was sometimes very helpful to have specialists work on a part-time or shared-time basis over either a long or short period of time. One of my points of gratitude to the SU administration is that such flexibility was allowed and even rewarded in the Hendricks Chapel operation.

Earlier I mentioned that volunteers were sometimes part of the staff operation at Hendricks Chapel. This list did not often go beyond the members of the choir and the Hendricks Chapel Board members and sometimes other committees. We were able to use the time of our student employees in tasks that might well have been done by volunteers in other religiously constituted organizations. Please see appendixes A and B for the names of university faculty and administrative staff serving over the years as members of the Hendricks Chapel Board.

At one point we were hard-pressed to cover the evening operations of the chapel with a staff presence, and as a result we tried using a volunteer, a retired individual by the name of Ernie Dumars. He was also our general repair man, fixing things like furniture that were in need of repair but not worth the cost of having it done by either the SU Physical Plant or a local repair shop. This arrangement worked well for about four semesters, and then we discovered it was too difficult to work around Ernie's schedule to keep the building covered, so we made other arrangements. I am very fond of volunteer arrangements and would like to have used that model far more than we were able.

Our custodian for some fourteen years was a woman named Effie Clark. Though not a member of our staff, she worked closely with the staff. I give some special attention to Effie's years of service and her death in chapter 61.

I close this chapter by repeating some of my charges to the staff of Hendricks Chapel year after year:

• The customer is not always right, but insofar as possible we are going to treat them as if they are.

Another valued member of the Hendricks Chapel "family" was Effie Clark, whose love for the chapel was evident in the care she lavished on it in her fourteen years as its custodian. Courtesy of Richard L. Phillips.

- Try your best to treat everyone who walks into your office the way you would like to be treated when you walk into an office and need service.
- Never show anger if you can help it. Wait until you can come to me and tell me what the anger is all about.
- Do not reprimand an employee, student, or any other person in public. Do it, as I will if necessary with you, in private.
- Do not speak for a chaplain. Refer the person directly to the chaplain or, if that remedy does not work, to me.
- Don't butt in, but on the other hand do not hesitate to help one another out.
- I am busy, but I am not too busy for you if you have a question or a problem.
- We exist to serve. Remember that service is why we are paid. This includes everyone from the chancellor to the part-time worker getting the fewest hours of work per month! Enjoy servant status!

I do not recall a single moment when I was not proud to be a part of the Hendricks Chapel staff.

56. Other Group Ministries at Hendricks Chapel

THE CORE CHAPLAINCIES and the Hendricks Chapel staff work detailed in the previous chapters constitute only a portion of the religious-life programs conducted at Syracuse University. During my years as dean there was each year an average of seventeen to eighteen group ministries. They ranged from those ministries with professional paid staff to ones with a volunteer faculty or staff adviser. Some were present from year to year, and others came and went as the semesters rolled by. Most were small and met with "their" students irregularly. Some were large and had regular meetings one or more times per week during each semester. Very few had any activity during summer school sessions.

Many groups like Campus Crusade for Christ (a national nondenominational organization) required their permanent staff on campus to be responsible for raising part if not all of the support money necessary for the operation. The fundraising was often done in local churches with a similar theological (usually conservative) orientation. In all cases any ministries on campus had to be approved by the dean and formally registered with Hendricks Chapel and the Office of Student Affairs. In all cases they had to agree to follow the rules of operation of both SU and Hendricks Chapel and to support the purposes of higher education.

Many such groups are very evangelical in nature, often recruiting with aggressive and sometimes cultlike activity. One of our rules made it clear that proselytizing from other campus religious organizations, including all the denominations having ministries on campus, was off-limits. As a result, some consistent and careful monitoring of such groups was an important task for the office of the dean. Several staff members and all the chaplains were lookouts for inappropriate activity.

Although I site this caution I must say that we experienced very little in the way of problems with these groups and never with ones representing the more standard but smaller religious bodies—an example would be the ministry to and for the Christian Science people on campus. For almost all my years this group was led by faculty member, neighbor, and friend Samuel Clemence. In my eighteen years only three groups had to have their activities curtailed for violations of the rules, and only one was barred from the campus.

I will not go into detail about the operation of any of the groups or organizations listed later in this chapter. Any library can provide ample information on those groups with national organizations with a minimum of research. The leadership of these groups is usually not identified in this chapter or this book. For the most part they were fun to work with, cooperative, and a positive presence on the campus. As stated earlier, my own philosophy was to welcome any group wishing to go through the proper registration process and to abide by the rules. From time to time cultlike groups tried to operate on campus without registering. I believe we were successful in all such cases in seeing to it that such unregistered operation was very brief. I firmly believe that the open-arms policy for accepting such groups is the only way to go. When we had to expel The Way International group from campus they were very understanding. Their parting comment essentially was that their purposes did not allow them to comply with the rules so they expected to be expelled.

The northeastern part of the United States is well known for not being very fertile ground for many of the theologically conservative, sometimes fundamentalist, sometimes very exclusivist, groups. What I found over the years was that each group oriented to persistent if not heavy recruitment of members found themselves competing for the participation of a very small percentage of our students. Because there were so few available students, many attempts at forming a group failed or were of short duration. An example would be the Maranatha Christian Fellowship. They sent two young men as full-time staff to create a permanent ministry at SU. Their ministry is conservative in theology, and they work with heavy recruitment effort. The young men in question as well as their national organization agreed to the rules and followed them pretty well while they were on our campus. After two full years they could account for only five participants. As a result, they then pulled out and were not heard from again.

Over the years, particularly in the late 1980s and the early 1990s, the office of the dean and the chaplains found it necessary to hold major programs aimed at alerting the campus to cultlike groups and their practices. On three occasions we invited national experts on the subject to come to campus for the programs we sponsored. It does not seem to be possible to permanently eradicate the problems inherent in cultlike practices and in keeping students informed about them, for what we came to believe was their own safety and their own good. Such practices crop up each year—in some years with considerable intensity. Constant vigilance on the campus and educational efforts that are "ready to go" whenever cultlike tendencies reappear are, I believe, the only responsible stances possible.

Again, the above paragraphs spend more time on the exception rather than the rule. Most of our group ministries at Syracuse University and within Hendricks Chapel were carried out year after year with no complaints from students, chaplains, faculty, or staff, and I came to see almost all of them as legitimate ministerial expressions of their particular faith or orientation and as complying fully with our regulations.

Before providing a list of the ministries, this is a good place to write about Jed Smock! His traveling "ministry" came to Syracuse three times while I was in office. His approach was essentially the same each time but bringing with it different problems. His was a one-day-and-gone approach, and he always wanted to be surrounded by a big crowd of students in the middle of whatever campus he was visiting. He usually came to Cornell in Ithaca, New York, the day before coming to SU, so we had some warning. His orientation was to the public campus rather than the private one, so our rules were of some frustration to him. His was not the only traveling ministry we experienced, but I believe his was one of only two that did not ask for permission ahead of time.

Smock identified himself as part of a ministry called "the Destroyers." He claimed a biblical passage about being destroyers of the works of the devil as the inspiration for the ministry. His technique, once surrounded by students, was to be very loud and very confrontational with much sexual reference in the content of his preaching. Calls from faculty that the noise was disturbing classes were usually the impetus for our efforts to control him. His visits to our campus became somewhat legendary. After the third visit he understood our position, and he did not return again.

Two brief Jed Smock stories are memorable enough to repeat here. On one visit, when we were alerted to his noise with a group of students just south of a classroom building, Peter Baigent from the Office of Student Affairs and I went to greet him, explained that he was causing a disturbance, and took him to my office to "work things out." This part of our effort was duly recorded and broadcast by a local TV station. Once in my office we asked Smock what his purpose was. Was it entertainment or religious in nature? We explained that if it was entertainment, then Baigent would take the lead; if it were religious, then I would be doing so. At this point he became calm and as easy to deal with as he was difficult when in his circle of performance. Smock stated, "There is an element of entertainment in what I do, but the basic purpose is religious." This time we moved him to the area just west of Hendricks Chapel, away from any classrooms, and allowed him to, in the name of freedom of speech, continue his "performance." Before it was over one of our students threw a cream pie in his face, and that issue was as hard to resolve as was the one of whatever to do with Jed!

During the next visit, two or three years later, the noise complaints were such that we limited him to the inside of the main chapel of Hendricks Chapel for his "performance" (it is far too limiting to call it a sermon). Students who heard his first words, many of whom were familiar with his reputation, passed the word, and very soon the chapel was filled to capacity. Whenever Smock tried to speak, the catcalls and jeers literally obliterated his very strong voice. What happened next was, as far as I know, a one-time thing in the history of Hendricks Chapel. The crowd started doing the wave. It started in the south balcony and moved to the center and then the north balconies. The next round, those students on the main floor joined in proximity to the above balcony. For many minutes we had the wave going in Hendricks Chapel with far more enthusiasm that ever I saw it done in the Carrier Dome! When I detected that things might get out of hand I moved to the stage, took the microphone, and motioned and asked for quiet—a request that was granted but with some reluctance on the part of the students. I appealed to fair treatment for Mr. Smock on the grounds of free speech and not as an endorsement for what he was to say. If any individual was not willing to grant Smock the right of free speech I asked that they leave so the rest of us could hear and judge for ourselves what he would say. That did it. Order prevailed and after some ten minutes of his performance, the chapel started to empty until only a handful of students stayed to hear him out. I was tired when I got home late that afternoon.

Other outside groups usually asked for permission to come on campus. In the case of the Gideons who distributed Bibles we limited them to the public sidewalks on the perimeter of the campus so that we did not establish a precedent that then would be expected by other less peaceful groups. Some groups, such as Jews for Jesus, were not so noble. They would sneak on campus and in the surrounding areas, like Marshall Street, and leave their literature and be gone before either staff or campus security could confront them in their practice. And so it goes in campus ministry!

Several local churches also tried to create student ministries in their church and to draw students to their off-campus facilities. Some had moderate success, but I know of none that existed for more than a year or two. Many students did, however, participate in the life of a local church, and we encouraged that practice, especially with married students. As far as I know, this pattern of participation was always an individual choice. The other side of that coin is that local persons either joined or frequently participated in some of the campus groups, again as individuals. Only in two ministries was there group participation from outside of the university. One we have already discussed was Koshy's worshiping community; the other was during a brief time when an Orthodox priest brought in local congregants when the ministry was registered only as a student ministry.

What follows is a comprehensive list of the groups that existed on campus over the eighteen-year period of my deanship. When there was consistent campus-based leadership I have added names. Most of the groups changed leadership regularly enough that locating all the names would be very difficult and I trust of limited interest. Some of the groups spanned the entire time, some were on and off, and some were present for only one or two seasons. Even the names of some groups changed from time to time, so I have not attempted to put them in alphabetical order, instead ordering them roughly by size from largest to smallest:

Campus Crusade for Christ (national affiliation);
Chi Alpha (a ministry of the Assembly of God Church);
Campus Bible Fellowship (Paul Jewell, mentioned earlier);
Brothers and Sisters in Christ (chapter of a regional group);
Athletes in Action (connected with Campus Crusade for Christ);
Chabad House (the ministry of Rabbi Yaakov Rapoport);
Inter-Varsity Christian Fellowship (national affiliation);
Graduate Christian Fellowship (connected to Inter-Varsity Christian Fellowship);
Asian Christian Fellowship (connected to Inter-Varsity Christian Fellowship);
University Christian Fellowship (local, with ties to a few churches);
Maranatha Christian Fellowship (national affiliation);
Chinese Christian Fellowship (tied to T. E. Koshy's ministry);
Christian Science Organization (led for years by Professor Clemence);
Fellowship of Christian Athletes (national affiliation);

Zen Center of Syracuse (led by S. Chayat);

Korean Buddhist Association (local);

Alcoholics Anonymous (local group with national ties);

Kundalina Yoga Club (local with national ties);

Church of Jesus Christ of Latter-day Saints (local congregation of the Mormon faith);

New Birth Christian Fellowship (local, mostly African American);

Pan-Orthodox Christian Fellowship (local, mix of orthodox churches);

Society of the Holy Mother (local, possibly with outside ties);

Bible study groups (local and with many names, usually for one year);

Prayer groups (same as above);

Unitarian Universalist (when not represented by an intern);

The Way International (national, here only briefly before being expelled).

In addition to these groups, we had inquiries from:

several of the Moonie groups (none ever filed with us);

the Pagan Society (which did not follow up with an application);

Spirit of Satan (this inquiry was, I think, a joke);

Syracuse Church of God (Boston Church of God, which made many approaches but never filed);

Korean Presbyterian Church (did not file after consultation);

several local churches asking for a ministry without knowing that they were already represented by their denomination;

several clergy asking for chaplain status not knowing they were already denominationally represented on campus; and

a few local clergy asking for permission to come on campus and actively recruit members for their church (requests not granted).

Some of the ministries that did have registered campus status wanted to have open access to the living centers on the campus for their recruitment and their meetings. In some instances this practice took place without our knowledge. It was never granted. The officials associated with SU housing and those of us at Hendricks Chapel believed we had no right to expose students to such practices in their private living space. This rule was, of course, a real blockage to the desired access advocated by both local and national representatives of some of the groups. In fact, one group had to be severely disciplined for consistent violation of this restriction. I always referred to our position as the campus expression of the Green River Ordinance. That ordinance is common in the western parts of the United States and simply outlaws any kind of peddling without a proper permit from the city to do so. Religious "peddlers" were simply denied, for ethical reasons, access to our living centers. Of course, any student had the right to request a visit from a representative of a religious group, and there were proper procedures for doing so.

I offer one more matter for this chapter. I encouraged all groups and campus ministries to do joint or cooperative programming and to join the chaplains and the office of the dean in such joint efforts when a common agenda was possible. At times I offered budget assistance to do such cooperative programming. On several occasions this arrangement worked beautifully but was usually possible on only the most basic and common of concerns. For example, on several occasions a limited number of groups joined together for certain holy day celebrations. On rarer occasions there would be joint sponsorship of a film to be shown on campus. I always advocated as much intergroup contact as possible. I believe it leads to better understanding, which in turn often leads to more neighborliness. At the same time I am fully aware that our religious convictions are often real and powerful reasons for noncooperation! Being dean of Hendricks Chapel is often a very delicate balancing act, and sometimes falling from the balance beam is inevitable. Usually it is good to try to walk it!

57. The Lockerbie Air Disaster

ON DECEMBER 21, 1988, Pan Am Flight 103 was brought down by a terrorist bomb after leaving London, England. The plane's parts and the bodies of its passengers and crew came down on the town and the area surrounding Lockerbie, Scotland. On board that flight were thirty-five Syracuse University students on their way home from a semester or a year of study abroad, all but one of them from the SU program in London. It was and is the single greatest tragedy to be inflicted upon Syracuse University and in addition some families in the Syracuse area. Of course, other passengers left relatives and loved ones from around the world. There were also eleven citizens of Lockerbie who died in the village as the wreckage came down. There was also much damage both from the debris and several resulting fires.

My purpose in this chapter is not to retell the whole story. Indeed, it has over these many years been a major international news item, and some readers will personally remember the events of that time. What I want to do is to tell the story of the involvement of the chaplains, staff, and dean of Hendricks Chapel. It will also involve a bit of the story of a Lockerbie pastor by the name of Alan Neal, who became, quite literally, the minister to so many of those individuals who lost children, spouses, other relatives, and friends as a result of the bombing of the plane.

On that very day, December 21, Ethel and I arrived, having driven from Syracuse, in Clearmont, Missouri, where we planned to spend the holidays with our family. Only one day of the semester's final exams remained, and most of the students were already home or on their way home for the semester break and the holidays. For all intents and all expectations the semester was over, or we thought it was, for Hendricks Chapel.

Just past midafternoon my brother-in-law came into the living room where I was stretched out on the floor saying there was something on the television about Syracuse students killed in a plane crash. I went immediately to view the news, which at the time was confirming the downed plane and the involvement of SU students; all other details were very vague. Within minutes the telephone rang, and it was Lori Heath, one of our DIPA officers who administered our study abroad program. She had gotten my location from the Hendricks Chapel staff and immediately briefed me on what was known at that time. It was estimated that between seventeen and forty of our students might have been aboard the flight. For the next twenty-four hours I was on the phone almost half the time.

Lutheran chaplain Michael S. Rothermel took the lead with the other chaplains and began arranging a number of things. Within the first hour after confirmation of the tragedy the chapel was filling with students, staff, and faculty. Michael and I talked of the basketball game to be held in the Carrier Dome that night, and I asked him to call Athletic Director Jake Crouthamel on my behalf and to request that, if the game was held, Rothermel be asked to offer a prayer before the start of the game. By game time the news was still sketchy, and when the announcement was made about the fate of Pan Am Flight 103 and that many SU students were aboard it was obvious that it was the first time many in the crowd had heard the news. Our request for the saying of a prayer was granted, and I am told Michael did a fine job in a very tough situation.

All the chaplains and most of the staff who were in town gathered at the chapel and began to manage and participate in the unfolding events. The news media became omnipresent, and their behavior that night caused some of the most disrespectful behavior we have ever experienced in Hendricks Chapel. Newhouse faculty member Joan Deppa was later, along with several colleagues, to publish the book *The Media and Disasters: Pan Am 103* (New York University Press, 1994), detailing the events and the issues surrounding the practice of journalism in times of human crisis. Ethical behavior by journalists became a hot topic everywhere in the months that followed. I am told there has, in general, been significant improvement as a result of Deppa's book and the efforts of many teachers in the field. The journalism piece of the story is well documented in other places, and it is not my purpose to repeat more of it here.

The unplanned service in Hendricks Chapel that evening was somewhat chaotic owing both to the behavior of the press and the uncertainty surrounding the specifics about the passenger list. All of the chaplains who were there participated in the service and did their best to comfort everyone present. Many there knew that a sorority sister or a fraternity brother or a classmate was supposed to be on the flight, but an early, unauthorized passenger list had several mistakes, even listing a few names who were not on the flight.

Rabbi Milton Elefant and his family had gathered in New York City on December 21 to celebrate the Jewish holidays. When he saw the news that evening, which featured a mother in agony in a waiting room the airport had provided for relatives, he said, "I must go to the airport." When he arrived and explained that he was a Syracuse University chaplain he was allowed into the room and was our first direct contact with the families of our students. Some of the families were Jewish, some were not, but Milton became our presence with all of them in the midst of that agony and sorrow.

Announced at that first service in Hendricks Chapel and planned the next morning was the service held the second night, also with a full house. By that time the passenger list and the names of the thirty-five students and three others from the Syracuse area were known. That second night the press was restricted to a specific area of the chapel (many of them were very unhappy about it) and did somewhat better in terms of less disruptive and disrespectful behavior. Even so, there were many reports of aggressive, high-pressure interviewing inside but chiefly outside after the service. Again the service itself was interfaith in makeup, with many chaplains and several staff members participating.

During those two days most of my telephone conversations were with staff members Mary Farnsworth, Nan Jensen, and Alice Keefe and with chaplains Rothermel and Paul Kowalewski, the new interdenominational Protestant who did not yet know the university well and was just beginning to be familiar with the operation of the chapel. Lori Heath continued to be my main contact with DIPA personnel, but I also talked with others in that office. We stayed in Missouri until after our Christmas celebration and then returned earlier than planned, in late December, to Syracuse.

In telephone conversations with Chancellor Eggers we decided to have the first memorial service planning meeting as soon as possible after my return. My memory is that it took place on December 31. He put together a planning committee of five administrators, including myself. We had by phone debated both the date and the place for a major memorial service. By phone I had indicated that I thought the Carrier Dome was the only real possibility. Producing an event of any kind in the dome was and is expensive, and I wanted Mel to have some time to think about it before our first committee meeting. As for timing, we soon agreed that the service must take place a soon as possible after the start of the second semester. January 18, 1989, was tentatively set as the date.

At our first planning meeting three major decisions were made, and a few guidelines for the service were established. It was decided that January 18 would be the date, the easiest of the decisions. Mel, at first, wanted to have the service in Hendricks Chapel but was soon convinced by the rest of us that only Manley Field House and the Carrier Dome were large enough campus facilities. We discussed the War Memorial and other community possibilities and soon decided the service would be in the Carrier Dome. It proved to be a wise decision because approximately thirteen thousand people attended the service. They could not have been accommodated in any other indoor facility in Syracuse. Our final firm decision was to start the service at noon. We knew the time and the place should both be set in the original press release to avoid future confusion about those two matters. The noon service would allow travel time both before and after. Mel decided he himself would head up the Carrier Dome arrangements subcommittee.

In that first meeting we discussed who should be on the platform to address the service and in what capacity, how many persons we thought was the maximum number, and what the arrangement for music should be. It was tentatively agreed that the Protestant, Catholic, and Jewish chaplains would be asked to make statements of no more that three minutes each. I was to contact them concerning their willingness to be so involved. It was thought by all that I should open the service with greetings and an invocation but to speak in addition only if one or more of the chaplains were unwilling to do so. We anticipated inviting Syracuse mayor Tom Young and New York governor Mario Cuomo and assumed other public officials would be invited to speak. Eggers himself would give the closing remarks and do the benediction. At this first meeting the platform-people issue was not finalized. We were of a mind that six platform persons was probably the optimum number.

Mel, near the end of the first meeting, asked, "What will we do for music?" At first there was no response, but I was ready to make my suggestions and soon did. "Of course, we will have the Syracuse Symphony Orchestra." Michael Sawyer almost immediately said, "That won't work. There is no way we can get them to come." We briefly discussed issues of getting permission of the musicians' union, the expense involved, and the appropriateness of having them anchor the musical aspects of the service. I got everyone to agree to two things, first that the Syracuse Symphony Orchestra would be the most appropriate choice for music and second that they would let me make the effort to get them to come. If they come, I argued, we should have Burt Harbison lead the combined choirs of SU and members he might get from the Syracuse University Oratorio Society (which Burt directed). Burt was at the time our School of Music choral director but not yet the director of the Hendricks Chapel Choir. The music question was put on hold until we learned about the symphony orchestra possibility.

I first contacted the Syracuse Symphony Orchestra concertmaster, Andrew

Zaplatinsky, and he with some enthusiasm for the idea presented it to the members of the orchestra, the union steward, conductor Kazuyoshi Akiyama, and the orchestra's management staff. Within two or three days we had an enthusiastic affirmative response. Not only would they come but they also earnestly wanted to come and would even bear the expense of moving their equipment except for a few items to be provided by Hendricks Chapel and the School of Music. Special permission was attained for Hendricks Chapel and Syracuse University organist Katie Pardee to play with the orchestra on the shared items and for Burt to direct the combined choirs. The musical piece was soon set, and I was proud of the planning committee and of my efforts.

In our subsequent committee meetings we polished what had emerged as a very sound plan. Oops—both Young and Cuomo were Democrats. Thus we discussed inviting Alfonse D'Amato, New York Republican U.S. senator and Syracuse Law School graduate, to round out the public-official platform participants. We soon received word that New York Democratic senator and former SU Maxwell School faculty member Daniel Moynihan would like to be involved. Done! We discussed who among the students should participate, and that decision was easy. John M. Mandyck was president of our Student Government Association, was doing a fine job, and was the logical choice. He agreed to be involved. Eggers, while we were discussing a representative of the faculty as a speaker, indicated that he had a letter from professor of English Douglas Unger that would make a marvelous memorial service statement. We all soon agreed.

Most of the memorial services in both the United States and in Scotland and England had featured a Scottish pipe band, and we added that feature to our musical program. That arrangement was made by Syracuse University staff member Neil Appleby, also a member of the Syracuse Scottish Pipe Band. Soon the slate was set, the plans finalized, and the preparations under way.

The Hendricks Chapel staff and the chaplains were creative in a number of ways, and we all worked overtime as we prepared. The staff prepared thirty-five memorial books to have on tables around the perimeter inside of the main chapel on January 18 for anyone who wished to do so to write notes and share their good-byes to any or all of the thirty-five victims. They proved to be so much in demand that we had to leave them up for several days to accommodate everyone who wished to write something.

The *Syracuse Record* came out on January 17 with all the information about the service. Featured on the front page was an article I had written on Christmas Eve while in Missouri. I had spent so much time and energy in relationship to the Flight 103 aftermath that I found myself at the typewriter trying to express my thoughts, however profound or not profound. The *Record* published the article with the title "Reflections on Our Tragedy: Christmas Eve 1988." In an effort to have that record and to highlight the feel of those days the article is reproduced here.

S Y R A C U S E   U N I V E R S I T Y

Hendricks Chapel

Reflections on our Tragedy
Christmas Eve 1988

The Pan Am 103 disaster leaves all of us at Syracuse University experiencing agony, shock, a profound sadness and keen empathy with all who have lost loved ones. Nothing we can do will make the pain go away; time will bring its healing touch but we (and things) will never be "all right again" in some important ways. We join thousands of others in living with an emptiness created by this dramatic and fateful tragedy.

An inner nagging pain will not and should not let us forget the laughter and tears these youths will never again experience. The family circles which will never again be complete at Christmas or Passover or birthday time are also our family circles. The children they will never bear are our loss also. They are gone and can never be replaced. We stand in awe and anger at the same time.

There are those who say the current generations are not capable of experiencing the sacred. Playwright Thornton Wilder used death to bring us to an understanding of the sanctity of life. What we have experienced here is not theatre, it is stark reality. It has, for all age groups, confronted us with the sacred depth, wonder and beauty of life. If any good can come it surely lies here in the increase of our awareness of how precious life is (in Thornton Wilder's words) "every, every minute."

Our prayers are to bless the memories of those gone and we pray the richest of blessings on those who now live with their loss.

Finally a word of caution. There are those uttering the word Islam in taking credit for this dastardly deed. If it proves true I ask you to remember that they no more represent the true spirit of Islam and Muslims around the world than similarly dastardly deeds of Christians, Jews and others represent their faiths. Our histories unfortunately contain many examples of similar mistaken appropriation of religious fervor. The faithful of every religion are destined to suffer such plagues as this. Terrorism is terrorism no matter to what religion or philosophy it appeals.

Richard L. Phillips
Dean of Hendricks Chapel

Syracuse, New York 13244-1110 • 315-443-2901

"Reflections on our Tragedy: Christmas Eve 1988," by Richard L. Phillips. Article published in the Syracuse Record, vol. 19, no. 17 (January 17, 1989). Courtesy of Matthew Snyder.

There was to be, in connection with the memorial service, a two-day conference of the parents, grandparents, and siblings of the thirty-five students. All the chaplains and others who might provide counseling assistance were included as participants in the conference. It was headquartered in a local hotel and proved to be a very rewarding time for all of us. Most noteworthy is the discovery of a simple but unexpected two-way street of providing support. We were all prepared to bring as much comfort, sympathy, and support to the families as we could possibly convey. The strength of the families was amazing, and in the end they brought to all of us as much ministry as we provided for them. It was most rewarding.

The program on January 18 went extremely well. The Carrier Dome staff had made the most beautiful arrangement imaginable, with white chairs on the floor for family members and close friends of the students. The Syracuse Symphony Orchestra was in the lower stands on the northwest corner with the combined choirs next to them. Katie's rented electronic organ was nearby. The Syracuse Scottish Pipe Band was in the ambulance entrance to the dome on the southwest corner. The platform provided ample space and was beautifully decorated, and when we took our places in the procession to the platform we were a little overwhelmed by the size and tenor of the crowd. I believe all of us who participated received a copy of the video of the service, and of course there is one in the SU Archives.

On the day the Carrier Dome became an annex to Hendricks Chapel we all experienced what has to be the largest memorial service ever held in Syracuse. It did not bring to a close but attempted to deal with our loss and our needs in as powerful a manner as possible. The program for the service was also provided for each person in attendance and is reproduced below.

The Lockerbie air disaster, as it is called in most parts of the world, proved to have a life of its own. For several reasons it could not be "put to rest" and is still frequently the topic of new items as this book is written. We at SU continue to know, year by year, the impact. Several of our colleges lost scholars. Many students were from the Newhouse School and several from Visual and Performing Arts, particularly the Drama Department. At Hendricks Chapel we also felt a personal blow because Kesha Weedon was a member of the Black Celestial Choral Ensemble and Tim Cardwell a member of the Hendricks Chapel Choir. I knew four of the students; many of our staff and chaplains knew even more.

Hendricks Chapel conducts one and is involved in another annual service at Syracuse University. On December 21 each year the chaplains and staff plan a brief prayer service in the small chapel at the very minute the bomb is calculated to have gone off aboard Flight 103. Before his retirement Chaplain James Taylor led this service. The group gathered for the service carries a lighted symbol of life from the chapel to the Place of Remembrance north of the Hall of Languages. There flowers are placed on the memorial itself and the light left to burn as it will.

The other annual event is a convocation conducted in Hendricks Chapel by an all-university committee. There the thirty-five Memorial Scholarship recipients (selected each year for the awarding of the grants) are featured, each placing a flower or lighting a candle for one of the thirty-five students in whose honor the

IN MEMORIAM

Steven R. Berrell	Wendy A. Lincoln
Kenneth J. Bissett	Alexander Lowenstein
Stephen J. Boland	Suzanne M. Miazga
Nicole E. Boulanger	Richard P. Monetti
Timothy M. Cardwell	A. Lindsay Otenasek
Theodora E. Cohen	Sarah Philipps
Jason M. Coker	Frederick S. Phillips
Eric M. Coker	Peter R. Peirce
Gary L. Colasanti	Louise Rogers
Scott M. Cory	Thomas Schultz
Gretchen Dater	Amy E. Shapiro
Shannon Davis	Cynthia J. Smith
Turhan M. Ergin	Mark L. Tobin
John Flynn	Alexia K. Tsairis
Pamela Herbert	Nicholas A. Vrenios
Karen L. Hunt	Kesha Weedon
Christopher A. Jones	Miriam L. Wolfe
Julianne F. Kelly	

SYRACUSE UNIVERSITY
Memorial Service

Twelve O'Clock Noon
Wednesday, the Eighteenth of January
Nineteen Hundred and Eighty-Nine
The Carrier Dome

PROGRAM

Organ Prelude	Dr. Katharine F. Pardee
Lament for the Children (Traditional)	Arr. by J. Avery Head
Syracuse Scottish Pipe Band	

Words of Welcome and Invocation The Reverend Dr. Richard L. Phillips
Dean of Hendricks Chapel

Cast Thy Burden Upon the Lord (from *Elijah*) Felix Mendelssohn

Lacrymosa (from *Requiem*) W. A. Mozart
Syracuse University Combined Choruses
The Syracuse Symphony Orchestra
Kazuyoshi Akiyama, Conductor

In Tribute	The Honorable Thomas G. Young
	Mayor of the City of Syracuse
In Tribute	The Honorable Alfonse M. D'Amato
	Senator of the United States
In Tribute	The Honorable Daniel P. Moynihan
	Senator of the United States
In Tribute	The Honorable Mario M. Cuomo
	Governor of the State of New York

Nimrod (from *"Enigma" Variations*) Edward Elgar
The Syracuse Symphony Orchestra
Kazuyoshi Akiyama, Conductor

In Tribute	The Reverend Monsignor Charles Borgognoni
In Tribute	Rabbi Milton H. Elefant
In Tribute	The Reverend Dr. Paul J. Kowalewski

Salvation is Created Paul Tschesnokoff
Syracuse University Combined Choruses
G. Burton Harbison, Conductor

In Tribute	John M. Mandyck
	President of the Student Government Association
In Tribute	Douglas A. Unger
	Professor of English
In Tribute	Melvin A. Eggers
Benediction	Chancellor
Organ Postlude	Dr. Katharine F. Pardee

AFTER THE SERVICE

Hendricks Chapel will be open for quiet reflection and prayer until 5:30 p.m. Messages to the families may be written in individual memorial books located in the Main Chapel.

Refreshments will be served in the Noble Room of Hendricks Chapel until 4:00 p.m.

At 4:00 p.m. in the Noble Room, there will be a discussion session for those who would like to talk together.

ACKNOWLEDGEMENTS

Syracuse University Combined Choruses
The Hendricks Chapel Choir
Dr. Katharine Pardee, Director

The Black Celestial Choral Ensemble
Ervin Allgood, Director

The Syracuse University Choral Union
Martha Sutter, Director

The Syracuse University Vocal Jazz Ensemble
Diana Spradling, Director

The Syracuse University Singers
G. Burton Harbison, Director

The Syracuse University Oratorio Society
G. Burton Harbison, Director

Students, Faculty, Staff and Friends of
The School of Music and the Drama Department

The Syracuse Symphony Orchestra
Kazuyoshi Akiyama, Music Director

We are grateful for the contribution of the musicians of The Syracuse Symphony Orchestra and Local 78 of the American Federation of Musicians.

Program for the memorial service held January 19, 1989, for the thirty-five students killed the previous month in the terrorist bombing of Pan Am Flight 103. The service, which included U.S. Senators Alfonse D'Amato and Daniel Moynihan, New York State Governor Mario Cuomo, and Syracuse Mayor Thomas Young as well as SU Chancellor Eggers, drew more than thirteen thousand people and had to be held in the Carrier Dome. Courtesy of Richard Phillips.

scholarships were developed. So, in these two and in other more private ways, the magnitude and the memory of our loss are regularly called to our attention.

At Syracuse University funds were raised for the Place of Remembrance mentioned above. It was dedicated in the fall of 1990 with a Sunday service in Hendricks Chapel followed by the presence of a very large crowd for the service of dedication at the place itself. Hendricks Chapel chaplains, the Reverend Alan Neal from Lockerbie who preached at the Hendricks Chapel service that day, myself, and several members of the Hendricks Chapel staff joined a large platform of university officials, including Chancellor Eggers, in dedicating this impressive memorial. Now when I visit the campus I always stop there, and for years before I retired I walked past it almost every day. I can still see those faces and those students moving on the campus as I allow my mind to drift a bit into the past.

The tenth anniversary of the bombing was the occasion for something of a repeat of the original memorial service. The service was held in Hendricks Chapel, this time before the end of the first semester. For the Hendricks Chapel service of worship that week of December 13, 1998, Alan Neal was again the preacher. Doug Unger, now teaching elsewhere, returned at the committee's request to reflect on the events of ten years earlier. He was again a brilliant representative, expressing our institutional and individual sense of loss.

Chancellor Eggers and many Syracusans have found their way to the very impressive memorials created in the village and surrounding areas of Lockerbie. Ethel and I made our pilgrimage there in the spring of 1993. We went to welcome the two new Lockerbie scholars who would be coming to Syracuse University to study for the next academic year. A fund was created in Lockerbie from all the donations that came from all over the world after Flight 103. The rebuilding of the damage in the village and other things, such as the scholarship program, have been financed by the fund. An evening banquet at the Lockerbie Manor turned out to be a delightful experience, the hospitality of the Scots there was superb, the event filled with the good spirit that has developed between the village and Syracuse University.

We went to Lockerbie for another reason: we had to see where it had happened. The memorials and the cemetery where some of our students are buried are so very well and tastefully done. Those persons who took us on the tour were so kind and so sensitive to our needs and interests that the personal interactions themselves were worth the trip. Five distinct memorials have been created. All are very special. Many readers will remember the pictures of the nose cone of the plane that, in a field near a country church known as Tundergarth, had become the "signature" of the disaster. Also in this area many of the victims and body parts fell to the earth. Behind that church is a former toolshed that has been made into one of the memorials. In the building, when we visited, were two very large volumes where each of us could record our names and any comments we might like to make. One volume was already filled, the other about half full. I was most impressed with the comments and amazed as I took the time to page through the names in one of the volumes. What amazed me was that I did not find a single page that did not have at least one name on it of someone I either personally knew or had met because of the Flight 103 connection. It is indeed a small world, and that world had responded with much love and concern in the face of this disaster.

While we were there we were again together with Alan Neal, by now and continuing to be a very close and dear friend. Alan, since retiring from his Lockerbie church, has been serving rural churches in West Virginia. He continues to do much follow-up pastoral work on the aftermath of the Lockerbie air disaster. He himself was in the village when the plane came down, and his was a narrow escape. He labored, with many others, all through the night to put out fires, comfort the villagers, and try to assess the damages. His stories of that night and the years to follow testify to the preciousness of what we know as life itself. Alan is a priest in the Church of England and was on loan to the Anglican church and community in Lockerbie at the time of the disaster. Lockerbie had two other churches, and I was pleased on our trip there to meet both of those pastors. They were also very much involved but did not take up the international role that Alan did.

We are fortunate at Syracuse University to have the ties we do with Lockerbie. It even extended to athletics when Coach Roy Simmons, Jr., took the lacrosse team there (one of the students lost had been on the team) and started a lacrosse program in the area. Our relationship with the village is one of the positive things that grew out of the impact of the bombing of the plane, and there were others. It was a momentous time in the life of Syracuse University and Hendricks Chapel. Eggers has said it was the most important time and a watershed time in the history of his twenty-year chancellorship. It certainly played the same role in my eighteen years at Hendricks Chapel. Before Flight 103 and after Flight 103 has become one of the ways Syracuse University measures time. For a long time it heightened awareness and sensitivity on our campus and in the lives of most Syracusans. It made us more aware of the sacred nature of life and the deep value associated with human relationships. It also brought, as crises do, people together in a common concern and in a common healing effort.

Here is a final note in the Hendricks Chapel relationship to Flight 103 and its aftermath. One of our students on the flight, Alexander Lowenstein, is the son of a mother who is an artist. Almost by accident Suzie Lowenstein began to create metal and fiberglass sculptures representing the positions she and various other mothers of our students assumed when they first learned of their child's death on the plane. The project grew and became known to the point that it was in demand as an art and memorial exhibit. The Lowensteins brought it to Syracuse University through the efforts of a committee approved by Eggers. Judith O'Rourke, the staff member who had the awesome responsibility of talking by phone with the families immediately following the bombing, and Joan Deppa, a faculty member already mentioned in connection with the book dealing with the media, joined me on the committee. We went to see the sculptures being exhibited in New Jersey and started making the arrangements for the sculptures to come to our campus. They were placed on the lawn near the northeast corner of the main central campus and were here in 1995 and 1996 for a number of months.

Our university relationship to the Lockerbie air disaster is deep, it has some wonderful dimensions to it, and it will last into the foreseeable future. One of my favorite photojournalists in Syracuse once asked me why we continue to hold these mini memorial events. "Why not let it die?" My answer was twofold. First, we could not let it die if we wanted to—indeed, it does have a life of its own, in our history and the history of terrorism and the history of the world. The second answer: we still need to feel the pain, to grieve and be ministered unto because of our loss, because of our love, because of their loss of all their human potential. Their loss is our loss. None will ever have children that would have someday come to Syracuse and our sister institutions.

58. Hendricks Chapel Events and Auxiliary Organizations

OVER THE YEARS of its history many of the events in Hendricks Chapel were sponsored by Syracuse University or some department or program within the university other than Hendricks Chapel.

Convocations and other events planned by SU's schools and colleges are regularly scheduled. On a space-available basis we tried to accommodate the needs of all SU and ESF programs and from time to time the needs of the medical and the nursing schools. Hendricks Chapel has housed everything from Greek-organization ceremonies to academic classes and addresses by governors, senators, presidential candidates, first ladies, and government officials from virtually all departments, including high-ranking military officials. Authors, artists, journalists, entertainers, and experts from many fields of interest have certainly been frequent presenters from the Hendricks Chapel podium. Ever since my first year of acquaintance with Hendricks Chapel in 1961 I have heard a number of speeches and programs in all these areas. To try to list the names would only be to leave some important ones unmentioned. Nevertheless, such events in Hendricks Chapel are certainly a memorable and noteworthy part of our history.

I will risk recording one such example. In Hilary Clinton's address early in her tenure as first lady the Hendricks Chapel staff as well as the building became very involved. Members of both the Secret Service and the White House staff worked with us for three days prior to the speech. Not only was every inch of the chapel inspected in developing a security plan but photos and other information were also processed for anyone needing access to the chapel on the day of the event. I must say that I have never worked with more able and more considerate people, both the Secret Service and the White House staffs, than were with us for those days. They were pleasant, considerate, and delightful persons.

On the day of the speech Ethel and I were part of the delegation hosting Mrs. Clinton. She was equally gracious and made it a point to show considerable interest in everything and every chaplain and staff member she met that day, including our custodian, Effie Clark. Effie reminded her that her husband had been here as a candidate for the presidency. For the speech the chapel was packed and the crowd anxious to hear her speak. Her speech on the health plan being promoted was delivered to perfection, her interactions with the campus a model of good diplomacy. I should add that SU has always tried to balance the ticket with party leaders from Lyndon Johnson to Nelson Rockefeller, and Hendricks Chapel has welcomed them all. Controversial speakers have also received our hospitality, Louis Farrakhan being a recent example.

Entertainers, including comedians, have been included, although after one comedian's appearance we did our best to enforce a "no blue language" guideline! Scheduling the chapel building for campuswide events became less frequent and less problematic once the Goldstein Auditorium was in use, but it is still used for many campus events other than ones sponsored by Hendricks Chapel.

Events sponsored by the Hendricks Chapel family are held in many campus locations, certainly most often in the chapel. Such events fall into six broad categories: events planned and conducted by one of the chaplaincies or chapel groups; events sponsored by the office of the dean; events jointly sponsored by the office of the dean and one or more chaplaincies or Hendricks Chapel groups; events jointly sponsored by some segment of Hendricks Chapel and another department or program within the university; events generated by a society or worldwide situation such as the Lockerbie air disaster; and weddings and memorial services in which staff at Hendricks Chapel are involved.

Over the years many events, including art displays, have taken place in the chapel. The great sculptor Ivan Mestrovic came to the SU faculty after World War II and created many major works of art, mostly sculpture. *Job, Moses,* and *Persephone* are three hugh bronze works that now grace the campus sculpture garden. Thanks to research by Mary O'Brien, SU archivist, I learned that an extensive show of Mestrovic's art was exhibited in Hendricks Chapel. Mestrovic joined the faculty at the University of Notre Dame when he left Syracuse.

Art exhibits have frequently been held in the chapel, usually in the Noble

Room or the Strates Lounge. More often than not the exhibits have featured local artists. On two occasions the White Rose Society displayed photos and documents of their anti-Nazi work in World War II Europe. Their heroine, Maria Schultz-Jahn, also came and lectured at Hendricks Chapel.

Guest speakers have been common in the chapel; some have been sponsored by other segments of SU (also the Syracuse community), and some were Hendricks Chapel events. The following names are but a few, and this list is very unfair to dozens of guests with equally familiar names and national or worldwide reputations. Carl Sandburg in February 1939 and Robert Frost in May 1940 are especially well remembered by those who were here during those years. Other names known to readers include: Howard Thurman, D. T. Niles, E. Stanley Jones, Normal V. Peale, Ralph Sockman, William S. Coffin, Nelson Rockefeller, Jacob Javits, Chuck Willie, Hillary R. Clinton, Bill Clinton, Billy Graham, Andy Rooney, Colin Powell, Harry Belafonte, Andrew Young, Hans Küng, Jim Forbes, Rod Wilmoth, and Bob Costas.

Great care in scheduling all such events is a must for our staff. Schedule conflicts are a source of three-way unhappiness—the two parties scheduled at the same time and in the same space and the Hendricks Chapel staff!

It is helpful, of course, to have as many events scheduled as far ahead of time as possible, if nothing else because custodial work is critical. We usually had plenty of advance notice for weddings, but memorial services and crisis-produced events can and do happen with little and sometimes no advance notice. As a result, the guideline for staff and custodians serving Hendricks Chapel is that we must try to always be ready, on very short notice, to look and be at our best for a memorial service, be it for a first-year student, a faculty member, a chancellor, or a governor. We did not always find it possible to be in a perfect state of readiness, but it was always the goal. It was not always easy to convince everyone in the university to join us in this task, which is understandable because most of the campus operates on a more routine schedule. Even so, we have always experienced a special degree of consideration from essential SU services: custodial, physical plant, design and construction, campus security, campus fire marshals, food service, and that large contingent of administrators who has the ability to get it done and get it done now!

Events conducted in all of the above categories were sometimes religious in nature, sometimes secular. From a program on managing one's personal finances as a student (conducted by one of our business managers) to programs generated by the visit of a world-famous religious figure such as Hans Küng, the programmatic thrust of Hendricks Chapel was, I contend, greatly enriching to the communities of Syracuse University and central New York. Some programs were presented regularly, if not every semester. Examples would be programs dealing with theological issues, spiritual interests, social problems, moral and ethical matters, world events, Middle East peace, and always human sexuality. Some programming came and went with special needs. An example would be programs educating the campus on cultlike practices and the dangers associated during those times when cultlike activity was present on and around the campus. Yet other programs were scheduled only in times of major crises such as the deaths of marines in Lebanon, the Lockerbie air disaster, and certainly at the time of the death of a student or faculty or staff member.

I viewed the programming activity of the various branches of the Hendricks Chapel family to be part of the overall concept of ministry to the campus and the community. First and foremost, it is a sign that we are present and ready to stand with those individuals in need. Second, we were ready to take action that would speak to and be of service to the dignity, indeed the sacredness, of life in any of its entanglements. And, third, we were there to provide a variety of expert services in many of the areas of life where experience and some degree of wisdom might be called for. To facilitate all of these needs we staffed for counseling. We needed to know the areas of skill of each chaplain and staff member, and we all needed to be on the lookout for the right time for our special presence.

For our ability to do extensive programming I want to tip my symbolic hat to Chancellor Eggers. In the changes of 1980–81 he saw to it that the Hendricks Chapel budget was provided with fine programming potential and charged me with the responsibility of seeing that such programming be so broadly based that it would have value for every "corner" of the campus. That same tip of the hat goes to Chancellor Shaw, who with enthusiastic support continued in that tradition. If you, the reader, would like to survey the broad programming of one or many years of the chapel's life I refer you to the office of the dean, where you can view the current "scrapbook" where clippings are kept or go to the SU Archives where past years' scrapbooks are kept.

THOUGH NOT AN EVENT, the creation of a five-year plan produced some events and a great number of meetings in the life of the chapel family. In 1990, as the tenth year of my deanship was approaching, it became evident that we needed to update the Wiggins committee report and from it and our own perceptions develop a plan for the future operation of Hendricks Chapel. By 1991 we had made great progress, and the first draft was produced. Both staff and chaplains had given many hours, including summer picnic meetings, to the effort and to a second round of meetings to polish the plan. Copies of these documents and the record of the many meetings it took to produce them are contained in the SU Archives (in a box yet to be numbered), and anyone interested in our deliberations on the operation and future of Hendricks Chapel at that time would do well to look them up. Recently there were still copies in the Hendricks Chapel office in the dean's suite. A few years later a committee looked into updating the document, and only minor changes were made. The plan from that point forward was to review the document and update it every four years. Except for updating the wedding procedures and weddings "philosophy," we did not return to the update (Strasbourg and my upcoming retirement probably get credit for that). When we returned from France I did write a paper as a personal update of the five-year plan in response to a request from the chancellor's office. The effort was again renewed soon after Tom Wolfe became the fifth dean of Hendricks Chapel.

Programs

One of my Syracuse friends referred to some of our programs as "big-ticket items!" Big numbers, sometimes yes, but a big price tag was one thing we tried to avoid. During my deanship there were four such special efforts, three of which are still on-going. They have been mentioned before. I will deal with each here in this chapter. They are the International Thanksgiving Meal, the Martin Luther King Jr. Holiday Celebration, the Malmgren Concerts, and the Interfaith Hour (an experiment).

The birth of the International Thanksgiving Meal took place on November 21, 1980, under the joint chairmanship of Chaplain Koshy and Hendricks Chapel staff member Jean Baum. It was held in the Rockefeller United Methodist Church several blocks southeast of the campus. This event took place almost exactly one month before I became the dean designate of Hendricks Chapel. Invited to that event were all of our international students and their immediate families. The purpose was to introduce them to a slice of American life (Thanksgiving) and to let them know they were considered a valued part of the Syracuse University academic community. It was to become an annual event, one of considerable importance and emphasis in the life of Hendricks Chapel.

It was adopted as an official event of the office of the dean when planning for the second year got under way. Koshy and other chaplains served on the committee, but care was taken, at the request of the International Student Office (ISO), to be sure the event was not identified with any one chaplaincy or one religion.

Jean Baum continued to play the central role in the planning of the event, and I served as the chair of the committee responsible for the event. The ISO always provided their director or a senior staff person as a regular member of the committee. In addition to Gigi Torelli of ISO (and later Pat Burak), both the vice president for student affairs, Jim Morgan (later others in this office), and Chancellor Eggers (later Shaw) lent their names and offices to aid the event, along with the sponsorship of Hendricks Chapel.

One year, the year it was held in Manley Field House, the event was held in October, the actual day of Thanksgiving Day in Canada. Soon, because of student schedules and the fact that most of our international students were on campus the weekend before Thanksgiving, the date of the event soon became the Sunday before Thanksgiving. This move, for several reasons, fitted well with the students' schedules and the schedule of the university and Hendricks Chapel. It was, over the years, held in several different locations, including once at the Carrier Dome because we could take advantage of a setup the night before that allowed us to save on costs, and often in the larger student dining centers of campus until the Shine Center and Goldstein Auditorium were available. At that time Goldstein became the permanent site for the event.

On two occasions we were able to seat more than nine hundred at the meal but later had to comply with capacity limit in Goldstein and limit the number of tickets to six hundred. New international students were, from that time on, given priority status for tickets. Spouses and children of the students were always included, with the children always bringing a special charm to the event. Sometimes a mother or other close relative of the student in question was included.

A typical U.S. Thanksgiving meal was served with one exception. Rice was always included, thus satisfying many international diets for whom the typical Thanksgiving ingredients were often very strange. Each table of ten included one or two table hosts to help with the serving of the meal, to explain the tradition and the food, and to facilitate conversation. We enlisted about sixty-five table hosts in Goldstein for the event. Table hosts were mostly from the university community, faculty, administration, and chaplains and some members of the community. It became a tradition that the merchants who donated food were asked to be table hosts, and many over the years did so. We were able to keep costs down with such donations, but another very real plus was for the internationals to see the Syracuse community joining with us to provide for the meal and make them feel a welcome part of the student and domestic life in Syracuse. For years Peter's Grocery provided the turkeys and the Insera family the produce for the entire meal.

Programs for the event ranged from speakers to musical groups. As time passed it was agreed that speakers were not the right ticket, both because of the children and the holiday focus of the day. The university food service was always in charge of preparing and serving the meal, with David George usually being the person in charge of that part of the event. I think everyone who ever had anything to do with the International Thanksgiving Meal, and that included most everyone in the administration and on the faculty at one time or another, can testify that the event is a very important one in the life of Syracuse University and Hendricks Chapel and the lives of our international students.

Nicely printed invitations were sent to every international student at SU and ESF and sometimes the School of Medicine. It became so popular with the students that usually the tickets, once available, were gone in a forty-eight-hour span of time. Needless to say, the members of the Hendricks Chapel staff were the real workers making the event happen year after year.

As far as we know we are the only university in the country doing exactly this event for our international students. As it has from its beginning, Hendricks Chapel remains very active in embracing our internationals. The SU office for service to our internationals actually originally started as an extension of the work of Hendricks Chapel.

The Martin Luther King Jr. Holiday Celebration had its genesis as a Hendricks Chapel program almost three years before the national holiday was established. In the effort to encourage mixing of the African American community with the majority communities of Syracuse I saw the celebration of King's birth as having great facilitative potential. Conversations across the country were taking place about the possibility of a national holiday, and luckily I had the support needed to jump the date and start our celebration early.

We started with a personal friend, Dr. Paul Smith, then of Atlanta, as our chief speaker and resource person. Paul was later the first African American to become head pastor of the First Presbyterian Church of Brooklyn Heights, New York. In fact, he was the first black pastor of any First Presbyterian Church in the United States. Those modest first sessions in 1986 were held in the chapel and the Ernie Davis rooms of the Carrier Dome. Paul did an excellent job, and the idea was enthusiastically embraced by others in the university. A full listing of the speakers through 1999 is contained later in the chapter.

At the suggestion of Vice President Jim Morgan, the event was soon to become an all-university event but remained housed and budgeted through Hendricks Chapel. Both Chancellor Eggers and I agreed, and the Carrier Dome became the home of the event, with ever increasing numbers in attendance. In 1999 we had twenty-two hundred places set on the football field of the dome for the buffet-style meal that featured a southern-style African American (somewhat stylized) menu. Each year there is a community piece, usually in one of the churches, when the keynote speaker spends time in the community as well as on the campus with a seminar-type presentation. Always an extensive program surrounds the keynoter after the meal in the Carrier Dome.

I departed my service to the event at the end of January 1999, one month after retiring from Hendricks Chapel, which enabled me to complete my service as chair of the MLK Committee that last time! After it became an all-university event, the chairmanship of the MLK Committee was held by several different people. Except for the two years we were in France I served as treasurer of the event owing to the fact that the budget was housed in Hendricks Chapel. One of the delights, even if a bit of a time burden, was to serve on the Martin Luther King Commission of Central New York. That group of citizens always had a representative on the Syracuse University MLK Committee and supported the event in very tangible ways.

Over the years it has become a key event in the life of the university and of the Syracuse community. Early on we promoted it with the so-called black churches of Syracuse. Many complimentary tickets in the early years primed the pump that has become a very important, perhaps the most effective, mixer of the diverse populations of Syracuse and the university. After the first few years we added MLK recognition awards to community persons who were more or less unsung heroes in the general area of the King legacy, a very fine addition to the event.

The SU Food Service and the Carrier Dome staffs have been key to the planning and the success of the event. One of the first years in the dome some one hundred unexpected people arrived for the meal, the result of a ticket-procedure glitch. As soon as the problem was detected the dome staff was on the phone, and within minutes we had every piece of chicken from every Kentucky Fried Chicken in Syracuse on our buffet table. The folks at the Carrier Dome not only saved the event that year but were also the motivation we needed to be sure our ticketing was more professional in future years.

I have often been asked why we started and continue to hold the event. My personal answer has always been that the Martin Luther King nonviolent approach to the solution of our human problems is a message the white community needs to hear, know about, and celebrate even more than our black community. To bring the communities together to celebrate the dreams of Dr. King achieves more than twice as much! I remain proud of the event and very grateful to the dozens of students, faculty, and administrators who have given such faithful service to the MLK Committee and the event over the years, and I have many very fond memories of the people involved and the events themselves.

Martin Luther King Jr. Holiday Celebration

1986	Paul Smith
1987	Dorothy Cotton
1988	Judge Sandra Townes and Judge Langston McKinney
1989	Andrew Young
1990	Harry Belafonte
1991	Bernard Watson
1992	Johnetta Cole
1993	Charles Willie
1994	Julian Bond
1995	Charlayne Hunter-Gault
1996	Derrick A. Bell, Jr.
1997	Mary Frances Berry
1998	Kweisi Mfume
1999	Andrew Young

The Malmgren Fund

Esther Malmgren was one of those angels who come unexpectedly into the life of a dean or an institution very infrequently. And what an angel she was! The Malmgren Concerts at Hendricks Chapel are now, in perpetuity, in honor of her and her husband. Esther found me through our SU Development Office. She had been diagnosed with terminal cancer and wanted someone to be a pastor in that process and to visit with her about some religious issues she had. She told her story to Joel Katz, one of our staff members whom she knew, and Joel enlisted my services.

Esther's cancer, she was told, would eventually move to her brain and incapacitate her prior to her death. As a result, she wanted to get her estate in order—in quick order. We met at least twice a month, she, her pet parrot, and me, and discussed the full range of life's ups and downs. As it turns out she also wanted to leave her estate where it could honor her late husband and her with musical concerts featuring the organ, her favorite instrument. She was the owner of an Allen Theater Organ in her home that she gave to Hendricks Chapel before she died. With no offspring or close relatives, she left her entire estate to Hendricks Chapel to create the endowment for the Malmgren Concerts.

Esther's will specified two or three concerts a year, not all of them needing to feature the organ. We held the first two Malmgren Concerts, with her financial support, prior to her death. She was well enough to attend only one of them. During the remainder of my deanship Katie Pardee and Mary Farnsworth served with me as the Malmgren Concert Committee. The mailing list for the Malmgren Concerts includes many community people who were friends and supporters of Esther. For several years her theater organ was used at Syracuse University commencements in the Carrier Dome.

Esther's personal effects were sold at auction following her death. Several staff members purchased items, myself included. For a time I furnished part of the dean's office in Hendricks Chapel with some of her furniture. Her estate, including the sale of her house, became the largest single gift ever received by Hendricks Chapel. It was a blessing to me and to Hendricks Chapel, but my blessing also included the sharing of so many of life's concerns during Esther's final months. She denied being a particularly religious person but also believed the work of the chapel was very important, and she felt good about her plan to support it.

As mentioned earlier, the chaplains and staff at Hendricks Chapel, in secret, arranged for the final Malmgren Concert during my deanship to be a surprise in my honor. Both the program and the setting of a Malmgren Concert, including the musicians selected to perform that evening, honored me—to be sure!

The Interfaith Hour became an experiment on Sunday mornings at Hendricks Chapel almost by accident. Until the end of the spring semester of 1987 Carl Johnson was the interdenominational Protestant chaplain and had done a very fine job in that role. His move to a United Methodist Church in the Utica area created an opening that was not filled immediately, and as a result the Interfaith Hour experiment developed. There were many different influences bringing this experiment to reality in addition to the issue of a replacement for Carl.

The number of worshipers on Sunday mornings in Hendricks Chapel had been in decline since the mid-sixties, in serious decline during the seventies, and showing recovery only on special occasions in the eighties. As stated before in these pages no dean and no chaplain is to blame for the decline. Even so, there was often speculation about what might be a better use of the choir and the time on Sunday mornings. For one thing the members of the choir were restless about singing for a congregation often no larger in numbers than the choir itself. Chancellor Eggers was certainly one of the people concerned with the situation, as was I, and several discussions took place with the Hendricks Chapel Advisory Board members and others about what might be put in place that would be of benefit to the SU community. It was those discussions that soon produced the idea of "Interfaith Hour."

There was general agreement that much university-based talent, especially in the School of Music, could be used to try a religiously neutral "service" on Sunday morning. To make a long story short we moved the interdenominational Protestant services of worship to a Sunday evening hour, to the disgust of many who attended and those individuals who had responsibilities for that worshiping community. The possibility had been discussed off and on in the preceding years, but this time I, the dean, forced the move.

A United Church of Christ clergywoman, Elaine Cleeton, became chaplain for the first semester. Elaine was at the time a graduate student in the Maxwell School. The second semester, at Eggers's recommendation, a very popular and now retired Syracuse clergyman, Alex Carmichel, became the chaplain. This two-semester arrangement was approved by the United Methodist leaders but certainly without any real enthusiasm. There was some concern that the financial support for the chaplaincy might not be found in another year. That, fortunately, was not the case. The work of Cleeton and Carmichel with the interdenominational chaplaincy was spirited and blameless but nonetheless was seen by everyone as a holding action. Sunday evening was not a good draw for that chaplaincy. They did not have the services of the Hendricks Chapel Choir that were provided to the Interfaith Hour. When Paul Kowalewski became the interdenominational Protestant chaplain starting in the fall semester of 1988 he was called upon to rebuild the services, almost from scratch, as it were!

The flyer mailed to the entire campus announcing the September 13 start of the Interfaith Hour was sent in late August 1987 with lofty phrases of hope and expectation. Here are the three key paragraphs:

> The Hendricks Interfaith Hour is an attempt (following the move of the Interdenominational Protestant Service of Worship to Sunday evenings) to develop a university wide event which will, through great music and the sharing of our deeper concerns, make the S.U. experience richer for all of us.
>
> Reflections on September 13 will be by Music School Director George

Pappa-Stavrou, Rabbi Milton Elefant, Student Government Association president Franklin Redd and Dean Phillips. Music will be by Pappa-Stavrou on piano, Mary Webber on trumpet, Will Headlee at the organ and the Hendricks Chapel Choir. Please join us for this new beginning!

This series will range across the full spectrum of human concerns. It is designed for those with, as well as those without specifically religious interests and affiliations. We hope it will help us communicate within and across the various segments of the campus and be an aid to community building which will in turn enhance the Syracuse University experience for everyone.

These lofty thoughts along with some fine programming did not prove any more of a draw on Sunday mornings than had the previous twenty years of Protestant services of worship. In fact, it drew almost no students, its most regular supporters coming from the ranks of the central administration. In the end all agreed that though it had been an interesting experiment, it had basically failed to reach its goals. We spent more than a little time and money, had some excellent speakers from both inside and outside of Syracuse University, and provided especially professional music. I am certain, however, that no degree of excellence in programming would have edged it into the success category. By the end of the fall semester it was clear we could not save the program, so the last session was on December 13 and the plans for the spring semester were canceled.

Eggers told me, in private, that he was glad we had tried but that he was now convinced that Sunday morning was not a time in Hendricks Chapel that would ever again feel or look like it did under Powers and Noble! The Sunday morning time slot again became the possession of the Protestant chaplaincy. The "loan" of the choir was also reinstated.

Over the years the programs sponsored by the various entities within the chapel have had their influence on both persons and the university. It is not ever possible to predict when a given program will be successful. Sometimes we spent a great deal of money on a program that ended up costing far more that it seemed to be worth—sometimes as much as forty or fifty dollars per eventual participant. At other times we floated a program for almost no budgetary outlay that drew good participation and audiences for a cost of pennies per person, often having more lasting impact that the high-priced ones. One cannot predict the outcome, but programming of a very diverse nature went on and must go on at Hendricks Chapel. We always tried to target human, religious, or social needs or some combination of the three with our programs.

Hendricks Chapel Organizations

Several of our Hendricks Chapel operations were auxiliary in nature. The word *auxiliary* is descriptive in its use here and not really technical. We needed some term to categorize the following aspects of our operation. The Hendricks Chapel Choir, People's Place, the Black Celestial Choral Ensemble, and the Students Offering Service were lumped together under "auxiliary." Each had a director, and all were members of the Hendricks Chapel staff, except BCCE and People's Place, both of which were student administered and, in the case of BCCE, also administered by volunteers. The choral groups have already received some attention in chapter 50 and in other chapters, as has Students Offering Service to a lesser degree.

The Students Offering Service came into existence in 1990 and 1991 with leadership from a graduate assistant. Its value was evident immediately, and soon it was administered by a part-time staff person, Francis Parks, who became a full-time staff member and director for most of its existence and still is at this writing. It has resulted in countless student volunteer hours over its many years of existence and cooperates closely with the SU Volunteer Office that came into existence a year or two after the Students Offering Service.

The other three operations were up and running when I became dean, with the Hendricks Chapel Choir dating from the start of the chapel. During much of its existence it was a large choir of excellent reputation. In fact, during Arthur Poister's years it gained the reputation of being one of the finest college choirs in the nation. Much mention has already been made of the choir and its work in other sections of the book, so I will not add to it here. The same is true of BCCE. Both choirs have done much touring and have been a source of social life for their members. The Hendricks Chapel Choir has, for the most part, been characterized by singing classic church music but with some contemporary literature as well. It has been a choir in service to a worshiping congregation almost all of its existence. The BCCE specializes in a style of music called contemporary gospel. Though made up primarily of African American students, it has usually had one or more members who were not African American.

I have felt a close identification with both of these choral groups. I served as adviser for the BCCE and worked closely with its leadership over the years. The Hendricks Chapel Choir was always directly related to the office of the dean, and I was responsible for being sure each operation was budgeted at a level necessary to operate effectively. Each raised some of the funds necessary, BCCE on a matching basis, the Hendricks Chapel Choir underwriting a significant portion of their tours. Each choir has produced a limited number of recordings over the years. Tragically, each group lost a member in the Lockerbie air disaster.

People's Place is unique in that it is the only food operation within the bounds of Syracuse University that is not administered by the SU Food Service. On several occasions in its history it has been suggested that it shift to that operation. We were able to keep it in-house on the basis of the educational value it has for its student managers, its unique style of operation, and the fact that is has existed as a Hendricks Chapel operation for its whole history and has no plans to expand beyond its base of operation on the lower level of the chapel.

Originally started as an offshoot of the University Religious Council of Hendricks Chapel in the fall semester of 1971, it has been in operation every semester since. Two students, Ted Scheuler and Jeff Richards, were the personalities and workers behind the start of People's Place. Richards worked hard to find and in a real sense create space for People's Place to function, while Scheuler (later to marry and change his name to Ted Finleyson Scheuler) became its first administrator, serving as director for the 1971–72 and 1972–73 academic years. Student leadership, under the ultimate responsibility of the dean, has always provided the People's Place administration. In more recent times two students have usually shared codirector responsibilities, one for personnel and one for business.

In the early years cookies were a popular item (at first made by Scheuler's mother). People's Place can best be described as a coffee and donut shop. It has never been licensed to sell or serve food prepared on-site. Purchase for resale is its style of operation. Pricing is designed to make enough profit to provide for its necessary equipment and to contribute a little to Hendricks Chapel for its overhead expenses. Most years the latter has been the case. On only three occasions have there been problems with their budget. Two were minor and undoubtedly resulted from skimming. One year's problem was very serious, with the skimming having been discovered by the university deposit office alerting us to the fact that receipts were far too low. Several thousand dollars was never recovered, and it was discovered that one of the directors was guilty of the deed. Afterward, a system was established with the necessary supporting cash register to keep very close accounting of the financial aspects of the operation. The Hendricks Chapel graduate assistant business manager was also given more responsibility to monitor and train workers dealing with the flow of money.

The People's Place philosophy of operation was twofold: first, to provide the products at the best bargain possible and still meet the financial goals and, second, to be the most friendly place on campus to get coffee, tea, and snacks. It has been very successful in fulfilling both goals. Many of the managers over the years have been students at ESF; in fact, a significant portion of participants in most Hendricks Chapel activities and operations have come from ESF over the years.

A few times in the history of People's Place it has remained open or reopened to support Hendricks Chapel evening programs, coffee house-type programs to be specific. Student workers at People's Place for the most part have not been hard to recruit, and indeed some of the chapel's finest student employees have been based at People's Place. Summer operation has seen a normal pattern, with vacation times and final-exam times finding the shop closed. People's Place has a very loyal clientele that includes students, staff, administration, faculty, and those individuals who work in other capacities at Hendricks Chapel. Although People's Place does create both custodial and administrative work, it is a very important part of the identity and the operation of Hendricks Chapel.

Over the years there have been other activities and programs that might be called auxiliary. The ones mentioned above are certainly the chief ones in recent years, and they are a very significant part of the overall impact of Hendricks Chapel on the campus community.

59. Phillips to Strasbourg and Pickett to Hendricks Chapel

FOR SEVERAL YEARS I had been in light conversation with the staff at the Department of International Programs Abroad at Syracuse University. We had agreed that someday, when it was right for both them and us, I would teach for a semester in our study abroad program in London, England. We had visited the London center, and the DIPA staff and I had cooperated on other programs on the SU campus. They from time to time wanted to offer some courses in religion, and I had said I would be interested if and when our Department of Religion did not have someone available.

In the middle of the fall semester of 1994 a call came from DIPA asking me to come for a meeting with Director Nirelle Galson and other staff members about the possibility of my teaching a semester the next academic year. During the meeting with Nirelle I asked how our good friends Goodwin and Barbara Cooke were doing in Strasbourg. He was directing the program there for one year. Nirelle said she had a problem in that she could not find someone to take Cooke's place that coming summer and that she hoped it would be for a two-year directorship. I responded, probably half in jest, "That is something I could get interested in." I told her my French language skills had been pretty good twenty years earlier (we had spent a sabbatical year in Montpellier while I was on the faculty at Baker University) but that I would have to work at it for such an assignment.

We went on with the meeting, and soon, working with Sue Shane, we had planned two courses that I might teach in London. I was to prepare outlines for the courses, and we were each to talk with Jim Wiggins, chair of the Religion Department, to see if that department would grant me adjunct status for the teaching of the courses. Having once been a member of the department I was pretty sure they would, providing they did not have a regular member who wanted to go to London at the time proposed. I was also to talk with Chancellor Shaw about having someone substitute for me during the semester in question.

At the end of the meeting Nirelle asked me if I was serious about the Strasbourg possibility. I said I would need to talk with both Ethel and Chancellor Shaw but that I would indeed be interested if it could be worked out with all parties.

After the consultations I called to say yes. I told her we were interested and that I thought it could work for both Hendricks Chapel and our family. After a few days of checking on my academic and teaching background, seeing if Wiggins could provide the adjunct status in the Religion Department for teaching in Strasbourg, and discussing the possibility with the DIPA staff and with Vice President Ron Cavanagh within whose responsibility DIPA fell, Nirelle called to ask if Ethel and I could meet with her right away. The agreement for me to become director of the SU program in Strasbourg, France, for two years starting in the summer of 1995 was, by December, a done deal. It was also a great surprise!

The arrangements were complicated, to be sure. When I talked with Shaw about the possibility of a two-year rather than a one-semester absence, I made the following offer. First, I would be willing to retire from the chapel right away, effective the summer of 1995, and allow a search to begin immediately. Second, I would be willing to retire from Syracuse University (somewhat before I reached age sixty-five) in the summer of 1997 unless he, Shaw, had a better idea. In that meeting Shaw immediately made it clear that he did not want me to think about such a two-stage retirement but to return to Hendricks Chapel after the two years. He thought Strasbourg was right for me, I for it, and that if I could find the right person to fill the chapel role as an interim administrator it would have his blessing.

Earlier in the year I had told Shaw of my interest in an administrative sabbatical for either a semester or a year because I needed a change from the years at Hendricks Chapel to, as they say, "recharge my batteries." He had, for budgetary reasons, not been able to consider such a leave. It was a time of budget cuts and belt-tightening throughout the university, thus difficult to justify, and I understood. Therefore, Shaw was aware of my need to break the routine, but neither of us had thought it might involve a two-year deal.

We developed a short list of persons we thought would be good candidates, mostly persons who knew Hendricks Chapel and were either recently retired from the university or staff members who might be shifted to fill such a temporary role. I had decided the person selected should probably not be a clergy person. I had come to that opinion after considering the various implications of such a two-year role. The search to fill the role took several weeks. After many conversations within the university and with people associated with Hendricks Chapel, I started to focus on three possibilities who Shaw and I could agree could be the interim director of Hendricks Chapel. I was to retain my title and to continue to be responsible for the budgeting process and for regular consultation with the person selected.

When Dr. Robert Pickett became the choice, I placed calls to him in London where he and Jane were living while he was teaching in that program for the spring semester of 1995. Bob had just retired from Department of Child and Family

Studies in the College of Human Development, where he had also had several administrative responsibilities. The Pickett family and the Phillips family had been close friends since our days together as graduate students at SU in the 1960s. Bob and Jane had both been supporters of the chapel and knew its operation very well. A layman with a keen interest in religion, Bob was an excellent prospect for the interim role. Several calls failed to reach him at their London apartment or Bob's office at the SU London Center.

Therefore, Bob's call asking him the key question about becoming the interim director of Hendricks Chapel came at about one in the morning London time. I just knew he and Jane had to be at home to sleep sometime! A few days later he accepted. What a relief to have everything in place for an early July departure for France.

During the spring semester and early summer of 1995 many things were taking place. Here is a brief list: special French lessons; visiting and reading up on the Strasbourg program; selling the dean's residence at 315 Berkeley Drive; exploring with the Sheraton University Inn the possibility of our living in the hotel for three or four semesters when we returned from France; working with the Picketts for two to three weeks to introduce Bob to his interim roles; packing and moving our household goods into storage in a building adjacent to our log cabin in Clearmont, Missouri (it took two trips with rental trucks); and bringing several roles we were playing in Syracuse to a close as best we could, some not easy to do. In addition, Bob was listed on several of the SU committees upon which I was serving; duties associated with the Martin Luther King Jr. Holiday Celebration were passed to others; required shots and vaccinations were endured; French visas were obtained, along with relearning what French-life red tape is all about; and we had to take care of all the domestic things from mail to banking, health plans, and figuring out what to take on a two-year trip, other than tennis rackets, of course!

It is important to relate that the rumor mill was very active as we prepared for the Strasbourg experience. Almost as soon as the appointment was announced the rumor was afoot that I was being sent to Strasbourg to close the program there. It was running with far fewer students than in previous years and fewer than were needed to balance its share of the DIPA budget. In the end I hope we were part of a renewal effort that brought more students—the place is still alive and very active as this book goes to press.

A second aspect to the rumor mill had it that I was leaving because Hendricks Chapel was soon to be changed and all the campus ministries would be moved to the edge of campus and the history of Hendricks Chapel as we know it was at an end. The same anxieties that had been expressed during the Eggers-McCombe controversy were again alive and creeping into a good many conversations. In fact, Shaw had, during his second year as chancellor, told me he had become fully aware of the value of the chapel on campus and that he could be counted as one of its great supporters. I hope, in the end, my two-year leave strengthened Hendricks Chapel as a key facility and program in service to both its clientele and the institution of Syracuse University itself. Because of the efforts of both Bob Pickett and then my successor, Tom Wolfe, I believe that Hendricks Chapel is now as strong and important a part of Syracuse University as it has ever been.

We flew to Strasbourg on the Fourth of July, 1995, with a full load of luggage. The wonderful staff at our SU Center there welcomed us with open arms, even though the office was closed and most were on summer schedule, some on vacation. We moved into the apartment the two previous directors, Marshall Segall and Goodwin Cooke, and their wives had rented.

We fell in love with Strasbourg immediately. Our landlady, Francine Hildebrand, helped us settle in, took us hiking in the Vosges Mountains west of the city and to her family mountain villa, and gave us good advice on life in this rather unique area of France. Fortunately, her English was better than our French. The third-floor apartment did not give us the room we thought we needed to entertain students and faculty, but it was cozy and provided us with nice views of the city from its upper deck.

In far eastern France, Strasbourg is located on the Rhine River just across from Kehl, Germany. The riverbanks make up part of the famous Maginot line of World War II and are dotted with delightful parks and bike and hiking trails. I had known that a relative had served there with the U.S. Army in World War II, and we visited the park where some one million troops were assembled for the move into Germany. A city of culture, mixed French, German, and Alsatian, almost all the people speak both French and German and a good percentage also speak, often reluctantly, English. The climate includes all four seasons, with winter being relatively mild. There is some but generally not too much summer heat. We had a wonderful introduction to the area as we prepared for the fall semester.

Goodwin Cooke had taught, each of his two semesters, one of the key courses required of all the students in the program. It was called the European Policy Seminar, and Marshall Segall had taught it for the previous four semesters. One of my first tasks was to locate someone to teach that course for the upcoming semester. The person who had once taught the course was no longer at the Council of Europe offices in Strasbourg. Our local faculty members and our staff helped, but we could not find a qualified teacher for this course. In the end the Maxwell School gave me adjunct status to teach the course for one semester only. DIPA arranged for Goodwin Cooke to make a videotape in Syracuse of his wonderful and insightful introduction to the course. From there I thought I could get myself ready and did so. Basic to my confidence was the fact that many of the sessions were filled with guest lecturers in respective specialties (one even came from Syracuse that first semester just to give two lectures) related to the history of European unification efforts since World War II, the chief thrust and purpose of the course.

I have the Maxwell School to thank for extending permission for me to teach the course for all four of my semesters as director. We did not ever locate someone to take my place, even though for the second and third semesters we tried mightily to do so. As for the fourth semester—tradition had taken over! Thanks to Cooke's help, the Maxwell School's kindness, perhaps better called a kindness of necessity, and my willingness to drop the religion course for which I had prepared, I learned a new field and a great deal about the Europe of today and the past fifty years, and I was really rather delighted with the result.

It is not the purpose of this chapter to go into more detail about these two years. The reader already has the flavor, so a few summary comments will close this effort. Someday, if DIPA asks me to write a history of those two years, you can read more about them then!

Life in France is difficult in part because it is exhausting to work in a place where one's language skills are minimal. By the end I was proud that some local merchants were asking me if I was German or American. I did make real progress but not until the end of the assignment did I reach the level I had more than twenty years before. One reason I am sure was because all of our business at the center was in English. Probably another key reason was something called aging! Only after being back in Syracuse for a year and having my hearing tested at the SU Hearing Clinic did I realize that I was unable to hear some of the sounds so essential to learning and using another language. Hearing aids followed a few years later.

Life in France is difficult for a number of other reasons, but it is also wonderful for a number of reasons. Notoriously difficult is the already mentioned French red tape about all matters of life both for the French and for those of us in the expatriate category. The French reputation of not being very hospitable is warranted, but it is enough of a surface problem that it begins to be of less concern as the weeks roll by. Cultural difference are always evident and can cause both frustration and pleasant reflection on dimensions of one's home culture. The positives also include the wonderful food (this area of France is pure delight in this arena) and the opportunities to make fast friends far from home. Travel was without doubt one of the rich parts of the duties, as we traveled a great deal in much of Western and a little of Eastern Europe in seminars with our students. Private travel both on the German side of the river and in the Strasbourg area of France is a delight to experience, the villages of the wine district of Alsace perhaps the highlight. We are anxious to return for a visit with friends and to again experience some of the places we loved to visit.

The work at the SU Center was very demanding, with the director playing all the roles of administration found in a collegiate setting. I had, over the years, experienced most of these roles, which was of great help. We were understaffed and had it not been for Ethel's volunteer help in the office, I am not sure any of us would have remained sane through it all. In a very difficult budgetary time we took over everything we could, including the care for the center's lawn. One of the real budgetary successes was that I was able to bring to a close our commitment to rent a second facility that we had contracted, when we had more students, for an extended period of time. Normally in French law, one cannot get out of such a contract without the full cooperation of the landlord, which we were finally able, after a number of failures, to negotiate.

Relationships with Hendricks Chapel during the two years were a delight. Jane and Bob Pickett came to visit us during the university's spring break both years we were in Strasbourg. The joy inherent in those visits was beyond what can be expressed in a short paragraph. My budgetary duties were minimal, as Bob proved to be fully equal to that task. Perhaps the most time I spent on Hendricks Chapel business during the two years was in helping with the wedding issues that were taken under consideration and are mentioned elsewhere in this book. Returning to the duties at Hendricks Chapel late in the summer of 1997 proved easy because of Bob's excellent administration during our absence. Even so, I did have both jet and cultural lag for several weeks after returning. Ethel had not as severe a case as I.

Professor John Western of the Maxwell School became my successor as director of the Strasbourg program. Before he arrived in the summer of 1997 Ethel and I were able to organize and cull all the files in the director's office. We had time after John's arrival to give him a brief introduction to the program and the center before our July flight back to the United States. During the two years we had not visited Syracuse. I am pleased I had made that decision before we traveled to France. During the two years Ethel made four trips back to visit family; I made two.

After the first year in Strasbourg I was to let Chancellor Shaw know if for any reason I had reached the decision to retire in the summer of 1997 rather than return to the deanship. At that time I told him I wished to continue my deanship until June 1999, at which time I would have just passed the age of sixty-five. Why retire so early? he inquired. I told him I had always had an eye on the age of sixty-five so that while still young and healthy I could do other things and also not risk too much fading of my skills as dean of Hendricks Chapel. One other important aspect to the plan had to do with our conversation when I had asked for an administrative sabbatical. Shaw, at that time, had indicated that rather than such a sabbatical he might be able to grant the final semester "on leave" when I did decide to retire. In that summer of 1996 I asked if that idea was still a possibility, and the answer was yes.

As a result we returned to Syracuse in the summer of 1997 to serve Hendricks Chapel for three more semesters. According to plan I was to retire from Hendricks Chapel at the end of December 1998, to chair the January 1999 Martin Luther King Jr. Holiday Celebration, and to have the rest of that spring semester off and then officially retire from Syracuse University at the end of June 1999. That plan worked to perfection. During the months back at Hendricks Chapel I had duties associated with the search for my successor, which is reported in a subsequent chapter.

The plan to live in the Sheraton University Inn materialized when they changed a large conference room on the third floor into an apartment and had it ready by August for us. The rent cost the university and Hendricks Chapel less than would have the rental of a house plus utilities as replacement for the dean's residence, now long in private hands. Ethel and I thoroughly enjoyed our three-plus semesters in the hotel with a wonderful staff and the many conveniences associated and with very few domestic responsibilities.

As I have indicated, Bob Pickett did an excellent job as interim director of Hendricks Chapel. This judgment comes from individuals and programs throughout the university in addition to my own assessments both during and after his interim service. And, equally important, talking such a close friend into taking on some very heavy responsibilities has not harmed one bit a wonderful family friendship.

One more observation. Of great delight for the two-year period was the fact that Bob and the chaplains serving Syracuse University became close friends, and the chaplains were to a person solid fans of Bob's time as administrator of the place where they in turn exercise their professional service and leadership. How very gratifying to have such a person in the chair during our two years away from Syracuse.

To have been in Strasbourg for two of our last four years before retirement was a marvelous part of the end game to my eighteen-year career with Syracuse University.

60. "A Sacred Trust"

ROBERT S. PICKETT

IN THE SPRING SEMESTER of 1995, while I was teaching in the Syracuse University Semester Abroad program in London, I received a telephone call from Dean Richard Phillips, whom I had known ever since our graduate days in Syracuse. After a brief exchange of greetings, Dick asked me if I would consider the prospect of serving the university in the capacity of interim director of Hendricks Chapel. This possibility had arisen because Dick intended to assume responsibility for the Syracuse program in Strasbourg, France.

It took a bit of time for me to process Dick's comments and to think about how I might respond to his request. I knew about Hendricks Chapel through my long association with Dick and my years as professor and chairperson in the Department of Child and Family Studies, but the thought of serving as the administrator in charge of Hendricks had never occurred to me. Professors, outside of religion departments, are generally not given to participating extensively in organized religion. Even so, I was interested in the nature and scope of religious practices. Earlier on, when I was a graduate student at Harvard University, I was baptized in the Methodist-related Church of All Nations in Boston and later became active in the University Methodist Church in Syracuse. Near the end of the 1980s I became a member of the Unitarian Universalist Society. I knew that the various deans had always been Methodist clergymen, and I was no longer a Methodist, but the idea of serving as the administrator of an interfaith organization had a certain appeal. It suited my Universalist orientation. After a period of discussion with my wife, Jane, and some reflection, I accepted the appointment to serve as interim director of Hendricks.

A Tradition of Leadership at Hendricks Chapel

Hendricks Chapel was not a bastion of religious exclusivity bent on preserving itself and guarding against the inroads of rampant iconoclasm. Nevertheless, the various clergy who had occupied the deanship never shirked from the desire to champion the importance of a strong faith tradition. Through their preaching and people skills, earlier deans, such as Charles Noble, sought to maintain a central presence on the campus in the same fashion that the building itself occupied a central position. Every dean could be said to have inherited a different historical situation with respect to the changing role of organized religion and university life, but there was also the matter of the specific orientation and strengths each one brought to the position of the deanship. As I stepped into the position I knew I would be briefly inheriting a setting strongly influenced by the personality and achievements of Dr. Richard L. Phillips.

As one might expect, any dean's approach to chapel matters would be influenced by his own background as well as his knowledge of what had gone on before. When Dick assumed the role of dean of the chapel he could look back on the early part of the twentieth-century mainline Methodist churches that had been at the forefront of the so-called social gospel movement. Syracuse University had grown considerably during that period in the history of American Methodism. Dick also knew of the mid-twentieth-century period in which religious participation was still a strong component of university activities. Chapel services had been heavily attended, and mainline American Protestantism had been a central element of campus life, particularly at Syracuse and other Methodist-related institutions. He also knew by his own experience that by the end of the 1960s major changes had taken place. Even though the values inherent in liberal religion were being car-

Robert S. Pickett served as interim director of Hendricks Chapel from July 1995 to July 1997, allowing Dean Phillips to oversee Syracuse University's semester abroad program in Strasbourg, France. Courtesy of Syracuse University.

ried out in student involvement against racism and sexism as well as the antipoverty movement, other aspects of religious activity had diminished. Participation in organized religious worship had declined. Yet Dick and others engaged in working with students knew that when the uprisings of the late 1960s and early 1970s occurred, the front steps of the chapel was one of the places where the country's internal conflict over Vietnam was exposed for all the world to see.

Dick adapted well to living in New York State and relating to the ways of eastern schools, but he never shook the openhanded western manner in which he grew up. He still maintained his membership in the Rocky Mountain Methodist Conference, even though Syracuse University and the community of Syracuse had become very much a part of his consciousness. Dick's formative years as a young minister at University Church, just down the hill, as well as his experiences as a graduate student at the university and briefly as an instructor within the Religion Department had provided him with an opportunity to blend his western ways with upstate New York.

When Dick returned to Syracuse to assume the mantle of deanship he brought with him the prior experience with the Syracuse community combined with a set of valuable experiences gained from his position as chief administrator of the American Youth Foundation, a position that he had taken after a stint as a professor and eventually as registrar at Baker University in Kansas. Upon Dick's arrival to serve as dean of the chapel, Chancellor Melvin Eggers gave Dick the understanding that he should be active in as many spheres of campus activity as he could manage. The deanship was not to be strictly related to narrowly defined religious activity within the confines of the chapel. He was expected to be anywhere as well as everywhere. This idea suited Dick. A gregarious person by nature, he thrived in communicating with as many publics as possible. He saw his role as multifaceted, and he truly appreciated that challenge.

In addition to the dean being omnipresent on campus and in the community there had to be a systematic approach to maintaining the chapel's role as a visible and viable force on campus. Dick believed that the keys to the chapel's success would be clearly visible outreach types of programming and the encouragement of student voluntarism. Such programming was to be directed toward the betterment of the campus through an emphasis upon involvement in social concerns, particularly in addressing matters such as race relations, sexuality, and economic inequality. Dick knew that this focus would require a staff person who reflected these concerns in every way possible. One of his tasks was to find such a person. That person would need to be unusually gifted in responding to suggestions from many different places and would need maximum ability and sensitivity to reach students as well as citizens in the community at large. Whoever it was, the person should not be easily discouraged if grand designs failed to be achieved. As the years passed at Hendricks Chapel, Dick began to follow his plans and find his people. When I arrived in May 1996 to assume the interim director position, Dick had already established his own place in the tradition of leadership at Hendricks Chapel.

The Academic Year 1995–1996

When I returned to Syracuse I began to orient myself with respect to both the responsibilities entailed and the personnel involved in working in Hendricks Chapel. My orientation began when Dick and I went to have a chat with Chancellor Kenneth Shaw. Afterward, I came to the dean's office and began my encounters with the chapel staff, beginning with Dr. Katharine Pardee. As the Hendricks Chapel and university organist, Pardee worked with Associate Professor G. Burton Harbison, the university's director of choral activities and conductor of the Hendricks Chapel Choir. These two, along with Protestant chaplain the Reverend Thomas V. Wolfe, were key figures in conducting the Sunday morning Protestant services in the sanctuary. I also conferred with Imam Ahmed Nezar Kobeisy, the Islamic chaplain. Kobeisy was the essential person in charge of prayer services at Hendricks as well as the imam at the Islamic Society of Syracuse.

No administrator can function well without the assistance of an energetic and competent staff. As I met the various staff members and began to work with them I concluded that if I did not succeed at Hendricks, it would not be because of inadequacies on the part of the staff. I discovered that they were both competent and caring in every sense of these words. On the same day that I conversed with Dr. Pardee and Imam Kobeisy I met with Mary Farnsworth, who had oversight with respect to a variety of activities within the chapel. I also met Virginia Yerdon, who carried out the important function of scheduling activities within the chapel, and Kikuko Nishiguchi, the graduate assistant who took care of many of the business transactions of the chapel. One of her chief responsibilities was to exercise oversight with respect to the student managers of People's Place, the student-run snack bar operating a brisk business in the chapel basement area next to the Noble Room. In time, I would meet the student managers themselves. The final meeting of the day was with Susan Martini, who had come to interview for the position of the dean's secretary. In passing, I met other people, such as the student proctors who carried out various functions. They were the front line of chapel communication. They answered the main telephone and occupied the central desk in the dean's office foyer. As such, they were in contact with the various publics who came to the dean's office. In my early conversations with them and during a more formal meeting, I found the proctors to be a courteous and helpful group. They did an excellent job of representing both the chapel and the university.

The Community of Religious Workers at Hendricks Chapel

As time went on, I had the opportunity to meet a number of chapel-related people involved in the so-called group ministries and the affiliated groups. The group ministries were conducted in a variety of settings, both inside and outside the chapel proper. In addition to Rabbi Rapoport of Chabad House, there were religious workers such as Scott and Sherri Dalton, of BASIC, Paul and Sandy Jewell of the Campus Bible Fellowship, Nick DeCola of the Campus Crusade for Christ and Athletes in Action, James McCullough, staff worker for the Inter-Varsity Fellowship and worker with the Graduate Christian Fellowship, and, finally, members of the Southern Baptist Ministry.

Hendricks has always supported a number of religious groups who have established a legitimate presence on the campus. The category of affiliated groups contains a wide range of religious orientations. The Christian Scientists, Unitarian Universalists, Buddhists, Pan-Orthodox Christians, Society of Friends, and Zen Buddhists all have students with whom they work. In addition to these groups there are organizations such as Alcoholics Anonymous and various denominationally oriented student groups that do not maintain full-time chaplains on campus.

In time, I had plentiful opportunities to encounter people involved with various aspects of the chapel's activities. I met other members of the corps of chaplains from the mainline faith traditions. One of the first was Rabbi Toby Manewith, who worked with Jewish students and attended to the Hillel organization's functions within the chapel. She served as the chief contact with the conservative and Reform students, and like the other chaplains she received financial support from sources external to the university. I also had an audience with the Reverend

Thomas V. Wolfe, whose work was sponsored by the American Baptists, United Church of Christ, United Methodists, and Presbyterian Church (USA). Either in my office or in their quarters, I met Lutheran chaplain Dr. George J. Koch, Evangelical chaplain T. E. Koshy, Assemblies of God and Chi Alpha Christian Ministries chaplain the Reverend E. Andrew Mitchell, Roman Catholic chaplain the Reverend James P. Lang, and Episcopal chaplain the Reverend James K. Taylor. I discovered that in addition to Taylor's chaplaincy he served Grace Episcopal Church, an inner-city parish just down the hill from the university. Neither Mitchell nor Lang maintained offices within the chapel, but Lang was in and out of the chapel a great deal because he often conducted a daily mass in the sanctuary. His base of operations was the Alibrandi Catholic Center, which he generously offered on many occasions as an alternative space for occasional chapel programming.

As I interacted with the various people whom I saw during this early period, it became abundantly clear how Hendricks Chapel differed from the other parts of the university. The personnel in the chapel honored academic pursuits and enjoyed the stimulating activities of campus life, but their major orientation was directed toward service to others. By contrast, individual faculty and even some academic departments might have a strong concern for service in a broader sense, but they were basically oriented toward demonstrating competence in teaching and research. I found that with the exception of people employed in an area such as Student Affairs, administrative personnel within the university had to be primarily concerned with obtaining and handling economic resources of one kind or another. Every unit of the university had its mission, but as I looked at Hendricks I surmised that no other unit demonstrated the type of activity I was witnessing. The arrangements of the financial support for the people who worked in the chapel marked it as clearly different from the other parts of the university. The various religious organizations outside the university believed sufficiently in the importance of university work that they were willing to supply salary and benefit supports. In its turn, the university agreed to provide space for religious activity and fringe benefits such as the provision of tuition hours for full-time chaplains. As for the staff of the chapel, from the various people in the office of the dean to the person who provided janitorial service, the university provided the funds.

My first opportunity to observe the collective sense of responsibility displayed by chapel workers occurred a week or so after my arrival when I was invited to the Chaplains Council meeting. The meeting took place at the Islamic Society of Central New York mosque on Comstock Avenue. Dick Phillips, who had returned from out of town, introduced me to the assembled chaplains and allowed me to listen to their deliberations, most of which originated from actions having taken place during the past academic year. The great tragedy ensuing from the bombing incident in Oklahoma as well as the negative "fallout" from that event were still omnipresent. The chaplains were still in the process of preparing a document in which they expressed their concern about underlying racism and religious intolerance that had emerged in the early responses to the tragedy. After the document had received its final revision and we all signed it, I reflected on the strong interfaith cooperation displayed by the chaplains.

I found the chaplains to be very cordial to one another. Later on, I talked to them on the matter of how well they got along. It seemed to me that the chaplains got on exceedingly well. Evidently, they differed only when it came to theology, and I was not sure about that. I never heard them argue about such matters. As a group, they were very much concerned with the welfare of the university as a whole. They were clearly involved in serving their particular constituencies, but their actions revealed the fact that they saw their role as larger than that function. The chaplains clearly assisted the dean's office in many ways and worked in a cooperative fashion with one another to enhance the effectiveness of the chapel. This fact proved to be true many times over, particularly when crises arose within the campus community as a whole. When a disturbed student in one of the dormitories on Mount Olympus plunged to his death, the chaplains mobilized to provide needed support to the student's friends and family as well as the university staff. None of the chaplains demonstrated territorial behavior.

It is reasonable to expect that administrators will have varying styles of relating to persons with whom they work in close proximity. Nevertheless, to be effective, administrative approaches need to dovetail with the administered organization's known aims and values as well as its general character of communication. Some executives are very much given to using telephones or computers as well as memoranda. Others prefer face-to-face contact. While working in Hendricks Chapel, I soon found it necessary to be one of the latter. I sensed that the chapel thrived on a free-flowing communication pattern. Thus, if the need arose to talk with chaplains or staff members I went to wherever I could find them. Unless I was working on the budget or in a meeting that required confidentiality, my door was open. As time went on I learned that my open-door policy was appreciated.

The Social Gospel at Work in an Academic Setting

When I met Francis Parks, who had followed Millie Woods as a staff member, I discovered that Dick's efforts to achieve visible and effective programming were still highly operative. As the person in charge of the African American programs at the chapel and as the director of the Students Offering Service component, Francis Parks had inherited a major role in Dick's effort to achieve a maximum impact through programming. She operated out of an office squeezed into a corner of the Noble Room, but her activities there and elsewhere created a constant hum of activity throughout the university. With the assistance of her able graduate assistant Fred Boehrer, Francis conducted an extraordinary range of programming that involved the students, faculty, and staff in outreach within as well as beyond the campus. Assisted by the chaplains and staff, Francis spearheaded a number of activities related to enhancing awareness of the values of diversity and the necessity to engage in enlightened voluntarism. She proved to be highly effective in supporting initiatives developed by students, but she also developed programs that reflected her own concerns for the betterment of the university community and the community of Syracuse at large. The values that her work symbolized would eventually prove to be key elements within the university's goals espoused during the administration of Chancellor Kenneth Shaw. The programs developed under her guidance did not need any administrative urging, but they did require consistent support.

Some Notes on the Practical Side of Working in an Altruistic Setting

Journeying outside the office I had the opportunity to learn a number of things about the university that had seemed somewhat remote during the years in which I had served as a faculty member and chairperson of the Department of Child and Family Studies. I also developed a few new abilities. I expected to deliver invocations and benedictions, and I was glad to do so. Going to various functions and delivering such utterances provided the opportunity to establish contacts with people throughout the university and the community. Also, I found these short statements to be an important way for me to express my own thoughts about serious matters affecting the university and society at large. Whether the occasion was the "commencement exercises" of the international students attending the English Language Institute, an alumni banquet for the fifty-year class, or the dedication of a new structure at the university's sports complex at the outer Comstock location, I considered such occasions to be important. In passing, I also discovered that my presence and my role at these functions might have been appreciated, but they liked it when I kept my utterances short.

As I expected, some of my time as an administrator was taken up with stewarding the chapel's resources, and some of it was dedicated to the possibility of seeking additional economic support. Thus, I sought to adhere closely to budget guidelines while at the same time discovering worthwhile projects and seeking potential support for them. Early on, I had the opportunity to confer with people at the Skytop offices and to relate to the university's Development Office. I met Barbara Wessell and others in the latter, and before long we were exploring contacts with potential benefactors. I welcomed the opportunity to meet those individuals who in the past had contributed generously from their resources to help the chapel achieve its goals. One of those persons was Marjorie Pierson. She had been involved very early on as a participant in Hendricks Chapel activities and eventually became a financial contributor to the creation of the small chapel. The chapel had relatively little in the way of endowment funds, but what it had proved to be very useful. The Esther Malmgren Fund was the most sizable source of endowed moneys available, and I was eventually able to take advantage of this source by helping to coordinate some of the Malmgren Concerts.

With respect to raising funds, the chapel was at a disadvantage. Research projects, a major source of financial augmentation within the departments and colleges of the university, were not a part of the chapel's agenda. Alumni giving to the chapel was also more problematic than in the various schools and colleges. Many alumni had fond memories of their connection with the chapel, yet they tended not to think of it when the university made its annual requests for financial support. The chapel could not summon up the kind of specific college loyalties so typically found within the colleges. Nevertheless, there were a number of people among both the university's former employees and its former students who maintained a strong sense of obligation to the chapel because it had helped them or their families in some way. Others knew that the chapel often met needs that the university's regular offices did not. There were some benefactors, such as Dr. Roy Stegeman, an elderly retired professor from the College of Environmental Sciences and Forestry. During my time at the chapel I corresponded with Dr. Stegeman and received annual contributions to support the dean's Benevolence Fund. Financial resources obtained in this way were limited, but they proved to be helpful in aiding students and people who needed a small amount of economic assistance.

During my years at the chapel, the chancellor's office embarked on an effort to improve the quality of services delivered to students. It was clear to me that by contrast to some other units of the university, Hendricks was already a high achiever in delivering such services, but I discovered that the personnel within the chapel took the quality-improvement program very seriously. Along with other chapel staff and even the chaplains, I became engaged in the university's quest for quality improvement by attending training sessions. I was also a member of the chancellor's Area Quality Council. This participation immersed me in the administrative and financial concerns of other units within the university.

As the administrator of the chapel, I was an integral part of the chapel's system of care. Sometimes, care meant seeing that the building was ready for whatever might happen. It meant attending to things that might not be thought of as care but still needed to be done. As a mundane illustration of this point, I had to learn to raise and lower the sanctuary's pulpit for religious services and secular activities. The sound system had to be ready for different types of events. There was always the sense that the chapel had to be ready for a variety of activities that might take place, whether they were carefully planned and scheduled ahead of time or relatively spontaneous due to unforeseen events.

Various spaces within the chapel have been altered over time and very likely will continue to be altered as resources and imagination permit, but during the period of my service the logistics of preparing for activities and carrying them out within these spaces were generally not a problem. The personnel involved knew how to use what resources the building offered, and they knew how to respond to the needs of various publics. I attended weddings and observed how the student wedding coordinators and resident chaplains assisted visiting clergy. There were protocols to be met, and each ceremony received meticulous attention. Fortunately, the efficient and gracious manner of the chapel staff made my job easy. People such as Mary Farnsworth and Virginia Yerdon were always vigilant in seeing that required materials were in place and that the students appointed as proctors or wedding coordinators were thoroughly trained.

Becoming acquainted with the character of the building as a structure was instructive as well as inspiring. Before he left, Dick gave me a grand tour of the building, all the way to the top. He had enormous respect, almost reverence, for the structure and its many spaces. I observed that same feeling of respect on the part of Effie, the custodian. With her hands and heart she devoted loving care to the building every day in which she worked. If she found students expressing disrespect by the way they handled the furnishings they would be duly chastised. I had no choice but to agree that it was a magnificent structure, and later on, as I walked through its hallways and climbed its stairs, I felt the same sense of appreciation that Dick and Effie had expressed.

During my first summer as director, I attended a higher education conclave in Nashville, Tennessee, where I had the opportunity to meet with persons who held a position similar to mine. There was still much to absorb about serving the university in such a capacity. Upon my return from the conference, I became acutely aware that my responsibilities were considerably different from what they had been as a professor and department chairperson. Things could happen to jeopardize the chapel programs or even the chapel building itself, as was the case during an electrical storm. Upon returning from an out-of-town engagement I saw smoke issuing from the chapel steps. Some type of contact from the electricity in the atmosphere had been made just minutes before my arrival. Fortunately, Chaplain Tom Wolfe had been nearby attending to a wedding ceremony. He had alerted campus security, and with the help of the Fire Department the potential fire was extinguished. Thus, as I arrived I discovered that the building for which I was responsible and which Dick and Effie had taught me to revere had been in jeopardy but was no longer in danger. Breathing a sign of relief, I mused about the fact that both the young couple getting married and I had started out our respective new journeys in what might be thought of as a blazing fashion.

The summer is often one of those periods on campus when one can put the finishing touches on matters related to the past academic year and some last-minute planning for the coming year. There is also the opportunity and a bit of time to quietly enjoy the beauty of the campus in full bloom while observing happy wedding parties and students throwing Frisbees. Within the chapel staff, there is still work to do, but it is interspersed with some moments of spontaneous jollity and a more relaxed style of operation. One could look backward in recognition of events, both good and bad, yet, on a college campus, there is the tendency to look forward positively to the prospect of new beginnings. As a harbinger of things to come, the university's Preview '95 took place on the weekend of July 15–16. Receptions occurred in the student center, and I was on hand to greet and mingle with parents. There was still time for the annual Strawberry Festival and a jazz and reggae concert, but there was also time to acknowledge a momentous and somber anniversary. Early in August, the chapel staff and others conducted a remembrance service in which the fiftieth anniversary of the release of the atomic bomb on Hiroshima was reconsidered and reflected upon.

Eventually, the midsummer's idyll came to an end, and the campus population suddenly increased many times over. Like most universities in the country, mid- to late August heralded the return to full activity. On August 22 I went to South Campus to appear at the new faculty meeting, and on the twenty-fifth I joined the chapel staff and the chaplains in welcoming the incoming students. Greeting and hosting the eager freshmen students, who began to overrun the campus, the chapel staff and the religious workers were all on hand to share in the excitement that so often accompanies the start of a new academic year. The first day of classes was August 28.

In many ways, chapel life reflects personal events, whether positive or negative, within the entire university community. Along with the anticipation and optimism accompanying the beginning of the full university schedule, there is also the awareness that during the summer there are always some people in the community who have experienced personal tragedy. As Chancellor Melvin Eggers once indicated to me, when a tragedy strikes one of the university personnel or their families, it becomes a tragedy for the university as a whole. During my first summer, Kevin Van Doren, a talented and promising young professor in the Biology Department, had been killed during a violent thunderstorm in the Adirondacks. This tragedy meant meetings with the family and the Biology Department to discuss an appropriate memorial service for Kevin.

Hendricks Chapel is closely connected with the various other units who deliver personal services within the university. Of all its units, the relationship to the Office of Student Affairs is the closest. Thus, during the period prior to and during the school year, I became acquainted with a large number of people who worked in areas such as the Parents Office, the student center, and the residence halls. I joined in the monthly meetings of Student Affairs personnel and others involved in the delivery of a variety of services to the students. We met together in what was known as Director's Plus. At these meetings, chaired by the vice president of student affairs, we all reported on activities within our special areas of programming.

This relatively large and somewhat diverse group proved to be an invigorating assemblage of talent and goodwill. I also had my first meetings with the Hendricks Chapel Board, a helpful group made up of professionals and students who gave me wise counsel and good support. I had my first conference with Eleanor Gallagher. As the vice president to whom I reported, she was a direct conduit to Chancellor Shaw. In all of my dealings with Eleanor I found her to be helpful and supportive. As a unit, we did not constitute a source of great trouble for her. She seemed to enjoy my relating stories of chapel activities, and when asked to support needed elements of the chapel's functions she did so.

During the registration period and into the first day of classes, there were many campuswide events and receptions to attend. The chapel itself held an open house and collaborated with other units in conducting an extended evening program for new students. Between these larger events, the days were filled with meetings in which I met the people in charge of other important parts of the campus support system, one of whom was Pat Burak, head of the Office for International Students. Pat would prove to be a splendid associate in my dealings with international students and as a collaborator in conducting the annual Thanksgiving meal for international students. This fine relationship was also the case for Schine Student Center people such as Bridget Talbot and Tom Elmore. In time, I had a conference with James Heffernan, vice president at the School of Environmental Science and Forestry, who served on the Hendricks Chapel Board and participated in the Thanksgiving event. Donald Koten was also involved with us with respect to the students in forestry who participated in planning the Habitat for Humanity trip. In addition to meeting valuable contact persons, I had the opportunity to join with other members of the chancellor's Area Quality Council, such as Robert Robinson, the head of campus security, and Beth Rogeux, who had major responsibilities with the various external governmental relationships. Beth recognized me as one of her former professors. Whatever their areas of responsibility, I found that the opportunity to talk with the heads of various units provided me with valuable information and an opportunity to establish connections that would be important for later collaborations.

As might be expected, the early days of fall were largely devoted to start-up activities. I found myself even returning to the classroom for spot lectures. Professor Lissit of the Newhouse School of Public Communications invited me to make a presentation to freshmen students in his class. Lissit, like others, sought to familiarize the freshmen with different parts of the university that they might not otherwise appreciate. Therefore, he invited me to explain how the chapel operated and how it dealt with religious concerns on campus, not the least of which was the matter of off-campus fringe religious groups who might have designs on recruiting unsuspecting students. I welcomed Professor Lissit's invitation. Protestant chaplain Tom Wolfe, Catholic chaplain Jim Lang, and others had gathered data on various off-campus efforts by groups such as the so-called Moonies and members of The Way International who had sought to develop footholds on campus. Neither of these groups could produce a slate of students and neither had any faculty sponsorship, so those of us in the chapel maintained a close watch on their activities.

As the interim director of the chapel, I was expected to participate in campus committees. Through my earlier experiences as a faculty representative to the University Senate, I was familiar with meetings with people from a number of different places on campus. The first meeting of the University Senate Committee on Diversity, which occurred early in the fall, typified this type of involvement. Because I was in charge of a unit that by its very nature had to be considered as supporting the values of diversity, I was a logical member of this committee. What differed from my earlier situation was the number and the range of committees in which I became involved. The Martin Luther King Committee exemplified the difference. Its composition was large and complex. It held year-round meetings. Participation in this committee meant substantial input directed toward a large event taking place at a specified time. The chapel's role and the allotment of its resources were significant because of its long-term involvement in the King celebration. Dick Phillips had been a moving spirit in the event ever since its beginning. The Thanksgiving celebration with international students was another example of a campuswide event that required collaboration among various groups. It was also similar in the fact that the chapel had been a founding force in contributing to its development. Expanding on the original activity of Chaplain T. E. Koshy, Dick Phillips and the chapel staff had creatively collaborated with the Office of International Students, the Schine Center administrators and staff, and several Syracuse merchants, including Peter's Grocery that for many years contributed the turkeys. All worked tirelessly to host this wonderful event for the international students and their families.

Dark Elegy

One of the most significant of collaborations with others was the series of events that would once again call attention to the bombing of Flight 103, the university's greatest tragedy. In order to continue to deal constructively with that wrenching experience, an all-campus committee—including Judy O'Rourke, from the office of the vice president for undergraduate affairs, Pat Burak, and others—was organized to develop appropriate commemorative programs in cooperation and sometimes conjunction with the parents of students who had been the innocent victims of the disaster. From the outset, Hendricks Chapel had been drawn upon to help deal with the pain associated with that event. Thus, I followed Dick as a member of the committee. One of the committee's chief activities in the fall was planning for the program surrounding the installation of a set of sculptures titled *Dark Elegy.*

Suzie Lowenstein, the mother of one of the student victims, sculpted the powerful figures, for which some of the mothers of the victims had posed.

I regarded the prospect of involvement in preparing for *Dark Elegy* as a distinct honor. Shannon Davis, a victim of the crash, was one of my undergraduate advisees. Also, back in March, Jane and I had joined Syracuse University Drama Department faculty member Donna Inglima in journeying to Lockerbie, Scotland. As members of the American faculty in the university's London program, Donna and I were designated as university representatives involved in the selection of remembrance scholars. We also served in a liaison fashion with respect to people in Lockerbie, particularly in regard to the selection of Lockerbie secondary school students who were to receive scholarships at the home campus in Syracuse. We met with the students, visited their school, and talked with their parents.

On the weekend of September 23–24 the campus filled with activity. On Saturday afternoon the Syracuse football team hosted the University of Minnesota team. The installation and dedication of *Dark Elegy* also took place. On that same weekend, the African American and Latino alumni came once again to celebrate their "Coming Back Together" weekend. As a result of the tightness of scheduling, I found myself actually running from their exhilarating Sunday service in the chapel sanctuary to the *Dark Elegy* dedication on the corner in front of Lyman Hall. The event was a moving experience, especially for the two Lockerbie students, Katrina Bogie and Lucy Gibson. They had been to my house for dinner on the previous Thursday evening. In talking with them, both Jane and I surmised that the dedication service would be difficult for them. It was. A newspaper photographer from a local paper insisted on taking a close-up photo of the two saddened young girls in the midst of the emotionally draining service.

Dark Elegy had a powerful impact on the whole community. Even a sideways glance at the stark figures raising their hands to the sky as if imploring an uncaring deity caused many motorists to stop their cars and gaze solemnly at the angst represented on that quiet green space. It is often said that college fraternities are totally focused on party life. *Dark Elegy* broke through any such veneer of frivolity. Early one morning on my way to work, I passed by a group of young men clustered near the figures. By looking at them I could see that they were students of a fraternity, not generally thought to be advocates of early rising. They were holding a large framed photograph of a group of fraternity brothers. I suspected that at least one of the young men in the photograph had been lost over Lockerbie.

The involvement of Hendricks in regard to *Dark Elegy* and the programs surrounding it during the annual observance of the Lockerbie tragedy constituted the most obvious example of the chapel's tendency to try to alleviate agony on a personal level as well as an international level. From the outset, the chapel personnel engaged in cooperative programming and participation in a broad range of events, joining with others in coming together to remind the world of the harrowing occurrence that the Syracuse family itself had experienced in a most traumatic fashion. On November 3, Jane and I journeyed to Washington, D.C., to join others involved in the work of the university committee at the installation of the memorial cairn at Arlington National Cemetery. That event provided us with another opportunity to join with the families who had lost their children, and it also provided us with another contact with Lockerbie folks. Donald Bogie, Katrina's father, was involved in constructing the cairn, and he was on hand to witness the ceremony. In addition to active involvement in the programming developed by the university and the subsequent creation of the student scholarship program and hosting the students from Lockerbie, the chapel itself still held an annual vigil on December 21. Together with others, a small group came to the small chapel at the time in the day when the destruction had originally occurred and then processed to the memorial place at the head of University Avenue.

Hendricks Chapel: A Holy Beehive, a Quiet Space, and a Temple for Ideas

I thought that I was busy attending meetings all over campus and sometimes in the community, but I quickly discovered that the building for which I was responsible was even more busy than I. The chapel had many calls on its space, and dealing effectively with them was an important matter. Near the end of his tenure as the chancellor of the university, when I was still teaching, Chancellor Melvin Eggers said that he had never realized that the matter of dealing with space needs would be such a difficult part of his job. Clearly, the needs of the various religious groups had to be met, but the university as a whole often needed Hendricks as a space for some of its many functions. Fortunately, the chapel lent itself to quite a variety of activities, both religious and secular. The commodious nature and excellent acoustics of the sanctuary made it an important auditorium for prominent speakers and musical concerts as well as functions such as commencement convocations. The two wings of the sanctuary provided uniquely suitable spaces for smaller gatherings, most notably for the Jewish services on one side and the daily Roman Catholic masses on the other. On Sunday afternoons, Chaplain Andrew Mitchell used portions of the sanctuary. The sanctuary was not just for collective use; it was also a private haven. As I passed through its space it was not unusual to see a person quietly sitting or kneeling alone in quiet contemplation or prayer.

Throughout the year, the other rooms and spaces in what some might refer to as a "rabbit warren" of offices and the larger open spaces proved their worth by being in nearly constant use. The Strates Lounge, a flexible space as well as the small chapel, fulfilled the needs of small groups of people who needed to meet. Various religious groups such as the Buddhists and the Christian Scientists met in the small chapel. Of all the spaces, the situation with respect to the Noble Room proved to be the most varied in terms of who used it and how it was employed. It was one of those places on campus that could be counted on to be a center for a range of disparate meetings. No one knew that better than Ginny Yerdon, who ably kept tabs on all the possible meeting spaces within the building. The chaplains found the Noble Room to be very suitable for their functions. During regular Sunday mornings and during religious holy days I had an opportunity to see how valuable the Noble Room could be. Dr. Koch employed it for regular Sunday morning Lutheran services, and Rabbi Manewith used it for Reform services during Yom Kippur. It was heavily used by religious groups on Thursdays. At noon Dr. Koshy and his group transformed it into a free luncheon presentation space for international students. On Thursday evenings Nick DeCola held Campus Crusade for Christ meetings in the Noble Room. It was a place where a chaplain could conduct a forum or a professor like Sanford Sternlicht could give a talk on his latest book. On any given day or evening, Francis Parks or Fred Boehrer could be found helping students engineer the next Green Up day or lining up details for the next Habitat for Humanity road trip. During the evenings the room might become a setting for an interfaith discussion group, a planning committee, or a quilt-making session for a number of industrious and creative women. It also constituted a place where one could study or sit and chat with some cronies over coffee and bagels.

Even though I was impressed by the grandness and utilitarian character of the building, my appreciation for Hendricks Chapel transcended its physical characteristics. Hendricks Chapel was more than a building. It was a living community of active people operating within the context of a history of service to others. It was not a set of classrooms, but it was a learning environment. In order to know that, all one had to do was spend some time walking about and experiencing the hum of activity connected with programs both old and new. I attended meetings for projects and programs that had been in existence for some time, and I went to meetings connected with the birthing of new projects. I participated with them as they sought to make their plans and ideas operational. One initiative was the Chaplain's Forum, which the chaplains collectively designed to allow each chaplain to have an opportunity to explore issues with students. Hendricks chaplains also made contacts with various professors within the university and sought the dean office's support in developing worthy events. In a collaborative effort to bring Gil Bailee to the university for a colloquium during the spring term, Chaplain Jim Lang and Department of Religion professor James Williams met in my office to bring that prospect to fruition. A series of Sunday evening "Jazz Vespers" was put forward by Francis Parks in collaboration with Episcopal chaplain Jim Taylor and the Reverend Bill Coop, the pastor of a nearby Presbyterian church on the corner of South Salina and Colvin Streets. The vespers constituted an attempt to illustrate how the creative arts blended with religion in producing an alternative worship experience.

I discovered that the concept of service that the chapel represented was not lost on other campus organizations. There were always projects or events on campus, often generated by students or faculty. Frequently, these projects needed support, either through financial resources or through people power. Within our ability, we sought to be helpful. As the administrator of some limited funds, I could release moneys for worthy programs or events. As for our people power, the chaplains and staff provided a willing and resourceful set of allies for any useful project. Also, interspersed with contacts dedicated to meeting with organizations on campus with whom we expected to carry on programs, there were contacts with others whom we did not expect to see but whose creators knew that we were their allies.

Observations on Organizations: A Case Study of Hendricks Chapel

James Conant was once asked what he thought about running Harvard University, and Conant responded that Harvard ran itself. I believed the same was the case for Hendricks Chapel. Throughout the two years or so that I served as the administrator in charge of Hendricks I had a sense that it ran in an autonomous fashion. Initiatives were not a "top-down" matter in Hendricks Chapel. My administrative approach centered on trying to assist staff and chaplains who wanted to try something new. The modus operandi for the entire staff and chaplains was to see something that needed to be done and then to go ahead and do it. Fortunately, the staff and chaplains had the courtesy to ask my advice and counsel when they wanted to do something. I was never left out of the information network. On occasion, this relatively open style of operations had its problems, but they were minimal. I thought that it led to an atmosphere of innovation and trust.

I know of no organization or institution that is without problems. Hendricks Chapel was no exception. Nevertheless, my experience with Hendricks suggested that it had far fewer problems than most such entities. Throughout my administration I convened meetings, both regular staff sessions or focused meetings with larger groups, to deal with various aspects of chapel functioning. Some of these meetings proved to be only a matter of establishing an informed relationship that would allow for continued smooth functioning. In addition to conducting regular staff meetings in my office, I met individually with staff persons, such as Mary Farnsworth. She was a fount of energy and experience with respect to much of the dean's office activities. I also met often with Ginny Yerdon and Sue Martini. Kikuko Nishiguchi, the graduate student who served as the business manager, was also a frequent visitor to my office.

Meetings were often convened to address a specific ongoing problem or dilemma. We arranged one set of meetings to conduct an intensive examination of racism in its many insidious forms. Another set of meetings focused on the practical need to formulate a wedding policy that would help us deal with interfaith marriages. Occasionally, requests came from people who wanted to use the chapel for an interfaith wedding, but they often misunderstood the chapel's character. They failed to understand the interfaith nature of the chapel's composition and instead perceived it as simply a nondenominational place where clearly delineated faith concerns would not be central. This was not the case. Thus, people eager to bypass the specific concerns of relevant chaplains occasionally became disappointed or the corps of chaplains themselves became disturbed by what they considered as the callous behavior of some of the outside clergy invited to officiate at such marriage services. Disputes could arise because a couple sometimes wanted to design services incorporating a horrendous mishmash of different rituals and behaviors that resulted in trivializing long-honored faith practices. Thus, it fell to the chaplains and me to devise protocols that could provide the type of guidance that might be acceptable to all concerned. As the year progressed, the Committee on Wedding Policy deliberated a number of times, created and revised a number of drafts, and finally came up with a fairly suitable set of guidelines for weddings. Although these guidelines could never accommodate all of the concerns involved, they were at least a reasonable effort to deal with a problem that would never quite go away.

It should not have surprised me, but I never ceased to be astonished by the amount of altruism the chapel personnel continually displayed. From the most senior people down to the student proctors and the students who ran the coffee concession at People's Place, no one was interested in conducting strong ego demonstrations. Their behavior reminded me of James Q. Wilson's discussion of morality in which he argued that in an age of supposed moral relativism many people have still managed to operate with a seemingly inherent "moral sense."* These people certainly did. This background had not always been my experience in dealing with people in academic or religious institutions. I supposed that part of the cooperative and constructive manner in which the staff and chaplains operated could have been related to the fact that they had what I perceived as a talent for knowing how to build and maintain a sense of community. As a partial explanation of the origins of the unique Hendricks zeitgeist, I concluded that the staff and chaplains had either come to the chapel with an intrinsic sense of mission coupled with a strong orientation toward altruism or had developed it by osmosis. I also believed that their commitment might have developed as a result of sustained cooperation in the face of tragedy. When the student in the Mount Olympus complex of dormitories leaped to his death the chaplains immediately combined forces to bring solace and compassionate support to the students and staff who lived within those buildings. On occasions that called for either sadness or joy they operated as a concerted force. Whatever causes one might assign to their behavior, I considered myself to be truly fortunate to be in the midst of such a stalwart group.

---

*See James Q. Wilson, *The Moral Sense* (New York: Free Press, 1993), 2.

A great deal of Hendricks activity, both on and off campus, grew out of the need to respond to deeply felt concerns coming from people within the university as a whole as well as society at large. This need was not something new for the chapel. Through various student generations, Hendricks had been the place where pain could be expressed and dealt with and causes could be pursued. Even during the campuswide excitement generated by athletic events and eagerly anticipated yearly events such as Parents Weekend, Hendricks was a place for the expression of various social and economic concerns and the perceived need to respond to those concerns, whether they emanated from students, staff, or faculty. Historically, the chapel steps provided a rallying point for the airing of fractious issues even as they existed as a place for the beginnings and conclusions of joyous festivities such as commencements and weddings. In the midst of the usual ebullient backdrop of university life with its classes and its myriad social activities, Hendricks was both a haven for people in need and a repository of its own brand of lively involvement.

In addition to the desire to address the Lockerbie tragedy as it continued to resonate through the years, the Hendricks staff and the chaplains, as well as the students involved in the chapel, remained sensitive to individual tragedies and on-going patterns of injustice and exploitation wherever they found it. The chaplains and the staff could be great jokesters and full of joy, but their underlying motivations were empathic and permeated with the desire to help others and be involved in the healing process. Whether the activity grew out of the need to participate in an externally organized activity such as Crop Walk or a response to an unpredicted event that suddenly presented itself, the staff and the chaplains sought to provide enabling hands for the initiation and carrying out of appropriate action.

The chaplains and staff joined students and faculty in calling attention to the need to be cooperatively involved in understanding and dealing with the horrendous phenomenon of AIDS. The chapel staff and chaplains opened up several offices and the Strates Lounge to view and conduct an informed discussion on the film *Philadelphia*. It brought home the seriousness of AIDS and resulted in creative responses, one of which was an interfaith service commemorating the lives of AIDS victims. Violence also drew the attention of the students and the Hendricks staff. They joined others in addressing the matter of violence and became involved in the Zero Tolerance Vigil.

In some instances a chapel program emerged out of awareness of the specific needs of a group of people. One example was the Haitian Children's Project. In this case, Francis Parks and her allies, including several gifted students, responded to the needs of newly immigrated Haitian families by developing an innovative project directed to assisting the educational efforts of the Haitian children in Syracuse. While the Carrier Dome was filled with enthusiastic football fans on a Saturday afternoon Francis and her group hosted a dinner for the Haitian families. When cooperative activity was called for, the Students Offering Service was likely to be involved, whether it might be participating in a nationally recognized program such as Habitat for Humanity or providing assistance to the families in the local Ronald McDonald House.

The locale for cooperative action could be almost anywhere. The chapel steps often constituted a traditional rallying point for many activities, but the Noble Room and even the Strates Lounge often served as places for developing an understanding of issues, such as when Professor Arthur Parris moderated a discussion on the significance of the Million Men March. Even though the chapel had limited space, there always seemed to be someplace where people could talk and plan. The activities generated under the Students Offering Service and the African American programs of the chapel resisted containment in any building. One cold and frosty night in late November a chapel-led contingent lighted their candles and processed throughout the quadrangle in commemoration of the historic occasion in which Rosa Parks defied the authorities of Birmingham, Alabama. Often, the students under the leadership of Francis Parks or the Students Offering Service graduate assistant Fred Boehrer went further afield.

This commitment was the case with the Habitat groups whose members took their spring vacation to help build houses in poor areas in the South or neighborhoods and institutions in close proximity to the university. Nearly any place could and did constitute an opportunity for developing and carrying out programs. Francis Parks, Chaplain George Koch, and I met with a group of community people in the Martin Luther King School and its environs. This meeting and others that followed created a joint community project focused on honoring the famed African American folk singer and left-handed guitarist Libba Cotton. Eventually, this initiative blossomed into a collectivity known as the Libba Cotton Conservancy. This project was an example of how the chapel could interface in a reciprocal manner with the community of Syracuse.

Chapel staff members often took responsibility in aiding faculty members and students if they wanted to call attention to major societal issues as well as campus concerns. Chaplains and staff also came together to organize interfaith responses to tragedies of international import. Their response to the assassination of Yitzhak Rabin was one such example. On receiving news of Rabin's death, the chaplains organized and conducted an interfaith service. Faculty and student presentations as well as a program of organized open forums developed by the chaplains took place in the Noble Room and in other campus buildings. Students often demonstrated able, and creative leadership and the chaplains and staff supported them by providing wise counsel and appropriate resources. The chapel-sponsored Student Interfaith Council was an important conduit for responding to potentially divisive issues involving religious differences.

During the administration of Dean Phillips, the university conducted its first Martin Luther King Jr. Holiday Celebration. With this development, the university made a step forward in acknowledging the contributions of African Americans

as well as Dr. King. Since that time the university has continued to devote more resources to providing this increasingly significant program. Over the years this
event has increased in complexity and grandeur. During my two years at Hendricks, two marvelous dinner celebrations took place in the Carrier Dome and two
worthwhile sets of events took place throughout the community. I considered myself to be truly fortunate to participate in the yearlong planning sessions with the
all-university committee as well as a Syracuse-area Martin Luther King committee.
It was also a privilege to be in the midst of an audience of slightly fewer than two
thousand people singing James Weldon Johnson's stirring "Negro National Anthem," eating delicious soul food prepared by the university's staff, and meeting
and hearing Derrick Bell, a wonderful speaker who continued Dr. King's legacy by
articulating and elaborating upon his vision and relating it to the changing social
and economic context of American life for African Americans.

Because of its size and its prominence on the quadrangle, the chapel has always
been a valuable venue for public events and presentations. Throughout the spring
of 1996, Hendricks opened the doors of its spacious sanctuary to provide a venue
for a range of lectures, drama, and music. In addition to occasional presentations
featuring artists and lecturers and its own regularly scheduled Malmgren Concert
Series, there were many other musical treats. The Hendricks Chapel Choir, under
the direction of G. Burton Harbison, presented well-attended seasonal concerts,
and the Black Celestial Choral Ensemble, under the leadership of Evelyn Hoskins,
held a concert in the chapel as well as the community.

Throughout the year Hendricks Chapel also continued to be the site for many
testimonial celebrations as well as significant memorial services for faculty, staff,
and community citizens. One of the most important during my administration
took place on February 11, 1996, when the university held the memorial service
for Dr. William Pearson Tolley. As the last chancellor to have been an ordained
Methodist clergyman he frequently attended Sunday morning services in the
chapel. Over a very long period before and after his retirement, Dr. Tolley was
closely connected with Hendricks Chapel. From its earliest days until the end of
Tolley's administration, only one chancellor had not been an ordained Methodist
minister. Although Dean Richard Phillips and Dean Thomas Wolfe, as well as Professor Wiggins and active Chapel Board and university trustee the Reverend Vernon Lee are all Methodists, the sustained leadership relationship of Methodism to
Hendricks Chapel is no longer guaranteed.

Near the end of a busy spring semester filled with the completion of various
projects and much sustained activity with respect to developing new initiatives, the
chapel staff came together to plan for its annual Minnowbrook Retreat. In addition to laying out plans for the coming academic year, the staff and chaplains devised some strategies to support their desire to provide greater service to the
university community. When the chapel staff and chaplains finally went to Min-

nowbrook, they carried out some model exercises that they had developed to facilitate their sense of cohesiveness as a community of caring. The program that they devised also took time in the schedule that ordinarily would be devoted to some recreation and turned it into a service project in the nearby community. The entire retreat including the service project proved to be a joyous occasion that somehow captured the spirit of the year just passed.

The Academic Year 1996–1997

During the first part of August, Jane and I traveled to Omagh in Northern Ireland where we presented a scholarly paper on events in northern New England in relation to the migration of Protestant clerics from eighteenth-century Northern Ireland. Upon our return, I immediately became immersed in the round of activities associated with the beginning of the academic school year. My first meeting was with the Chaplains Council, followed by a conference with Physical Plant personnel. The doors of the chapel were thrown open to the newly arrived freshmen. On the evening of August 26 the chapel cooperated with others in a freshman orientation session titled "The Truth about Cats, Dogs, and Otto." In the meantime, the calendar filled with meetings and events. As per usual, I met with Eleanor Gallagher for our first conference of the new year, and hoping for more active interfaith activity I went to the Alibrandi Center to talk with the Interfaith Student Council. The chaplains met with their various constituencies, and Dr. Koshy held his usual welcome dinner for new international students. In the middle of it all, many of the chapel staff went to Mary Farnsworth's daughter's wedding reception.

In keeping with my activities of the previous year, I met regularly with Eleanor Gallagher as well as the dean's office staff, the Hendricks Chapel Advisory Board, and the Chaplin's Council. These meetings were always fruitful, as were the meetings with Director's Plus. I particularly enjoyed the opportunity to collaborate with Vice President Barry Wells and his able staff as we engaged in the various aspects of working with students.

As in any organization, some changes of personnel could be expected to occur. It happened at Hendricks Chapel, but, fortunately, the changes were minimal. The office staff of Mary Farnsworth and Ginny Yerdon, augmented by Sue Martini, who had taken the secretarial position, all remained. Francis Parks also continued to soldier on, even becoming involved in a number of new projects. A number of new students stepped forward to replace the ones who had graduated. Fred Boehrer moved on to Albany to support the Catholic Worker movement, and Sascha Milligan took over to fill the Students Offering Service assistantship while Sean Hynes assumed the business manager assistantship held during the previous year by Kikuko Nishiguchi.

As I thought about the changes in personnel that took place at the end of my first year at Hendricks, I sensed that the people who left to go on to other things had enjoyed their work with us as much as we enjoyed their presence. I looked forward to working with their replacements who, in their turn, eventually maintained the same standard of competence and good spirit.

But there was one person who could no longer be present, and her absence left a great hole in the chapel community. That person was Effie Clark. During the year Effie became ill. As the spring semester progressed, she grew worse. Her strong constitution broken, Effie died in late May. Not since the tragic death of a student worker in Chaplain Andrew Mitchell's Chi Alpha group had there been such a sense of bereavement within the chapel. On June 4 the staff and chaplains attended Effie's funeral at the New Salem Church on South Avenue, and on the following day the chapel held its own memorial service in the sanctuary. In November members of the chapel community and others who knew Effie came together again in the narthex. At that point a photographic image of Effie with an accompanying plaque was dedicated and placed on the south wall.

I have often thought that the early autumn months and the month prior to commencement are the busiest times of the college year, and 1996–97 bore out this belief. In addition to the many planning meetings and the onset of the Jewish holidays, there were new projects being developed. Some of the projects, as before, arose, almost spontaneously, out of the need to address an emotionally charged event. An example was the "Anti-Hate Rally" in which the students and chaplains played a major role. In September Khalid Muhammed, a outspoken man given to making inflammatory statements, had been invited to speak on campus. The local press had managed to increase acrimony by seeking opinions from local leaders who were very antagonistic toward Muhammed, thus ratcheting up the possibility of conflict. Because of this potentially explosive situation the chaplains and students worked to form a team with the specific purpose of bringing about a coalition of different religious groups to defuse the situation and turn it into a constructive interfaith experience. Following the Muhammed episode, the Student Interfaith Council sponsored dormitory interfaith panels in an effort to increase interfaith and interracial understanding. Visiting speaker Rhami Khouri also delivered an informative presentation that helped to provide information about the religious crosscurrents in the Middle East.

In keeping with the chapel's function with respect to assisting people in their rights of passage, weddings again took place, and a number of memorial services occurred. It was a particular honor to be of assistance at the services for people such as Phyllis Hunt, Bob Boney, and Max Casper.

Having enjoyed participating the previous year with the many scheduled religious holidays and the series of events that took place, I looked forward to being involved again. As always, it was a pleasure to hear the enthusiastic singing of the Black Celestial Choral Ensemble, and it was a special treat to hear the Hendricks

Chapel Choir sing from the new hymnals that we purchased with a generous grant from an anonymous donor. I also had the privilege to hear and meet with Dr. Mary Frances Berry, the speaker for the 1997 Martin Luther King Jr. Holiday Celebration. Her presentation and the surrounding activities and contributions of others amply repaid for the yearlong efforts of the committee to continue bringing this major event to the campus.

Once again, I had the opportunity to meet and hear other speakers and talented individuals who came to the university and connected with Hendricks Chapel. Religious leaders such as the Buddhists Eido Shimano Roshi and Jo Wang Kim came to deliver sage commentaries, and international activists such as Ron Young provided insights into interfaith opportunities for peace. Other speakers, such as Millard Fuller, the founder of the Habitat for Humanity program, came to the chapel to provide a vision of what voluntary efforts could achieve. Some who came to Hendricks were creative artists of international renown who displayed their talents to support an important cause. Two of the latter joined to perform one of the most unique and compelling concerts I witnessed while serving at Hendricks. Samite, the Ugandan musical phenomenon, and Joanne Shenandoah, the nationally prominent Native American singer, joined hands as feature performers, and the proceeds went to support an effort to publicize the atrocities that were taking place in Uganda.

Given the impetus of Chancellor Shaw to develop quality improvement within the university, the chapel staff and I were involved in seeking ways in which we could improve our attempts to deliver services to the students and the university as a whole. With the help of resource persons in Financial Aid Services and the Office of Student Affairs, we adopted new forms and procedures with respect to the ways in which we provided financial assistance to students. Also, although communication within the chapel and from the chapel to others was exemplary, we sought to enhance our efforts by upgrading our computer stations and developing materials to insert in the chapel's home page. In addition to these changes there was a distinct need to deal with the building itself. Such a building always experiences considerable wear and tear. In addition to standard maintenance there was a need to upgrade the facilities. This upgrading meant the refurbishing of some of the furniture, the installation of air-conditioning in selected areas, and the improvement of the washrooms. The alterations in the men's washrooms was particularly timely owing to the long-standing need to obtain a more suitable arrangement for ritual washing facilities utilized by the Muslim students and staff.

As I noted earlier, a collegiate chapel might be regarded as essentially a place where the conduct of a set of specifically defined religious worship functions is the only prominent activity, but such a perception would fail to encompass the character of Hendricks Chapel during the period in which I was present. In the planning taking place during that period, the people on the staff and the chaplains saw themselves as involved in "the life of the mind and the spirit."

Understandably, the chapel could be expected to be a natural ally of the Religion Department, and so it was during October. They jointly sponsored and hosted a conference titled "Death, Violence, and Transcendence: Ernest Becker and Rene Girard." Those individuals who attended were treated to an opportunity to examine and consider the impact of these two seminal thinkers.

This collaboration was not the only one under way during the year. While the Becker-Girard conference was going on, representatives from the natural sciences and engineering were meeting with the chapel people for the purpose of developing a national conference dealing with the interface between science and religion. This groundbreaking conference held in August 1997 was the brainchild of Dr. George Koch, the Lutheran chaplain at Hendricks. In many ways, the planning meetings that took place during the spring and eventually on into the early summer demonstrated how the chapel could be a uniting force between realms of discourse that are ordinarily assumed to be in opposition to one another. I thought back to the nineteenth-century discourse of Andrew Dickson White, the first president of Cornell University, who once wrote a treatise on the "warfare between science and theology." This conference, which Dr. Koch had worked so hard to bring about, was no war. It was a meeting of minds that earnestly desired to make sense of the relationship between the human condition and the universe.

This truth was brought home to me one evening in the spring when I was working in my office. My light was on and the door was open. I heard a slight noise, and I looked up from my desk to see a trim bald man dressed in a running costume. It was the astronaut Story Musgrave, one of Syracuse University's most outstanding alumni. He had come to participate in an event at the College of Engineering. We talked for a time, and then we began to discuss the mysteries of the universe that he had seen and filmed from his spacecraft. He described his experiences in a way that I regarded as profoundly spiritual. He invited me to attend an illustrated presentation he was going to make, and I happily agreed to go see it. I eventually summoned up the courage to ask him if he would participate in the conference that George and his scientific collaborators had been planning. He said he would consider that prospect, and he eventually agreed to come.

With the arrival of May 11, the academic year 1996–97 came to an end. It was Commencement Day, a day that many look forward to as that day in spring when parents arrive and the green grass of the quadrangle is covered with happy students and their families. Oddly enough, as Chancellor Shaw and Douglas Barclay, chairman of the Board of Trustees, stepped out on the quadrangle early in the morning, they were greeted with a quadrangle carpeted in snow. Syracuse had a reputation to maintain.

Preparing for the Next Year

In the weeks shortly before commencement and afterward, the chapel staff and the chaplains busied themselves with more planning meetings across campus. The Fall

Orientation Committee came together, and the Martin Luther King Committee convened a meeting to determine if they were on schedule for the next year's celebration. At the same time, the dean's office staff was busy preparing for its annual Hendricks retreat to the Minnowbrook Conference Center in the Adirondacks. This opportunity afforded the chaplains and staff time to grapple with big issues in an informal setting. It was also a time for planning the yearly calendar yet appreciating the relaxed surroundings.

Upon returning from Minnowbrook there was time for individual conferences and time to get caught up with paperwork before late summer when Dick Phillips would be returning. It was time to pass on whatever information I had with respect to the state of the chapel. The chapel was still active in its summer pattern. Weddings, alumni events, and memorial services continued, including the service for Bettina Chapman, a staunch university supporter and an active participant in the Syracuse community. Between all of these events there were ice cream socials and potluck picnics. There were receptions for people who would be leaving as well as interviews and meetings for ones who would be coming. After participating in the Science and Religion Conference and congratulating Chaplain George Koch for his achievement, I left. Dick Phillips was back and primed for the fall semester. I wished him well and thanked him for that telephone call he made in the early spring of 1995.

61. Challenges and Reflections after Strasbourg

WE RETURNED FROM FRANCE in July 1997, and on August 1, after a couple of weeks of briefings and conversations with Bob Pickett, I again took up the duties of dean. It had already been set with Chancellor Shaw that I would work through December 1998 and then retire from Hendricks Chapel. We added a January schedule to my work a bit later. That spring semester I was to be on leave before officially retiring from SU the last day of June 1999. That scheduling developed as planned.

Chancellor Shaw and Vice President Eleanor Ware asked me to focus on three things during my remaining three semesters as dean. The first was to help with the search for my successor, the fifth dean of Hendricks Chapel. The second was to arrange to back away from some of the traditional duties of the deanship so that I would have time to help select a successor. The third was to prepare for and help with the transition to and with the new dean. The second of these tasks was the most difficult for me: it was hard to simultaneously try to reimmerse myself in the duties of the deanship and to step back enough to free some time, especially since the drive to respond affirmatively to demands for my time is a deep-seated characteristic of mine.

While we were still in France, Shaw and Ware had requested that I give some serious thought to how to prepare Hendricks Chapel to best serve at the university in the twenty-first century. I did so, consulting with others, and on returning from Strasbourg I presented my suggestions in a paper representing my personal updating of the five-year plan, which I discussed earlier. Copies of that paper are in the SU Archives.

I have mentioned earlier that it took me longer than I had expected to recover from both jet lag and reverse cultural adjustment. Perhaps the most telling was difficulty adjusting to Syracuse time (waking up at strange hours lasted for well over a month), but equally difficult was getting back into all the routines that make life flow smoothly. I doubt if having been born in 1934 had anything to do with it. Yes, I did notice that energy levels were lower than just a few months earlier!

We started to work immediately on a plan for transition and the search for a new dean. I was to be a resource for the Search Committee but not to serve on the committee itself, which was as it should be. One of my first tasks was to write the description for the deanship, a description to be used in the news releases for the open position. I found this job difficult until several meetings with Shaw and Ware confirmed that they, as did I, wanted to continue the pattern associated with the history of the deanship, including the changes Eggers had implemented as a result of the work of the Wiggins committee between 1979 and 1981. That there was to be no major change in the style or character of the deanship made the job both easier and more comfortable.

In order to cut back on my involvement I did not rejoin several committees on which I had previously served and asked other SU committees to work with a chapel staff or chaplain substitute until such time as a new dean was in place. I had reduced my recreational activity just before going to Strasbourg. I had dropped team basketball but still played some recreational basketball. My tennis schedule returned to the same as before, and Ethel and I added a bit more bike riding and hiking. The normal institutional demands on my time did not seem much different from before. Living a short block from campus saved some time, which was helpful.

With a great deal of staff help I started getting the files and the office routines ready for my retirement and the arrival of my replacement. A good number of boxes of files and records were prepared, again with staff help, for the SU Archives, and I began sorting and filing things in preparation for the research and writing that would be required, after retirement, for the writing of this book. In our focus on all these matters the three semesters seemed to fly by all too fast. Even so, most of the work seemed fresh and rewarding.

I was particularly pleased with the last two International Thanksgiving Meal preparations and events and the last two times of working with the MLK Committee. That I was asked to again chair that committee in my last year was for me very confirming. It was that MLK involvement that caused Shaw and me to extend my work time through January 1999. While retaining my chairmanship of the Malmgren Committee I passed the real work on to Katie, Burt, and Mary and asked one of the chaplains, Tom Wolfe, to join the committee.

Working with students has always been both a joy and a privilege. By now I was keenly aware of the joy I found in working with the many wonderful people in the administrative staff and faculty ranks at SU. My retirement reflections have confirmed that I miss the people the most, as they in a very real way were the heart and soul of my understanding of the work of the dean. Indeed, when work and joy are combined the reward is not just good, it is a very special blessing.

The Honors Program of SU invited me to teach the Senior Honors Seminar in the spring semester of 1998. I had done so once before, in the mid-eighties. With the approval of Shaw and Ware, I accepted. The course dealt with issues being raised by the arrival of the twenty-first century. Thus, in both Strasbourg and Syracuse I was able to cap my career with a lifelong love: teaching.

Domestic life during those last eighteen months, in the apartment (suite 330) at the Sheraton University Inn, also proved wonderful. The dean's residence at 315 Berkeley Drive had been sold when we moved to Strasbourg, and it had already been determined that the fifth dean would receive a housing adjustment in salary rather than a parsonage. The interim arrangement at the Sheraton allowed us to live close to campus and the chapel while saving the university some money over the cost of renting a house or apartment and paying for utilities there. We found the staff of the hotel wonderfully accommodating.

One adventure during that period illustrates this point. On Labor Day, 1997, a devastating storm hit Syracuse, causing extensive damage to campus buildings and trees. It also knocked out the electricity to the university area for more than a week. The staff of the Sheraton moved all the other residents to hotels outside the affected area, but we asked to stay put. For a week we lived by candlelight in our hotel apartment; the manager was the only other person to spend the nights on site. Late in the week the hotel rented a generator, so we did have some electricity in the last days of the outage.

Early the morning after the storm I walked to Hendricks Chapel. I found little damage but a considerable amount of water: rain driven horizontally by the wind had found its way through doors and windows. I mopped water for most of an hour and then went to help on South Campus, where the storm had caused serious property damage to some housing units. All in all, Syracuse got off pretty lightly, considering the severity of the storm. Only two people died, both crushed by falling matter at the state fairgrounds. No students were killed or seriously injured, but many campus trees were damaged, and Oakwood Cemetery just south of the campus required more than a million dollars' worth of cleanup as a result of damage to its trees. It was no small storm!

I mentioned in chapter 55 that I would be saying some things about Effie in this chapter. Effie Clark was our custodian, and though she was not a Hendricks Chapel employee she was a valued member of the Hendricks Chapel family. We were more than fortunate when she was assigned to us. For years she did the work in Hendricks Chapel, work that was estimated to require one and one-half custodians. There were tasks once or twice a year, like stripping the wax from the stage and the floors, when extra staff came from Custodial Services to help. We kept Effie when she was slated to move to another campus facility by making a fervent appeal for the administration of Custodial Services not to change her assignment. Such an appeal, on more than one occasion, was fortunately granted.

In other chapters I have mentioned the importance of custodial work in a place that has the heavy and constant use characteristic of Hendricks Chapel. In my long career I have usually had stewardship responsibilities for one or more buildings. I have never known anyone who cared for a facility better or with more love than did Effie. Here in this chapter she is receiving more ink than otherwise might be the case, in part because, as Pickett has reported, she died as a member of our "family." There are so many Effie stories, they all deserve to be told but for now only a tribute must do.

Just weeks before Ethel and I left for France Effie was diagnosed with cancer. She, her doctor, and her Hendricks Chapel family all had every hope that she would be victorious in the fight to defeat it. It was not to be, however; she died while we were in France. Following her death the staff asked Custodial Services to join in a short memorial service to Effie in the narthex of the main chapel. Others from the university were also in attendance. A permanent plaque with her picture and a tribute on it is located in the southeastern part of the narthex. From Strasbourg I faxed the following four paragraphs. They were read by Bob Pickett in the service.

I know those who are assembled here to dedicate this plaque to you will understand if I talk with you just a bit. I did not have the opportunity to do that face to face between the onset of your illness and your death. Now I have forever missed that opportunity; this dedication is as close as I will come.

When I reenter the Chapel late this summer it will be the first time in over fourteen years that it will not have been while serving this community along with you, along beside you. That development is most unwelcome. I shall, as a result, visit some of your places. I shall stand before your closet, your home away from home as you once called it. I shall sit in the back pew on the south side where I often found you when you were on break. From there you and I viewed with pride the polished results of your work on many occasions. I will walk the halls and again feel your hand on my shoulder. I will reenter your world with a sense of reverence, and respect, and a love which often blossoms when co-workers have labored together when the "co" has been a real part of the relationship.

Most of all, Effie, I just want to say a simple thank you. Not just thank you for your splendid work, not even just thank you for loving us all as if we were family. To these I add thank you for your perception about the critically important nature of your work and your roles, thank you for caring for people (members of your own family, your former employers, members of my family, your fellow workers, and the new student and the stranger who entered these doors).

There is not much else to say, Effie. Thank You.

In July and August I paid my homage to Effie as indicated above. For months Hendricks Chapel was just not the same place without Effie. My memories of Effie are some of the shining beacons in my reflections on my own years at Hendricks Chapel.

In December 1998 we celebrated the tenth anniversary of the loss of our students on Flight 103. Some of that story is told in chapter 57. It was a bittersweet event. Many of our 103 families returned for the service in Hendricks Chapel. It was a full house, well covered by a very sensitive press. Some of it was broadcast live in Scotland and England. It was one of four services that took place that day, one each in Washington, D.C., London, Lockerbie, and Syracuse. Frances Parks had overseen the making of a quilt with a panel for each student, each panel containing something from that student's personal effects. One of my prize photographs is a picture of the quilt taken by Steve Sartori of the SU Photo Shop.

One thing I missed in those last months was a chance to attend another meeting of ACURA, the nationwide organization of those people in a similar position as mine. I had served just over two years as president in the late 1980s and had a number of colleagues and friends whom I would like to have been with for a final meeting. It seemed the ACURA schedule, both academic years, conflicted with something for which I needed to be in Syracuse. Our Syracuse University Archives are the official depository for the records and history of ACURA. I hope someday someone will write a history of this fine organization of professionals.

While we were in Strasbourg, Syracuse University and Hendricks Chapel lost one of our longtime number-one citizens. Born in 1900, retired chancellor William Tolley was both a legend at Syracuse University and a major contributor to our growth and development in the forties, fifties, and sixties. Both in France and after returning to Syracuse I found myself reflecting on him as administrator, chapelite, and friend. I had been, while a graduate student at SU, a member of his tennis group. He was chancellor when I got my first graduate assistantship and my first full-time teaching job. As a friend he was a real boost to my athletic endeavors and my professional development. I had many visits with him in his living room after I became dean; we lived only a long block from each other on the Berkeley Drive hill. I found his writings advocating for higher education filled with inspiration as well as love for learning.

I had seen in full flower his close friendship with Charlie Noble and regretted very much the conflict that had developed between them. I admired Tolley for his honesty in confessing that it was he who was wrong and Charlie who was right about the issue involved in that conflict. I only wish the confession had come much earlier. Both before and during my deanship I experienced his loyalty to Hendricks Chapel and knew how much he had contributed to both the existence of the chapel and its operation from his own student days at SU and through his long tenure in leading this academy. He served as the honorary chair of Hendricks Chapel fund drives under Dean McCombe and me. It was through him that I learned how to get tickets at Wimbledon for that grand-slam tennis tournament in London just before we went there to celebrate my parents' fiftieth wedding anniversary; for many years Tolley had attended that tournament every year. I felt his loss, and I am very grateful to have shared some of the extensive variety of his career and his life.

During my last months in office I found myself often in a reflective moment. This contemplation motivated me to ask several others at SU, persons who had some length of experience but were not directly connected to Hendricks Chapel, to share their reflections on the role and presence of Hendricks Chapel in the life of the university. Here I share two for this record. The first is from Dr. Gershon Vincow, a chemist by profession who served long in the Syracuse University administration, first as dean of the College of Arts and Sciences and then as vice chancellor for academic affairs. In a memo written in June 1999 he shared his thoughts with me.

Perhaps the most salient feature on the Syracuse University Quad, Hendricks Chapel makes an important institutional statement by its central location and majestic physical appearance—inside and out. In the latter half of the twentieth century, dominated as it is by science and technology, Hendricks reminds us that there are vast and important realms of human experience outside the bounds of the positivist approach to knowledge and meaning. This is a comfort—often unconscious—to secessions of eighteen-year-old students coming to face the many challenges of the Syracuse undergraduate experience.

Within the walls of the Chapel, I recall many significant personal experiences of a kind shared by many—High Holyday Jewish religious services, lectures by the Dalai Lama, Elie Wiesel, and James Baldwin, the service immediately following the Pan Am 103 disaster, the annual ROTC commissioning ceremonies, and annual presentations to the faculty by Chancellor Kenneth A. Shaw and me on the State of the University. Hendricks is the main campus locus for experiencing community and communication on all subjects and levels.

Programmatically, Hendricks is a safe haven for students. Its outstanding staff offers programming, counseling, and friendship—all in the warm environment of a particular faith community but, also significantly, in the rich ambiance of the diversity of such communities.

On a final note, as a member of the academic community for three decades, Hendricks Chapel has offered me the opportunity to celebrate the lives and bid farewell to many colleagues. Some of the memorial services more directly reflect a particular faith while others do not, but all present the richness of the lives of members of the Syracuse community in a way that is fitting, meaningful, and ultimately fulfilling.

Hendricks Chapel is the heart—if not the soul—of Syracuse University.

The second memo, summarized below, was written by Dr. William Pollard on July 26, 1999. Dr. Pollard served at the university for ten years as dean of the School of Social Work.

It is essential to have a Chapel at the heart of an institution like Syracuse University. . . . Students . . . bring an array of religious values and attitudes which ought to be nurtured and shared. . . . Syracuse ought to be helping its students confront the many spiritual/religious issues that shape our world. The confrontation I speak of is not one that is designed to proselytize, but to inform.

And as for the deanship, Pollard has these reflections:

The Dean serves. . . . [Y]ou don't direct, you lead. . . . [M]odel the compassion and caring that seems to be an intrinsic feature of most of the world's religions. . . . The Dean should insure the opportunity for religious expression. . . . The Dean should serve the moral/religious/spiritual fabric of the University. And finally, the dean . . . should recognize and honor the religious diversity of our college community.

After Tom Wolfe was selected to become the fifth dean of Hendricks Chapel, the nature of the workweek again changed at Hendricks Chapel. I met with Tom regularly as part of the transition process. Our staff also met with him and as much introductory ground was covered as possible. He was invited to regular staff meetings. Essentially, he was included as much as possible as a member of the operation of the Office of the Dean, even through he was not to officially become the dean until January 1, 1999.

In his eight and a half years as the interdenominational Protestant chaplain, Tom had long been a valued member of the Hendricks Chapel family and a trusted

Dean Phillips at the final college convocation before his retirement. Photograph by Steve Sartori, courtesy of Syracuse University.

friend. The chaplaincy he had filled so well went right to work on finding his replacement through a committee made up of the members of the advisory committee Tom had created years before. The United Methodist officials did not have a ready candidate for appointment to Tom's position, and they approved, an exception to normal procedure, a national search endeavor. I was invited and reluctantly agreed to serve as an adjunct member for the search. It turned out, like all committee work with an important charge, to involve a rather heavy time commitment. That search ended before the end of the semester with the selection of Thomas Davenport, a United Methodist minister from Ohio.

On December 15, 1998, at the Drumlins banquet facility, the chancellor's office held a farewell reception for Ethel and me that I found most memorable. More than six hundred colleagues, friends, and family members attended. Although declining health prevented my parents from making the trip from Boulder, Colorado, my brother, Keith, and his partner, Sharon, came from Colorado; our daughter, Cynthia, came from Boston; and our son, Ken, came from New York City. Gifts were presented, amazingly exaggerated statements were made about my work, wishes for a joyous retirement were extended, and much spirited conversation took place in a decidedly party atmosphere.

One very unique gift was presented by the Carrier Dome and the Athletic Department—the gift of the three-seat section of the aluminum bench where we had our season basketball tickets throughout my deanship. They had put a nice plaque on the back, and the bench is now in use on our town house patio in Boulder. So unique is this gift that when Pat Campbell uncovered it on the stage there were gasps of surprise from everyone assembled.

At the final Malmgren Concert mentioned earlier, the chaplains and the staff had presented to me yet another very unusual and very precious gift. They had commissioned Dr. Joe Downing of the School of Music to compose and write the text of a hymn in my honor. It is one of the most touching gifts any group has ever given to me. It expresses not only my own orientation to my ministry at Syracuse but, I believe, the nature of Hendricks Chapel's role on campus. The hymn is called "This House Shall Be a House of Prayer for All." It is to be found in appendix D of this volume.

I would like to end this chapter by expressing my own gratitude. I can but hope that I was of as much value to Hendricks Chapel and Syracuse University as these remarkable entities have been to me. The five years between 1961 and 1966 as a graduate student and Department of Religion faculty member, my eighteen years as dean, and the two academic years of directing our study abroad program in Strasbourg, France, gave me an identity, challenging work, and other rewards that I treasure beyond expression. My career has proved very fulfilling for both Ethel and me! Each relationship it has given me, from those with our chancellors to those with our custodians, has been precious. When we reflect upon our friendships, the Syracuse pages are very full. Thank you!

62. The Search for the Fifth Dean

THE FALL SEMESTER of 1997 found a committee of Chancellor Kenneth Shaw, Vice President Eleanor Ware, and me working regularly on a plan for succession. We established a timetable and decided on the extent we would advertise the position, what documents needed to be developed, and what criteria would be used for the position. I was asked to draft a description of the position and a letter to solicit nominations.

By the end of the semester, Shaw and Ware had appointed a search committee. Serving on it were retired faculty and chair Robert Pickett; Barry Wells, the vice president for student affairs; Pat Burak, director of the Office of International Students; faculty member Sari Biklen; Tiffany Tchakirides, an undergraduate student; and Dana Banks, a graduate student. I was asked to be a resource for the committee but not to attend their meetings.

After Shaw and Ware did some editing the following was released as a "position summary":

> Since 1930 Hendricks Chapel and its deanship have been a central part of the operation of Syracuse University. This position reports to the central administration. The fourth and current Dean (for seventeen years) will retire at the end of 1998. The fifth dean, it is planned, will assume the position on January 1, 1999. Approximately 85 percent of the responsibilities are administrative, with "chaplaincy" type duties accounting for the other 15 percent. The role involves helping facilitate the work of all chaplaincies and ministries and religious groups having any presence on the campus. Chaplains are "hosted" but not paid by the University. Involvement in community outreach and the promotion of volunteerism is traditionally part of the role. The dean administers a set budget and a small staff and is responsible for a variety of programming operations which are sometimes focused on the entire campus. The deanship does not involve serving as the pastor to a congregation or worshipping community. It does involve some campuswide "ombudsperson" responsibility.
>
> Qualifications: An earned doctorate and clergy status is desired. Administrative skill in administering budgets and personnel is very important, general counseling experience is also desirable. Experience in a university setting, while not required, will be considered important in the selection process.

Nominations were to be sent to Dr. Pickett's attention by March 16, 1998. It was assumed that the interview process would be complete before or by the end of the spring semester and an appointment be designated in the summer. The statement was released to a number of newspapers and journals, including academically and religiously oriented publications, with the goal of publication in December and January.

We had also determined that direct nominations would be solicited from people known to be in touch with persons with the qualifications we were seeking. In late January, approximately eleven months prior to the anticipated starting date for the new dean, some two hundred letters went out soliciting nominations. These letters went to ACURA members (that is, persons serving in similar positions around the country), denominational leaders having responsibilities for campus ministries, a limited number of college administrators, and individuals known to one or more of us as likely contacts for qualified candidates. In addition, nominations were sought from anyone within Syracuse University wishing to forward a nomination to the committee.

By mid-March we had an excellent pool of applicants and nominees, including three already related to Hendricks Chapel and one or two others from the central New York area. The search process, by regulation, had been submitted to and approved by the Human Resources division of SU, and the Search Committee soon started the process of prioritizing the candidates. Our goal to have an appointment by the summer of 1998 seemed a bit tight, but the Search Committee work went rapidly.

The pool of candidates was reduced to ten and then to six or seven before references were called. By mid-April it was determined that three top candidates would be asked to come to campus for interviews and to make public presentations; others would be added later if none of the three was to be recommended to the chancellor for appointment. All three candidates were already serving in one form or another of campus ministry, two as administrators (including one who was also teaching at his university), and one, Tom Wolfe, already working at Syracuse University as interdenominational Protestant chaplain, representing his denomination and three others. The three interviews were scheduled for separate days in late April. This schedule allowed us to meet our timetable and to make a decision before the campus community broke for the summer in early May.

With a single voice the committee chose Tom Wolfe, recommending to Chancellor Shaw that he be designated as the fifth dean of Hendricks Chapel beginning in January. I was not just pleased, I was delighted. My knowledge of my peers across the country and of the campus ministers who attended conferences that I also attended, and of the schools having programs similar to ours, made me confident, even before the search was at midpoint, that Tom was probably the best candidate in the country, let alone the best in our pool of prospects.

Although Tom had not yet completed his doctorate from our School of Education, he was close to the dissertation stage and has since completed it. In eight and a half years of ministry at Syracuse University and Hendricks Chapel he had demonstrated his abilities to a very broad range of constituencies. His years as a United Methodist clergyman, combined with his interfaith and ecumenical sensitivities, enriched his performance as the interdenominational Protestant chaplain, and I felt fortunate that he was now to become our dean.

Both Hendricks Chapel and those individuals responsible for replacing Tom in the chaplaincy he occupied were fortunate to have all summer and the fall semester as a time of transition, and both got right to work.

One key supporter in bringing about a smooth transition was Bob Pickett. Over three and a half years he had twice served Hendricks Chapel with distinction, first as my replacement while I was in Strasbourg and then as the chair of the committee recommending Tom to the deanship. I can only assume that he enjoyed these capstone experiences to his own long Syracuse University career as much as Hendricks Chapel and SU benefited from his involvement.

63. The Stewardship of a Meaningful Tradition, 1999–2005

THOMAS V. WOLFE

I CAME TO HENDRICKS CHAPEL on July 1, 1990, to serve as the interdenominational Protestant chaplain. Recognizing that I would quickly become accustomed to the chapel and the university, I believed it important to experience it much as a first-year student would. On a bright, sunny summer day, my second day on campus, I made a point to walk all around the chapel and view it with one question in mind, "What would it be like to be a new student approaching this building?" I wanted to know if I would feel welcome, put off, or something else. I stood on the front sidewalk for a long time contemplating the imposing steps of the chapel. They felt to me simultaneously impressive and inhibiting. I imagined the stories of the events that had happened on the steps. I also imagined a first-year student who might not be altogether comfortable seeking out the services of the chapel but being curious and wanting to go in. In my mind's eye, I saw that person ascending the stairs and approaching the big oak door. "Is it unlocked? What's going on inside? Is there someone to greet me? I feel so exposed now that I am on the quad's stage for all to see where I am headed."

At that moment I made a decision. When I welcomed students to worship, the door would always be fastened open. I wanted to meet their commitment to come here with a spirit of hospitality. I wanted them to see that there was activity inside and a person ready to welcome them. I wanted them to have easy access not so much to a building but to a series of relationships.

To this day, the open door is our central image. It is our hope that all students, faculty, staff, and visitors will feel warmly and meaningfully received. It is our way of being good stewards of the rich inheritance we know as Hendricks Chapel.

THIS CHAPTER BEGINS with a changing of the guard. An ordained elder in the United Methodist Church, I became the fifth dean of Hendricks Chapel on January 1, 1999. I succeeded my own dean, Richard L. Phillips, who had successfully served in the position for eighteen years. I served with Phillips when he came to Syracuse University in 1990 as the interdenominational Protestant chaplain. During my tenure as a chaplain, my love for the interface between religious institutions and higher education was confirmed. When the opportunity to serve as dean arose, it was a challenge I felt was the logical next step toward putting into practice this love for these two institutions.

Thomas V. Wolfe, current dean of Hendricks Chapel, in September 2004. Wolfe took over the post in January 1999. On September 11, 2001, he presided over a university gathering in the chapel to mourn the terrorist attacks on New York City and Washington, D.C. More than 2000 people attended, spilling out of the chapel onto the Quad outside. Courtesy of Syracuse University Art Collection.

I was very familiar with Syracuse University: many members of my family were graduates. My own father, John Wolfe, recently deceased at the time of my installation as dean, was a member of the Syracuse class of 1953. After graduation and seminary, he spent his career as a United Methodist pastor. During my installation address, I took a personal privilege to remember my father as a person who was always reaching out to the members of different faith communities in the places he served. He befriended and initiated collaborations with the priests and rabbis of these communities. John Wolfe attributed his commitment to interfaith relationships directly to the influence of Charles Noble, the second dean of Hendricks Chapel who served during my father's student years. In my remarks at the installation, I said, "My appreciation for building relationships between faith communities comes, in part, from observing my own father's commitment. He learned it while a student here. In that way, Hendricks Chapel has been an influence on me all of my life."

The beginning of my tenure was marked by the creation of a new five-year strategic plan. The Chaplains Council, comprising all of the university chaplains and the Hendricks staff, adopted a nine-month process for assessing the role of the chapel at the university, within the community, and in relation to other chapels on campuses throughout the nation. To guide the process, several questions were posed:

• What is unique about Hendricks Chapel from all other entities at SU?
• What campus relationships does it need to develop?
• What university initiatives exist that we can join?
• What university needs do we know of that we can initiate on behalf of?

- When has Hendricks Chapel been most effective? Why?
- What has been a barrier to effectiveness at other times?
- What does Hendricks Chapel have to contribute to the national community of chapels on university campuses?
- Where rests our authority in shaping the campus culture?
- What does Hendricks Chapel have to offer the culture of higher education?

Over the next months, the Chaplains Council and the Hendricks Chapel Advisory Board contemplated these questions under the facilitation of Dr. Robert and Jane Pickett. The Picketts were intimately knowledgeable of Hendricks Chapel. Bob was a retired member of the Department of Child and Family Studies faculty and had recently served as the interim dean of the chapel while Richard Phillips served a two-year position as director of the university's international program in Strasbourg, France.

In June 2000 the Chaplains Council and the Hendricks Chapel Advisory Board presented to Eleanor Ware, vice president of Human Services and Government Relations, the new five-year plan of initiatives and a new mission statement for the chapel. The mission statement set the tone for the initiatives that followed:

> Hendricks Chapel is a diverse religious, spiritual, and cultural learning environment seeking to generate a welcoming and caring community within Syracuse University. The Chapel values differences as a resource for enrichment.
>
> The Chapel supports the University's core values by creatively promoting interfaith understanding and cooperation through program and example. The Chapel honors religious traditions and encourages spiritual introspection while at the same time promoting active voluntarism. The Chapel is a source of constructive efforts to deal responsibly with personal and cultural pain as well as issues of social justice and reconciliation.

The new initiatives were divided into three distinct types: global, strategic, and administrative. Global initiatives set an agenda for the chapel to be responsive to contemporary issues through creative programming. They sought to acknowledge global issues, notably racism and other forms of discrimination and poverty, and to address them on a university level by creating activities designed to bring diverse groups together and foster a deeper understanding among them.

The chapel's strategic initiatives were intended to demonstrate an openness to all persons: not only those individuals defining themselves as religious but also those defining themselves as nonreligious. Articulating the chapel's commitment to fostering many different types of learning experiences, the planners sought to maintain the chapel's traditional role in student support while more fully integrating chapel activities with the academic mission of the university. Not only would

Hendricks Chapel be a place for diverse experiences of worship and meditation, but it would also be a forum for difficult discussions between groups struggling with opposing views. It would be a place where students could connect to service opportunities and in the process learn about the history of poverty and the effects of racism. The planners also sought to incorporate the arts, viewing them as a means of expressing meaning and purpose in ways not confined to only the spoken word. To this end, the chapel would host many artistic endeavors.

The administrative initiatives were designed to address organizational issues. To enhance the chapel's ability to effectively communicate its mission to the campus community and beyond, the planners sought to review its organizational structures across its many relationships and upgrade technology and other communications systems where needed. Another initiative addressed the diversity of the chaplains. Because the chaplains are appointed by their various sponsoring bodies, there is no direct control for ensuring diversity. This initiative would explore ways to create a more racially diverse staff of chaplains.

A strategic plan is worthless if it is not embraced by the people entrusted to put it into practice. The new five-year plan was designed to be a living document, fostering sustained and varied dialogue over the designed period of impact. Every administrative action and programmatic emphasis needed to reveal the heart of Hendricks Chapel. There was no sense of entitlement in its spirit. Those individuals in leadership of the chapel and its various chaplaincies and programs knew that the tradition from which the chapel formed its identity was a gift of which they must be stewards. As the vision of the five-year plan took hold, reimagining the chapel's program and direction, the growing recognition that change was inevitable was balanced by the understanding that it should never be at the expense of the inherited tradition of interfaith collegiality and dialogue. This plan was designed to build a new future based on the impressive past.

During the initial transition some of the staff changed positions. Ginny Yerdon was promoted to administrative assistant in charge of managing not only the daily flow of the office but also special events, including the International Thanksgiving Meal hosted each year in collaboration with the Slutzker Center for International Services. She was also given responsibility for organizing the table and ticket logistics of the Martin Luther King Jr. Holiday Celebration held each January in the Carrier Dome.

Sue Martini was promoted from secretary to the dean to scheduling secretary. She is responsible for the daily scheduling of the various rooms of the chapel and for the myriad details related to the scheduled events. Sue's cheery, can-do attitude is a staple of Hendricks hospitality and has engendered a good measure of trust and a spirit of welcome to all using the chapel.

Agnes H. Magnarelli joined the chapel staff as the dean's secretary in late 1998 in anticipation of the transition of deans. Agnes coordinates my comings and goings and much of my communications. She is well known by all members of the various listservs. Her consistently happy greetings have become a tradition. Members of these groups have asked me to bring Agnes to their meetings so they can meet her and thank her for all her work on their behalf.

To provide long-term stability and consistency for the business affairs of the chapel, a permanent business manager position replaced the previous graduate assistant position. Collette Fay is the first to serve in the new post. Drawing on her wealth of expertise, she has set up many organizational schemes to streamline procedures and organize and fine-tune accounting processes. The chapel has also benefited from her expertise in computer technology; she organized a three-year plan to upgrade the chapel computers.

Long-range planning set the course, but the mission of the chapel continued to emphasize response to campus crises. As early as May 1999, the chaplains were called into action after the annual block party held by off-campus student residents on Livingston Avenue got out of control with drunkenness and violence. After party goers set bonfires in the street using apartment furniture, the Syracuse Police and Fire Departments responded, only to have their personnel accosted by drunken students. A fire truck was damaged when bottles and other hard objects were thrown at it. The riot-control squad was called to break up the party.

There was chaos on campus the next day. University officials took a very hard line with the students charged in the incident. They were suspended from classes and thus could not take finals. Implicated seniors on the verge of graduating were told they might be denied the privilege if they were found guilty of the charges against them. Feelings were running very high.

That morning I was informed by telephone that four Latino students had been charged with involvement in the riot. The four, claiming that they had been unjustly charged, sought help from a community organizer in their neighborhood. Each of them represented the first generation of their families to attend college. All were seniors looking forward to commencement just a few days later. The community organizer believed their story of innocence and asked me to advocate for them. She announced that they intended to protest their charges publicly from the steps of the chapel.

This demonstration certainly was not the first such protest. I called Bridget Talbot, the director of the Schine Student Center and the person overseeing the office responsible for scheduling events on the steps of the chapel, since they are considered part of the quad space. Talbot reported that although no other protest was on the schedule for the steps, they had been reserved for an annual step-dancing event held by one of the African American student groups. I feared that the protestors would be removed by the university's public safety officers because they had not scheduled their event. This action might deepen the wound and further polarize the students and the university, impeding efforts to discover the truth.

Meanwhile, the media had already been told that this protest would take place at the chapel, and all three local network affiliates had set up their remote broadcast trucks on the side lawn and brought live crews to the scene. They were taking footage of the step-dancing event and mistakenly calling it the protest they had come to cover.

I intercepted the aggrieved Latino students and their supporters and invited them into the Noble Room. I and Francis Parks, director of the Students Offering Service and African American Programs at the chapel, had assembled a variety of people from across the campus and from the region to hear their concerns. They included Robbie Robinson, chief of public safety; Irma Almirall-Padamsee, director of the Office of Multicultural Affairs; representatives from Onondaga County's Civil Rights Commission; and other concerned neighbors. I insisted that the media not be allowed in the room for this conversation; I wanted the talk to focus on solving a problem, not posturing to the world. However, I reassured the students that after the meeting, they were welcome to exit the chapel and talk to the awaiting media. The four students, in the presence of these people and their supporting peers, told their stories.

After all of the stories were told, it was clear to all that these students truly were innocent. They had not even been on the street, but because their apartment was in proximity to the riot they had been accused. The university and community leaders at the meeting helped the students find the resources to formally clear themselves of the university charges against them. Confident that they had been heard, the students left the building and reported to the media that the university had been responsive to their concerns. The next day the charges were dropped, and all four graduated on time.

This incident and many like it illustrate a major role of Hendricks Chapel at the university—that of independent mediator in times of crisis. This role had been assessed and reaffirmed in 1980, in a meeting chaired by Professor James B. Wiggins of the Religion Department. The meeting concluded that the chapel had to remain autonomous within the university so that it could function without a conflict of interest during times of campus unrest. According to its report—a document that lives to this day in the body of each successive strategic plan—the chapel is to be "a keeper of the questions" and "a nerve exposed to pain." It is charged to ask questions of the world and the university itself that seek to clarify the nature of justice. It is also charged with supporting people who experience personal or cultural pain arising from their disfranchisement from existing structures and resources. Incidents such as the Livingston riot and its aftermath point to the chapel's usefulness to the university in times of tension and unrest.

Throughout the first couple of years of this period, plans were being made to renovate the lower level of the chapel to enhance another kind of usefulness. The main offices of the dean's suite needed upgrades and new workstations. At the same time, a plan was put in place to update the office technology. The first phase was completed by early spring semester 2000. The second phase focused on the Noble Room. It continues to be affectionately called "the university's living room." It serves as a venue for some of the larger chapel and outside groups. On any given moment, a visit to the space will show its popularity. Individuals or small groups of students study together there. They might get a cup of coffee and something to eat from People's Place and have quiet conversation or read. It was decided that it was not to be overscheduled so as to not cut in to this relaxed purpose. However, with an overall shortage of space available within the chapel, it was necessary to rethink its purpose. The Office of Design and Construction assisted in imagining it as a multipurpose space without harming the living room feel. The space retained its general function. The two offices that were located on each end of the room were reconfigured and made into storage. A moveable wall was installed so the room could be used without cutting off the traffic flow on that end of the building. A large-screen projection system was installed for video and DVD viewing. A curtain was hung on one end to serve as a backdrop for coffee-house musical performances and speakers. Simple stage lights were hung from the ceiling to illuminate that area. The walls were fitted to accommodate the hanging of art. This phase of renovation was completed by opening weekend 2000.

At the same time, the university was making a large investment in the building by putting on a new roof. This work was projected to take two outdoor seasons. From March 2000 until November 2001, workers climbed all over the roof area. Many of them were artisans with specialties in working on historic sites. They carefully matched the new mortar to the old. The dome area of the roof had to be created by individually hand-cut pieces of a special tin and then fabricated into place. Once fitted, the joints were soldered by hand.

I was fascinated by the extensive project and made a point to visit the site as often as I could. During one visit to the roof, I made the offhand comment that it would be fun to stand on the very peak of the building. On a sunny day in the second year of the project, I was summoned from my office. The day before I had been told to wear appropriate footwear in anticipation of my ascent. I climbed the stairs of the scaffolding and climbed out on the first ledge. I was handed a harness and instructed how to wear it. I clipped on the guide wire that led to the top and hand over hand pulled myself to the top. I was joined there by several of the workers. Photographs were taken as evidence.

Renovations to the Rena Pierson Dankovich Chapel were also completed. This site also has multiple uses. The Buddhist community uses it for Zen meditation, the Episcopal community uses it for their weekly liturgy, and other groups regularly schedule it. Two new altars were created for the space. One was dedicated exclusively to the Buddhist community. The renowned Japanese artist Thomas Matsuta was commissioned to create a Buddha for it. Another altar was created for Christian use and designed particularly for the Eucharist. Attention was given to the details of the room to be sensitive to a variety of uses. Because meditation is usually conducted while sitting on the floor, an extra pad was installed below the new carpet to make people on the floor more comfortable.

All of the renovations that took place were one way to make obvious the mission of Hendricks Chapel. Creating a space that addresses the interests of a diversity of people and experiences makes all feel welcome and invites them to have a sense of ownership for it. Additional renovations included installation of the campus wireless network AirOrange on the main and lower levels of the chapel. By October 2003 students could bring their laptop computers into the chapel and have full wireless Internet access.

In March 1999 I received a call from Chancellor Shaw, who was traveling at the time in southern California. He reported the intentions of an alumna to give a major gift toward the building of a new Hillel center. Chancellor Shaw requested that I investigate Tufts, Brown, and Cornell Universities, which had all been offered similar gifts. Brown and Tufts each built the buildings, but Cornell declined the gift, citing its "all religious groups under one roof" policy.

Since its beginning, Hillel had occupied a major portion of the lower level of Hendricks Chapel. I wrote a memo regarding my findings, offering support for the idea of accepting the gift. Toward the end of the memo, I reflected with the chancellor that on the surface, some might think the Jewish presence moving out of Hendricks would harm the constellation of interfaith relationships within the chapel. I observed that for many years there has been a separate building for the Roman Catholic community located on Walnut Park. Additionally, the mosque is located on Comstock Avenue, across from the Women's Building. The chapel had already faced the precedent-setting issues of affiliated groups having their own space apart from the chapel. In my response to Chancellor Shaw, I stated that "collegiality is not dependent on geographical location but rather on a spirit of chosen mutuality." The history of the chapel and its rich relationships could continue with Hillel in its own building. In fact, the role of the dean was to support the growth of all groups, and this phase appeared to be the "logical next step." Strong groups make for better collegiality. The Hillel Winnick Center was opened in July 2004 and dedicated in October of that same year. It was built on the corner of Walnut Park and Harrison Street, just two doors down from the Alibrandi Catholic Center. A year before, all of the chaplains gathered at the site with members of the Hillel governing council to dedicate the site. Prayers and best wishes were offered in many traditions, and the genuine good feeling was palpable. At the formal building dedication, I was asked to speak for the university.

> The university is committed to diversity, and the chapel is a special place that serves to acknowledge and support each faith tradition that is represented on cam-

pus. At the same time, it is charged with creating an environment of dialogue and creative interaction between those traditions. Over many years, we have come to know that healthy collegiality among religious groups begins by encouraging and supporting each one to first claim its uniqueness by providing its constituents with a full expression of its religious and cultural life. That individual strength then becomes a source of enrichment for all of our students, faculty, and staff as it contributes to the religious diversity of our learning environment.

This center represents the natural and timely next step in enriching Jewish life at Syracuse University. Hillel provides a "home place" for students who wish to practice and explore their faith and cultural identity. The establishment of the Winnick Center provides Hillel with a place to grow into, and their increased strength will contribute in even greater ways to the full spectrum of religious life at Syracuse University.

We know from our own wonderful experience that collegiality is never a product of simply sharing space. Rather, it is in the quality of "chosen-ness" that our relationships reflect. We celebrate these relationships, today.

Once Hillel was relocated, it did provide the opportunity to put the old space to a new purpose. The chapel programs continued to outgrow the chapel's physical space. At no time in history did the chaplains have a common suite of offices or any comprehensive shared space. In the summer of 2004 the former Hillel space was renovated into a suite of offices to house all of the chaplains. Six offices were created in that space to be shared by eight chaplains. If the chaplain had no external location, that chaplain received an office to him- or herself. If the chaplain had a location outside of the chapel, that individual was asked to share. This new configuration was intended to make a statement about the collegiality of the chapel and its relationships. At the same time, it was designed to offer larger offices that would support the chaplains' programming needs. The shared offices were not-so-subtle statements in and of themselves. Imam Ahmed Nezar Kobeisy, the Muslim chaplain, shared an office in the suite with Hillel director Joel Miller. This arrangement was welcomed by the two of them in an age of increasing tensions in the Middle East. Father Tim Mulligan, the Catholic chaplain, shared an office with Evangelical Christian chaplain T. E. Koshy. Even though these chaplains had space in other locations, it was important to everyone that they also have physical space in Hendricks Chapel. It affords them the possibility of daily contact and gives students who enter the space a visual sense of the diversity of the chapel.

This creation of the Chaplains' Suite made it necessary to relocate the offices of the Hendricks Chapel Choir director, G. Burton Harbison, and the university organist, Christopher Marx. They were relocated into the center core of the chapel in order to create a choir rehearsal space and a new music library. A lounge adjacent to the music office serves as the gathering space for the choir. When the choir is not using it, the space divides into two rooms, one being the Strates Lounge, given by alumnus James Strates in the eighties.

This center core of music-related rooms reflects a reaffirmation of the historical role played by the Hendricks Chapel Choir and the organist. The choir is as old as the chapel and has come to represent a tradition of choral excellence. The choir continues to provide the music for the interdenominational Protestant service each Sunday morning at eleven. From 1999 until 2002 the service was led by the Reverend Thomas Davenport, and from 2002 until 2004 it was led by the Reverend Kathryn Fraser Bell. The choir performs concerts twice a year. The holiday concert in December finds the chapel full to the brim with people wanting to hear the sounds of the season. Burt Harbison directs a host of music and also acknowledges the season of Hanukkah in the repertoire. The choir also sings a spring concert and with that occasion typically ends its year.

I am committed to making it possible for the Hendricks Chapel Choir to travel on an international tour every four years. In 2001 the choir traveled to Poland and the Czech Republic. The forty-voice choir sang in churches throughout Poland, with one concert in Prague. The crowds were enormous and very appreciative. Often a local singing group would take a turn during the concert to share a native piece and add to the feeling of cultural exchange. By the end of the evening the choir members were exchanging addresses, promising to share music and stay in touch. Any language barrier was overcome with music. The students benefited from this exchange, and the university benefited by being represented internationally.

In 2000 Dr. Katharine Pardee, the university organist, announced she was leaving her position to move to England. Dr. Christopher Marx was hired as the university organist and given the responsibility of continuing the development of the annual Malmgren Concert Series begun under Dean Phillips and Dr. Pardee. The Malmgren gift is the largest bequest given to Hendricks Chapel to date. Its primary purpose is to be used for a free concert series offered at Hendricks Chapel. One concert a year must feature the organ, Esther Malmgren's favorite instrument. Chris Marx set out to develop the Malmgren Concert into a premier and known series. He scheduled performances of the leading groups in the nation, including Chanticleer from San Francisco, the Boston Brass, and the Waverly Consort from New York. In addition, he commissioned several pieces of music for organ as a way to add to the contemporary organ literature. Each year one of the series features a rising star in organ performance as recognized by the American Guild of Organists. To help facilitate the increasing prominence of this series, a Steinway grand piano was purchased for the main sanctuary.

Another performance group at Hendricks Chapel is the Hendricks Handbell Ringers. They have been a tradition at the chapel for years. During the summer of 2003 bells were purchased to complete the full five octaves. Under the direction of alumna Jessica Bowerman, the handbell ringers were transformed. At the 2004 spring concert they began their set of music by processing in from all corners of the chapel, antiphonally ringing back and forth to each other until they had assembled together in the front. The audience loved it, and the musicians were met with enthusiastic applause.

During this same period the Black Celestial Choral Ensemble celebrated its twenty-fifth anniversary. Evelyn Walker, an original member and later its director, stepped down from her leadership of the organization. Shayla Adams assumed the directorship, and the choir continued to grow in numbers and stature within the university community and throughout the Northeast. They continually travel to local churches on weekend tours throughout the academic year. A Jewish student who happened by the open doors of the chapel one night during one of the performances was taken by the sheer joy being expressed in the sanctuary. It prompted him to write a letter to the editor of the *Daily Orange,* the student newspaper, describing his delight at witnessing such a celebration of music. He came away from that event with a new appreciation and awareness of a type of music he had never been exposed to.

Over the years Hendricks Chapel has been the site of visits by numerous prominent figures. On February 9, 2000, Hillary Clinton came to the chapel, sponsored by the College Democrats. During her speech she announced her intentions to run for the available U.S. Senate seat in New York. This occasion was not the first time she had been to the chapel. She promoted the Clinton health care bill during the early years of the Clinton administration, and before that trip she campaigned with her husband during his run for the presidency.

Recognizing the importance of Hendricks Chapel as a university and community venue, a state-of-the-art sound system was installed in the main sanctuary during the summer of 2002. This installation was intended to expand the options of the use of the main chapel. As a result, the university lecture series chose the chapel as its primary venue. A host of speakers immediately began to draw crowds, nearly filling the chapel on each occasion. In the academic year 2002–2003, lecturers included *New York Times* columnist William Safire, Nobel Peace laureates Betty Williams and Jody Williams, Middle East expert Shibley Telhami, MacArthur Foundation "genius" fellow Robert Sapolsky, former surgeon general David Satcher, *New York Times* correspondent Judith Miller, violinist Joshua Bell, dramatist August Wilson, and psychologist Daniel Goleman.

The building improvements were drawing more events to the chapel and filling the sanctuary more frequently. At the end of the 2003–2004 academic year more than thirteen hundred events were held at the chapel with more than forty-three thousand people in attendance! These events are only the ones held in the chapel and do not reflect some of the chapel groups that meet outside of the building. In that same year the chapel registered eight chaplaincies and twenty-six religious groups.

People's Place experienced a very large upturn in business. Just a few years ago, it had been a struggling student-run business and was running a significant deficit. New marketing and a new menu turned the place around. Still under student operation, People's Place saw sixty-five thousand customers in the 2003–2004 academic year. The student employees who had been around for a while could remember quiet times in the business day. Now they were serving customers more frequently. Much of the transformation can be credited to one of the student managers. K. C. Duggan took on the job with an extraordinary zeal. She redecorated the front, introduced new foods, interviewed customers, and even promoted a new line of handmade all-original People's Place mugs. K. C. was such an outstanding employee that the Hendricks Chapel staff nominated her for student employee of the year for the university. She won and the banner hung in the reception area for the year.

Physical space has been important to the chapel from the beginning in 1930 when it was strategically located at the geographic center of the campus. But space has also meant something to the chapel beyond its physical dimensions. At Hendricks Chapel there has always been value in the kind of space that is safe for exploration of difficult questions. This space is reserved for the questions of meaning and purpose as marked by an examination of the spiritual life. The chapel has always provided the space for worship where some of this questioning is explored. The chapel has also provided space for individual exploration. To this end, in 2001 the Chaplains Council adopted the document "Ethical Framework for Religious Life at Syracuse University." The document describes the expected behavior of all registered religious groups in regard to their own members and to the community as a whole. It ensures that they will behave in such a way that students will not be pressured to accept certain beliefs. It ensures that all groups have the right to full expression of their beliefs and further stipulates that no group will publicly demean another group. No group can act exclusively, meaning that membership in that particular faith tradition cannot be an expectation for participation. As with the creation of physical space, the safe space created by the document put into practice the chapel's commitment to students exploring their own spiritual questions without having to fear being taken advantage of in the process. It established healthy boundaries about how religious groups were to relate to students and each other.

Perhaps the most defining moment for Hendricks Chapel since its response to the December 21, 1988, bombing of Pan Am Flight 103 over Lockerbie, Scotland, was its response in the wake of the terrorist attacks of September 11, 2001. On that morning I and administrative assistant, Ginny Yerdon, were attending a meeting at the Slutzker Center for International Services to begin planning the annual International Thanksgiving Meal. News spread quickly of the attacks, and we were called out of the meeting to watch the live news reports on the television located in the Slutzker Center lounge. Realizing the gravity of the situation, I called my secretary, Agnes H. Magnarelli, to summon the chaplains to an emergency meeting in my office. Ginny and I arrived back at the chapel where a message was awaiting me to join a meeting of university officials to plan a response. The chaplains' meeting was combined with the other and relocated to the Noble Room. Before the end of the meeting nearly seventy persons, including the chancellor and his wife, Mary Ann Shaw, were identifying the concerns and planning a course of action.

The staff, chaplains, and I offered to host a community gathering at three o'clock that day. It would be a moment for people to come together and draw strength from university leaders, readings from various sacred texts, and simply being together.

In the meantime, the chapel doors were fastened opened, and Sue Martini, the scheduling secretary, lit a candle in a floor stand and placed it at the head of the aisle. News was broadcast via e-mail, word of mouth, and flyers that the chapel would remain open twenty-four hours a day for the foreseeable future. The chapel was wired to broadcast via the Internet the daily messages of the chancellor as to the state of the university and update people with accurate information about how the university was responding and any developments that would impact the university.

At three o'clock on the day of the attacks, more than two thousand people filed into the chapel, a structure designed to hold eleven hundred. Students sat in the aisles and on the floor in front. The choir loft was given to general seating. Not a single square foot was left. Several hundred more waited on the steps or tried to hear from the open doors of the front porch. The chancellor's cabinet members sat together near the front. As I ascended to the pulpit to open the gathering, there was absolute silence. To those individuals gathered, I spoke these words:

> I want you to feel this room. I want you to feel what it is like to be together at this moment in the history of our world, nation, and university. I want you to feel what it is like to be in a room with this many people who have feelings similar to yours. But more than anything, I want you to feel what it is like to care so deeply about something that you could not have not come here, today. . . .
>
> This morning, our experience of the world changed forever. The tragedies of this day have left us in shock and fear and in a chaos of other emotions. We may feel more vulnerable. We may feel that what we once thought we controlled is now beyond our control. No one is left unaffected. It is important that we are here. It is important that we are here, together. In these moments we draw strength from each other, and the whole community serves to sustain and support each individual.
>
> At this all-university gathering, we will acknowledge our thoughts and feelings. We will begin to account for their impact on us. Before we can understand or comprehend the scope of this day, we simply present ourselves in this place as we are. It is a good thing.
>
> So this gathering is about finding others with whom we can share. It is a time

to pause, reflect, and find ourselves again. It is a time to hear readings that contain centering wisdom that have been uttered at other critical times in history and from which other generations have found strength. In this place we will share these words, prayers, and the wisdom from our global community. May we know, from having been together, that through it all, the center holds.

Be present to each other at this moment. Let us begin this gathering in a time of respectful silence. Let us be in prayer, meditation, and reflection.

Chancellor Shaw was the next to speak. His words were calm and determined. He assured the students that the university would provide support to them and their various needs. As the service was being quickly planned, it was determined by the chaplains that there needed to be readings from the three major faith traditions. Imam Ahmed Kobeisy was home ill that day but agreed to come in and read a passage from the Qur'an. I asked him to first read the passage in Arabic and then translate it into English. Because the word in the news was that the attacks had been committed by "Islamic terrorists," it would be important to hear Arabic spoken associated with a message of peace and reassurance. He spoke following the chancellor. After the service an individual in attendance stopped me and confessed that hearing the Arabic spoken was personally jarring. Then when the translation was offered, the person acknowledged that she realized that resistance was her own bias reacting.

Kevin Morrow, the university spokesperson, shared an information update that served to quell rumors and misinformation. Father Tim Mulligan, serving in his first year as the Catholic chaplain, read the Prayer of St. Francis. Christopher Marx, the university organist, played an interlude so everyone could absorb the words and reflections thus far. Vice Chancellor Deborah Freund spoke to the gathering, offering more words of support, and announced that classes would continue to meet. She wisely perceived that it was important for students to have the opportunity to talk about this event and get out their feelings, and the classroom was a good resource for keeping students from becoming isolated. She also said that if students could not attend classes for reasons of personal distress, there would certainly be leniency, and she recommended that they avail themselves of the many campus resources.

The university at that time was in search of a Hillel director. Rabbi Shelley Ezring from the nearby Temple Society of Concord assisted interim Hillel director Mark Rothchild in reciting the Kaddish in English and Hebrew. As the gathering neared an end, Dr. T. E. Koshy, the evangelical Christian chaplain, read the Twenty-third Psalm, and Thomas Davenport, the interdenominational Protestant chaplain, offered the benediction. I shared a final closing word encouraging students to reach out to each other. The chaplains who had participated in the service joined the remaining chaplains: Mike McQuitty, Southern Baptist; Fritz Lampe,

Lutheran; and Sister Pat Larkin, codirector of the Alibrandi Catholic Center. Together, they lingered in the chapel to listen to the students' fears and calm anxieties.

After the gathering the candle remained lit at the head of the aisle for three days. The doors that had been fastened open on the morning of September 11 remained that way all through the night and the following night. Chaplains took shifts throughout the days and nights so that there would be someone to receive anyone who wanted to seek the peace of the chapel.

As the campus gradually came back to normal in the days following the tragedies, the reality of those tragedies also came home to everyone. Reports of our alumni who had been killed in either the World Trade Center or the Pentagon began to accumulate. In all, forty-three alumni had been killed. One faculty member had lost her pregnant daughter in New York City; when her memorial service was held in the chapel two months later, an urn containing the soil from Ground Zero was placed on the altar table. Her body was later found intact and interred in New Jersey.

Robert Dewey, the director of Lubin House, the alumni center in New York, invited me to meet with a gathering of New York City alumni for a reception and brief time of common prayer. The Greenberg House in Washington, D.C., held a similar reception at which I led a time of remembrance for four alumni killed in the attack on the Pentagon. In both places, families and friends of the victims were given an opportunity to pause and remember.

The chapel staff and chaplains continued to work collaboratively on all of the many efforts of the university to respond to the tragic events of September 11. The university created the Critical Incident Management Team and charged them with creating an emergency-response protocol to guide the university in any kind of crisis. I was asked to cochair the team with Mary Jo Custer, director of student affairs. We had worked together many times on various crises and even cotaught a graduate course in critical incident management in higher education for the Higher Education Administration Program in the School of Education.

One year later the chapel organized an all-university six-day event around the first anniversary of the attacks. Every school and college offered symposia, and the chapel hosted the Reverend Dr. Stuart Hoke as the keynote speaker. Dr. Hoke was the executive assistant to the rector of Trinity Church at Wall Street and was at Trinity's St. Paul's Chapel next door to the World Trade Towers when they collapsed. He described in detail his experience of surviving and then offer assistance to the people affected. The chapel also hosted a service at noon on September 11, 2002. Again, the chapel was filled to capacity. The Reverend Christine Day, the Episcopal chaplain, took the lead responsibility for ordering the interfaith service. The Hendricks Chapel Choir sang, as did the Alibrandi Catholic Center singers. The names of the deceased alumni were read, and a candle was lit for each one of them. Chancellor Shaw was asked to read a prayer that was punctuated by the reading of the names. I offered a reflection on the occasion. Again, the candle was lit at the head of the aisle when the chapel opened in the morning and remained lit throughout the service and until ten o'clock when the chapel closed that night. All through the day students, faculty, and staff found a bit of quiet time there.

Simultaneous to the events and aftermath of September 11, 2001, was another major Hendricks Chapel program. During the 2000–2001 academic year I had begun to create an experience in which fifteen students representing Islam, Judaism, and Christianity, along with their respective chaplains, would prepare for and carry out a travel study experience to Israel and Palestine. I had long believed that the everyday collegiality that the chaplains and staff enjoyed needed to be modeled and lived out in a deeper way with students.

The various religious groups enjoyed regular encounters of exchange with dialogue groups and even fun times like the Hendricks Chapel Cup sporting series. The cup series was a friendly competition among Muslims, Jews, and Christians and all the diverse types within each of those categories. They agreed to a yearlong set of sports competitions depending on the season. They competed in softball, soccer, ultimate Frisbee, and many other sports. At the end of the year they added up the points, and the winner was awarded the Hendricks Chapel Cup, a real but not-too-expensive trophy. That group then possessed it until the next year's competitions. These and many other interfaith interactions were established. But there was room in the chapel program for a sustained kind of interfaith interaction that would focus on how diverse groups engage difficult issues and remain respectful and bonded despite their differences.

I proposed to the Chaplains Council the creation of the Interfaith Middle East Experience. The idea was simple: Form a group with five students from each of the traditions, their chaplains, and a few selected others. Create a curriculum with content that allows the group to learn about each other's traditions. Study the history of the region of the Middle East with emphasis on how that history has been impacted by the presence of these traditions. Create opportunities for the group to visit each other's sacred sites and also commit to doing community service together. The goal was to form a group with a well-established history of trust that could visit sites in Israel and Palestine without breaking apart when the discussion points got tough.

In the process of outlining this experience, I heard a presentation on the university's Vision Fund. This fund granted money to academic units for the purpose of promoting the study of diversity through all disciplines. The chapel was not an academic unit but had a commitment to participating in the university's academic mission. A seminary student at the Colgate Rochester Crozer Theological Seminary in Rochester, New York, was interning that year at the chapel. Naomi Annandale was a former journalist and gifted writer. She accepted the task of writing each successive draft of the request. The chapel was awarded the maximum grant of

ERRATA

Donors

P. [vii] "Nawel Obeid" should read "Nawal Obeid"

Chap. 55

P. 315: "Chris Marx" should read "Chris Marks."

Chap. 63

P. 397: "Christopher Marx" should read "Christopher Marks."

P. 398: "Dr. Christopher Marx" should read "Dr. Christopher Marks."

"Chris Marx" should read "Chris Marks."

P. 402: "Christopher Marx" should read "Christopher Marks."

P. 474: "Marx, Christopher" should read "Marks, Christopher."

thirty thousand dollars. This amount would cover a great portion of the students' travel expenses and allow for other costs related to the preparation of the group. Chris Walsh, director of financial aid, heard of the project and called me to express his support for the undertaking. He asked what expenses remained, and I told him that there was still a balance each student was responsible for that was not covered by the Vision Fund grant. Walsh announced that he would donate funds to cover the rest of the students' travel expenses.

Forty-two students applied for the fifteen positions. At the end of April 2001, the names selected were posted on the door of my office. The group was a balance of the three traditions, included both genders, and had both undergraduate and graduate students. They came together for the first time in May just before the end of the semester. It was simply a time of meeting before everyone scattered for the summer. The first formal meeting of the group in the new semester was announced for September 12.

The date arrived and in one regard many of the participants agreed the timing was ironically tragically perfect. With the events of the day before still raw, the group could not see the curriculum as simply an exercise of the mind but instead saw it as having a deeply important context. Into the fall, the group met for the course sessions and an occasional meal at one of the leader's homes.

The group was still committed to traveling, but increasingly their thoughts turned to the wisdom and practicality of traveling to the Middle East in light of recent events. A new level of conflict was escalating between Israelis and Palestinians. There were increased reports of violence. The group monitored the news daily and made contact with people who were on the ground in the region. By the end of the semester, after a meeting with a number of university officials whose concern was growing, it was decided to postpone the travel portion until tensions in the region eased. The decision was based not only on the increased tensions but also on the very practical issue of access to the sites that were necessary to visit. The group had decided early on that they would go to each location together in order to teach the others about their respective sacred sites. There was also a hope to visit Gaza and refugee camps. Access to many sites was severely restricted.

On December 15 I made the sad determination that the trip had to be delayed. By this time the students and the other leaders felt a strong connection and commitment to the purpose of the group and decided to stay together and work on the experience. Certainly, some would graduate before any travel was possible, but the value of working toward it seemed to pervade, especially in light of the current events. The students wanted to process the September 11 attacks and the looming war on terror in Afghanistan from this uniquely diverse setting. As time went on and the relationships deepened, the conversation became more honest.

By the fall of 2002 it was clear that the group would have to travel by the following spring or lose the funding that had already been generously extended to them past the deadline because of the unique circumstances of the project. The group was also having its members called away by other life pulls, such as graduation and the demands of dissertations and job searches. The remnant gathered to assess its options. The Middle East was still in turmoil, and visiting it was no longer seemed an option. Where would they travel? In the course of their study of Islam as part of the curriculum they had studied the influence of Muslims in Spain during the medieval period. It was a place governed by a succession of Islamic rulers from roughly 750 to 1492. During that time, Muslims, Jews, and Christians forged a culture of tolerance and collaboration. The evidence remains to this day in the architecture and cultural advancements from that period.

Permission was granted by the Vision Fund administrators to travel to Spain as a fulfillment of the grant. The group brought together many campus resources to study Spain in light of their intended purpose. During spring break 2003 the group spent eight days traveling through Madrid, Cordoba, Granada, and Seville. They climbed on ruins of earlier Islamic architecture and saw evidence of what happens when one faith group attempts to dominate another. The group visited a synagogue that was built by Muslims for Jews and cathedrals that were once mosques. They ate meals together and negotiated the complexities of diverse religious dietary laws. The group found itself sensitized to how history is often recounted by conveniently leaving out significant elements. As they toured the Alhambra in Granada, the tour guide was heard to say, "There was a mosque located over there, but then it disappeared." Imam Kobeisy gently asked, "Sir, how does a mosque disappear?" The Eurocentric guide did not even comprehend the nature of the question that had to do with a history of domination that had undermined that seven hundred-year era of tolerance. That ignorance led to much discussion among the group members during their evening discussion when they gathered to ponder their day's experience. Upon returning home, the group reflected on a significant experience of negotiating diversity, having examined models where diversity worked to enrich everyone, as well as when differences were not appreciated and succumbed to forms of dominance. The group was made up of students who will one day hold significant power and responsibility. This kind of in-depth exposure to religious diversity generalizes to other experiences when differences are encountered.

In the same spirit Hendricks Chapel joined the university in supporting a seamless environment for learning. Since 2000 the university had been examining ways that it could enrich the out-of-classroom environment by understanding that students learn a great deal just from the environment and their daily encounters with other students and activities on campus. One of the strategies was the creation of learning communities in the residence halls. They were intentional communities offered for students to join that are centered on a common theme. They are focused around multicultural living, leadership, various specific majors, and many other interests.

Again, seeking to serve the academic mission of the university, the Chaplains Council decided to create a learning community that allowed students the opportunity to live in an interfaith setting. The Interfaith Living Learning Community took in its first residents in the fall of 2003. Ten students agreed to live together for a year for the purpose of learning about other faith traditions from each other. They lived in a wing in Shaw Hall, chosen because it was the site of the kosher and *halal* kitchens. The idea was that they were to witness each other practicing their traditions and have an opportunity to inquire of each other on a daily basis.

The chaplains led four sessions each semester based on a curriculum they created to explore the issues in interfaith exchange. The students visited the various chaplains' worship sites and were known to stay up into the early morning hours in spontaneous discussions about their different experiences. At the end of the first year, they reported how informed they thought they were in the beginning and how uninformed they really had been. As they reflected on that first year, they laughed among themselves about the questions they asked each other that might have gotten them in trouble under any other circumstances. One of the students told the chaplains that he had come to be able to appreciate another member's faith tradition, not by believing in it but by realizing the other genuinely respected his. They discovered that what they had in common was mutual respect for each other's deep faith. That one commonality was enough on which to build a relationship. Another student thought that her dilemma would be in finding a faith community after graduation that would allow her to deepen in her tradition without having to be exclusive toward others.

That same year a group of students made up of the various chaplaincies and other religious groups on campus formed the Interfaith Student Council. The work had begun at the end of the previous academic year when Jennifer Bevilacqua, a practicum student in the higher education graduate program, took the assignment to assist in organizing the students. The intention was that the council would be self-governing and initiate interfaith opportunities among students. They started small but persisted into the year. By midyear they had assembled several other students and had taken on a determined series of discussions on a variety of topics. At the meetings they each came prepared to discuss the topic of the week, be it about how their respective traditions understood the nature of suffering, sexuality, worship, or other important issues such as war and peace. As with the learning community, the students came to a deeper appreciation of their own beliefs, discovered by having to articulate them to someone from another faith group. They also reported an increased appreciation and awareness of the other faiths represented by the membership.

In all of these interfaith initiatives, the environment of the chapel continued to serve to reveal assumptions that people carry around with them. In several situations, these assumptions were challenged as to make way for a deeper understanding of another person's experience.

Religious diversity is not the only concern of Hendricks Chapel. As it serves the university community, it has always seen itself as responsible to the larger issues of the campus. Diversity is one of the institutional core values, and it is expressed in many ways. There were times when the values of a particular religious community clashed with the Syracuse University values. For several years it had been university policy to grant benefits to same-sex partners of employees. The religious communities affiliated at the university through Hendricks Chapel represented a full spectrum of opinion and theological outlook on their relationship to the lesbian, gay, bisexual, and transgender communities. Typically, the issues centered on whether to allow avowed members of those communities to be ordained into their bodies and also about the blessing of their relationships. Some of the chaplains defended their traditions' positions, while other chaplains wrestled with the reality that their own positions conflicted with their tradition's position.

Because the university had taken a clear position in recognizing same-sex partnerships, I believed it was important for Hendricks Chapel to reflect the university's position by creating a formal policy regarding the use of Hendricks Chapel for gay-union services. I drafted a policy for discussion by the Chaplains Council. Once it was approved by that body, I planned to present it to the Hendricks Chapel Advisory Board comprising students, faculty, staff, and alumni. The goal was to have it finally approved by the Board of Trustees. I proposed the following policy in the fall of 1999:

> Gay or lesbian couples are welcome at Hendricks Chapel for ceremonies of commitment. These ceremonies cannot be considered marriages because there is at present no provision in New York State law making same-sex unions legally binding.
>
> Syracuse University claims diversity as one of its core values. In that spirit, Hendricks Chapel affirms the full range of diversity of faiths and provides space for each of these traditions and their particular practices. Thus, it opens its doors to the blessing of relationships between gay and lesbian couples in accordance to those faith traditions that affirm such relationships and to those individual chaplains who, after sincere reflection, wish to officiate such ceremonies as an act of conscience. The University chaplains retain the right to accept or decline officiating at ceremonies of commitment or marriages based on their assessment of the integrity of the relationship as it stands in connection to their particular faith tradition.
>
> Each couple desiring to have a ceremony of commitment is invited to contact the scheduling secretary at Hendricks Chapel to select a time and determine arrangements.

As anticipated, it created a great deal of discussion among the chaplains. Some were delighted to see it. Others accepted it in principle but were concerned that their denominations might cease to fund their programs if they were perceived in any way to be mandated to do these ceremonies or endorse a same-sex lifestyle. The point at which there was unanimous agreement was in the basic premise of the policy. It was based on the fact that Hendricks Chapel affords each religious group full expression of its religious rites and practices. There were some religious groups that affirmed same-sex-union ceremonies. None of the chaplains wanted any single group to be denied one of its practices. Even though different theological perspectives still permeated the conversation, the idea of affording all groups' full expression of their traditions gave rise to the chaplains passing the policy unanimously. The advisory board also approved the policy unanimously, and the trustees of the university affirmed it as well. Since its adoption, other universities have used it as a model for writing or defending their own policies.

Hendricks Chapel continues the tradition of participating with the Martin Luther King Jr. Holiday Celebration committee. This group works to create an annual MLK celebration near the birthday of Dr. King. It is held in the Carrier Dome in January. More than twenty-two hundred people share a meal of southern cuisine. Following the dinner there is a program that includes honoring various unsung heroes in the community. The tradition of gathering a mass choir from the campus and the community results in more than 150 voices. The program leads to the keynote speaker, who is always a prominent national figure in the civil rights movement. Andrew Young was the speaker in 1999. He was followed by Lani Guinier in 2000, Cornell West in 2001, and Randall Robinson in 2002. Suzan-Lori Parks was the speaker in 2003. It was a very special year for the campus and the committee. Parks had just recently been awarded the Pulitzer for her play, *Topdog, Underdog*. She was the first African American woman to win this award for drama. But what made her presence more special was that she was the daughter of Francis McMillan Parks, director of Hendricks Chapel's Students Offering Service and African American Programs. Francis had served on the MLK Committee for years and been charged with opening each meeting with a historical reflection that would ground the committee in the history of the civil rights movement. Geoffrey Canada was the speaker for the celebration in 2004.

Another established program of Hendricks Chapel continued to flourish during this period. The International Thanksgiving Meal is cosponsored by the Slutzker Center for International Services. Five hundred international students from eighty countries are introduced to a traditional American Thanksgiving meal. Each table is hosted by a member of the university community, and all are served family style. There is always a program of a dance group that represents how Americans continue to celebrate their original heritages.

The chapel's sense of responsibility to issues of campus diversity is also reflected in the office of the Students Offering Service and African American Programs. Francis McMillan Parks is the director, and Rachel Gazdick serves as the graduate assistant to the program. The service programs build grassroots community networks on and off campus.

On its tenth anniversary in 2000, the Students Offering Service reaffirmed its work by creating a new mission statement. "The Mission of Students Offering Service of Hendricks Chapel is to generate and enhance a commitment to service by all people—providing for a more caring, just, and democratic university community and community at large." The group also established goals to accomplish its mission:

• To broaden the learning experience of students, faculty, staff, and community members and to encompass civic virtue by providing forums where volunteers can practically apply their skills, resources, time, and energy, in a manner that aids others.

• To facilitate communication about the historical context of social justice movements and how they interact with current initiatives toward "life, liberty and the pursuit of happiness" for all people.

• To empower and challenge student leaders to emerge and take responsibility for new or existing service projects and activities.

Each program is educationally grounded in a historical context. Students who volunteer at an agency on the south side of Syracuse not only have a hands-on experience of service but also learn about the impact of the 1930s practice of redlining neighborhoods and the long-term poverty that resulted. Cross-cultural activities are always framed in terms of the dynamics of race and how society structures privilege. Francis and Rachel operate programs that bring young children to campus to expose them to university life and to instill in them at a very early age that a university is a place that includes them. The Students Offering Service joins forces with local refugee resettlement activities and provides the International Young Scholars Program. Each week, children from the community, many of whom have just arrived in Syracuse sponsored by a refugee program, find tutoring by an SU student who will help them with their homework. The children are introduced to a variety of university disciplines and are generally assisted with the cultural adjustment, including language development.

Francis, an avid believer that chess is a game that teaches critical thinking skills while also providing a community experience among a diverse group, created a summer program called Chess Camp for Kids. She managed to corral a group of faculty and staff to donate their mornings for a week to teach basic and advanced levels of chess to the eager participants. Kids from inner-city neighborhoods mingle with children of faculty and staff while learning and teaching each other chess. At the end of the week, all of the kids assemble on the sidewalk out in front of the chapel where they find a large chessboard drawn on the cement. Each child is given a hat representing a chess piece. They assemble a human chess match, and two of the advanced kids stand at the top of the steps calling out moves in a match to the end.

Throughout the year, students march on the Church World Service Crop Walk to raise money for local and global hunger. They also participate in green-ups throughout the region. In 2004 the Students Offering Service and African American Programs led the way in creating a campuswide collaboration to commemorate the fiftieth year of the Supreme Court decision of *Brown v. Board of Education*. After a year of planning a conference took place that gave a thorough examination of the landmark decision and its impact. Dr. Charles Willie of Harvard, who earned his doctorate at Syracuse, delivered the opening address framing the issues. Several panel discussions followed throughout the day. The keynote speakers were the Brown sisters, Linda Brown Thompson and Cheryl Brown Henderson. Their father had been one of the plaintiffs in the case and the one for whom the case had been named.

The programming of the Students Offering Service and African American Programs serves a concrete purpose, but it also helps create a spirit at the chapel. The attempt is always to communicate safe space to individuals and groups on the campus so they will seek out the chapel during critical times. Such a time was when a student was spotted moving from bar to bar on Marshall Street wearing blackface. The students of color along with many white students were deeply disturbed by the event. A group of African American students sought to have a lengthy meeting with the chancellor so their concerns would be heard. Chancellor Shaw received them and listened in depth to their concerns. But in the early morning hours before that meeting, when tensions on campus were about to explode, several African American students sought out Francis Parks for her wisdom and support. At six o'clock the morning after the incident she met the students on the steps of the chapel for conversation and provided them with a basket of apples to help keep their strength up. Later in the next two days the chapel was the site of a listening session as groups gathered in the safe space of the sanctuary to voice concerns and feelings of hurt and disappointment.

In the 2004–2005 academic year a new internship was created to begin with the traditionally black churches of the south side of Syracuse. Each year an African American student from Colgate Rochester Crozer Theological Seminary will serve the spiritual needs of our students of color who identify with the traditions of these churches with the hope that one day this position will develop into a full chaplaincy.

Hendricks Chapel will celebrate its seventy-fifth anniversary in 2005. A year-long celebration is being planned to take place from January to December. The beginning of the celebration will be marked by the introduction of a new five-year strategic plan. During the year a major new initiative with the south side neighborhood will be announced. The Hendricks Chapel Choir will tour China in May. Major speakers and concerts are planned for the year, along with a weekend dedicated to a very specific celebration and homecoming for all former chaplains, staff, and students. There will be an interfaith convocation of rededication, a special Malmgren Concert, and a banquet with a keynote speaker. Those events will have to be accounted for at the beginning of the next writing of the history of Hendricks Chapel.

The tradition with which we have been entrusted runs deep. Each successive generation draws life from this well and engages the university community in a spirit of service. It is the hope that this special place will continue to remind the community of the questions of meaning and purpose and that all will know they have a place inside. Though this chapter must finally end, it is really only just the beginning. The door remains open.

APPENDIXES

INDEX

Officers, Staff, and Board Members, 1929–1963

This appendix contains lists of Hendricks Chapel staff and Hendricks Chapel Board members and chaplains, by year, compiled by Dr. Wright in his original manuscript. Not every year is included, and his lists for some years are not complete, probably because he lacked access to some of the information. Nevertheless, the lists do give an overview of the administrative structure of the chapel.

The Hendricks Chapel Board

1929–1930

Members Ex-Officio

Charles W. Flint, Chancellor of the University
William H. Powers, University Chaplain
Whitney M. Trousdale, Assistant to the Chaplain

Administration and Faculty Members

Harold Butler, Dean of Fine Arts
Helene W. Hartley, Professor, Teachers College
Karl C. Leebrick, Dean of Liberal Arts
Mabel C. Lytton, Associate Dean of Women
Herbert Shenton, Head, Sociology Department
Donald Watt, Personnel Director
Clyde Wildman, Professor, Bible Department
George Wilson, Head, Philosophy Department

Student Representatives and At-Large Members

Glen Loucks (class of 1930), Men's Senate
Dean Henderson (1930), Men's Senate
Alice Evans (1930), Women's Senate
Nancy Ferguson (1930), Women's Senate
Marion Diamond (1930), Convocation Committee
Ewart Blaine (1930), Convocation Committee

Ivan M. Gould (1930)
Dorothy Flood (1931)
Marjorie O. Bronner (1931)
Douglas Petrie (1930)
Ellamae Merrick (1930)
John Leininger (1930)

1930–1931

William H. Powers, Dean

Chapel Staff

Mabel C. Lytton, Associate Dean of Women
Bernice H. Meredith, Executive Secretary, Syracuse-in-China
Earl D. Stout, Chapel Music Director
Reverend Whitney M. Trousdale, Men's Student Counselor

Administration and Faculty Members

Dwight M. Beck, Professor, Bible Department
Harold Butler, Dean of Fine Arts
Helene W. Hartley, Teachers College
Karl C. Leebrick, Dean of Liberal Arts
Mabel C. Lytton, Associate Dean of Women
Raymond F. Piper, Head, Philosophy Department
Herbert Shenton, Head, Sociology Department
Donald Watt, Personnel Director

Student Chairmen

Marjorie Farley, Sunday and Special Services
Marjorie O. Bronner, Daily Chapel Services
Irwin Hannum, Church and Chapel Relations
Margaret Iglehart, YWCA
Helen Laidlaw, Social Relations
Brewer Burnett, Oxford Fellowship
Mildred David, Syracuse-in-China
Joseph Hogben, Discussion Groups
Wellington Truran, Ushers
Ewart Blaine, Publicity
Dorothy Flood, Secretary
Donald G. Wright, Inter-University Conferences

1931–1932

William H. Powers, Dean

Chapel Staff

Bernice H. Meredith, Executive Secretary, Syracuse-in-China
Earl D. Stout, Chapel Music Director
Reverend Whitney M. Trousdale, Men's Student Counselor

Administration and Faculty Members

Dwight M. Beck, Professor, Bible Department
William L. Bray, Dean
Leslie A. Bryan, Professor, Dean
Ernest S. Griffith, Dean
Ross E. Hoople, Professor
Annie Macleod, Dean
Charles L. Raper, Dean
William E. Smallwood, Professor

Student Chairmen

Marion Wilner, Sunday and Special Worship
Florence Fenner, Daily Chapel Services
Wellington Truran, Church and Chapel Relations
Donald Wright, Inter-University Conferences
Helen Laidlaw, YWCA and Women's Student Senate
Mildred David, Syracuse-in-China
George Reifenstein, Student-Faculty Relations and Men's Student Senate
Ruth MacDonald, Social Relations
Ralph Laidlaw, Ushers
Walter Wakefield, Men's Discussion Groups
Webster Keefe, Freshman Camp
Ida Marie Sayers, Publicity
Brewer Burnett, Men's Fellowship
Helen Loggie, Secretary

1932–1933

William H. Powers, Dean

Chapel Staff

Marjorie O. Bronner, Secretary to the Dean
Helen D. Laidlaw, Student Loan Counselor
Bernice H. Meredith, Executive Secretary, Syracuse-in-China, and Women's Student Counselor
Earl D. Stout, Chapel Music Director
Whitney M. Trousdale, Men's Student Counselor

Administration and Faculty Members

Dwight M. Beck, Professor, Bible Department
William L. Bray, Dean, Graduate School
Leslie A. Bryan, Professor
Ernest L. Griffith, Dean
Ross E. Hoople, Professor
Annie L. Macleod, Dean
Charles L. Raper, Dean
William E. Smallwood, Professor

Student Committees

Margaret Elwood, Sunday and Special Worship
Annabel Nichols, Daily Chapel Services
Edward Meacham, Men's Chapel Association
Adelaide Ayling, YWCA
Lenore Rousseau, Social Relations
Albert Gutzman, Student-Faculty Relations
Winthrop Long, Church and Chapel Relations
Benjamin Moses, Inter-University Relations
William Bedford, Music
Virginia Rand, Dramatics
Helen Hand, Syracuse-in-China
Philip Ryder, Ushers
Robert Merritt, Men's Discussion Groups
Herbert Ross, Freshman Camp
Edna Askwith, Publicity
Helen Koford, Secretary

1933–1934

William H. Powers, Dean

Chapel Staff

Marjorie O. Bronner, Secretary to the Dean
Helen D. Laidlaw, Student Loan Counselor
Bernice H. Meredith, Executive Secretary, Syracuse-in-China, and Women's Student
Counselor
Earl D. Stout, Chapel Music Director

Administration and Faculty Members

William L. Bray, Dean
Leslie Bryan, Professor
Charles L. Raper, Dean
Ross Hoople, Professor

Student Members

Benjamin Moses and Annabel Nichols, Chairmen
Daniel Soper and Louise Ulrich, Chapel Worship
Lester Rounds and Edith Bishop, Deputation
Earl Stone and Vivian Whyte, Discussion Groups
John Hafer and Margaret Short, Freshman Commission
Anthony Fantaci and Martha Odell, House Representatives
William Bedford, Music
Pearle Spiro, Publicity
Julie Iglehart, Secretary
James Cadwallader and Elizabeth Decker, Social Relations
Elizabeth Clark, Social Service
Lloyd Hartman and Martha Dence, Special Programs
Donald Shetland, Syracuse-in-China
James Shenton, Ushers
Leslie Nichols and Dorothy Applin, World Relations

Denominational Pastors

Leland A. Barnes, Methodist
David Braun, Presbyterian
Charles Paterson-Smyth, Episcopalian

1934–1935

William H. Powers, Dean

Chapel Staff

Marjorie O. Bronner, Secretary to the Dean
Helen D. Laidlaw, Student Loan Counselor
Bernice H. Meredith, Executive Secretary, Syracuse-in-China, and Women's Student
Counselor
Annabel Nichols, Interim Secretary to the Dean
Earl D. Stout, Chapel Music Director

Administration and Faculty Members

Kenneth Bartlett, Professor
Ross Hoople, Dr.
Lewis Mitchell, Dean
Harry P. Smith, Dr.
Samuel Spring, Dean
Bess Templeton

Student Members

Ernest Fowler
Dorothy Applin
Fred Shippey
Edith Bishop
Lester Rounds
Elizabeth Koehler
James Shenton
Jeannette Birdsall
Malcom Rowe
Ola Woodward
Russell Anderson
Mildred Wicke
William Mattledge
Dorothy Ulrich
James Cadwallader
Doris Newton
Leroy Silverman
Jane Bradley
Earl Stone
Ruth Kaletsky

Lyman Hurd
Phyllis Field
Bill Hafer
Claudia Terry

Denominational Pastors

Leland A. Barnes, Methodist
David Braun, Presbyterian
Charles Patterson Smith, Episcopalian

1935–1936

William H. Powers, Dean

Chapel Staff

Ethel M. Armstrong, Executive Secretary, Syracuse-in-China
Marjorie O. Bronner, Secretary to the Dean
Helen D. Laidlaw, Student Loan Counselor
Benjamin H. Moses, Graduate Assistant
Earl D. Stout, Chapel Music Director
Adelaide A. Webster, Women's Student Counselor

Administration and Faculty Members

Eric Faigle, Professor
Hermann Kirhofer, Professor
Lewis Mitchell, Dean
F. Gordon Smith, Director
Harry Smith, Professor
Samuel Spring, Dean

Student Members

James Cadwallader and Marjorie Gwyne, Chairmen
James Skillen and Mary Church, Deputation
Raymond Jeffries and Eunice Green, Discussion
Robert Van Arnam and Marion Walker, Freshman Commission
Arthur McKean and Phyllis Haderup, Graduate Students
Walter Kieback and Nancy Miller, House Representatives
Lyman Hurd and Ola Woodward, Music
Jane Foley, Publicity
Richard Brungart and Fanny Rogers, Social Relations

Webster Haight and Alice Hardin, Social Service
Leroy Silverman, Ushers
George Mohlenhoff and Elizabeth Thompson, World Relations
James Mitchell and Catharine Mathews, Worship

Denominational Pastors

Lloyd R. Stamp, Methodist
David Braun, Presbyterian
Charles Patterson-Smyth, Episcopalian
Gannon F. Ryan, Roman Catholic

1936–1937

William H. Powers, Dean

Chapel Staff

Ethel M. Armstrong, Executive Secretary, Syracuse-in-China
Marjorie Bronner Pierson, Secretary to the Dean
Helen D. Laidlaw, Student Loan Counselor
Benjamin H. Moses, Graduate Assistant
Earl D. Stout, Chapel Music Director
Adelaide A. Webster, Women's Student Counselor

Administration and Faculty Members

Frank Bryant, Director
Finla Crawford, Professor
Eric Faigle, Professor
H. Kirchhofer, Professor
D. Walter Morton, Dr.
F. Gordon Smith, Director
M. L. Spencer, Dean

Student Members

Roy Terry and Beth Maxwell, Chairmen
Dick Dower and Nancy Welch, Vice Chairmen
George Stratton and Anna Lou Carmichael, Church and Chapel
Elwin Davey and Miriam Decker, Deputation
Donald Darrone and Margaret Kevand, Freshmen Commission
Raymond Yoh and Mildred Wharton, Graduate Students
George Rockrise and Lemoyne Markham, House Representatives

Charles Odell and Rita Silberstein, Inter-Faith
William Stevens, Music
Margaret Magie, Publicity
Dick Dower and Marjorie Frick, Social Relations
John Gough and Alice Babcock, Social Service
William Nichols and Jane Beeler, Special Programs
Thomas Lalor and Flower Sheldon, Student Emergency Loan Fund
Thomas Gable and Elsieanna McClure, Syracuse-in-China
Clarence Backwold, Ushers
Darrison Sillesky and Frances Martin, World Relations
Charles Ellison and Marie Freese, Worship

Denominational Pastors

Lloyd Stamp, Methodist
David Braun, Presbyterian
Charles Patterson-Smyth, Episcopalian
Gannon F. Ryan, Roman Catholic

1937–1938

William H. Powers, Dean

Chapel Staff

Ethel M. Armstrong, Executive Secretary, Syracuse-in-China
Benjamin H. Moses, Graduate Assistant
Florence E. Perry
Carol I. Simons
Earl D. Stout, Chapel Music Director
Adelaide A. Webster, Women's Student Counselor

Administration and Faculty Members

Kenneth Bartlett, Professor
Dwight M. Beck, Professor
Leslie Bryan, Professor
Finla Crawford, Dean
George B. Cressey, Professor
Eric Faigle, Professor
M. Eunice Hilton, Dean
Ross Hoople, Professor
Blair Knapp, Director
William T. Melchoir, Professor

Douglass W. Miller, Professor
Katherine Sibley, Professor
Ernst Thelin, Professor
Maurice E. Troyer, Professor
Herman G. Weiskotten, Dean

Alumni Representatives

J. Winifred Hughes
Charles Lee, Jr.

Graduate Student Representatives

John Gough
Ellen Peterson

Student Representatives

Newell Rossman and Jane King, Chairmen
Richard Shaw and Marian Jane Morgan, Vice Chairmen
Virginia Crate, Secretary
Morton Winters and Isabelle McDivitt, Church and Chapel
Clark Hunt and Anne Herrington, Deputation
Richard Wichlei and Jane Gardner, Freshmen Commission
Jack Meeks, Barbara DeLong, John Major, and Geraldine Mayer, House Representatives
Kern Ulrich and Winifred Bisgyer, Inter-Faith
Ruth Kaufman, Librarian
Kendall Doman and Betty Farber, Music
Elizabeth Donnelly, Public Relations
Gustave Milkey and Muriel Baas, Social Relations
John Olver and Lila Jones, Social Service
Millard Roberts and Isabelle Ballantyne, Special Programs
Cheste Hansen and Dorothy Skerritt, Student Emergency Loan Fund
Robert Grant and Helen Young, Syracuse-in-China
George Sierwald, Ushers
Rodney Fisher and Margaret Benedict, World Relations
Robert Terwilliger and Kathleen Walker, Worship

Denominational Counselors

Rolland McKee, Baptist
Hermann K. Kirchhofer, Episcopalian
Rabbi Irwin Hyman, Jewish
Rollin Shaffer, Lutheran

Lloyd Stamp, Methodist
Egbert M. Jayes, Presbyterian
Gannon F. Ryan, Roman Catholic

1940–1941

William Pratt Graham, Chancellor
William H. Powers, Dean

Chapel Staff

Ethel M. Armstrong, Executive Secretary, Syracuse-in-China
Benjamin H. Moses, Graduate Assistant
Florence E. Perry
Earl D. Stout, Chapel Music Director
Jean M. Templeton

Administration and Faculty Members

M. Eunice Hilton, Dean
A. Blair Knapp, Dean
Katherine Sibley, Director
Finla G. Crawford, Dean
Kenneth G. Bartlett, Professor
Ross E. Hoople, Professor
Dwight M. Beck, Professor
William C. Lehmann, Professor
Leslie A. Bryan, Professor
William T. Melchior, Professor
George B. Cressey, Professor
Douglass W. Miller, Professor
Eric H. Faigle, Professor
Graeme O'Geran, Professor
Harry J. Heltman, Professor
Warren Shepard, Professor
Reeves Baysinger
Ernst Thelin, Professor
Herman G. Weiskotten, Dean

Alumni Representatives

J. Winifred Hughes
Charles Lee, Jr.

Graduate Student Representatives

N. Virginia Avery
Newell Rossman

Student Representatives

Arnold Fellows and Marion Covell, Chairmen of the Board
George Bailey and Winifred Kob, Vice Chairmen
Shirley Weingrad, Secretary
Mary Mathieson, *Chapel News*
Kenneth Forbes and Elizabeth Peck, Deputation
Douglas Cagwin and Lucille Baker, Freshman Commission
Richard Hill and Martha Morrow, House Representatives
Drew Morris and Helen Panarites, Inter-Faith
Mary E. Williams, Library
Stuart Hallock and Myre Williams, Music
William Torrence and Martha Wright, Public Relations
Dewey Holcombe and Jeanette Talmadge, SELF
Bruce Chamberlain and Jane Hooper, Social Relations
John Wilson and Elizabeth Tracy, Social Service
Eugene Panhorst and Mary M. Hopkins, Special Programs
John Skeirik and Lucia Mason, Syracuse-in-China
Charles Lapham, Ushers
Ernest Grant and Evelyn Coman, World Relations
Joel Shippey and Beryl Ball, Worship

Denominational Counselors

Reverend Lloyd R. Stamp, Methodist
Reverend Egbert M. Hayes, Presbyterian
Professor Herman Kirchhofer, Episcopalian
Professor Roland C. McKee, Baptist
Rabbi Irwin Hyman, Jewish
Reverend Gannon F. Ryan, Roman Catholic
J. Benner Weaver
Chauncey Sampsell

1942–1943

William H. Powers, Dean

Chapel Staff

Agnes L. M. Gasch, Women's Counselor
Mary Alice Gates, Office Secretary
Eleanor W. McCurdy, Loan Counselor, Syracuse-in-China
Lloyd R. Stamp, Associate Minister
Leon Verrees, Organist and Director of Music

Student Officers

Tom Banfield and Doris Perry, Chairmen
Charles Brown and Barbara Reid, Vice Chairmen
Muriel Rosen, Secretary

Denominational Counselors

Reverend Lloyd R. Stamp, Methodist
Reverend Egbert M. Hayes, Presbyterian
Reverend Gannon F. Ryan, Roman Catholic
William Ward, Lutheran
Reverend John Schroeder, Baptist
Rabbi Irwin Hyman, Jewish

1943–1944

Student Members

Dorothy Pendleton and Daniel Hoag, Chapel Association Chairmen
Betty Tracy, Secretary
Janice Beck and Jason Blundon, Deputation
Gertrude Gates and Elman "Buzz" Gibson, Freshman Commission
Harriet Monroe, Graduate Commission
Wynne Cotton, House Representative
Marjorie Ehrenreich and Chester Galaska, Interfaith Committee
Dorothy Spencer, Music
Irene Hughes and James McCurdy, Public Relations
Gertrude Lane, Social Relations
Grace McCarthy, Social Service
Shirley Jeffords, Ruth Bisgrave, and Albert Lew, Syracuse-in-China
Robert Everson, Ushers
Marjorie Tonks, Volunteers
Alice Webster and Walter Turner, World Relations
Shirley Bowman and Robert Woodfield, Worship

Other Student Members

Edgar Everett
Charles Albright
Franklin Callender
Edwin Ellis
Hale Hubbard
Sterling Mayo
Richard Thompson
Ellsworth Stone

1944–1945

Student Chairs

Philip Dunning and Harriet Hoffman, House Representatives
Archer Andrews and Billy Burdett, Deputation
Robert Herr and Marjorie Ehrenreich, Freshman Commission
Clarence Steinberger and Frances Radford, Graduate Commission
Elinor Lewis, Intercollegiate Coordinator
Jason Blundon and Renee Engel, Interfaith Committee
Samuel Bingham and Janet Schomo, Music
James McCurdy and Laura Coman, Syracuse-in-China
James Norton, Ushers
Franklin Callender and Sally Harrison, Volunteers
David Bauer and Joyce Somers, World Relations
Arthur Blackburn and Carol Foote, Worship

1946–1947

The Hendricks Chapel Student Board

Romayne Brown and David Bauer, Chairmen
Margery Knapp and Edward Hanna, Vice Chairmen
Jeanne Waage and Philip Dunning, Secretaries
Rosalind Glickman and Arthur Andrews, Recording Secretaries
Helen Budd and Clyde Jones, Campus Relations
Esther Stevenson and Malcolm Calman, Chapel Service
Dorothy Laird and Daniel Adair, Deputation
Marcia Taylor and Ronald Green, Freshman Commission
Mary Winshurst, Graduate Commission
Wilma Jepson and John Shaver, Interfaith Committee
Claire Smith and Samuel Bingham, Jr., Music
Fred Wolk, Ushers

Marilyn Baum and Robert Britton, World Relations
Dorothy Schambacher and Robert Fehlman, Worship
Ruth Tannenhaus, Group Social Work
Patricia Younkins, Personal Social Service
Eva Teichman, Religious Education

1947–1948

Charles C. Noble, Dean

Chapel Staff

Ruth Hoople, Syracuse-in-China
Marguerite MacKinnon, Loan Counselor
Charlotte Welling, Secretary

Denominational Counselors

Reverend Charles H. Schmitz, Baptist
Melville Clark, Christian Science
Reverend Donald Tarr, Congregational
Reverend James A. Rockwell, Episcopal
Elizabeth Riley, Episcopal
Catherine Condon, Inter-Varsity
Rabbi Luitpold Wallach, Jewish
Reverend Donald W. Prigge, Lutheran
Reverend Thomas J. Van Loon, Methodist
Reverend Wilbert B. Smith, Jr., Presbyterian
Reverend Gannon F. Ryan, Roman Catholic
Reverend Theodore Kondratick, Russian Orthodox
Reverend Glenn O. Canfield, Unitarian
Reverend Ellsworth C. Reamon, Universalist

The Hendricks Chapel Student Board

Edward Hanna and Claire Smith, Chairmen
Elton Ridge and Esther Stevenson, Vice Chairmen
George Daigneault and Dorothy Schambacher, Secretaries
Ed London, Jeanne Markham, and Alice Reid, Campus Relations
Bud Howard and Betsy Hudson, Chapel Service
Ralph Coon and Mary Lou Street, Freshman Commission
Barbara Jones, Graduate Commission
Gregor Calender, Betty Daley, and Joan Troyer, Group Social Service
Ben Carroll and Molly Buckingham, House Representatives

Jerome Tobias and Judy Gregg, Interfaith Committee
Robert Quentin and Irene Engel, Music
Anne Vandenberg, Personal Social Service
Frances Weiss, Religious Education
Robert Malkmus and Penny Foster, Senior Commission
Ed Rothrock and Dorothy Scott, Syracuse-in-China
Ted Leverett and Don Cahoon, Ushers
Cicely Davenport, Vocations
John Ballentine and Ethel Greene, World Relations
Robert Youngs and Mary Lou Kiefer, Worship

1948–1949

Hendricks Chapel Student Board, First Cabinet

Alice Reid and Elton Ridge, Chairmen
Anne Vandenberg and John Ballentine, Vice Chairmen
Molly Buckingham and Bill Wilson, Recording Secretaries
Betsy Hudson and George Daigneault, Comptrollers
Ruth Spoor and John Hess, Chapel Service
Lorraine Lichty and Mark Shepard, Freshman Commission
Emily Jennings, Graduate Commission
Betty Daley, Elizabeth Illick, and Gregor Calender, Group Social Service
Mary Lou Street and Frank Meduna, House Representatives
Jeannine Saul and Dick VanDuser, Human Relations
Joan Morford and Earl Bolton, International Students
Irene Engle, Music
Marilyn Foster and John Heaslip, Personal Social Service
Honey Aberson, Barbara Blumenstiel, and Yale Newman, Public Relations
Judy Gregg and Nancy Philips, Radio
Marjorie Roberts and Don Wright, Senior Commission
Barbara Love and Henry Strock, Syracuse-in-China
Charles Hill and Ted Leverett, Ushers
Ellen Twining and Don Parker, Vocations
Margaret Noble and Glenn Wagner, World Relations
Betty Ruth Scott and Milan Slahor, Worship

Second Cabinet

John Ballentine and Anne Vandenberg, Chairmen
Mary Copeland, Secretary
Constance Banta, Paul Van Wicklen, Audrey Hardy, and Letitia Rotondaro, Chapel Service
Viola Sabia and Eric Heiberg, Freshman Commission

Wallace Many, Bert Kosloff, Jane Grimm, Lois Lipa, Thelma Tuttle, Christine Teale, Ken Roberts, Isabel Rockmore, Dick Kelly, and Judith Rothmore, Group Social Service
Anne Hyde and Jay Halio, House Representatives
Karen Packard and Ben Turner, Human Relations
Martha Jacobs and Abdul Ralin Dadi, International Students
Mary Bru Bard and Ruth Nies, Personal Social Service
Nancy Widrig and Lorraine Palmeter, Public Relations
Millicent Howells and Stan Hinden, Radio
Rita Gertner and Martin Pray, Syracuse-in-China
George Lee, Ushers
Nancy Livermore and James Collison, Vocations
Esther Van der Wart, Erwin White, Bob Troyer, and Bernard Hoyt, World Relations

1949–1950

Hendricks Chapel Student Board, First Cabinet

Betty Ruth Scott and John Hess, Chairmen
Ruth Spoor and Milan Slahor, Vice Chairmen
Barbara Love and Mark Shepard, Recording Secretaries
Jeannine Saul and Henry Strock, Comptrollers
Betty Coulter and Chet Seymour, Chapel Service
Billie Howells and Leo Rosenbaum, Freshman Commission
Peggy Lusk and Leonard Millner, Graduate Commission
Mary Lou Baird, Group Social Service
Ann Hyde and Jay Halio, House Representatives
Karen Packard and Ben Terner, Human Relations
Joan Morford and David Rosen, International Students
Arthur "Tex" Alpert, Jewish Fellowship
Dorothy Miner and Gerald Smith, Music
Bruce Bishop, Overseas Relief
Bob Sturge, Protestant Council Representative
Honey Aberson and Hy Nissenbaum, Public Relations
Nancy Phillips and Harold Venko, Radio
Ruth Surbeck and Arthur "Tex" Alpert, Senior Commission
Mary Bru Baird and Thelma Tuttle, Social Service
Rita Gertner and Marty Pray, Syracuse-in-China
Bernard Hoyt, Thompson Road Representative
Duncan Harkin and George Baker, Ushers
Carolyn Teeson, Minnie Telson, and Allen Berger, Vocations
Ester VanDerWort and Irwin White, World Relations
Gloria Mogel and Larry Welch, Worship

1950–1951

Charles C. Noble, Dean

Chapel Staff

Ruth Hoople, Syracuse-in-China
Marguerite MacKinnon, Loan Counselor
Arthur Poister, Choir Director and Organist

Chaplains

Reverend Charles H. Schmitz, Baptist
Mary Lent Ayer, Congregational
Walter C. Herget, Christian Science
Reverends Walter M. Welsh and Robert M. Cook, Episcopalian
Catherine Condon, Inter-Varsity Fellowship
Rabbi William Schwartz, Jewish
Dorothy Nieman, Lutheran
Reverend Arthur Hopkinson, Methodist
Reverend Wilbert B. Smith, Jr., Presbyterian
Professor Norman Whitney, Quaker
Reverend Gannon F. Ryan, Roman Catholic
Reverend Glenn O. Canfield, Unitarian
Reverend Ellsworth C. Reamon, Universalist
Hendricks Chapel Board, First Cabinet

Betty Coulter and Merph Smith, Chairmen
Sally Stephens and Allen Berger, Vice Chairmen
Marty Harkin and David Rosen, Recording Secretaries
Audrey Facius and Ben Terner, Comptrollers
Danna Steele and Bob Wright, Chapel Service
Carmen Snoke and Dick Stone, Design and Decorations
Sarah Lee Beard and Nick Carter, Freshman Commission
Rita Gertner and Margaret Forsythe, Graduate Commission
Carol Duemler and Mary Ann Buell, House Representatives
Joan Faigle and Seymour Sacks, Human Relations
Sally Stevens and David Rosen, International Students
Jean Birnbaum and Len Brown, Jewish Fellowship
Pat Miller and Weller Crandell, Music
Pat Lyons and Mark Shepard, Personnel Committee
Betty Weibezahl and John Olafson, Powers Club
Kathy O'Hara and John Marsh, Protestant Council Representatives
Renee Lurie, Bob Johnsrud, and Fran Nolan, Public Relations

Ruth Selsky and Dick Schaeffer, Radio
Nancy Widrig and Sherman Lieber, Senior Commission
Jean Hayes, Gretchen Weber, and Ann Berry, Social Service
Betty Bergen and Bill Kliber, Syracuse-in-China
Edward Rook and Tom Dunham, Ushers
Virginia Gray, Marianne Sarter, E. V. Howells, and Bob Nelson, Vocations
Doris Olson and Larry Fuerst, World Relations
Clara Weeks and Howard Hull, Worship Committee

1951–1952

The Student Chapel Board

Joan Faigle and William Kliber, Chairmen
Ginny Gray and Howie Hull, Vice Chairmen
Dana Steele and John Olafson, Recording Secretaries
Betty Weibezahl and Seymour Sacks, Comptrollers
Wilma Stegeman and Everett Gertner, Chapel Service
Dorothy Orr and Ray Johnson, Graduate Commission
Phyllis Kallenberg and Robert Wright, House Representatives
Ruth Ann Genner and Dorothy Winer, Human Relations
Ruth Fellows and John Olafson, International Students
Judith Rascover and David Ben-Asher, Jewish Fellowship
Pat Miller, Dave Essom, and Lila Greenberg, Music
Pat Lyon, Personnel
Ken Brown and Verne Nichols, Powers Club
Doris Maxeiner and Robert Beacham, Protestant Council
Marcia Moskowitz, Joyce Hallett, and Robert Vernoo, Public Relations
Joanne Williams and Al Hutin, Radio
Doris Freitag and Burton Weisberger, Senior Vocations
Diane Davis and Miriam Hopkins, Social Service
Elaine Davis and Richard Jeffries, Syracuse-in-Thailand
Ray Wilson and Dave Laine, Ushers
Bernice Rothenberg, World Relations
Nancy Rankin, Phillip Hallen, and Helen Berowotz, Worship

1952–1953

Executive Committee

Margaret Wolcott and John Olafson, Chairmen
Diane Davis and Everett Gertner, Vice Chairmen
Constance Pierson and Robert Wright, Secretaries
Judith Rascover and Vernon Lee, Jr., Comptrollers

First Cabinet

Nancy Knapp and Bruce Gibbs, Chapel Service
Sandra Kerry and Lee Sunstead, COR
Judith Kreisberg, Design and Decorations
Nan Kendall and Al Dilthey, Graduate Commission
Jane Miner and Warren Miller, House Representatives
Sora Getmansky and Anne Zehner, Human Relations
Jane Dempsey, International Students
Gus Uhry and Stanley Leff, Jewish Fellowship
Gail Hoadley and Nancy Reed, Library Committee
Carolyn Ober and Tom Scott, Music
Mary Ellen Furbush and John Snead, Powers Club
Harriet Kellogg and Milton Stevenson, Protestant Council
Dorothy Hopkins and William Kagler, Public Relations
Daisy Sherwood and Alice Bell, Radio
Georgia Obrist and Joyce Ruso, Social Service
Hannah Hillen and Bruce McCarthy, Syracuse-in-Thailand
Ray Wilson and Edwin Gros, Ushers
Patricia Roden and Edward Snyder, World Relations

Second Cabinet

Gail Kepner, Sally Koby, and Marcia Michelbacher, Chapel Service
Marcia LeFevre and Herbert Walker, COR
Jane Williams and Barrie Gray, House Representatives
Lee Blumberg and Ken Frederick, Human Relations
Alice Daltz, International Students
Mary Ann Lana, Library
Rolf Thorkildsen, Powers Club
George Van Volkenburg, Radio
Nona Brierley, Secretary
Caroline Hussing, Greta Alexander, and Margaret Andersone, Social Service
Robert Armitage and Donald Fryer, Ushers
Cynthia Reed and Dean Lavender, Worship

1953–1954

Chapel Board Directory

Deanne Lavender and Patricia Roden, Chairmen
Mary Ellen Furbush, Hanako Hillen, and William Kagler, Vice Chairmen
Nona Brierley and Constance Pierson, Recording Secretaries

Marcia Heath and William Connolly, Chapel Representatives
Gail Kepner and Dorothy Cole, Chapel Service
Margaret Hoar, Human Relations
Betsy Wright, International Students
Linda Polloch and Henry Einhorn, Jewish Fellowship
Madeline Chambers and Marilyn Day, Library
Jane Williams and Robert Roberts, Music
Ann Forest, Edward Snyder, and Carolyn Ober, Protestant Council
Ethel Smetts, Public Relations
Lucille Stitzenberger and Ransom Place, Radio
Mary Ann Lana, Skeptics Corner
Caroline Hussing and Dorianne Bright, Social Service
Ruth Schmidt and David Crossman, Syracuse-in-Asia
Robert Armitage, Donald Connolly, and Don Fryer, Ushers
Marcia LeFevre, World Relations
Ann Cross and James Fellows, Worship

1954–1955

Student Board Leaders

Betsy Wright and James Fellows, Chairmen
Ann Cross, Ethel Smetts, and Arthur Kinney, Vice Chairmen
Mary Ann Lana, Secretary
David Crossman, Comptroller
Joan Bosworth and Marjorie Clark, Chapel Service
Gayle Kepner and James Manibo, House Representatives
Barbara Watson and Edward Eberding, Human Understanding
Audrey Lous Benn, International Students
Louise Garretson, Library
Lou Ann Muller and Lawrence Steiner, Music
Marilyn Campbell and Barbara Anderson, Public Relations
Gail Kepner and Robert Martingale, Radio
Beverly Nason, Skeptics Corner
Lynn Pierce, Elsa Shyman, and Barbara Elwood, Social Hygiene
Sherry Woolever and Ann Schafale, Social Service
Barbara Pritchard, Syracuse-in-Asia
James Ferguson and Harold Vicora, Ushers
Ann Wiegreffe and Lee Pierce, Worship

1955–1956

Chapel Board

Jean Bosworth and John Husband, Chairmen
Barbara Pritchard and Lee Pierce, Vice Chairmen
Marion Campbell, Secretary
Sherrell Wolever, Comptroller
Melvin Scott and Nancy VanSchaich, Chapel Receptionists
Richard Coulter and Marilyn Swanson, Chapel Representatives
Gerald Frutchey and Elinor Hussey, Choir
Mary Lee White and Jean Banincasa, Human Understanding
Ellen Baer and Kay Wallace, International Students
Carolyn Gilbert and Arlene Speed, Mental Hygiene
Lois Black and William Classen, Powers Club
Katherine Bell and Theodore Speck, Radio
Ann Goddard, Skeptics Corner
Barbara Robinson, Social Relations
Marcia Smelin and Lila Rosen, Social Service
Elizabeth Cougler and Paul Ackerman, Syracuse-in-Asia
John Robinson and George Bulin, Ushers
Virginia BeVard and David Beuton, Worship

1957–1958

Student Leaders on the Chapel Board

Donald Tetmeyer and Roger Greenlaw, Chairmen
Barbara Dubin, Vice Chairman
Ann Phillips and Betty Fulton, Receptionists
Carolyn Snyder, Secretary
Barbara Zschiesche, Treasurer
Toby Sue Shapiro and Carol Lee Harmeson, Chapel Representatives
Katherine Radcliff and Warren Powers, Choir
Susan Goldberg, Human Understanding
Barbara Templeton and Ruth Vivian, Library
Hugh Gregg and Barbara Statlander, Public Relations
Ginger Gerkin and James Barker, Radio
Marcia Zahn, Skeptics Corner
Jean Mayo and Alice Nielson, Social Service
Helen Kneider and Joseph Singer, Syracuse-in-Asia
Charles Hill and Maxwell Pounder, Ushers
Robert Craig and Dick Heimburg, Worship

1958–1959

Student Officers

Hugh Gregg and John Colley, Chairmen
Judy Bloomingdale and Susan Goldberg, Secretaries
Barbara Zschiesche, Treasurer
Laura Wood, Chapel Representative
Barbara Trimmer, Choir
Carol Eaton, Human Understanding
Eunice Kent, Library
Robert Spies, Public Relations
Betty Goetzin and Garry Schlesser, Radio
Iris Fortang, Skeptics Corner
Bob Rhodes, Stewardship
Carol McDougal and J. W. Singer, Jr., Syracuse-in-Asia
Nat Rhodes and David Singerland, Ushers
Patricia Ellis and Jeanne Irene, Worship

1962–1963

Rinna Block, Chairman
Judith Shoenborn, Secretary
John Opperman, Social Service
Joan Richardson, Freshman Commission
Jan Hillegas, Worship

Chaplains and Staff, 1980–1999

Chaplains and staff members who served Hendricks Chapel between 1980 and 1999 are listed in this appendix, roughly by academic year, even where individuals' specific dates of service may vary from the academic calendar. Persons who assisted or worked for chaplains are not listed because they were not formally part of the structure of Hendricks Chapel. For the same reason, volunteers, substitutes, and very short-term workers on the staff are likewise not listed.

1980–1981

James B. Wiggins, Interim Dean (July 1, 1980-February 28, 1981)
Richard L. Phillips, Dean (as of March 1, 1981)

Chapel Staff

Jean Baum, Programs
Geoff Drutchas, UU Intern
Tione Gausman, Secretary
Ed Griffin, Mutuality in Mission Intern
John Jones, Chaplain-at-Large
Nina Sardino, Secretary
Winston Stephens, Jr., Organ and Choir

Chaplains

Rick Bair, Lutheran
Jean Baum, Methodist
Charles Borgognoni, Roman Catholic
Rafil Dahfir, Islamic (part-time)
Milton Elefant, Jewish
Norm Keim, Chaplain-at-Large
T. E. Koshy, Evangelical Christian
Ed Ondrako, Roman Catholic
Robert Raspberry, Empire State Baptist (on call)
Jacqueline Schmitt, Episcopal

1981–1982

Richard L. Phillips, Dean

Chapel Staff

Jean Baum, Counseling and Events
Judy Crane, Secretary
Diane Heller, Mutuality in Mission Intern
Dan Hoversten, Graduate Assistant Business Manager
William Johnson, Graduate Assistant to Dean
Rosemarie McGinnis, Secretary
Richard Shprecher, UU Intern
Winston Stephens, Jr., Organ and Choir
Millie Woods, Minority Programs

Chaplains

Rick Bair, Lutheran
Charles Borgognoni, Roman Catholic
Rafil Dahfir, Islamic (part-time)
Milton Elefant, Jewish
Norm Keim, Chaplain-at-Large
William Kliber, Interdenominational Protestant
T. E. Koshy, Evangelical
Kathy Madigan, Presbyterian (part-time)
Ed Ondrako, Roman Catholic
Robert Raspberry, Empire Baptist (on call)
Jacqueline Schmitt, Episcopal

1982–1983

Richard L. Phillips, Dean

Chapel Staff

Jean Baum, Counseling and Events
John Baros-Johnson, UU Intern
Will O. Headlee, Organ and Choir
Diane Heller, Mutuality-in-Mission Intern
William Johnson, Graduate Assistant to Dean
Rosemarie McGinnis, Secretary
Todd Root, Graduate Assistant Business Manager

Millie Woods, Minority Programs
Myrtle Zacharek, Secretary

Chaplains

Rich Bair, Lutheran
Charles Borgognoni, Roman Catholic
Rafil Dahfir, Islamic (part-time)
Milton Elefant, Jewish
Carl Johnson, Interdenominational Protestant
Norm Keim, Chaplain-at-Large
T. E. Koshy, Evangelical
Ed Ondrako, Roman Catholic
Robert Raspberry, Empire Baptist (first semester only)
Dennis Winslow, Episcopal

1983–1984

Richard L. Phillips, Dean

Chapel Staff

Mark Allstrom, UU Intern
Jean Baum, Counseling and Events
Kathy Blossom, Music-Bell Choir (part-time)
Kristine Christlieb, Graduate Assistant to Dean
Michael Durrer, Graduate Assistant Administration
Will O. Headlee, Organ and Choir
Rosemarie McGinnis, Secretary
Paul Simonet, Graduate Assistant Business Manager
Corinne Sopchak, Secretary
Millie Woods, Minority Programs

Chaplains

Rick Bair, Lutheran
Charles Borgognoni, Roman Catholic
Rafil Dahfir, Islamic (part-time)
Malcolm Dawes, Assembly of God (part-time)
Milton Elefant, Jewish
Carl Johnson, Interdenominational Protestant
T. E. Koshy, Evangelical
Ed Ondrako, Roman Catholic
Dennis Winslow, Episcopal

Chapel Staff

Mary Farnsworth, Secretary and Office Coordinator
Nansie Jensen, Counseling and Events
Christopher Koliba, Graduate Assistant Administration
Rosemarie McGinnis, Secretary
Katharine Pardee, Director of Music
David Parkhurst, Graduate Assistant Administration (first semester)
Thomas Platt, Graduate Assistant Business Manager (second semester)
Marilyn Schultz, Director of Students Offering Services (SOS) (part-time)
Janet Shortall-Bates, UU Intern
Peter Shumski, Graduate Assistant Business Manager (first semester)
Karla Ver Bryck, Graduate Assistant Administrative SOS (second semester)
Millie Woods, Minority Programs

Chaplains

Charles Borgognoni, Roman Catholic
Alan Iser, Jewish
Ahmed Kobeisy, Islamic (part-time)
T. E. Koshy, Evangelical
Ed Ondrako, Roman Catholic
Michael S. Rothermel, Lutheran
James Taylor, Episcopal
Tom Wolfe, Interdenominational Protestant

1991–1992

Richard L. Phillips, Dean

Chapel Staff

Mary Farnsworth, Secretary and Office Coordinator
Nansie Jensen, Counseling and Events Coordinator
Christopher Koliba, Graduate Assistant Administration and SOS (second semester)
Rosemarie McGinnis, Secretary
Katharine Pardee, Director of Music
Thomas Platt, Graduate Assistant Business Manager (first semester)
Marilyn Schultz, Director of SOS (first semester part-time)
Karla Ver Bryck, Assistant Director of SOS
Millie Woods, Minority Programs

Chaplains

Alan Iser, Jewish
Ahmed Kobeisy, Islamic (part-time)
T. E. Koshy, Evangelical
James Lang, Roman Catholic
Ed Ondrako, Roman Catholic
Michael S. Rothermel, Lutheran
James Taylor, Episcopal
Tom Wolfe, Interdenominational Protestant

1992–1993

Richard L. Phillips, Dean

Chapel Staff

Mary Farnsworth, Secretary and Office Coordinator
Nansie Jensen, Counseling and Events
Christopher Koliba, SOS Graduate Assistant (part-time)
Sue Martini, Secretary
Katharine Pardee, Organ and Choir (part-time)
Francis Parks, Graduate Assistant African American Programs
Tom Platt, Graduate Assistant Business Manager
Julie Pretzat, Choir (part-time)
Ginny Yerdon, Secretary

Chaplains

Alan Iser, Jewish
Ahmed Kobeisy, Islamic (part-time)
T. E. Koshy, Evangelical
James Lang, Roman Catholic
Ed Ondrako, Roman Catholic
Michael S. Rothermel, Lutheran
James Taylor, Episcopal
Tom Wolfe, Interdenominational Protestant

1993–1994

Richard L. Phillips, Dean

Chapel Staff

Tom Bell, Graduate Assistant Business Manager
Mary Farnsworth, Secretary and Office Coordinator
Nansie Jensen, Counseling and Events
Christopher Koliba, SOS (part-time)
Sue Martini, Secretary
Katharine Pardee, Choir (part-time)
Francis Parks, Graduate Assistant African American Programs and SOS
Julie Pretzat, Choir (part-time)
Ginny Yerdon, Secretary

Chaplains

Michael and Michele Dean, Southern Baptist
Craig Herrick, Lutheran
Ahmed Kobeisy, Islamic (part-time)
T. E. Koshy, Evangelical
James Lang, Roman Catholic
Toby Manewith, Jewish
James Taylor, Episcopal
Tom Wolfe, Interdenominational Protestant

1994–1995

Richard L. Phillips, Dean

Chapel Staff

Fred Boehrer, Graduate Assistant SOS
Rob Donihue, Graduate Assistant Business Manager (first semester)
Mary Farnsworth, Secretary and Office Coordinator
Burt Harbison, Choir (part-time)
Nansie Jensen, Counseling and Events
Sue Martini, Secretary
Kikuko Nishiguchi, Graduate Assistant Business Manager (second semester)
Katharine Pardee, Organ (part-time)
Francis Parks, African American Programs and SOS
Ginny Yerdon, Secretary

Chaplains

George Koch, Lutheran
Ahmed Kobeisy, Islamic (part-time)

T. E. Koshy, Evangelical
James Lang, Roman Catholic
Toby Manewith, Jewish
Michael McQuitty, Southern Baptist
James Taylor, Episcopal
Tom Wolfe, Interdenominational Protestant

1995–1996

Richard L. Phillips, Dean (on leave)
Robert S. Pickett, Interim Director

Chapel Staff

Fred Boehrer, Graduate Assistant SOS
Mary Farnsworth, Events Coordinator
Burt Harbison, Choir (part-time)
Sue Martini, Secretary
Kikuko Nishiguchi, Graduate Assistant Business Manager
Katharine Pardee, Organ (part-time)
Francis Parks, African American Programs and SOS
Ginny Yerdon, Secretary

Chaplains

Ahmed Kobeisy, Islamic (part-time)
George Koch, Lutheran
T. E. Koshy, Evangelical
James Lang, Roman Catholic
Toby Manewith, Jewish
James Taylor, Episcopal
Mary Tuney, Southern Baptist
Tom Wolfe, Interdenominational Protestant

1996–1997

Richard L. Phillips, Dean (on leave)
Robert S. Pickett, Interim Director

Chapel Staff

Mary Farnsworth, Events Coordinator
Burt Harbison, Choir (part-time)
Sean Hynes, Graduate Assistant Business Manager (second semester part-time)

Sue Martini, Secretary
Sascha Milligan, Graduate Assistant SOS
Kikuko Nishiguchi, Graduate Assistant Business Manager (first semester)
Katharine Pardee, Organ
Francis Parks, African American Programs and SOS
Ginny Yerdon, Secretary

Chaplains

Sivan Kaminsky, Jewish (second semester)
Ahmed Kobeisy, Islamic (part-time)
George Koch, Lutheran
James Lang, Roman Catholic
Toby Manewith, Jewish (first semester)
Michael McQuitty, Southern Baptist
James Taylor, Episcopal
Tom Wolfe, Interdenominational Protestant

1997–1998

Richard L. Phillips, Dean

Chapel Staff

Mary Farnsworth, Events Coordinator
Burt Harbison, Choir (part-time)
Sean Hymes, Graduate Assistant Business Manager
Sue Martini, Secretary
Sasha Milligan, Graduate Assistant SOS
Katharine Pardee, Organ
Francis Parks, African American Programs and SOS
Ginny Yerdon, Secretary

Chaplains

Sivan Kaminsky, Jewish
George Koch, Lutheran
Ahmed Kobeisy, Islamic (part-time)
T. E. Koshy, Evangelical
James Lang, Roman Catholic
Michael McQuitty, Southern Baptist
James Taylor, Episcopal
Tom Wolfe, Interdenominational Protestant

1998–1999

Richard L. Phillips, Dean (retired December 31, 1998; retired SU June 30, 1999)
Thomas V. Wolfe, Dean (as of January 1, 1999)

Chapel Staff

Matthew Dean, Graduate Assistant Business Manager
Mary Farnsworth, Special Secretary (first semester)
Burt Harbison, Choir (part-time)
Agnes H. Magnarelli, Secretary (October 1998)
Sue Martini, Secretary
Katharine Pardee, Organ (part-time)
Francis Parks, African American Programs and SOS
Sally Valentino, Graduate Assistant SOS
Ginny Yerdon, Events Coordinator

Chaplains

Thomas Davenport, Interdenominational Protestant (late second semester)
Adam Keltos, Roman Catholic (second semester)
George Koch, Lutheran
Ahmed Kobeisy, Islamic (part-time)
T. E. Koshy, Evangelical
James Lang, Roman Catholic (first semester)
Michael McQuitty, Southern Baptist
James Taylor, Episcopal
Tom Wolfe, Interdenominational Protestant (first semester)
TBA, Jewish

Organizational Information

Although the following organizational information is based on the operation of the Office of the Dean of Hendricks Chapel during the 1989–90 academic year, it is representative of the structure and operation of that office throughout the tenure of Dean Phillips. In 1990, Chancellor Eggers shifted authority over the Hendricks Chapel Advisory Board (HCAB) from his own office to the Office of the Dean. Technically, this shift changed the HCAB from a chancellor's committee to a dean's committee. (See chapter 51.)

Hendricks Chapel

Chancellor, President
Vice Chancellor, Executive Assistant
Office of the Dean
Hendricks Chapel Advisory Board (a committee of the Office of the Chancellor made up of faculty, administrators, staff, students, trustees, and one chaplain)
F = Full-time
P = Part-time
GA = Graduate Assistant Part-time

Chapel Staff

Chapel Secretary, F
Dean's Secretary, F
Director of Music, F
Assistant to the Dean, P
Minority Ministries, P
Business Manager, GA
Coordinator of Council and Events, P
Administrative Assistant, GA
Dean, F

Chaplaincies (not funded by Syracuse University)

Episcopal, F
Evangelical Christian, F
Islamic, P
Jewish (Hillel and Chabad), 2F
Lutheran, F

Protestant Interdenominational, F (Amercan Baptist, United Christian Council, United
Methodist, United Presbyterian)
Roman Catholic, 2F

Group Ministries (not funded by Syracuse University)

Baptist Campus Ministries (Southern Baptist)
Campus Bible Fellowship
Campus Crusade for Christ
Chi Alpha (Assembly of God)
Inter-Varsity Christian Fellowship

Affiliated Groups (self-funded)

Alpha Phi Omega
Christian Science Organization
Hindu Samaj
Korean Student Fellowship
Kundalini Yoga Club
Latter-day Saints Student Association
Muslim Student Association
New Birth Christian Fellowship
Pan-Orthodox Christian Fellowship
Society of the Holy Mother
Society of Friends (Quaker)
SU Buddist Association
Unitarian Universalist Society
Zen Center of Syracuse

Auxiliary Operations (self- and organizationally funded)

Alcoholics Anonymous
Black Celestial Choral Ensemble
Hendricks Chapel Choir
Hendricks Chapel Handbell Choir
People's Place (food)
Students Offering Service (volunteer projects)
Chaplains Council (all chaplains and most members of the Office of the Dean; meets
monthly)

The Operation of the Office of the Dean of Hendricks Chapel at Syracuse University

This chart represents Hendricks Chapel's position in the administrative structure of Syracuse University and also shows the various "departments" answering to the dean of Hendricks Chapel. Like any administrative chart, it tells an incomplete story. The present administrative structure of Hendricks Chapel came into existence in 1980, following a thorough study of the operation of the chapel and the Office of the Dean of Hendricks Chapel. Shortly after that study was completed, Richard L. Phillips became the fourth dean, beginning his tenure on March 1, 1981.

The dean of Hendricks Chapel is a university administrator charged with several responsibilities. All chaplains, and all groups with any religious purpose whatsoever must come under the administrative umbrella of Hendricks Chapel, whether or not they use the chapel building. The dean must approve any chaplaincies, group ministries, or affiliated groups, including the personnel assigned to such operations. The Office of the Dean is expected to facilitate the successful operation of the constituent groups of the chapel and to ensure that each is in compliance with university procedures and regulations.

Each chaplaincy representing a denomination or major religious group (based on negotiation with the dean) is supplied with office space without charge. Each is given a telephone, although calls made on it must be at the expense of the chaplaincy involved. Each chaplain and most members of the dean's staff are members of the Chaplains' Council, which meets monthly, both to review the entire operation and to facilitate as much cooperative work as possible. The dean serves as convenor and coordinator of the Chaplains' Council. The dean will receive a report at least once each year from each group and chaplaincy operating within the structure of Hendricks Chapel.

The dean of the chapel collaborates with various judicatories and religious bodies in the selection of new or replacement chaplains and the review of those chaplains already in place. In addition, the dean is the administrative officer responsible for all relationships between the university and religious organizations or bodies as directed by the chancellor.

The chaplaincies are not the only ministries having full-time staff people. Most of the group ministries noted on the chart have one or more full-time staff person; moreover although they are not granted office space, these staff members are granted certain privileges similar to those enjoyed by the chaplains, such as university staff ID cards. Like the chaplaincies, these ministries are expected to operate with funding from outside the university, except for the small portions of their budgets that may derive from free-will offerings within their constituent groups. The dean meets at least once each semester with the workers affiliated with these group ministries and attempts to maintain good working relationships with all parties.

Groups listed on the chart as affiliated groups consist for the most part of student groups that form on an annual basis and are led either by a student or by a volunteer from the university's faculty or staff. Each of the group ministries and the affiliated groups must have a faculty or administrative sponsor as a part of the system of accountability that characterizes the group structure of the entire university.

Any group can be removed from the campus for noncompliance with university regulations; however, this has happened only once, when, in 1989, a group known as The Way International lost its campus status for refusing to comply with the basic regulations.

The auxiliary operations of the chapel are either self-sustaining or operate using a portion of the budget of the Office of the Dean. People's Place is a good example. A food service operating part-time from a room in the chapel about the size of a chaplain's office, it is managed by students and offers simple, nonprepared foods. Approximately twenty-five students work on a part-time basis in People's Place.

The Office of the Dean of Hendricks Chapel is also charged with the mission of improving the quality of life for all members of the Syracuse University campus community; engaging the entire university in the consideration of questions dealing with moral and ethical issues; and considering such things as meaning, purpose, and values. It seeks to create programming to facilitate interdisciplinary and cross-college dialogue as well as to foster general awareness of the world in which we live and the problems of the larger society of which we are a part. To these ends, the chapel staff is charged with the responsibility of serving all members of the campus community—both those with religious affiliations and those without.

The programming emanating from the Office of the Dean of Hendricks Chapel is carefully planned so that it does not in any way interfere with or appear to usurp the ministries or traditional roles of the chaplains and religious workers on the campus. For example, this office does not engage in sponsoring services of worship, prayer or fellowship groups, Bible study, or similar activities that the chaplains might regard as an "invasion" of their territory by the Office of the Dean.

Finally, the dean of Hendricks Chapel is charged with the responsibility of serving as a campus ombudsperson for the entire university community. In order to facilitate that mission the dean sits on many university committees, notably the chancellor's Administrative Group, the Office of Student Affairs Management Group, the University Senate, and the Academic Deans and Directors Council.

The chancellor of Syracuse University has formed a committee known as the Hendricks Chapel Advisory Board, created to give advice and counsel both to the dean of Hendricks Chapel and to the chancellor in matters pertaining to the overall operation of Hendricks Chapel. The membership categories for this board are prescribed by the chancellor, with the board itself serving as its nominating committee for the rotation of membership and each election requiring confirmation by the chancellor. The board normally meets from two to four times each semester to hear reports from the dean and to discuss issues pertinent to the operation of the chapel and the ways in which the chapel, the chapel staff, and the chaplains can best serve the needs of the individuals who make up the entire university community.

With some frequency, the dean of the chapel is called upon to function in official capacities at major university events. When appropriate, such roles can be passed on to chaplains, and where practical a system should be used so that over a period of time all chaplains are able to interact with the broader scope of the university community.

"This House Shall Be a House of Prayer for All"

Hymn written for and dedicated to Dean Richard Phillips of Hendricks Chapel, on the occasion of his retirement, by Joseph Downing; copyright 1998 by Joesph Downing; courtesy of the composer.

Index